FRANCE by TRAIN

Simon Vickers

has travelled widely in France and has lived in Paris and
Périgord. He is the author of *Between the Hammer and the
Sickle*, an account of a 7,500 mile journey by bicycle through
Russia from St. Petersburg to Vladivostok. He is currently
writing a book about a boat journey down the Dordogne
through the vineyards of Monbazillac and St-Emilion to the
Atlantic.

Fodor's

FRANCE *by* TRAIN

BY SIMON VICKERS

Fodor's Travel Publications, Inc.
New York • Toronto • London • Sydney • Auckland

Published in the United States by Fodor's Travel Publications, Inc.

Published in the United Kingdom by Hodder and Stoughton, a division of Hodder and Stoughton Ltd.

Fodor's is a registered trademark of Fodor's Travel Publications, Inc.

ISBN 0-679-02826-9

First Edition

Library of Congress Cataloging-in-Publication Data
Vickers, Simon, 1960–
    Fodor's France by train / by Simon Vickers.
        p.   cm.
    Includes index.
    ISBN 0-679-02826-9 (pbk.) : $16.00
    1. France—Guidebooks.   2. Railroad travel—France—Guidebooks.
I. Fodor's Travel Publications, Inc.   II. Title.   III. Title: France
by train.
DC 16.V52   1994
914.404'839—dc20   94-6875
                                                                CIP

Maps by Alec Spark

Typeset by Hewer Text Composition Services, Edinburgh, Scotland.

Special Sales
Fodor's Travel Publications are available at special discounts for bulk purchases for sales promotions or premiums. Special editions, including personalized covers, excerpts of existing guides, and corporate imprints, can be created in large quantities for special needs. For more information, contact your local bookseller or Special Markets, Fodor's Travel Publications, 201 E. 50th Street, New York, NY 10022. Inquiries from Canada should be directed to your local Canadian bookseller or sent to Random House of Canada, Ltd., Marketing Dept., 1265 Aerowood Drive, Mississauga, Ontario L4W 1B9.

MANUFACTURED IN THE UNITED STATES OF AMERICA

10   9   8   7   6   5   4   3   2   1

Contents

Introduction

Only 30 years ago drastic cuts were being made to railway networks in Europe and the railways seemed to have no future worth speaking of. But as the year 2,000 approaches train travel is enjoying a revival as trains become ever faster, smoother and more comfortable. In France, TGV's have revolutionized the patterns of internal travel, even to the extent of putting airlines out of business on a number of domestic flights between Paris and provincial cities. The comfort, ease and speed of traveling via the Channel Tunnel now makes air travel from London to Paris seem the slow option. Flying to Paris requires 4 hours from central London to central Paris (one hour's travel from central London to Heathrow, one hour check-in time spent hanging around, one hour flight and then another hour getting to central Paris from Roissy-Charles de Gaulle airport), whereas trains using the Channel Tunnel take exactly 3 hours.

Train travel in France is not only comfortable and straightforward but tremendously enjoyable. True, you cannot get to every single village and monument of interest but that is really a blessing in disguise. What is more remarkable is just how many places you can get to. Railway lines lead high up into the Pyrenees and the Alps, offering superb panoramic views of dramatic mountain scenery and snow-capped peaks. They climb steeply through the wild uplands of the Cévennes and the dramatic volcanic landscape of Auvergne. In Provence, they cross the deserted stone plateau of La Crau and climb through the dry aromatic hills of Basse-Provence. In the west, they skirt the craggy shores of Brittany and meander through enchanting Norman towns. Small branch lines thread through the fortified towns and villages of Aquitaine and Languedoc, and follow the enchanting valleys of the Dordogne and Isle. Dramatic routes lead up into the Pyrenees, and in Roussillon a narrow-gauge railway line takes one up in open carriages from Perpignan to the Spanish border and the highest railway station in France at a height of 1,592 metres. In winter, snow-ploughs keep this spectacular route open for weekend skiers.

France probably has a more varied landscape than any other country in Europe, as becomes apparent from the moment you begin to explore the country by train. Routes in the guide combine visits to historic towns and cities with journeys through beautiful countryside. Traveling by train puts one in mind of Robert Louis Stevenson's maxim that 'I travel not to go anywhere, but to go. I travel for travel's sake. The great affair is to move'.

There is no reason of course why you should not abandon the train from time to time to take the occasional bus or ferry. Many of the routes include excursions to nearby places which can be reached by bus. As SNCF operates buses which are co-ordinated with train arrivals, this is often very simple. Only the most worthwhile excursions have been suggested, however, for the emphasis is naturally on train travel. With the exception of Paris, which is dealt with in depth, the guide concentrates on the main sights, museums and monuments and steers you gently in the direction of the most interesting part of the town. As important as the place you visit are the experiences you will have on the train itself. Train travel still has an aura of romance and excitement – even with TGVs traveling at 300 kmph. The vast majority of French trains are efficient and modern, allowing you to travel quickly and comfortably from place to place, but there are also the provincial lines with older trains which are slower but very rewarding.

The French tend to be more convivial than the British and it's quite possible you will be engaged in conversation by a stranger, especially in the south. Remember that local people often will have interesting suggestions about what to visit or where to get the best meal in a town – so don't be too shy, you might miss out on some wonderful experience!

How to use this book

FRANCE BY TRAIN is divided into 18 chapters, the first 2 covering general background information, the rest rail journeys divided into 5 regions which have been ordered alphabetically. If you don't know France, the first chapter, *General Information*, describes some of the basic information you will need before visiting the country, concentrating on the various rail tickets and passes that can be bought in the United States.

The second chapter, *The Train Network*, covers the practical aspects of French train travel. Much of the information is common sense, much of the detail more than you will probably need. It's worth reading through if this is going to be your first journey on French railways. Some of the vocabulary might be useful, and odd tips will save time and money. As for the main chapters, the aim is to help you to decide what to see, how to see it and how and where to spend the night. Each chapter has a brief **introduction**, designed to point out what a region has to offer. This is followed by a summary of the **route**, which may be circular or linear. Of course there is no reason why routes cannot be done in reverse order, and towns or villages can be skipped altogether to save time or if one town interests you more than another.

Each chapter starts with a **major city**, often the center of the rail network for the

whole region, with details of the important things to see in the city and all the practical information you will need. The cities that every journey starts from are easily accessible from Paris, and information about how to reach the city is given at the head of the section.

The chapter then moves on to the next town of interest, starting with information on how to reach it by train, with details of the frequency of trains and the duration of the journey. A description of the journey to the next destination usually precedes the description of the next town. Virtually every city and town entry has a separate **Practicalities** section. Look first at the entry for the railway station, which tells you how to reach the town center, either by walking or taking a bus. Then look for the tourist office entry, which should be your first port of call to pick up maps and lists of local events or festivals, or for help with accommodation. We also recommend a selection of hotels, and the best neighborhoods in which to look for others. Restaurants and a few bars are listed, together with a miscellany of information about foreign exchange, buses, travel agents, and so forth.

Some journeys contain excursions – short trips (usually by bus) you can make from towns on the railway network. Some take you to towns, some to individual buildings, others to notable scenic regions of the country.

General Information

Because the railways were built in the 19th century, when French towns were much smaller, train stations are virtually always close to the center of cities and the most interesting sites are within easy walking distance. Nor is train travel expensive in France thanks to the French government's policy of investment and modernization. By attracting a large volume of business, SNCF has been able to keep fares to a reasonable level.

The opening of the Channel Tunnel in May 1994 has revolutionized travel between Britain and the continent, offering a whole new dimension to visitors wishing to explore France by train. Very soon direct trains will be leaving London not just for Paris but for the Mediterranean beaches of the Côte d'Azur, the ski resorts of the French Alps and the Pyrenees. Never before has visiting France been so simple. And as roads become ever more congested never has it been more attractive to travel by train. With the most efficient, modern and extensive rail network in Europe, France is the natural country to explore by train.

There are many excellent reasons for leaving the car behind and exploring France by train. Instead of having to concentrate on the road, it is possible to look at the landscape instead. After all, the point of traveling around a country is to see it – not to be constantly worrying about such alarming French road procedures as *priorité à droite*. Traveling by train you do not have the dilemma of where to park or have to puzzle out parking restrictions. Nor do you run the risk of coming back to find that your car has been towed away for some parking infringement you were unaware of – or that it has been broken into. And because the railways were built in the 19th century when French towns were much smaller, train stations are virtually always close to the centre of cities and towns are within easy walking distance of the most interesting sites.

Before You Go

Climate
Though France is hospitable most of the year, there are some dramatic regional and seasonal variations, with the north some 20 degrees centigrade cooler in the summer than the Mediterranean coast. July and August are the hottest months when the average daily maximum temperature reaches 84°F on the southern coast. Paris in summer is often only a little cooler, at 80°F. Western and northern France are

usually much cooler, with an average daily maximum in July and August of 72°F at Boulogne and 70°F at Brest in Brittany. Humidity in cities can also be unpleasant in late spring and early autumn. Mountain regions are cooler in summer and the Massif Central, the Auvergne, the Pyrenees and the Alps are generally cooler than other parts of France. The worst of the heat can be avoided by traveling in the morning and reserving the afternoons for sight-seeing, drinks in cafés, swimming or siestas. Persistent rain in summer is rare but powerful thunderstorms can affect all areas. These, however, are generally short-lived. As in England, however, the weather is difficult to predict and the summer months can pass without a drop of rain. In winter the Riviera has a milder climate than most of France, but winter is not really a season to visit; the towns can have a deserted feel and the temperature is not conducive to sunbathing on the long, sandy beaches.

Apart from the high Alps and Pyrenees, where abundant snowfall provides for skiers, few towns or areas have an average daily minimum for January more than one or two degrees below freezing. Winter is short-lived, except in the Alps and Pyrenees, where snow can fall from as early as the beginning of October. The winter ski season runs from late November to March.

When to go

Bearing in mind the crowds and the weather, the ideal time to vist France is around April – June and September – October. Other spring and autumn months are often fine but can be wet or surprisingly cold. From April to June mild weather is certain everywhere, except for the occasional shower. This is perhaps the ideal time to be on the Mediterranean before the crowds arrive. June to September is perfect weather in the north of France and the best time to be on the coast, except for the Côte d'Azur, which is then packed with tourists, French and foreign alike.

July is perfect weather in the mountains but August can be stormy. Crowds are at their worst, and the trains busiest, during July and August, months when the main tourist cities seem to be inhabited almost entirely by visitors. July and, even more so, August are the main holiday months for the French, who depart from Paris and the other big towns to the beaches on the coasts or to their families in the countryside. These are the months when the death-toll on the roads jumps up faster than the temperature – not something the train traveler has to contend with. In August the departure of millions of inhabitants gives the cities a different feel – it's quieter and slower, despite the influx of foreign visitors.

From September to November, the days are often summery. Forests are clothed in golden autumnal colors and wild-game hunting begins in Eastern France. Beajolais Nouveau arrives to cheer people up in the autumn. Then comes winter, and from December to March the ski runs of the Alps are open for winter sports.

Passports and Visas

U.S. citizens need a passport to enter France; a visa is not necessary for stays of up to 90 days. For further informatnio, contact the Embassy of France (4101 Reservoir Rd., NW, Washington, DC 20007, tel. 202/944–6000).

You can pick up new and renewal passport application forms at any of the 13

U.S. Passport Agency offices and at home post offices and courthouses. Although passports are usually mailed within two weeks of your application's receipt, it's best to allow three weeks for delivery in low season, five weeks or more from April through summer. Call the Department of State Office of Passport Services' information line (1425 K St. NW, Washington, DC 20522, tel. 202/647–0518) for fees, documentation requirements, and other details.

Canadian citizens need a valid passport to enter France. Application forms are available at 23 regional passport offices as well as post offices and travel agencies. Whether applying for a first or subsequent passport, you must apply in person. Children under 16 may be included on a parent's passport but must have their own passport to travel alone. Passports are valid for five years and usually mailed within two weeks of an application's receipt. For fees, documentation requirements, and other information in English or French, call the passport office (tel. 514/283–2152).

If your passport is lost or stolen abroad, report it immediately to the nearest embassy or consulate and to the local police. If you can provide the consular officer with the information contained in the passport, they will usually be able to issue you a new passport. For this reason, it is a good idea to keep a copy of the data page of your passport in a separate place, or to leave the passport number, date, and place off issuance with a relative or friend at home.

Customs

There are two levels of duty-free allowance for travelers entering France: one for goods obtained (tax paid) within another European Community (EC) country and the other for goods obtained anywhere outside the EC or for goods purchased in a duty-free shop within the EC.

In the first category, you may import duty-free: 300 cigarettes or 150 cigarillos or 75 cigars or 400 grams of tobacco; five liters of table wine and (1) 1½ liters of alcohol over 22% volume (most spirits), (2) three liters of alcohol under 22% by volume (fortified or sparkling wine), or (3) three more liters of table wine; 90 milliliters of perfume; 375 milliliters of toilet water; and other goods to the value of 2,400 francs (620 francs for those under 15).

In the second category, you may import duty-free: 200 cigarettes or 100 cigarillos or 50 cigars or 250 grams of tabacco (these allowances are doubled if you live outside Europe); two liters of wine and (1) one liter of alcohol over 22% volume (most spirits), (2) two liters of alcohol under 22% volume (fortified or sparkling wine), or (3) two more liters of table wine; 60 milliliters of perfume; 250 milliliters of toilet water; and other goods to the value of 300 france (150 francs for those under 15).

Provided you've been out of the coutry for at least 48 hours and haven't already used the exemption, or any part of it, in the past 30 days, you may bring home $400 worth of foreign goods duty-free. So can each members of your family, regardless of age; and your exemptions may be pooled, so one of you can bring in more if another brings in less. A flat 10% duty applies to the next $1,000 of goods; above $1,400, the rate varies with the merchandise. (If the 48-hour or 30-day limits apply, your duty-free allowance drops to $25, which may not be pooled.) Please note that these are the *general* rules, applicable to most countries, including France.

Travelers 21 or older may bring back 1 liter of alcohol duty-free, provided the beverage laws of the state through which they reenter the United States allow it. In addition, 100 non-Cuban cigars and 200 cigarettes are allowed, regardless of your age. Antiques and works of art more than 100 years old are duty-free.

Gifts valued at less than $50 may be mailed duty-free to stateside friends and relatives, with a limit of one package per day per addressee (do not send alcohol or tobacco products, nor perfume valued at more than $5). These gifts do not count as part of your exemption, unless you bring them home with you. Mark the package 'Unsolicited Gift' and include the nature of the gift and its retail value.

For a copy of 'Know Before You Go,' a free brochure detailing what you may and may not bring back to the United States, rates of suty, and other pointers, contact the U.S. Customs Service (Box 7407, Washington, DC 20044, tel. 202/927–6724).

Money

In the main tourist destinations – Paris, Nice, Cannes, Strasbourg – costs can be higher for accommodation and food than in provincial towns, but costs vary little outside the large cities. Food is marginally cheaper in the south, especially fruit and vegetables. The cheapest possible budget for an economical backpacker, occasionally sleeping in cheap hotels and occasionally camping and buying food from shops and markets would be around $25 per day. A more realistic daily budget, allowing for eating out once a day and staying in an average one- or two-star hotel, would be in the region of $45 – $60 per day (excluding train fares). Staying in comfortable two- or three-star hotels and eating out at good and typical local restaurants would require a budget of $55 – $80 a day.

Currency The French unit of currency is the franc (plural francs), which is itself divided into 100 centimes. The rate of exchange at press time was around 5.6 FF to the US dollar. Notes come in denominations of 20FF, 50FF, 100FF, 200FF and 500FF, coins as 10FF, 5FF, 2FF, 1FF, 50 centimes, 20 centimes, 10 centimes and 5 centimes.

Cash and Traveler's Checks Try to carry some French francs with you for emergencies, delays, closed banks and other unforseen circumstances. To avoid lines at airport currency-exchange booths, arrive in France with some francs in your pocket. Thomas Cook Currency Serice (630 Fifth Ave., New York, NY 10111, tel. 212/757–6915) supplies foreign currency by mail.

The most widely recognized are **American Express, Barclay's, Thomas Cook,** and those issued by major commercial banks such as **Citibank** and **Bank of America.** American Express also issues *Traveler's Cheques for Two,* which can be signed and used by you or your traveling companion. Some checks are free; usually the issuing company or the bank at which you make your purchase charges 1% of the checks' face value as free. Be sure to buy a few checks in small denominations to cash toward the end of your trip, when you don't want to be left with more foreign currency than you can spend. Always record the numbers of checks as you spend them, and keep this list separate from the checks.

Banks and bank-operated exchange booths at airports and railroad stations are usually the best places to exchange money. Hotels, stores, and privately run exchange firms typically offer less favorable rates.

Before your trip, pay attention to how the dollar is doing vis-à-vis French currency. If the dollar is losing strength, try to pay as many travel bills as possible in advance, especially the big ones. If it is getting stronger, pay for costly items overseas, and use your credit card whenever possible – you'll come out ahead, whether the exchange rate at which your purchase is calculated is the one in effect the day the vendor's bank abroad processes the charge, or the one prevailing on the day the charge company's service center processes it at home.

Credit Cards Credit cards are widely accepted in shops, hotels and restaurants, especially American Express, Visa, Diners Club and MasterCard. Some credit cards are also accepted at highway restaurants, many gas stations and some supermarkets. When paying by credit card, check the amount which appears on the receipt: in France, no decimal point is shown between francs and centimes.

Nearly 800 banks in France marked with the sign CB/VISA ou EC will allow you to withdraw money from a cash-dispenser with a Visa or American Express card. Visa cash machines are also widespread in France, and American Express cards can be used in automated teller machines at Crédit Lyonnais banks. Credit cards are useful in an emergency – for a sudden ticket home or unexpected hospital bill – which may leave one without access to other sources of money. Some credit cards offer other useful services, ranging from insurance to emergency assistance. American Express cardholders can cash up to US $1000 in personal checks at any American Express office in France.

Banks Banks often offer the best rates of exchange but usually charge a commission, which can be as much as $3 per exchange. Large local or national banks, such as Crédit Agricole or Crédit Lyonnais, have decent rates and charge the smallest commission. Avoid exchanging money at hotels, airports, restaurants or tourist offices: their rates are usually considerably worse than those of banks or currency exchange bureaus. Banks are open only on weekdays, usually 9 am–12 noon and 2–4 pm; make sure you have enough cash to get you through the weekend, especially in areas off the beaten track. Many banks are closed on Mondays and early on the day before a bank holiday.

Check the rate at several banks, as the commission varies as well as the rate. The service is usually fast and efficient; remember that your passport will be required if you are cashing traveler's checks. Traveler's checks in French francs purchased in your home country are clearly the simplest option, but checks in dollars are equally widely accepted.

In large cities, the main post office usually exchanges foreign currency. 'Change' is the sign to be on the lookout for in banks and on the streets. Outside banking hours, large city railway stations often have exchange facilities open at weekends and in the evening, but at poorer rates. Airport exchange bureaus are the place of last resort, generally having the worst possible rates.

Health and Insurance

First aid, medical advice and night service are all available from pharmacies, recognizable by their green cross. French pharmacists are well-trained, able to diagnose many minor problems and able to sell a wide range of medicines over the counter, including many for which a prescription would be needed at home. They are usually open on a rotation system, so if one is closed the address of the nearest one will be posted in the window. The *pharmacie de garde* is also noted in the local newspapers.

Minor, first-aid problems are usually dealt with free and promptly at the local public hospital (*l'hôpital*); head for the emergency room (*le service des urgences*). American, Canadian and British embassies and consulates can also help you to find English-speaking doctors.

For more serious medical complaints find the local doctor (*le médecin*) in the nearest village or town. The French have a reputation for being a nation of hypochondriacs so doctors are thick on the ground. Faith in conventional medicine is strong while less interest has been shown in France in homoeopathic and alternative medicine. Even quite small villages have their local doctor. The doctor's surgery is *le cabinet de consultation*; his surgery hours are *heures de consultations*. Most doctors have a basic grasp of English and some speak it excellently.

Most tour operators, travel agents, and insurance agents sell specialized health-and-accident, flight, trip-cancellation, and luggage insurance as well as comprehensive policies with some or all of these features. But before you make any purchase, review your existing helath and homeowner policies to find out whether they cover expenses incurred while traveling.

Disabled Travelers   The French Tourist Board issues free handbooks and guides to travelers with disabilities but these cannot always be relied upon for accuracy, not being compiled by people with disabilities. All TGV trains have been built to accommodate wheelchairs, and guide dogs accompany blind people free of charge. Other trains have a special compartment and a lift for boarding, but it is advisable to write to the railway station you are heading to for further information before traveling. In the Paris metro, seats are reserved for the disabled but some stations have stairs rather than escalators or elevators. A number of stations on the RER system in Paris have elevators or ramps allowing easy access to the platforms. Otherwise, station staff are likely to help as best they can. Contact the **Comité Nationale Français de Liaison pour la Réadaptation des Handicapés** (38 blvd Raspail, 75007 Paris, tel. 45–48–90–13); the **Association des Paralysés de France** (17 blvd. Auguste-Blanqui, 75013 Paris, tel. 40–78–69–00), which publishes a useful Paris hotel list.

Information and Maps

Before you travel to France, visit or write to the **French Government Tourist Office**, 610 Fifth Ave., New York, NY 10020 (tel. 212/315–0888); 645 N. Michigan Ave., Chicago, IL 60611 (tel. 312/751–7804); 2305 Cedar Springs Rd., Dallas, TX 75201 (tel. 214/720–4010); 9454 Wilshire Blvd., Suite 303, Beverly Hills, CA 90212 (tel. 310/271–2358); 1981 McGill College, Suite 490, Montreal, Quebec H3A 2W9 (tel. 514/288–4264); 30 St. Patrick St., Suite 700, Toronto,Ontario M5T 3A3 (tel. 416/593–4723). In France itself, virtually every town of any size has a tourist office, known either as *le syndicat d'initiative* or *l'office de tourisme*. In fact there are over 5,000 of them in France, many of them brimming with information on accommodation, restaurants, entertainment and local transport. They are especially useful for the train traveler wishing to make the occasional bus excursion to nearby châteaux and vineyards that may not be accessible by train. In the text below the address and telephone number of each local tourist office is given in the **Practicalities** section. More detail on the services provided by tourist offices is given under **Sleeping**.

In Paris, the main tourist office is at 127 Champs-Elysées, in the 8th arrondissement. (Open daily 9 am–8 pm). Tourist offices in Paris' main railway stations are open daily except Sundays and bank holidays, from 9 am–8 pm (8 am–9 pm between Easter and October 31).

Maps of the train routes in this book are good for basic planning but it's worth carrying a general map of France as well. Michelin produce a whole range of maps including a series of detailed regional ones in the *yellow* series, with a scale of 1:200,000. These are excellent if you're visiting not more than 2 or 3 regions, otherwise, they begin to become too bulky. Hallwag produce a single-sheet map of France which marks the train lines clearly, on a scale of 1:1,000,000. The Institut Géographique National, or IGN, produces various series of maps of excellent quality and legibility. *IGN 901* is a general road map to France, while the *IGN Topo guides* and *IGN Red regional maps* are the best for walking tours, covering 40,000 km of long-distance footpaths. IGN also produces the more detailed *Green* series. Some tourist offices, notably of the larger towns and cities, provide useful town and city plans, and some have reasonable free regional maps as well. Some SNCF timetables have a good map of the French railway network which marks virtually all the lines and all the main stations. Plans of Paris and a Paris atlas are published by Lascelles and available from Stanfords and other bookshops.

Getting to France

By Air from the United States

Since the air routes between North America and France are among the world's most heavily traveled, passengers can choose from many different airlines and fares. But fares change with stunning rapidity, so consult your travel agent on which bargains are currently available.

Flights are either nonstop, direct, or connecting. A **nonstop** flight requires no change of plane and makes no stops. A **direct** flight stops at least once and can involve a change of plane, although the flight number remains the same; if the first leg is late, the second waits. This is not the case with a **connecting** flight, which involves a different plane and a different flight number.

The U.S. airlines that serve France are **TWA** (tel. 800/892–4141), **American Airlines** (tel. 800/433–7300), **Delta** (tel. 800/241–4141), **United Airlines** (tel. 800/241–6522), and **Continental** (tel. 800/231–0856), and **USAir** (tel. 800/428–4322). American and Continental fly to Paris's Orly Airport (tel. 49–75–52–52), the others to Charles de Gaulle (Roissy) Airport (tel. 48–62–22–80).

The flying time to Paris from New York is 7½ hours; from Chicago, 9 hours; from Los Angeles, 11 hours.

The Sunday travel section of most newspapers is a good source of deals. When booking, particularly through an unfamiliar company, call the Better Business Bureau to find out whether any complaints have been registered against the company, pay with a credit card if you can, and consider trip-cancellation and default insurance.

All the less expensive fares, called promotional or discount fares, are round-trip and involve restrictions. The exact nature of the restrictions depends on the airline, the route, and the season and on whether travel is domestic or international, but you must usually buy the ticket – commonly called an APEX (advance purchase excursion) when it's for international travel – in advance (seven, 14, or 21 days are usual). You must also respect certain minimum- and maximum-stay requirements (for instance, over a Saturday night or at least seven and no more than 30, 45, or 90 days), and you must be willing to pay penalties for changes. Airlines generally allow some changes for a fee. But the cheaper the fare, the more likely the ticket is nonrefundable; it would take a death in the family for the airline to give you any of your money back if you had to cancel. The cheapest fares are also subject to availability; because only a certain percentage of the plane's total seats will be sold at that price, they may go quickly.

Consolidators or bulk-fare operators – also known as bucket shops – buy blocks of seats on scheduled flights that airlines anticipate they won't be able to sell. They pay wholesale prices, add a markup, and resell the seats to travel agents or directly to the public at prices that still undercut the airline's promotional or discount fares. You pay more than on a charter but ordinarily less than for an APEX ticket, and, even when there is not much of a price difference, the ticket usually comes without the advance-purchase restriction. Moreover, although tickets are marked nonrefundable so you can't turn them in to the airline for a full-fare refund, some consolidators sometimes give you your money back. Carefully read the fine print detailing penalities and charges for cancellations. If you doubt the reliability of a company, call the airline once you've made your booking and confirm that you do, indeed, have a reservation on the flight.

The biggest U.S. consolidator, C. L. Thomson Express, sells only to travel agents. Well-established consolidators selling to the public include UniTravel (Box 12485, St. Louis, MO 63132, tel. 314/569–0900 or 800/325–2222); Council Charter

(205 E. 42nd St., New York, NY 10017, tel. 212/661–0311 or 800/800–8222), a division of the Council on International Educational Exchange and a longtime charter operator now functioning more as a consolidator; and Travac (989 6th Ave., New York, NY 10018, tel. 212/563–3303 or 800/872–8800), also a former charterer.

Charters usually have the lowest fares and the most restrictions. Departures are limited and seldom on time, and you can lose all or most of your money if you cancel. (Generally, the closer to departure you cancel, the more you lose, although sometimes you will be charged only a small fee if you supply a substitute passenger.) The charterer, on the other hand, may legally cancel the flight for any reason up to 10 days before departure; within 10 days of departure, the flight may be cancelled only if it becomes physically impossible to operate it. The charterer may also revise the itinerary or increase the price after you have bought the ticket, but if the new arrangement constitutes a 'major change,' you have the right to a refund. Before buying a charter ticket, read the fine print for the company's refund policy and details on major changes. Money for charter flights is usually paid into a bank escrow account, the name of which should be on the contract. If you don't pay by credit card, make your check payable to the escrow account (unless your dealing with a travel agent, in which case, his or her check should be payable to the escrow account). The Department of Transportation's Consumer Affairs Office (I–25, Washington, DC 20590, tel. 202/366–2220) can answer questions on charters and send you its 'Plane Talk: Public Charter Flights' information sheet.

Charter operators may offer flights alone or with ground arrangements that constitute a charter package. Well-established charter operators include Council Charter (205 E. 42nd St., New York, NY 10017, tel. 212/661–0311 or 800/800–8222), now largely a consolidator, despite its name, and Travel Charter (1120 E. Long Lake Rd., Troy, MI 48098, tel. 313/528–3570 or 800/521–5267), with Midwestern departures. DER Tours (Box 1606, Des Plains, IL 60017, tel. 800/782–2424), a charterer and consolidator, sell through travel agents.

Travel clubs offer their members unsold space on airplanes, cruise ships, and package tours at nearly the last minute and at well below the original cost. Suppliers thus receive some revenue for their 'leftovers,' and members get a bargain. Membership generally includes a regular bulletin or access to a toll-free telephone hot line giving details of available trips departing anywhere from three or four days to several months in the future. Packages tend to be more common than flights alone, so if airfares are your only interest, read the literature before joining. Reductions on hotels are also available. Clubs include Discount Travel International (114 Forrest Ave., Suite 203, Narberth, PA 19072, tel. 215/668–7184; $45 annually, single or family), Moment's Notice (425 Madison Ave., New York, NY 10017, tel. 212/486–0503; $45 annually, single or family), Travelers Advantage (CUC Travel Service, 49 Music Sq. W, Nashville, TN 37203, tel. 800/548–1116; $49 annually, single or family), and Worldwide Discount Travel Club (1674 Meridian Ave., Miami Beach, FL 33139, tel. 305/534–2082; $50 annually for family, $40 single).

By Train from the United Kingdom

After 2 centuries of dreaming and 6 years of tunnelling, the world's longest tunnel and most expensive engineering project, the Channel Tunnel, opened in 1994 revolutionizing travel to the Continent at a stroke and making train travel around France and Britain an even more attractive proposition. Nothing could be easier than stepping on to the train at Waterloo and stepping out at Paris Gare du Nord.

Not only does the Channel Tunnel revolutionise travel to Paris but also to countless other destinations in France. Over 5 hours have been cut off the time previously required to travel between the 2 capitals, eliminating the need to transfer on to and off ferries and trains. Direct **London–Paris** trains depart from the sophisticated new international station at Waterloo.

The **Channel Tunnel** – the Chunnel – consists of 3 separate tunnels: 2 single-tracked rail tunnels with a service tunnel between them, each 50km (31 miles) long. Eurotunnel trains, called *le Shuttle*, carry passengers and vehicles from Folkestone to Calais at speeds of up to 160k mph (100 mph) while Eurostar operates the London–Paris service. The time spent actually under the Channel between the Folkestone and Calais terminals is a mere 26 minutes, dropping to only 21 minutes for the faster London–Paris trains. Terminals with toll booths, frontier controls, shops and other facilities are located at Folkestone and Calais.

Eurostar Eurostar is the brand name for the daytime high-speed service between London Waterloo International and Paris Nord. By 1996 Eurostar is expected to carry around 15 million passengers a year, and 19–23 million by the year 2000.

To put these figures in perspective, about 3 million seats per year are currently being flown between London and Paris. Market research has shown that travelers from Britain to Paris will increasingly choose to travel by train to Paris to avoid the inherent hassle associated with air travel. The same research shows that the Channel Tunnel will win not just take a significant share of the existing market from air but will also generate a large segment of new travel by people who will use the service simply because it is there. Assuming that the Great Western and Midland main lines were electrified, it is very likely that direct services will be operated by the end of the decade to such cities as Bristol, Reading, Swindon, Cardiff and Leicester.

Departure Times: Day Services For Paris Trains leaving from Waterloo International for Paris Gare du Nord are scheduled to depart hourly at 23 minutes past the hour, with the first train leaving at 6.23 am and the last one at 7.23 pm. From Paris Nord departure times are scheduled to be at 13 minutes past the hour, with hourly departures, the first train leaving at 7.13 am and the last at 8.13 pm. One question – as yet unresolved – is the issue of clock harmonization with the rest of Europe. The British Government has been considering eliminating the one-hour time difference which persists between Britain and the rest of Europe for the greater part of the year.

The difference between British and mainland Europe daytime saving inevitably distorts the arrival times which are given in 'local' times. Services between Waterloo International and Paris Nord – and those trains from points North of London – will make selected stops at Ashford or Lille-Europe in northern France.

The entire North-of-London service is based on outward departures from Britain in the morning with return services from Paris in the afternoon. Approximate departure time from Edinburgh to Paris-Nord is 8.20 am, arriving at Paris Nord at 5.35 pm; departing from Paris at 2.40 pm and arriving at Edinburgh at 10.24 pm.

Other French Destinations Initially, direct services from Britain to France will only be to Paris Nord and to Lille. Soon however, with just one change at Lille-Europe, it will be possible to go from London to Lyon by train in 5 hours, and to Marseille, Nantes and Bordeaux in 6 hours.

From 1994 a new high-speed rail link in northern France allows TGVs from Northern France to bypass Paris and run to points on the south-east and Atlantic TGV lines. A new fleet of trains – TGV Réseau – has been built to link Lille-Europe with important centers such as Lyon, Marseille, Nice, Bordeaux, Nantes and Rennes.

Night Departures: European Night Services With trains taking only 3 hours from London to Paris, there is no need for night trains between the 2 capitals. Night trains, however, will be of particular interest for travelers from Scotland, with departures, from 1995, from Glasgow and Edinburgh. Night departures will probably also leave from Swansea, Cardiff, Bristol and Plymouth. Sleeping cars will have cabins of two types, one with WC, washing facilities and showers, the other without shower facilities.

Prices Prices are calculated on the basis of different demands according to the time of day, week and year. The price for a 1st class ticket on a prime morning business service from Waterloo International to Paris is the highest charged and is around the level of a competitive airline ticket. At the other end of the scale, 2 senior citizens traveling at mid-day, mid-week in mid-November are able to travel 1st class at very competitive prices. 1st class fares include a full meal service and all drinks. As with air travel, the cheaper the fares the more restrictive the choice of journey. To travel the cheapest way, the date and time of outward and return journeys are decided on and fixed at the time the reservation is made.

On-Board Service and Facilities All staff on board Eurostar trains to Paris – British, French or Belgian – speak at least 2 languages. Full meals are included with the 1st class ticket and are served to passengers at their seats. There is a bar and trolley service for 2nd class passengers on a cash basis. Payment is accepted in British, French or Belgian currency. Computer-displayed information panels give details of departure times, destination, carriage number and so on. Facilities are provided for parents with infants and areas are reserved for families and passengers with disabilities.

Taking Your Car Those taking their car to France will pay at the Eurotunnel booth at Folkestone, pass through the British customs check, then through France's customs check before their vehicle is loaded on to the shuttle train. Once on the French side therefore there are no checks – motorists simply drive away, thus avoiding congestion and delay.

By Train via Folkestone, Dover and Newhaven

The standard route from London to Paris by train, which continues to operate, is from London Victoria to Paris Gare du Nord, via one of the Channel ports, the most common crossing being from Dover to Calais. Evening departures leave at around 8.40 pm from Victoria and bring travelers into Paris Gare du Nord via New Heaven and Dieppe at Jam the following day. Such a journey however involves climbing on to the ferry at around midnight, and disembarking from the ferry and climbing on to a French train at about 3 in the morning – not the most attractive proposition. A more attractive alternative is to leave early in the morning from Victoria and arrive at Paris in the late afternoon or early evening.

Three different routes are currently available (1994):

(1) The fastest: via Folkestone and Boulogne, traveling by SeaCat. 2 departures daily from Victoria (6½ hours). $90 ordinary single, $135 return, valid for 2 months.

(2) Via Dover and Calais, traveling by ferry. 3 departures daily in summer, 2 in winter from Victoria (8½ hours). $66 ordinary single (discount fare for those under 26), $128 return, valid for 2 months.

(3) Via Newhaven and Dieppe, traveling by ferry. 2 departures daily in summer from Victoria (10 hours). $71 ordinary single, $105 return, valid for 2 months.

Information, departure times, tickets and reservations available from **British Rail International,** *Platform 2, Victoria Station, London SWIV 1JY (Tel. 071 834 2345). For advance booking Mon–Fri 8 am–6 pm, Sat 8 am–4 pm. Closed Sundays. For some day travel, open 7 days a week, 7 am–10 pm.*

By Train from the Continent

Cities like Brussels, Rome, Frankfurt, Geneva, and Madrid have regular daily services to Paris, as well as regular night trains with couchette and sleeper accommodations. Use the *Thomas Cook European Timetable* to plan routes to France from more obscure towns. There are, for instance, 17 through departures from France to Italy, 7 of them from Paris (to Rome, Milan, Florence, Turin, Brindisi and towns in between).

From Paris **Gare du Nord**, direct trains lead to Belgium (Brussels), the Netherlands (Amsterdam), Scandinavia, the Commonwealth of Independent States (Moscow), Denmark (Copenhagen) and northern Germany (Cologne, Hamburg). The **Gare de l'Est** sends out direct trains to Switzerland (Basel, Zurich, Lucerne), southern Germany (Munich) and Austria (Vienna); the **Gare de Lyon** to Switzerland (Geneva, Lausanne, Berne) and Italy (Venice, Florence, Rome, Genoa); and the **Gare d'Austerlitz** to Spain (Barcelona, Madrid) and Portugal.

By Air from the United Kingdom

Even if you are on a train holiday, you may want to maximize your time by flying to France before boarding a train, especially if you are heading to the extreme south. Charter deals are about comparable with standard 2nd class rail fares from London but cheaper than traveling on trains through the Channel Tunnel.

France's 2 national carriers, Air France and SNCF have got together to offer a bargain price ticket which combines the speed of air travel with the flexibility of the train. Under this scheme it's possible to fly direct from one of 7 airports in Great Britain and Ireland to Paris, and then continue your journey by train to any of the 3,000 stations in France, all for a highly competitive, inclusive fare.

For Air-France Rail tickets and information, once you're in Britain, contact **French Railways**, *179 Piccadilly, London W1V OBA (*Tel. 081 571 1413*)*.

Scheduled Flights In summer British Airways and Air France between them fly direct from London Heathrow to Paris, Bordeaux, Nice, Marseille, Toulouse, Lyon, Nantes and Strasbourg. British Airwyas also flies from Birmingham and Manchester to Paris and Nice. Both Air France and British Airways fly from Edinburgh and Glasgow to Paris. Air France also has flights to Paris from Bristol, Gatwick, Southampton and Stanstead. If you have a fixed schedule the cheapest ticket is an APEX return fare. Its conditions require that you make a reservation and pay at the same time, book at least 14 days in advance, spend a Saturday night abroad, and that you specify precise departure and return dates. Occasionally you can find cheaper flights on other airlines making stop-overs at Paris on the way to Asia, Africa or the Middle East.

By Ferry from the United Kingdom

Ferries are a slow way of getting to France but can be a wonderful experience in their own right, especially in summer on a fine day. All ferry crossings arrive in ports connected to the French rail network, and the Channel ports have quick connections with Paris.

P & O European Ferries (Channel House, Channel View Road, Dover, CT16 3BR, Tel. 0304 203388) have several Dover – Calais daily departures: every 45 minutes in winter and every 75 minutes in summer. Faster crossings are provided by hovercraft by **Hoverspeed** (Eastern Docks, Dover, CT17 9TG, Tel. 0304 240241): 12 departures daily from Dover – Calais (35 minutes) in summer. Hovercraft by **Sea-Cat** (for booking Tel. 0304 204241) have 6 Folkestone – Boulogne daily departures (55 minutes). **Sealink Stena Line** (Charter House, Park Street, Ashford, TN24 8EX, Tel. 02333 647047) also run ferries: 20 daily departures on the Dover – Calais route (90 minutes); 1 – 3 daily departures in summer from Southampton – Cherbourg (5 – 8 hours); and 4 daily departures from Newhaven – Dieppe (4 hours).

Routes avoiding Paris include **Brittany Ferries** services direct from Portsmouth to Caen (6 hours) and **St-Malo** (9 hours) and from Poole to Cherbourg (4 hours 30 mins), all very convenient destinations from which to begin exploring Normandy by train. They also operate a ferry from Plymouth to Roscoff (6 hours), an ideal jumping-off point for exploring Brittany. P & O also have 3 ferries daily all year from Portsmouth to **Le Havre** (5 hours 45 mins) and 2–3 ferries daily (April–Oct) to Cherbourg (4 hours 45 mins), both excellent destinations for the start of a Normandy tour.

Tickets and Rail Passes

Buying a rail pass can same you money if you plan to do a lot of traveling by train. The French Flexipass allows you unlimited train travel on any four days within a one-month period; cost is $175 in first class, $125 in second. The France Rail 'n' Drive Pass buys you three days of unlimited train travel and three days use of an Avis car within a one-month period; cost is $189 in first class, $149 in second class, with up to six additional days' use of the car available at $35 per day. With both passes, you can buy up to six additional days of train travel for $40 a day in first class, $29 a day in second class. The BritFrance Rail Pass covers both France and Britain (and Hovercraft Channel crossings); cost for unlimited travel on any 5 days of a 15 day period is $359 in first class, $269 in second class; $539 and $409 for any 10 days in a 30-day period. All these passes must be purchased stateside and are sold by travel agents as well as Rail Europe (226–230 Westchester Ave., White Plains, NY 10604, tel. 914/682–5172 or 800/438–7245 from the East, 800/848–724 from the West).

France is also one of the 17 countries in which you can use EurailPasses, which provide unlimited first-class rail travel during their period of validity. If you plan to rack up the miles, they can be an excellent value. Standard passes are available for 15 days ($460), 21 days ($598), one month ($728), two months ($998), and three months ($1,260). Eurail Saverpasses, valid for 15 days, cost $390 per person; you must do all your traveling with at least one companion (two companions from April through September). Eurail Youthpasses, which cover second-class travel, cost $508 for one month, $698 for two; you must be under 26 on the first day you travel. Flexipasses allow you to travel for five, 10, or 15 days within any two-month period. You pay $298, $496, and $676 for the Eurail Flexipass, sold for first-class travel; and $220, $348, $474 for the Eurail Youth Flexipass, available to those under 26 on their first travel day, sold for second-class travel. Apply through your travel agent, or Rail Europe (226–230 Westchester Ave., White Plains, NY 10604, tel. 914/682–5172 or 800/438–7245 from the East and 800/848–7245 from the West).

Don't make the mistake of assuming that your rail pass guarantees you seats on the trains you want to ride. Seat reservations are required on some trains, particularly high-speed trains, and are a good idea on trains that may be crowded. You will also need reservations for overnight sleeping accomodations. Rail Europe can help you determine if you need reservations and can make them for you (about $10 each, less if you purchase them in Europe at the time of travel).

France's SNCF is generally recognized as Europe's best national train service: It's fast, punctual, comfortable, and comprehensive. The high-speed TGVs, or *Train à Grande Vitesse* (average 255 kph/160 mph on the Lyon/southeast line, 300 kph/190mph on the Bordeaux/southwest line), are the best domestic trains, operating between Paris and Lyon/Switzerland/the Riviera, and Agers/Nantes and Tours/Poiters/Bordeaux. As with other main-line trains, a small supplement may be assessed at peak hours. Unlike other trains, the TGV *always* requires a seat reservation – easily obtained at the ticket window or from an automatic machine. Seat reservations are reassuring but seldom necessary on other main-line French trains, except at certain busy holiday times.

If you are traveling from Paris (or any other station terminus), get to the station half an hour before departure to ensure that you'll have a good seat. The majority of intercity trains in France consist of open-plan cars and are known as *Corail* trains. They are clean and extremely comfortable, even in second class. Trains on regional branch lines are currently being spruced up but lag behind in style and quality. The food in French trains can be good, but it's poor value for the money.

It is possible to get from one end of France to the other without traveling overnight. Otherwise you have the choice between high-priced *wagons-lits* (sleeping cars) and affordable *couchettes* (bunks, six to a compartment, with sheet and pillow provided, priced at around 80 francs). Special summer night trains from Paris to Spain and the Riviera, geared to younger people, are equipped with disco and bar.

Various reduced fares schemes are available. Senior citizens (over 60) and young people (under 26) are eligible for the Carte Vermeil (165 francs)and Carrissimo (190 francs for four trips, 350 for eight) respectively, wth proof of identity and two passport photos. The SNCF offers 50% reductions during 'blue' periods (most of the time) and 20% the rest of the time ('white' periods: noon Friday through noon Saturday; 3 PM Sunday through noon Monday). On major holidays ('red' periods), there are no reductions. Every station can give you a calendar of red/white/blue periods and sell you the appropriate tickets. Note that there is no reduction for buying a round-trip (*aller-retour*) ticket rather than a one-way (*aller simple*) ticket.

Student and Youth Travel

For students, France holds special allure, particularly Paris. During the summer, young people from all over Europe congregate in the French capital. During the school year, students dominate the Left Bank. Cheap food and lodging is easy to find throughout the country, so there's little need to scrounge. In addition, there are student bargains almost everywhere, on train and plane fares, and for movie and museum tickets. All you need is an International Student Identity Card (*see below*).

The foremost U.S. student travel agency is Council Travel, a subsidiary of the nonprofit Council on International Educational Exchange. It specializes in low-cost travel arrangements, is the exclusive U.S. agent for several discount cards, and, with its sister CIEE subsidiary, Council Charter, is a source of airfare bargains. The Council Charter brochure and CIEE's twice-yearly *Student Travels* magazine, which details its programs, are available at the Council Travel office at CIEE headquarters (205 E. 42nd Street, New York, NY 10017, tel. 212/661–1450) and at 37 branches in college towns nationwide (free in person, $1 by mail). The Educational Travel Center (ETC, 438 N. Francis St., Madison, WI 53703, tel. 608/256–5551) also offers low-cost rail passes, domestic and international airline tickets (mostly for flights departing from Chicago), and other budgetwise travel arrangements. Other travel agencies catering to students include Travel Management International (TMI, 18 Prescott St., Suite 4, Cambridge, MA 02138, tel. 617/661–8187) and Travel Cuts (187 College St., Toronto, Ont. M5T 1P7, tel. 416/979–2406).

For discounts on transportation and on museum and attractions admissions, buy the International Student Identity Card (ISIC) if you're a bona fide student, or the International Youth Card (IYC) if you're under 26. In the United States the ISIC and IYC cards cost $15 each and include basic travel accident and sickness coverage. Apply to CIEE (*see* address *above*, tel. 212/661–1414; the application is in *Student Travels*). In Canada the cards are available for $15 each from Travel Cuts (*see above*). In the United Kingdom they cost £5 and £4 respectively at student unions and student travel companies, including Council Travel's London office (28A Poland St., London W1V 3DB, tel. 071/437–7767).

Traveling with Cameras, Camcorders, and Laptops

Buy your film and camera in the U.S. as prices are about half of those in France. If your camera is new or if you haven't used it for a while, shoot and develop a few rolls of film before leaving home. Pack some lens tissue and an extra battery for your built-in light meter, and invest in an inexpensive skylight filter, to both protect your lens and provide some definition in hazy shots. Store film in a cool, dry place – never in the car's glove compartment or on the shelf under the rear window.

Flims above ISO 400 are more sensitive to damage from airport security X-rays than others; very high speed films, ISO 1,000 and above, are exceedingly vulnerable. To protect your film, don't put it in checked luggage; carry it with you in a plastic bag and ask for a hand inspection. Such requests are honored at American airports, up to the inspector abroad. Don't depend on a lead-lined bag to protect film in checked luggage – the airline may very well turn up the dosage of radiation to see what you've got in there. Airport metal detectors do not harm film, although you'll set off the alarm if you walk through one with a roll in your pocket. Call the Kodak Information Center (tel. 800/242–2424) for details.

Before your trip, put new or long-unused camcorders through their paces, and practice panning and zooming. Invest in a sky-light filter to protect the lens, and check the lithium battery that lights up the LCD (liquid crystal display) modes. As for the rechargeable nickel-cadmium batteries that are the camera's power source, take along an extra pair, so while you're using you camcorder you'll have one battery ready and another recharging. Most newer camcorders are equipped with the battery (which generally slides or clicks onto the camera body) and, to recharge it, with what's known as a universal or world-wide AC adapter charger (or multivoltage converter) that can be used whether the voltage is 110 or 220. All that's needed is the appropriate plug.

Unlike still-camera film, videotape is not damaged by X-rays. However, it may well be harmed by the magnetic field of a walk-through metal detector. Airport security personnel may want you to turn the camcorder on to prove that that's what it is, so make sure the battery is charged when you get to the airport. Note that although the United States, Canada, Japan, Korea, Taiwan, and other countries operate on the National Television System Committee video standard (NTSC), France uses SECAM technology. So you will not be able to view movies bought there in your home VCR. Blank tapes bought in France can be used for

NTSC camcorder taping, however – although you'll probably find they cost more in France and wish you'd brought an adequate supply along.

Security X-rays do not harm hard-disk or floppy-disk storage. Most airlines allow you to use your laptop aloft but request that you turn it off during takeoff and landing so as not to interfere with navigation equipment. Make sure the battery is charged when you arrive at the airport, because you may be asked to turn on the computer at security checkpoints to prove that it is what it appears to be. If you're a heavy computer user, consider traveling with a backup battery. For international travel, register your laptop with U.S. Customs as you leave the country, providing it's manufactured abroad (U.S.-origin items cannot be registered at U.S. Customs); when you do so, you'll get a certificate, good for as long as you own the item, containing your name and address, a description of the laptop, and its serial number, that will quash any questions that may arise on your return. If your laptop is U.S.-made, call the consulate of the country you'll be visiting to find out whether it should be registered with customs in that country upon arrival. Some travelers do this as a matter of course and ask customs officers to sign a document that specifies the total configuration of the system, computer and peripherals, and its value. In addition, before leaving home, find out about repair facilities at your destination, and don't forget any transformer or adapter plug you may need.

Traveling with Children

The easiest way to break down any gallic arrogance is to show up with a child. Normally stiff salesmen go ga-ga and become immediately helpful. Bakers are often known to give young children free sweets, and children are accepted in both fancy and informal restaurants with little fuss. Changing compartments for infants are available on all TGV trains. In short, don't worry about bringing a child into France.

Family Travel Times, published 10 times a year by Travel With Your Children (TWYCH, 45 W. 18th St., 7th Floor Tower, New York, NY 10011, tel. 212/206–0688; annual subscription $55), covers destinations, types of vacations, and modes of travel.

Great Vacations with Your Kids, by Dorothy Jordan and Marjorie Cohen ($13; Penguin USA, 120 Woodbine St., Bergenfield, NJ 07621, tel. 800/253–6476) and Traveling with Children – And Enjoying It, by Arlene K. Nutler ($11.95 plus $3 shipping per book; Globe Pequot Press, Box 833, Old Saybrook, CT 06475, tel. 800/243–0495, or 800/962–0973 in CT), both help plan your trip with children, from toddlers to teens. *Innocents Abroad: Traveling with Kids in Europe*, by Valerie Wolf Deutsch and Laura Sutherland ($15.95 or $4.95 paperback, Penguin USA, *as above*), covers child- and teen-friendly activities, food, and transportation.

On international flights, the fare for infants under 2 not occupying a seat is generally 10% of the accompanying adult's fare; children ages 2–11 usually pay half to two-thirds of the adult fare. On domestic flights, children under 2 not occupying a seat travel free, and older children currently travel on the 'lowest applicable' adult fare.

In general, infants paying 10% of the adult fare are allowed one carry-on bag, not to exceed 70 pounds or 45 inches (length + width + height). The adult baggage allowance applies for children paying half or more of the adult fare. Check with the airline for particulars, especially regarding flights bwteen two foreign destinations, where allowances for infants may be less generous than those above.

The FAA recommends the use of safety seats aloft and details approved models in the free leaflet 'Child/Infant Safety Seats Recommended for Use in Aircraft' (available from the Federal Aviation Administration, APA–200, 800 Independence Ave. SW, Washington, DC 20591, tel. 202/267–3479). Airline policy varies. U.S. carriers must allow FAA-approved models, but because these seats are strapped into a regular passenger seat, they may require that parents buy a ticket even for an infant under 2 who would otherwise ride free. Foreign carriers may not allow infant seats, may charge the child's rather than the infant's fare for their use, or may require you to hold your baby during takeoff and landing, thus defeating the seat's purpose.

Airlines do provide other facilities and services for children, such as children's meals and freestanding bassinets (to those sitting in seats on the bulkhead, where there's enough legroom to accommodate them). Make your request when reserving. The annual February/March issue of *Family Travel Times* gives details of the children's services of dozens of airlines ($10; *see above*). 'Kids and Teens in Flight' (free from the U.S. Department of Transportation, tel. 202/366–2220) offers tips for children flying alone.

The **Novotel** hotel chain (tel. 800/221–4542) allows up to two children under 15 to stay free in their parents' room. Many Novotel properties have playgrounds. **Sofitel** hotels (tel. 800/221–4542) offer a free second room for children during July and August and over the Christmas holidays. **Club Med** (40 W. 57th St., New York, NY 10019, tel. 800/CLUB–MED) has a 'Baby Club' (from age four months) at its resort in Chamonix; 'Mini Clubs' (from ages four to six or eight, depending on the resort), and 'Kids Clubs' (for ages eight and up during school holidays) at all its resort villages in France except in Val d'Isère. In general, supervised activities are scheduled all day long. Some clubs are only French-speaking, so check first.

The **French National Railways** (SNCF) allows children under four to travel free (provided they don't occupy a seat) and children four to 11 to travel at half fare. The *Carte Kiwi* (395 francs) allows children under 16 and up to four accompanying adults to travel at half fare.

Your best is to check with the hotel concierge. Baby-sitting agencies usually charge a hefty 'finder's fee.' The going rate in Paris for a babysitter is up to $7 an hour.

In France

Finding a Place to Stay

Finding a pleasant hotel for the night in France is usually straightforward and simple. The exception is likely to be in the major cities of Paris, Nice, Cannes, Bordeaux, Lyons, where hotels are in demand all year round, and at the major tourist resorts which are full most of the summer. But in the majority of French towns there should be few problems, and none at all if you are traveling out of season or off the beaten track. As a rail traveler, you have the advantage of always being able to move on, and indeed it may be more pleasant sometimes to stay in a small town on the outskirts of a city and visit the city on day trips.

The range of accommodations available to visitors in France is vast, with a choice from thousands of delightful small family-run hotels to sumptuous château hotels and charming bed and breakfasts. The secret to finding the ideal hideaway – whether it is a country farmhouse or a modest town hotel – is booking in advance, especially in July and August, when the French themselves are on holiday, along the Mediterranean and Atlantic coasts; and in major tourist destinations, such as Avignon and Mont St Michel.

Hotel prices *in this guide are indicated by stars, and refer to the cost of a double room with bathroom (where available). Remember that hotels will very often have rooms without bathrooms at cheaper rates.*

No star	up to 150 FF		
☆	120 – 250 FF	☆☆☆	300 – 450 FF
☆☆	200 – 300 FF	☆☆☆☆	400 – 700 FF

Booking Your first option is to phone hotels recommended in this book. Booking is advisable, especially in summer – even if it's only a call the night before to say you're coming. Calls to cheaper hotels and hostels, however, don't always ensure a firm booking. If you have a set itinerary and you have knowledge of French and intend to stay in only a few towns, you might try writing from home or faxing to book a hotel. A deposit in the shape of an International Money Order or a credit card number will help to secure a room but isn't usually neccesary.

When booking or looking for a room, a single room is *une chambre pour une personne* and a room with a double-bed is *une chambre avec un grand lit*. For a room with 2 single beds ask for *une chambre à deux lits*. At the reception it is quite likely that you will not be offered the cheapest room of the type you have asked for. If necessary, ask for something cheaper (*moins chère*) or without a bathroom (*sans salle de bain*).

Tourist Offices If you have no reservation in a big city, especially in peak season, try to arrive in the morning. By late afternoon the empty rooms are often snapped up. In such circumstances it's worth heading first to the station's tourist office (usually found in larger cities). If it's crowded, it's probably best to head to the less hectic main tourist office, usually in the center of town. Without exception, every French town and city has a tourist information office (*Syndicat d'Initiative* or *Office de Tourisme*). In all there are over 5,000 tourist offices in France, usually open from 9 – 12 am and 2 – 7 pm.

Those marked *Accueil de France* will help to find you a hotel room for a small fee. At the very least, tourist offices have lists of all the hotels, rooms and prices within their town or district. Many are in daily contact with hotels and know what rooms are available. They may also have lists of rooms in private houses, places which are often hard to find simply by walking around the streets. Lines for the accommodation service, however, can be long, and obviously you have no chance of looking at the room or the area in which the hotel is located. If everything else is booked up, the hotel they find for you may be some distance out of town. The great majority of personnel working in these tourist information offices speak English; most are extremely patient, helpful and polite.

If you have not booked accommodation and arrive when the tourist office is already shut, or if you want to find a place for yourself, get hold of a street plan and set off to look for accommodation. Your luggage can usually be left at the station in a locker or in the left-luggage office if you do not feel like taking it with you. Hotels near railway stations are convenient and usually among the cheapest available; in the largest cities, such as Paris, such locations often leave something to be desired and may be a little dangerous at night. In the vast majority of towns, however, hotels near stations are generally clean, comfortable and cheap, even if some are a little lacking in character. In a small town try asking locals where the nearest hotel is (*Où est l'hôtel le plus proche ?*) or if there is anyone who rents rooms (*Est-ce qu'il y a quelqu'un qui loue des chambres ?*)

Hotels

With the exception of a few small villages which have no accommodation facilities, we have recommended a handful of hotels in different categories for every town and city that appears in the guide. They are chosen for their convenience for the train traveler, being either in the heart of the town close to the principal sites or within a short distance of the railway station. All are generally pleasant, clean and comfortable; only a few could be classified as luxurious or grand. Most fall into 1- or 2-star categories with the occasional 3-star in the larger towns and cities; cheaper hotels with no star are also included from time to time. The assumption is that people want to stay somewhere central and modestly priced, but whenever possible with character, a warm welcome and pleasant atmosphere. Most hotels therefore fall into the category of traditional French family-run hotels, offering visitors a small room but a big, warm welcome.

It is worth noting that almost without exception the cheapest hotels are always grouped round or close to the railway station. Many of these are very simple and functional, with little time or money spent on decoration or furniture. They are, however, the best value for money, almost without exception, and are almost always immaculately clean and perfectly acceptable (though occasionally some-what less so in the big cities – Paris, Marseille, Lyon, Bordeaux). It doesn't take long to have a look inside, and it is perfectly acceptable and reasonable to ask to see a room before making a decision on whether or not to take it.

In France, the usual practice is to charge a set price for a room – irrespective of whether one or two people share it. Most rooms come with double beds. If your room has no shower, you'll usually have to use a hall shower, for which there may be a small charge (10–20 FF). Many French hotel bathrooms still have a *bidet*, which is not a lavatory! It is a French invention, designed for the saving of water, and is best given a wide berth by Anglo-Saxons. By law, prices have to be displayed outside a hotel, and these give details of the different rooms available and their corresponding prices. Prices also have to be displayed in the room itself, usually on the back of the door. Breakfast is seldom included in the price and does not have to be taken in the hotel unless *petit déjeuner obligatoire* is stipulated on the price list; nor does the evening meal. Occasionally a hotel proprietor may turn away the visitor who says he doesn't intend to eat in the hotel's restaurant. So if accommodations are scarce, it's probably better to indicate that you're going to eat in the hotel restaurant – you can always change your mind and go out and eat elsewhere. Check prices before staying in a hotel that requires *demi-pension* (i.e. an obligatory evening meal).

Over 5,000 mostly 1- and 2-star family-run hotels are grouped together under the name of Logis et Auberges de France; these are selected for their attractiveness, warm welcome, comfort and reliability. Almost without exception they are good old-fashioned traditional hotels, well-run, clean and comfortable – a safe bet almost anywhere in France. You can obtain information on these from: 25 rue Jean-Mermoz, 75008 Paris. Tel. 43–59–86–67.) Another group, often with slightly more modern buildings, is France Accueil, which runs a chain of inexpensive 1- and 2-star hotels throughout the country. (For information contact: 85 rue du Dessous-des-Berges, 75013 Paris. Tel. 45–83–04–22.).

Youth Hostels Auberges De Jeunesse

The cheapest accommodation in towns is usually the youth hostel or Auberge de Jeunesse, costing generally between 40 and 80 FF per person/per night, with breakfast an additional 15 FF per person. Only camping is cheaper. In theory you are meant to be a member of the YHA before you arrive, but in fact you can often join on the spot. In 1992 the International Youth Hostel Federation (IYHF) changed its name to Hostelling International (HI), HI now being the new symbol. Membership is available in the United States through American Youth Hostels (AYH, 733 15th St. NW, Washignton, DC 20005, tel. 202/783–6161), the American link in the worldwide chain, and costs $25 for adults 18–54, $10 for those under 18, $15 for those 55 and over, and $35 for families. Volume 1 of the two-volume *Guide to Budget Accommodation* lists hostels in Europe and the Mediterranean ($13.95, including postage). IYHF membership is available in Canada through the Canadian Hostelling Association (CHA, 1600 James Naismith Dr., Suite 608, Gloucester, Ont. K1B 5N4, tel. 613/748–5638) for $26.75. Membership purchased in France costs 100 FF per person and in England £9. The HI can be joined in France at all major hostels and in Paris at the head office at 10 rue Notre Dame de Lorette.

The quality of the youth hostels and the facilities they provide varies widely; some sell groceries and supplies; all have kitchens. Some hostels are well-managed, clean and in good central locations; others can be run-down or far from the center of town. There are a few disadvantages to staying in hostels: many have a curfew of around 11 or 12 pm, almost all are closed to everybody between 10 am and 5 pm, most limit your stay to a maximum of 3 days, and most offer beds in single-sex dorms that can be noisy. The advantages, however, are that they are cheap and often an excellent meeting place, convivial and fun. Addresses are listed in the French section of the international handbook and in the **Practicalities** section of this guide book. Sheet sleeping bags are required and can be bought or hired at all hostels.

During July and August try to book a hostel bed well in advance, either by calling a week or two in advance, or by using the International Multi-Lingual Booking Cards, available from youth hostels or the YHA head office. You must post the cards with an International Reply Coupon (available from post offices). Reserved beds are only held until 6 pm. Youth hostels are listed in the text but for full details buy the new HI handbook (available in bookshops and from the YHA head office).

Foyers des Jeunes Travailleurs

Another type of hostel accommodation available to YHA members in some towns are the Foyers des Jeunes Travailleurs/Travailleuses, which are residential hostels for students and young working people living away from home. Accommodation is usually in single-sex dorms but single rooms are sometimes available. Foreign travelers are usually accepted if there is space available. The Accueil des Jeunes en France (AJF) has hostels throughout France with several thousand beds in Paris alone while the Union des Centres de Rencontre(s) Internationale(s) de France (UCRIF) is a smaller organization which also operates hostels throughout France.

Camping

France is an ideal country for camping, with its beautiful landscapes, delightful rivers and uncrowded countryside, and its campsites are generally well-organized and equipped. Traveling by train, however, the number of campsites that can be easily reached is quite small; often they are a few kilometers from the station. Leaving a city on public transport slightly defeats one of the main attractions of train travel – that you are carried right into the heart of the city and do not have to trouble with getting through the suburbs. When campsites are easily reached or are situated very close to the town center, we have listed them below.

Though campsites may be hard to reach, virtually every town and village in France has one that caters to the thousands of French people who camp during their summer holiday. The cheapest are the Camping Municipal, run by the local municipality; out of season there is rarely someone around to collect the fee; when officially open they are clean, have plenty of hot water and are often beautifully situated. Superior campsites with swimming pools are a great deal more expensive. Remember that all campsites are likely to be packed in July and August; on the Côte d'Azur reservations need to be made months in advance. Like hotels, French campsites are classified by a star system. Three- and 4-star sites are usually large and shady, with good washing facilities, a restaurant or shop and either a lake or a swimming pool within the grounds. These superior sites are not cheap, however, and can easily cost as much as a budget hotel. Prices range from 15FF to 40FF per person per night, plus 20 – 40 FF per tent, depending on the rating of the campsite. Camping unofficially in fields and forests is at your own risk; it's better to ask permission, which may result in an interesting and enjoyable encounter and an offer of a glass of the farmer's home-made apéritif. If you intend to rough it, travel with a good light tent, small stove, utensils, thin insulating mat and lightweight sleeping bag. Be discreet, don't light fires (unless with permission) and make sure that you leave nothing to show that you have been camped there.

Tourist offices have details of local sites and information on camping in France. Lists of campsites are available from the French Government Tourist Office.

Gîtes d'Etape

Gîtes d'étape are rustic, rural houses, of more use to the cyclist and walker than to the train traveler. Tourist offices, however, have details of all the *gîtes d'étape* in their area; and for anyone heading into the hills who wants a base from which to walk, they provide excellent, simple accommodation, with bunk beds and reasonable kitchen and washing facilities. These self-catering accommodations are in or near small country villages and are usually rented by the week. Prices range from $140 to $250 for a week for a house able to sleep 4 – 6 people comfortably.

Refuges

Several of the routes in the text take you into the mountains, and with a short bus ride from the stations it's possible to be in superb walking country. In some places, trekking and mountain walking can begin right at the station door. Most national parks and areas in the French Alps and Pyrenees have a system of refuges which are cheap, friendly and often dramatically situated high in the mountains. Most mountain refuge huts are not normally open before the beginning of June and generally close at the end of September. Although most of them belong to the Club Alpin Français, you do not have to be a member of any club to use them. They cost in the region of 60 – 80FF per person per night and less to members of affiliated climbing clubs. No refuge will turn you away, which means that in summer you may end up sleeping on the floor of the more popular places. Tourist offices in mountain areas have full details of the refuges.

Eating in France

One of the principal reasons for coming to France is the food. Here, for anyone with the taste-buds to notice, food is cooked and prepared as it should be – with real interest and enthusiasm. As a result, France has the most memorable and delicious cuisine of Europe and wines to match. The tradition of good French cooking dates back a long way. Under the *ancien régime* the king and his court ate gargantuan meals, prepared by the best chefs of the day with access to the best and freshest ingredients. The extreme richness and elaborate presentation of *haute cuisine* derived from this rich fare eaten by the nobility and the court. *Cuisine bourgeoise* is high-quality French home cooking based on provincial and country dishes, refined and modified with experimentation over time. *Nouvelle cuisine* was in vogue during the 1980s, but after its initial novelty it has lost some of its appeal and followers. The movement in many French homes today is alas slowly but inevitably towards more prepared foods, but the vast majority of the population still take the time to shop daily, prepare fine meals and sit down and enjoy them.

Breakfast in France (*le petit déjeuner*) is a simple affair – usually a coffee with milk (*un café crème* or simply *un crème*) or small black coffee (*un café noir* or simply *un noir*) with either bread (*pain*), butter (*beurre*) and jam (*confiture*) or croissants or brioches (a cross between a pastry and a light bread). People can afford to eat small breakfasts for at twelve noon they head for the restaurants for **lunch** (*le déjeuner*). In small towns and villages, an almost complete hush descends for two hours, but even in cities the pause is noticeable. *Le déjeuner* is often the largest meal of the day, and most shops, government offices and businesses close for the two hours between 12 and 2pm.

Dinner (*le dîner*) begins quite late, usually not before 8pm. Lunch or dinner will usually start with an *apéritif*, a light drink to whet the appetite and get the gastric juices going, followed by *l'entrée* (first course), *le plat* (main dish), which may consist of meat (*viandes*), a fish dish (*poisson*) and *légumes* (vegetables) and/or *salad* (salad). In France *fromages* (cheeses) precede the dessert which may be followed by *un expresso* (a strong black coffee) and possibly a *digestif* (after-dinner drink, usually a cognac or local brandy, such as Calvados in Normandy). The digestif aids digestion and settles the stomach, a much-needed aid, especially if there have been five, six, or seven dishes even in a relatively simple meal.

There are five main apéritifs – *kir*, chilled white wine served with cassis, a blackcurrant liqueur; *kir royale* which substitutes champagne for wine; *pastis*, a liquorice liqueur diluted with water; *Suze*, a bitter-sweet liqueur made from the mountain flower gentiane; *Picon-bière*, a mixture of beer and sweet citrus liqueur; and Martini. **Wine**, naturally, accompanies every meal; finding out about wine is one of the pleasures of any visit to France. Very occasionally the set menu might be marked *boisson comprise*, indicating that a quarter of a liter of house wine is included in the price. Water too is drunk with the meal, virtually always mineral water (*eau minérale*), of either the bubbly (*gazeuse*) or still (*plate*) variety. If you want tap-water, order *une carafe d'eau*.

Most **restaurants** offer a menu *à prix fixe* (fixed-price meal) which is less expensive than ordering *à la carte* and usually includes a first course (*entrée*) such as *pâte*, *crudités* (raw vegetables), *jambon* (ham), or *rillettes* (a rich thick pork pâté); a main course (*plat*) such as *agneau* (lamb), *porc* (pork), *boeuf* (beef), *poulet* (chicken) or *veau* (veal); and *fromages* (cheese) and/or *dessert*. Usually you get a much better deal by ordering a menu *à prix fixe*; you will be eating what the chef has decided to make a speciality of that day, probably because he has just secured an excellent local supply of certain ingredients.

Bread, like wine, accompanies every meal and it is eaten in large quantities; usually it consists of slices of long thin *baguette*. The meal ends for most people with a strong black coffee (*express*). Before you leave, the bill (*l'addition*) will arrive, marked either *service compris* (service included) or *service non compris* (service not included.) When not included, the tip is at your discretion but 10 per cent is normal. A cover charge (*le couvert*) is sometimes charged but often absorbed into the price. Prices naturally vary according to what you eat (and drink). For 90FF you should be able to eat an excellent meal, but you don't need to pay a lot to eat well. The cheapest set menus at 60 and 70 francs can be extremely good; everything depends on the chef. Restaurants recommended in the text have been selected on the basis of providing good local food, for those wanting to eat well but not break the bank. In large towns we recommend various places; in smaller towns the best place (on the assumption that you are probably going to stay only one night). If you find a place you like, it's probably worth going back. In a small restaurant you will certainly be recognized and your implied appreciation of the cuisine will probably win you a particularly friendly welcome.

Cafés Cafés are places for breakfast, for dawdling and for leisurely breaks when you have had enough of sight-seeing and just want to watch the world go by. Small snacks available in cafés or brasseries often seem poor value when compared to the meal available in simple restaurants at 60 or 70 francs. Café meals are generally simple but often good – such as grilled goat's cheese on toast (*chèvre chaud*). A beer (*bière*), coffee (*café*) and other drinks generally cost twice as much if taken at a table than standing at the bar, but if you order a drink at the table you can usually sit there for hours undisturbed.

Museums, Galleries and Archaeological Sites

Admission prices for museums, galleries and archaeological sites are increased annually and are not given in the text. At present in small town galleries and minor archaeological sites you can expect to pay about 15–20FF per adult. At more major museums such as the Louvre or the Panthéon in Paris the price is in the region of 30–40FF per adult. The Eiffel Tower is one of the most expensive sites in France, at 51FF per adult. There are often reductions for students (an ISIC card is required) and for those under 12 and over 60 years of age. (The Louvre is free to everybody under 18). Somey museums, such as the Musée d'Orsay in Paris, have reduced rates on Sundays or are completely free on certain specified days.

LIGNES À GRANDE VITESSE

en service

en construction

AUTRES LIGNES

The Train Network

SNCF provides an extremely efficient service. Trains usually run on time; they are clean and many have excellent facilities. For example many trains on the important lines have a car expressly designed and reserved for small children that is in effect a playroom! The rail system is also well co-ordinated with a bus system run by SNCF, so that many small villages and outlying places can be reached by SNCF buses whose departures are timed to coincide with the arrival of trains. Naturally enough, such buses leave from the SNCF stations. What could be more intelligent or convenient?

The SNCF staff is exceptionally courteous and helpful. Many, especially on the main lines, are able to speak some English, but even so, visitors should not expect them to do so as a matter of course. Some of the main line stations in Paris announce train departures in English; unlike British Rail announcements mumbled over some antiquated loudspeaker system, those in France are clear and audible. Some Paris railway stations also have automatic multi-lingual railway timetable computers which will give free print-outs of train times, connections, etc. in the language of your choice.

Almost every station has an information desk and *consignes automatiques* – coin-operated left-luggage lockers which are big enough to take a suitcase or rucksack. Often, for security reasons, the room where these are located is locked overnight, so check on closing times before you set out to explore a town or city.

The French railway network – SNCF – revolves around 9 principal lines. Between them they link France's major cities and provide the arteries from which the network's spurs and branch lines operate. Trains often run the entire length of one or more of these lines – from Nice to Paris, for example – allowing you to cover huge distances without having to change trains.

- *Paris–Amiens–Lille–Calais*
- *Paris–Nancy–Strasbourg*
- *Paris–Lyon–Avignon–Marseille*
- *Paris–Orléans–Vierzon–Limoges–Brive–Cahors–Montauban–Toulouse*
- *Paris–Tours–Poitiers–Angoulême–Bordeaux–Bayonne–Biarritz*
- *Paris–Le Mans–Angers–Nantes*
- *Paris–Le Mans–Rennes–Brest*

- *Marseille–Toulon–Nice–Cannes–Ventimiglia*
- *Biarritz–Bayonne–Pau–Lourdes–Toulouse–Narbonne–Montpellier–Avignon*

Trains

French Railways have four main categories of train: Trains à Grande Vitesse (TGV); intercity trains referred to as **express** or **rapide** trains; local **autotrains**; and **EuroCity** trains. Check the timetable carefully as the type of train determines not only how long a journey will take but also what it will cost and whether you'll need to reserve seats.

TGV trains For 10 years France has been actively building a whole new rail network for high-speed trains – the TGVs, or Trains à Grande Vitesse – laying some 4,000 kilometers of new track with the ambition of providing the fastest and most efficient rail service in Europe, and securing for Paris the position as the rail hub of Europe.

TGVs run from Paris to Lyon, Avignon, Marseille, Nice and other destinations on the Côte d'Azur; Quimper and Brest in Brittany, to Bordeaux and the Spanish border on the Atlantic coast; and to Calais and London to the north. Each year more and more stations are served by TGVs as the lines extend south and east towards the frontiers of France. A new TGV line is now being completed along the Mediterranean coast from Nice to Perpignan and the Spanish border. From Paris, Avignon can be reached in only 3 hours 45 minutes, Brest in 3 ½ hours, Nantes in 2, Bordeaux in less than 3. This service is the fastest in Europe. With trains traveling at up to 300 kmph (190 mph), this means that it is possible to reach the Mediterranean, the Alps and the Pyrenees in an astonishingly quick time. On some routes, TGVs provide a quicker service than flying because of the need to check in at airports half an hour or an hour before flying and the need to get to the airport in the first place. Traveling on a TGV is an experience in itself but it also makes it easy and quick to get to a city at the start of one of the regional tours outlined in the following chapters.

Tickets for TGVs cost the same as regular SNCF tickets except for the cost of reservations. The price of TGV tickets varies according to the time of travel and day of the week (for example, they are highest at rush-hour, on Friday evenings leaving Paris and Sunday evenings returning to Paris). In order to travel on any TGV, passengers must have a seat reservation before boarding the train; a reservation is automatically made when buying an ordinary TGV ticket in France. People using a rail pass must make a reservation before boarding the train. Reservations can be made at the last minute at a train station; by phone you must allow nine days advance notice. Most French railway stations have two telephone numbers – one for information and advice, the other solely for reservations.

Rapide trains One down from the TGV, these are the standard rapide trains – extremely modern, comfortable, air-conditioned, usually with a buffet-bar and making only limited stops. Many of the trains are marked Corail, the apellation given to the new-style rolling stock introduced in the 1970s. As with all French trains since 1993, smoking is prohibited in the bar and restaurant cars. Reserving a seat is compulsory only for the TGV but it is strongly recommended for other trains during the school vacations and at peak hours on main lines.

Express trains These are virtually identical to rapide trains but are slightly slower, making more stops along the line. The same Corail cars may be used and no distinction is drawn in timetables between express or rapide trains.

Autotrains These are the slow local or regional trains connecting country villages and small towns. Generally only a few of these trains run each day, usually at the hours when people are traveling to or returning from work in neighboring town. Quite often the trains consist of only a couple of cars. Some stop at every station, travel very slowly and are an excellent way of seeing the local scenery, in particular the mountains, but they can be frustratingly slow if you have only very limited time at your disposal. For those with plenty of time they provide a fascinating way to travel as the trains often pull into charming country stations where the station master has time for a quick chat with the conductor. These trains are usually the only ones on which you can take a bicycle as free accompanied luggage. Details of local or regional trains are provided in the TER (Transport Express Régional) Timetables, available locally in France.

EuroCity trains These are all trains with international destinations, virtually all departing from Paris. They conform to the highest European standard of speed, comfort and service, making very few and very short stops only at major cities en route to their destination. A supplement is payable on almost all such trains.

Autocars When listed on a French Railways timetable this indicates that the service will be provided by a SNCF bus and not a train. This has been introduced on a number of very minor lines in country areas.

Couchettes and Night Trains
There are advantages to traveling by night. It can solve the problem of accommodation and effectively adds a day to your journey by allowing you to arrive first thing in the morning. Some journeys within France are very long, and these are served by a number of night departures. These allow you to make some long trips without stirring – direct from Paris to Perpignan or Paris to Nice, for example. In addition there are regular night departures to numerous international destinations.

One of the main disadvantages to night travel is that you miss the scenery en route. Night trains also travel more slowly than the daytime equivalents so you will take longer to reach your destination. You may gain a day but you won't necessarily have a great night's sleep. Ear plugs and a mild sleeping pill or a half-bottle of wine are also a good investment. If you decide to travel overnight on a French train, there are three ways of passing the night: in an ordinary seat, a couchette, or a voiture-lits (a sleeper).

The Seat It's free, but unless you're a great sleeper you will arrive with a stiff neck and in no state to face the following day. A small inflatable neck cushion will make all the difference. Carriages can be crowded, with people getting on and off all through the night. At the very least, reserve a seat when buying your ticket. Double-check on timetables that your train does have ordinary seating; the vast majority of night trains do have seats but a few will have only sleeper and couchette coaches. If you board a train in the middle of the night you may have to try several compartments before finding a seat. Don't be intimidated, but ask if there is an empty place (*C'est libre?*) and watch out for bags occupying seats. There are reclining seats in rapide trains, but in first class only.

Couchettes   Couchettes are comfortable, and getting a good night's sleep means you will be ready for sightseeing when you step off the train in the morning, rather than feeling exhausted from having sat up all night. One indispensable article for night-time travel is a miniature alarm clock; there is nothing worse than panicking all night with fear that you are going to oversleep your destination.

Couchettes must be booked in advance, and you must of course also have a valid ticket for the journey in addition to the couchette voucher. If you have a rail pass you will be given a separate couchette voucher; if you are buying a ticket in France, the couchette reservation is marked on the ticket itself. Each voucher shows the train number, time of departure, time of arrival, number of the car containing your couchette and the number of your berth within the coach. The cost of a couchette, in first or second class, is 86FF.

Try to reserve your couchette at least the day before you need it, and, in high summer, on weekends and before public holidays, preferably several days in advance. The closure time for reservations of couchettes is two hours before departure.

There are six berths to a couchette compartment in 2nd class, four in 1st class. Each comes with a sheet, blanket and pillow. Top berths are less claustrophobic, less stuffy and offer a little more privacy; bottom berths have marginally less room because of arm rests at either end. None are segregated, but for women traveling alone this is rarely a problem as the compartments are usually full. If you have doubts about the person, or people, in your compartment, and there's room elsewhere, the *contrôleur*, who will have checked your ticket on arrival, will usually move you elsewhere on request. Women traveling alone rarely need to do this but it's advisable to avoid compartments occupied by men only and to look instead for families or other women traveling alone. At the end of each carriage there are lavatories and washrooms; the water is not for drinking. It's obviously a good idea to have the things you need for the night, plus music, books and so on, in a separate bag so that you can stash away your main bag or pack. At night be careful of your possessions, keep your valuables on you and lock the door of your compartment. To prevent thefts, night trains now have a double locking system; one of the locks can only be opened from the inside. Even the *contrôleur* can only open the door a few inches – enough to request a passenger's ticket; night trains have therefore become much safer. But although berths have a small personal luggage rack, it's obviously not the place to put your valuables.

Obtaining a couchette on the train is occasionally possible but don't rely on it. Your best chances are increased if you're joining the train at its station of departure. Approach the attendants of one or more of the carriages and let them know you are looking for a couchette. (*Est-ce-qu'il y a par hasard une couchette libre?* Is there by any chance a spare couchette?) During busy times the chances are that all will be booked. Remember that officials are likely to be busy, so be patient; if, as often happens, someone hasn't arrived to take his place, it can be given to you. Have cash to pay for the seat as attendants won't always be able to accept traveler's checks or credit cards. If you're boarding a night train part-way through a journey, speak to the *contôleur* as soon as the train pulls in. He will almost certainly know if a couchette is available.

Voitures-lits (Sleepers) *Voitures-lits* are the ultimate way to spend the night, providing a much higher standard of privacy, comfort and service than a couchette. Each cabin has its own washing facilities and each coach has its own *conducteur* to look after the needs of the passengers. Reservations are made in the same way as for couchettes. *Voiture-lits* come in a number of different combinations; these prices are in addition to the cost of a ticket. A single compartment costs 905FF (a slightly smaller version on some trains called a *Spécial* costs 647FF); a double costs 388FF per person (1st-class ticket also required); a T2 is also for two people but is slightly smaller and is available for people traveling 2nd class (388FF per person); a Touriste T3 is for three people traveling 2nd class and costs 259FF per person.

Safety on Trains Theft on trains is just as likely as theft elsewhere. Obviously it makes sense to take precautions and keep an eye on your baggage. Most French trains, during day-time travel, have three places to put luggage: at the end of the compartment, in the space between the backs of the seats and on the overhead rack. The last two are the safest, and the gap between the seats is big enough to take large suitcases without difficulty. If you leave your suitcases in the space at the end of the compartments, it's difficult if not impossible to keep an eye on them, and they could be removed without your noticing. It's better to keep your luggage close to you.

Reports of people being drugged and robbed in their sleep on night trains are now, thankfully, a thing of the past, although it was a problem a few years ago. As basic precautions in any situation, however, you should ensure that the door to your compartment is locked from the inside once everyone has settled down for the night. Keep money and valuables close to you in a pouch or money belt. Obviously avoid letting people see where you have put your camera, wallet or other valuables. Be more wary if you are sitting up all night rather than taking a couchette. Don't accept food or drink if you're at all unsure of a person. And remember that in a couchette you can usually ask the attendant to move you if you are worried.

Food and Drink on Trains The vast majority of night trains do not have a restaurant or buffet-bar so it's advisable to bring your own food and drink. The assumption is that if you are departing between 9 pm and midnight you will already have eaten. The more prestigious international trains and long-distance overnight *Voitures-lits* trains, however, do have restaurant cars. The restaurant coach will close at around midnight, and on international journeys the restaurant car may have disappeared altogether by the time you wake up the next morning. Night trains can become stuffy and dry although the vast majority are air-conditioned; it is essential to carry a bottle of water with you. Water in the lavatories and washrooms is not drinkable (*eau non potable*), but many stations have a tap or drinking fountain.

International Services

From Paris, trains reach out to places as far afield as Rome, Warsaw, Madrid, Vienna, Prague, Cologne, Hamburg and Moscow. While other international train departures from France are less far-reaching, it's still possible to take a direct train from many French cities to almost any country in Europe. France has consciously striven to achieve a position as the international transport hub of Europe, with the construction of an impressive high-speed rail and road network. With the new Channel Tunnel open, France's position at the crossroads of international rail routes will be confirmed. With a Eurail pass or its equivalent, France is an ideally located country to be explored by train before you move on to the easily-reached countries near by.

International destinations are served by **Intercité** or **Eurocité** trains, which are the top class of international train, usually requiring a supplement and often a reservation.

Destinations To such destinations as Italy, Switzerland, Belgium, Holland, Germany, Austria and Spain – all served by through trains from France – can now be added the eastern European countries of Hungary, the Czech Republic, Poland and Russia, all of which can be reached direct from Paris. Don't feel that foreign journeys beginning in France require an enormous amount of time. You can, for example, leave Paris in the morning and be in Florence 11 hours later, or leave Paris at 6 pm and step out for a late breakfast in Copenhagen at 10 am. Munich and the Bavarian Alps are only 9 hours away; Madrid 12–16 hours away; Barcelona 11–14 hours away. Brussels is 3 hours away, Amsterdam 6 hours away and Geneva only 3½ hours away.

Planning For detailed planning *Thomas Cook's European Timetable* is the best source of information. The SNCF *Ville à Ville Timetable*, a handy digest of main line and important international services, can be bought in France at news-stands in the major stations. Main line stations have individual timetables for specific routes, and station platform timetables identify international departures.

Remember that tickets for international departures are usually sold from a separate window at the ticket office. Tyr to make a reservation, especially in summer or near public holidays, and book a couchette in good time before the journey. Check to see if overnight trains have cars with seats; many offer couchette and sleeper accommodation only.

Train Splitting Before boarding a train for another country check that you are getting on to the right section of the train. Trains on European routes make complicated journeys and often contain a hotch-potch of rolling stock belonging to several countries. Some trains are split up as they leave France and at key stations en route, with perhaps only one or two cars making the whole journey to your final destination. Be sure that you're in the right compartment and stay in it religiously. Nothing is worse than strolling down a train during a long wait at a station to find that you car has been shunted off to be hitched onto another train. TGVs have destination information electronically displayed on a screen on the sides of cars; other international trains have destination boards on the side of trains. Each car also has a number, with which your ticket should correspond if you have a reservation. If in doubt, ask! (*Est-ce que cette voiture-ci va à Rome ?*)

Tickets and Rail Passes

The ticketing system on French railways is fairly straightforward, the main principle being that you pay more if you travel at peak times and less at times of low use. On top of the standard single and return tickets (1st and 2nd class) there is only one specific rail pass, the Eurodomino Pass, and various cards that give discounts on the majority of journeys.

Fares Prices are determined according to a complicated formula which consists of a constant element and a kilometric element. First class is around 50 per cent more than 2nd class; 50 per cent reductions are available to people under 26 years (with a Carissimo Card), under 16 years (with a Kiwi Card) and over 60 years (with a Vermeil Card).

Single and Return Tickets A standard, one way ticket in French is *un aller simple*; a return ticket is *un aller et retour*. First class is *première classe*; 2nd class is *deuxième classe*. Thus for a 2nd class return ticket to Bordeaux you'd ask for '*Un aller et retour pour Bordeaux, deuxième classe*'. Generally return tickets (*un aller et retour*) are simply the price of two single tickets for each leg of the journey. There are no equivalents to round trips. Only return journeys of over 1,000 kilometers qualify for a *Séjour* ticket which may cost slightly less than two single tickets.

Ticket Supplements The system of supplements has largely been done away with, except on very few trains—EuroCity trains, the Capitol which runs from Paris to Toulouse, the Barcelona–Geneva Talgo, certain trains starting or ending in Lyon and a few trains in Normandy. A supplement is generally marked on timetables with a small black star. The cost of any journey will, however, vary according to the day and time of day of your departure, but the higher figure for traveling at a peak time is not expressed in terms of a supplement. It would be more accurate to say that you are given a discount for traveling at off-peak times of the day and week.

Standard Train Fares – The Red, White and Blue Periods SNCF has designed a system to encourage people to travel at times when the rail network is underused and to dissuade them from doing so when the trains are most in demand.

Passengers pay a higher price for traveling at a peak time (*période rouge*), a slightly lower price for traveling at less busy times (*période blanche*) and the lowest price available for traveling during quiet times of the day, week and month (*période bleue*).

Blue period: usually from Saturday 12 noon to Sunday 3 pm, from Monday 12 noon to Friday 12 noon.

White period: usually from Friday 12 noon to Saturday 12 noon; from Sunday 3 pm to Monday 12 noon and on a few public holidays.

Red period: the few days corresponding to the peak departure periods (ie. Friday evenings and Saturday mornings). A free leaflet, *Calendrier Voyageurs*, showing the blue, white and red periods is available at all SNCF railway stations.

Travel is free for children under the age of 4 and half-price for children between the ages of 4 and 12. Senior citizens are entitled to half-price tickets (with a Carte Vermeil) except on some peak trains.

Examples of a few standard single fares (without reservation fee).

	1st class	2nd class
Paris–Amiens	128FF	86FF
Paris–Bordeaux	410FF	274FF
Bordeaux–Toulouse	229FF	153FF
Paris–Nice	664FF	443FF

Remember that several cards exist which enable cardholders to get a 50 per cent discount on the majority of journeys.

TGV fares A similar system has been devised for traveling by TGV. Colors are shown on the TGV timetables. Yellow indicates TGVs with many seats usually available in 1st and 2nd class; grey indicates TGVs with heavily oversubscribed 1st class seats; green indicates TGVs with heavily oversubscribed 2nd class seats, and pink indicates TGVs with both classes heavily oversubscribed. The cheapest TGVs to travel on are obviously those marked in yellow. To work out the exact cost of a TGV ticket from Paris to a destinaton, read the back of the timetable at the page headed *Index des gares et Prix des billets au 9 Mars 1994* (or whatever date it is); here you will see the basic cost of the ticket (*prix du billet, plein tarif*) and the price of a reservation (*prix des RESA TGV*) marked in the 4 different colors. For example, if you want to go from Paris to Chambéry in the Alps you will see that the basic 2nd class single ticket costs 203FF. A reservation in a yellow period will cost 16FF, in a grey period 40FF, in a green period 80FF, in a pink period 88FF. To travel in the most over subscribed (pink) period will therefore cost you 72FF more than if you travel in the little used (yellow) period – it is about 30 per cent more expensive.

Validity of Tickets All tickets are valid for two months from the moment of purchases, but once they have been *composté* or punched in the orange boxes in a station, the journey must be completed within 24 hours. If you wish to stop off somewhere en route to your destination, you must tell the clerk at the ticket office when buying the ticket. The date and destination are printed on each ticket.

Reservations A reservation (*une réservation*) is made at the same time and at the same window as you buy your ticket. The present fee for a seat reservation is 18FF, and bookings can be made up to 20:00 (8 pm) the day before departure for trains leaving between 00:00 (midnight) and 17:00 (5 pm) and up to 12:00 (noon) the day of departure for trains leaving between 17:01 and 23:59. To avoid the worst of the queues, visit ticket offices at the quietest time (usually 3–5 pm) and not on weekends or lunchtimes, when the offices are besieged. Be sure to specify 1st class (*un billet de première classe*) or 2nd class (*de deuxième classe*), smoker (*fumeur*) or non-smoker (*non fumeur*) and window (*une place côté fenêtre*) or aisle (*une place côté couloir*). If you want you can specify facing the direction of travel (*face à la marche*) or with your back to the direction of travel (*dos à la marche*).

Virtually every town and city has travel agents which act as ticket agencies for the state railways – look for the SNCF logo in the windows. Where relevant, these are listed in the text below. Most large towns and cities also have student travel agencies which issue domestic and international tickets, reservations and couchettes for students and non-students alike; CTS is the best known.

International Tickets Standard 1st and 2nd class tickets are easily available over the counter from virtually every station in the country. Some big city stations have separate offices which deal specifically with reduced rate under-26 fares. If not, visit the nearest CTS student travel agents for discounted tickets.

Buying a Ticket Unless you are buying a French rail pass before you set off (see below), you'll probably buy tickets from the ticket office, or *le bureau de vente des billets* or *le guichet*. This is a perfectly straightforward undertaking, especially if you know the time of departure of the train you intend to catch.

The most common problem is not so much long as slow-moving queues; computerization hardly seems to have speeded up the process of issuing tickets and you should allow plenty of time. Friday evening, Saturday morning and Sunday evening are notoriously bad at main line stations. Aim to buy your tickets in the middle of the afternoon or in the evening for travel on the following day. If you rush for a train without a ticket you will have to pay a hefty surcharge to the *contrôleur*. Payments for tickets can be made by cash, Carte Bleue, Visa, Eurocard, MasterCard and American Express.

French Rail Pass: Eurodomino French Railways offers one rail pass that allows unrestricted travel to people of any age on a set number of days within any one month – the Eurodomino pass. A new scheme introduced in 1993, Eurodomino allows unrestricted travel on any 3, 5 or 10 days during a month. It's a totally flexible arrangement enabling you to begin your holiday on any day of the week and at any time of the year. The only thing Eurodomino pass-holders have to pay once in France is the reservation fee for travel on TGVs.

After having bought your Eurodomino pass, you have to simply write in the date you intend to begin traveling, and then you can travel as far as you like on the railway network until midnight at that day. Tickets must be purchased in France.

Discount Cards Not only do the French have relatively low rail fares, but they also have a whole range of discount cards which give them further reductions. There are bargain travel cards for everyone, it seems. Most can be used in either 1st or 2nd class. They can either be valid for any amount of travel or alternatively for a specific number of journeys. Nearly all discounted journeys must commence in the *période bleue*, the off-peak blue period. Americans must buy these tickets in France

Carissimo This is SNCF's new card for those aged under 26 years and it offers great advantages. It comes in two versions, both valid for one year, and both giving 50 per cent off fares in *période bleue* and 20 per cent off fares in *période blanche* – not only for the cardholder but up to three traveling companions all under the age of 26. The difference between the two versions is that one is valid for any four journeys and costs 190FF, while the other can be used for any eight journeys and costs 350FF.

Carte Kiwi Kiwi cards are for children aged under 16 years and they entitle the cardholder to a 50 per cent reduction on all rail fares. Not only that, they also give the same reduction for up to four accompanying passengers – of any age. Although the card is geared to families, to forestall difficulties of definition the four travelers don't even have to be related to the cardholder. It costs 395FF and is valid for a year, for any number of journeys started in either the blue or white periods. You can buy the Carte Kiwi in the United Kingdom, at the French Railways shop in Piccadilly; all you need is a photograph and a passport.

Carte Vermeil This card offers low-cost rail travel to anyone aged over 60 years. This card also comes in two types, both valid for one year on journeys started in *période bleue* and both giving a 50 per cent reduction on rail fares within France. **Carte Vermeil Quatre Temps** (currently 135FF) allows the holder to make any four single journeys within France, or two return journeys. When the card is used up, you may buy another – it's as simple as that. **Carte Vermeil Plein Temps** (currently 235FF) entitles travelers to make any number of journeys and not just within France; it also gives a 30 per cent reduction on cross-border journeys to more than a dozen other European countries. Plein Temps can therefore be used to travel from Britain to France and vice-versa. Both these cards can be purchased at most railway stations and are valid for one year.

Carte Couple The Carte Couple is designed for couples. As a Carte Couple cardholder you pay full fare but your companion or spouse travels at half fare. Photograph and passport required.

Motorail Motorail enables you to travel to your destination by train with your car. It allows motorists to save precious vacation time by cutting out a long, tiring drive at the beginning and end of a holiday, and is not as expensive as might initially appear when the cost of gas, motorway tolls, hotels, restaurants and wear and tear on the car are taken into account. Motorail services are currently provided to some 30 of the largest French cities.

When your car is driven on to the flat-bed wagon at its point of departure, SNCF officials will inspect your car with you and make a note of any dents and scratches so that in the unlikely event of damage you will both have a record to consult. If you are traveling by Motorail, do not expect to have easy access to your car; you may well be traveling on a completely separate train and you are not likely to see it again until your arrival at your destination.

Stations

French railway stations range from the gargantuan and cavernous, as at Toulouse, Bordeaux or Metz, to the tiny sun-drenched single platforms of villages in Provence and the deserted stations of Savoie or the Auvergne. Some of your time will be spent negotiating these fascinating worlds – teeming and cosmopolitan in the cities, often isolated and idyllic in the countryside. This section aims to make the business of stations as straightforward as possible.

Ticket Offices The ticket office, or *bureau de vente des billets*, is usually easy to spot and well-marked. Tickets, reservations of seats and reservations of couchettes or *voitures-lits* are normally purchased at the same window. Tickets for international departures are usually sold from a separate window or at a different office – so check the heading above each window to make sure that you are standing in the right queue. The hours that offices are open varies with the size of city and station; in large towns most open daily at 5:30 am and close at midnight; in cities they are open longer hours.

Train Information Train information offices, marked with a blue letter *i*, are found in the largest stations. Some mid-size stations may have a separate window dealing with information and enquiries. In the smallest stations the ticket office or station master or mistress can usually find time to help with information. In large cities staff at the ticket windows – *guichets* – will direct you to the information office if there is one. More and more towns and city stations are installing computerized multilingual information units, with a TV like screen where you can type in your query and wait for an on-screen answer or a print-out of the information you require. At many of Paris's railway stations train departures are announced in English.

Station Timetables When information offices are open they are sometimes crowded with people standing in queues. You can, however, usually find the information you need either in the current *Ville à Ville Timetable* or the white station timetables pasted to boards near the ticket office. In main line stations these may cover the entire SNCF network. The lists in smaller stations are usually restricted to timetables for local lines and stations.

Most of the time, though, all you need are the large station timetables posted up on boards at various points on the platforms, waiting-rooms and main terminal. These show all the arrivals (**Arrivées**) and departures (**Départs**) from the station in question.

Each major town and city entry in chapters 1–15 includes information on the railway station, such as its address, telephone numbers for information and reservations, directions (for getting to the center of town and the main tourist office), and locations of offices for tickets, left-luggage, lost property, foreign exchange and showers.

Time And Train Category Timetables run chronologically on a 24-hour clock from 0 hr. to 24 hr. The categories of trains marked on a station timetable are TGVs (marked TGV), Eurocity trains (marked EC), InterCity trains (marked IC), Rapides (R) and Expresses (E). There are also a number of trains specifically for business travelers which are marked **Euraffaires** in grey and red. If a train is replaced by a bus on a particular local service it will be marked **Autocar**.

Train Number And Name All trains in France are given numbers by which you can identify them and these can be found on all timetables. They will also appear on the information screen on the platforms of large stations and also on the main departure board and they will be mentioned in loudspeaker announcements. Only prestige trains, domestic or international, are assigned names – such as *Le Capitole* for the fastest Paris–Toulouse service. Every train however has its number.

Always check any other symbols and small print on the timetable, including in the small print, to see if reservations are necessary: R1.2 under the heading **Places** indicates that reservations are recommended in 1st and 2nd class. (Remember that seat reservations on all TGVs are compulsory.) Check to see whether a train carries couchettes and sleeping cars only or has seats as well.

The Route To the right, alongside the time, number and category of the train, is the route the train will take, with the main stops and the time of arrivals in brackets for each stop. These are not, however, necessarily the only stops the train will make en route.

Platform Number On the right of each entry is the number of the platform (quai) on which the train is arriving or from which it is leaving. Very occasionally, due to operating difficulties or a late arrival, the platform may be changed. Changes are announced on the loudspeaker, but you can always simply follow the crowds as they move platforms. Otherwise double-check with the information screens at the head of each platform or with the station's main departures board.

IMPORTANT: always keep behind the yellow line marked on the platform one meter from the track; TGV trains sometimes race through stations at 200 kmph. Their arrival is announced on the loudspeaker (*Le TGV Paris–Lyon va entrer en gare; éloignez-vous du quai*), but if you don't understand French and are standing one foot from the track, you literally won't know what's hit you.

Electronic Departure Boards The electronic departure noticeboard in larger stations, marked Départs, lists, from left to right, the time of departure, the destination, the category of train, the number of the train and the platform (**quai**).

Ticket Control French Railways no longer control tickets at platform barriers. Rail passengers MUST insert their ticket into one of the many odd-looking orange machines, marked *compostez votre billet*, that stand at the entrance to the platforms. These punch or *composter* the ticket and validate it for a journey. (The main ticket as well as the seat reservation voucher – if separate – has to be punched.) Those who forget, or simply don't have time to do this because they're rushing for a train, will find that they still have to pay an on-the-spot fine (*une amende/une contravention*) to the ticket conductor on the train.

Left-Luggage All large stations have a manned left-luggage depot (*Consigne*) – invaluable institutions that allow you to wander a city unencumbered, whether to look for a room or to get in a day's sightseeing before picking up a train in the evening. Most depots open around 5 am and close at midnight, although times can vary according to the season, especially in the more popular tourist cities such as Paris, Nice and Cannes. Make sure you have everything you need out of your bags before leaving them; you'll not be able to remove them to dig out a forgotten toothbrush – at least not without paying. It's unwise, of course, to leave valuables, tickets or passport in left-luggage.

You will be given a ticket for each bag which you must hand in when reclaiming your luggage, and you will be charged a fee for every piece of luggage. You will also pay by the day, so that even a portion of a day counts as a full 24 hours. Fees are 30FF per suitcase or piece of luggage per day. Bicycles and wheelchairs can be left for 35FF per day.

All but the smallest stations have automatic left-luggage lockers, often in addition to the manned depots. Clearly these are the solution if your train leaves while the depot is locked. Lockers come in several sizes so make sure your suitcase or pack is going to fit before paying to use the locker. There are two different types and prices of lockers: mechanically-operated ones costing 5 or 20FF per 24 hours, and electronic ones costing 15, 20 or 30FF per 72 hours.

Lost Property Most main line stations have a lost property office (*bureau des objets trouvés*), usually annexed to the left-luggage depot. In smaller stations or in emergencies ask station staff whether anything has been handed in. Ask the Station Master (*le chef de gare*) as a last resort. In theory he or she is responsible for trains rather than passengers but as the head of the station, they're the ones who can get things done in a real emergency.

WCs, Washrooms and Waiting Rooms WCs vary greatly; sometimes they are looked after by attendants, in which case you are expected or have to pay. On all stations they are marked; look for the blue **W C** symbol. It's a wise precaution to bring your own supply of toilet paper (*papier hygiénique* in French).

Some large stations have shower facilities (**Douches**). Recently some 'maternity' units have been built where parents with small babies can change diapers, etc. (SOS Voyageurs).

Waiting-rooms (**Salles d'attente**), often closed at night, are usually perfectly pleasant except for those at main line stations after dark when there are often unsavoury characters around. It is not allowed to spend the night sleeping in waiting-rooms, nor is it likely to be a particularly pleasant experience.

Assistance Larger stations have first aid posts (**Poste de secours**) as well as station staff qualified to give first aid. If you obviously need help, concerned French people will usually take you to the appropriate spot. In emergencies or where there is no help, head for the Station Master's office.

The police or the semi-military gendarmerie patrol on or near most larger stations.

Emergencies *Emergency telephone numbers*: 15 *for SAMU (Ambulance)*, 17 *for the police*, 18 *for fire services*.

Eating and Drinking Prices for food and drink in station bars and restaurants are slightly above the norm but the food is often suprisingly good and service reasonably fast. Ideally, if you want to create your own meal, you should try and buy provisions in shops or markets away from the station. Counter service in bars is always cheaper – although often there's nowhere to sit. At stand-up bars you usually pay when your order arrives; at sit-down restaurants, expect to pay when you are ready to leave.

If there are tables, simply sit down and wait for the waiter. You will pay almost twice as much this way, but if things are quiet you also buy the right to sit at the table for hours – useful if you have time to kill between trains and have done all the sight-seeing you want to. In smaller stations, with the odd bar table and no waiter, you can usually buy from the bar and sit down without paying extra, but it is better to ask at the bar first. (*Puis-je m'asseoir?*)

All bars serve coffee, tea, alcoholic and soft drinks and various rolls and sandwiches. Larger stations may well have a restaurant. Bars also often sell tickets for the shuttle buses which connect the station with the town center. If, as is usually the case, the bus terminal is itself outside the station, the bar may also operate as the general ticket office. In smaller stations, the bar is also home to telephones, WCs, a shop and a news-stand.

Shops and Foreign Exchange City stations always have news-stands (*un kios-que*), usually selling timetables and a selection of English-language newspapers and magazines. There is also often a pharmacy as well. Prices of articles in shops in or near the station precincts are usually higher than those in the town. Most large stations have foreign exchange facilities (*Change*); these are mentioned in the text below. Rates are invariably poorer than in banks and queues may be long, but they have the advantage of being open on weekends, unlike banks, and outside normal banking hours during the week.

Telephones All stations have telephones – look for the **blue telephone symbol**. In small stations the telephone is usually in the bar. Telephone calls from cafés, hotels and restaurants cost up to 30 per cent more than from a telephone booth. Telephone booths using coins are being phased out rapidly and are now few and far between. Virtually all booths now only take phonecards (*télécartes*), which can be bought from post offices, newsagents, and tobacconists (*tabac*). Cards come in units of 50 (costing 50FF) and 120 (costing 120FF). Calls can be received at phone boxes where the blue bell sign is shown.

France has a simplified telephone system so that there are now only two regions: Paris and the Provinces. All subscribers have an 8-figure number. All Paris numbers should begin with a 4, numbers to the Paris outskirts begin with a 3 or a 6. For calls within Paris, or from province to province, dial the 8-figure number. From Paris to any province, dial 16 then the 8 figure number. From a province to Paris, dial 16 – 1 and then the 8 figures. From France to the UK, first dial 19, wait until the continuous tone recurs, then dial 44 followed by your STD code minus the first 0, and the number you wish to call.

At off hours (weekdays between 10:30 pm and 8 am, and weekends starting 2 pm on Saturdays) rates are cheaper and you can speak longer for the same price.

To make international calls, use a telephone booth or go to the post office. The post office clerk will indicate a booth from which you can dial direct and you pay for the call afterwards. A call is *un coup de téléphone* or *un appel*, to dial is *composer*, a reverse-charge call is *en PCV*. To make a reverse-charge call tell the international operator: *Je veux faire un appel en PCV en Angleterre* (I want to make a reverse-charge call to England). Tel: 13 for operator, 12 for directory enquiries, 19 33 11 for international operator.

Post Most stations have a letter box (small yellow boxes fixed to walls). In larger cities many stations have a fully-functioning post office. Opening hours are usually Monday to Friday 8 am–7 pm and 8 am–12 pm on Saturday mornings. Mail can be received in France through the **Poste Restante** system and should be addressed to the recipient with his surname first, first name second, followed by Poste Restante, R.P. (Recette Principale), Postal Code, City Name, France. A passport or other proof of identity is required to pick up mail and there is a very small fee for the service. Stamps (*timbres*) can also be bought in tobacconists (*tabacs*) and in the odd gift shop in some tourist resorts.

Buses The location of a city's main bus terminal is given below in the Practicalities sections for major cities. Often it is just outside the station itself. Where it's not, there is almost always a shuttle bus which runs to the town center. Tickets usually cost between 3 and 6 FF and are often sold at the station bar or news-stand. The text below occasionally gives details of longer-haul buses that might be useful for excursions. Generally you cannot get on a bus without having bought a ticket beforehand.

Taxis Taxis naturally congregate outside main line stations. Never take rides from people who approach you in the station itself and only take a ride in a registered cab.

Make sure the meter is on zero and running, and be prepared to pay legitimate surcharges for luggage, and weekend, holiday and late-night travel. By law there should be a list of such surcharges in the taxi. For very long journeys try to establish the price beforehand. (*Ça va coûter combien pour aller à . . . –* How much would it cost to go to . . .) If in doubt, ask the driver to write the price down. In the case of any dispute stay calm and polite and try to find a policeman. At smaller stations you may have to call a taxi. Often a variety of numbers will be posted near the public telephones. If not, ask at the bar. Taxis in cities are only allowed to pick up from taxi ranks (*stations de taxis*) or will go to an address to which they have been called by phone. Flagging down taxis in the streets of Paris, in particular can be difficult. In Paris the pick-up charge is 11FF and automatically 5FF higher from a station.

Car Rentals In most big cities there are car rental offices close to mainline stations. Look for advertising within the station, ask at the bar or ticket office or look through the local Yellow Pages (*Les pages jaunes* in French). Avis, Hertz, Solvet, Budget and Europcar have networks in France, the latter two being the least expensive. Europcar has an office at 145 ave Malakoff, 75016 Paris (Tel 45 00 08 06).

Timetables Investing in a timetable will whet your appetite for travel, allow you to plan your routes – or embellish those suggested here – and save you an immense amount of time queueing for information. It's important to remember that the French railway network, like all others in Continental Europe, moves from winter to summer schedules on the last Sunday in May, and from summer to winter schedules on the last Sunday in September. When buying a timetable in France, be sure you are purchasing a current timetable – either late May to late September or late September to late May.

There are two basic schedules which are invaluable if you intend to spend any time traveling by rail.

Thomas Cook's European Timetable The first is *Thomas Cook's European Timetable*, the bible of European rail travelers and an essential handbook if you have a Eurail pass. It contains the timetables for all main line trains and a few minor services on all the European rail networks. It also lists ferry services and a few tables from the *Thomas Cook Airports Guide Europe*.

The June to September issue contains the full European Summer schedule, the issues from February to May contain forecasts of the Summer timetables, thus allowing you to indulge in some pre-planning. The Winter schedules are covered in the October to May issues, with forecasts in the preceding August and September issues.

The timetable is available from Forsyth Travel Library, 9154 West 57 St., Box 2975, Dept. TCT, Shawnee Mission, KS 66201, tel. 800–FORSYTH or 913/384–3440. You might also think about buying the *Thomas Cook Rail Map of Europe*, published every 2 years.

Ville à Ville Timetable The *Ville à Ville*, literally the 'town to town' timetable, is absolutely essential if you're traveling on French trains. The size of a paperback, grey with a green silhouette of France on the cover, it's issued twice yearly at the beginning of May and beginning of September to coincide with the SNCF Summer and Winter schedules. The *Ville à Ville* costs £8 and contains all the major train services in France, plus a map of the entire French rail network. It gives details in a clear, easily understood layout of all the main services with the number of the train, their types or categories, their times of departure and arrival and the services available on board. It also gives the distance of each journey in kilometers and a table showing the price per kilometer which, in conjunction with the 'constant' prices table, can be used to calculate the cost of any trip. It indicates whether couchettes are available, what the facilities are for persons with disabilities, whether bicycles can be taken on board as accompanied luggage, whether there is a supplement to be paid and if necessary, where and when a change has to be made. The *Ville à Ville Timetable* is available from virtually every station kiosk or newsagent in France. You can order it from Bureau de Vente, des Documents, Tarifaires, 212 rue de Bercy, 75571, Paris, tel 011/331/401 96881.

Other Timetables SNCF publishes a whole host of timetables, for which the formats vary.

(1) *Grandes Lignes* timetables: these detail the standard intercity trains and may include some TGV services. The yellow, grey, green and pink squares indicate the level of passenger use, which are the basis for determining fares. *Semaine type* indicates the color code (and therefore fare) that usually applies for the different trains Monday to Sunday. The section below, in yet more yellow, grey, green and pink squares, is marked *Jours particuliers*. This indicates the exceptions, for example it might show that it is usually cheap to travel on a train leaving on Wednesdays at 16:21 hours, but on 3rd April 1995 a higher fare will apply (because, for instance, Easter falls on the 4th that year and everyone will be leaving for their holiday the day before).

Some Grandes Lignes timetables only give details of TGV services in which case they are so marked.

(2) **Guide Régional des Transports:** These brightly colored regional timetables can be picked up from stations within each region in France. These give details of all major and minor local lines, train departures divided into weekly departures (*semaine*) and Sunday and public holiday services (*dimanches et fêtes*).

(3) **Single-line timetables:** stations usually carry all the relevant single-line time-tables for their area. These are small leaflets that give details of the service of one line only (e.g. Paris–Nantes, Paris–Bordeaux or Bordeaux–Périgueux).

Reading a Timetable Please refer to above for reading station timetables. For a key to the symbols which appear in French railway timetables with their English translation, see below. On a regional timetable a blue dot indicates that a train runs from Monday to Friday; a thin blue circle that it runs on Saturdays only; a blue dot with a thin blue circle around it that the train runs from Monday to Saturday. 'Car' indicates that the service is provided by an SNCF bus. Numbers refer to footnotes,

How to use the Timetable

Finding the train you require

Select the timetable you require and check that the train actually runs on the day you have chosen.

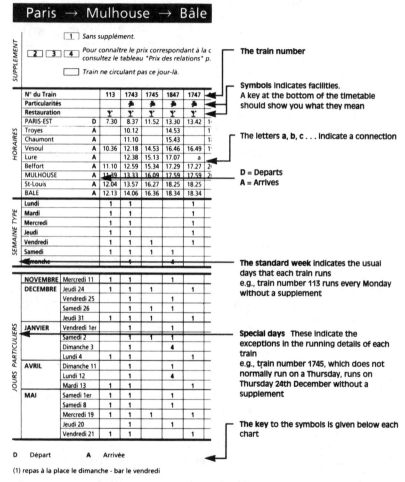

Paris → Mulhouse → Bâle

SUPPLEMENT

☐ 1   Sans supplément.

☐ 2   ☐ 3   ☐ 4   Pour connaître le prix correspondant à la c → The train number
consultez le tableau "Prix des relations" p.

☐   Train ne circulant pas ce jour-là.

Symbols indicates facilities.
A key at the bottom of the timetable
should show you what they mean

HORAIRES

N° du Train		113	1743	1745	1847	1747	
Particularités			♣	♣	♣	♣	
Restauration		⊻	⊻	⊻	⊻	⊻	
PARIS-EST	D	7.30	8.37	11.52	13.30	13.42	1·
Troyes	A		10.12		14.53		1
Chaumont	A		11.10		15.43		1:
Vesoul	A	10.36	12.18	14.53	16.46	16.49	1·
Lure	A		12.38	15.13	17.07	a	
Belfort	A	11.10	12.59	15.34	17.29	17.27	2·
MULHOUSE	A	11.39	13.33	16.09	17.59	17.59	2·
St-Louis	A	12.04	13.57	16.27	18.25	18.25	
BALE	A	12.13	14.06	16.36	18.34	18.34	

The letters a, b, c . . . indicate a connection

D = Departs
A = Arrives

SEMAINE TYPE

	113	1743	1745	1847	1747
Lundi	1	1			1
Mardi	1	1			1
Mercredi	1	1			1
Jeudi	1	1			1
Vendredi	1	1	1		1
Samedi	1	1	1	1	
Dimanche			1	4	

The standard week indicates the usual
days that each train runs
e.g., train number 113 runs every Monday
without a supplement

JOURS PARTICULIERS

NOVEMBRE	Mercredi 11	1	1		1	
DECEMBRE	Jeudi 24	1	1	1		1
	Vendredi 25		1		1	
	Samedi 26		1	1	1	
	Jeudi 31	1	1	1		1
JANVIER	Vendredi 1er		1		1	
	Samedi 2	1	1	1		
	Dimanche 3		1		4	
	Lundi 4	1	1			1
AVRIL	Dimanche 11		1		1	
	Lundi 12		1		4	
	Mardi 13	1	1			1
MAI	Samedi 1er	1	1		1	
	Samedi 8	1	1		1	
	Mercredi 19	1	1	1		1
	Jeudi 20		1		1	
	Vendredi 21		1			1

Special days These indicate the
exceptions in the running details of each
train
e.g., train number 1745, which does not
normally run on a Thursday, runs on
Thursday 24th December without a
supplement

The key to the symbols is given below each
chart

D   Départ   A   Arrivée

(1) repas à la place le dimanche - bar le vendredi

♣   Possibilité de réserver un compartiment Famille en
2e classe tous les jours de circulation du train.

Having decided on your train, note the number and departure time and then you can obtain your ticket either through a travel agent, by phone, by minitel, from a ticket machine or from a station booking office.

which indicate the particularities of that train. For example, a train marked with a 5 might indicate under note 5: *Circule du 4 jan au 22 fév les lun.* (Runs from 4th Jan. to 22nd Feb., Mondays.)

Public Holidays

Trains running either side of public holidays are much busier than normal and are likely to be heavily reserved. Christmas, Easter and around Bastille Day (14th July) are especially hectic periods. Extra trains are added, some of them listed in timetables, others posted at main line stations. On the holidays themselves there are fewer trains, and on smaller lines often no service at all. Trains which do run are often full. Watch out for the French habit of *le pont* or 'bridge', whereby days or half days on either side of an official holiday also become days off, especially if the holiday falls on a Tuesday or Thursday. If you're traveling close to a national holiday check with the stations for changes, try to make a reservation of your own, and arrive earlier than usual for your train.

Public holidays in France *1st January, New Year's Day (le Jour de l'an)*; Easter Monday (*Lundi de Pâques*); Ascension, Whit Monday (*Lundi de Pentecôte*); 1st May, Labour Day (*Fête du Travail*); 8th May (Armistice Day 1945); 14th July, National Bastille Day (*Fête Nationale*); 15th August, Assumption (*Assomption*); 1st November, All Saints (*Toussaint*); 11th November (Armistice Day 1918); 25th December, Christmas Day (*Nöel*).

Timekeeping

French trains are among the most efficient and reliable in Europe. Weather has little effect on French services, not even snow. In fact, there are fast direct trains which sweep through the Alps from Paris straight to towns nearest to the ski resorts. Announcements on trains and in stations are made in clearly articulated French (and at most Paris stations in English as well for certain trains). The vast majority of trains are perfectly punctual; on TGVs refunds are made of the cost of part of the ticket if a train is more than 30 minutes late. Not only are main line trains on time but local ones usually are too. Strikes are rare, pride among staff in the service is high, and so is morale, for French Railways have been the beneficiary of a massive investment program and the management is determined to create one of the fastest, most efficient and reliable train services in the world. Staff are well trained, efficient, polite and well-dressed.

On The Train

Food and Drink

A meal or snack on a train can be a pleasure worth treating yourself to – particularly if you're looking out at great scenery. The classic restaurant cars have become rarer in recent years and a meal is much more likely to be eaten in the buffet-bar. On international trains or TGVs, however, the restaurant car is usually comfortable and smart, with excellent service and surprisingly good food. On one of these, a modest three-course lunch will probably cost about $35 while the same meal in a buffet-bar coach will cost about half as much. Some trains no longer have restaurant cars, in which case meals are brought and served to you in your seat. If you want this service you should request it when you buy your ticket; you will then be allocated a seat in the appropriate part of the train. To check out if your intercity or international train has a full-fledged restaurant car, read the timetable for the appropriate symbols. Announcements are made on trains stating when the buffet-bar or restaurant is open.

Overcrowding

Overcrowding is largely a thing of the past on French trains, except perhaps for the days preceding national holidays when everyone is on the move. On such days, reserve well in advance or stay put, unless you are in the provinces where there will be fewer people moving around. TGVs are never crowded because all seats are reserved. On local trains it is rare for any seats to be booked, and seating is on a first-come-first-seated basis.

There are several ways to escape the problem of overcrowding, at least partially. The most obvious is to make a reservation and to avoid traveling on Friday and Sunday evening or mid-morning on Saturday. Try to take a train that starts at your station and arrive as early as possible if you have not booked a seat.

If papers, magazines, handbags and briefcases are spread out but you feel sure that some places are vacant, the only thing to do is to ask (*Excusez-moi, Madame/ Monsieur, est-ce que ce siège est libre?* – Is this seat vacant?). The likelihood is that it will be and that people will make room. Remember that the buffet-car has seats which are often free when the rest of the train is packed. The price of a cup of coffee lets you sit in peace for a good while.

If there are two or more of you with a lot of luggage it makes sense for one of you to hop on board swiftly, unencumbered by bags. He or she can secure seats – checking the top of the seat to see if it is reserved – and you can follow at leisure with the luggage. Also try the obvious trick of standing at the far ends of the platform where the crowds waiting to get on tend to be thinner. Each platform has a board with colored diagrams of trains, indicating exactly where each car is going to come to rest.

Hazards

Theft of luggage, money or passport is the obvious hazard you face as a rail traveler. In France the danger is much less than, for instance, in neighboring Italy, but care should be taken at stations in Marseilles, Nice, Cannes and Paris late at night. Due to the new double-locking systems on couchette coaches, French night trains are among the safest in Europe. Crowded streets and markets, tourist traps, and the larger cities of Mediterranean France provide the richest pickings for pick- pockets (*voleurs à la tire*). So too do crowded railway stations.

For the most part common sense will ensure that you have no problems. Be discreet and don't parade anything of value. Don't carry money in wallets bulging out of back pockets – keep it in a money belt or something similar – and keep it on your person, especially at night, which is when most thefts occur. Keep a close eye on bags and packs, especially at stations and during the confusion of getting on and off trains. Putting a bag on the platform and turning to take another one from a friend is all the time someone needs to make the snatch. In a big city station keep your camera close to you or put it into a bag. At night women should carry handbags or shoulder bags as French women do, slung across the body.

On the vast majority of trains you can no longer lean out of windows; most are air-conditioned. Even if you can, don't; it's not worth it with a TGV approaching at 300 kmph.

In emergencies, or if you need to report a theft, go first to the ticket inspector (*le contrôleur*) on the train. He will summon the person in charge of the train who in turn will alert the police. At stations go to the Station Master's office (*le chef de gare*), contact a policeman or call 17 for the police.

Women Travelers In the vast majority of places and on the vast majority of trains in France women traveling alone or in pairs are most unlikely to come across any sexual harassment. To avoid unwanted attention it is usually enough to simply move places and find a seat next to a French woman. Introduce yourself and explain why you are changing seats; most will understand immediately and be helpful.

Smoking and Non-Smoking French cars are increasingly either entirely smoking (*fumeurs*) or non-smoking (*non fumeurs*), although some are still divided in the middle. Smoking is still fashionable in France in a way that it has long since ceased to be in the United States, although moves have recently been made to restrict the number of public places where people can smoke. Smoking is now prohibited in the buffet-bars and restaurant cars, and fines for flouting the regulations are severe and immediate.

Some Useful Words and Phrases

La Gare	Railway station
Arrivées	Arrivals
Départs	Departures
Horaire, indicateur	Timetable
Quai	Platform
Correspondance pour	Connection for
Voiture-lits	Sleeper
Voiture-restaurant	Restaurant-car
Vente ambulante	Snack trolley on train
Numéro du train	Train number
Notes à consulter	See footnotes
Le train circule. . .	The train runs . . .
Tous les jours sauf	Every day except
Les sam, dim et fêtes	Saturdays, Sundays & holidays
Circule jusqu'au 18 mai 1995	In service until 18 May 1995
Navette	Shuttle
Excusez-moi, Monsieur/Madame. . .	Excuse me . . .

A quelle heure part le train pour Bordeaux ?	When does the train to Bordeaux leave?
De quel quai part le train ?	Which platform does the train leave from?
Est-ce que le train est direct ?	Is it a direct train?
Est-ce qu'il faut changer ?	Do I have to change?
Où est-ce qu'il faut changer ?	Where must I change?
A quel heure arrive le train à Nice ?	When does the train arrive at Nice?
Combien coûte un aller simple pour Lyon ?	How much is a single ticket to Lyon?
Un aller simple	A single ticket
Un aller et retour	A return ticket
Je veux un aller simple	I want a single ticket
Est-ce que je peux l'acheter ici ?	Can I buy it here?
Où puis-je acheter le billet ?	Where can I buy the ticket?
Je veux réserver une place assise/des places assises	I want to reserve a seat/some seats.
Je suis très pressé	I'm in a hurry.
Mon train va partir!	My train is about to leave!
Est-ce que ceci est le train pour . . .?	Is this the train for . . .?
Est-ce que ce train s'arrête à Arles?	Does this train stop at Arles?
Eloignez-vous du quai!	Stand back from the platform!
Je ne trouve pas mon billet!	I can't find my ticket!
J'ai perdu mon billet!	I've lost my ticket!
Je l'ai acheté à Grenoble.	I bought it at Grenoble.
Est-ce que vous avez un horaire, s'il vous plaît?	Do you have a timetable please?
Composition des trains	Order of train carriages.

Bicycles

Taking bicycles on French trains is not a straightforward matter, for they may take five days to arrive at your destination. Since there is usually no special compartment for them, bicycles have to travel separately and are classified as registered luggage. This is quite safe and not expensive but SNCF does not guarantee delivery in less than five days, although in practice it is sometimes faster. On the smaller local trains, which have a special compartment, it is possible, however, to take a bicycle with you and such trains are marked with a bicycle symbol in the timetable.

To make up for this inconvenience, and as a service to the visitor, SNCF instituted a bicyle rental system at 250 stations a few years ago. Problems with the bicycles and with their maintenance, however, meant that this idea was not a great success and some SNCF stations have abandoned the scheme altogether. Bicycles are hired out at 44 or 55FF per day or 33 or 44FF per half-day depending on the type of bicycle, with lower rates applying from the third day onwards. A deposit of 1,000FF per bicycle is required (1,500FF for mountain bikes). In the Parisian region, RATP (the French equivalent of London Transport) rents bicycles on the A line of the RER (regional rail network) at such places as Saint-Germain-en-Laye.

Dogs and Other Creatures

It's unlikely that Americans will be traveling around with their pets but one never knows. Dogs and other domestic animals pay 50 per cent of the price of a normal 2nd class ticket irrespective of whether the animal (and you) are traveling 1st or 2nd class. If, however, your domestic animal is on the small side (weighing no more than 6 kg!) and you transport it in a box not exceeding 45 × 30 × 25 cms, you only have to pay a flat fee of 28FF. *Et voilà!* What hasn't SNCF thought about!

Arriving in Paris

The French railway system, like so much else in France, is centered on Paris. This is natural enough, Paris being the capital, but it does mean that it is sometimes easier to return to Paris and take another train from there than to attempt to cross the country east to west across the center. Paris therefore forms the hub of the railway network, with radiating spokes leading out in all directions. Different railway stations in Paris serve different parts of the country; all of them are on Metro lines and most have the facilities required by the traveler, including left-luggage offices (*consigne*) or lockers and information bureaus. The main railway stations in Paris and the regions they serve are:

(1) **Gare d'Austerlitz** Serves the Région Sud-Ouest (the Loire Valley and south-western France): La Rochelle, Tours, Bordeaux, Toulouse, Bayonne, the Pyrenees etc. and Spain (Barcelona, Madrid) and Portugal. Information: Tel. (1) 45 82 50 50; Reservations: (1) 45 65 60 60.

(2) **Gare de l'Est** Serves the Région Est (eastern France): Reims, Metz, Nancy, Strasbourg etc. and Switzerland (Geneva, Lausanne, Bern), southern Germany (Munich, Frankfurt) and Luxembourg.
Information: Tel. (1) 45 82 50 50; Reservations: (1) 45 65 60 60.

(3) **Gare de Lyon** Serves the Région Sud-Est (southern and south-eastern France): Lyon, Dijon, Provence, Côte d'Azur, including the new TGVs. Also serves Switzerland, Italy and Greece.
Information: Tel. (1) 45 82 50 50; Reservations: (1) 45 65 60 60.

(4) **Gare Montparnasse** Serves the Région Ouest (western France): Brittany, parts of Normandy and TGV departures for south-western France (Bordeaux), and Spain (Barcelona, Madrid).
Information: Tel. (1) 45 82 50 50; Reservations: (1) 45 65 60 60.

(5) **Gare du Nord** Serves the Région Nord (northern France): Lille, boat-trains to Boulogne, Calais, Dunkirk and Belgium, Netherlands and northern Germany.
Information: Tel. (1) 45 82 50 50; Reservations: (1) 45 65 60 60.

(6) **Gare St Lazare** Also serves the Région Ouest (western France): Normandy lines, Rouen, and boat trains to Dieppe, Le Havre, Cherbourg.
Information: Tel. (1) 45 82 50 50; Reservations: (1) 45 65 60 60.

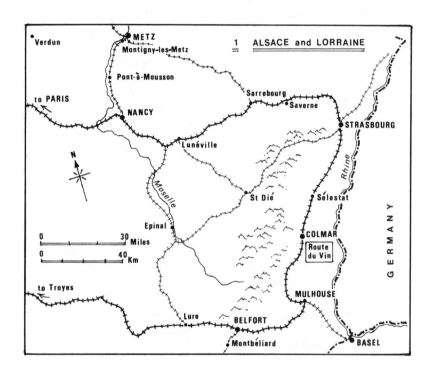

1 = ALSACE and LORRAINE

1 Alsace-Lorraine

Occupying an unenviable position mid-way between the historic heart of France and that of the Teutonic races to the east, Alsace and Lorraine have been in the path of eastern invaders since the 3rd and 4th centuries when barbarian tribes first swept across the Rhine. That the population stems from both Gallic and Teutonic origins however gives the region its unique and intriguing flavour. The border has long been an area of dispute; the Gauls claimed the Rhine as their natural frontier while the Teutons preferred the heights of the Vosges. The area was under German rule for 7 centuries until conquered by Louis XIV between 1648 and 1697. The people of Alsace then inclined towards Protestantism which had been widely accepted in the northern half of the Holy Roman Empire. The connection of Alsace with France was strengthened during the Revolution in the 18th century and there was little popular support for the annexation of the province by Germany in 1871 after France's defeat in the Franco-Prussian war. The Treaty of Versailles in 1919 returned the province to France.

The history of Lorraine differs from that of Alsace primarily in being more closely allied to the Catholic cause, particularly under the sons of René II, the Duc de Guise and his brother Jean, Cardinal of Lorraine in the 17th century. The Duchy of Lorraine was occupied by France at the end of the Thirty Years War, the Treaty of Westphalia confirming French possession of the Three Bishoprics of Toul, Verdun and Metz. French forces invaded the province again during the War of the Polish Succession in the early 1730s. The northern part of the province was annexed by Germany in 1871 but it was later returned to French rule after the First World War.

Alsace-Lorraine is a region of great scenic and artistic interest. Gutenberg, who revolutionised the social and political face of Europe by inventing a printing press using movable type, lived in Strasbourg from 1437 to 1447. An important city throughout the Middle Ages, today the city is the home of the European Parliament and the Council of Europe. The wooded hills of the Vosges mountains, which run from north to south parallel to the Rhine as far as Thann, form the backbone of Alsace. And from here on these undulating slopes covered with vineyards and picturesque villages come a number of white wines and the dry rosé Pinot Noir.

Riesling and Gewurtztraminer are the most famous wines from these vineyards, the latter in particular having a superb fragrance.

The cuisine too is unmistakably German in influence. Pork dishes abound and wine is used frequently in the traditional dishes such as *choucroute garnie* and *coq au Riesling*, while the use of goose or pork fat gives many of the dishes a superb taste. Sausages and ham play an important role in Alsace cooking and *foie gras* is as relished here as it is in Périgord. Poultry from the farmyards of Alsace, especially those of Wantzenau, are fine and delicate and often cooked with cream, butter or lard. Other specialities include *tarte à l'oignon*, the famous *quiche Lorraine*, *pâté de foie gras* and *baeckaoffe*, a casserole of marinated beef, pork and lamb. From the rivers of the Vosges come trout, often served with a cream sauce or cooked in Riesling. Local cheeses include Munster and Emmental.

The early domestic architecture of Alsace and Lorraine is primarily half-timbered houses with steep roofs, the balconies loaded with geraniums. Spring, early summer and autumn during the grape harvest are the best times to go, but also the most crowded.

The route *Nancy – Toul – Metz – Saverne – Strasbourg – Sélestat – Colmar – Route du Vin – Mulhouse – Belfort – Epinal – St-Dié*

*Easily accessible from Paris and one of the most perfect examples in France of 18th-century town planning, with huge public squares and magnificent public buildings, **Nancy** is an elegant, dynamic and historic city which for 6 centuries was the capital of the dukes of Lorraine. The valley of the Moselle is then followed north to **Metz**, a German stronghold during the first World War, which has retained its historic heart of cobblestone streets and tranquil canals. Heading south-east a narrow gap in the Vosges leads to **Saverne**, a little town on the Zorn and Marne-Rhine canal, and on to the magnificent city of **Strasbourg**, the old capital of Alsace, with its fabulous cathedral and historic centre surrounded by canals and branches of the river Ill. A short distance south is **Colmar**, calmer than Strasbourg and surrounded by vineyards and the wooded Vosges mountains. Further south lies **Mulhouse**, an industrial city of interest primarily for its unusual museums devoted to trains and vintage cars. The Vosges mountains are then skirted to **Epinal**, an attractive little town situated on the Moselle and famous throughout Europe in the 18th century for its prints and caricatures.*

From Epinal one of the few railway routes through the Vosges can be followed to St-Dié, a small town with a delightful cathedral and Gothic cloisters which have been painstakingly restored after severe damage in 1944. The route then lies either north-west to Nancy or back to Strasbourg, descending through the foothills of the Vosges. Many of the villages on the famous wine route through Alsace – the **Route du Vin** *– are not accessible by train; some, however, can be reached by bicycle, which can be hired from some of the stations en route, or by bus excursions from tourist offices. (Approximately* **4–6 days.***)*

Nancy

Trains *Frequent daily trains from* **Paris** *Gare de l'Est (2½–3½ hours); every 1–2 hours from* **Strasbourg** *(1½ hours); every 2 hours from* **Metz** *(2¾ hours).*

Nancy, the old capital of Lorraine, lies in the broad valley of the Meurthe at the foot of wooded hills. Today Nancy consists of the **medieval town**, located around the church of the Cordeliers and the old palace of the dukes of Lorraine, and the **new town** laid out in the 17th and 18th centuries. Above all, Nancy is famed for its magnificent 18th-century Baroque architecture.

From the 12th century Nancy was the capital of the Dukes of Lorraine but it was Stanislas Leszczyński, the ex-King of Poland and father-in-law of Louis xv, who was responsible for the chief embellishments of the town. He was given the Duchy to console him for his loss of the Polish throne under the Peace of Vienna after the War of the Polish Succession (1732–38) and on his death, in 1766, Louis xv incorporated the province into France. Under Stanislas the town became the seat of a brilliant court which attracted many distinguished artists, the most famous of whom were the architect Emmanuel Héré, the iron-worker Jean Lamour and the sculptor Nicolas Adam. Using their talents to the full, Stanislas laid out large areas of the town, combining squares and grand vistas in an elegant, formal and geometric plan.

What to see

Place Stanislas
Stanislas's greatest legacy is the square named after him. Designed by Emmanuel Héré, it is one of the most beautiful squares built anywhere in Europe in the course

of the 18th century. The square is enclosed by palatial buildings of uniform design, the largest being the **Hôtel de Ville** to the south, decorated with Corinthian pilasters and magnificent banisters by Jean Lamour, a native of Nancy. Others include the **theatre** and the **Grand Hôtel** to the north and the Musée des Beaux-Art on the West. In the northern angles of the square stand 2 exquisite fountains. The leaden statues are backed by the most characteristic feature of the square – the magnificent gilded wrought-ironwork, also by Lamour and considered to be a masterpiece of 18th-century metalwork. The statues of Neptune and Amphitrite surrounded by their allegorical retinue are the work of an artist from Nîmes, Barthélemy Guibal. In the centre of Place Stanislas stands a bronze statue of the Polish King by Georges Jacquot.

Musée des Beaux-Arts

In the Musée des Beaux-Arts, on the west side of Place Stanislas, Nancy possesses an unusually fine provincial art collection with works by Monet, Dufy, Manet, Modigliani, Matisse, Poussin, Claude-Lorrain, Ruisdael, Perugino, and others, including Fauvist paintings and one of Delacroix's great historical paintings, the *Death of Charles the Bold at the Battle of Nancy*, a painting of particular interest to the city. (Open Wed–Sun 10:30 am–12:30 pm and 1:30 pm–5:45 pm; Mon 1:30–5:45 pm.) Adjoining the Musée des Beaux-Arts is the **triumphal arch** which leads onto the Place de la Carrière lined by 2 palaces, built in 1715 and 1753 and a series of elegant town houses.

Arc de Triomphe

To the north of Place Stanislas lies the triumphal arch built by Héré in honour of a visit made to the town by Louis XV. It was modelled on the arch of Septimus-Severus in Rome and has panels dedicated to the gods of war and peace, where Louis XV appears enshrined in a medallion. At the northern end of Place de la Carrière, a long straight boulevard which was used as a tournament ground in the 16th century, stands the Palais du Gouvernement, the former home of the governors of Lorraine.

Palais Ducal

Adjoining the Palais du Gouvernement is the huge but ugly Palais Ducal, the most important secular building of the late-Gothic period in Lorraine. René II began building this around 1495 and it was continued by his son Antoine in the florid flamboyant style between 1508 and 1544. The palace was thoroughly sacked in 1792 before being unfortunately restored in the mid-19th century and then burnt again by a fire in 1871. The only genuinely noteworthy part of the palace is the main gateway, the Renaissance **Porterie**, which dates from the beginning of the 16th century. This finely sculpted and elaborate gateway incorporates a restored equestrian statue of Antoine, Duc de Lorraine.

The Palais Ducal now houses the **Musée Historique de Lorraine** devoted to the history of Lorraine, with archaeological finds, Stone Age tools, Roman coins, Roman and medieval sculpture and rich collections of material on the culture of the province. On the first floor is the **Galerie des Cerfs**, with relics of the ducal period, tapestries, etchings by Jacques Callot and pictures by Georges de la Tour. An interesting collection of historical portraits has been gathered together in the Historical Museum of Lorraine. (Open Wed–Mon 10 am–noon and 2–6 pm).

Eglise des Cordeliers

Behind the ducal palace is the Eglise des Cordeliers, a huge but unremarkable church built by king René II in the 1480s to mark the deliverance of Nancy from the Burgundians. Their attempt to seize the city collapsed when their Duke, Charles the Bold, was killed in a battle before the city in 1477. The church contains the tombs of the Dukes of Lorraine carved by the Renaissance artists Mansuy Gauvain, Ligier Richier and Florent Drouin. Richier's masterpiece is the recumbent effigy of Philippa de Gueldre, Duchess of Lorraine, where a grim naturalism is conveyed through the alarmingly realistic rendering of her drawn, gaunt face. Such naturalism was an element of the late-Gothic preoccupation with death which manifested itself in funereal art through the portrayal of skeletons and the macabre. Profoundly affected by the religious conflict and controversy of the day, which was particularly severe in Alsace and Lorraine, Richier eventually converted to Protestantism, an action that forced him to flee to Geneva where he died in 1566. The octagonal Ducal Chapel, begun in 1607 in a classical style, was modelled on the chapel of the Médicis in Florence. Around the ducal palace are a number of fine town houses, especially the 18th-century **Hôtel Ferrari** by Boffrand at 29 rue Haut-Bourgeois, the **Hôtel de Lillebonne** at 12 rue de la Source and the **Hôtel du Marquis de Ville** at 10 rue de la Source.

Parc de la Pépinière

East of the ducal palace and the Eglise des Cordeliers is the huge Parc de la Pépinière, created in 1765, in the middle of which stands a sculpture by Rodin of the painter Claude le Lorrain. Opposite the gardens is the neo-Gothic church of St-Epvre with superb stained glass from the Geyling workshop in Vienna. The street opposite the church, **Grand Rue**, is the principal thoroughfare of the city.

Cathedral

Situated south of Place Stanislas in the 18th-century part of the city, Nancy Cathedral is a disappointing building, despite being the work of Hardouin-Mansart. It is built in a ponderous classical style which has little warmth and is of interest more for its superb interior ironwork by Lamour and Jean Maire than for its architecture.

Chapelle de Bonsecours

Of greater interest than the cathedral is the Chapelle de Bonsecours, some distance to the east of the cathedral, a pretty little Baroque chapel built for King Stanislas who is buried inside with his wife. It was designed by Héré in 1738 and decorated in a rich Italian Renaissance style. King Stanislas's tomb, sculpted by Vassé, is coldly classical: the King appears to be rising awkwardly from his tomb while beneath him stand figures consumed by grief. The mausoleum of his wife, Catherine Opalinska, which is altogether more lyrical and joyous in spirit, is the work of

Lambert Adam. The heart of their daughter Marie Leszczyńska, wife of Louis XV, lies beneath a nearby tablet.

Practicalities in Nancy

Tourist Office 14 Place Stanislas, on the main square, close to the triumphal arch (Tel. 83 35 22 41); accommodation service; daily city tours in French during summer.

Railway Station Place Thiers. For the town centre, turn left out of station, then right down Rue Stanislas to the heart of Nancy – Place Stanislas. (Tel. 83 56 50 50); lockers; information office; open Mon-Sat 5.30 am–7.30 pm; Sun 6.30 am–8.30 pm.

Buses *Rapides de Lorraine*, Place de la Cathédrale (Tel. 83 32 34 20). To Verdun battlefields (2½ hours), Vittel, Lunéville.

Festivals *Festival de Jazz*: mid-October in the Parc de la Pépinière.

Markets Outside Eglise St-Sébastien, Mon–Sat.

Post Office Rue Pierre-Fourier, behind Hôtel de Ville (Tel. 83 36 51 47), currency exchange. Open Mon–Fri 8am–7pm, Sat 8am-noon.

Hotels *Hôtel Jean Jaurès*, 14 blvd Jean Jaurès (Tel. 83 27 74 14). Quiet and pleasant.

Hôtel Pasteur, 47 rue Pasteur, off rue Graffigny, not far from the centre but nicer than the cheap hotels in Rue Jeanne d'Arc (Tel. 83 40 29 85).

Hôtel Moderne, 73 rue Jeanne d'Arc (Tel. 83 40 14 26). Very basic and very cheap!

☆ *Hôtel Résidence*, 30 blvd Jean Jaurès (Tel. 83 40 33 56). Close to station, welcoming and good value.

☆ *Hôtel Cigogne*, 4 bis rue des Ponts, near Eglise St-Sébastien (Tel. 83 32 89 44).

☆☆ *Hôtel Ibis*, 3 rue Crampel (Tel. 83 37 84 61). Modern and close to sation.

☆☆ *Central*, 6 rue Raymond Poincaré (Tel. 83 32 21 24). Next to the station, modernised, double-glazed to keep out noise; delightful courtyard.

☆☆☆☆ *Grand Hôtel de la Reine*, 2 place Stanislas (Tel. 83 35 03 01). The most magnificent hotel in Nancy, in a superb 18th-century building on Place Stanislas; Louis XV style.

Restaurants *La Miltonne*, 2 rue St-Michel, near St-Epvre. Tel. Specialises in fondues.

L'Elephante sous la Tonnelle, 47 Grande Rue. Unusual flavours and mixtures in this curious and lively restaurant.

☆ *L'Entracte*, 123 Grand Rue (Tel. 83 36 62 71). Good, traditional French country cooking.

☆☆ *Mirabelle*, 24 rue Heré (Tel. 83 30 49 69).

☆☆ *Petit Gastrolatre*, 7 rue des Maréchaux (Tel. 83 35 51 94). Excellent *nouvelle cuisine* from chef Patrick Tanesy.

☆☆☆ *Cap Marine*, 60 rue Stanislas (Tel. 83 37 05 03). Modern setting and excellent food in one of the best restaurants in Nancy.

Excursion from Nancy
The Verdun Battlefields

Trains *2 trains daily from Nancy, changing at Conflans-Jarny (2 hours).*

No battlefield in France is more famous or more symbolic of the devastating human loss of human life incurred by France than that of Verdun. In the eight months between January and October 1916 over 335,000 German and 360,000 French soldiers died here in the bloodiest battle in recorded history.

Built at a strategic crossing point on the Meuse, **Verdun** was an important military town from the Middle Ages to 1918. Most of the town was flattened during the First World War but some of the town's finest monuments were painstakingly rebuilt in the 1920's. Most impressive is the 14th century fortress, the **Porte Chaussée**, which guarded the passage over the Meuse, its massive round towers capped by crenellations and machicolations. Like the Porte Chaussée, the 15th century Porte Châtel was also once incorporated into the city walls.

Verdun's cathedral has been extensively restored but retains the impressive Romanesque buttresses of its two apses which are carved with attractive figures. The tympanum in the round arch of the 12th century Porte du Lion is of interest for its beautifully carved figure of Christ in Majesty in Burgundian style.

Above all however, Verdun should be

visited for its **battlefields**, a sombre reminder of the scale of human destruction in the trenches of the Picardy battlefields. The peaceful fields of ripening grain belie the carnage and horror of the scene some 80 years ago. The only way for train travellers to explore the battlefields is to take one of the excellent 4 hour bus tours which leave from the tourist office on Place de la Nation. (April–Sept, 4 hours round trip). The chilling 'Tranchée des Baïonettes' marks the spot where an entire company of French infantry were buried alive in their trench while waiting to go into attack; only discovered after the war, the trench has been preserved as a monument for posterity.

The two most impressive forts at the heart of the battlefields are **Fort Vaux** and **Fort Douaumont**. Fort Douaumont fell to the Germans on 25 February 1916 after the collapse of communication left it with a garrison of only 57 men. From the top of the fort there is an excellent view out over the battlefield, still irrevocably pitted three quarters of a century later. Nearby is a small war museum, the **Musée de Fleury**, with models, uniforms and military equipment. (Open daily 9 am–6 pm; mid-Sept – mid March 9 am–noon and 2–6 pm). A short distance away is the massive ossuary with a rocket-like tower, the **Ossuaire de Douaumont**, which holds the bones of 100,000 French soldiers, while another 15,000 lie in the adjacent cemetery. It is impossible not to be overwhelmed by the sense of waste and terrible loss, walking round the vast cemetery, perfectly aligned rows of white crosses tailing away into the distance. The graves of British and Commonwealth soldiers were laid out and have been beautifully maintained by the War Graves Commission since the 1920's. (Open daily 9 am–12:30 pm and 2–6:30 pm).

Practicalities in Verdun

Tourist office Place de la Nation, opposite the medieval Porte Chaussée (Tel. 29 86 14 18); maps, details of bus tours of battlefields.
Railway station Place Maurice Genevoix (Tel. 29 86 25 65). To reach tourist office from station, walk down ave. Garibaldi, turn right through the Porte St Paul (passing the Rodin monument), then left into rue Chaussée and across bridge.
Accommodation *Hôtel de la Porte Chaussée*, (Tel. 29 86 00 78), overlooking the Meuse close to the Porte Chaussée; simple but good and clean and in convenient central location.
☆☆ *Bellevue*, rond-point de Lattre-de-Tassigny (Tel 29 84 39 41). Hotel and restaurant open Easter-end October; located on roundabout on far side of Meuse from railway station over Pont Chaussée.
Restaurants *Des Deux Gares*, 23 ave. Garibaldi. Simple brasserie with a choice of cheap menus.
Markets Wed. and Fri. mornings on rue du Rû.

Toul

Trains *4 trains daily from* **Nancy** *(20 mins).*
Only a short distance away from Nancy lies the lovely old town of Toul. Situated within impressive ramparts Toul is a quiet town with ramshackle streets. There are 2 fine Gothic buildings which survived despite severe bombing to the town during the Second World War.

The **Cathedral of Saint-Etienne**, begun in 1204 and not completed until the 16th century, is a masterpiece of Flamboyant architecture. Its 15th-century façade incorporates 2 octagonal towers which soar 60 metres from the ground. Inside there are 2 exquisite Renaissance chapels on either side of a rather austere nave lit by sunlight which pours through the beautiful 13th–15th century stained glass. On one side of the cathedral are the attractive 14th-century cloisters, on the other the Hôtel de Ville which was originally built in 1740 as the Archbishop's Palace. In Rue Gouvion St Cyr is the small **Musée Municipal**, housed in a former medieval hospital. The Salle des Malades was built in the 13th century as the patients' ward. (Open Wed–Mon 10am-noon and 2–6pm.)

Old houses in Rue de la Boucherie and its continuation lead to the **Church of St-Gengoult**, with its graceful 15th-century west door. Its choir contains some of the most attractive 13th-century stained glass in eastern France and its Flamboyant Gothic cloister has elegant and intricate stellar vaulting.

Practicalities in Toul

Tourist Office Parvis de la Cathédrale (Tel. 83 64 11 69).
Railway Station (Info: Tel. 83 56 50 50; Reservations: Tel. 83 35 08 58.)

Restaurants ☆ *Belle Epoque*, 31 ave Victor Hugo (Tel. 83 43 23 71). Good, standard dishes in intimate restaurant located between the station and the old town.

Metz

Trains *10 trains daily from* **Nancy** *(40 mins); 9–10 from* **Strasbourg** *(1½ hours); 5 from* **Lyon** *(5 hours).*

The landscape between Nancy and Metz is characterised by the flat plain of the Moselle, much of it devoted in summer to hop-growing. Mid-way between the 2 cities is **Pont-à-Mousson** which was an important bastion of Catholicism in the religious debates of the 16th and 17th centuries. The vast building visible on the far bank of the river is a **Premonstratensian Abbey** which dates from the 18th century. Charles III established a university there in 1572 to combat the spread of Protestantism. Run by Jesuits it was eventually transferred to Nancy in the 18th century. **Pont-à-Mousson** was the scene of fierce fighting in September 1944 when German forces attempted to resist General Patton's Allied crossing of the Moselle from a strongpoint on the hill east of the river known as the butte de Mousson.

Metz railway station probably qualifies as the most hideous and grandiose in Europe; it was built under the Germans in 1908 in a bizarre neo-Romanesque style. More attractive than the German quarter of Metz, built between the Franco-Prussian war and the First World War, is the historic quarter with its narrow streets and lanes and old houses situated around the **Place d'Armes** and the cathedral.

Although an industrial city, Metz is one of the greenest cities in France, with many leafy gardens, parks and shady squares. At its heart, soaring above the **Hôtel de Ville** and the 18th-century **Place d'Armes**, is the Cathedral of St-Etienne. The town centre is divided into islands linked together by bridges.

What to see

Cathédrale St-Etienne

The cathedral of St-Etienne is a handsome Gothic building of yellow sandstone flanked by 2 slender towers. Built between 1250 and 1380, it originally consisted of 2 entirely separate churches; these were joined together, the nave being added in the 13th and 14th centuries, the transept in the 15th and the choir in the 16th. One might therefore expect it to form an unsatisfactory ensemble but somehow it all hangs together with remarkable fluidity. The northern and southern façades are flanked by a tower that creates an image of order and symmetry, and the body of the church has a wealth of flying buttresses of great beauty.

The windows cover an area of over 7,000 square metres and make the interior of the cathedral unusually bright. The stained glass that fills these windows spans 7 centuries: some of the earliest stained glass, by Herman von Muster, dates from the 14th century while the most modern, by Jacques Villon, Bissière and Marc Chagall, dates from the early 20th century. The nave which soars to a height of 45 metres is one of the tallest in France and is a fine example of Gothic art. In the south aisle are the Chapelle Notre-Dame, once the choir of the older church of Notre-Dame-la-Ronde and the Chapelle du St-Sacrement with stained glass by Jacques Villon. North-east of the cathedral is the **Musée d'Art et d'Histoire** in the former convent of the Petits Carmes, with a small collection of Gallo-Roman artefacts and medieval art and sculpture. In the 1930s Roman baths were uncovered in the basement of the convent and they now form part of the museum's exhibits. Religious works of art are exhibited in the **Grenier de Chevremont**, a stone granary built in 1457.

Porte des Allemands

Most of the city's medieval walls and defences have been dismantled but the Porte des Allemands is a formidable double fortification straddling the river Seille. The first gateway, closest to the town, consists of 2 round 13th-century towers with pepper-pot slate roofs. A fortified bridge leads across to a second gateway defended by 2 massive strongly machicolated 15th-century towers. The four towers are linked by a covered passageway which enabled troops to supply the forward defensive tower. Lying at the very heart of the town is the large **Place de la République** facing the formal gardens of the **Esplanade** which descend west to the Moselle. From the beautiful terrace of the Esplanade there are superb views of the Moselle valley and Mont St-Quentin.

Palais de Justice

North of the Esplanade stands the large, classical Palais de Justice built in the 18th century in an attractive yellow stone. It stands on the site of the Hôtel de la Haute

Pierre which at one point was the residence of the Duke of Suffolk, Queen Mary's 'favourite' (ie. secret lover). One of the sculpted bas-relief panels in the interior courtyard celebrates the peace concluded between England, France, the United States and Holland in 1783.

St-Pierre aux Nonnains

South of the Esplanade stands the little church of St-Pierre-aux-Nonnains, one of the oldest churches in France. In the 4th century it was a Roman basilica but it was sacked in 451 by Attila and fell into disrepair before being converted into a church in the 7th century. The stonework dating from this period is now conserved in the **Musée d'Art et d'Histoire**. Close to St-Pierre-aux-Nonnains is an unusual little octagonal chapel, the Chapelle des Templiers, built by the Knights Templar at the beginning of the 13th century (Open Tues-Sun, 2 – 6.30 pm).

Although one of the best fortified towns of northern France – Metz successfully resisted 2 sieges in 1814 and 1815 – the French General Bazaine surrendered the city to the Germans in the Franco-Prussian war of 1870 after putting up resistance for only 10 weeks. The surrender of the city, together with some 179,000 men, 6,000 officers and 1,600 guns was a catastrophic defeat for France. The city, and a large part of the Lorraine, then became part of Germany and 43 years later the city played a crucial role in the German offensives of the First World War. The front lines stabilised only a few miles from the city and as a result the town received the occasional bombardment. Just before an offensive was begun to outflank the city by the Allies, however, the Armistice was signed and the city capitulated to Petain who entered the city on 19th November 1918.

Practicalities in Metz

Tourist office Place d'Armes, almost opposite the cathedral (Tel. 87 75 65 21); accommodation service; daily city tours, some in English.
Railway station Place Général de Gaulle. For town centre take bus 11 from opposite the station to Place d'Armes, or turn right and walk past gardens, left onto Rue Haute-Seille and left onto En Gournirue. (Info: Tel. 85 56 50 50; Reservations: Tel 87 63 50 50). Open Mon– Sat 8 am–7.30 pm; Sun 9.30 am–noon and 2– 6.30 pm.)
Buses Place Coislin (Tel. 87 75 73 73) to Verdun (4 daily, 2 hours).
Markets Place St-Jacques: Tues and Thurs mornings; Place de la Cathedrale: Sat mornings.
Festivals *Festival Etonnante Musique*: end Aug, beginning of Sept, contemporary music celebrations. *Fête de la Mirabelle* One week in Sept, hot-air ballooning, processions, music. *Recontres Internatinales de Musique Contemporaine* November, contemporary choral and classical music concerts throughout city.
Hotels *Hôtel Moderne*, 1 rue de la Fayette, a

stone's throw from the station but simpler and cheaper than Hôtel Métropole (Tel. 87 66 57 33).
Hôtel de France, 25 Place de Chambre (Tel. 87 75 00 02). A little faded but superb location right behind the cathedral.
☆☆ *Hôtel Métropole*, 5 Place Général de Gaulle, opposite the station (Tel. 87 66 26 22). Large, simple, clean, well-modernised, and convenient to station. Brasserie downstairs provides quick, simple meals.
☆☆ *Hôtel de la Gare*, 20 rue Gambetta, right opposite the station (Tel. 87 66 74 03).
Hostels *Auberge de Jeunesse* (HI), 1 allée de Metz Plage, opposite end of town from station. Bus 3 or 11 from station to **Pontiffroy** on Moselle River (Tel. 87 30 44 02). Clean, simple, good facilities.
Camping *Metz-Plage* (Tel. 87 32 05 58). Beautiful, shady location beside the Moselle River and Auberge de Jeunesse. Showers, swimming pool.
Restaurants *Albion*, 8 rue de Père-Potot, off Rue de la Fontaine (Tel. 87 36 55 56). Good fare at cheap prices.

☆ *A La Ville de Lyon*, 7 rue des Piques (Tel. 87 36 07 01). Tucked behind the cathedral. Superb dishes and magnificent wine list.
☆ *La Gargouille*, 29 Place Chambre (Tel. 87 36 65 77).
☆☆ *La Dinanderie*, 2 rue de Paris (Tel. 87 30 14 40). Intimate restaurant overlooking River

Moselle from the cathedral. Imaginative chef Claude Piegiorgi creates memorable dishes.
☆ *Le Chat Noir*, 30 rue Pasteur (Tel. 87 56 99 19).
☆☆ *Le Bouquet Garni*, 10 rue Pasteur (Tel. 87 66 85 97).

Saverne

Trains 3–5 *trains daily from* **Metz** *(1 hour 5 mins);* 7–9 *trains daily from* **Paris** *Gare de l'Est (4 hours 20 mins),* **Nancy** *(1 hour) and* **Strasbourg** *(30 mins).*

Saverne is the first Alsatian town on the Paris to Strasbourg railway line, occupying a strategic position at the mouth of a valley which opens from the Vosges mountains onto the plain of Alsace.

Initially a Roman settlement called Tres Tabernae, Saverne became the residence of the bishops of Strasbourg from 1414 to 1789. There are many fine Renaissance houses in the **Grand Rue**, the 17th-century Maison Katz being an especially fine example with its rich wood carving. The houses have the steep-pitched roofs, dormer windows and window-boxes full of brightly-coloured geraniums. In the 16th century Saverne was the scene of an infamous revolt by the peasants of Alsace which was brutally stopped when they were massacred by the troops of the Duke of Lorraine. Known as the *Rustauds*, the rebellious peasants had negotiated a truce with the noble Duke but were cut down to the last man by his soldiers the moment they had disarmed and left the defences of the city.

What to see

Château des Rohan

The bishops of Strasbourg ruled the town from the 13th century until the Revolution, residing in a luxurious palace which was visited by Louis XIV in 1681, Marie Leszczyńska in 1725 and Louis XV in 1744. When the palace burnt down in 1779 the extravagant Cardinal, Louis René de Rohan, spent a fortune rebuilding the enormous sandstone château that still stands today. It had barely been completed when the Revolution took place, by which time the cardinal had been disgraced after being implicated in the *Affaire du Collier* scandal at Versailles in 1785.

Goethe described the Louis XVI château as 'an ecclesiastical outpost of a powerful monarch'; it is an imposing but somewhat severe structure of pink sandstone and was completed by Napoleon III who turned it into a residence for the widows of civil servants. It now houses a museum of archaeology, art and history, a theatre, a primary school and a youth hostel.

Saverne is an attractive town with a number of old buildings and a pretty 15th-century church and it makes an excellent centre from which to explore the large

Parc Naturel Régional des Vosges du Nord. Forests of chestnut, beech and larch extend for miles around. Through these woods a track leads up to the precariously sited Château du Haut-Barr which crowns some craggy rocks 450 metres up to the south-west. A Romanesque building occupied in the 16th century by a bishop of Strasbourg, it was damaged during the Thirty Years War and sold off by the state following the Revolution.

Practicalities in Saverne

Tourist Office Château des Rohan, on place Gen. de Gaulle. (Tel. 88 91 80 47). **Railway Station** (Info: Tel. 88 22 50 50; Reservations: Tel. 88 32 07 51). For the town centre walk to the bottom of the Rue de la Gare which leads to the main street, the Grand Rue. **Festivals** *Son-et-lumière* performances at château during summer. **Hotels** ☆ *Hôtel Boeuf Noir*, 22 Grand Rue (Tel. 88 91 10 53). Clean rooms plus attractive restaurant offering good, regional cooking. ☆☆ *Hôtel Chez Jean*, 3 rue de la Gare, 2 minutes from the station (Tel. 88 91 10 19); with excellent restaurant. ☆☆*Hôtel Europe*, 7 rue de la Gare, close to Chez Jean (Tel. 88 71 11 43). **Restaurants** ☆ *Zum Staeffele*, 1 rue Poincaré, just off Place Général de Gaulle (Tel. 88 91 63 94).

Strasbourg

Trains *2 or 3 trains daily from* Saverne *(15 mins);* 12 from Nancy *(1 hour 20 mins);* 12 from Paris Gare de l'Est *(4 hours);* 12 from Frankfurt *(2½ hours);* 6 from Zurich *(3 hours);* 2 from Vienna *(11 hours).*

Strasbourg, the ancient capital of Alsace, is one of the most attractive cities in France, situated with its historic centre encircled by branches of the river Ill. Every style of building can be found in the city, reflecting Strasbourg's varied history and critical geographic location on the borders of Germany and France. A university town, the See of a bishop, seat of the Council of Europe, the European Commission on Human Rights and the meeting place of the European Parliament, Strasbourg is the symbol of a new united Europe. With its spectacular cathedral and numerous 16th and 17th century burghers' houses Strasbourg still retains something of the character of an old free city of the Holy Roman Empire but is also typically French with its elegant buildings in Louis xv style.

For much of its history Strasbourg was nominally part of the Holy Roman Empire but in practice it was governed by the bishop of the city and, after 1322, by a guild of citizens, making it one of the most democratic cities in Europe. The freedom this created attracted leaders of the Reformation, some of whom, like Calvin and Martin Bucer, settled temporarily in the city. From the 14th to the 17th centuries the city benefited from the wise and democratic rule the Guilds provided and enjoyed an almost uninterrupted period of peace and prosperity. Its long history of freedom and toleration came to an end, however, when the city was seized by Louis XIV in 1681, with the support of the Catholic faction. France's annexation of the city was confirmed by the Treaty of Ryswyck in 1697 but it was not until the Revolution, a century later, that the city lost its many and ancient privileges.

During the Franco-Prussian war Strasbourg was bombarded and endured a 7-week siege before surrendering to the Prussians, after which it became the capital of the German province of Elsass-Lothringen for 47 years. It was occupied a second time by the Germans in 1940 and liberated by the Allies on 23rd November 1944 after having suffered artillery fire for nearly 5 months.

What to see

Cathédrale Notre-Dame

On the south-east of the island on which the old city of Strasbourg is situated rises the magnificent Gothic cathedral of Notre-Dame. Above its magnificent red sandstone façade soars its single spire which was completed in 1439.

The western façade is enriched by innumerable statues and covered with a veil of the most exquisite tracery, the design of Erwin of Steinbach. Strasbourg Cathedral is almost unique in possessing the plans of the façade, known as 'Plan B', which are preserved in the Maison de l'Oeuvre Notre-Dame next to the cathedral. After the nave had been largely rebuilt in French Gothic style, work began on the façade in 1277 and continued for 60 years.

The western façade has 3 portals, the central one with a tympanum in 4 horizontal panels, the first 3 of which are 13th-century and the top one is modern. The tympanum scenes depict the Life of Christ, above which are a line of lion cubs, 2 of which support a 19th-century statue of the Virgin and Child. Either side of the tympanum are prophets in 5 concentric arches, most of which are 19th-century, the medieval ones having been destroyed during the Revolution. The portal on the right is flanked by statues of the Wise and Foolish Virgins, only some of which are original, and that on the left of the Virtues triumphing over the Vices. Above these, amongst the buttresses, are equestrian statues of Merovingian, Carolingian and Capetian kings and above the graceful pinnacle of the central gable is the delicate rose window, surmounted by a gallery of apostles.

The original plan was to build 2 towers above the western façade but this idea was abandoned in the 1420s; instead what had already been built was joined together by the existing platform on the 3rd storey and a massive openwork spire, decorated with statuary, built above it to the dizzying height of 141 metres.

The exterior of the cathedral is more successful than the interior for the nave seems to lack proportion, being rather too wide for its height while the beauty of the choir is impaired by ugly frescoes in Byzantine style which were executed in the 19th century.

The stained glass however is superb, much of it dating from the 13th and 14th centuries. Princes and emperors of the Holy Roman Empire are depicted in the stained-glass windows of the northern aisle, and the western façade is pierced by a delicately carved rose window of brilliant colour. Apart from stained glass, the interior is chiefly of interest for the **Pilier des Anges**, a 13th-century column decorated with exquisitely carved figures of the Evangelists and angels blowing trumpets. Gazing down on this heavenly scene from above is a little man carved of stone, his elbows leaning on the choristers' gallery. Nearby is a large and garish astronomical clock that intrigued Thomas Coryate, the inveterate traveller, on his visit to the cathedral in 1608. At midday the Apostles emerge jerkily and bow stiffly to the figure of Christ, while a cock beats its wings and crows raucously, much to the surprise of the unwary tourists passing beneath it. For some reason, never satisfactorily explained, the clock is always kept half an hour slow. It is possible to follow in the footsteps of Victor Hugo and Goethe, both of whom climbed the soaring tower of the cathedral, the highest building in Christendom for several centuries (Tower open daily 8.30 am–7 pm.)

Château des Rohan

Outside the cathedral, on the southern side of the Place du Château, stands the magnificent classical palace designed in 1730 by Robert de Cotte for Armand Gaston de Rohan, the Prince-Archbishop of Strasbourg. Cotte, who had earlier designed the dome of Les Invalides in Paris, was 75 by the time he came to design this new palace for the Rohan family, 4 members of which became bishops of the city during the 18th century. On the ground and 1st floors are the bishop's apartments but the palace now contains an impressive **Musée des Beaux-Arts** with an excellent collection of Italian, Spanish, Flemish, Dutch and French paintings and a **museum of archaeology**. Some of the finest rooms facing south over the Ill were beautifully decorated by Jean-Auguste Nahl.

The superb **Musée d'Art Moderne** is in the Ancienne Douane, with paintings and sculpture by Klimt, Chagall, Klee and Arp, the latter a native of the city (All museums open Wed–Mon 10 am–noon and 2–6 pm.)

Maison de l'Oeuvre Notre-Dame

Another outstanding building faces the Place du Château and the cathedral. This edifice, the Maison de l'Oeuvre Notre-Dame, consists of 2 starkly contrasting buildings – a crenellated Gothic one dating from the 14th century and a late 16th-century one in German Renaissance style. La Maison de l'Oeuvre is unique in France, having been established in the 14th century as a residence for the mason-architects of the cathedral, and as a headquarters that managed and directed work on the cathedral, received donations, supervised accounts and legacies, undertook repairs and supervised major architectural projects. It now contains an outstanding collection of medieval and Renaissance art in over 40 rooms clustered in buildings overlooking 4 internal courtyards. Amongst its many treasures are the original 14th- and 15th-century drawings made by the architects of the cathedral, including 'Plan B' which is the master-plan of the façade. Other treasures include one of the oldest known stained-glass windows in existence, the 'Wissembourg Head', dating from the 11th century. (Open April–Sept Wed–Mon 10 am–noon and 2–6 pm; Oct–Mar Wed–Sat, Mon 2–6 pm, Sun 10 am–noon.)

Old Town

Making a great contrast to the grandeur of the Palais Rohan are a whole series of old houses characteristic of Strasbourg with extremely steep tiled roofs that appear to accommodate 2 and often 3 attic floors in their cramped confines. The finest of these is the **Hôtel du Corbeau** on the south side of the River Ill, a hostelry with a picturesque courtyard where Turenne lodged in the middle of the 17th century and Frederick the Great dined a century later. Convicted criminals used to be taken to the nearby **Pont du Corbeau** to be drowned.

Musée Alsacien

Facing the river on the Quai Saint-Nicolas is the Musée Alsacien in an old building with a delightful galleried courtyard; local interiors have been reconstituted to reveal a glimpse of the way Alsatians used to live and local trades and crafts are represented through exhibitions with tools and equipment.

Ancienne Douane

Opposite, on the north bank, is an exhibition space in a 14th-century customs building that has been rebuilt since the war. Works from the city's Musée des Beaux-Arts have been exhibited here while the art museum is being relocated opposite the cathedral, in the former Château des Rohan. Only a few items of the collection, largely 19th-century French paintings, can be seen. However the collection includes works by Renoir, Monet, Boudin, Sisley, Monticelli and Degas. A 3rd museum in the same locality, devoted to the history of Strasbourg, occupies a fine 16th-century market building, on the delightfully named square, Place du Marché-aux-Cochons-de-Lait. (All museums open Wed–Mon 10 am–noon and 2–6 pm.) Running north from the museum is the **Rue du Vieux-Marché-aux-Poissons** where Goethe lodged at number 36 as a student while attending the university in 1771. This leads to Place Gutenberg, where the famous printer worked in Strasbourg for a year in conjunction with Peter Schoffer in 1434.

It was in this square, onto which faced the Hôtel de Ville, that Arthur Young, the English agronomist, witnessed an early outbreak of revolutionary fervour directed against the authorities. He gives a description of it in the account of his journey *An agricultural tour of France*. The date was 21st July 1789:

the mob were breaking the windows with stones . . . Perceiving that their numbers not only increased but that they grew bolder and bolder every moment, I thought it worth staying to see what it would end in, and clambered on to the roof of low stalls opposite the building against which their malice was directed . . . Perceiving the troops would not attack them, except in words and menaces, they grew more violent and furiously attempted to beat the door to pieces with iron crows, placing ladders to the windows. In about a quarter of an hour, which gave time for the assembled magistrates to escape by a back door, they burst all open, and entered like a torrent with a universal shout of the spectators. From that minute a shower of casements, sashes, shutters, chairs, tables, sofas, books, papers, pictures, etc, rained incessantly from all the windows of the house . . . which was then succeeded by tiles, skirting boards, banisters, frame-work and every part of the building that force could detach. The troops, both horse and foot, were quiet spectators.

Quartier des Tanneurs/Petite France

One of the most delightful quarters of the city, easily overlooked, lies in the south-western corner of the town between the church of St-Thomas and the Ponts Couverts. Until the revocation of the Edict of Nantes Strasbourg was a leading city of the French Reformation and St-Thomas was the principal Protestant church in the city. Martin Bucer preached regularly in the church which contains the tomb of the Maréchal de Saxe executed by Pigalle in 1777. A remarkable statue, it portrays the Marshal philosophically descending the steps of a grey marble pyramid towards an open coffin below.

The area to the west of the church, a maze of half-timbered houses with gables, rambling roofs and cobbled courtyards, many facing onto the docks and quays, is known as the 'Petite France'. This area was once occupied by fishermen, tanners and artisans. Strongly fortified towers overlooking the once-covered 14th-century bridges that span the Ill, the Ponts Couverts, guarded the port upon which the prosperity of the city depended. In the 17th century further fortifications, visible upstream, were built across the river by Vauban.

Practicalities in Strasbourg

Tourist Office Place de la Gare, opposite the station on arrival (Tel. 88 32 51 49); another at Place de la Cathédrale, opposite the cathedral (Tel. 88 32 51 49).
Railway Station Place de la Gare. For town centre from station, walk down Rue du Maire Kuss, over Pont Kuss, and along Rue du 22 Novembre to *centre ville*; information office open Mon–Fri 7.30 am–8 pm; Sat–Sun 7.30 am–7 pm; lockers; (Info: Tel. 88 22 50 50; Reservations: Tel. 88 32 07 51).
Buses Place des Halles (Tel. 88 32 36 97); buses to towns along the Route du Vin, such as Obernai.
Currency Exchange *Change Cathédrale*, 7 Place du Marché-aux-Cochons-de-Lait, behind cathedral (Tel. 88 23 26 46); open 9am–6pm.
Festivals *Festival International de Musique*: June, jazz and classical music (Tel. 88 32 43 10) *Music Festival* Sept, contemporary music.
Hotels ☆ Hôtel de l'Ill, 8 rue des Bateliers, near Eglise Ste-Madeleine (Tel. 88 36 20 01). Quiet location near the river but 30-mins walk from station.
Hôtel de la Cruche d'or, 6 rue des Tonneliers, off Place Gutenberg. (Tel. 88 36 10 60). Spacious, clean and close to cathedral

☆ *Michelet*, 48 rue du Vieux-Marché-aux-Poissons (Tel. 88 32 17 15). Rooms small but clean, and in excellent location near the cathedral.
☆☆ *Hôtel du Rhin*, 8 place de la Gare (Tel. 88 32 35 00). Clean and convenient, opposite station
☆☆ *Hôtel Vendôme*, 9 place de la Gare, close to the Hôtel du Rhin (Tel. 88 32 45 23).
☆☆ *Hôtel Royal*, 3 rue du Maire Kuss (Tel. 88 32 28 71). Modern, but conveniently situated on way to *centre ville* from station
☆☆ *Hôtel Pax*, 24–26 rue du Faubourg National (Tel. 88 32 14 54). South of the station off Petite Rue de la Course.
☆☆ *Hôtel Gutenberg*, 31 rue des Serruriers (Tel. 88 32 17 15). Delightful hotel in old mansion just off Place Gutenberg; rooms vary widely in price.
☆☆☆ *Hôtel Hannong*, 15 rue du 22 Novembre, on way in towards centre (Tel. 88 32 16 22).
Hostels *Auberge de Jeunesse René Cassin* (HI), 9 rue de l'Auberge de Jeunesse, off Route de Schirmeck. Bus 3, 13 or 23 from Rue du Vieux-Marché-aux-Vins or ½ hour walk down Blvd de Metz, Blvd de Nancy and Blvd de Lyon; good facilities (Tel. 88 30 26 46).

Camping *La Montagne Verte* (Tel. 88 30 25 46) on Rue du Schnokeloch, near youth hostel. Bus 3, 13 or 23 to **Nid de Cigogne**. Open Mar–Oct.

Restaurants *Au Pont St-Martin*, 12–15 rue des Moulins (88 32 45 13). Generous platters of good seafood and salads.

Restaurant au Petit Tonnelier, 16 rue des Tonneliers, off Rue de la Douane (88 32 53 54). Small busy restaurant serving good French and Alsatian dishes.

☆☆ *Maison Kammerzell*, Place de la Cathédrale (Tel. 88 32 42 14). An old favourite, in 15th-century building serving excellent traditional Alsatian food.

☆ *Zum Strissel*, 5 place de la Grande-Boucherie (Tel. 88 32 14 73). Classic Alsatian restaurant with delicious regional specialities. Snails and sauerkraut served with jugs of local white wine.

☆ *Au Rocher du Sapin*, 6 rue du Noyer (Tel. 88 32 39 65). North of Place Kléber, specialising in Alsatian dishes; popular and animated.

☆☆ *Au Romain*, 6 rue du Vieux Marché aux Grains, just off Rue des Grandes Arcades (Tel 88 32 08 54). Delicious meals can be eaten outside.

Sélestat

Trains *8 – 10 daily from* **Strasbourg** *(25 – 40 mins) and* **Colmar** *(15 mins); 7 trains from* **Obernai** *(30 mins).*

An ancient town on the River Ill, once an early residence of the Frankish kings, Sélestat possesses one of the finest Romanesque churches in Alsace. It is a quiet little town, its unprepossessing suburbs giving no indication of the delightful little squares and narrow, crooked streets that characterise the centre. After Strasbourg, the tranquillity of Sélestat comes as a welcome surprise.

What to see

Many of the buildings are timber-framed and white-washed, with dark shutters, balconies and window boxes full of red geraniums. But the local stone is a strong pink and this colour is the dominant one in the town. In the 15th and 16th centuries the town was an important centre of learning, with a renowned Latin School which was endowed with a fine library. The earliest of its manuscripts, on display in the **Musée et Bibliothèque Humaniste** at 1, rue de la Bibliothèque, is the *Book of Miracles of Ste-Foy*, dating from the 12th century (Open weekdays 9am-noon and 2 – 5pm.) The Protestant reformer Martin Bucer, who was born in the town, was invited to England by Cranmer in 1549 where he became professor of divinity at Cambridge.

Eglise Ste-Foy The church of Ste-Foy was rebuilt in the 12th century and has a fine Romanesque façade but its 2 western towers were added in 1889. The interior gives an impression of weight, the great arcades of the nave being supported by thick, round columns which are capped by cubical capitals decorated with unusual rope and ribbon motifs. The Romanesque bas-relief next to the baptistery was originally the lid of a sarcophagus. Rue de Babil leads to the Gothic church of **St-Georges** with a fine tower built in 1490 and beautiful medieval stained glass in the rose window above the south door.

Hôtel d'Ebermunster Near the church of St Georges is an early Renaissance mansion, the Hôtel d'Ebermunster. Of the original fortifications of the town only 2 remnants remain – the **Tour des Sorcières** and the massive 14th-century tower, the **Tour de l'Horloge**, which faces the Rue du Président Poincaré.

Practicalities in Sélestat

Tourist Office La Commanderie, Blvd du Général Leclerc (Tel. 88 92 07 84).
Station Info. Tel. 88 22 50 50; Reservations Tel. 88 92 05 36). For town centre from station walk down Rue du Babil which leads to Eglise St-Georges.
Hotels ☆☆ *Hôtel Vaillant*, Place République, facing the fine square (Tel. 88 92 09 46); restaurant offers good regional dishes.

☆☆*Auberge des Alliés*, 39 rue des Chevaliers, right in the centre, close to the Place d'Armes (Tel. 88 92 12 88). Modernised and attractive, with good restaurant
Restaurants ☆ *Vieille Tour*, 8 rue Jauge (Tel. 88 92 15 02). Delicious local dishes in rustic restaurant down side-street off the Place d'Armes.

Colmar

Trains *Frequent trains daily from* Sélestat *(15 mins);* Strasbourg *(35 – 50 mins) and* Mulhouse *(30 mins); 6 from* Paris *(5 hours); 3 from* Nancy *(2 hours); 4 from* Lyon *(4½ hours).*

The landscape from Sélestat to Colmar is flat while away to the west rise up the dark hills of the Vosges. Situated on the plain of Alsace near the vine-covered foothills of the southern Vosges, Colmar is a typical Alsatian town which grew up around the river Lauch from obscure origins to become a free Imperial city in 1226. It fell to the Swedes in the Thirty Years War and was taken under temporary French 'protection' in 1635.

The beauty of the city, the capital of Upper Alsace, lies less in any particular building than in the general ensemble of narrow and irregular streets onto which face countless delightful and picturesque half-timbered and painted houses. With its picturesque old burghers' houses, it is one of the most beautiful towns of Alsace. Some houses have ornate and fanciful façades, others are plastered and painted with various pastel shades. Not everyone, however has taken to the charms of Colmar. Voltaire described it as an ugly place 'half-German, half-French, and altogether bizarre'.

What to see

Old Town

The old town is scattered between the Rue des Têtes and the Musée Unterlinden in the north and the river Lauch in the south. Along the latter river spreads an area known as the **La Petite Venise**, a charming area which was once the tanners' quarter, spread out along tranquil branches of the river Lauch. Flat-bottomed barges formerly carried the produce of the market gardens into the heart of the city and to the steps of the market buildings and the Customs House.

The Ill was navigable as far as Colmar and one of the boasts of the citizens was that they could travel as far as Amsterdam via the Rhine simply by stepping onto a boat tied up at the Customs House in the heart of the city.

Customs House

The oldest civil building in the city, the Customs House is a remarkable structure on 3 floors built in 1480, capped by a yellow-, green- and red-tiled roof characteristic of the region. Representatives of the 10 free towns of Alsace, the Decapolis (a confederation of free Alsatian cities) met on the 1st floor, while the ground floor was used as a warehouse for the city's customs officials where taxes were assessed and levied on goods coming into the city. The most important merchants had their premises in the street that runs away to the west, the **Rue des Marchands**, one of the most picturesque and impressive streets of Colmar.

The finest examples of Alsatian architecture are to be found in the **Quartier des Tanneurs** and close to the canals in La Petite Venise. The **Maison des Têtes**, in the street of the same name, is a superb Renaissance mansion on 5 floors, with an elaborately carved doorway and magnificent enclosed balconies, ornately carved and decorated with numerous characterful faces.

Maison Pfister

Another superb mansion is the Maison Pfister, constructed in 1537 and ornamented with frescoes and medallions and wooden galleries which are very elaborately carved and sculpted.

Musée Unterlinden

On the northern edge of the old town stands the Musée d'Unterlinden on the site of a former Dominican convent which was an important centre of German mysticism. The museum (Open daily 9 am–6 pm; Wed–Mon, 9 am–noon and 2–5 pm, in Nov–March), housed in buildings that surround the cloister of the old convent, is one of the most magnificent provincial art collections in France. Its many treasures include an outstanding collection of the German primitive school, with masterpieces by Martin Schongauer, Gaspard Isenmann and Mathias Gothardt Nithardt (better known as Mathias Grünewald), author of the Issenheim altar piece.

The 3 churches of Colmar however are not the greatest works of religious architecture. The **Dominican church** was built in Rhenish Gothic style between the 13th and 15th centuries and was once used as a corn market. At the entrance to the choir hangs an exquisite painting by Martin Schongauer, La Vierge au buisson de roses. (Altar open for viewing April–Oct 10 am–6 pm.) The church of St Martin, begun in 1250 and completed by 1375, betrays the influence of the Ile-de-France on local architectural styles. On the south side the **Portail St-Nicolas** has some fine grotesques and the interior is lit by attractive 15th-century stained glass. Opposite the church is the **Ancien Corps de Garde**, a 16th-century building with a Renaissance balcony formerly used by the city magistrates to make announcements. Next to it is the oldest house in Colmar, la **Maison Adolphe**, dating from

1350. The final church, **St-Matthieu**, was once a Franciscan church and later divided in 2, one end being Protestant and the other Catholic, in a remarkable display of religious toleration. It contains an exceptionally fine stained-glass window of the Crucifixion, probably the work of Pierre d'Andlau in the 15th century.

Practicalities in Colmar

Tourist Office 4 rue des Unterlinden, opposite the Unterlinden Museum (Tel. 89 20 68 92); accommodation service; city tours in French; currency exchange.

Railway Station Place de la Gare (Info: Tel. 89 24 50 50; Reservations: Tel. 89 23 17 00); lockers; information office open Mon–Fri 7.30 am–7.30 pm; Sat 8 am–10.30 pm; Sun 9 am–8 pm (Tel. 89 41 66 80). For town centre from station follow Rue de la Gare from station, follow its continuation, Rue de Lattre de Tassigny, right onto Rue des Unterlinden to tourist office.

Buses Place de la Gare (Tel. 89 41 40 27); local buses to Riquewhir, St-Hippolyte, Ribeauvillé and Eguisheim on the Route du Vin. Schedules from tourist office.

Post Office 36 ave de la République, opposite public gardens; currency exchange and *poste restante*. Open Mon-Fri 8am-7pm, Sat 8am-noon.

Markets *Place de l'Ancienne Douane* on Thurs mornings and *Place St-Joseph* on Sat mornings.

Festivals *Alsatian Wine Festival*: early Aug, *Jours Choucroute*: early September. Alsatian wines, costume, dancing and music fill the streets.

Hotels *Hôtel St-Lauren*, 1 rue de la Gare: (Tel. 89 41 45 19). Clean and attractive, close to station.

La Chaumière, 74 ave de la République, near station (Tel. 89 41 08 99); basic but clean.

☆☆ *Hôtel Colbert*, 2 rue des Trois-Epis (Tel. 89 41 31 05). Excellent location between station and centre. Quieter rooms overlook Rue des Tallandiers.

☆☆ *Hôtel Rapp*, 1 rue Weinemer, at junction with Rue Molly (Tel. 89 41 62 10). Close to place Rapp and the old town.

☆☆ *Hôtel Amiral*, 11 blvd Champ de Mars (Tel. 89 41 54 54). Stylish and comfortable hotel opposite place Rapp.

Hostels Maison des Jeunes (*Centre International de Séjour*), 17 rue Camille-Schlumberger, well-run and clean, 10 mins from station (Tel. 89 41 26 87).

Restaurants *La Pergola*, 24 rue des Marchands (89 41 36 79). Cheap but good cooking; meals can be eaten outside on terrace.

☆ *Buffet de la Gare*, 9 place de la Gare (Tel. 89 41 21 26). Stained-glass windows and superb cuisine distinguish this from most station restaurants.

☆ *Le Petit Bouchon*, 11 rue Alspach, off Rue Vauban (Tel. 89 23 45 57).

☆☆ *Aux Trois Poissons*, 15 quai Poissonnerie, just south of the river Lauch (Tel. 89 41 25 21).

☆☆☆ *Maison des Têtes*, 19 rue des Têtes (Tel. 89 24 43 43). Superb regional specialities in this beautiful 17th-century mansion, itself one of the sights of Colmar.

La Route du Vin

One of the most enchanting features of the countryside between Colmar and Strasbourg is the labyrinth of tiny back roads which meander through the picturesque vineyards of Alsace known collectively as the 'Route du Vin'. Many of the smallest and most delightful villages are not accessible by train but most can be reached by bus or – from Colmar – by bicycle, albeit through fairly hilly country. One of the larger towns accessible by train from Strasbourg is **Molsheim**, 10 trains daily (30 mins). The town's handsome townhall, the '**Meitzig**', has a tower, clock and charming sixteenth-century moondial. Molsheim also has a small **Musée Régional**, with a display of wine equipment in the centre of the town. Guided tours of the surrounding vineyards leave from the town hall between June and August on Mondays and Thursdays at 10 am.

Riquewihr

From Colmar buses leave for Riquewihr, St Hippolyte, Ribeauville and Eguisheim, four of the most delightful villages on the Route du Vin. (Details and timetables of bus departures are contained in the *Actualité de Colmar*, issued free by Colmar tourist office).

Riquewihr is perhaps the most enchanting town on the *Route du Vin*, an ancient walled village lying at the foot of the vine-covered slopes of the Vosges. It is also one of the most popular destinations for foreign and French tourists alike and as a result is thronged with visitors in summer, especially at weekends. Of the many medieval houses in Riquewihr, the finest is the **Tour du Dolder**, which now houses a good firearm museum (Open May–Oct daily 9 am–noon and 1.30–6.30 pm). The beautiful exterior of the **Tour des Voleurs** hides a hideous torture chamber still equipped with many of its original torture instruments. (Open Easter–Oct, daily 9:30 am–noon and 1:30–6:3–pm).

Practicalities in Riquewihr

Tourist office 2 rue de la 1ère Armée (Tel. 89 47 80 80); open in summer 10am–7pm; issues lists of private rooms to rent.
Accommodation ☆☆☆ *Hotel Couronne*, 5 rue Couronne (Tel. 89 49 03 03); excellent, comfortable and modernised hotel, no restaurant.
Restaurant *Au Petit Gourmet*, 5 rue de la 1ère Armée (89 47 98 77); excellent Alsatian dishes in an authentic Alsatian setting, very close to the tourist office.

Kayserberg

Only a few kilometres south of Riquewihr at the mouth of Weiss valley is the picturesque and flower-bedecked town of Kayserberg, clustered around a fifteenth-sixteenth century fortified bridge under the ruins of an ancient castle. In 1944 Kayserberg was a stronghold of the SS in their attempt to stem the advance of French and American troops but luckily escaped the destruction of December 1944. The castle was rebuilt in the thirteenth century by a son of Emperor Frederick II Hohenstaufen and flourished as a free Imperial city before being sacked by the Swedes in 1636.

Fine old houses line both sides of the very long main street, the half-timbered ones around the bridge dating from the fifteenth-century. Not to be missed is the twelfth-fifteenth century church of **Ste-Croix** which possesses an elaborate carved and gilded retable or altar-piece, the work of Jean Bogartz in 1518, and naive Romanesque sculpture in its portal. Nearby is the **Hôtel de Ville**, dating from 1604, in German Renaissance style while a medieval courtyard at 62 rue Gén. de Gaulle leads to a small museum housing a collection of attractive polychrome statues and a fourteenth-century statue of the Virgin. (Open July–August, daily 10 am–noon and 2–6 pm; June and Sept–Oct 10 am–noon and 2–6 pm).

At 126 rue Gén. de Gaulle is a small **museum** devoted to the doctor, missionary, musician and physician, Albert Schweitzer, a native of the town, who won the Nobel Peace Prize in 1952. (Open May–Oct, daily 9 am–noon and 2–6 pm).

Practicalities in Kayserberg

Tourist office Town Hall, at entrance to the town. (Tel. 89 78 22 78).
Bus 3–5 buses daily from Colmar's Place de la Gare (25 mins).

Accommodation *Hôtel Constantin*, 10 rue Père Kohlman (Tel. 89 47 19 90); modernised, pleasant and comfortable; no restaurant.

Mulhouse

Trains 12–16 *trains daily from* **Comar** *(30 mins) and* **Strasbourg** *(1 hour–1 hour 20 mins).*

Mulhouse is not a beautiful town by any standard, nor is it particularly interesting in terms of historic monuments although the central Place de la Réunion has a number of fine buildings.

From 1308 to 1515 Mulhouse was a free imperial city and a member of the league of 10 Alsatian free cities. From 1515 to 1648 it was ruled by the Swiss, from 1798 to 1871 by the French, from then until 1918 by the Germans and since then, except for a brief interlude during the Second World War, by the French again. Mulhouse is an industrial city, its fortunes long tied to the manufacture of printed calico or 'indiennes'. A museum devoted to this will be of interest to the *cognoscenti*. But as this book is devoted to the exploration of France by train, it would seem ungrateful to skip over Mulhouse without paying homage to its railway museum. This superb museum is a little difficult to reach, being 3 kilometres from the town centre in the suburban district of Dornach, but this will not deter the rail enthusiast.

What to see

Musée Français du Chemin de Fer

This unusual museum, the Musée Français du Chemin de Fer, consists of a vast station crammed with locomotives and steam engines, many of which once broke speed records, including locomotive 33 *Saint Pierre* at 40 mph in 1844 and locomotive 5 *Suzanne* which scraped the same speed 3 years later. Other fine trains include the saloon car used as his moving headquarters by General Joffe in 1914–15 and a luxuriously appointed dining-car from the Golden Arrow. (Open April–Sept, daily 9 am–6 pm, Oct–March, daily 10 am–5 pm; 15 mins walk west down Rue J. Hofer).

Musée National de l'Automobile

The most unusual museum in Mulhouse is the national car museum, the Musée National de l'Automobile, at 192 Avenue de Colmar. It developed out of the private

private collection of 2 Swiss brothers by the name of Schlumpf. Here more than 500 vehicles are displayed over an area of 17,000 square metres. The collection is nothing short of breath-taking: 122 Bugattis, 14 Panhards, 31 Mercedes, 12 Gordinis, 22 Peugeot, 26 De Dion, 14 Renault, 8 Alfa Romeos, Hispano Suizas and Benzs, 15 Rolls-Royces, 5 Bentleys . . . The earliest vehicle is the steam-driven Jacquot complete with wooden wheels dating from 1878; the largest a Bugatti Royale. Car enthusiasts are unlikely to be disappointed (Open Wed–Mon 10 am–6 pm.)

Practicalities in Mulhouse

Tourist Office 9 ave Maréchal Foch (Tel. 89 45 68 31).
Railway Station Ave du Général Leclerc (Info: Tel. 89 46 50 50; Reservations: Tel. 89 45 62 83).
Hotels ☆ *Hôtel Bâle*, 19 Passage Central, off Rue du Sauvage (Tel. 89 46 19 87).
☆ *Hôtel Wir*, 1 porte de Bâle, off Place de la République (Tel. 89 56 13 22).
Restaurants *Aux Caves du Vieux Couvent*, 23 rue du Couvent, near church of Ste-Marie. (Tel. 89 46 28 79). Good value for money at this popular tavern.
☆☆☆ *Au Quai de la Cloche*, 5 quai de la Cloche (Tel. 89 43 07 81). 15 mins walk north-west of the centre, beyond Rue Franklin.

Belfort

Trains *10–15 trains daily from* **Mulhouse** (30–50 mins) and **Strasbourg** (1½ hours).

Lying between the Jura and the Vosges, Belfort was historically the greatest strategic weak point in France's natural eastern border. The countryside west of Mulhouse to Belfort is fertile and wooded; the Vosges drop away to the north while west of Belfort begins a vast plain drained to the south by the Saône and to the north by the Meuse and Moselle. Belfort is primarily an industrial town, of limited interest to the tourist, but its central square, faced by handsome 17th-century houses of red sandstone, is very attractive. In the Place des Bourgeois, the huge Lion of Belfort, sculpted from red sandstone by Félix-Auguste Bartholdi, rises over the heart of the city. The lion was commissioned to celebrate Belfort's heroic resistance during the Franco-Prussian War of 1870–71 when French forces, under General Denfert-Rochereau, withstood a 100-day siege.

What to see

Dominating the town is the 13th-century feudal **castle**, situated on the top of a 60-metre-high cliff. In the 17th century Vauban turned it into a defensive Citadel surrounded by an ingenious system of fortifications. Most were levelled at the end of the 19th century but the **Porte de Brisach** is one of the original gateways which pierced the double wall which surrounded the city. It led to the Citadel which now houses the **Musée d'Art et d'Histoire** in which there is Vauban's 1687 scale model of the town. From the Citadel there are superb views over the town towards the Vosges mountains to the north and the Jura to the south.

Basilique Saint Christophe The Basilica of St-Christophe, dating from the 18th century, is a massive, solemn building, lightened inside by elegant wrought-iron grille work and a charming frieze of angels' heads in the nave.

Practicalities in Belfort

Tourist Office Rue Jules-Vallès (Tel. 84 28 12 23).

Railway Station (Info: Tel. 84 28 50 50; Reservations: Tel. 84 28 50 50). To town centre from station, follow Rue Thiers, turn left after crossing Savoureuse River.

Markets Rue Dr Fréry, on riverbank, Wed, Fri and Sat mornings; Marché des Vosges, on Ave Jean Jaurès, Tues, Thurs and Sun mornings.

Hotels Hôtel Vauban, 4 rue du Magasin (Tel. 84 21 59 37), cheap accommodation in centre. ☆☆ Hôtel des Capucins, 20 Faubourg de Montbéliard (Tel. 84 28 04 60). Good,

comfortable hotel with pleasant, bright rooms, short walk from station.

☆☆☆ Château Servin, 9 rue du Général de Négrier (Tel. 84 21 41 85). Lovely grounds and comfortable rooms in quiet, classic, hotel; outstanding cuisine.

Camping Camping Municipal, promenade d'Essert (Tel. 84 21 03 30). Cool, shady location in park 10 mins from station.

Restaurant ☆ Pot au Feu, 27 bis Grande Rue (Tel. 84 28 57 84). Good, tasty dishes served at rustic, simple restaurant at foot of the Citadel.

Epinal

Trains 2–4 trains daily to **Lure** (20 mins from **Belfort**); change at Lure for Epinal (1 hour).

The journey to Epinal and St-Dié requires a couple of changes onto minor lines, with infrequent trains, but these lines do allow the train traveller to climb up into and through the beautiful Vosges mountains, before descending eventually either to Strasbourg or Nancy.

West of Belfort a small branch line heads north to **Remiremont**, a delightful town looking out over hilly and wooded country. It once had an important house of canonesses who held the title of countess and took an active military part in the 16th-century religious wars.

Further north lies **Epinal** straddling the Moselle, an important town in the Middle Ages, at a strategic crossing point on the river. Its once vast château is now reduced to a pile of masonry on top of a hill to the east of the town.

What to see

Basilique St-Maurice

Most of the town remains clustered around the Basilica of St-Maurice, a curious building of white and red sandstone with a Germanic bell-tower, 13th-century Burgundian nave and wide Gothic choir. On its western side is a deep vaulted porch, the Portail des Bourgeois, once elaborately carved.

Print Museum

Since the 18th century Epinal has been famous for the manufacture of popular prints known as *images* which were sold by peddlars and hawkers throughout

France, modern versions of which are still printed in the town. Hundreds of examples of these early prints are exhibited in the **Musée départmental des Vosges et Musée international de l'Imagerie** which is at the southern end of the island created by a division in the waters of the Moselle. The prints were produced in a factory on the east bank of the Moselle, some 17 million being produced here during the Second Empire.

Place des Vosges

Close to the church, in the centre of the town, lies the Place des Vosges, a handsome square lined with arcaded houses, one of which is ornamented with an elegant Renaissance loggia.

Practicalities in Epinal

Tourist Office 13 rue de la Comédie, close to the basilica (Tel. 29 82 53 32).
Railway Station Ave Dutac, almost opposite Notre-Dame (Tel. 29 82 50 50). Ave. Maréchal de Lattre leads down to the Moselle and old centre.
Hotels ☆ *Hôtel de l'Europe*, 16 rue F. Blaudez, close to the basilica and Pont Sadi Carnot (Tel.

29 82 21 04).
☆☆ *Hôtel Ariane*, 12 ave Général de Gaulle, virtually opposite station (Tel. 29 82 10 74).
Restaurants ☆*Le Petit Robinson*, 24 rue Poincaré (Tel. 29 34 23 51). A short walk north from the basilica, offers a good range of economical menus.

St-Dié

Trains 4 – 6 *trains daily from* **Epinal** (1 hour) and **Strasbourg** (1 hour 20 mins).

St-Dié has been twice destroyed by fire: in 1757 by accident and in 1944 when it was deliberately set alight by retreating German soldiers, only the little 12th-century church of Notre-Dame escaping the flames.

What to see

Cathedral

The cathedral was dynamited and has had to be rebuilt almost from scratch – a labour of love that has restored the Romanesque nave and 14th-century choir and transept to their former appearance. Most of the stained glass is the work of 10 modern artists but a little 13th-century glass survives in one of the side chapels.

The little church of **Notre Dame-de-Galilée** is built in Rhenish Romanesque style and has a simple, well proportioned nave and free-standing bell tower.

Gothic Cloisters

Notre-Dame-de-Galilée is linked to the cathedral by an enchanting Flamboyant cloister of pink stone built at the turn of the 15th century.

The town has an unusual connection with the new world. In the 16th century a group of geographers working in St-Dié decided on the name '*Amérique*' for the newly-discovered continent on the far side of the Atlantic which they named after the explorer, Amerigo Vespucci. The first time the word appears in print is in the *Cosmographiae Introductio* printed in the town in 1507, a copy of which is exhibited in the town library. The small **museum** contains interesting objects found at the nearby Celtic camp of Bure.

From St-Dié, trains can be caught north-west to **Lunéville** (40 mins), with its vast 18th-century **château** designed by Boffrand for the Dukes of Lorraine in a magnificent park, and back to Nancy (1 hour 5 mins), or north-east skirting the northern flanks of the Vosges in a picturesque journey to Strasbourg (1 hour 20 mins).

Practicalities in St-Dié

Tourist Office 31 rue Thiers (Tel. 29 56 17 62).
Railway Station South of the river Meurthe and Place St-Martin (Tel. 29 82 50 50).
Hotels ☆ *Hôtel de France*, 12 rue Dauphine. (Tel. 29 56 32 61). Very close to tourist office, just off Rue Thiers. No restaurant.

☆ *Hôtel le Globe*, 2 quai de Lattre de Tassigny, with views of the River Meurthe (Tel. 29 56 13 40). No restaurant.
Restaurants ☆☆ *Voyageurs*, 22 rue Hellieule, between the station and the river Meurthe (Tel. 29 56 21 56).

2 Aquitaine

One of the largest and oldest provinces of France, Aquitaine is also one of the most fascinating and beautiful regions to visit in France. First settled in the mid-Paleolithic era 150,000 years ago, Aquitaine has more Stone Age sites than anywhere else in the world. At the centre of this area is **Les-Eyzies-de-Tayac**, 'the capital of pre-history'; where grottoes with 20,000-year-old rock paintings, depicting bison, wild horses and hunting scenes, were first discovered in the 1860s.

Aquitaine is now divided into 6 *départements*: the Gironde, the Dordogne, the Lot-et-Garonne to the west and the Aveyron, Lot and Tarn-et-Garonne to the east. The 3 western departments roughly represent, the old districts of Bordelais, Périgord and Agenais while the 3 eastern ones correspond to the old areas known as Rouergue and Quercy. Travelling inland from Bordeaux and the Gironde to the uplands of the central mountains of France, the **Périgord** uplands are characterised by extensive woods of chestnut and oak trees, in which thrive the truffles for which the cuisine of the region is famous. The valleys of the Lot, Dordogne and Isle flow westwards from the Massif Central, cutting deeply into the uplands which, in the south, fade away into the rich but dreary plain of the Garonne.

The Roman province of Aquitania, that part of Gaul which lay between the Garonne and the Pyrenees, was subdued by Julius Caesar but not finally conquered until 28 BC. The borders of Roman Aquitania stretched as far north as the Loire and when the Romans left the province was claimed by Clovis the Frank. In the 7th century the Vascones (ie. the Basques or Gascons) invaded the land from the south and occupied what is now Gascony. In the 8th century the Gascons united briefly with Charlemagne against the Moorish invasion and the crowning of Charlemagne's son as King of Aquitania in 778 marked the first acknowledgment of the supremacy of the French crown.

In the struggles that followed between the nascent kingdoms of the south, the dukes of Aquitaine increased their power by conquest and marriage, even posing a threat to the counts of Toulouse by the late 11th century. When William IX's granddaughter, Eleanor, married Henry II of England she brought as her dowry the whole province of Guyenne with

Gascony, Limousin and Poitou, so that the King of England, already the Lord of Normandy, Anjou, Touraine, Maine and Saintonge, was master of the whole of western France.

The reaction of the local people to their English rulers varied greatly according to the proximity to the headquarters of English Government at Bordeaux. The wine-shippers and growers, benefitting from the lucrative wine trade with England and the stability imposed by English government, favoured the new rulers but inland, where the native barons took advantage of the unsettled state of affairs to pillage the countryside, English rule was naturally seen as oppressive. The crusade in the 13th century against the Albigensian heretics on the eastern borders of Aquitaine further destabilised the region; a whole series of new fortress towns sprung up on a regular plan, with streets at right angles and an arcaded central space. Edward I built such *bastides* all over Aquitaine in an attempt to protect English possessions against the French.

King John was responsible for the loss of most of the English domains in France but in 1259 Louis IX, by the Treaty of Saintes, left Aquitaine and

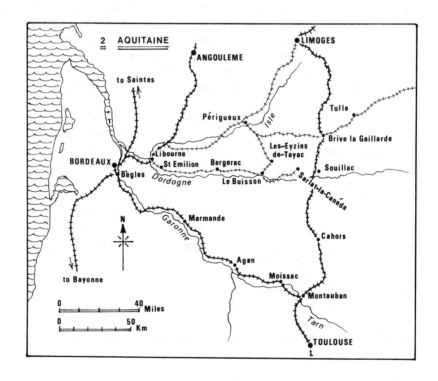

Gascony from the Charente to the Pyrenees to Henry III. The Black Prince was virtually King of Guyenne but from 1360 French power increased and, despite the solid support of the people of Bordeaux, the English were finally crushed at the battle of Castillon in 1453. In the 16th century Aquitaine was often the battleground between Protestants and Catholics, until Henri IV brought peace and prosperity to the province. In the 18th century the misgovernment so prevalent elsewhere in France was felt less in Aquitaine because of the wise administration of such men as Turgot, Tourny and Etigny. The Revolution was, correspondingly, less savage, the Girondin party standing for moderate reform.

Quercy in the east, once a fief of the counts of Toulouse, was ceded by St-Louis to Henry III of England in 1259 but the English were driven out in the 14th century while the district of Rouergue passed through the Armagnac family to the French crown. In the 16th century both districts were bitterly divided during the Religious Wars: Cahors was a stronghold of Catholicism while Montauban was a centre of reform.

Gastronomically, the **Périgord** district of Aquitaine has only one rival – Burgundy. *Foie gras*, the liver of goose and duck, is a speciality, eaten alone or in pâtés, as is that other mysterious ingredient of Périgord cooking – the black truffle, known as the *diamond noir* of Périgord. For centuries pigs were used to search out the elusive truffles which grow underground in the vicinity of the small holm oaks which grow on the limestone *causses*. Now pigs are a rare sight but local knowledge and a good 'nose' for the soil are indispensable qualities for anyone setting out to find one. Not quite so elusive is the boletus mushroom, *cèpe*, which can transform the simplest omelette into a gourmet's delight. Other local dishes include the *confit de canard* and *confit d'oie*, duck or goose cooked in its own fat. Goose fat, and garlic, is also used in the preparation of *pommes sarlaidaises*, while walnut oil, ground in local mills, is used on salads. The wines of Cahors are new and strong but the finest red wines are those from the vineyards around Bordeaux and St-Emilion while sweet white Monbazillac wines are the perfect accompaniment to the delicate flavour of *foie gras*.

The Route *Bordeaux -St-Emilion – Bergerac – Beynac-et-Cazenac – Sarlat-la-Canéda – Les-Eyzies-de-Tayac – Périgueux – Brive-la-Gaillarde – Souillac – Cahors – Montauban – Moissac – Agen*

The capital of the old province of Aquitaine or Guienne, and laid out in an elegant 18th-century plan, **Bordeaux** *is one of the great ports of*

France, its wealth stemming largely from the wine trade. As far back as the 14th century, some 10,000 English wine merchants wintered in the town, purchasing and sampling wine to be exported to England. From Bordeaux a beautiful journey can be made by train through the vineyards to **Saint-Emilion** and along the most magical stretches of the Dordogne River to the spectacularly sited château of **Beynac-et-Cazenac**, beyond which lies **Sarlat**, the capital of Périgord Noir, full of 14–16th-century houses. **Les-Eyzies-de-Tayac**, sprang into fame when the world's best-preserved prehistoric cave paintings came to light in the limestone cliffs above the town. **Périgueux** has some interesting buildings, the most curious of which is the vast Byzantine cathedral, but it is famous above all for its truffles and pâtés de foie gras. **Brive** is an attractive little market town on the Corrèze river and **Souillac**, on the Dordogne, has a beautiful 12th-century abbey church famous for its highly realistic Romanesque sculpture. A little to the south, on the Lot, is **Cahors**, the capital of the old province of Quercy, with one of the finest ancient bridges in Europe. Crossing the Aveyron and the Tarn, **Montauban** is reached, its old red-brick buildings a foretaste of the architecture of Toulouse. A little to the east, in a small village is the 6th-century **Abbaye de Moissac**, with one of the most exquisite cloisters in southern France and a superbly carved Romanesque portal. **Agen**, on the bank of the Garonne at the foot of the steep Coteau de l'Ermitage, has long been famous for its stuffed plums and the Roman antiquities found in the locality which have been collected in its museum. A short journey brings us back to Bordeaux from where there are fast connections with Paris, Toulouse and Avignon. (**Approximately 7–11 days.**)

Bordeaux

Trains 6–7 trains daily from **Paris Austerlitz** (5½ hours); night trains (8 hours); also 10–12 TGVs from **Paris Montparnasse** (3 hours); 5–8 from **Nantes** (4 hours); 9–11 from **Toulouse** (2½ hours); 2 from **St-Emilion** (45 mins).

A splendid city, and still a thriving port, Bordeaux is one of the noble cities of France, resplendent with Gothic churches and cathedrals and a wealth of superb domestic and civic architecture which stem from the enormous wealth the city acquired through foreign trade, in which wine has always taken an important place.

Bordeaux is not only the third largest town in France but one of its most beautiful provincial cities, with the distinction of having more refined civic buildings and a nobler general layout than any city except Paris and Lyon. Bordeaux has been a prosperous city since Roman days when it flourished under the name of Burdigala. From the middle of the 12th century it was held by the English for 3 centuries and the Black Prince, when not engaged in sacking towns in France, held his court here. His son, later Richard II, was born here. With the defeat of the English forces under Talbot at Castillon in 1453 Bordeaux rejoined the French crown. In the 17th century the Bordelais – the people from Bordeaux – were the chief supporters of the Fronde insurrection and the city withstood a lengthy siege by the troops of Louis XIV and Mazarin. The 18th century saw a further flourishing of the city, based on a huge trade with overseas colonies, that funded the erection of so many of the fine buildings in the city. Bordeaux is distinguished by the brilliance of its eighteenth-century town planning and nowhere is this more evident than in its magnificent squares, Place Gambetta, Place de la Comédie and the Place Tourny. Each of these is outstanding for its layout or the individual buildings which embellish it.

What to see

Place de la Comédie
The hub of the city is the busy Place de la Comédie, on the site of the Roman forum. In this square stands the superb Grand Théatre, one of the finest theatres in France. Its façade consists of a great classical colonnade composed of 12 Corinthian columns supporting a balustraded gallery crowned with statues of the Muses and Graces. The staircases, foyers and theatre itself are all fabulously decorated. North of the Place de la Comédie is the **Esplanade des Quinconces**, the largest square in Europe, covering some 30 acres. Laid out in the 1820s, it contains a monument to the Girondists and statues of Montaigne and Montesquieu, both closely associated with the city, the essayist and philosopher Michel de Montaigne being mayor of the city in the 16th century.

Place Gambetta
Place Gambetta is a superb example of Louis XV architecture. Although moderate leaders held sway in Bordeaux at the time of the French Revolution, forming the nucleus of the Girondist party, 300 citizens were guillotined in the centre of the Place Gambetta during the brief period of the Terror.

Place Tourny
Place Tourny is named after Aubert de Tourny, a governor appointed by the crown, who was chiefly responsible for the spectacular lay-out of the city in the 2nd half of the 18th century. Place Tourny leads to the spacious Places des Quinconces on the Quai Louis XVIII in the middle of which lies the Monument des Girondins, a bronze Art Nouveau sculpture that was almost melted down for scrap

in 1943 and has only recently been restored. Visits to wine caves can be arranged through the **Maison du Vin** in the Cours du 30 Juillet just off the place des Quinconces.

Place de la Bourse

Another outstanding square is that of the Place de la Bourse, facing the Garonne, built by Jacques Gabriel between 1738 and 1755, and flanked on either side by 2 pavilion-like buildings, the Stock Exchange and the Customs House. The latter contains the **Musée des Douanes**, which traces the history of the port of Bordeaux and displays many marine articles and models of ships. A fountain of the Three Graces stands in the middle of the square from which 3 streets radiate, the Quai de la Douane leads to the delightful Porte de Caillau, a machicolated Gothic gateway with pointed tiered roofs.

Hôtel de Ville

Opposite the west front of the cathedral stands the Hôtel de Ville, a fine classical building erected by Etienne for Archbishop Rohan at the end of 18th century. It is approached through a beautiful screen ornamented with Doric columns and high ironwork grilles of great delicacy. Opposite the cathedral is the **Musée des Beaux-Arts** in the Cours d'Albret, a small collection with works by Titian, Perugino, Veronese, Jordaens, Rubens and a good collection of 17th-century Dutch art. (Open Wed–Mon 10am–6pm.)

Cathédrale St-André

Facing the former Archbishop's Palace is the Cathedral of St-André, most remarkable for its huge choir begun by Bertrand de Got, later Pope Clement V. The nave, built in the 12th century, was altered in the 13th and 15th centuries; the finest feature of the cathedral is the north doorway, the **Porte Royale**, with some exquisite 13th-century sculpture of the Apostles on either side of the doorway, the Resurrection of the Dead on the lintel and the Last Judgement in the tympanum. Beside the cathedral is a finely decorated free-standing 15th-century tower, the **Tour Pey Berland**, from which there are superb views over the city.

Eglises Ste-Croix

More interesting are the churches of Ste-Croix, which has some of the finest Romanesque capitals in France, and the elaborately ornate **Notre-Dame**, a late 17th century Baroque church that was once part of a Dominican convent. It contains a library, foremost amongst its collection being Montaigne's own copy of the 1588 edition of his *Essays* with his annotations and corrections and 3 manuscript volumes of Montesquieu's *Pensées*.

Museums

Bordeaux has 2 other museums of note, the **Musée d'Aquitaine** (Open Tues–Sun 10am–6pm, free on Wed, guided tour on Sat at 3.30pm), in Cours Pasteur, which vividly illustrates the history of the city and region from prehistoric times to the present day, and the **Musée des Arts Décoratifs** (Open for guided tours Wed–Mon

2pm–6pm; free on Wed), housed in the attractive 18th-century mansion, Hôtel de Lalande, an appropriate setting for its exhibits of furniture, ceramics, glass, jewellery and everyday luxury articles from the 16th to 18th centuries. (Tel. 56 10 15 62).

Jardin Public

A superb break from the museums and noise of the town centre, the 25,000 acres of the Jardin Public can be enjoyed. (Open daily 7am–8pm).

Bordeaux Wines

Bordeaux is still the centre of the flourishing Bordeaux wine trade. Red Bordeaux wines belong to 3 distinct groups, each related to a specific geographical area. They include the Médoc and Graves appellations, from the north and south-west; St-Emilion, Pomerol and Fronsac from the Libourne region above Bordeaux and the Bordeaux and Côtes de Bordeaux. There is only one place in Bordeaux that offers free wine-tasting or *dégustations*, which are run by professional wine experts or *sommeliers* who are knowledgeable about all aspects of wine production: the **Maison du Vin**, at 1 cours du 30 Juillet, is open Mon – Fri 8.30 am – 6 pm; Sat 9 am – 12. 30 pm and 1.30 pm – 5 pm.

Practicalities in Bordeaux

Tourist Office 12 cours du 30 Juillet (Tel. 56 44 28 41); bus 7 or 8 from station and descend at Grand Théatre; hotel listings; maps; bus tours to local vineyards; city bus passes.

Railway Station Gare St-Jean, Rue Charles Domercq; 30 min walk from centre or bus 7 or 8 to Place Gambetta; information office open 5 am – 11 pm; showers open until 10.30 pm; lockers; (Info: Tel. 56 92 50 50; Reservations: Tel. 56 92 60 60).

Buses Citram, 14 rue Fondaudège (Tel. 56 43 04 04); buses to St-Emilion and other local destinations.

Currency Exchange *Thomas Cook* (Tel. 56 91 58 80) at train station. Open daily 8am–8pm.

Public Transport CGTE: tickets, maps, information from tourist office or from CFTE, 4 rue Geroges Bonnac, off Place Gambetta.

Bicycle Rental *Cycles Pasteur*, 42 cours Pasteur (Tel. 56 92 68 20).

Post Office 52 rue Georges Bonnac; open Mon– Fri 8 am–6:30 pm, Sat 8-am noon.

Markets Numerous daily markets, including *Place des Grands Hommes*; *Marché aux Capucins*, off Cours de la Marne; *Place de la Ferme de Richemont*, on Cours Victor Hugo.

Hôtels *Hôtel la Boétie*, 4 rue de la Boétie (Tel. 56 81 76 68). In quiet street between Place Gambetta and Musée des Beaux-Arts.

Hôtel d'Amboise, 22 rue de la Vieille Tour (Tel. 56 81 62 67). Right in the heart of the city, off Place Gambetta.

☆ *Hôtel Relais Bleus*, 68 rue Tauzia, convenient for station (Tel. 56 91 55 50).

☆ *Hôtel des Quatre Soeurs*, 6 cours 30 Juillet. Every close to the tourist office, good, clean and central. (Tel. 56 48 16 00)

☆ *Hôtel Gambetta*, 66 rue Porte Dijeaux. Comfortable little hotel just off the Place du Parlement. (Tel. 56 51 21 83)

☆ *Hôtel California*, 47 rue E. Leroy. Modern, clean and comfortable; 2 mins walk from station. (Tel. 56 91 58 97)

☆☆ *Hôtel Royal St-Jean*, 15 rue Ch. Domercq (Tel. 56 58 10 35). Superbly situated between Eglise Notre-Dame and the Grand Theatre.

☆☆ *Hôtel des Pyrénées*, 12 rue St-Rémi (Tel. 56 81 66 58). Pleasant turn-of-the-century hotel; comfortable, relaxed and homey. No restaurant.

☆☆☆ *Royal Médoc*, 5 rue de Sèze (Tel. 56 81 72 42). Elegant 18th-century hotel near the beautiful Esplanade des Quinconces.

Hostels *Auberge de Jeunesse* (HI), 22 cours Barbey (Tel. 56 91 59 51). Close to station but 30 min walk from *centre ville*.

Restaurants *Café des Arts*, 138 cours Victor Hugo. A busy little brasserie good for a light lunch.

☆ *La Tenarèze*, 18 Place du Parlement (Tel. 56 44 43 29).

☆☆ *Le Loup*, 66 rue Loup (Tel. 56 48 20 21). In central location in street behind the cathedral.

☆☆ *Clavel*, 44 rue Charles-Domercq (Tel. 56 92 91 52). Modern setting near the station. Superb dishes, ranging from salmon to pigs' trotters and lobster.

☆☆ *La Tupina*, 6 rue Porte de la Monnaie, between the churches of St-Michel and Ste-Croix (Tel. 56 91 56 37). Excellent restaurant, serving specialities from south-west France.

☆☆☆ *Le Vieux Bordeaux*, 27 rue Buhan (Tel. 56 52 94 36). Outstanding cuisine from chef Michel Bordage; specialities include *foie gras de canard*, steamed turbot and eel sautéed with mushrooms.

Bordeaux – Bergerac – Beynac-et-Cazenac

Part, if not all, of the **Dordogne valley** can be visited by train and the journey is one of exceptional interest and beauty as the little local train weaves its way slowly up one of the most entrancing and romantic river valleys of France. The lower Dordogne is a succession of towns made rich by wine. Following the acquisition of Aquitaine by the English crown, by the marriage of Eleanor to Henry Plantagenet in 1154, vast quantities of wine were exported to England. Indeed, some of the best-known Bordeaux wine merchants trading at the end of the 20th century can trace their ascendants to English merchants trading from Bordeaux at the end of the 14th century.

Libourne, the very first town in the Dordogne valley, takes its name from a Kentish nobleman, Roger de Leybourne, who accompanied Henry III to Gascony for the Crusades, but although once the foremost town of the Dordogne wine trade, today it is largely an industrial city. Beyond the town, however, vineyards soon dominate the landscape.

St-Emilion

Trains 2–4 trains daily from *Bordeaux* (½ hour).

A 2 kilometre walk leads from the station to St-Emilion, the most picturesque and unspoilt town in the department of the Gironde. This small town, situated on a slight hill adorned with beautiful buildings, enclosed by its medieval walls, has a fine 12th-century collegiate church with an impressive Gothic cloister. Not far away lies the magnificent **Château du Roi**, built by Louis VIII in 1225 which is almost the only Romanesque fortress in the Gironde.

Below the château lies the **monolithic church of St-Emilion**, carved out of the rock in the 8th century by the ascetic saint who has given his name to one of the finest red wines in the world. The subterranean Eglise Monolithe is carved from a single piece of rock; adjacent to it are ancient catacombs with open sarcophagi. (Tours from tourist office, hourly in summer.) The worn stone steps of the 12th-century Clocher de l'Eglise Monolithe lead up to the top of the belfry, from where there are the most magnificent views over the vineyards of St-Emilion. In autumn the town is scented with the aroma of grape-juice as the wine-harvest is collected. Frescoes of Ste-Valérie, the patron saint of wine-growers, are visible in the Benedictine chapel above the church.

Practicalities in St-Emilion

Hotels ☆☆*Auberge de la Commanderie*, rue des Cordeliers (Tel. 57 24 70 19). No restaurant. ☆☆ *Hotel Otelinn*, 5 Champs du Rivallon, D670 (Tel. 57 61 52 05). Modern hotel with pool, just outside village. ☆☆☆ *Hotel Palai Cardinal*, Place du 11 Novembre 1918 (Tel. 57 24 72 39). Restaurant with menus between 80–130ff.

Tourist office Place des Créneaux, at foot of church; arranges tours to different châteaux, wineries and degustations (Tel. 57 24 72 03). Open Apr–end Oct.

Restaurants *Bar Le Clocker*, Place du Clocker (Tel. 57 74 43 04). Wide range of menus in excellent central location.

Buses *Citram*, 5 daily to Bordeaux (20 mins) and 7 daily to Libourne (10 mins).

Market Flower market on Sunday mornings.

A little distance upstream on the banks of the Dordogne lies **Castillon-la-Bataille**, where the English were defeated in the last battle of the Hundred Years War. It was here too that the Earl of Shrewsbury, immortalised in Shakespeare's *Henry V, Part 1* as Old John Talbot 'who was so renowned in France that no man in that kingdom dared to encounter him in single combat' met his death. Sent out to help the Bordelais resist the armies of Charles vii, Talbot attacked the French forces just to the east of the village of Castillon on 17th July 1453 under the misapprehension that the French army was in disarray. For the first time however the French army was well equipped with cannon which decimated the ranks of English and Gascon infantry and cavalry. Talbot, still commander of the English forces at the age of 82 was struck down, and with his death the English hold on Aquitaine was severed for ever. For nearly 2 centuries Périgord and Quercy had been ravaged by almost constant warfare, quite apart from the periodic visitations of black death and plague which decimated the population, particularly that of the towns. A monument to Talbot stands down near the river east of the town.

Montaigne's Château

On the hills to the north, half shrouded by forest, lies the tower of Michel de Montaigne, the greatest and one of the few voices of moderation to be heard during the Wars of Religion that raged through France in the 16th century. The only part of the home of the philosopher that survives is the library tower in which he wrote his incomparable *Essays*, the adjacent château having been entirely rebuilt during the Second Empire. On one of the beams Montaigne wrote what almost seems to read as his obituary:

Michel de Montaigne, wearied long since of the slavery of courts and public pomps, has taken his entire refuge in the arms of the learned sisters. He wishes, free from care, to finish there the course of his age, already more than half run, and he has consecrated to repose and liberty this lovable and peaceful building, the heritage of his ancestors.

After studying at the universities of Bordeaux and Toulouse, Montaigne moved to Bordeaux where he met Etienne de la Boétie, a compassionate humanist who, like Montaigne himself, was able to rise above the intrigues and passionate conflicts that racked 16th-century France. Montaigne once remarked of la Boétie that he was closer to him than to his own wife.

Bergerac

Trains *2–4 trains daily from* **St-Emilion** *(1–1½ hours) and* **Bordeaux** *(2–2½ hours).*

Bergerac and Ste-Foy-la-Grande were Protestant towns in the 16th century and as such were the scenes of intense fighting. Ste-Foy, a 13th-century *bastide*, preserves its grid of streets and still retains some timber-framed houses. Bergerac, on the other hand, was razed to the ground and after the Revocation of the Edict of Nantes, which laid Protestants open to persecution, virtually the entire population emigrated overseas. Little by little it fell into decay and only in the last 50 years has it prospered again, thriving on the growing demand for the red Bergerac wine. Wine was taken downstream to Libourne to avoid Bordeaux which tended to monopolise the export trade, even introducing regulations on the size of barrels in an attempt to compel wine to be exported through the city.

What to see

Old Quarter

An idea of Bergerac's appearance in those times can be gained by a walk through the area behind the port. In the 15th and 16th centuries Bergerac was also an important centre for trading salt which was hauled up the river in boats by teams of oxen. Although the biggest town on the River Dordogne, Bergerac is not particularly picturesque but it has a pleasant relaxed atmosphere, especially on market days. In the old quarter north of the Dordogne, there are still a few narrow streets with timber-framed houses topped by corbelled towers and decorated with medieval and Renaissance bays.

Maison des Recollets

One of the oldest buildings in Bergerac is the Convent of Recollets, which survived the religious wars. Built of brick and stone over 5 centuries, the Maison des Recollets now houses a small **wine museum**, which traces the history of local wine production from the Middle Ages to the present day. Wine-tastings are held in vaulted cellars. The inner courtyard of the monastery has 2 beautiful galleries, built in the 14th and 16th centuries, and from the exquisitely decorated great hall on the 1st floor you can look out over the Monbazillac vineyards to the south. The town has long been the centre of the wine industry of the Dordogne department but even the best Bergerac wines are no match for the St-Emilions and Bordeaux of the neighbouring Gironde.

Musée du Tabac

One of the oldest houses in Bergerac, once belonging to the Peyrarède family, is now a tobacco museum, which traces the influence of the weed over 5 centuries as well as the manners and customs of using it. Tobacco was widely grown in the department of the Dordogne and is still grown today on small farms but the amount of work involved in picking, drying, deleafing and sorting by hand, means that fewer and fewer farmers find it economic to farm. The museum also has an interesting collection of pipes and snuff boxes. Bergerac was once home to the experimental Insitute of Tobacco but this closed due to the dwindling level of tobacco production.

A statue of **Cyrano de Bergerac**, made famous by the playwright Edmond Rostand stands in Place de la Myrpe. Rostand's Cyrano was a fine swordsman and accomplished poet whose honour and worldly success were blighted by his large ugly nose that led men to insult him and women to spurn him. Constantly fighting and winning duels to defend his honour, he fell in love with a girl called Roxane who felt nothing for him. In the end, despairing of ever being successful in love, he assisted a friend to woo her by writing love letters to her in his friend's name. Tragically, Roxane fell in love with her handsome lover, unaware that it was in effect Cyrano de Bergerac who had been wooing her all along. Rostand's fictional character was based on a real native of Bergerac who was born in the town in 1619. A *'libertin'* or free-thinker, Cyrano was in constant conflict with the church, largely due to his satricial works which mocked contemporary orthodox religious beliefs. One of his best works, *Histoires comiques des états de la lune et du soleil*, consisted of satirical, almost lunatic, descriptions of journeys to the moon and the sun. Swift may well have been inspired by Cyrano's writings when he sat down to compose *Gulliver's Travels*.

Bergerac's small **cathedral** is only a creation of the last century but it houses 2 16th-century paintings, the *Adoration of the Magi* by the Venetian Pordenone and the *Adoration of the Shepherds* by a student of da Vinci's called Ferrari.

Practicalities in Bergerac

Tourist Office 97 rue Neuve-d'Argenson (Tel. 53 57 03 11).
Markets Wed and Sat mornings; livestock market: 1st and 3rd Tues of the month.
Festivals *Easter Fair*; *Fair of St-Martin*: Nov.
Hotels ☆☆ *Hôtel Cyrano*, 2 blvd Montaigne (Tel. 53 57 02 76). Lovely and inexpensive old-style hotel with terrace and excellent restaurant serving Périgord specialities.
☆☆ *Bordeaux Hôtel*, 38 Place Gambetta (Tel. 53 57 12 83). Attractive hotel with swimming pool. Good regional cooking and value for money.

Six kilometres to the south, but not visible from the river valley, lies the distinguished **Château de Monbazillac** surrounded by its vineyards where the famous white grape is grown.

A little further east the **Château de Lanquais** can be seen south of the river – an Italianate Renaissance building standing beside a massive round tower, all that remains of a medieval fortress almost entirely destroyed by the English during the Hundred Years War. The medieval tower retains its battlemented sentry walk.

The tiny village of **Badefols** on the southern bank of the Dordogne is overlooked by the ruins of a 15th- and 16th-century castle perched high on a cliff. In the Middle Ages it served as a base for lawless local lords who descended to the river to loot barges heading downstream but the castle was destroyed during the Revolution by Lakanal.

At **Mauzac** the train reaches the Cingle de Tremolat, a massive loop in the Dordogne River which can be explored on foot by alighting at **Tremolat**, a delightful village with a curious Romanesque church. The huge horseshoe-shaped meander of the Dordogne encloses a vast chequer-board of cultivated fields and meadows that can best be seen by walking along the steep road north of the village.

Beynac-et-Cazenac

The train then traverses the river 5 times in the next few kilometres, giving unsurpassed views of the villages bordering the river and the châteaux of Les Milandes and Fayrac before arriving at **Beynac-et-Cazenac**, where the massive castle rests like an eagle's aerie on a limestone cliff high above the Dordogne river. This redoubtable stronghold, rising up like an extension of the rock on which it is built, was a French castle for most of the Hundred Years War when the river marked the front between the English and the French.

In the Middle Ages Beynac was the senior of the 4 baronies of Périgord, the others being Biron, Bourdeilles and Mareuil. In the 12th century the château was the stronghold of Mercadier, a liege of Richard the Lionheart, until Simon de Montfort seized and dismantled most of the château in 1214. Rebuilt by the barons of Beynac shortly afterwards, the château dramatically overhangs the climbing village, itself full of fascinating buildings. The château is enclosed by a double line of ramparts except on the south side where a precipitous cliff drops abruptly 60 metres to the river. A bridge over a dry moat leads to a guardhouse, beyond which is a courtyard overlooked by a powerful, quadrangular Keep dating from the 13th century and surmounted by small corner watch-towers. A machicolated sentry walk links the Keep to a 14th-century tower. The living quarters face west toward the river and contain a number of beautiful rooms, notably the great State Hall with its 2 tall lancet windows. (Open Mar–mid-Nov 10 am–noon and 2.30–6.30 pm.) Behind the castle stretch extensive oak and beech forests which make excellent walking country, while the chateaux of **Les Milandes, Fayrac** and **Castelnaud** are but a short walk south of the river.

The **Château de Castelnaud**, half an hour's walk upstream, is a fine example of a medieval castle which was further strengthened in the 15th century. Carefully restored since 1958, the château, which has a superb panoramic view of the Dordogne flowing beneath and of its rival château – that of Beynac – it now houses one of the best museums of early warfare in France. Amongst the artefacts are reconstructions of the primitive rock-throwing devices used in medieval warfare.

Hidden in the trees between Castelnaud and Beynac is the romantic **Château de Fayrac**. Although not open to the public, it can be approached on the small valley road running to the west of the Dordogne River. The 2 fourteenth-century towers which face the road are the oldest part of the chateau – the later buildings date from the 19th century.

The delightful **Château de Milande**, once the home of the black American singer and dancer Josephine Baker, is an hour's walk from Beynac on the southern side of the river. The side of the château facing the road has some elegant Renaissance windows and is partly hidden by a huge magnolia tree while the side facing the river is altogether more medieval and military.

The River Dordogne is left behind at Beynac and the train climbs through oak and chestnut forest to **Sarlat**, once the capital of Perigord Noir and an episcopal city of great importance.

Practicalities in Beynac-et-Cazenac

Hotels *Hôtel de la Poste*, on road climbing up to château (Tel. 53 29 50 22). Small, clean rooms and spectacular views from this enchanting family-run hote. *Hôtel Bonnet*, 'le bourg'. Facing the Dordogne, with delightful shady terrace (Tel. 53 29 50 01).

A delightful, small and friendly family-run hotel. *Taverne des Remparts*, Place du Château (Tel. 53 29 57 76). A tiny place with only 4 rooms, opposite the château; excellent local cuisine. **Tourist office** , in small kiosk beside the river.

Sarlat-la-Canéda

Trains *3 – 4 trains daily from* **Bordeaux** *(2½ hours)*; *3 from* **Périgueux** *(1½ hours) via Les Eyzies-de-Tayac (1 hour)*; *4 from* **Le Buisson** *(1½ hours)*; SNCF *buses from* **Souillac** *(3 per day, 2 hours), from where there are trains to* **Paris**.

Situated within a narrow valley, its houses climbing the valley sides, Sarlat is one of the most attractive medieval town in France and one of the few places where virtually all its ancient buildings are preserved intact.

What to see

Old Quarter

The old quarter is to be found down the quiet, old back-streets on either side of the Rue de la Republique, the street that was built through the heart of this medieval city in 1837. Most of the houses, cut from honey-coloured stone, with their gables and turrets and roofs of stone slates, date from the 14th to the 16th centuries. The most remarkable is the home of Etienne de la Boetie, Place du Peyrou, opposite former bishop's place. Montaigne's dearly beloved friend and the author of *Voluntary Servitude*, a discourse against tyranny which inspired Jean-Jacques Rousseau while he was writing his *Social Contract*. The house has a fine sculptured façade, facing the cathedral square, with Renaissance bays and mullioned windows set within pilasters adorned with medallions and lozenges. Above are handsome gables decorated with rose motifs.

Lanterne des Morts

Immediately behind the Church of St-Sacerdos is the curious conical grey-stone building, the Lanterne des Morts. It is believed to have been built as a lantern to the dead but the reasons for its construction are not fully known. Some legends assert that it was built to commemorate St-Bernard's visit to Sarlat in 1147, on his return from the Albigensian Crusade during which he wrought miracles with bread that he had blessed.

Sarlat was inhabited in Gallo-Roman times but the town only became important when Pepin the Short founded a monastery here which was enriched by Charlemagne with the relics of St-Sacerdos, Bishop of Limoges. The abbey ruled the town until 1298 when the citizens of Sarlat won the right to govern themselves. Although little is to be seen of its medieval walls, Sarlat was one of the few towns that was not captured during the Hundred Years War. Nor was it forced to surrender to besieging armies during the Wars of Religion despite the attentions of the Protestant leaders, Coligny and Turenne.

The main artery of the old quarter is the Rue de la Liberté which links the cathedral square with the Place de la Liberté. Adjoining the 16-century cathedral are 2 courtyards, onto which faces the **Chapel of the Blue Penitents**, a Romanesque building around which medieval Sarlat grew. The crazy roofscapes and ancient buildings of mellow golden stone make Sarlat one of the most picturesque towns in France. As a result it is inevitably crowded with visitors in summer and best visited out of season.

L'Hôtel Plamon

The most remarkable of the town's many enchanting turreted houses are the *Hôtel Plamon* in the Rue des Consuls, built in the 14th century for the de Plamon family combining Gothic and Renaissance styles, and the *Hôtel de Maleville* in early Renaissance style with mullioned windows, small slender columns and corbelled towers. Some of the steeply pitched roofs are weighed down with heavy stone tiles or lauzes, a characteristic roofing style of Périgord and Quercy.

Practicalities in Sarlat-la-Canéda

Tourist Office Place de la Liberté, in the Renaissance Hôtel de Maleville (Tel. 53 59 27 67); accommodations service; emergency currency exchange; free maps and booklet.

Railway Station Ave de la Gare (Tel. 53 59 00 21). If travelling to Paris, it's better to take the SNCF bus to Souillac, from where fast trains run north (see page 000).

Markets Wed and Sat, spreading through many streets and squares. The *Marché des Oies* is the historic goose market, where live geese and fresh and tinned *foie gras* are for sale.

Festivals Classical drama festival: end July, early Aug.

Hôtels *Hôtel des Récollets*, 4 rue Jean Jacques Rousseau, on west of town (Tel. 53 59 00 49). Beautiful hotel, quiet and central.
Hôtel Marcel, 8 ave de Selves (Tel. 53 59 21 98). Cheap – for Sarlat – but a little noisy.
☆☆*St-Albert et Montaigne*, Place Pasteur (Tel. 53 59 01 09). A pleasant and comfortable hotel;

restaurant offers wide range of regional specialities and wines.
☆☆*Couleuvrine*, 1 Place Bouquerie (Tel. 53 31 26 83). A delightful, simple hotel backing onto the medieval ramparts with small charmingly decorated rooms. Superb dining-room in the former guard-room of the castle.
☆☆*Hôtel Salamandre*, rue Abbé Surguier, located in a tiny street between rue de Cahors and ave Thiers (Tel. 53 59 35 98).
☆☆☆*Madeleine*, 1 Place Petite Rigaudie (Tel. 53 59 10 41), A pleasant, old-fashioned and quiet hotel; with restaurant serving good Perigord dishes.

Hostels *Auberge de Jeunesse* (HI) 15 bis, ave de Selves; ½ hour walk from station, down Rue de la République and Gambetta; close to centre (Tel. 53 59 47 59).

Restaurant *Auberge de la Lanterne*, 18 blvd Nesmann (Tel. 53 59 05 54). A simple restaurant but with rich Perigordin dishes.

☆*Jardins des Consuls*, 4 rue des Consuls (Tel. 53 59 18 77). The shady courtyard offers a welcome retreat for light, refreshing meals in summer.

☆☆*St-Albert*, 10 Place Pasteur (Tel. 56 59 01 56). classic, restrained cooking; specialities *la mique*, a rich pork and vegetable dumpling.

Les-Eyzies-de-Tayac

Trains *3 trains a day from* **Sarlat** *(1 hour), some require you to change trains at Le Buisson; 3–5 from* **Périgueux** *(30–45 mins); 4 daily from* **Agen** *(2 hours) 3 daily from* **Paris** *(6–8 hours).*

From Sarlat the valley of the Dordogne descends west to Le Buisson, beyond which the enchanting valley of the Vezère, a tributary of the Dordogne, is followed north to Les-Eyzies-de-Tayac.

Situated in a wooded river valley hemmed in by imposing cliffs, the village of Les-Eyzies is generally known as the 'capital of prehistory'. From the mid-19th century an unparalleled number of prehistoric paintings, drawings and engravings have been discovered in the surrounding caves half-way up the high limestone cliffs flanking the Vezère and Beune rivers. The most famous sites of the area are the Abri du Cap-Blanc, the Grotte des Combarelles, the Grotte de Font-de-Gaume, the Grotte de la Mouthe and the Abri du Poisson.

The retreat of the Ice Age during the Upper Paleolithic period, some 40,000 years ago, left exposed a large sheltered region that stretched roughly from central France to northern Spain. The greatest examples of prehistoric art in the world are to be found in this region and in particular in the Dordogne. The valley of the Vezère, whose bed was then 25 metres above its present level, attracted prehistoric man because of its easily accesible natural caves, sheltered position, and over-hanging rock in which shelters could be hollowed out more easily than from the limestone of the Dordogne valley itself. The richest concentration of prehistoric finds has therefore been in the valley of the Vezère of which Les-Eyzies-de-Tayac is the main village. It was from here, in 1863, that 2 eminent antiquarians, the Frenchman E. Lartet and the Englishman H. Cristy, began a systematic exploration of the area's caves and rock shelters that led to a number of important discoveries.

What to see

Font-de-Gaume Caves

The most magnificent find close to Les Eyzies was that of the cave of Font-de-Gaume which, except for those at Lascaux, contains the finest cave paintings in the Dordogne. Those of Font-de-Gaume however have the advantage that they can be visited unlike those at Lascaux where an identical copy, known as 'Lascaux 2' has been recreated for visitors. (Open Wed – Mon 9 am – noon and 2 – 6 pm; Oct– Mar Wed–Mon 10 am–noon and 2 – 4 pm; only 340 people admitted daily, in groups; arrive by 8am for chance of securing an entrance ticket for same day.)

Grotte des Combarelles

The Grotte des Combarelles, 2 kilometres away, consists of a winding passage of which 140 yards are covered with engravings of nearly 300 animals, including horses, bison, bears, reindeer, mammoths, a giraffe and a lion. Open Thurs–Tues, 9 am-noon and 2–6 pm; Oct–Mar. 10 am–noon and 2–4 pm; groups only; tickets on sale at 9 am for morning tours and 2 pm for afternoon tours.)

The dating of prehistoric art presents its own dilemmas but most of the prehistoric paintings and drawings close to Les Eyzies date from between 35,000 and 15,000 BC. Those arriving by train can enjoy the thought that the discovery of the rock shelter of Cro-Magnon was made by accident in 1868 when the railway from Sarlat to Les Eyzies was being constructed. The work revealed the first burial sites ever found of upper paleolithic man, from which originates the anthropological term of a distinct prehistoric race, Cro-Magnon man.

Virtually all the major cave paintings and engravings are found in cave sites too deep and cold for human habitation and it is probable therefore that they had some religious significance. As prehistoric man lived largely from hunting it is likely that the portrayal of animals was believed to assist, through some kind of sympathetic magic, with the killing of the animal itself. Humans themselves are therefore very rarely represented in prehistoric cave art. One notable exception is at Lascaux where a scene shows a man apparently in the act of falling under a bison, but apart from this human representation is restricted to carved female figures that served almost certainly as fertility symbols. The decorated caves are generally found half-way up the cliffs but prehistoric man himself lived in the shelters cut out at their base. Some of these cave dwellings were inhabited for tens of thousands of years and reveal traces of prehistoric man's way of living. Bones, ashes from fires, tools, weapons, fragments of pottery, utensils and decorative items all reveal vital clues to building up a picture of prehistoric life.

Musée National de Prehistoire

The archaeological museum, located in the 12th-century castle of a former baron of Beynac, is probably the finest museum of prehistory in Europe. The castle, built beneath an overhanging rock, has rich collections of prehistoric objects and works of art, its collections including numerous bones, flints, tools, together with engravings and bas-reliefs of animals and crude fertility figures. (Open Wed–Mon 9.30 am-6 pm; April–June and Sept–Nov Wed–Mon 9.30 am–noon and 2–6 pm; Dec–Mar Wed–Mon 9.30 am–noon and 2–5 pm.)

Practicalities in Les-Eyzies-de-Tayac

Tourist Office Place de la Mairie, 5 mins walk from station (Tel. 53 06 97 05); currency exchange; bicycle rental; tours of nearby grottoes and caves.

Railway Station 1 km from centre of town (Tel. 53 06 97 22)

Markets Mon.

Hotels Hotels and restaurants in Les-Eyzies are on the expensive side. All the hotels have excellent restaurants serving traditional Périgord cuisine: foie gras, confits, dock and truffles.

Hôtel des Falaises, short walk from tourist office (Tel. 53 06 97 35). One of the few affordable hotels.

Hôtel du Périgord, on D47 near the Grotte de

Font-de-Gaume (Tel. 53 06 97 26). Quiet location near woods.

☆☆ *Hôtel Centre*, Place Mairie (Tel 53 06 97 13). Welcoming and comfortable Logis de France in a lovely old Périgord house with delightful gardens; excellent restaurant.

☆☆ *Hôtel de la Beune* (Tel. 53 06 94 33). Pleasant cool rooms in a lovely old watermill in a delightful setting on the river.

☆☆☆ *Hôtel Centenaire*, Rocher de la Penne (Tel. 53 06 97 18). Delightful, elegant and comfortable hotel with outstanding cooking. Old and new Périgourdin cuisine.

☆☆☆ *Hôtel Glycines*. (Tel. 53 06 97 13). Delightful country house, well furnished with lovely garden stretching down to the river; excellent regional cuisine.

☆☆☆ *Hôtel Les Roches*, route de Sarlat (Tel. 53 06 96 59).

Hostels Gite d'Etapes, Ferme des Eymaries, route de St-Cirq (Tel. 53 06 94 73). Delightful hostel accommodation in idyllic location in valley 4km from town.

Camping *La Rivière*, just out of Les-Eyzies, down by the river on the Périgueux road (Tel. 53 06 97 14).

Périgueux

Trains *4–5 trains daily from* **Les-Eyzies-de-Tayac** *(30 mins); 2–3 from* **Sarlat**, *change at Le Buisson (1 hour); 6 from* **Paris** *(6–7 hours); 10 from* **Bordeaux** *(2½ hours); 7 from* **Toulouse** *(4 hours).*

Périgueux, capital of the ancient province of Périgord, is very much dominated by its cathedral, one of the most curious churches in France.

What to See

Cathédrale St-Front

St-Front, topped by its 5 massive domes – one over the crossing and one over each transept –, presents a strangely Eastern appearance. Byzantine in influence, it is constructed on the plan of a Greek cross like St-Mark's at Venice, after which it is said to have been copied in the 12th century. The interior was unsympathetically restored by Abadie in the 19th century and is remarkably cold but its bare walls and enormous pillars pierced with passages impress by their grandeur, the exterior is a superb combination of Romanesque and Byzantine styles.

Roman Périgueux: La Cité

Perigueux has often been destroyed because of its vulnerable location next to the River Isle, from which it has no natural protection other than a slightly raised bank. Until the 13th century Périgueux consisted of 2 towns – Puy St-Front, a commercial and monastic centre gathered round the hilltop abbey, and La Cité, a town in a nearby loop of the Isle on the site of the original Gallo-Roman settlement. There are still impressive remains of the Roman city, notably the **Tour de Vesone**, a 25-metre-high brick tower that was once the cella of the Roman temple to Vesunna, the tutelary deity of the city. An excavation of the amphitheatre, which held 20,000 spectators, has revealed seating stair wells and vaulted passages. The great bulk of the amphitheatre was carted away for house building in medieval times but many interesting sculptures have been collected in the **town museum**. Close by is an impressive section of the Carolingian wall, built at speed using vast blocks of stone dragged from the amphitheatre, to erect hasty defences for La Cité. Perched high on the Gallo-Roman ramparts is the ruined **Château Barrière**, with its 12th-century Keep virtually intact.

St-Etienne

Although the town stands on the right bank of the Isle, the river is hardly noticed in the town, the medieval nucleus being grouped on a hill around the cathedral. The former cathedral of St-Etienne was partly destroyed by the Huguenots in 1577 as a result of which St-Front became the cathedral when the city returned to Catholic hands. But the mutilated old cathedral is altogether more interesting – a great hulk of a building with tiny windows, more Byzantine in spirit than St-Front itself.

After St-Front, Périgueux is best known as a gastronomic centre, famous for the truffles and *foie gras* that are brought into its weekly market by peasants from the surrounding villages. In summer the **Allées de Tourny** 5 minutes walk north of the cathedral up rue St Front give welcome shade from the sun under their pollarded plane trees and here the Périgourdins gather to wile away afternoons playing *boules*.

The Old Quarter

In the old quarter around St-Front there are some fine Renaissance houses, most notably in Rue Limogeanne, Rue de la Clarté, Rue du Plantier, Rue de la Sagesse, Rue de la Miséricorde and Rue de la Constitution, some with internal courtyards, turrets and towers. The **Maison Lajoubertie** in Rue de la Sagesse has a magnificent internal Renaissance staircase. Facing the River Isle itself there are 3 ancient houses with wooden balconies and in the southern part of the old quarter the **Tour Mataguerre**, a 14th-century fortified tower that was once part of the town's ramparts.

But without a doubt Périgueux is seen at its best on market day when the town comes alive with colour as stallholders with flowers and fruit ripe to perfection crowd in in front of the primitive façade of St-Front before dispersing punctually for a sacrosanct meal at midday.

Practicalities in Périgueux

Tourist Office 26 Place Francheville (Tel. 53 53 10 63); guided city tours in summer; tourist office for the region of Périgord itself is at 16 rue Président Wilson (Tel. 53 53 44 35).
Railway Station Rue Denis Papin (Info: Tel. 53 09 50 50; Reservations: Tel. 53 08 23 00).
Markets Wed and Sat, near cathedral.
Festivals *International Mime Festival* July–August; *Fair-Exposition*: late September.
Hotels *Hôtel du Lion d'Or*, 17 cours Fénelon, near tourist office (Tel. 53 53 49 03). Bright and friendly.
Hôtel du Midi et du Terminus, 18–20 rue Denis Papin, opposite the station (Tel. 53 53 41 06). Comfortable, modern and impeccable.
☆☆ *Hôtel Périgord*, 74 rue Victor Hugo, at junction with rue Kléber (Tel. 53 53 33 63). A delightful hotel with pleasant rooms, lovely courtyard and garden with tables. Restaurant serves good Périgordian food at reasonable prices.
☆☆ *Domino*, 21 Place Francheville (Tel. 53 08 25 80). A lovely old *Relais de Poste* building in town centre; delightful courtyard and good restaurant serving local specialities.
☆☆☆ *Hôtel Bristol*, 37 rue A. Gadaud, off rue Gambetta (Tel. 53 08 75 90). Calm location right in the centre of town.
Camping *Barnabé-Plage*, 80 rue des Bains, 1.5 km from centre in Boulazac. Bus D (direction **Cité Bélaire** from cours Montaigne as far as **Rue des Bains**. Delightful site but very crowded

in mid-summer (Tel. 53 53 41 45).
Restaurants ☆ *L'Amandier*, 12 rue Eguillerie, just off Place St-Louis (Tel. 53 04 15 51). Good regional cooking and superb value for money. ☆ *Le Fromage à Malices*, 5 rue Porte de Graule. Every dish features cheese in this imaginative and delightful little restaurant. A

must for cheese connoisseurs.
☆☆ *Flambée*, 2 rue Montaigne (Tel. 53 53 23 06). A good old restaurant well-known to locals; in a 16th-century house. ☆☆☆ *Oison*, 31 rue St-Front (Tel. 53 09 84 02). One of Périgueux's best restaurants; the cheapest menu is excellent value.

Brive-la-Gaillarde

Trains 5 *trains daily from* Périgueux *(1 ¼ hours); 12 from* Toulouse *(2 ½ hours); 12 from* Paris *(4 hours); 4 from* Bordeaux *(3 hours); 8 from* Cahors *(1 ½ hours); 6 from* Souillac *(25 mins).*

Brive, on the Corrèze, is an attractive, busy town with a wide, shady boulevard that encircles the lively and crowded streets of the old quarter. The centre of an immensely fertile alluvial basin, Brive's prosperity in recent times stems from its export of early vegetables and fruit by train to Paris. It acquired its suffix, literally 'the sprightly', from the vigour with which in medieval times it defended itself against the ambitions of neighbouring lords.

What to see

The town runs downhill from the railway station to the Corrèze, pausing at the interesting little **Church of St-Martin** with its lofty nave and high pillars. South of the church is a Renaissance building, the **Tour des Echevins**, and a fine turreted 16th-century mansion and in Rue Blaise Raynal is the attractive 16th-century **Hôtel de la Benche**, with an internal courtyard containing the local museum.

The 12th-century **Collégiale St-Martin**, named after the Spaniard who introduced Christianity to Brive in the 5th century, dominates the centre of Brive; the crypt contains sarcophagi recently unearthed in excavations. The **Musée Edmond Michelet**, 4 rue Chamanatier, has an interesting section devoted to the Resistance movement; Michelet was a Resistance leader who was a native of Brive and went on to become a Minister under de Gaulle. (Open Mon–Sat 10 am–noon and 2–6 pm.)

Practicalities in Brive-la-Gaillarde

Tourist Office Immeuble Château d'Eau, on Place du 14 Juillet (Tel. 55 24 08 80).
Railway Station (Info: Tel. 55 23 50 50; Reservations: Tel. 55 74 23 97.)
Markets Brive has long been famous for its markets which take place on the Place du 14 Juillet every Tues, Thurs and Sat.
Festivals Foie Gras and Truffle Fair: early Jan; Festival de la Bourrée: July; *Melon Fair*: last Sun in Aug; *Walnut Fair*: Sept; *Book Fair*: Nov.
Hotels *Hôtel Champanatier*, 15 rue Dumyrat

(Tel. 55 74 24 14). Some noise from railway line but cheap.
Hôtel de l'Avenir, 39 ave Jean Jaurès, close to train station (Tel. 55 74 11 84).
☆☆*Crémailière*, 53 ave de Paris (Tel. 55 74 32 47). Delightful Logis de France hotel, with superb, hearty local fare in restaurant and an attractive garden.
☆☆*Hôtel Truffe Noire*, 22 blvd Anatole France (Tel. 55 74 35 32). Pleasant hotel with authentic regional cooking and a few modern dishes.
Hostels *Auberge de Jeunesse* (HI), 56 ave du

Maréchal Bugeaud, off Blvd Voltaire (Tel. 55 24 34 00).
Restaurants *Périgourdine*, 15 ave Alsace-Lorraine (Tel. 55 24 26 55). Delightful restaurant with garden; good value for money.

Souillac

Trains *7 trains daily from* **Brive-la-Gaillarde** *(45 mins); 7 from* **Toulouse** *(1 hour 45 mins); 4 from* **Paris** *(5–6 hours); 5 from* **Limoges** *(1½ hours).*

Souillac, the only town in the upper valley of the Dordogne accessible by train, is a small rural town at the confluence of the rivers Borrèze and Dordogne. The town developed in the 13th century, growing up around the abbey which was a dependant of the Benedictine abbey at Aurillac.

In the 12th century the land around Souillac was marshy and had to be drained by the monks to create the rich land we see today. During the Hundred Years War the English plundered and sacked the abbey a number of times but each time it recovered. The ravages of the Wars of Religion were more extensive and permanent. In 1562 Protestant bands pillaged the abbey and later it was set on fire, only the abbey church escaping the conflagration. It was rebuilt in the 17th century but it ended its life as a working monastery after the Revolution.

What to see

Eglise Abbatiale

The abbey church that remains however is, with the cathedral of Cahors, the finest church built in the Périgordian Romanesque style. Built at the end of the 12th-century, it bears a resemblance to the Romanesque-Byzantine cathedrals of St-Front at Périgueux, Angoulême and Cahors. Inside the church is so proportioned as to give an impression of mysterious space, serenity and shelter. Inside there are parts of a Romanesque doorway rescued after the Protestant depradations of 1562, with a magnificent bas-relief depicting the life of the Monk Theophilus, Deacon of Adana in Cicilia. According to the legend, popular in medieval times, Theophilus had a burning desire to build a church but this was forbidden by his superiors. Out of resentment, Theophilus signed a pact with the devil and then built his church which he dedicated to the Virgin Mary. Later repenting his ways, he begged forgiveness of the Virgin who flew down to snatch the fatal contract from Satan and give it back to Theophilius. The carvings are remarkable for their vitality and strength, and the terrifying portrayal of Satan, a skeleton consumed by evil. The right hand pillar, originally in the centre, is carved with figures of animals representing the Seven Deadly Sins, only Pride being represented by man in the process of being eaten and strangled by bizarre Romanesque devil-beasts. The carvings of the 2 Messianic figures, Isaiah and Hosea, are remarkably flowing and poignant.

At first Souillac can seem rather disappointing – appearing to consist of little more than a busy main street with heavy traffic which is the main Limoges–Toulouse road. Between this road and the Dordogne however is the old quarter with the fine old stone market building, a labyrinth of medieval streets, the magnificent Byzantine-Romanesque abbey church, and the ancient belfry of an old church which has now been transformed into a cultural hall/theatre behind the tourist office. The junk shop opposite the old market building is an Aladdin's cave filled with fascinating rooms of junk sold by an engaging but volatile proprietress.

Practicalities in Souillac

Tourist Office Blvd Louis-Jean Malvy (Tel. 65 37 81 56); maps, hiking info., organises excursions to Rocamadour and the Gouffre de Padirac and to Sarlat, La Roque Gageac and Beynac.
Railway Station Place de la Gare, (Info: Tel. 55 23 50 50; Reservations: Tel. 65 32 78 21); to centre, walk downhill, turn left onto Ave Jean Jaurès, after 800m turn right onto Ave Général de Gaulle, continue to tourist office. Markets Mon and Wed morning on Place Doussot; also first and third Fridays of the month.
Festivals Annual Jazz Festival: 3rd week of July.
Hotels Hôtel l'Escale, 4 ave Général de Gaulle, at Place de la Laborie (Tel. 65 37 03 96). Very simple, if not basic, but central.

☆ Auberge du Puits, 5 Place du Puits (Tel. 65 37 80 32). Pleasant ivy-covered hotel; quiet and comfortable.
☆☆ Hôtel Vieille Auberge, Place Minoterie, near the river (Tel. 65 32 79 43)
☆☆ Grand Hôtel, 1 Allée Verninac, very close to the tourist office, in the centre (Tel. 65 32 78 30).
Camping Camping Municipal les Ondines, ave de Sarlat, on the Dordogne River; leaving town on Ave de Toulouse (Tel. 65 37 86 44).
Restaurants Hôtel Beffroi, Place St-Martin. Good, hearty servings in informal restaurant popular with locals.
La Crêperie, 33 rue de la Halle. Simple crêpes in a quiet street.

Cahors

Trains 10 trains daily from **Montauban** (45 mins); 10 from **Brive-la-Gaillarde** (1 hour); 10 from **Toulouse** (1¼ hour); 10 from **Souillac** (40 mins); 5 from **Paris** (5½ hours); SNCF buses from train station to **St-Cirq-Lapopie** (4 daily, 30 mins).

Leaving Souillac, the train heads south through green undulating countryside known as the Bouraine, where dark chestnut and walnut trees stand out against the light green pastures, passing the hilltop town of **Gourdon**, situated on the borders of Périgord and Quercy. The Causse de Gramat, a high limestone plateau almost devoid of trees and grazed by sheep, stretches away to the east. Passing through a tunnel the train emerges into a bright valley directly under the magnificent **Château de Mercuès**, before arriving at **Cahors** located on an isthmus formed by a sharp bend of the River Lot. Across the river strides the Pont Valentré, an early 14th-century fortified bridge defended by 3 towers, one of the finest medieval bridges in Europe.

Cahors, the capital of the province of Quercy, is a natural stronghold. It lies in a loop of the Lot on a peninsula surrounded on 3 sides by the river. To make up for the one drawback of its location – a poor water supply – an aqueduct was built to the river Vers to the east and from a spring across the river once called by the name

Divona, from which the Gallic town first took its name. In the 8th century the town was briefly occupied by the Moors and in the 12th century was part of Eleanor of Aquitaine's dowry at the time of her marriage to Henry Plantagenet. The arrival of Lombard merchants and bankers in the city, perhaps at the instigation of the Templars, led to enormous prosperity based on usury. For a century the city became one of the banking centres of Europe; borrowers included the Pope, the Kings of France and foreign princes.

During the Hundred Years War English troops attempted to seize all the towns of Quercy which were nominally part of the Duchy of Aquitaine. Few resisted except Cahors despite the onslought of the Black Death which decimated half the population. Cahors was ceded to the English in 1360 by the Treaty of Brétigny, but the town refused to be handed over. The King of France compelled the keys to the city gates to be delivered up, which they ultimately were. By the time the English left Quercy, in 1450, Cahors was a ruined city with a depleted population. In the 16th century it was a Catholic stronghold until besieged successfully by Henry of Navarre in 1580, its nominal suzerain, against whom it had rebelled.

What to See
Pont Valentré

The most distinctive and arresting sight of Cahors for which it is justly famous is the Pont Valentré with its 3 slim towers, its 6 great Gothic arches and the diamond-shaped buttresses of its piles. Winter or summer, the reflection of its outline in the rippling waters of the Lot is remarkable; it hardly seems possible that the town had 2 other medieval bridges, one guarded by 5 towers, until they were pulled down as recently as the 19th century. How many barrels of rich Cahors wine must have been transported into the city since the Pont Valentré was built in 1308 defies belief. The deep red wine Vieux Cahors is one of the few constants in the life of the town.

The university, established by the Bishop Jacques d'Euse in 1331, was closed during the 18th century. Later Jacques d'Euse went on to become John XXII, the second of the Avignon popes.

Cathédralé St-Etienne

The other glory of Cahors is the cathedral of St-Etienne, an impressive building presenting a fortified façade to the market square. Its glory lies in its north door, with an intensely moving figure of the Ascension in the tympanum that was carved around the year 1135. The west façade consists of 3 adjoining towers which gives it the stark appearance of a military building; it was completed early in the 14th century at the time when the English were attempting to seize the city. The interior of the church is of interest for the 2 great domes and 14th-century frescoes depicting the stoning of St-Stephen, his executioners, and 8 giant-sized saints.

La Maison de Roaldes

The old town lying east of the main street is full of ancient houses, the Maison de Roaldes, dating from the end of the 15th century, being one of the most interesting with its wooden walls, a large round tower, mullioned windows, a rose window and Flamboyant suns.

City Walls

Cahors is an ideal town for wandering around for everything is neatly enclosed within the banks of the Lot. At the north end of the town can be found the 14th-century ramparts which completely cut the city off from the surrounding country-side on the only side not protected by the river. These fortifications include a massive tower at the west end containing a powder-mill and the Porte St-Michel which is now the entrance to a cemetery. On the east side are more impressive fortifications: the **Barbican** or guardhouse which defended the Barre gateway and **St John's Tower**, or the Tower of the Hanged Men, which is built on a rock overlooking the River Lot. Further to the south is the **Tour de Jean XXIII**, all that is left of the palace of Pope John XXIII's brother, Pierre d'Euse.

Practicalities in Cahors

Tourist Office Place Aristide Briand, off rue Gambetta (Tel. 65 39 09 56); daily tours of the *vieille ville*; bus excursions to Rocamadour, Pech-Merle, Château of Bonaguil.
Railway Station Ave Jean Jaurès; information booth; (Info: Tel. 65 22 50 50; Reservations: Tel. 65 35 20 41).
Buses SNCF buses from station to nearby villages and Figeac.
Markets Wed and Sat mornings; on 1st and 3rd Saturdays of the month, markets extend throughout the *vieille ville*.
Festivals *Festival de Blues*, jazz: end of July.
Cycles *Combes*, 117 blvd, Gambetta (Tel. 65 35 06 73) and *Cycles 7*, 417 quai de Regourd (Tel. 65 22 66 60)
Hotels *Hôtel de la Paix*, Place St-Maurice (Tel. 65 35 03 40) Overlooking the old market.
☆☆*Le Melchior*, Place de la Gare (Tel. 65 35 03 38). Comfortable hotel, conveniently close to station.
☆☆*Hôtel Terminus*, 5 ave Ch. de Freycinet

(Tel. 65 35 24 50). Small, *fin-de-siècle* hotel, close to station; chef Gilles Marre and wife Jacqueline use local truffles to brilliant effect in superb, light cuisine.
☆☆☆*Hôtel La Chartreuse*, fg St-Georges, on the southern bank of the Lot over Pont Louis Philippe (Tel. 65 35 17 37).
Hostel *Foyer des Jeunes Travailleurs Frédéric Suisse* (HI), 20 rue Frédéric Suisse: youth hostel; singles and dorms (Tel. 65 35 64 71).
Camping *Camping Municipal St-Georges*, on bank of the Lot, across Pont Louis Philippe, up path to Mont St-Cyr; open April–Nov (Tel. 65 35 04 74).
Restaurants *Le Baladin*, 163 rue Clément Marot (Tel. 65 22 36 52). Specialises in *crêpes* and salads; the perfect place to be refreshed on a hot summer's day.
Le Coq & La Pendule, 10 rue St-James (Tel. 65 35 28 84). Small, animated and popular café with good home cooking.

Montauban

Trains *10 trains daily from* **Cahors** *(45 mins); 7–9 from* **Paris** *(5½ hours); 10 from* **Toulouse** *(25 mins); 9 from* **Bordeaux** *(2 hours); 7–9 from* **Agen** *(1 hour); 4–5 from* **Moissac** *(50 mins).*

From Cahors the train heads south skirting the western edge of the Causse de Limogne passing through Caussade and following the old Roman road to Montauban, a pleasantly situated town with an interesting square and a fine old brick bridge over the River Tarn. Montauban was a Protestant stronghold in the 16th century, being one of 4 cities in which Huguenots were given freedom of worship by the treaty of St-Germain in 1570. Despite such assurances however it was besieged by Royalist forces in 1629 and later surrendered to Louis XIII after the fall of La Rochelle.

Although failing to create a harmonious architectural ensemble there are many attractive red-brick houses which reveal the influence of the architecture of Toulouse.

What to see

Eglise St-Jacques

The fortified church of St-Jacques, which dominates the town, has a superb octagonal tower and makes a startling contrast to the vast and severe classical cathedral of Notre-Dame. The belfry is still scarred by the cannon-balls of Louis XIII's artillery fire during the king's unsuccessful siege of the town in 1629. Only when neighbouring towns surrendered to royal forces was Montauban too finally conquered. After the revocation of the Edict of Nantes in 1685, which had guaranteed religious freedom to protestants, Louis XIV ordered the construction of the cathedral which is only really of interest for the painting by Ingres of the *Vow of Louis XIII* depicting the king offering his kingdom to the Virgin Mary.

Musée Ingres

The great Classicist artist Jean Auguste Dominique Ingres was a native of the town and the **Musée Ingres**, in the brick fortress overlooking Place Bourdelle, contains the superb collection of drawings that he bequeathed to the city. Amongst the drawings are many preliminary sketches of paintings and canvases, including *Jésus et les Médecins*, *Madame Gonse* and *La Rêve d'Ossian*. The former **Archbishop's Palace** also contains contemporary furniture and a basement still home to numerous torture instruments. (Open July–Aug, Mon–Sat 9.30 am–noon and 1.30–6 pm; Sun 1.30–6 pm; Sept–June, Tues–Sat 10 am–noon and 2–6 pm.)

Place Nationale

The most pleasant place in which to linger is the enchanting square, Place Nationale, surrounded by 17th-century arches. The square was rebuilt after having been badly burnt by fires in the early 17th century. Behind the cathedral is a small public garden through which the little river Tescou runs into the Tarn.

Practicalities in Montauban

Tourist Office 2 rue du College (Tel. 63 63 60 60); organises walking tours in summer.
Railway Station Rue Salengro, (Info: Tel. 63 63 50 50; Reservations: Tel. 63 63 05 14); for town centre from station, walk down Ave Mayenne, cross Pont Vieux, walk uphill on Côte de Bonnetiers past church, turn right onto Rue Princesse and continue to Rue du Collège.

Markets Place Nationale, daily except Sunday.
Hotels The hotels close to station are not very attractive, even if they are cheap. *Hôtel du Commerce*, 9 Place Roosevelt (Tel. 63 66 31 32). Simple and cheap.
☆ *Hôtel de la Poste*, 17 rue Michelet, off Place Nationale (Tel. 63 63 05 95). Clean and simple rooms.

☆☆ *Hôtel et Restaurant Orsay*, opposite the station (Tel. 63 66 06 66).
☆☆ *Hôtel Midi*, 12 rue Notre Dame (Tel. 63 63 17 23). Delightful, rambling provincial hotel close to cathedral with spacious rooms; delicious cuisine and good-value menus.

Restaurants ☆ *Toulousian*, 2 rue Gillaque, cheap and hearty regional dishes.
☆ *Ambroisie*. 41 rue Comédie, off Rue Mary Lafon. (Tel. 63 66 27 40)
☆☆ *Chapon Fin*, 1 Place St-Orens, virtually at the Pont-Neuf near the Tarn (Tel. 63 63 12 10).

Moissac

Trains *4 – 6 trains daily from* Montauban *(15 mins);* Agen *(35 mins) and* Bordeaux *(2 hours);* 5 *from* Toulouse *(45 – 60 mins).*

Moissac is a quiet place with a southern air, built between the Tarn and the edge of the causse. What at first may seen an unremarkable little town possesses one of the masterpieces of Romanesque sculpture. It lies, almost hidden, tucked away on the south doorway of its old abbey church.

What to see

L'abbaye St-Pierre

Moissac abbey, which is believed to have been founded by a Benedictine monk from Normandy, was at the height of its fame in the 11th century. Its fortunes stem from the day in 1047 when St Odilon, the Abbot of Cluny, attached Moissac Abbey to his own abbey at Cluny, giving it an influence that was to stretch as far as Catalonia. Inevitably the abbey was pillaged both during the Hundred Years War and the Wars of Religion and today only the massive belfry-porch dates from the original 12th-century building. It was built as massively as a Keep with a watch-path running along the inside from which defenders could attack assailants.

The chief glory of the church is the **tympanum** over the south doorway which was carved between 1100 and 1130 on the theme of the Vision of the Apocalypse according to St John. In the centre is the seated figure of Christ, majestic, crowned and haloed, dominating all other figures by his size. In his left hand he holds the Book of Life while his right hand is raised in benediction. His features are sharply defined, his eyes brilliant, the sculpted locks of his beard and hair accentuating the severity of his expression and sense of strength and majesty. Around him are gathered the Evangelists: St Matthew as a winged man, St Mark as a lion, St Luke as a bull and St John as an eagle, all turning towards the figure of Christ enthroned. Outside the 2 tall figures of seraphims are the 24 Old Men of the Apocalypse ranged in 3 rows, their eyes turned towards Christ as if in amazement and fear.

The lintel is held up by a magnificent column incorporating 3 pairs of intertwined lions, with the figures of St Peter and Isaiah carved to either side. On either side of the door there are further carvings, notably scenes from the life of the Virgin and, on the left, scenes of damnation.

Cloisters An inconspicuous door opens into the abbey cloisters which are among the most beautiful in Europe. The elegant, alternate single and double columns, cut from white, pink, green and grey marble, are headed with exquisitely carved capitals portraying scenes from the Old and New Testaments and remarkable details of animals and foliage. At the corners and on the sides are columns with the bas-reliefs of abbots and saints including a bust of Abbot Bredon who was largely responsible for the construction of the abbey and who consecrated the church in 1053. (Cloister open July–Aug daily 9 am–7 pm; Sept–Oct and April–May 9 am–noon and 2–6 pm; Nov–Mar 9 am–noon and 2–5 pm.)

Practicalities in Moissac

Tourist office Place Durand-de-Bredon, next to the cloister (Tel. 63 04 01 85).
Festival Classical concerts held in cloister from June–August (Tel. 63 04 06 81).
Hotels ☆☆ *Hôtel le Chapon Fin*, Place Récollets. Comfortable, reliable and friendly hotel in the heart of the town. (Tel. 63 04 04 22); with an excellent restaurant.
☆☆☆ *Mapotel Moulin de Moissac*, Place Moulin (Tel. 63 04 03 55).

Agen

Trains *4 – 5 trains daily from* **Moissac** *(35 mins); 8 – 12 trains daily from* **Bordeaux** *(1 hour 20 mins); 8 – 12 from* **Toulouse** *(1 hour 10 mins), including* TGVs.

Agen is an old town on the right bank of the Garonne near the foot of steep wooded slopes of the Coteau de l'Ermitage. It is famed above all for its plums which grow in profusion on the hillsides north of the Garonne, the plum-trees thriving from warm locations, freedom from spring frosts and strong winds and guaranteed spring sunshine.

The **old quarter** of Agen is bisected by two 19th-century streets the Boulevard de la République and Boulevard President Carnot that run south from the railway station. North-west of their intersection stands the **cathedral** with an imposing 12th-century apse but a hideous 19th-century interior.

What to see

Musée des Beaux-Arts

The old streets repay quiet wandering, especially the area around the museum on Place Esquirol which is housed in a group of elegant Renaissance mansions. The museum houses a magnificent marble sculpture, the *Venus of Le Mas*, thought to be a 1st-century copy of a Greek original, that was discovered by a local farmer ploughing his fields at the end of the 19th century. On 4 floors, thousands of Gallo-Roman antiquities are displayed, including swords and a fine bronzed Celtic horse. There is also a good collection of delightful Impressionist paintings and works by Goya. (Open Wed–Mon 11 am–6 pm.)

Practicalities in Agen

Tourist Office 107 blvd Carnot (Tel. 53 47 36 09); free guided tours of the old town.
Railway Station Blvd Sylvain Dumon (Tel. 53 66 50 50).
Markets Covered daily market on Place des Laitiers; weekend market on Place du Pin.
Hotels ☆☆ *Hostellerie des Jacobin*, 1 ter Place Jacobins, next to church of same name (Tel. 53 47 36 09). Comfortable and stylish hotel. No restaurant.
☆ ☆ *Stim'Otel*, 105 blvd Carnot (Tel. 53 47 31 23). Modernised and comfortable, adjacent to tourist information.

Hostels *Auberge de Jeunesse* (HI) 17 rue Lagrange, 2km from centre. Bus (direction Lalande) from station to Léon Blum stop (Tel. 53 66 18 98).
Camping *Camping Municipal*, near Auberge de Jeunesse (Tel. 53 68 27 18).
Restaurants *Les Mignardes*, 40 rue Camille Desmoulins (Tel. 53 47 18 62). Generous hearty home cooking; packed with locals at lunchtime. *Lamanguié*, 66 rue C. Desmoulins, traditional French dishes in popular local restaurant (Tel. 53 66 24 35).

From Agen to Bordeaux the landscape is a delightful succession of orchards, a picturesque ocean of blossom in spring, and vineyards, bottle-green in summer and rich golds, reds and yellows in autumn. Close by are the small vineyards of **Sauterne**, from which comes Château Yquem, one of the wonders of the oenopole world, and then the vineyards of **Graves**. To the west of this great tract of grape-producing country the endless lowland forests of **Les Landes** stretch a hundred kilometres to the Atlantic coast.

Aiguillon is a small *bastide* town with a ducal château partly rebuilt in the 18th century. Close to **Fauguerolles** lies Le Mas d'Agenais where the Venus of Le Mas was found. The train then passes through the little towns of Marmande and La Réole, once a place of exile for the Parlement of Bordeaux, and Langon before arriving at Bordeaux.

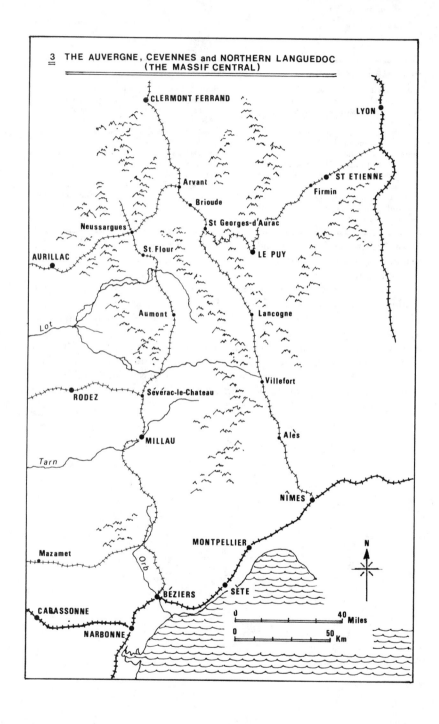

3 THE AUVERGNE, CEVENNES and NORTHERN LANGUEDOC
(THE MASSIF CENTRAL)

CLERMONT FERRAND

LYON

Arvant

Brioude

ST ETIENNE

Firmin

Neussargues

St Georges-d'Aurac

St Flour

LE PUY

AURILLAC

Lot

Aumont

Lancogne

Villefort

RODEZ

Sévérac-le-Chateau

MILLAU

Alès

Tarn

NÎMES

Mazamet

MONTPELLIER

N

Orb

BÉZIERS

SÈTE

CARASSONNE

0   40 Miles

0   50 Km

NARBONNE

3 The Auvergne, the Cévennes and Northern Languedoc

Massif Central is the broad name given to the vast central plateau of France west of the Rhône, east of Limoges, north of Languedoc and south of the plains of Orléans. From this large area of high ground spring the sources of almost all the rivers of France, with the exception of the Rhône, the Saône and the Seine. This large upland area includes the extraordinary volcanic landscape of Le Puy and range on range of hills running into another at confused angles, but in general lying in a north-south direction. There is a strange air about this great central plateau which isolates it from the surrounding plains; geographically it is the heart of France but in a curious way, it feels essentially un-French. The explanation lies perhaps partly in the fact that the indigenous people of the central Massif Central and Auvergne are of Celtic origin and have, by and large, maintained the characteristics of their race. Until the 2nd half of the 20th century there was little movement of population outside the region and tight family bonds were necessary to work the land in face of a harsh climate and often rather thin, poor, soil. The unique feel of this region may also be due in part to the geological formation of the hills, the result of violent volcanic activity, which has led to a landscape quite different, and harsher, than any to be found elsewhere in France.

The history of the region is somewhat different from other regions of France too. Apart from a brief period in the 11th century, when Peter the Hermit preached the First Crusade at Clermont-Ferrand, the towns of the Massif Central have rarely been in the forefront of political or economic change. News from the outside filtered through slowly to the remote towns and villages of the Auvergne, and when outsiders arrived it usually spelt trouble. The first such intruders to break in on the peace of the Auvergne were the Romans. Vercingetorix nearly succeeded in destroying the Roman legions under Julius Caesar before surrendering and being carried off as a prisoner to Rome. He was probably born in the vicinity of Clermont-Ferrand and Gergovia, nearby, was his headquarters during his campaign against Julius Caesar in 53 BC. In the 12th century part of the Auvergne passed to the English crown through the marriage of Eleanor of Aquitaine to Henry Plantagenet, but in 1190 King Philippe Auguste conquered the area. Sub-divided between the royal dukes, centred on Riom, the counts of Auvergne and the bishops of Clermont, the Auvergne was too divided amongst itself in petty jealousy ever to play an important role in medieval history.

The history of the **Cévennes** is one of even greater isolation and harshness. During the Middle Ages and religious wars of the 16th and 17th centuries many religious refugees, fleeing from persecution, settled in the secluded valleys of the Cévennes. Campaigns against the Camisards in particular, went on for decades until all had been killed, deported or were languishing in prisons.

The Route *Nîmes – Brioude – Le Puy – Clermont-Ferrand – St-Flour – Chaudes-Aigues – Béziers – Sète – Montpellier*

This journey is one of extremes for nothing could be more different than the sun-drenched vineyards that trail down to the Mediterranean coast at **Nîmes** *and the huge expanse of forested hills and valleys of the Cévennes and uplands of Auvergne. While there are a number of magnificent Roman buildings to be seen at Nîmes and a handful of interesting Romanesque churches elsewhere, this route is primarily scenic rather than cultural. Most of the route lies in the narrow valleys of the* **Cévennes** *and the upland plateau of the* **Massif Central**. *The railway lines that run north from Nîmes to* **Clermont-Ferrand** *and south to* **Béziers** *are little used and it is perhaps even surprising that they are still kept open. While they are, it is a real joy to sit back and watch the landscape of the Cévennes and Auvergne unfold. Often the railway is far from any road and takes the traveller into valleys and through mountains to places inaccessible by car and difficult to reach by foot.*

Nîmes, famous for its wonderful relics of the Roman occupation of Gaul, is as flourishing a city today as it was in Roman times, although in medieval times it was far smaller than the Roman settlement. The Cévennes are quickly reached, a wild forebidding area, harsh and closed but also with a strange haunting beauty, brought closer to peoples' hearts since the late 19th-century by Robert Louis Stevenson's enchanting journey with his donkey, Modestine. **Clermont-Ferrand**, *shut in by hills on 3 sides, has the feel almost of a lost and forgotten city, far from where history is being made. Nevertheless this important town has some fine old houses and an intriguing coal-black cathedral built of local volcanic stone. Around*

it lies the volcanic landscape of the Monts Dômes, volcanic masses which
hardened almost immediately after being thrown up. The train then heads
south to **St-Flour,** *a picturesque old town strikingly built on a precipitous*
rock 90 metres above the little river Lander. A magnificent twisting journey
is then made through the limestone causses before emerging once again on
the Mediterranean coastline at **Béziers,** *a prosperous wine town of the*
Hérault and Aude, dramatically sited on a bluff above the river Orb.

   Languedoc *is the name given to the area ruled over by the Counts of*
Toulouse which now includes the départements of Ardeche, Lozère, Gard,
Hérault, Aude and Tarn. In the north it stretches as afar as **Le Puy,** *in the*
east as far as the Rhône, incorporating the coast strip between **Aigues-**
mortes *and* **Narbonne** *known as Bas-Languedoc or 'the land of sand and*
ruin and gold'. It is therefore a country of contrast, its climate ranging from
the barren wintry slopes and plateaux of the Cévennes and Causses to the
sun-baked plain of Carcassonne, while upper Languedoc was for centuries
among the most backward parts of France. Nîmes however was known as
the 'little Rome in Gaul' on account of its splendour and civilisation.
(**Approximately 4–7 days.**)

Nîmes

Trains *5–6* TGVs *daily from* **Paris** *(4½ hours); frequent trains from* **Avignon** *(30 mins);* **Montpellier** *(30 mins);* **Narbonne** *(1 hour 50 mins);* **Arles** *(35 mins); 16 daily from* **Toulouse** *(3 hours 20 mins).*

Elegant, vivacious, Mediterranean and cosmopolitan, Nîmes lies on a gently shelving plain where Languedoc merges imperceptibly with Provence. Surrounded by vines, close to the sea and the wild limestone garrigues of the Cévennes to the north, Nîmes is a vibrant city which enjoys an almost idyllic climate and superb geographical position.

   When Christ was born in Bethlehem, Nîmes was already an important and flourishing Roman town on the Domitian Way, the road which linked Italy with Spain. Founded by Augustus with a colony of veterans of the Roman campaign in Egypt, the Roman city covered a huge area of almost 500 square acres surrounded by fortifications. Under Agrippa, the **Pont du Gard**, one of the finest and tallest Roman aqueducts in existence was built to bring water from the river Eure to the heart of the city.

What to see

Amphitheatre

The 1st century AD also saw the construction of a vast amphitheatre, the finest in France, which could hold 20,000 spectators; although fractionally smaller than the one at Arles it is in better condition. As at Arles it was turned into a defensive bastion by the Visigoths and then became a rabbit-warren of alleyways and houses in medieval times. Even when Smollett visited Nîmes in 1763 people were still carting away stones for their own use. It has recently been restored as close as possible to its former appearance and is used in summer for bull-fighting. High up on the inside can be seen the sockets that held posts carrying the huge adjustable awning, the velum, that could be closed to shelter the spectators from sun and rain. (Open mid-June–mid-Sept, daily 8 am–8 pm; mid-Sept–Oct and Apr–mid-June, daily 9 am–noon and 2–6 pm; Nov–Mar, daily 9 am–noon and 2–5 pm.)

Maison Carrée

But even if the amphitheatre is impressive, nothing can compare with the Maison Carrée, a small Roman temple of exquisite beauty probably built around 20 BC by the architect of the Pont du Gard. The beauty of its proportions, the delicacy of its decoration and its statuesque nobility make it the most important intact building of its kind extant. Arthur Young, touring France just before the Revolution found it beyond comparison the most light, elegant and pleasing building I ever beheld . . . one perfect whole of symmetry and grace. What an infatuation in modern architects that can overlook the chaste and elegant simplicity of taste manifest in such a work and yet rear such piles of laboured foppery and heaviness as are to be met with in France.

It was built as a temple and dedicated to Lucius and Gaius, sons of Agrippa, adopted by Augustus as his heirs.

The enormous pottery jar on the pronaos was found at the site of a Roman villa near the city; originally it would have been half buried in the earth to obtain a cool even temperature and used to store provisions. (Open mid-June–mid-Sept, daily 9 am–7 pm; mid-Sept–Oct and Apr–mid-June, daily 9 am–noon and 2–6 pm; Nov–Mar, daily 9 am–noon and 2–5 pm.)

Carré d'Art

The noble majesty of the Maison Carrée would be hard to equal and therefore the choice of a building to replace the early 19th-century theatre opposite that was burnt to the ground in 1952 cannot have been easy. But the town council have chosen with confidence, commissioning a superbly restrained rectangular glass building designed by the English architect Sir Norman Foster, which serves as the new museum of contemporary art. This elegant building houses the city's *médiathèque* a combined museum of modern art, library and musical and video facility, as well as housing the municipal archives and having a superb rooftop café which looks out over the Maison Carrée.

An astute solution was found to keep the building within proportions harmonious with the Maison Carrée: 5 of the 9 floors are below ground. Foster's design for a 'modern temple of art and learning' shows sympathy for its classical neighbour, the pale slim pillars of the façade respecting the spirit of the Corinthian colossi opposite. Whether glass and thin pale blue metal piping will weather as well over 2,000 years as the golden sandstone of the Maison Carrée time alone will tell.

Jardin de la Fontaine

Nîmes is also fortunate in possessing some of the most attractive public gardens of any city in France. The beautiful 18th-century gardens, les Jardin de la Fontaine, are laid out around the source of the Nemausus, a once-sacred spring, on the site of the Roman baths. The spring water is collected in a mirror-like pool surrounded by delightful balustraded walks, before flowing through a series of pools to the canal. Within the gardens are the remains of a Roman temple known as the **Temple of Diana** and above is the old stump of a tower, the **Tour Magne** which is in fact of great antiquity, its Roman superstructure resting on ramparts that date back to the 16th-century BC. From the summit there is an excellent view of the Garrigues, stony scrub-covered hills, to the north through which the railway line climbs into the Cévennes.

Cathédrale St-Castor

Two of Nîmes' most enchanting little squares are the **Place du Marché** and the **Place aux Herbes** next to the cathedral, with its cast-iron fountain, flower beds and cafés. Although the interior of Nôtre-Dame and St Castor cathedral is entirely 19th-century, the west façade facing the Place aux Herbes retains a fascinating Romanesque frieze with scenes of Adam and Eve, Cain and Abel, stone-masons at work and a cathedral in the process of being built. Next to the cathedral, in the old Archbishop's Palace behind elegant wrought-iron railings, is the excellent **Musée du Vieux Nîmes**, with beautifully arranged exhibits in a superbly restored 17th-century interior. (Open daily 10 am–6 pm.) Among the clothes and embroidered garments on display are early specimens of denim, the tough blue cotton cloth *de Nîmes* – of Nîmes – which has become the world's single largest selling item of clothing.

Practicalities in Nîmes

Tourist Office 6 rue Auguste (Tel. 66 67 29 11); accommodation service.
Railway Station (Tel. 66 23 50 50); information office; automatic lockers. For town centre from station walk along Ave Feuchère, up to semi-circular Esplanade de Gaulle, follow it round to left, cross blvd and walk round to far side of Roman arena, then head up Blvd Victor Hugo, and turn right on Rue du Général Périer. Rue Auguste faces the Maison Carrée.
Buses Rue Ste-Félicité, behind station (Tel. 66 29 52 00). Information office open Mon–Fri 9 am–noon and 2–6 pm. Buses to Pond-du-Gard (5 daily; 30 mins), Aigues-Mortes (6 daily, 1 hour).
Festivals *Bull-fighting 'corridas'*: in Feb, June and Sept; *Ferria de Pentecôte*: early June.
Markets Outside Maison Carrée, Wed and Sat mornings.

Hotels Hôtel de France, 4 blvd des Arènes (Tel. 66 67 47 72). Central location, close to arena. *Hôtel Majestic*, 10 rue Pradier (Tel. 66 29 24 14). Near station, bright and friendly.
☆☆*Hôtel le Cheval Blanc*, Place des Arènes (Tel. 66 76 32 32). Close to arena.
☆☆☆*Louvre*, 2 sq de la Couronne (Tel. 66 67 22 75). Cool, spacious rooms in lovely 17th-century house near the Roman arena; very good restaurant.
Hostels *Auberge de la Jeunesse* (HI), off chemin de la Cigale, 3km from station on bus 20. (direction l'Auberge de Jeunesse').
Restaurants *Nicholas*, 1 rue Poise (Tel. 66 67 50 41). Fun, animated regulars arrive early for local specialities such as *bourride*, a thick garlic fish soup. *Les Hirondelles*, 13 rue Bigot (Tel. 66 21 38 69). Busy little bistro serving good Provençal fare.

Through the Cévennes: Nîmes – Brioude – Clermont-Ferrand

Trains *4 slow trains daily to* **Brioude** *(3 ½ hours) and* **Clermont-Ferrand** *(5 hours).*

The moment the train pulls out of Nîmes it enters the **Garrigues**, a limestone formation of low hills which sweep along the foot of the Massif Central, between it and the level plains of Languedoc. This area was once densely covered with holm oaks and Aleppo pines, most of which had already been felled by medieval times. Rain, frost and wind have carried away much of the topsoil over the centuries and the area now tends to have a dry and somewhat barren appearance. Where soil still exists scrub oak, gorse, asphodel and wild aromatic plants have taken hold while the valleys and flat plains are devoted almost exclusively to vines. In autumn the colours of the vines are breath-taking.

Very quickly the train passes through the Garrigues into thick forested country of ash, rowan and oak. Over the Gardon River, the **Cévennes** slowly come into view in the distance – bluey-green in colour with barely a house to be seen on the hillsides. **Alès** is a dreary industrial town on the River Gardon where coal has long been mined; it was also once an important centre of the silk trade. Having finished his walk and sold Modestine his faithful companion in the village of St-Jean-du-Gard, a little to the west, Robert Louis Stevenson left the Cévennes from Alès railway station. Alès forms the gateway to the mountains – a frontier town between the arid Garrigues to the south and the watery uplands of the Auvergne.

The Cévennes

The Cévennes, a huge mass of igneous and limestone mountains, form the backbone of central France. Overlooking the Rhône valley in the east and the Mediterranean basin in the south, the Cévennes merge gradually in the west with the long narrow valleys of the Loire, Dore, Allier, Lot and Tarn. The heart of the Cévennes however centres on the old *pays* of 'La Cévenne' between the sources of the Allier and the Gard. Due to the wide spread of their foothills on the north and the steepness of their slopes on the south, the Cévennes are crossed by only one railway – the Nîmes-Clermont line – which crawls slowly up to the **Col de la Bastide** (1,077 metres), the principal gap in the main chain.

The people of the Cévennes, hardened by continual struggle with the barrenness of the soil and the rigours of the climate, have always been famous for their sturdy independence, especially in questions of religion. In the 13th century the persecuted Albigensian heretics founded a refuge in the Cévennes and later the mountain valleys were peopled by the Waldensians fleeing from Lyon. The attempt to oppress Protestants following the revocation of the Edict of Nantes led to an outbreak in 1702 amongst the Cévenols – the insurrection of the Camisards. At first the Cévenols were successful, forcing the Comte de Broglie to retreat within the walls of Nîmes. But the Camisard leader was induced to meet with Villars at Nîmes in 1704 and, given assurances of safety and inducements, none of which were kept, the Camisards were hunted down, tortured and buried alive at Nîmes or imprisoned for years in the dungeons of Aiguesmortes.

Beyond Alès the train passes a twin-turreted medieval château on a rocky outcrop and follows the valley of the Gardon upstream, steadily climbing in height. Despite its exotic name **Grande Combe la Pise** is not a beautiful town but beyond it the railway enters a deeply incised river valley of reddish rock. Waterfalls, dramatic rocky outcrops and mountainous torrents become more frequent and the train passes through a number of short tunnels. The valleys are cool and refreshing in summer and rather dark and forebidding in winter but the landscape begins to open out, as at **Chamborigaud**, giving magnificent views over the purply brooding hills of the Cévennes.

A spectacular 19th-century viaduct is crossed before **Genolhac**, giving superb views of the valley far below, the train stopping at tiny stations that appear to be deserted. It's necessary to inform the guard if you want to get off the train and to wave at the incoming train if you want to be picked up. Otherwise the train is quite likely to amble through the station without stopping at all.

National Park of the Cévennes

The little town of **Villefort**, on the eastern edge of the National Park of the Cévennes, is the best place from which to begin a walking trip. From here Grandes Randonnées footpaths 44, 66 and 68 radiate out across the heart of the Cévennes. During the summer the information centre on the National Park is open and watersports can be enjoyed on the adjacent lake which is crossed by the train on an impressive viaduct.

The oak forests further south have long since disappeared, having given way to vast expanses of pine and larch while silver birch and chestnut are scattered amongst the pine on the lower slopes and in the valleys. From time to time the valleys open out into wild country of short grass, grazed by sheep, and high open hills. In winter the landscape can be cold and austere, in spring the valleys are briefly scattered with wild flowers. The contrast with the Mediterranean coast is extraordinary.

Owing to the high altitude of the Massif Central the seasons are almost a month behind that of the surrounding plains, and never is that more noticeable than when coming from the south. One may leave Nîmes basking in the full beauty of early summer and find, 200 kilometres north on the plateau, that the trees are still black and leafless. The atmosphere also changes: the deep, warm colour of the southern sky gives way to a clear, cold blue suggestive of frosts and icy winds. But if winters in the uplands of the Massif Central are long, dark and cold, in summer the sparkling air and mountain streams come as a welcome relief from the heat-laden towns of Provence and Languedoc.

The medieval heart of the village of **Langogne** reflects 15th- and 16th-century concerns for defence with its medieval rampart towers, gateway and houses built shoulder to shoulder in a tight protective circle around its Romanesque church.

Beyond Langogne the train crosses the huge **resevoir of Naussac** on a viaduct high above the water. The landscape then becomes noticeably more dramatic, the Allier river flowing fast and turbulent between abrupt rock-faces, and entering narrow chasms, as it plunges downstream. For at Langogne we have crossed the watershed and follow the Allier, a tributary of the Loire which flows north for 150 kilometres to Nevers. The river is characterised by jagged rocks and quiet pools, caves eroded by torrential spring rivers and foaming rapids. North of Langogne the landscape slowly opens out, the valleys become broader and the pine forests recede as the train descends to **Langeac**, a centre for kayaking on the Allier river, and **Brioude**. The small towns and villages are built of hard grey granite and gneiss and can appear uninviting, especially in winter. Few have churches or works of art of distinction for this area has never had wealth enough to be disputed for long. Brioude, however, the most important town on the upper reaches of the Allier, is the exception.

Brioude

Trains *4 slow trains daily from* **Nîmes** *(3½ hours) and* **Clermont-Ferrand** *(1½ hours).*

For centuries Brioude was a pilgrimage centre with pilgrims coming to pray at the tomb of St-Julian, the 4th-century martyr. It is here that the Allier enters an inaccessible gorge which extends for many kilometres, so from very earliest times Brioude was the natural crossing place on the River Allier, whose plain it dominates. Brioude is also famous to all students of Froissart as the headquarters of the fictional brigand Louis Raimbaut who ravaged the Auvergne in the days of Edward the Black Prince. So remote were the castles of Auvergne that for centuries their lords were able to oppress their subjects and extort exorbitant taxes with impunity. It was not until the capricious behaviour of the Auvergnat lords came to the attention of Louis XIV that any attempt was made to curtail their excesses. Many of their castles were equipped with *oubliettes* or dungeons into which their enemies were dropped and left to die pitiable deaths from starvation. The **Château of La Mothe**, close to Brioude, has not one but several such wells with smooth perpendicular walls and a deep bottom from which no steps ascend.

What to see

Basilica de St-Julien

There is very little to see at Brioude other than the Basilica of Saint Julien but this is one of the finest examples of Byzantine Auvergnat Romanesque architecture and the largest Romanesque church in the Auvergne. It is remarkable for its apse, the upper part of which is decorated with magnificent polychrome masonry. Here are to be seen 'flowers which no land has ever been able to produce and creatures still more extraordinary, blossoming and amusing themselves over the walls. All the lavas which our soil produces have lent the monks their greys and blacks, their reds and whites. This splendid covering of many-coloured mosaic clothes the outer walls of the apse and hangs like a veil of Syrian embroidery above the entrances.' Within there is a feeling of breadth, power and harmony of colour. The beauty of the polychrome masonry is matched by the variety of finely-sculptured capitals and rich frescoes which reveal the dexterity, sensitivity and fertile imagination of the Auvergnat artists and masons.

According to legend, it was to Brioude that 2 shepherds carried the body of Saint Julien who had been beheaded nearby at Saint-Ferreol, in 403 by a troop of Roman soldiers. The first shrine to St Julien was razed to the ground by the Saracens and the present basilica not built until the end of the 11th century. Within the basilica is a moving sculpture of a leprous Christ, a 15th-century work almost certainly executed in a local leper house. The doors of the north porch are reputed to be covered with human skin.

Practicalities in Brioude

Tourist Office Place Champanne (Tel. 71 74 97 49).
Railway Station (Information and Reservations: Tel. 71 02 50 50).
Hotels ✩✩ *Hôtel Moderne*, 12 ave Victor Hugo, on way into town from station (Tel. 71 50 07 30).
Hôtel Poste et Champanne, 1 blvd Dr Devins (Tel. 71 50 14 62).

St-Georges d'Aurac is the junction for trains to Le Puy, St-Etienne and Lyon; Arvant, a little further north, is the junction for trains heading south-west to Toulouse.

Le Puy

Trains *4 daily from* **St-Georges d'Aurac** *(50 mins) and* **Clermont-Ferrand** *(2–3 hours); 9 from* **St-Etienne** *(1 hour 20 mins) and Lyon (2½ hours).*

Le Puy or Le-Puy-en-Velay is one of the most remarkable towns in France, both on account of its strange position surrounded by the fertile slopes of extinct volcanoes and of its many interesting buildings.

It is the centre of the ancient district of Velay, the mountainous region inhabited by the Gallic Vellavi, and was noted for centuries for the manufacture of lace. The most superb view of the town is reserved for those arriving by train from Nîmes or Clermont-Ferrand via St Georges d'Aurac. Everywhere around rise up volcanic rocks of fantastic shapes which were thrown up by a terrific upheaval. The old town clings to the steep slopes of the **Rocher Corneille**, on the side of which rises the cathedral. To the north and west are the fantastic pinnacles of **Aiguilhe** and **Espaly**, the first topped by a delightful little chapel. To the south lies the modern town in a green and fertile basin overlooked by the grim forbidding outline of the Cévennes.

Famous since the 12th century because of cures effected by a 'fever stone', Le Puy suddenly became famous when a statue of the Virgin was brought here by St-Louis in 1254, probably from the Crusades. Thousands of pilgrims on the route to Santiago de Compostela came to worship the statue of the Virgin in the glorious Romanesque cathedral.

What to see

Old Quarter

From the spacious **Place du Breuil**, the heart of Le Puy, the old town is entered along the Rue Porte-Aiguière, passing the 18th-century **Hôtel de Ville**. The most interesting part of old Le Puy centres on the street leading from the **Tour Pannesac** which has many houses form the 15th, 16th and 17th centuries. Down a narrow alley, called 'du Charmalenc' is the 17th-century **Maison des Connards**, the meeting place of the Le Puy company. The cathedral can be approached via the Place du Plot, the Rue Chenebouterie and the Rue Raphael; the steep Rue des Tables then mounts in steps past a graceful 15th-century fountain to the cathedral steps.

Cathédrale Notre-Dame

Set on a rock, somewhat forebidding and austere, stands the Cathédrale Notre-Dame, one of the largest and most beautiful buildings in the Auvergne. The cathedral is a remarkable building, unique in plan, approached by a flight of 60 steps which lead up to the triple porch of the polychrone façade. On the left are the late Gothic **Hôtel-Dieu** and the **Machicoulis**, a curious building which formed part of the defensive fortifications of the bishop's palace. For the cathedral is but one part of a whole network of religious buildings which make up a city within a city.

The cathedral is largely built on a rock and is unusual in incorporating Islamic features. The staircase continues under the porch and beneath the floor of the nave before dividing into 2, the left branch leading to the cloister. The interior is spacious and plain, the choir and transepts and 2 eastern bays of the nave dating from the 11th century, the rest from the 12th century. On the high altar is the statue of Notre-Dame-du-Puy, a black Virgin, a copy by a local artist of the original pilgrimage statue which was destroyed during the Revolution. The origins of the Black Virgins, found all over central France, are believed to stem back to the 12th century when Crusaders in the Middle East first came across images of the Virgin with a dark complexion painted by local artists. In the south transept a door leads out to the **Porte du For**, a beautiful example of late-Romanesque art showing Arab influence in its embossed columns and pierced arches; outside it is the little Place du For, the terrace of the former bishop's palace.

Cloisters
The 12th-century Romanesque cloister, betraying Islamic influences with its alternating black and white stone arcades and mosaics of coloured lozenges, is extremely beautiful. The arches are supported by magnificent pillars, each surrounded by 4 columns, while the cornice is richly decorated with grotesque heads. The whole ensemble, with its variegated colour, fine capitals, red tiled roof and 12th-century iron grille, is very picturesque. A 13th-century fresco on the Byzantine arches depicts the crucifixion amid a bright black volcanic landscape evocative of the area. Nearby is the **Trésor d'Art Religieux** and the **Chapelle des Reliques** with a head of Christ in beaten copper, a reliquary, silverware, and the remarkable 9th century Théodulphe Bible, the work of monks from St-Bénoit-sur-Loire. (Open daily 9.30 am–7.30 pm.)

Rocher Corneille
From the Porche St-Jean, close to the baptistery with its antique font and columns, a road leads up the Rocher Corneille, the eroded core of an ancient volcano. A 130 metres climb takes one to the summit from where rises a colossal statue of the Virgin, made in 1860 from the metal of 213 cannon captured by the French at Sebastopol; other military equipment lies at the foot of the Rocher. (Open daily 9 am–7 pm, off season 9.30 am–noon and 2–5.30 pm.)

Rocher d'Aiguilhe
Even more impressive is the other pinnacle of Le Puy, the Rocher d'Aiguilhe, a vertical pinnacle of 85 metres, crowned by a **chapel**, from where there are panoramic views of the town and surrounding country. The chapel, dedicated to St-Michel d'Aiguilhe, is a charming little 10th-century oratory with a spectacular trefoiled doorway and capitals which are masterpieces of Romanesque sculpture. A parapet walk round the church reveals the oriental influence in the arch and the 2 sirens on the lintel. At its foot is the 12th-century baptistery or **Chapelle de Ste-Claire**. (Same hours as for Rocher Corneille.)

Musée Crozatier
At the back of the Jardin Henri Vinay, the Musée Crozatier houses a small collection of archeological finds but also an interesting collection of lace, with exhibitions on lace-making, which was the most important activity of the town for 400 years. Until the 1950s women could be seen working on the lacework outside their homes, producing either 'dentelles du Puy', silk-thread lace, or 'dentelles de Craponne', cotton-thread lace, but the mechanisation of lace-making at the turn of the century dealt a death-blow to this labour-intensive craft. (Open Wed–Mon 10 am–noon and 2–6 pm; off season Mon and Wed–Sat 10 am–noon and 2–6 pm.)

L'Atelier Conservatoire National de la Dentelle

A conscious attempt to preserve the tradition of lace-making led to the creation of the Atelier Conservatoire National de la Dentelle, at 2 rue Duguesclin, in 1976. The exhibition displays many different types of lace, from France and abroad, and has demonstrations of traditional lace-making techniques. (Open Mon–Sat 9 – 11.30 am and 2 – 5.30 pm; Oct–May, Mon–Fri. 9 – 11.30 am and 2 – 5.30 pm.)

Practicalities in Le Puy

Tourist Office Place du Breuil (Tel. 71 09 38 41); accommodation service; city map; hotels and restaurants list; guided tours in French. Open daily 8.30 am–7 pm; branch office open at 23 rue des Tables near cathedral in summer (71 09 27 42).

Railway Station Place Maréchal Leclerc (Tel. 71 02 50 50). Information centre open daily 9 am–1 pm and 2.30 – 6 pm; lockers. To town centre from station, turn left along Ave Charles Dupuy and past Place Michelet to Place de Breuil.

Buses Beside station (Tel. 71 09 25 60); to local destinations.

Markets Sat mornings across the town, especially *Place du Plot* (animals); *Place du Clauzel* (antiques); *Place du Breuil* (clothes and household goods).

Festivals *Fête du Roi de l'Oiseau*: 3rd week Sept, week-long Renaissance festival with period costume, feasts, music, theatre; *Festival Carnavalesque de Musique de Rues*: early spring, 100s of street musicians from all over Europe congregate for two day celebration; *Festival International de Folklore*: 3rd week July, musicians and dancers in traditional costumes from most European countries take to the streets.

Hotels *Hôtel le Veau d'Or*, 7 Place Cadelade (Tel. 71 09 07 74). Near junction of blvd Maréchal Foyolle and Ave Dupuy. Small, simple, friendly and cheap hotel. *Hôtel le Régional*, 36 blvd Maréchal Fayolle (Tel. 71 09 37 74). Simple, cheap, hall showers and animated bar on ground floor.

☆*Hôtel des Cordeliers*, 17 rue des Cordelieres, off rue Crozatier (Tel. 71 09 01 12). Excellent, clean, attractive. Restaurant downstairs offers good hearty cheap meals.

☆☆*Hôtel Chris'tel*, 15 bd. Alex. Clair (Tel. 71 02 24 44). Quiet location and comfortable; high standard and good restaurant.

☆☆*Hôtel Bristol*, 7 ave Maréchal Foch (Tel. 71 09 13 38). Pleasant, comfortable hotel on left beyond St-Pierre-des-Carmes with plenty of rooms.

Camping *Camping Municipal Bouthezard*, Chemin de Roderie (Tel. 71 09 55 09), 2km from station. Bus No. 7 (7 daily, 10 mins).

Restaurants *Café le Palais*, 27 place du Breuil (Tel. 71 09 00 28). Smart café on the main square offering simple meals and snacks.

☆*Bateau Ivre*, 5 rue Portail d'Avignon (Tel. 71 09 67 20). Excellent local cuisine in relaxing, attractive, setting.

Clermont-Ferrand

Trains *4 – 8 trains daily to* **Paris** *(4 hours); sleeper trains at night; 4 daily to* **Nîmes** *(5 hours) and* **Marseille** *(6 hours); 2 – 3 daily to* **Toulouse** *(6 hours) via* **Issoire** *(27 mins),* **Arvant** *(50 mins) and* **Neussargues** *(1 hour 33 mins) (some involve changing at Issoire); 3 daily to* **Béziers** *(around 6 hours, change required at Neussargues); 7 daily to* **Lyon** *(3 hours); 3 daily to* **Bordeaux** *(3 hours).*

It seems that almost no one has ever had a good word to say about Clermont-Ferrand. Even in the 17th century the French writer Fléchier remarked disparagingly 'there is scarcely a town in France more disagreeable'. He found the situation inconvenient, the streets too narrow and the drivers 'more accomplished in the art of swearing than those of any other city'. But if its attractions are few, they are all located close together in the centre, clustered around the cathedral; and the surrounding country-side more than makes up for what the city lacks.

What to see

Cathédrale Notre-Dame de l'Assomption

The black stone from which the cathedral is built is volcanic tufa from nearby Volvic and even if the cathedral strikes one as severe, it is the finest example of Gothic architecture in the Auvergne. Somehow its severity seems in keeping with its history and the rigours of the local climate. Approached on a black night, up rue Phillippe Marcombes with the dim candlelight shining through the brilliant colours of the stained glass, it is a strangely impressive and haunting sight. On other days, when the sun shines strongly through the 13th-century stained glass, the lava walls are turned to purple as the light floods in. Patches of amethyst, emerald and ruby lie in pools on the floor and flicker on the arches, dazzling and brilliant. The western façade of the cathedral dates from the 19th century, but from its steps there is a superb view down the Rue des Gras to the Auvergnat hills beyond.

Rue des Gras

The Rue des Gras contains many interesting and characterful old houses, one near the cathedral incorporating a 12th-century bas-relief of Christ washing the feet of his apostles. The most interesting quarter is small and lies around the cathedral on a steeply sloping hillside. Behind the town rises up the great bulk of the **Puy-de-Dome**, a volcanic plug reaching up to a height of nearly 1,500 metres.

Notre-Dame-du-Port

Although the exterior of the Romanesque church, Notre-Dame-du-Port, is not exceptional, the church is the earliest example of Romanesque Auvergnat architecture and was built in the 11th and 12th centuries on the site of an earlier church destroyed by the Normans. It is not built of the sombre Volvic stone which makes Clermont rather gloomy but of a warm-coloured stone which has mellowed well over the years. The interior, however, is quite extraordinary and in itself repays any visit to Clermont-Ferrand. For here are some of the most grotesque and fascinating Romanesque capitals in France – elaborately carved with crowded groups of figures that give an accurate picture of customs and costume of the early 12th century. Adam can be seen being dragged out of Paradise by his beard; Eve has fallen, physically and spiritually, and is being trampled on by her husband in the most graphic manner. It is also possible to distinguish the Annunciation, the Assumption and the struggle of the Vices and the Virtues. The church is illuminated by light from 3 beautiful rose windows and the magnificent 13th-century stained glass in the chapels behind the altar.

Although the choir is marvellously arranged and flooded by light which illuminates the capitals, the real focus of the church is the crypt which houses the Black Virgin, a reproduction of the vanished original, Byzantine in style, which for centuries was venerated by crowds of pilgrims. Saint Avit, Bishop of Clermont, ordered the church of Notre-Dame-du-Port to be built at the end of the 10th century in thanksgiving for the deliverance of the city from the Black Plague. It was outside this same church, then in the process of construction, that Pope Urban II proclaimed the First Crusade to the assembled nobility of France in 1095. In the centre of Place de la Victoire to the south of the Cathedral stands a sculpture of Urbain II by Gourgouillon, executed to mark the 800th anniversary of the First Crusade.

Hôtel de Chazarat

The pedestrianised streets behind the cathedral contain a number of delightful houses, of which the most unusual is the 18th-century Hôtel de Chazerat in **Rue Blaise Pascal** with its tiny and curious oval cobbled courtyard. The **Rue du Port** and **Rue des Chaussetiers** also possess interesting houses with richly-decorated inner courtyards, carved doorways and balustraded windows dating from the 15th, 16th and 17th centuries. Not far away is an enchanting Renaissance fountain, built of dark Volvic stone, decorated with small naked figures and a hairy figure of Hercules carrying the coat-of-arms of the Amboise family.

Musée Bargoin

The best museum in Clermont-Ferrand, the Musée Bargoin, at 45 rue Ballainvilliers, has a splendid collection of Gallo-Roman artefacts, particularly ones discovered during excavations of the Temple of Mercury on the Puy de Dome. Other exhibits include Roman wall paintings, mummified babies and a selection of the thousands of Gallo-Roman wooden votive offerings which were discovered in 1968 in the nearby town of Chamalières. (Open Tues–Sat 10 am–noon and 2–6 pm; Sun 2–5 pm; off-season Tues–Sat 10 am–noon and 2–5 pm.)

Montferrand

Now part of the city, the old town of Montferrand was for a long time the rival of Clermont. In the Middle Ages the Kings of France lent their power to the neighbouring town of Montferrand, in an attempt to restrain the growing power of the Bishops of Clermont and it was only in 1731 that the 2 towns were finally joined.

To a greater extent than Clermont, Montferrand has retained its medieval appearance and its Gothic and Renaissance houses have been very well restored. In the 12th century the town was laid out on the regular *bastide* plan of southern France: 2 main streets at right angles cutting the town into 4 quarters. The 16th century saw Montferrand at its height and its finest buildings, built for the nobility and wealthy citizens, date from this period. One outstanding example is the Renaissance **Hôtel Vachier-Fontfreyde** in the Rue du Port, a fine Renaissance building, with exceptionally beautiful wrought-iron balconies and a Gothic doorway with the Vachier coat-of-arms to be found in the inner courtyard. In the same street is the **Hôtel Ribbeyre**, its 2nd internal courtyard reached via a vaulted passage, while the 16th-century **Hôtel Savaron** in the Rue des Chaussetiers has a charming courtyard and a beautiful carved door leading to a staircase turret. Another fine mansion is the **Hôtel de Lignat** with its Italianate doorway. The **Hôtel d'Albiat** is of special interest for the superb **Porte des Centaures** located in its courtyard. At the intersection of Rue des Cordeliers and Rue Séminaire is the **Maison de l'Apothécaire**, with some humorous 15th-century wood carvings. The new *Musée des Beaux-Arts*, located in a former convent, contains a wealth of works of art and archaeological finds, all attractively presented.

Practicalities in Clermont-Ferrand

Tourist Office 69 blvd. Gergovia (Tel. 73 93 30 20); branch office at station (Tel. 73 91 87 89) and Place de Jaude; maps; hotel and restaurant lists. Open Mon–Sat 8.30 am–7 pm, Sun 9 am–noon and 2–6 pm; off-season Mon–Fri: 9 am–6.30 pm, Sat 9 am–noon and 2–6 pm.)
Railway Station Ave de l'Union Soviétique (Tel. 73 92 63 00); lockers; information office. To reach town centre take bus **2, 4**, or **145** from station to Place de Jaude.
Buses Bus station located just behind main tourist office; buses to Le Puy; buses on Monday morning from station to Puy de Dome, the massive flat-topped volcanic plug in the Parc Naturel Régional des Volcans d'Auvergne.
Hiking Information From *Comité Départemental de Tourisme du Puy-de-Dome*, 26 rue St-Esprit (Tel. 73 42 21 21), open Mon–Thurs. 8.30 am–12.15 pm and 1.45–5.30 pm.
Markets *Marché St-Pierre*, huge daily covered market which takes up the entire old market place.
Festivals International Festival of Short Films: late Jan–early Feb; *Fête de la Musique*: 21st June, a cacophony of music of every description hits the streets.
Hotels *Hôtel Foch*, 22 rue Maréchal Foch, off Place de la Jaude (Tel. 73 93 48 40) Quiet, attractive rooms, some overlooking courtyard.

Hôtel d'Aigueperse, 4 rue Aigueperse (Tel. 73 91 30 62). Near station, off ave Albert et Elisabeth, spacious, clean rooms.
☆☆ *Hôtel Albert-Elisabeth*, 37 ave. Albert et Elisabeth, on a street leading from station to *centre ville* (Tel. 73 92 47 41).
☆☆ *Hôtel Lyon*, 16 Place de Jaude (Tel. 79 93 32 55). Attractive little hotel in a delightful square, close to branch tourist office.
Hostels *Auberge de la Jeunesse* (HI), 55 ave de l'Union Soviétique, next to train station; basic (Tel. 73 92 26 39).
Camping *Le Chanset*, ave Jean-Baptiste Marrou (Tel. 73 61 30 73); bus **4** from station to **Préguille.**
Restaurants *Le Relais Pascal*, 15 rue Pascal, (Tel. 73 92 21 04). The best place for auvergnat specialities; good, tasty cuisine and wine-list but not expensive.
☆ *Brasserie*, Gare Routière Gergovia, 69 blvd (Tel. 73 93 13 32). The restaurant on the 1st floor of the bus station: surprisingly good fare.
☆☆ *Clos St-Pierre*, Place Marché St-Pierre (Tel. 73 31 23 23). Superb cooking on the ground floor of the old market place.
☆☆ *Gérard Anglard*, 17 rue Lamartine (Tel. 73 93 52 25). One of the best restaurants in Clermont-Ferrand offering delicious regional dishes.

St-Flour – Chaudes Aigues

Trains *3 – 4 trains daily from* Clermont-Ferrand *(2 – 2½ hours): change at* Neussargues *(1 hour 35 mins).*

To the south of Clermont-Ferrand the high, bleak plains of the Massif Central stretch away without a tree to break the monotonous prospect of endless grass and arable fields. Here and there a village clusters on a steep, volcanic hill below the ruined towers of a medieval castle. The farmhouses and buildings cluster together closely for protection for in winter most of this high upland plain is whipped by icy winds and covered with deep snow for months at a time.

Just before the village of **Andelat** the railway circles a small fortified château standing at the head of a valley on an elevated outcrop of rock, its 5 circular towers dominating the hamlet at its feet. To the east lies the long north-south range of mountains, the Montagne de la Margeride, in the foothills of which lies the picturesque fortified town of **St-Flour**.

St-Flour

As the train approaches St-Flour from the north all signs of the modern town at the foot of its rocky outcrop are hidden from view and the impression gained is that of a medieval town springing up tightly within its own natural walls. From the precipitous basalt bluff on which the Citadel stands there is a drop of 90 metres to the River Lander flowing below. The old town, a steep walk up from the station, clusters around the cathedral built in a commanding position 900 metres above sea level on the edge of a basalt plateau.

What to see

Cathédrale Saint-Pierre

The fortress-like appearance of the 15th-century Cathédrale de Saint-Pierre-et-Saint-Flour is accentuated by the forbidding dark stone of which it is built. The defensive appearance of the cathedral is not misleading, for it is in truth a fortified building, with 2 strong square towers, the northern one long being used as the town prison. The interior of this severe Gothic cathedral is more graceful than the exterior would lead one to expect and contains a beautiful wooden statue of Christ that dates from the 15th century – the *Bon Dieu Noir* of St-Flour.

The town occupies a remarkable position but it is also the most attractive – perhaps the only really attractive – town between Clermont-Ferrand and Béziers in which one is tempted to linger. Not only does it have a ring of ruined ramparts but a number of pretty streets lined by fine mansions, some retaining their tongue-shaped roof slates.

Maison Consulaire

One of the finest mansions is the Maison Consulaire, a Renaissance house on the Place d'Armes with a pretty staircase turret in its courtyard, and now home to a small museum, the *Musée Douet*. The house is richly furnished with contemporary furniture, paintings and arms. (Open daily 9 am–noon and 2–7 pm; Oct–May, Mon–Sat 9 am–noon and 2–7.30 pm.)

The 16th-century Bishop's Palace has been transformed into the *Musée de la Haute Auvergne*, an attractive museum devoted to Auvergnat folklore, which contains examples of the traditional auvergnat musical instrument, the *brette*, which has many similarities to the bagpipe.

When English soldiers began to ravage the Auvergne, St-Flour became the obvious place of retreat for, standing as it does on its height, it is the natural acropolis of the district. All attempts to take the town failed however and in the early 15th century the town contributed 200 horsemen to assist Joan of Arc's campaign against the English. The town was rewarded, after the expulsion of the English, by a visit from Charles VII and his mistress Agnes Sorel, 'La Belle des Belles'. Legend has it that Charles took a sudden fancy to a local girl, Marguerite Bedon, whom he planned to visit at night. Arriving without apparent detection in her bedroom he found himself, much to his own discomfort, face to face with her father and his own mistress, Agnes Sorel.

Practicalities in St-Flour-Chaudes-Aigues

Tourist Office 2 Place d'Armes, next to cathedral (Tel. 71 60 26 29).
Railway Station *Haute ville* is a steep 2km climb from the station: turn right onto Ave de la République, then left onto Rue du Pont Vieux at Place de la Liberté. Turn right onto chemin des Chèvres and climb steeply.
Hotels *Hôtel Les Orgues*, Ave. des Orgues (Tel. 71 60 06 41). Simple, basic hotel; cheapest available.

☆ *Grand Hôtel Voyageurs*, 25 rue Collège, on central street in the *haute ville* (Tel. 71 60 03 45).
☆ *Auberge La Providence*, 1 rue Château d'Alleuze, in the *ville basse* (Tel. 71 60 12 05).
☆☆ *Hôtel Europe*, 12 cours Ternes (Tel. 71 60 03 64). In the *haute ville* with superb view over valley and excellent cooking.
Camping *Camping de l'Ander*, rue de Massales, next to covered market (Tel. 71 60 44 01).

South of St-Flour the famous **Garabit Viaduct** takes the train over the dammed barrage of *Les gorges de la Truyère*. This superb viaduct was built by Eiffel in 1882 and crosses the river at a height of 120 metres. A little beyond lies **St Chély d'Apcher**, an old fortified town on a bleak granite upland, vainly besieged by the English in 1362. A few other viaducts and tunnels bring the train to **Marjevols**, a market town with a battlemented fortress and 3 ancient fortified gateways, that date back to its role in the religious wars of the 16th century. The valleys roundabout are grazed by sheep and Charollais and Limousin cattle while plantations of pine cover much of the high hills.

A little beyond Marjevols lies **Le Monastier** from where Robert Louis Stevenson set out across the Cévennes with his donkey Modestine. The town, he noted, was 'notable for the making of lace, for drunkenness, freedom of language and unparalleled political dissension . . . except for business purposes or to give each other the lie in a tavern brawl, they have laid aside even the civility of speech.' The train no longer stops there, however, so anyone determined to follow in Stevenson's footsteps through the Cévennes needs to alight at Marjevols and make their own way south.

Beyond Le Monastier the landscape begins to change and for a short while the train follows the lovely valley of the upper Lot before twisting and turning as it climbs the **Causse de Sévérac**. The *causses* consist of fragmented uplands that were once part of a vast plateau of Jurassic limestone that stretched between the

Cévennes in the east and Lodève in the west. Dissected by the powerful vertical erosion of the rivers Lot, Aveyron, Tarn and Dourbie, they now appear as high uplands separated from each other by huge chasms, the most famous and scenic being that of the **Gorges du Tarn**.

As the train heads south it descends in height, the soil and stone taking on a reddish hue and fortified manors and farms becoming more frequent. The landscape too becomes softer and gentler, a patchwork of carefully-tilled fields and deciduous woods taking the place of the open pasture and pine forest to the north. **Sévérac-le-Château** is aptly named and behind the town a ruined castle rises up on a plug of rock that was the scene of a battle fought by the Maquis against the Germans in 1944.

South of Sévérac-le-Château there is a spectacular approach to the Gorges du Tarn which is joined a little upriver from **Millau** at Aguessac, an ideal point from which to explore the valley of the Tarn. Millau, the capital of the leather glove industry since the Middle Ages, is not the most attractive of towns but it has a pleasant arcaded central square with an Empire-style fountain, the Place du Maréchal Foch, surrounded by a maze of quaint old streets. On arriving and on leaving Millau there are unrivalled views of the jagged ochre teeth of the limestone escarpment of the Gorges du Tarn as well as the green fast-flowing waters of the Tarn itself, bordered by bright green poplar and willow.

The town of Millau is of little interest except to connoisseurs of Roquefort, the centre of production of which lies at the tiny village of **Roquefort-sur-Soulzon**, through which the train passes as it skirts the western edge of the massive Causse de Larzac. This distinguished cheese, France's rival to England's Stilton, is made from the milk of ewes grazing on the neighbouring causses or limestone uplands. The cheeses are left to ripen in caverns, which can be visited, carved out of the limestone cliffs against which the village itself clings.

From Millau south to **Bédarieux** the train at first keeps high on the **Causse de Larzac** and then descends to the valley of the Orb before meandering through isolated valleys and deciduous woods, stopping or passing through tiny villages, slowly descending in height. After passing through the thickly wooded forests of **Mont d'Orb**, one suddenly comes across the first vines and fruit trees that cling tentatively to a few south-facing slopes. And as one pulls into Bédarieux one is aware that the light is brighter, the colours of stone and soil warmer, and that the houses have once again taken on that reddish hue of the south. These vines are the first since having climbed into the Cévennes north of Nîmes. South of Bédarieux the stone begins to soften and lighten, the roofs are once more clothed with the red Roman roof-tile and umbrella pines reappear again as if by magic in the landscape. A tunnel is entered, from which the railway line bursts forth onto the plain of **Bas Languedoc**, into a familiar landscape of dry, dusty garrigues, scattered with gnarled olive trees, and a sea of vines that stretch to the very edge of the city of **Béziers**.

Béziers

Trains *3 – 4 trains daily to* **Marseille** *(2½ hours) via* **Sète** *(30 mins); 12 – 20 daily to* **Montpellier** *(40 – 60 mins);* **Nîmes** *(1½ hours);* **Arles** *(2 hours); 12 – 20 daily to* **Narbonne** *(20 mins) and* **Toulouse** *(1 hour 33 mins); 15 from* **Paris**, *changing at* **Avignon** *or* **Montpellier** *(5½ hours by* TGV, *8 hours others).*

Built proudly on a bold bluff above the River Orb, old Béziers has a sleepy and contented air. Once the headquarters of the wine-trade of the Hérault and Aude, 2 large and important wine-growing *départements*, its vineyards were ravaged in 1907 by *phylloxéra* (an American louse which was accidentally imported), it has now re-acquired its role in the wine trade. An important Roman colony in 120 BC, Béziers prospered for 1,000 years until its destruction at the hands of the Crusade against the Cathar heresy. Today, with the sea some distance away and the Canal du Midi no longer bringing business and wealth to the town, Béziers now has the feel of a calm and tranquil backwater.

What to see

Cathédrale St-Nazaire

The steep and narrow streets of the old town lead to the formidable battlemented cathedral of St Nazaire which, from a high bastion atop a conical hill, stares menacingly out towards the distant foothills of the Pyrenees. It was here that the Cathars who had taken refuge against the advancing crusaders led by Arnald-Amaury, the implacable Abbot of Citeaux, and Simon de Montfort, were burnt to death as the cathedral collapsed in flames. Although only 200 odd Cathars had sought refuge in the city, the refusal of the town authorities to hand them over to the Crusaders spelt the end of the city and its inhabitants. It was taken by storm and its citizens slaughtered indiscriminately. When the Crusaders hesitated, not knowing which were heretics and which orthodox Christians, the Abbot of Citeaux urged them on with the scriptural text 'Kill all! The Lord will know his own!' As many as 20,000 people died in the ruins of the city, the worst massacre of a Crusade not given to mercy.

The cathedral of St-Nazaire was rebuilt after the razing of the city in 1209 and only small parts of the choir and tower ante-date its destruction. From the 14th-century there remain some attractive stained glass, the portal with the symbols of the Church Triumphant and the Synagogue Overwhelmed, and a few murals. From outside on the terrace there are superb views over the vineyards that stretch almost uninterrupted west to Carcassonne.

Canal du Midi

Since its destruction in the 13th-century Béziers has enjoyed a relatively uneventful history, the most important development being the construction of the **Canal du Midi**, the brainchild of Paul Riquet, a native of Béziers, in the 17th-century. This canal, the most important in southern France, connects the Garonne with the Mediterranean, ending in the Etang de Thau near Agde. It is at Béziers that the canal required the greatest undertaking – the construction of 9 massive locks that allowed for a 25-metre drop in water levels. By any reckoning the work is impressive; by the standards of the time the undertaking is prodigious. On seeing the canal during his tour of France at the outbreak of the French Revolution, Arthur Young remarked, 'Here, Louis xiv, thou art truly great.'

Allées Paul Riquet

It is therefore not surprising that the delightful promenade in the heart of the city, the Allées Paul Riquet, lined with plane trees, should be named in his honour. In the heat of summer, it is here that people gather to meet and wile away the evening hours and fêtes, flower markets and Bastille Day celebrations take place. The Allées Paul Riquet leads to another delightful garden, the Plateau des Poètes, ornamented by numerous busts of distinguished French writers, from where there is a panoramic view. For centuries Béziers saw little in the way of development, other than Ricquet's project, until the 19th century. Then, with the arrival of the railway line in 1857 and the planting of vineyards in the surrounding area, the population grew rapidly, quadrupling in number between 1850 and 1900. In recent times the town has become the prosperous centre of a flourishing wine trade based on the nearby vineyards of Hérault and Aude. The local museum, housed in a former Dominican church, traces the history of the city and of wine production in the region.

Musée St-Jacques

Most prized of all the exhibits in the Musée St-Jacques are 3 outstanding silver Gallo-Roman dishes found as recently as 1983 in a vineyard close to the city.

Practicalities in Béziers

Tourist Office Hôtel du Lac, 27 rue du 4 Septembre (Tel. 67 49 24 19); lists of vineyards offering tours and *dégustations*.
Railway Station Open 6 am–12 pm; (Information: Tel. 67 62 50 50); Reservations: Tel. 67 58 43 06).
Buses From Place Général de Gaulle, to Valras beach; bus station at Place Jean Jaurès (Tel. 67 28 23 85) for buses to Narbonne and Montpellier.
Festivals *Féria*: end of August, *corridas*, traditional dancing and the running of the bulls. Tickets available at the arènes, Ave Emile Claparède, *Classical music and opera*: end of July, held in the town's churches. Tickets from Théatre Municipal, allées Paul Riquet, *Fête du vin nouveau*: 3rd Sunday in October.
Canal du Midi Boat cruises through the locks and local vineyards, departure at 8.30 am, return 5pm (Tel. 67 37 13 96).
Association Propagande pour le Vin 18 rue 4

Septembre (Tel. 67 49 22 18); information on the wine producing regions of Minervois, St-Chinian, Pinet, Faugères and Cabrières.
Hotels *Hôtel de Paris*, 70 ave Gambetta (Tel 67 28 43 80). Clean and close to station.
La Dorade, 10 rue André Nougaret, off Place du Général de Gaulle, warm welcome from Spanish proprietors (Tel. 67 49 35 39).
Hôtel Angleterre, 22 Place Jean Jaurès (Tel 67 28 48 42). Quiet, clean and central.
☆ *Hôtel Paul Riquet*, 45 bis allées Paul Riquet (Tel. 67 76 44 37).
☆ *Hôtel Poète*, 80 allées Paul Riquet, between Plateau des Poètes and the main stretch of the boulevards (Tel. 67 76 38 66).
Restaurants *L'Hacienda*, 14 bis, rue des Balances (Tel. 67 49 01 06). Good cooking at low prices.
☆☆ *La Potinière*, 15 rue Alfred de Musset (Tel. 67 76 35 30). Extremely good regional cooking, off the lower end of Allées Paul Riquet.

Sète

Trains *12 – 20 trains daily from* **Béziers** *(25 mins)*, **Agde** *(30 mins) and* **Montpellier** *(20 mins).*

The route to Sète lies between the Mediterranean and the inland Bassin de Thau, a large expanse of water trapped by the growth of a spit that links it to **Agde**. In medieval times Agde was a prosperous town but as its port silted up it sank progressively into gentle decay; glimpses may be had in passing of its fortress-like cathedral.

Sète, perched on a stony slope between the Etang de Thau and the sea is not architecturally distinguished but the maze of wide canals which pass through the town make it extremely picturesque. It owes its existence to Louis XIV's finance minister, Colbert, who settled on Sète as the site for a new port, and the Mediterranean terminus of the Canal du Midi. To encourage settlement and trade Louis XIV gave Sète a special privilege, freeing all trade and building from the requirement to pay taxes. Within a short time a thriving town had been created, stimulated by the completion of the Canal du Midi that brought exports to Sète from all over southern France. Ever since then the inhabitants, the Setois, have celebrated the creation of their city with naval jousting in which rival teams manoeuvre in an attempt to lance their opposite number into the water.

What to see

Espace Brassens

Paul Valéry, the poet, and Georges Brassens, the popular singer, were both natives of Sète and at 67 blvd Camille Blanc is the Espace Brassens, a **museum** devoted to the life and works of the much-loved poet, singer and musician. (Open daily 10 am–noon and 3 – 7 pm; Oct–May Tues–Sun 10 am–noon and 2 – 6 pm.)

The most picturesque part of the old port, **La Marine** is adjacent to the Canal de Sète; a huge new port has been built away to the south and east. A steep climb leads to the summit of **Mont St-Clair**, from where there are superb views along the coast.

Practicalities in Sète

Tourist Office 60 Grand rue Mario-Roustan, behind quai Général Durand (Tel. 67 46 51 00); currency exchange.

Railway Station Quai M. Joffre (Tel. 67 46 51 00 or Tel. 67 58 00 00); 15 mins walk to centre from station: walk down Ave Victor Hugo, right down Montmorency and left along Quai Maréchal de Tassigny.

Buses 13 quai de la République; buses to Montpellier and Pezenas.

Markets *Les Halles*, off rue Alsace-Lorraine, daily, mornings only.

Festivals *Fête locale de la St-Louis*: last weekend in Aug, a wild celebration with traditional music, dance, fireworks and nautical jousting.

Hotels *Hôtel le Valéry*, 20 rue Denfert Rochereau, close to station (Tel. 67 74 77 51).

Hôtel Family, 20 quai Lattre de Tassigny (Tel. 67 74 05 03). Friendly welcome and spacious rooms.

Hôtel Tramontane, 5 rue Frédéric Mistral (Tel. 67 74 37 92). Friendly, central and close to canals.

☆☆*Hôtel Hippocampe*, 3 rue Longuyon, at junction with rue Montmorency and adjacent to Eglise St-Pierre (Tel. 67 74 51 14).
☆☆*Hôtel Port Marine*, Mole St-Louis. (Tel. 67 74 92 34). Modern facilities and real comfort at far end of town from station, near Théatre Jean Vilar.
Restaurants *Le Skipper*, 24 promenade J. B.

Marty (Tel. 67 74 68 52). Good, hearty local dishes, including *bouillabaisse* as part of the cheap menu.
☆☆*Restaurant Alsacien*, 25 rue P. Sémard (Tel. 67 74 77 94). A pleasant and popular little restaurant on the island over Pont de la Civette, off Rue H. Euzet.

Montpellier

Trains *5 – 6* TGVs *daily from* **Paris** *(5 hours); frequent trains from* **Lyon** *via* **Nîmes** *(30 mins); 12 – 20 daily from* **Avignon** *(1 hour); and from* **Sète** *(30 mins),* **Béziers** *(1 hour),* **Narbonne** *(1 hour 20 mins); 4 – 8 daily from* **Marseille** *(2 hour 10 mins) and* **Nice** *(4½ hours).*

Inland from the salt-water lagoons along the coast, the gently undulating landscape of this part of Languedoc is planted thickly with vines which, broken by occasional groups of trees, stretch away to the horizon. Montpellier competes with Béziers for mastery of the wine trade and as the capital of the *département* of Hérault, it is a charming town of wide streets and spacious squares. Montpellier is one of those rare, fortunate towns that successfully combines a rich past with a lively present. Predominantly 17th- and 18th-century, it is the administrative capital of the Languedoc-Roussillon region, and one of the most beautiful and dynamic cities of southern France.

What to see

Vieille Ville
The *vieille ville* lies within the area enclosed by Blvd Pasteur and Blvd Louis Blanc to the north, the Esplanade Charles de Gaulle and Blvd Victor Hugo to the east, and Blvd Jeu de Paume to the west. Within these confines lies a labyrinth of attractive pedestrianised streets, handsome town-houses and little squares with cafés and bookshops. Henry James called Montpellier 'one of those places that please, without your being able to say wherefore'.

Place de la Comédie
The heart of the city, between the Place de la Comédie, with its theatre, cafés and fountains, and the triumphal arch of Le Peyrou, has innumerable interesting private mansions, many with internal courtyards. The **Place de la Canourgue**, centred on a garden in the middle of which is a Unicorn Fountain, was the centre of the town in the 17th-century. Of the many interesting and elegant old mansions to be found in the town, the best are to be found in Rue Embouque-d'Or, Rue des Trésoriers-de-France and Rue du Cannau but the entire district is full of quiet

squares where the splash of water from fountains cools the summer air. The finest of the mansions include the **Hôtel de Ganges**, the **Hôtel de Castries** in Rue Saint-Guilhiem, the **Hôtel de Saint-Come** – now the Chambre de Commerce, the **Hôtel Bonnier-de-la-Mosson** and **Hôtel de Lunaret** in Rue des Trésoriers-de-France and the **Hôtel de Sarret** in the place de la Canourgue.

A large marble-flagged open space, the Place de la Comédie is known affectionately by the citizens of Montpellier as 'L'oeuf' (the egg) on account of its rounded shape. Here, for most of the year, café tables and chairs stretch out languidly towards the central moss-covered fountain. Behind the Place de la Comédie lies another tree-lined promenade, the **Esplanade**, a handsome and peaceful quarter with exquisitely kept gardens overshadowed by huge flowing plane trees.

Musée Fabre

On the edge of the Esplanade stands the handsome building occupied by the Musée Fabre, at 39 blvd Bonne Nouvelle, with an excellent collection of Flemish, Dutch and Italian paintings and a number by Bazille, a native of Montpellier who was killed in the Franco–Prussian War.

Château d'Eau and Porte de Peyrou

The 18th century saw a huge explosion in the growth of Montpellier's population and a rapid building programme. The need for a decent water supply led to the construction of a magnificent aqueduct some 850 metres long which brings water from the neighbouring hills into a beautiful pavilion known as the **Château d'Eau**. This elegant temple, which rises from a stone-rimmed pool, is remarkable for the delicacy of its ornamentation and forms the central feature of a fine formal garden laid out by d'Aviler. Pleached lime-trees, gravel walks and stone balustrades lead through it to the **Porte du Peyrou**, a triumphal arch erected at the end of the 18th century in memory of Louis xiv. The Promenade du Peyrou consists of a series of terraces above Montpellier which were created between 1689 and 1776.

Jardin des Plantes

Close by, down Blvd Henri IV lies the Jardin des Plantes, the first botanical garden to be laid out in France. It was founded in 1593 by Richer de Belleval for students of botany at the university to study medicinal herbs, and is now a historic monument, open to the public. (Open April–Oct Mon–Sat 8.30 am–noon and 2–6 pm; 16th Nov–Mar 8.30 am–noon and 2–5 pm.) Opposite the garden stands the **Faculté de Médicine**, founded in 1221 and occupying the buildings of a Benedictine abbey founded by Urban v in 1364.

University

Although Montpellier is not an ancient town by the standards of southern France, only coming into existence in the 10th century, it flourished brilliantly under the kings of Aragon and Majorca. Even before the year 1000 a medical school had been established by Arab or Jewish physicians and in 1289 a university was founded. Here Petrarch began his studies before leaving for Bologna and it was here that

Rabelais obtained his doctorate in 1537. The medical faculty attracted students from all over the western world, including Sir Thomas Browne and Thomas Sydenham from England in the 17th century.

The **medical faculty** is now located in the former Bishop's Palace in Rue de l'Ecole de Médicine, on the 1st floor of which is to be found an outstanding collection of Italian and French drawings put together by Xavier Atger at the end of the 18th century. (Oct–May Mon–Fri 1.30–4.30 pm.)

Cathédrale St-Pierre

The medical faculty abuts directly onto the Cathédrale St-Pierre with its extraordinary portico consisting of 2 massive circular towers supporting a giant stone canopy – a bizarre combination which provoked Stendhal to describe its appearance as 'ridiculous'. There is certainly something immensely ponderous and ungainly about it.

In the 16th century Montpellier saw bitter fighting between Protestants and Catholics and blood was shed even within the cathedral walls. Every church and convent in the city was reduced to complete or partial ruins – with the exception of the cathedral. Even so, the cathedral's interior needed extensive restorations after the depredations of the Protestants in 1567. The end to the bitter dispute only came in 1622 when Louis XIII besieged the town, at that point held by the Protestants, forcing it to capitulate after 3 months. To dissuade the inhabitants from any idea of taking up arms yet again, a massive fortified fortress was built facing the city, opposite the Esplanade, on the orders of Cardinal Richelieu.

Water seems to flow in Montpellier as nowhere else in France and even today new fountains are being built, as in the Place de la Comédie, where 3 bronze male torsos appear to emerge from a tinkling hedge of water. Montpellier is almost alone among French towns in having given its name to countless squares and streets in London, Cheltenham and Bath. This distinction is due to the popularity of the town with English visitors during the 18th century who had visited Montpellier to take the waters.

Among 18th-century English visitors can be numbered Sterne, Smollett, Boswell, Thicknesse, Wraxall and Arthur Young. Smollett remarked that Montpellier was 'one of the dearest places in the South of France', due to 'the concourse of English who come hither and, like simple birds of passage, allow themselves to be plucked by the people of the country.' He came to the conclusion that the French seemed to believe that anyone English was 'a grand seigneur, immensely rich and incredibly generous' but he admitted that 'we are silly enough to encourage this opinion, by submitting quietly to the most ridiculous extortion, as well as by committing acts of the most absurd extravagance'.

Antigone

If the 18th century saw a burst of architectural activity, so too did the 20th century. Below the Place de la Comédie lies Antigone, an exciting neo-classical housing development designed by the Catalonian architect Ricard Boffil. The town is now working on another exciting project – Port Marianne – which plans to reunite the city with the sea, from which it had been severed by an accumulation of sand since the end of the Middle Ages.

Practicalities in Montpellier

Tourist Office Passage du Tourisme in Le Triangle; accommodation service (Tel. 67 58 67 58); branch office at railway station (Tel. 67 92 70 03).

Railway Station Place Auguste Gilbert; automatic lockers, currency exchange, information office open Mon–Fri 8 am–7 pm, Sat 9 am–6 pm (Tel. 67 58 50 50); For town centre from station, walk up Rue Maguelone and turn right onto Place de la Comédie. Tourist office in modern building Le Triangle.

Buses Bus station, rue Jules Ferry (Tel. 67 92 01 43); on 2nd floor of parking garage next to train station.

Markets *Place Cabane* and *place Jean Jaurès*: daily morning markets.

Festivals *Festival International Montpellier Danse*: late June, early July, brings a season of dance performances and workshops. Office at 7 blvd Henri IV (Tel. 67 61 21 11); *Festival de Radio France et de Montpellier*: 2nd half of July, opera, jazz and classical music (Tel. 67 61 66 81); *Theatre: Printemps des Comédiens*: early June (Tel. 67 61 06 30).

Hotels *Nova Hôtel*, 8 rue Richelieu (Tel. 67 60 79 85) Family-run hotel in delightful old town mansion.

Hôtel Plantade, 10 rue Plantade (Tel. 67 92 61 45). Simple but clean.

Hôtel Fauvettes, 8 rue Bonnard, near Jardin des Plantes (Tel. 67 63 17 60). 20 mins walk from station but with own garden.

Hôtel France, 3–4 rue de la République (Tel. 67 92 68 14). A huge hotel with nice spacious rooms, close to station.

☆☆*Hôtel George V*, 42 ave St-Lazare, in a side street off rue Maguelone, heading towards Place de la Comédie (Tel. 67 72 35 91).

☆☆☆*Hôtel Noailles*, 2 rue Ecoles-Centrales (Tel 67 60 49 80). Beautiful 17th-century mansion in superb location near Notre-Dame-des-Tables.

Restaurant *Le Stromboli*, rue du Faubourg St-Jaumes (Tel. 67 63 58 62). Good Italian dishes, some French; good value.

☆*Le Louvre*, 2 rue Vieille (Tel. 67 60 59 37). Close to the Rue and Hôtel des Trésoriers de la Bourse.

☆☆*Isadora*, 6 rue Petit Scel (Tel. 67 66 25 23). Near the church of St-Anne off rue Foch. Superb cuisine in delightful setting with meals served outside.

Trains from Montpellier *5–6* TGVs *daily to* **Paris** *(5 hours); frequent to* **Lyon** *via* **Nîmes** *(½ hour) and* **Avignon** *(1 hour); and to* **Béziers** *(45 mins),* **Narbonne** *(1 hour 20 mins) and* **Carcassonne** *(2 hours); 8 daily to* **Arles** *(1 hour) and* **Marseille** *(2 hours 10 mins).*

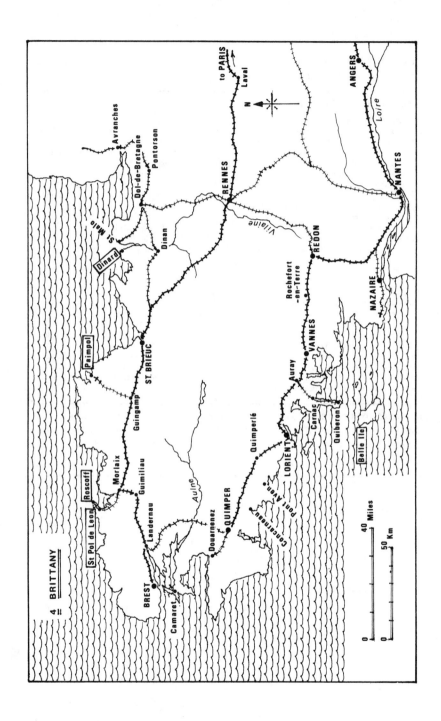

4 Brittany

The wild and rugged peninsula of Brittany, its coast lapped by blue water in summer and shrouded in mist at times in winter, bears many affinities with the south-western tip of England. The name Brittany itself derives from the Britons who arrived on the peninsula in the 5th and 6th centuries, fleeing from the Anglo-Saxon invasions of their island to the north. Their arrival seems to have been accepted peacefully by the people who were already settled in a kingdom of Armorica ('near the sea'). The original inhabitants, possibly of Ligurian stock, were responsible for the construction of the numerous megaliths, the most famous of which stand at Carnac on the southern coast of Brittany. Racially, therefore, the Bretons are quite different in origin from their neighbours the Normans, or the French, to the east.

The indigenous tribes were crushed by Julius Caesar but the region then prospered under the Romans until excessive Imperial taxation ruined the economy. The inflow of Britons led to 'Little Britain' or 'Brittany' becoming the fiefdom of British princes, held together by their Celtic origins. In the 9th and 10th century the Bretons established some authority vis à vis the Norman and French kings, especially under Nominoë, who was crowned king of the Bretons at Dol. After the Norman invasion of England, however, Brittany increasingly became the battlefield between the kings of England and France. In the 14th century this struggle crystallised into a trial of strength between the English king Edward III and Philippe VI of France. Playing one off against the other, Brittany maintained an uneasy and precarious independence until Anne of Brittany married 2 French kings in succession, Charles VIII and Louis XII. When her daughter married François I of France, the province was united once and for all with the French crown. Union with France however did not prevent the Bretons maintaining many of their former traditions and institutions. Until the Revolution the Bretons held their own *parlement* and rose against the French kings during the Religious wars while Quiberon, on the south coast, was the scene of an unsuccessful, counter-revolutionary expedition in 1795.

Until the 1950s the traditional Breton costume of black dress and elaborate white lace headdress, or *coiffe*, was a common everyday sight;

all such marks of the distinctiveness of Breton history have fast disappeared although traditional costume is worn on feast days and for the religious processions or *pardons* for which Brittany is famous. Held on the Feast of the Assumption and on local saints' days, the *pardons* consist of morning Mass followed by processions in which banners, candles and effigies of the saints are carried through the streets. Most famous amongst them are those at Quimper at the end of July, Ste-Anne d'Auray in late July, Perros-Guirec in mid-August and Ste-Anne-La-Palaud towards the end of the month. The traditional Breton dancing, which often follows the *pardons*, is occasionally accompanied by traditional instruments.

Gastronomically, the cuisine of Brittany is dominated by fish and seafood. Crabs, crayfish, oysters, shrimp and scallops are found throughout the region; so too is lobster, creamed or grilled. Ham and lamb are important dishes and fried eel is the speciality of Nantes. Brittany is famous too for its *galettes* and *crêpes*, thin pancakes served with sweet or savoury fillings. Delicious and quick to make, they are the closest to fast-food most Bretons want to get.

The route Rennes – St-Malo – Dinard – Dol-de-Bretagne – Dinan – Guingamp – Paimpol – Morlaix – St-Pol-de-Léon – Roscoff – Guimiliau - Landerneau – Quimper – Camaret-sur-Mer – Concarneau – Pont Aven – Auray – Quiberon – Belle-Ile – Vannes – Redon

The Journey through Brittany begins at **Rennes**, *the capital of the region, with its elegant 18th-century town centre, magnificent Law Courts and town hall, designed by Gabriel, the greatest of the architects of Louis XV's reign.* **St-Malo** *has been brilliantly restored since the Second World War, its cobblestone streets enclosed within massive stone walls, behind which the town is almost completely hidden from view. Surrounded by superb beaches and delightful scenery, St-Malo stands on a promontory at the mouth of the Rance opposite* **Dinard**. *Behind it lies* **Dol-de-Bretagne**, *a typical Breton town with ancient arcaded and gabled houses, some dating back to the 11th-century. Here one of the earliest Breton kings, Nominoë, was crowned in 848. At the head of the Rance estuary, in a spectacular position,* **Dinan** *is almost entirely surrounded by walls enclosing picturesque 15th-century houses which line the cobblestone streets. 'I have seen no town more beautifully sited,' Southey remarked of Dinan, the best preserved medieval town in Brittany. From Guingamp a short journey takes the* *traveller to the coast at* Paimpol, *a fishing village full of ancient granite houses and set in a beautiful position on Paimpol Bay. From here fishing fleets set out to Newfoundland and Iceland; now it is an ideal location from which to explore the eastern section of the Côte de Granite Rose. Heading west along the northern coast leads to* Morlaix, *an important port at the foot of a maze of steeply winding streets, overlooked by the massive viaduct and steep green hills which overlook the narrow valley. At* Guimiliau *stands one of the most famous stone calvaries of Brittany, a masterpiece of Breton religious architecture.* Landerneau, *occupying a delightful and tranquil position on the Elorn river, has some fine old houses, many faced with slates and gabled upper storeys, and boasts the only still inhabited medieval bridge in Europe. South of some of the wilder landscape of rugged western Brittany,* Quimper *is one of the most attractive towns of Brittany, its* vieille ville *full of half-timbered houses and overlooked by its magnificent cathedral. On market days and during the July Festival de Cornouaille the women still wear their traditional* coiffes. *Heading east along the southern coast of Brittany brings one to* Concarneau, *a walled port with superb beaches, the beautiful* Quiberon peninsula, *the little town of* Auray, *famed for its oysters, and* Vannes *on the Gulf of Morbihan. From Redon, trains run north to Rennes from where there are fast and frequent connections to Paris.* (**Approximately 6 – 10 days.**)

Rennes

Trains *13* TGVs *daily from* Paris *(2 hours); 3 slow trains daily from* Paris Montparnasse *(3¼ hours); 10 daily from* St Malo *(1 hour); 8 daily from* Nantes *(2 hours); 2 – 3 daily from* Caen *(3 hours); 5 from* Morlaix *(2 hours) and* Brest *(2¾ hours).*

Although Rennes was badly damaged in the Second World War the absence of very early buildings in the city is mainly due not to the bombing but to a devastating fire of 1720. Undaunted by the scale of destruction it caused, the city elders had the wisdom to decide on the design of a wholly new city, which was laid out on a spacious classical plan of fine streets and squares with long vistas up and down the gentle slopes of the town. Most of this elegant 18th-century city is still to be found today.

Central to the plan was a new town-hall in one of the main squares designed by Jacques Gabriel who produced one of the finest ornaments of the town, a building forming a wide semi-circle with elaborate pavilions at either end and a tall elegant central cupola. Opposite in deliberate juxtaposition is the convex façade of the mid-19th-century theatre.

What to see

Palais de Justice

One of the few important buildings to survive the fire of 1720 was the nearby Palais de Justice which was carefully incorporated into the new design of the city. This magnificent building had been designed by Solomon de Brosse, the architect of the Palais du Luxembourg in Paris, in 1618 as the seat of the Breton parliament. Its white stone and granite façade makes it one of the most striking buildings in the city. Within there are a series of fine rooms panelled in oak which culminate in the **Grande Chambre de Parlement**, decorated with perhaps the most magnificent 18th-century wood carving in the whole of France. The **tapestries** illustrating the most important events in the history of Brittany are modern ones from the Gobelins factory and took 24 years to produce. (Open Wed–Mon 10 am–noon and 2–6 pm.)

The rue Nationale and pedestrian rue Lafayette lead to the cathedral.

Cathédrale St-Pierre

The cathedral that replaces the one burnt in the fire of 1720 is a curious mixture of styles, its interior having been described as resembling more a Regency London club than a religious building. It was in the original cathedral that Henry of Richmond promised to marry Elizabeth of York once he won the English crown. Although only dating from the 18th century, it is richly decorated inside and houses an outstanding 16th-century Flemish altarpiece. (Open Sept–June, daily 8.30 am–noon and 2–5 pm; July–Aug Mon–Sat. 8.30 am–noon and 2–5 pm, Sun 8.30 am–noon.)

Rennes also witnessed another important liaison following the death of François II in 1489. Although at the age of 12 Anne de Bretagne, François II's successor, had been promised in marriage to Maximilian of Austria, Charles VIII journeyed to Rennes in 1491 to seek her hand in marriage. The chances that either would be attracted by the other were considered slim. Anne was small, thin and had something of a limp although she was vivacious and gracious and well versed in Latin and Greek. Charles was also something of an ungainly figure being short and weakly built. Contemporary accounts described him as having large white eyes and a wide drooping mouth that was permanently open. Although somewhat slow-witted, he was devoted to fasting and had ambitions of greatness. Against the odds, friendship developed into deeper affection whereupon their respective engagements were annulled by Papal dispensations, thus allowing them to marry. In fact their marriage was not to last long. Only 7 years later Charles VIII died accidentally and the following year Anne remarried Louis XII, becoming Queen of France while retaining her control of the Duchy of Brittany. There are still a number of houses which date from this era in the vicinity of the cathedral, especially in rue St-Guillaume, rue de la Palette and rue de Chapitre.

Musée de Bretagne

The long Avenue Janvier leads from the station over a bridge, beyond which to the west lies the heart of the city. But before the bridge is reached, on the left next to a small garden, is a former university building at 20 quai Emile Zola that houses 2 excellent museums. The Musée de Bretagne possesses the most comprehensive collection of material relating to Celtic Breton culture in Brittany while the **Musée des Beaux-Arts** has a fine provincial collection of French art, including works by Georges de la Tour, Chardin, Corot, Gauguin and Utrillo. (Open Wed–Mon 10 am–noon and 2–6 pm.)

Jardin du Thabor

In medieval times a Benedictine abbey dedicated to St Melanie existed just north of the city walls on a hill called Thabor, named by the monks after the mountain of that name in Palestine. Of the abbey only the tranquil cloister and the much rebuilt **church of Notre-Dame-en-St-Melanie** remains, of which only the tower and transepts date back to the original abbey. Just behind however lie glorious gardens, the Jardin du Thabor, beautifully laid out in the 19th century on the site of the former abbey gardens. These formal French gardens ornamented with fountains and statues give way to other ones specifically devoted to botanical rarities and roses. (Open June–Sept, daily 7 am–9.30 pm.)

Practicalities in Rennes

Tourist Office Pont de Nemours, in the middle of the main street south of the cathedral. Open Mon–Sat 9am–7pm, Sun 10am–1pm and 3–5pm; mid-Sept to mid-June: Tues–Sun 10am–12.30pm and 2–6.30pm, Mon 2–6.30pm (Tel. 99 79 01 98).

Railway Station Blvd Magenta. (Info: Tel. 99 65 50 50; Reservations: Tel. 99 65 18 65); information office; lockers; bike rental; luggage storage: 8 am–8 pm; to *centre ville*, walk down ave Janvier and turn left onto quai Emile-Zola. After 700 yards, turn right.

Buses Blvd Magenta, off Place de la Gare (Tel. 99 30 87 80); TIV buses (Tel. 99 82 26 26) to St Malo, TAE buses (Tel. 99 50 64 17) to Dinard, *Courriers Breton* (Tel. 99 56 79 09) to Mont-St-Michel via Pontorson.

Markets Mon–Sat, covered market, all day in Les Halles, behind post office; daily markets held in different place each day; details from tourist office.

Post office 27 blvd du Colombier; also currency exchange.

Festivals *Les Tombées de la Nuit*: early July, 9 days of continuous music, mime, theatre, danse, much of it in the streets. Details from tourist office, *Festival International des Arts Electroniques*: June, state of the art electronic and laser art.

Hotels *Hôtel le St Malo*, 8 rue Dupon des Loges (Tel. 99 30 85 37). In street to right off rue Janvier from station. Clean, bright rooms, all with showers.

Hôtel de Léon, 15 rue de Léon, near Vilaine River (Tel. 99 30 55 28). Welcoming and spacious.

Hôtel le Magenta, 35 blvd Magenta, close to bus station (Tel. 99 30 85 37).

☆ *Angélina*, 1 quai Lammenais (Tel. 99 79 29 66). Delightful rooms despite inauspicious entrance stairs; clean and quiet.

☆☆ *Central*, 6 rue Lanjuinais (Tel. 99 79 12 36). Stately 19th-century hotel close to cathedral; quiet rooms at back overlooking courtyard. No restaurant.

Hostels *Auberge de Jeunesse* (HI), 10–12 Canal St Martin, bus 20 or 22, in direction of **Centre Commercial Nord**. Descend at Pont de Legraverend; then 5 min walk away from centre (Tel. 99 33 22 33).

Restaurants *Restaurant des Carmes*, 2 rue des Carmes, off blvd de la Liberté (Tel. 99 79 27 52). Good value menus offering standard French cooking; crowded with locals.

☆ *Le Grain de Sable*, 2 rue des Dames (Tel 99 30 78 18). Succulent grilled meats and exquisite vegetables in nostalgic restaurant.

☆☆ *Le Palais*, 6 Place du Parlement de Bretagne (Tel. 99 79 45 01). One of the best restaurants in Rennes, imaginative menus include fried oysters in crab sauce and roast rabbit.

St-Malo

Trains *8–12 trains daily from* **Rennes** *(1 hour); 7–9* TGVs *from* **Paris** *via Rennes (3½ hours); 3 slow trains from* **Paris** *Montparnasse (5 hours); 3–5 from* **Caen** *via Dol- de-Bretagne (3½ hours); 5–8 from* **Dinan** *via Dol-de-Bretagne (1 hour).*

For centuries St-Malo played a vital role in the struggles between the Kings of France, the Dukes of Brittany and the English who raided and bombarded the town periodically in the 14th, 17th and 18th centuries. Lying as it does on a granite spur and sheltering a natural bay, the town has always had military and strategic importance. Its massive walls were built as a protection principally against the English, who succeeded in breaching them however under the Duke of Lancaster in 1378, but also against the French, from whom the town remained independent for a long time. At high tide the sea rises up to the very walls of the city, cutting off the little island du **Grand Bé** to the west.

Unfortunately the town was virtually razed to the ground during the Second World War but it has been carefully rebuilt in a style sympathetic to the original and the magnificent location of the town remains as beautiful and impressive as it ever was. Rocky islands lie scattered out to sea, a long beach of white sand stretches up to the walls of the town and the picturesque estuary of the Rance to the west delights the eye.

What to see

The City Walls
From the walls which encircle the city there are magnificent views across to Dinard and in fine weather to **Cap Fréhel** in the distance. The old walled town is a long but straightforward walk from the railway station down the Avenue Louis Martin through an active port humming with activity.

Château de la Duchesse Anne
High above the huge town walls rises the massive pentagonal castle built by Duke François II during the 15th century at the neck of the narrow isthmus joining the island with the mainland. The castle, known as the Château de la Duchesse Anne after Anne de Bretagne, the wife of Charles VIII and Louis XII, consists of 4 massive drum-like towers surmounted by battlemented keeps, one capped by 2 pepper-pot watch towers and a covered defensive parapet, the *chemin de ronde.* The castle houses 2 museums, the **Musée de la Ville**, devoted to local history, and the **Quic-en-Groigne**, a tower with models of St-Malo's celebrities. (Open daily 9.30 am–noon and 2–6.30 pm; April and Oct 10 am–noon and 2–6 pm.)

Virtually all the town and the cathedral has been rebuilt with local Normandy stone but some surviving old buildings are still to be found close to the castle and south of the bay close to the Fort St Servan.

Ile du Grand Bé

On the little island of rocks lying a short distance from the shore, the Ile du Grand Bé, lies the **tomb of Châteaubriand**, one of France's most distinguished Romantic poets. His childhood was spent in a modest flat that opens onto the courtyard of the hotel now named *France et Châteaubriand* adjacent to the Quic-en-Groigne tower of the castle. One cannot imagine a childhood setting more inclined to foster a Romantic sensibility. Living within earshot of the sea, in the shadow of a castle that had seen innumerable naval engagements, it comes as no surprise to learn that Châteaubriand dreamt of running away to sea and eventually did travel extensively abroad. After writing his memoirs, *Memories from Beyond the Grave*, he left a note requesting that he be buried on the Ile du Grand Bé, a rocky outcrop that is romantically severed from the town at high tide. Also offshore is the **Fort National**, accessible at low tide, a massive fortress with a dungeon designed by Vauban in 1689. (Open Apr – Sept, daily 9.30 am – noon and 2.30 – 6 pm.)

Very few trains now make the journey west from St-Malo to **Pontorson** which is the nearest railway station to **Mont-St-Michel**. It is far easier and quicker to visit Mont-St-Michel by bus from Rennes or St-Malo. Buses leave St Malo from the Syndicat Initiative building just outside the walls on Avenue Louis Martin.

Practicalities in St-Malo

Tourist Office Esplanade St Vincent, near entrance to walled city. Open Mon–Sat 8.30 am–8 pm, Sun 10 am–6.30 pm; Sept-June Mon–Sat 9 am–noon and 2–7 pm, Sun 10.15 am–12.15 pm and 2.15–5.15 pm (Tel. 99 56 64 48).
Railway Station Place de l'Hermine. (Info: Tel. 99 65 50 50; Reservations: Tel. 99 56 15 33); lockers; luggage storage; bike rental in July and August.
Ferries To Mont-St-Michel, Quimper, Cap Fréhel, Quiberon, Jersey contact *Voyages Pansart*: Esplanade St-Vincent (Tel. 99 40 85 96). *Emeraude Lines*: Gare Maritime de la Bourse (Tel. 99 40 48 40) organise trips to Jersey (1 or 2 sailings daily); Guernsey (1 or 2 sailings daily); Dinard (8 or more sailings daily), Cap Fréhel and to Dinan up the Rance estuary; *Brittany Ferries*: Gare Maritime du Naye (Tel. 99 40 64 41) 1 sailing daily (10.30–11 am), end March-6 Nov), sailing weekly (Saturday) 6 Nov–18 Dec. No sailings 19 Dec–18 Mar).
Markets Mon, Thurs and Sat morning behind Notre-Dame-des-Greves; Tues and Fri: *Marché aux Legumes*, within the city walls.
Hotels *Auberge au Gai Bec*, 4 rue des Lauriers (Tel. 99 40 82 16). Small, clean but friendly and within the old walls.
☆ *Hôtel Louvre*, 2 rue Marins (Tel. 99 40 86 62). In the walled town close to St Vincent.
☆ *Hôtel Brochet*, 1 rue Corne de Cerf (Tel. 99 56 30 00). In the walled town.

☆☆ *Hôtel l'Univers*, 12 place Châteaubriand (Tel. 99 40 89 52). Adjacent to the
☆☆ *Hôtel France et Châteaubriand* (Tel. 99 56 66 52). Unexceptional but comfortable rooms. Superb *art nouveau* décor and excellent central location. Once the home of the St-Malo Yacht Club, attractive dining-room and conservatory.
☆ *Hôtel Noguette*, rue de la Fosse (Tel. 99 40 83 57). Professionally run hotel right in the centre, with excellent restaurant.
☆☆ *Hôtel Jean-Bart*, 12 rue de Chartres (Tel. 99 40 33 88). Smallish rooms but clean and quiet, some rooms with sea-views over the ramparts.
☆☆ *Hôtel Bristol Union*, 4 Place Poissonnerie, off Grande-Rue, leading up from the Grande Porte (Tel. 99 40 83 36).
☆☆ *Hôtel Quic-en-Groigne*, 8 rue d'Estrées (Tel. 99 40 83 36). Delightful, tranquil hotel in the walled town, off rue de Dinan.
Hostels Auberge de Jeunesse/Centre de Rencontres Internationales (HI); bus 5 from station (direction **Paramet**) until you see hostel flags (Tel. 99 40 29 80).
Restaurants *Café de la Bourse*, 1 rue de Dinan (Tel. 99 56 47 17). Mussels, crab and oysters come by the bucketful in this hearty marine-style restaurant.
Café de Paris, Place Guy la Chambre (Tel. 99 56 46 75). One of the liveliest cafés in town, just opposite the Porte St-Vincent, with good bistro fare.

☆☆ *La Duchesse Anne*, Place Guy la Chambre (Tel. 99 40 85 33). Excellent and popular restaurant; traditional cooking, superb seafood and attractive décor.
☆☆ *A l'Abordage*, Place de la Poissonnerie (Tel. 99 40 87 53). Superb fish restaurant, located right in the heart of the fish market and usually crowded with locals.
☆☆ *Delaunay*, 6 rue Ste-Barbe (Tel. 99 40 92 46). Good dishes, especially fish, in this attractive restaurant just within the Grande Porte.

Excursion from St Malo

Dinard

Boats *Boats frequently across the estuary of the Rance which seperates St Malo from Dinard* (see Practicalities in St Malo)

Dinard is a stylish seaside resort made popular by the English in the Edwardian age. Until the late 19th century it was no more than a fishing village but its dramatic cliffs, mild climate and luxuriant vegetation attracted the attention of Edwardians bent on a good weekend on the continent. At the southern end of the town is the **Pointe de la Vicomté** from where there are panoramic views across the bay and Rance estuary. Nearby is a beach and the **Clair de la Lune Promenade** which hugs the coast north towards the English Channel, past the jetty used by boats crossing to St Malo.

Musée de la Mer The little museum devoted to the sea is surprisingly good with species of virtually every Breton bird and sea creature, a useful introduction to the natural history of the region. One room is devoted to the Antarctic explorer Jean Charcot who failed to return from his voyage to the Antarctic in 1936. (Open April–Sept, daily 10 am–noon and 2–6 pm.)

The Clair de la Lune Promenade, with its semitropical vegetation, leads to the **Prieuré beach** and then the quieter, sheltered **Plage de l'Ecluse**, below a casino and some smart hotels. The coastal path continues round the Pointe de la Malouine and Pointe des Etêtés before reaching Dinard's last beach, **Plage de St-Enogat**.

Practicalities in Dinard

Tourist office 2 bd. Feart (Tel. 99 46 94 12). **Ferries** from Gare Maritime, in St Malo, frequent crossings daily (10 mins). NB No railway station.

Dol-de-Bretagne

Trains *5 trains daily from St-Malo (10 mins); 14 daily from Rennes (40 mins); 5 daily from Dinan (30 mins).*

A short distance to the south of St Malo lies the ancient and little visited but delightful town of Dol-de-Bretagne healthily located on high ground rising above the surrounding marshy lowland. The town consists of little more than its cathedral and its central street but the latter is remarkable for its very early and rare Norman domestic architecture. The **Promenade des Douves**, laid out along the northern part of the former ramparts, gives wonderful views of **Le Marais** and **Mont Dol**, a 60-metre-high granite hill, the legendary scene of combat between St Michael and the devil.

What to see

Cathédrale St-Samson

At the end of the Promenade de Douves is the Gothic cathedral, a soaring and fortress-like building – evidence of the former wealth of the town which was an important bishopric and a leading religious centre until the 13th century. The massive cathedral is built of local granite and replaces an earlier church burnt down by King John in 1204. On the southern side there is a large and beautiful porch while the great east window contains fine 13th-century stained glass. The wooden statue of the Virgin, sculpted in the 14th century, is particularly fine. 800 years after it was built it seems doubtful that the present day population of the town is large enough to fill the cathedral, even if they were all to attend a service.

Grand rue des Stuarts

In the 13th and 14th centuries the merchants of Dol devoted a part of their substantial wealth to building solid houses carved from the hard local granite. Many of these, such as the **Maison de la Guillotière** which now houses the local museum, are still standing. Most are to be found in the **Grande Rue des Stuarts**, such as La Grisardière, and consist of timber-framed upper storeys resting on solid octagonal granite columns or pointed or rounded arcades. The finest amongst them is the Maison de Palets with its original round-arched windows which probably dates back to the first years of the 12th century.

Practicalities in Dol-de-Bretagne

☆☆ *Hôtel de Bretagne*, Place Chateaubriand (Tel. 99 48 02 03) Spacious, quiet, family-run, hotel, part of the Logis de France network, with good restaurant.

☆☆ *Logis de Bresche-Arthur*, 36 blvd Deminiac

(Tel. 99 48 01 44). Handsome white-washed family-run hotel-restaurant, popular and busy; superb cooking and choice of menus from imaginative and accomplished chef.

Dinan

Trains *5 trains daily from* **Dol-de-Bretagne** *(30 mins); 6 – 7 from* **Rennes**, *changing at Dol-de-Bretagne (1 hour 20 mins); 3 from* **St-Brieuc** *(55 mins); 3 from* **Morlaix**, *changing at St Brieuc (2 hours), 7 from* **St-Malo**, *changing at Dol-de-Bretagne (1¼ hours); 9 from* **Paris** *Montparnasse via Rennes (5 hours).*

The strongly fortified town of Dinan occupies an almost impregnable position above the River Rance at the head of a picturesque and wooded estuary. Fortified by the Dukes of Brittany, Dinan was besieged twice by the English in the 14th century. On the 2nd occasion, in 1364, the rival armies agreed that the fate of the town should be determined by the result of a duel between the English and French champions, Sir Thomas of Cantorbery and Du Guesclin respectively. In the duel that followed Du Guesclin won the day and the English army duly withdrew. Such were the rules of war.

What to see

Medieval Walls

Dinan is one of the most remarkable sights of Brittany, surrounded as it is by medieval walls punctured by no less than 15 imposing strongly fortified towers and battlemented gateways. The most impressive of these is the 14th-century **Porte du Jerzual**, through which a road leads steeply up into the heart of the old town centred on the Place des Cordeliers. The Porte St-Malo leads to the shaded **Promenade des Grand Fossés** which is the best preserved section of the town walls. To fix one's surroundings a climb up the **Tour de l'Horloge**, next to the tourist office, gives one a superb view of the town and the Rance estuary. (Open July–Aug Mon–Sat 10 am–noon and 2–6 pm.)

Basilique St-Sauveur

Nearby are the cloisters of the convent, the Couvent des Cordeliers, and St-Sauveur, a Romanesque and Gothic church with an unusual holy water stoup in which swims a carved fish. In the north transept is to be found the embalmed heart of Bertrand Du Guesclin, Charles V's most formidable ally in the internecine wars that racked Brittany in the 14th century. Having fought for the French crown for over 20 years, Du Guesclin died besieging Châteauneuf-de-Randon in the Auvergne. Although his request was to be buried at Dinan, competition to possess his remains was intense and only Du Guesclin's heart arrived at Dinan. His innards had been buried at Le Puy on the way north, while his embalmed body was taken to Montferrand, before being moved to Le Mans and eventually to Paris.

Jardin Anglais

Behind the church of St-Sauveur lies an attractive garden, known as the English garden, which overlooks the valley of the Rance. From St Catherine's tower there is an unparalleled view of the river, the medieval bridge spanning the river far below and the walls and ramparts encircling the city. Nearby the steep cobbled rue du Jerzual leads down through the massive Porte du Jerzual gateway to the river valley.

Château de la Duchesse Anne

At the southern edge of the town, in a commanding position high above the valley of the Rance, lies the superb 14th-century castle, consisting of a huge oval keep with outstanding machicolations and a massive circular tower, the **Tour de Coëtquen** that dates from the 15th century. At the end of September the château and town walls come alive as the city celebrates its history, using the towers and castle walls as a spectacular and authentic backdrop for historical re-enactments. The Coëtquen Tower and 30-metre-high, 14th-century Keep now house an interesting collection of medieval effigies and statues. (Open Wed–Mon 9 am–noon and 2–6 pm.)

To the south of Dinan the steep and wooded hills of the **Rance estuary** make for excellent walks, accessible in the direction of the little village of Lehon after passing through the Porte St-Louis.

Practicalities in Dinan

Tourist Office 6 rue de l'Horloge in a superb granite mansion dating from the 16th-century; guided tours (Tel. 96 39 75 40).
Railway Station Place du 11 Novembre 1918. (Info: Tel. 96 94 50 50; Reservations: Tel. 96 39 22 39).
Buses CAT/TV depart from train station to villages along northern coast – St Malo, Mont St Michel, Rennes, Dinard (Tel. 96 39 21 05).
Markets Place Du Guesclin, Thurs mornings.
Festivals *Fête des Remparts*: end September, recreation of Dinan's medieval past.
Ferries *Emeraude Lines*, quai de la Rance (Tel. 96 39 18 04); 1 sailing a day to St Malo (2½ hours); return by bus (45 mins).
Hotels *Hôtel du Théatre*, 2 rue Ste Claire, around corner from tourist office (Tel. 96 39 06 91). Dimly lit but central.
Hôtel de la Duchesse Anne, 10 Place du Guesclin. Attractive and central.
Hôtel Restaurant de l'Océan, place du Novembre 1918 (Tel. 96 39 21 51). A stone's throw from the station.
☆ ☆ *Hôtel Tour de l'Horloge*, 5 rue Chaux (Tel. 96 39 96 92). Down a little street off rue de la Ferronerie in the *vieille ville*.
☆☆☆ *Hôtel d'Avaugour*, 1 Place du Champ (Tel. 96 39 07 49). A beautiful hotel in a stunning position within the walls overlooking the Promenade des Petits Fossés and castle; excellent traditional cuisine in the restaurant.
Hostels *Auberge de Jeunesse* (HI). Moulin du Méen in Vallée de la Fontaine-des-Eaux (Tel. 96 39 10 83). Delightful youth hostel ½ hour walk from station.
Restaurants *Pélican*, 3 rue Haute-Voile (Tel. 96 39 47 05). Excellent value for money.
☆ *Relais des Corsaires*, 7 rue du Quai (Tel. 96 39 40 17). The cheaper menus are good value at this smart establishment down on the Rance River.
☆☆ *Restaurant des Terrasses*, le Port (Tel. 96 39 09 60). A superb restaurant in delightful situation beside the Rance River; offers excellent seafood.
☆☆ *Chez la Mère Pourcel*, 3 Place des Merciers (Tel. 96 39 03 80). Delicious cuisine, good service and a magnificent setting in a lovely 15th-century house.
☆☆☆ *D'Avaugour*, 1 Place Champs Clos (Tel. 96 39 07 49). Mouth-watering dishes from a talented chef in this superbly located old restaurant, its gardens high above the ramparts and castle lawns.

Guingamp via Lamballe and St-Brieuc

Trains 5 *trains daily from* Dinan *(1½ hours), changing at St-Brieuc; 8 daily from* Morlaix *(55 mins); 2* TGVs *daily from* Morlaix *(30 mins); 8 daily from* St-Brieuc *(20 mins).*

East of Dinan the Brittany plain has something of the character of Normandy with small grass fields, apple trees and poplars. A characteristic feature of the landscape are the severely pollarded trees which take the place of hedges, the intention of the pollarding being to maximise the growth of the central trunk. To the west the landscape becomes a little more broken and irregular but the wildest part of Brittany lies to the south in the centre of the peninsula – a central plateau of deserted stony moorland reminiscent of the bleaker moors of Yorkshire or Scotland.

From Dinan the train passes through the little village of **Plancoët**, where the poet Châteaubriand used to spend his holidays as a child. Beyond lies the Fôret de la Hunaudaie in which lie the massive ruins of the **Château de la Hunaudaie**, a romantic pentagonal castle surrounded by an impressive moat.

In the Middle Ages **Lamballe** was a town of consequence, being the capital of the counts of Penthievre, one of whose houses still stands in the rue Notre-Dame. Over the centuries the local nobility went quietly to seed, living a riotous life of leisure on their poorly maintained but extensive estates. Arthur Young came across 50 noble families in the town in 1788 living a life of 'foppery and nonsense', while the poor eked out a living in the most primitive of conditions. 'One third of what I have seen of this province,' he wrote of Brittany, 'seems uncultivated and nearly all of it is misery.' He went on to describe the housing of the peasantry as little better than 'miserable heaps of dirt'. It seems that Young's observations were not wide of the mark for in 1767 the 20-year-old Prince de Lamballe had led a life so dissolute that his father married him off to a 17-year-old princess from Piedmont in the hope that her gentle disposition would lead him to change his ways. It was a vain hope and the son died soon after, exhausted by his debauchery. The unfortunate Piedmontese princess seems to have been dealt a poor hand in life for she went on to become an intimate friend of Marie-Antoinette and was guillotined in September 1792, her severed head being borne aloft on a pike.

St-Brieuc, situated on a plain 3 kilometres from the sea, was once one of the most animated towns of Brittany for here were held agricultural fairs famous throughout France. Of the dozens that once took place only one, that of St Michel on the 29th September, still continues. St-Brieuc however has never been a town that greatly stirred the imagination. Even the Francophile, Augustus Hare described it in the mid-19th century as 'clean but exceedingly dull', and although much has changed, little to the town's advantage.

St-Brieuc's redeeming feature is its cathedral which still retains 2 austere fortified towers. In the 14th century the struggles between Jean de Montfort and Olivier de Clisson for the Duchy of Brittany led to the destruction of many towns in Brittany and St-Brieuc was no exception. Olivier de Clisson succeeded in entering St-Brieuc in 1375 but was quickly compelled to take refuge in the cathedral from where he successfully resisted the attempts by the Briochins to dislodge him until help arrived.

Crossing an artifically dammed lake the train passes through an open landscape of arable fields until the dense pine forest of the Fôret de Malaunay, beyond which lies the little town of **Guingamp**. Little remains of the ancient town which was once the home of the dukes of Penthievre, except for the Hôtel Dieu rebuilt in Renaissance style in 1699 and the interesting part-Gothic, part-Renaissance church, **Notre-Dame de Bon Secours**. This unusual building is flanked by 2 impressive towers while on the north side is a fine 14th-century porch now used as a chapel. Although little else of great interest is to be seen in Guingamp, from here a delightful journey can be made north by train to Paimpol.

Practicalities in Guingamp

Hotels ☆☆ *Hôtel d'Armor*, 44 blvd Clemenceau, near railway station in Guingamp (Tel. 96 43 76 16).

☆ *L'Hermine*, 1 blvd Clemenceau, a little further away from station in Guingamp, leading towards *centre ville* (Tel. 96 44 08 81).

Excursion from Guingamp
Paimpol

Trains *4 trains daily from* **Guingamp** *(40 mins).*

The delightful landscape of the **Côte d'Armor** can be seen to good effect from this journey north to Paimpol, a little traditional Breton fishing village now dependent on oyster farming rather than the Atlantic cod fisheries, which for centuries formed the basis of its livelihood, and yachting. Just beyond Pontrieux the railway line skirts the enchanting wooded estuary of the Trieux. On the far bank, across the still waters of the river, lies the early Renaissance **château of La Roche-Jagu**. This enchanting château is exquisitely sited above a meander in the Trieux guarding the passage of the river. A covered parapet or *chemin de ronde* runs the length of the eastern façade facing the river. From Frynaudor, opposite the château, the Grande Randonnée 341 affords magnificent walks through beautiful beach and oak forests along the valley of the River Leff.

Paimpol itself is a quiet little place, celebrated by Pierre Loti in his novel *Pêcheur d'Islande*. It was from here that Henry of Richmond set out on his abortive mission to England. The enchanting island of **Bréhat** can be visited by boat from Paimpol and there are delightful walks to be had by walking north to the **Tour de Kerroc'h**.

Another walk south leads to the romantic ruins of the Gothic **abbaye de Kerity**, also known as the abbaye de Beauport, most of which dates from the 13th century. The few monks occupying the abbey were forced to leave at the Revolution, since when the abbey has fallen into disrepair. The chapter-house is a particularly beautiful example of Gothic art.

Practicalities in Paimpol

Tourist Office Rue Pierre Feutren, in town hall near the church of Notre-Dame (Tel. 96 20 83 16).
Hotels *Hôtel Berthelot*, 1 rue du Port (Tel. 96 20 88 66). Curious décor but light attractive rooms.
☆ *Hôtel Le Goelo*, Quai Duguay-Trouin (Tel. 96 20 82 74) small hotel by the port.
☆ *Hôtel Chalutiers*, 5 quai Morand, beyond Place de la République (Tel. 96 20 82 15). By the port.
☆☆ *Hôtel Marne*, 30 rue Marne, short walk from station, off Ave Général de Gaulle (Tel. 96 20 82 16).

☆☆ *Repaire de Kerroc'h*, 29 quai Morand (Tel. 96 20 50 13), a superb old house in the harbour, once the home of the pirate and revolutionary Pierre Corouge Kersaux; good little restaurant downstairs.
Hostels *Auberge de Jeunesse/Gîte d'Etape* (HI) at Château de Keraoul, 25 min walk from station in direction of Keraoul (Tel. 96 20 83 60).
Camping *Municipal de Cruckin*, near Plage du Cruckin (Tel. 96 20 78 47).

Morlaix

Trains *7 – 9 trains a day including 2 TGVs from* **Guingamp** *(30 mins) and* **St-Brieuc** *(1 hour); 9 daily from* **Brest** *(45 mins); 2 trains and 4 buses a day from* **St-Pol de Léon** *(35 mins) and* **Roscoff** *(50 mins).*

Although some distance from the open sea, Morlaix has a tidal harbour and its fortunes have always been closely tied to the sea. Arriving by train there is a spectacular view of the city, tucked far below in its narrow valley, from the enormous railway viaduct which towers above and dominates the town. This massive piece of railway engineering was designed by Eiffel in 1864 and is one of the longest and most impressive railway bridges in France.

As an important port in medieval times, Morlaix inevitably attracted the attention of the English and during the Hundred Years War it changed hands innumerable times. Even after the English had been forced out of France, the wealth and proximity of the town to the south coast of England encouraged privateers and English naval squadrons to make surprise raids on the town. In 1522, as a reprisal for a raid on Bristol led by the corsair, John of Coetanlem, 60 English ships entered the bay led by the Earl of Surrey. It appears that the menfolk of Morlaix happened to be away at fairs in nearby Guingamp at the time and the English force was able to pillage the town unchallenged. According to Breton tradition however the English troops were ambushed as they attempted to regain their boats laden with booty, at a spot subsequently named the Fontaine des Anglais. In recognition of their feat of arms the town added the motto 'a bite for a bite' to their coat-of-arms. Perhaps as an additional precaution the **Taureau Castle** was built in a commanding position at the entrance of the bay to prevent the repetition of such an unwelcome surprise assault.

What to see

Place des Otages
The focus of the town is the broad tree-lined Place des Otages, in the centre of which is an elegant 19th-century band-stand. Behind the town hall lies the old town, the most striking street of which is the **Grande Rue**, a street of 16th-century timber-framed houses, many with interesting and curious carvings of medieval figures that reflect the sense of humour enjoyed by the medieval craftsmen. Among the many figures to be seen are a man with his bagpipes and a monk leading a pig. Almost all the houses have overhanging storeys that lean precariously inwards across the street and many are faced with traditional, small roughly-hewn slate-tiles characteristic of Brittany.

Maison de la Duchesse Anne

At the northern end of the old town, in the **Place des Halles**, is the 16th-century timber-framed mansion, the Maison de la Duchesse Anne, which rests on carved granite pillars. Like many of the wealthy merchants' houses in the Grande Rue it is constructed around a large chamber focused on a large central chimney off which other rooms radiate. (Open Mon–Sat 10.30am–noon and 2.30–6pm.)

When Mary Queen of Scots arrived in Morlaix in 1548 on her way to be betrothed to the Dauphin of France, later Francois II, she spent the night in the Jacobin convent, the sad remains of which are to be found in the **Place des Jacobins**. At the Revolution the convent was ransacked and used in turn as a Jacobin club and military barracks while the church was used as a shop. Over 200 years later the church is still in use as the market hall.

Below the viaduct, towards the sea, lie **Place Cornic** and **Place Charles de Gaulle**, where the harbour begins and one or two handsome 17th-century mansions can be found flanking the quays.

Practicalities in Morlaix

Tourist Office Place des Otages, at bottom of hill, near viaduct (Tel. 98 62 12 94); guided tours to the calvaries of St Thégonnec and Guimiliau. Open Mon–Sat 9 am–12.30 pm and 1.30–7.30 pm, Sun 10 am–12.30 pm; Sept–June Tues–Sat 9 am–noon and 2–6.30 pm

Railway Station Rue de la gare. (Info: Tel. 98 80 50 50; Reservations: Tel 98 31 51 64); follow signs to *centre ville*, short cut down steep steps on left.

Hotels *Hôtel le Saint Melaine*, 75–77 rue Ange de Guernisac (Tel. 98 88 08 79) *Hôtel le Port*, 3 quai du Léon (Tel. 98 88 07 54). Central and

newly renovated.
Hôtel Au Roy d'Ys, Place des Jacobins (Tel. 98 88 61 19). Central, basic and cheap.
☆ *Hôtel des Halles*, 23 rue du Mur (Tel. 98 88 03 86). Clean and quiet.
☆☆ *Hôtel de l'Europe*, 1 rue d'Aiguillon (Tel. 98 62 11 99). Stylish, comfortable and with an excellent restaurant; mouth-watering lobster, salmon and a fine cellar.

Restaurants ☆☆ *Marée Bleue*, 3 rampe St-Mélaine (Tel. 98 63 24 21). Superb seafood and a popular restaurant, just off the Place des Otages.

Excursions from Morlaix
St-Pol-de-Léon

Trains *2 – 5 trains and 4 buses daily from Morlaix (35 mins) and from Roscoff (10 mins).*

St-Pol-de-Léon is a delightful market town mistakenly overlooked by visitors hurrying south from the port at Roscoff but this is what makes it such a pleasant place in which to linger. Founded by a Welsh monk, St Paul Aurelian, in the 6th century, St-Pol-de-Léon became a prosperous religious centre that attracted the attentions first of Norman pirates and then of the English who burnt the Kreisker in 1375. Perhaps the latter was a blessing in disguise for the Kreisker built

to replace it is one of the most beautiful buildings in Brittany, with a soaring openwork spire of the utmost delicacy. Four massive piers support the 75-metre-high spire which served as the model for many Breton churches. It seems remarkable that such a masterpiece of lightness and audacity could be hewn from the steel-hard local granite. Quite apart from the Kreisker, there is another magnificent building in the **cathedral**, one of the most outstanding churches in Brittany. Apparently inspired by the cathedral of Caen the architects chose to build the nave of limestone from Normandy in the 13th century while granite was chosen for the choir, built 2 centuries later. The resulting building is an intriguing contrast of colour and texture.

Practicalities in St-Pol-de-Léon

Tourist Office Place de l'Eveché, opposite the cathedral (Tel. 98 69 05 69).
Railway Station (Tel. 98 80 50 50). From station walk down Blvd de la Gare to the left, turn right onto rue Pen ar Pont and down its continuation to *centre ville.*
Hotels *Hôtel du Cheval Blanc,* 6 rue au Lin, (Tel 98 69 01 00). Attractive, airy rooms.

☆☆ *Hôtel de France,* rue Minimes, comfortable and traditional hotel in good location. (Tel 98 29 14 14).
Restaurants *Crêperie Ty Korn* (Tel. 98 69 25 14), rue Vezen Dan. Excellent, inexpensive local crêpes.
☆ *Restaurant of Hôtel du Cheval Blanc,* 6 rue au Lin. Good standard fare.

Roscoff

Trains *3–5 trains and 4 buses daily from* **St Pol-de-Léon** *(10 mins) and* **Morlaix** *(45 mins).*

Ten minutes further on from St-Pol-de-Léon is the small port of Roscoff where Mary Queen of Scots landed in 1548 on her way to be betrothed to the Dauphin of France. Towards the beach is the little tower called **La Tourelle de Marie Stuart,** which allegedly marks the spot where the young Scottish Queen, then only 6 years old, landed after her rough trip from Scotland. Brought up at the French court until her marriage at the age of 16 to François II, she returned to Scotland 13 years later as the widowed Queen of France and Queen of the Scots. It was also to Roscoff that the Young Pretender fled to after the Battle of Culloden, stepping ashore here after being pursued down the English Channel by a corsair from St-Malo.

What to see

The important maritime role of the town is reflected in the fine stone carvings on exterior walls of the Flamboyant church, **Notre-Dame de Kroaz-Batz,** which portray ships and cannon. Although the church is Gothic, it has an unusual tiered Renaissance bell-tower which is one of the finest in northern Brittany. Adorned with galleries and lantern turrets and open work balconies, the tower is extremely ornate. The church itself, the sanctuary of Our Lady of the Cross of the Stick, is in Flamboyant Gothic style, the curious bas-reliefs on the walls recalling the principal occupations of the Roscoff men until the end of the Napoleonic era – commerce and piracy.

From the port at Roscoff short journeys can be made across to the unspoilt and delightful **Ile de Batz** with its rugged shoreline and rocky outcrops, separated from the mainland by violent currents. The town shelters an attractive beach, with Kayaking, windsurfing and sailing facilities, as well as an enormous and much celebrated fig tree that is reputed to have been planted about 1620. Boats leave daily in summer (details from the tourist information office). Farming and fishing still exceed tourism in importance on the island. A *pardon* honoring Ste-Anne takes place on the last Sunday in July, with an open-air mass and Breton *fête*.

Practicalities in Roscoff

Tourist Office Near port (Tel. 98 61 12 13); open March–Nov Mon–Sat 9 am–7 pm
Railway Station (Info: Tel. 98 80 50 50; Reservations: Tel. 98 31 51 64).
Ferries *Brittany Ferries* to Plymouth, 1–3 daily (6 hours); Cork, 1 weekly (15 hours); *Vedettes de l'Ile de Batz* (Tel. 98 61 78 87) and *Compagnie-Maritime Armien* (Tel. 98 61 77 75) both have ferries to the beautiful Ile de Batz, 13 daily in summer (15 mins).
Hotels *Hôtel les Arcades*, 15 rue Amiral Réveillière (Tel. 98 69 70 45). With animated bar and restaurant downstairs.
✩ *Hôtel Bains*, Place Eglise (Tel. 98 61 20 65); pleasant old hotel, overlooking the harbour. No restaurant.

✩✩ *Hôtel Régina*, rue Ropartz Morvan, immediately next to the station (Tel. 98 61 23 55).
✩✩ *Hôtel Bellevue*, rue Jeanne d'Arc, to east of main bay, in direction of the Chapelle Ste-Barbe (Tel. 98 61 11 80).
✩✩ *Hôtel Talabardon*, Place Eglise, next to Notre-Dame de Kroaz-Batz and the sea (Tel. 98 61 24 95).
Hostels *Auberge de Jeunesse*, 10 min walk from dock (Tel. 98 61 77 69).
Restaurants ✩✩ *Chardons Bleus*, 4 rue A Réveillière (Tel. 98 69 72 03). Superb seafood restaurant, close to Notre-Dame de Kroaz-Batz, serving many Breton specialities. Also has pleasant rooms for overnight accommodation.

Guimiliau

Trains *only 4 slow local trains from* **Morlaix** *(10 mins) and* **Landerneau** *(20 mins) make the stop at Guimiliau; easier to visit by* **bus from Morlaix**.

Guimiliau has one of the 3 most elaborate and striking of the Breton **calvaries**, one of the most remarkable and distinctive features of Brittany, another of which at **St Thégonnec** is to be found only 6 kilometres north-east of the town. The Breton calvaries, representing the scene of the Crucifixion, are outstanding for their graphic realism, poignancy and mastery of execution. They are also of great historical interest for the light they throw on contemporary costume, traditions and religious belief, as portrayed through the eyes of Breton craftsmen in the 16th century.

Guimiliau obtains its name from King Miliau of Cornouaille who was murdered by his brother in 531 and later canonised. The Calvary of Guimiliau has a carved frieze crowded with figures dressed in 16th-century costume, some representing scenes from the life of Christ. Nearby is an ossuary – a bone or charnel house – used to preserve the bones of those exhumed from cemeteries to make way for later arrivals. Like the calvaries, with their intriguing groups of sorrowful figures, they date largely from the 16th and 17th centuries. Quite what led to the dramatic proliferation of these spectacular calvaries at much the same time has not been fully explained but they remain the most moving testament to the faith of the rural Breton communities and the skill of Breton stone-masons.

Landerneau

Trains *4 trains a day from* **Guimiliau** *(20 mins);* 6 *trains a day from* **Morlaix** *(40 mins);* 8 *trains a day from* **Quimper** *(1 hour);* 13 *trains daily from* **Brest** *(10 mins)*

West of Landivisiau the beautiful wooded valley of the Elorn leads to Landerneau past the ruined **Château of La Roche Maurice.** Located in a pleasant and sheltered position at the head of the estuary of the Elorn, Landerneau makes a much pleasanter place to stop than the sprawling and ugly port of Brest to the west. Because of its provincial pretensions to importance Landerneau has long been the butt of jokes in Brittany, any piece of trivial news being said to be bound 'to create a stir in Landerneau'. It is a quiet uneventful town but has a number of attractive houses built from local golden stone and delightful promenades along the quays with emerald green hills rising directly behind. The finest mansion stands in **Place Général de Gaulle**, a magnificent gabled and turreted mansion, with its date of construction, 1664, chiselled elegantly on the façade.

What to see

Vieux Pont

Landerneau claims the distinction of possessing the last remaining inhabited bridge in western Europe. The Vieux Pont was rebuilt in 1510 to incorporate 2 fine mansions whose finely carved privvies of golden sandstone still extend out purposefully over the river. Beyond the bridge lies the little **church of Sir Thomas de Cantorbery** opposite which stands a delightful Renaissance ossuary of golden stone.

A 3-kilometre walk to the south of the town lies the *enclos paroissial* of **Pencran**.

Brest

A little to the west of Landerneau lies the capital of Finistère, Brest, an important naval base that has been largely rebuilt since its destruction in 1944. The position of the city is delightful, on the shores of the Rade de Brest, a wide indented bay which stretches far inland and has only a narrow opening to the sea. Of the old town however little survives except for parts of its 13th-century castle and the town offers little else in the way of sightseeing or amusement.

Practicalities in Brest

Tourist Office Pont de Rohan (Tel. 98 85 13 09).
Railway Station Ave M Donnart (Info: Tel. 98 80 50 50; Reservations: Tel. 98 31 51 64).
Hotel ☆☆ *Clos du Pontic*, rue du Pontic (Tel.

98 21 50 91). Modernised, comfortable rooms in quiet street south of the Elorn, off quai de Corouaille.
Restaurant ☆ *L'Amandier*, 55 rue de Brest off blvd de la Gare (Tel. 98 85 10 89).

Quimper

Trains *6 – 8 trains daily from* **Brest** *(1 ½ hours) and* **Landerneau** *(1 hour); 3 daily from* **Paris** *Montparnasse (6 ½ hours); 5* TGVs *daily from* **Paris** *(5 hours); 8 daily from* **Rennes** *(3 hours), 6 daily from* **Nantes** *(3 hours).*

South of Landerneau, Brittany assumes a gentler aspect as the countryside loses its rough, windswept look. The trees are larger, the fields more open, the earth less stony. Fruit trees begin to proliferate and gorse and bracken become scarcer. In some respects the landscape, of small fields enclosed by old hedges, is reminiscent of Devon and Dorset. The village church of **Daoulas** has a beautiful porch crowded with sculpted figures and animals. The nearby abbey is now chiefly of interest for its Romanesque cloister, decorated with geometric and foliate designs. Meandering and slowly climbing the train ascends to the **Fôret du Cranou**, entering the **Parc Régional d'Armorique**, a large expanse of oak and beech forest that stretches away to the east. After crossing the Douffine river by viaduct at **Pont-de-Buis** the train winds down to **Châteaulin**, a small town built around a loop in the river Aulne. The Aulne is one of the best salmon rivers in Brittany and here, during the months of March and April, thousands of salmon attempt to reach their spawning grounds further up-stream. From the viaduct there are superb views over the checkerboard of Breton forest and field. Beyond lies a whole series of small, sheltered valleys with isolated farmsteads surrounded by a mixture of arable land, forest and pasturee.

'Kemper' means 'meeting' or confluence in Breton and Quimper lies at the confluence of 2 rivers, the Odet and Steir. The Odet is the larger river and leads directly from the station, beside the Boulevard de Kerguelen, to the centre of town. The numerous elegant wrought-iron footbridges that cross and re-cross the Odet give Quimper the elegant and civilised flavour that one only expects to find in a much larger city. And there is no better, cooler or more agreeable spot to rest in Quimper in the hot summer months than beside this gurgling river.

What to see

Cathédrale St-Corentin
From every direction in Quimper the eye is attracted by the 2 lofty and delicate spires that rise from the cathedral. Closer inspection reveals that they date from the mid-19th century – paid for by the 600,000 faithful of the diocese who contributed

a shilling a week for 5 years – but they have weathered well and appear in harmony with the large and handsome Gothic building which was begun in the 13th and completed in the 16th century.

Between the 2 spires, and undetected at first, is a statue of Breton King Gradlon on his horse. Quimper is reputed to have been founded by him in the 5th century when he made the town the capital of his Breton kingdom, calling it *Cornouaille* after his native Cornwall. The sculptures on the western facade are severely worn except for their 19th-century replacements but the building is nevertheless the complete Gothic cathedral in Brittany. Behind it stands the Archbishop's Palace, a restrained Renaissance building that now houses a good **museum of Breton art and culture**. (Open Wed–Sun 9 am–noon and 2–5 pm.)

Nestling in the wooded estuary of the Odet, Quimper still has the feel of a market town. Today the steep hill west of the river is still partly covered with trees and is largely free from building, a fortunate occurrence that accounts for much of the charm and beauty of the city's setting. Should this hill be built over, Quimper would lose much of its attraction.

Medieval Quarter

The town has a remarkably well-preserved medieval quarter, spread between the cathedral and the rivers Odet and Steir, which is one of the most beautiful in Brittany. The streets and squares around the cathedral are bordered by picturesque timbered houses with high overhanging gables dating from the 15th and 16th centuries, notably in **Rue Kéréon** which leads to a bridge and a section of the fortified wall. To the north of the cathedral lies **Place St-Corentin** where you will find the **Musée des Beaux-Arts**, with paintings by followers of Gauguin and a small collection by Max Jacob, a native of the town. (Open Wed–Mon, 9.30 am–noon and 2–5 pm.) Famous in the 18th-century as the centre of imitation of Rouen faience earthenware, Quimper continues to produce hand-painted ceramics which come from the Faïencerie Henriot, on the banks of the Odet south of the old town. The pottery and its museum are open to the public. Open Mon–Thurs 9.30 am–11 am and 1.30 pm–4.30 pm (3 pm on Fridays).

Practicalities in Quimper

Tourist Office 7 rue Desee, off Place de la Resistance (Tel. 98 53 04 05); guided city tours; bus excursion tickets; accommodation service. Open Mon–Sat 8.30 am–8 pm, Sun 9.30 am–12.30 pm; Sept–June, Mon–Sat 8.30 am–noon and 1.30 pm–6.30 pm.

Railway Station Ave de la Gare (Tel. 98 90 26 21); information office open daily 9.30 am–7 pm; luggage storage; 24 hour lockers. For town centre from station, turn right onto Ave de la Gare and walk along banks of Odet River (blvd de Kerguelen) to the cathedral.

Buses Depart from Ave de la Gare, in front of SNCF station.

Post office and Currency Exchange Blvd de Kerguélen. Open 8.30 am–noon and 1.30–6 pm, Sat 8.30 am–noon.

Markets Animated covered market at *Les Halles*, off rue Kéréon; twice weekly market held on Wed and Sat.

Festivals *Festival de Cornouaille*, last week of July: processions, Breton music and traditional costume in the streets.

Hotels *Hôtel Terminus*, 14 ave de la Gare (Tel. 98 90 00 63). Unexceptional but clean, popular, cheerful and close to the railway station. *Hôtel de l'Ouest*, 63 rue le Dean, near the station, off rue Jean-Pierre Calloch (Tel. 98 90 28 35). Clean, welcoming hotel in quiet area. ☆ *Hôtel le Transvaal*, 57 rue Jean-Jaurès, on the left bank of the Odet down rue Aristide Briand (Tel. 98 90 09 91).

Hôtel Gradlon, 30 rue de Brest (Tel. 98 95 04 39).

Hôtel de l'Odet, 83 rue de Douarnenez, on edge of old quarter.

Hôtel Arcade, 21 ave de la Gare (Tel. 98 90 31 71).

Hostels *Auberge de Jeunesse* (HI), 7 ave des Oiseaux, 2 km from centre in quiet, secluded location; bus 1 to Chaptal (Tel. 98 55 41 67).

Camping *Camping Municipal*, ave des Oiseaux, adjacent to hostel; bus 1 to Chaptal.

Restaurants *Cariatides*, 4 rue Guedot (Tel. 98 95 15 14). The most popular *crêperie* in Quimper. In medieval building, with astonishing variety of crêpes.

Le St-Mathieu, 18 rue St Mathieu, near Eglise St-Mathieu; delicious seafood, cheap, popular and always busy.

Le Saint Co, 20 rue Frout, off Place St Corentin. Superb venue for mussels and oysters.

☆☆ *L'Ambroisie*, 49 rue Elie Fréron (Tel. 98 95 00 02). One of the best restaurants in Quimper with superb cuisine and a lovely setting.

Excursion from Quimper

Douarnenez

4 buses daily from Quimper in summer

There is nothing touristy about Douarnenez, a small village which sells, thrives on and smells of fish. If however you are prepared to get up at 6am for the Monday, Wednesday and Friday fish auctions, you will witness a sight that seems to have more in common with the 19th century than the approaching year 2000. Large quantities of fish are canned in the local factories or get sent to the Paris fish market or exported. The harbour itself is a hive of activity when the fishing fleet comes in, and the fish is unloaded, usually late in the evening. On rue Anatole France leading down to the harbour is a small 16th century chapel dedicated to Saint Helen. In summer boats leave from the harbour for Morgat on the Crozon Peninsula.

Concarneau

Trains *12 trains daily from* Quimper to Rosporden *(10–20 mins), then connecting* SNCF *buses south to Concarneau (20 mins).*

On leaving Quimper, the train follows the delightful valley of the river Jet, threading through rich water meadows and poplar plantations as far as **Rosporden**, a small town on the Aven river, once noted for the elaborate local headdress or *coiffes* worn by the women of the town until the 1950s. From here 3 or 4 SNCF buses run daily south to **Concarneau**, one of the most attractive towns on the south Brittany coast.

What to see

Ville Close

Situated on an island between Port Arvant and Port Arrière is a fortified island and medieval village, the Ville Close. The impressive gateways, separated by a barbican and massive battlemented ramparts of granite were originally built by the English in the 14th century and later strengthened in the 17th century by Vauban. Rue

Vauban runs the length of the small island and today it is packed with art galleries, restaurants and souvenir shops. During the 14th century the English were besieged 3 times by the French under the command of Bertrand du Guesclin; on the 3rd attempt the English were defeated, withdrawing in 1371. (Ramparts open Easter-Sept, daily 9am–7pm, winter 10am–5pm.) The third largest fishing port in France, Concarneau still has an important fish market, as well as a museum devoted entirely to fishing, the **Musée de la Peche**. Located in a vast hall which was once part of the town's arsenal on the Ville Close, the museum contains not only exhibitions on fishing techniques but has numerous aquariums stocked with turtles and fish. (Open Sept–Jun daily 10 am–12.30 pm and 2–7 pm, July and Aug. 10 am–6 pm.)

Practicalities in Concarneau

Tourist Office Quai d'Aiguillon (Tel. 98 97 01 44).

Buses Buses stop on the Quai d'Aiguillon, next to the tourist office.

Markets Daily fish market starting at 7 am on Quai Carnot.

Festivals 1st week of August: *Festival International de Folklore*; mid-August: *Fete des Filets Bleu (Blue Nets)*; traditional music, dance and costume in the streets.

Hotel ☆ *Hôtel des Voyageurs*, 9 Place Jean Jaurès (Tel. 98 97 08 06). Close to bus station, spacious attractive rooms.

☆ *Hotel Sables Blancs*, Place des Dables Blancs. (Te. 98 97 01 39). Traditional hotel, most rooms with sea view, rooms vary widely in price.

Hostels *Auberge de Jeunesse (HI), Quai de la Croix (Tel. 98 97 03 47). 10 mins from centre, over-looking the sea.*

Restaurants *L'Escale*, 19 quai Carnot. Popular with locals and hungry fishermen.

☆☆ *Le Galion*, 15 rue St-Guenole, Ville Close (Tel. 98 97 30 16). Henri Gaonach has made *Le Galion* a must for all seafood enthusiasts.

Excursion from Quimper
Pont-Aven

The picturesque little village of Pont-Aven is situated in a rocky valley at the head of a delightful estuary, behind which rises up the romantic **Bois d'Amour** and the simple chapel of **Tremaco**. Since 1888 Pont-Aven has become indelibly associated with the name of Paul Gauguin who encouraged other artists to the village, thereby establishing the 'School of Pont Aven'. In fact Gauguin left for Le Pouldu a year later but the area continued to attract artists tempted by the extraordinary brilliance and clarity of the light. The landscape around the town is exceptionally lovely and can best be appreciated on foot. Paths and small roads lead through the **Bois d'Amour** to the 16th-century chapel of Tremaco which features in Gauguin's startling painting 'The Yellow Christ'.

The little **Musée de l'Ecole de Pont-Aven**, located in the Hotel de Ville, does not have any important works of Gauguin's but an interesting little collection of his drawings, and letters, as well as paintings by other artists of the Pont-Aven School. (Open April–Sept; daily 10 am–12.30 pm and 2–6.30 pm).

Practicalities in Pont-Aven

Tourist Office Place de L'Hotel de Ville (Tel. 98 06 04 70).

Buses Cars Caoudal, 6 buses daily from Quimper, to Place Paul Gauguin in Pont-Aven

(45 mins).

Hotels ☆☆ *Hotel d'Anjoncs d'Or*, 1 Place de l'Hotel de Ville (Tel. 98 06 02 06).

Auray

Trains *12 trains including* TGVs *daily from* **Quimper** *(50–60 mins); 12 daily from* **Rennes** *(1 hour 20 mins); change here for Carnac and Quiberon.*

Leaving Concarneau and heading back to Rosporden, to connect with trains for Auray, one passes through the poor and rocky landscape of the south Brittany coast which supports little in the way of vegetation except the ever-thriving pine tree.

Inland from Rosporden to Quimperlé the land is carefully cultivated or devoted to pasture. To the south of Quimperlé is the forest of Carnoët in which can be glimpsed a ruined château, and **Lorient**, an important French naval base which was virtually levelled in 1943 in the Allied attempt to destroy the German submarine base located here. Leaving the modern town, the train passes over a viaduct and through gently undulating landscape of pine and silver birch forest. At *Hennebont* there is a good view of the 15th-century church before crossing the estuary of the Blavet and reaching the *Etang du Cranic*, a secluded stretch of water that is home to numerous wildfowl.

Auray is a small but picturesque town situated on the Auray river between the Quiberon peninsula and the Gulf of Morbihan. Auray is of greatest interest to oyster-lovers for the estuary of the Loc has long been famed for the excellence of its oysters. They were doubtless eaten by Jean de Montfort in the celebrations that followed the decisive battle that took place here in 1364 in which Du Guesclin was taken prisoner by Sir John Chandos and Charles de Blois was killed.

There is little of great interest to see in Auray but it is the station from which to head south to Quiberon, Carnac and the island of Belle-Ile. However the 15th-century fishing port springs to life at the beginning of July when the **Festival International** brings a medley of music and dance groups from all over the world, and a pleasant afternoon can always be spent in **Place St Sauveur**, where 15th century buildings house tempting cafes and restaurants with open-air terraces.

Practicalities in Auray

Tourist Office 20 rue du Lait (Tel. 97 24 09 75); located in an old chapel; guided tours; accommodation lists.
Railway Station Just off Ave General de Gaulle. To reach 'centre ville' follow Ave Gen de Gaulle and its continuation rue Aristide Briand and rue Clemenceau to Place de la Republique and the tourist office.

Hotels *Hôtel Celtic*, 30 rue Clemenceau (Tel. 97 24 05 37). Quiet, clean and cheap.
☆☆ *Hôtel Mairie*, 32 Place de la Republique (Tel. 97 24 04 65).
Restaurants *Auberge La Plaine*, rue du Lait (Tel. 97 24 09 40. Near ornate church of St-Gildas; good mid-price lunchtime menu.

Carnac

Trains *10 trains daily to* **Carnac-Ville**, *in July and August only; from* **Auray** *(30 mins) and* **Quiberon** *(35 mins); at other times* SNCF *bus;* 7 **buses** *daily from* **Quiberon** *(1 hour).*

To the south amongst the rather sad coastal plains around Carnac stand a group of stones which are perhaps the most remarkable megalithic remains in the world. The most extensive of the megalithic monuments is the **Alignment of Carnac** which consists of no less than 2,730 standing and fallen menhirs, and runs for almost 2½ miles parallel to the coast just inland from Carnac-Ville. To the north is another alignment, that of **Le Ménec**, with a semi-circle of menhirs partly embedded in the houses and gardens of the village of Le Ménec. Further east is the Alignment of **Kermario**, consisting of 10 rows graded in size, and the **Alignment of Kerlescant** with 13 rows preceded by an irregular ring of menhirs. Here and there are scattered dolmen and chambered tumuli, including the 120-metre-long **Tumulus de St-Michel**, above which sits a small chapel from which there are fine views of the megalith-strewn landscape.

The great grey monoliths are drawn up in even rows, forming long avenues which appear to march across the countryside. At one end they stand 3 – 4 metres in height, dwindling away at the end of their lines to no more than a metre. As the rows point to one another it is assumed that they were connected at one time and seems likely that they had a dual function: primarily to act as an astronomical clock, devised to indicate the direction of sunrise at the solstices and the equinox so as to fix the periods for ceremonies based on solar worship and for some kind of funerary purpose.

What to see

Musée de Préhistoire, 10 Place de la Chapelle (Tel. 97 52 22 04).

There is a good **beach** at Carnac (**Carnac-Plage**) and the town (Carnac-Ville) is quite interesting.

Practicalities in Carnac

Tourist office *Place de l'Eglise*, near church (Tel. 97 52 13 52); also at 74 ave des Druides at Carnac-Plage (same tel. no.); accommodation service.

Buses At bottom of rue St Cornely from Place de l'Eglise.

Hotels *Hotel d'Arvor*, 5 rue St-Cornely (Tel. 97 52 96 90). Cheap and convenient location.

☆☆ *Hotel La Marine*, 4 Place de la Chapelle, close to tourist office (Tel. 97 52 07 33); rooms smallish but modernised; good, quiet location. Excellent cooking, especially seafood, in stylish but pricey restaurant.

☆☆ *Lann-Roz*, 12 ave de la Poste (Tel. 97 52 11 01). On street connecting old town with Carnac-Plage and the beaches. Pricey but less so than most in Carnac. Expensive restaurant, also serving excellent seafood.

☆☆ *Hotel Alignements*, 45 rue St Cornely, in Carnac-Ville. (Tel. 97 52 06 30).

Camping *Alignements de Kermario*, opposite megaliths of same name; open June–Sept (Tel. 97 52 16 57). A pleasant campsite.

Quiberon

Trains *10 trains daily, in July and August only, from* **Carnac** *(30 mins) and* **Auray** *(1 hour 5mins); at other times of year* SNCF **bus from Auray** *(1½ hours).*

Half way down the Quiberon peninsula stands the 18th-century, **Fort de Penthievre** which guards the narrowest part of the isthmus. At the southern end of the peninsula lies **Quiberon**, a quiet fishing port and small resort which becomes crowded in summer. The landscape of the west coast lives up to its name, the **Côte Sauvage**, while from the south of the peninsula ferries can be caught over to the enchanting island, **Belle-Ile**.

It was at Quiberon that the Monarchists' last hopes for an end to the French Revolution were destroyed in 1795. Encouraged by the English, who agreed to provide the ships necessary for the expedition, 10,000 French *emigrés* were landed by the English Navy at Quiberon in June 1795, with the intention of driving the Republicans before them. Fated from the moment the expedition began, no sooner had the *emigrés* landed than some of the rank and file, whose allegiance to the monarchy was wafer-thin, began to mutiny. Due to insufficient secrecy having been observed prior to the fleet's departure, the Convention had had wind of the coming invasion and had made preparations, sending General Hoche to Quiberon in advance of the arrival of the invasion force. No sooner had the Royalists begun to disembark than they came under murderous fire and the mutiny of many of their men further added to the confusion and disarray. To make matters worse a storm arose, making it impossible for the English ships to approach the shore to assist and the Royalists were beaten back into the water and drowned or were compelled to surrender. Only 2 of the original 10,000 men managed to retreat to the safety of the boats; the others were taken prisoner, killed or lost at sea. Of those taken prisoner the 22 most notable and noble were led in chains to Vannes where they were sentenced to death by firing squad. Sympathy for the royalists however was still strong among much of the local population and when the local regiments refused to carry out the death sentence, Parisian volunteers had to be called in to execute the sentences which took place on the Promenade de la Garenne.

What to see

Beaches
The **Grande Plage**, extends from the harbour wall to the casino and the rocks to the east. If too crowded in mid-summer, smaller, rockier beaches can be found such as the Plage du Goviro, while the western coast of the Quiberon peninsula is rocky and wild, scattered with wildflowers in spring and superb walking country in summer. Due to strong tidal currents swimming is dangerous and forbidden on the Côte Sauvage. For *the best views of the Côte Sauvage*, which runs for most of the length of the western peninsula, go to the **Pointe du Percho**.

Practicalities in Quiberon

Tourist Office 7 rue de Verdun (Tel. 97 50 07 84); accommodation service.
Railway Station (Info. Tel. 97 42 50 50; Reservations: Tel. 97 42 50 10). For town centre from station, turn left, follow Rue de la Gare, pass to right of church, and follow rue de Verdun to tourist office.
Buses TTO buses (Tel. 97 47 29 64) to Carnac and Auray from central Place Hoche, train station and Port Maria.
Hotels Au Bon Accueil 6 quai de l'Houat (Tel. 97 50 07 92). Plain and simple.
☆ *Hôtel de l'Océan*, 7 quai de l'Océan (Tel. 97 50 07 58). Clean and simple.
☆☆ *Hôtel Druides*, 6 rue Port Maria (Tel. 97 50 14 74).
☆☆ *Hôtel Neptune*, 4 quai de Houat, in port Maria (Tel. 97 50 09 62).
Hostels *Auberge de Jeunesse* (HI), 45 rue de Roch-Priol, off rue de Lille (Tel. 97 50 15 54). Small and central.
Camping *Camping du Goviro*, Plage du Goviro (Tel. 97 50 13 54).
Camping Bois d'Amour, (Tel. 97 50 13 52). Good facilities, pool.
Restaurants *La Criée*, 11 quai de l'Océan. Good shellfish including seafood couscous.
☆☆ *La Roseraie*, 2 quai Houat, in the Port Maria (Tel. 97 30 40 83).

Excursion from Quiberon
Belle-Ile

Ferries *Ferries to Belle-Ile leave from Port Maria in Quiberon, 10 daily (30–45 mins) and to the islands of Houat and Hoedic (1½ hours), daily except Tuesday.*

Belle-Ile may be a little more touristy than the neighbouring island, Ile de Groix, but it is the largest, prettiest and most interesting of Britanny's islands and it has superb scenery with high cliffs, heather-covered moorland, fantastic beaches, and attractive walks and trails. Cycling is a good way to explore the island (cycles available from Didier Banet, quai de l'Acadie, in the harbour of St-Palais: Tel. 97 31 84 74).

15th-century walls protects the old port, **Le Palais**, which is now the island's largest and busiest town. Its **museum** tells the story of the island and some of its more famous inhabitants, notably Monet and Sarah Bernhardt. On the north-western coast of the island is a huge grotto, the **Grotte de l'Apothicairerie**, which it is dangerous to enter. Claude Monet painted the Aiguilles de Port-Coton during his sojourn on the island in 1886.

Practicalities on Belle-Ile

Tourist office Quai Bonnelle, Le Palais (Tel. 97 31 81 93); accommodation service.
Hostel *Auberge de Jeunesse* Near Citadel, 20 mins from port (Tel. 97 31 81 33). Comfortable and pleasant conversion from old prison; camping facilities.
Hotels *Hôtel La Désirade*, route Port Goulphar, Bangor (Tel. 97 31 64 65).
☆☆ *Bretagne*, quai Macé (Tel. 97 31 80 14). One of the few affordable hotels on the island, in old house in the harbour. Restaurant with good seafood dishes.
Restaurants *La Forge*, route de Port-Gouphar, Bangor (Tel. 91 31 51 76). Excellent shellfish and seafish in the old forge at Bangor.

Vannes

Trains *12 trains including* TGVs *daily from* **Quimper** *(1½ – 2 hours); 10 daily from* **Auray** *(10 mins); 8 – 11 from* **Nantes** *(1 hours); 4 – 6 express or 'rapide' trains from* **Paris** *(6 hours); 5 – 8* TGVs *from* **Paris** *(3½2 hours); 6 – 8 from* **Rennes** *(1¼ hours).*

Vannes, the capital of Morbihan is, with Quimper, among the prettiest and most interesting of Brittany's towns. At Vannes the long Boulevard Victor Hugo leads down from the station to the old port, a long canal full of yachts which joins Vannes to the **Golfe du Morbihan**. At the end of the canal is **Place Gambetta**, surrounded by lively cafes open well into the night and the medieval gate which leads into the ramshackle city with the perfectly preserved square, **Place Henri I V**, and timber-framed buildings.

What to see

Cathédrale St-Pierre

Twisting, narrow streets surround the attractive cathedral with a Renaissance chapel, Flamboyant Gothic transept portal and 19th-century neo-Gothic western façade. In the adjoining street is the archdeaconary where Queen Henrietta Maria, the daughter of Henri I V and wife of Charles I of England, sought refuge in August 1644 following the execution of her husband. Little more than a century later a French force assembled in the town during the Seven Years War for a projected invasion of England. 8,000 troops made preparations for the invasion but the defeat inflicted on the French navy off Quiberon by Admiral Hawke in November 1759 destroyed any plans.

Ramparts and Promenade de la Garenne

Nothing now remains of the original castle of l'Hermine built by Duc Jean IV de Montfort but the huge battlemented gateway of the Porte Prison with its doughty towers is the most impressive part of the fortified walls, the oldest part of which date from the 14th century. The ramparts are best seen from the **Promenade de la Garenne** outside the walls where royalist leaders were executed by firing squad following their disastrous attempt to land at Quiberon in 1795. This look down on to beautiful public gardens, which occupy the site of the moat which once ran around the walls from the oldest medieval gateway, the Porte Prison, to the Porte Poterne and the Porte Vincent in the south. A small river threads through the gardens past the timber-framed and slate-tiled public washhouse at Porte Poterne which was in use from the 15th century until after the Second World War.

Place Henry IV

Numerous, handsome timber-framed houses with overhanging gables surround the western facade of the cathedral. A steepish street leads down to the market square, the **Place des Lices**, which is overlooked by a fine turreted 17th-century mansion. General Hoche had his headquarters in the square during the Quiberon campaign. In the adjacent street, the Rue de Noe, is an unprepossessing but ancient building, the **Château Gaillard**, where the Breton parliament met from the mid-15th to the mid-16th centuries. It now houses a small archaeological museum.

Practicalities in Vannes

Tourist Office 1 rue Thiers in a 17th-century mansion (Tel. 97 47 24 34). Accommodation service; tours; currency exchange.
Railway Station Ave Favrel et Lincy, north off Ave Victor Hugo (Info. Tel. 97 42 50 50; Reservations: Tel. 97 42 50 10); to town centre, turn right out of station, walk down to major junction, turn left down ave Victor Hugo; then right into rue J. le Brix, left at *mairie* and continue to Place de la République and tourist office.
Buses TTO, 4 rue du 116ème R.I. (Tel. 97 47 29 64); local buses to Quiberon, Auray and Carnac.
Ferries *Vedettes du Golfe*, tours of the Gulf and to island of Ile-aux-Moines; 4 sailings daily departing from the Parc du Golfe, 10 mins south of the port. Ile d'Arz . . .
Markets Huge market Wed and Sat mornings, spilling out through Place Lucien Laroche, Place du Poids Public and Place des Lices.
Festivals *Les Fêtes d'Arvor*, 11th–15th August: Breton folkore festival; *Jazz Festival*, 4 days at beginning of August, in Jardins de Limur.
Hotels *Hôtel Le Moderne*, 2 rue de la Boucherie, Clean and pleasant.

☆ *Hôtel de Bretagne*, 34 rue du Méné, near the cathedral (Tel. 97 47 20 21). Simple, clean and friendly.
☆☆ *Hôtel Anne de Bretagne*, 42 rue O. de Clisson, near the station (Tel. 97 54 22 19).
☆☆☆ *Image Ste-Anne*, 8 Place de la Libération (Tel. 97 63 27 36). A very comfortable and charming hotel right in the centre; excellent affordable menus featuring sole in cider, duck, and oysters from Auray.
Camping Municipal de Conleau, 3 star, 3 km from town on bus 2 (direction **Conleau**) to Camping (Tel. 97 63 13 88).
Restaurant ☆ *Le Pavé des Halles*, 17 rue des Halles (Tel. 97 47 15 96). Smart but good value with imaginative, delicately cooked dishes.
☆ *La Varende*, 22 rue de la Fontaine (Tel. 97 42 57 52). Delicious meals. Restaurant just beyond St-Pattern, opposite another good place to eat, *La Morgate*, at number 21 (Tel. 97 42 42 39).
☆☆ *Lys*, 51 rue du Maréchal-Leclerc (Tel. 97 47 29 30). *Nouvelle cuisine* in smart, elegant restaurant in delightful setting close to the Promenade de la Garenne.

Excursion from Vannes
Golfe du Morbihan

From Vannes it is possible to see something of the beautiful tidal inlet, the **Golfe du Morbihan**, which means 'Little Sea' in Breton. Boats leave in summer from the little port just outside the old city walls and Porte St-Vincent and thread their way past many of the enchanting little islands which are scattered across the waters of the bay. (Vedettes du Golfe, 4 sailings daily between June and August, 1–2 sailings in spring and autumn. Tel. 97 46 60 00).

Ile-aux-Moines The largest and the most worthwhile island to visit is the Ile-aux-Moines, a thin 6-kilometre long island partly covered with pine trees. Lemon, orange and mimosa trees flourish in the sandy soil, benefitting from the sheltered south-facing location. The far end of the island from the little port is deserted and romantic, with dolmens and the largest cromlech (menhirs in semi-circular formation) in France scattered amongst the heather. The tiny little town of Ile-aux-Moines has a typically Breton flavour with its low-lying white-washed and thatched cottages.

Gavr'Inis To visit the island of Gavr'Inis ('Goat Island' in Breton) with its late Neolithic tumulus, it is neccesary to take a bus to Larmor-Baden (Wed and Sat only, 3 buses, 30 mins), then a Vedettes Blanches Armors boat to the island.

(Mar–Sept, 14 daily, 20 mins). The massive burial mount, some 100 metres in circumference, is approached by a gallery with inscribed menhirs and slabs. Estimated to be 7,000 years old, archaeological excavations continue.

The boat continues to Port Navalo, a little village with a pleasant campsite at the end of the penisula 'de Rhuys.' On the opposite side of the strait is Locmariaquer, near the mouth of the River d'Auray, one of the most picturesque villages in southern Brittany. A short walk beyond the village leads one to two impressive megalithic monuments – the **Grand Menhir**, the broken remains of a 350 ton menhir and the Table du Negociant consisting of 3 huge flat slabs resting on pointed standing stones. From the megaliths there is a lovely view across the mouth of the Golfe du Morbihan.

Redon

Trains *12 trains daily from* **Vannes** *(30 mins) and* **Quimper** *(2 hours); 8 daily from* **Nantes** *(45 mins); 10 from* **Rennes** *(45 mins); 10 – 15 from* **Paris** *Montparnasse, changing at Nantes or Rennes (2 – 3 hours).*

The trains runs parallel to the river Liziec which flows east from Vannes to the tiny train stop of Elven, 3 kilometres north of which lie the ruins of the **Fortresse de Largoët** with a massive 40-metre-high Keep. Henry of Richmond, later Henry vii, and his uncle the Earl of Pembroke were held prisoner here for 2 years after fleeing from England following the Battle of Tewkesbury in 1474. They found refuge in France but not of the sort they can have hoped for, being held prisoner in total for 14 years before being allowed to return to England.

Hills give way to watermeadows and marshland outside Redon, a pleasant little town at the confluence of the Vilaine river and the Nantes-Brest canal, with an interesting 12th-century tower and 17th-century abbey buildings and cloisters. The church of St-Sauveur was an important pilgrimage destination in the Middle Ages and this led to a number of important fairs being held in the town. The most famous, *la Teillouse*, devoted to chestnuts grown in the vicinity, still takes place on the 4th Sunday of October. Fine old houses are to be found close to the cathedral in the **Grande Rue** and along the Quai Dugauy-Trouin facing the Vilaine river.

Practicalities in Redon

Hotels ☆☆ *Hôtel-Restaurant Jean-Marc Chandouneau*, 10 av de la Gare (Tel. 99 71 02 24). Delicious cuisine and a comfortable old hotel.

Railway Station (Info. Tel. 99 65 50 50; Reservations 99 65 18 65); to centre, turn right out of station, follow street for 200 metres.

From Redon 12 trains daily lead north up the marshy valley of the Vilaine to **Rennes** (40 – 60 mins); 8 trains daily to **Nantes** (55 mins), the starting point of the Poitou Tour and from where there are fast TGVs direct to Paris Montparnasse (2 hours 10 mins).

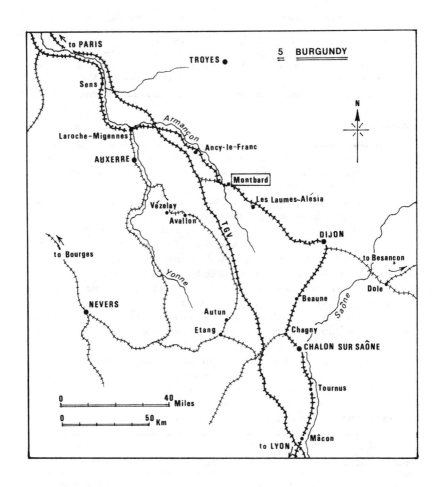

5 Burgundy

There is no other region of France that conjures up such a picture of plenty and prosperity as does Burgundy. Scenically, gastronomically and culturally, it has few peers; historically, no region is able to draw on such a rich history as that enjoyed by the Dukes of Burgundy who rivalled the Kings of France in power and influence, and at times equalled if not excelled them in the extent of their domains.

Best known for its Romanesque architecture and superb wine, it is an area of rich cultural history, stately rivers and renowned wines. Signs indicating free tastings (*dégustations*) beguile the traveller into sampling the dry Pouilly whites from Nievre and Chablis from L'Yonne, as well as reds from the Côte d'Or and Saône-et-Loire.

The Roman conquest of Gaul saw some of its fiercest engagements around Autun which has extensive Gallo-Roman remains and ruins. Excavation sites and archaeological museums reveal the region's early history while from the middle ages, innumerable Romanesque churches testify to the strength of the church and the skill and vision of medieval craftsmen.

The Dukes of Burgundy stemmed from the same royal blood as the kings of France for it was Henri I of France who first gave the duchy, which stretched from the Jura to the Saône, to his brother Robert in the 11th century. This line of Capet dukes came to an end in 1361 and the province reverted to the French crown. John II of France then gave the province to his son Philip the Bold who was the first of the second line of Capet dukes under whom, in the 14th and 15th centuries, the province achieved the height of its power. This period saw the acquisition by the Dukes of Burgundy of vast tracts of land in Flanders and Brabant.

The land of Burgundy itself is characterised by gentleness and domesticity, with none of the wildness of the Jura that borders it to the east, or the monotony of the plains of Champagne to the north. It is a fertile region, cultivated since antiquity, with rich soils and a mild climate conducive alike to vines and fruit. Unlike the Ile-de-France, Burgundy does not conform to the medieval sense of an *île* – a territory enclosed more or less on all sides by rivers which mark its extent. On the contrary, Burgundy cuts across those rivers in a more amorphous and less defensive fashion. It is the rising hills of Franche-Comté that separate it from the province of that name, with whom its fortunes have so often been tied, while to the west it is the Morvan and Nivernais hills that cut it off from the old province of Berry.

Dijon, the capital of Burgundy, lies strategically at its very centre and a little north of the slopes of the Côte d'Or which are crowded with vineyards, from which come some of the most famous Burgundy wines: Chambertin, Beaune, Clos-Vougeot, Nuits St Georges, Pommard and Meursaut, to name but a few. Not surprisingly, the most rewarding time to be in Burgundy is during the grape harvest, the *vendange*, which usually begins around mid-September and lasts but a few weeks. Then the fields, a mixture of gold and yellow, are alive with the grape-pickers working rapidly and enthusiastically, as they attempt to bring in the harvest at the exact moment when the grapes are deemed to have reached their ideal maturity. Too little rain in the crucial weeks preceding the harvest means the grapes will not swell; too much threatens to bring mildew and the loss of flavour whilst a heavy hailstorm can completely destroy a crop within a few minutes.

Wine however is but the complement for something of even greater importance in Burgundy – the food. Only Périgord can claim with justification to rival Burgundy for the excellence and quality of its cuisine. On gastronomic grounds alone Burgundy justifies not just visits but lengthy periods of residence. Frogs, crayfish, snails, pike, beef, cherries, currants, mustard and local cow and goat cheeses have long been staples of Burgundian cooking. *Boeuf bourguignon* and *coq au vin* are perhaps the most famous dishes to have originated from the region, but snails, rabbits, poultry and game are to be found widely, often accompanied by the most delectable sauces imaginable. The apéritif *kir*, a refreshing summer concoction of *cassis*, blackcurrant liqueur, and chilled white wine, stems from Burgundy. Other local specialities include *gougère*, a soft bread made with cabbage and cheese, and *quenelles*, savoury little dumplings. Dijon mustards, far milder than English ones, are made using white wine instead of the vineagar employed by manufacturers elsewhere.

The route *Sens – Auxerre – Avallon – Vézelay – Autun – Beaune – Chalons-sur-Saône – Dijon – Les Laumes – Alésia – Montbard – Ancy-le-Franc – Besançon*

This circular route through Burgundy samples all that is best in the province: Sens, *with its glorious stained glass in one of the earliest Gothic cathedrals in France; the lovely old town of* Auxerre *in a superb* location of the River Yonne and spectacular **Avallon** surrounded by medieval ramparts high on a granite mountain. A short distance from Avallon lies **Vézelay** which seems to breathe the very spirit of medieval Christendom in its magnificent basilica, once the wonder of the western world. **Autun** was founded by the Emperor Augustus and retains much of its Roman past; **Beaune** boasts superb town architecture and unrivalled food and wine while **Dijon** has magnificent Renaissance architecture and ducal palaces. On a smaller scale is the **Château of Ancy-le-Franc**, one of the most perfect Renaissance châteaux in France.

Sens

Trains *Frequent trains from* Paris *Gare de Lyon (50 mins–1½ hours); and* Laroche-Migennes *(20 mins); 9 from* Dijon *(1¾ hours).*

Through their title of Primate of the Gauls and of Germania, the Archbishops of Sens acquired an extraordinary power that enabled them to extend their ecclesiastical rule over Paris, Chartres, Orléans and Meaux until as late as the 17th century. An important religious council took place in Sens in 1140 at which the doctrines of Abelard were condemned as heretical; in 1234 Louis IX was married to Margaret of Provence in the cathedral.

England has a special link with Sens for the master-mason of the cathedral, William of Sens, was almost certainly responsible for the construction of the east end of Canterbury cathedral, and St Thomas à Becket spent part of his exile nearby at the Abbaye de Ste Colombe. William of Sens worked on Canterbury Cathedral for 5 years before falling from scaffolding and sustaining injuries which led to his death.

Cathédrale St-Etienne

What to see
The cathedral of St-Etienne was one of the first great Gothic churches of France: work was begun in 1130, the choir completed by 1164 and the nave by 1180, but the transept not until the end of the 15th century. Various chapels were added in the 16th and 18th centuries. The cathedral is an early example of the Transitional style in France but it has suffered severely both at the hands of the mob, which mutilated every statue bar one of the western façade in 1793, and at those of the architect and restorer, Viollet-le-Duc. What remains of the sculptures of the western façade is 12th-century work depicting the life of St John the Baptist and the Dormition of the Virgin. One of the few original statues to survive was that of St Stephen himself

who still stands on a pillar of the central doorway. The stained glass in Sens Cathedral is one of its greatest treasures. The rose-windows in the transept are among the largest in the world and date from the early 16th century. Two of the windows, one representing Augustus and the sibyl (1530), the other the life of St Eutropius (1536), are by Jean Cousin, a native of Sens, who worked at the same time as but was unaffected by the central stream of French painting – the Fontainebleau School, as represented by Primaticcio and Niccolo dell'Abbate.

The choir has a fine wrought-iron screen in Louis xv style; Louis xv's son, the Dauphin, is buried in a tomb in the Chapelle de Sainte-Colombe. Despite the pillaging that took place during the Revolution, the Treasury possesses some fascinating items that include pieces of silk cloth made in the 6th century for the wrapping of relics, and the mitre and vestments of Thomas à Becket which became the objects of veneration following his murder. There is a story that these vestments were tried on by Cardinal Manning, 19th century English Cardinal and Theologian, while on a visit to the cathedral. Adjacent to the cathedral is the elegant Palais Synodal, formerly an ecclesiastical court dating from the 13th century and beyond it, through a Renaissance doorway, the Archbishop's Palace. The ecclesiastical court sat in the great vaulted chamber and the bishops met in the grand 1st-floor hall, while heretics were imprisoned in the downstairs courtroom. In the gallery of the Archbishop's Palace there is the hat worn by Napoleon at Waterloo. (Open 10 am–noon and 2–6 pm.)

Profiting from its strategic location between the Ile-de-France and Burgundy, Sens developed as an important commercial centre, reaching the height of its prosperity in the 16th century. Many of its finest houses, such as the **Maison Abraham**, with its beautifully carved wooden beams, in the Rue de la République, date from this era. Back streets off the pedestrianised Grande Rue reveal old Renaissance *hôtels particuliers*, a few incorporating stone taken from Roman buildings.

Practicalities in Sens

Tourist Office Place Jean Jaurès (Tel. 86 65 18 49); currency exchange, accommodation service. Open daily 9 am-noon and 1.30–7.30 pm.
Railway Station (Info: Tel. 67 58 50 50; Reservations: Tel. 80 43 52 56). For town centre, follow Ave Vauban, cross bridge and then head left for cathedral.
Markets Most days.
Hotels *Hôtel Esplanade*, 2 blvd du Mail, just off Place Jean Jaurès (Tel. 86 65 20 95) ☆☆☆ *Paris et Poste*, 97 rue République,

opposite Hôtel de Ville (Tel. 86 65 17 43). Traditional hotel; excellent cuisine in restaurant.
Camping *Municipal Entre-deux-Vannes*, just outside town on road to Lyon (Tel. 86 65 64 71).
Restaurants *Le Soleil Levant*, 51 rue Emile Zola (Tel. 86 65 71 82). Burgundian dishes; situated in street leading from station to centre. ☆☆ *Potinière*, rue Cecile de Marsagny (Tel. 86 66 31 08). Good, modern regional cuisine.

Auxerre

Trains *13 trains daily from* **Paris** *(1 ½ hours), some will require you to change at Laroche-Migennes; 9 from* **Avallon** *(1 hour); 6 from* **Autun** *(3 hours).*

Auxerre, one of the most delightful and tranquil towns of Burgundy, stands on 2 hills that rise above the River Yonne. The city was once surrounded by 2 concentric defensive walls whose place has now been taken by boulevards. Governed in turn by bishops and counts, the town was part of the Duchy of Burgundy until the death of Charles the Bold signalled the end of Burgundy's independence of the French crown.

What to see

Tour de l'Horloge

One of the most characteristic features of Auxerre is the combined clock tower and gateway, the Tour de l'Horloge, which was built at the end of the 15th century, at which point it formed part of the town's fortifications. The 17th-century clock faces that now adorn it tell not only the time but the movement of the sun and the moon. In the 18th-century the bailiff, Roussel, who was the inspiration for the absurd figure in the song, Cadet-Roussel, lived in a house nearby.

Cathédrale St-Etienne

Even if the Tour de l'Horloge is the most distinctive feature of Auxerre, the most dominating one is the cathedral, a large Gothic structure, whose bulk is reflected in the waters of the Yonne. One of the earliest bishops of Auxerre was St Germanus who was ordered to Wales in the early 5th century to combat the Pelagian heresy and succeeded in defeating the heathen Picts and Scots near Mold in 430. The cathedral was never completed, no southern tower ever being built, and building extended from 1215 to the middle of the 16th century. Although the western façade was severely mutilated by the Huguenots in the Wars of Religion, its 3 portals preserve a little sculpture dating from the 14th century, representing scenes from Genesis, the Coronation of the Virgin and David and Bathsheba, while the central tympanum portrays the Last Judgement. One small bas-relief tells the story of Aristotle carrying the mistress of Alexander on his back – an unusual allusion to classical legend. The portals of the transepts are of later date and represent the life of St Germanus and the stoning of St Stephen, the saint to whom the cathedral is dedicated.

The exceptionally elegant choir is a fine example of early Gothic architecture and was constructed between 1215 and 1234. The ambulatory is also a remarkable architectural ensemble. Dating from the 13th century, it is extremely elegant with magnificent richly-coloured 13th-century stained glass illustrating 350 scenes from the Bible and early Christian legends. The crypt, part of an earlier 11th-century church, is decorated with early 12th-century frescoes.

Bishop's Palace

Not far from the cathedral stands the Bishop's Palace, its Romanesque arcades facing the river, part of which dates back to the 13th century. Another interesting building is the **church of St-Germain** which was damaged in the Wars of Religion. In 1810 the nave was destroyed so that the transepts and choir are now separate from the high clock-tower to which they were once attached. The fascination of St-Germain is not visible at first to a casual visitor for it is to be found below ground. Beneath the church is a 9th-century **crypt** with some of the earliest frescoes to be found in France. The crypt was constructed by Count Conrad, the uncle of Charles the Bald, one of the early Carolingian kings. Apart from the frescoes illustrating 3 episodes in the life of St Stephen, the crypt also contains the tomb of St Germanus, 2 Merovingian tombs and the remains of early Christian martyrs.

Old Town

The old heart of the town lies between the cathedral and the church of St-Germain. Here are to be found picturesque streets of old gabled houses and the local **museum**, containing furniture that belonged to Germain Soufflot, the architect of the Panthéon in Paris, which is located in an interesting town house at rue d'Egleny.

Practicalities in Auxerre

Tourist Office 1 quai de la République, just below the cathedral besides the River Yonne (Tel. 86 52 06 19); accommodation service.
Railway Station Rue Paul Doumer, east of the Yonne (Tel. 86 46 50 50).
Markets Sun morning, Tues and Fri.
Festivals *Jazz*: June; *St Martin's Fair*: early Nov.
Hotels *Hôtel de la Renomée*, 27 rue d'Egleny, (Tel. 86 52 03 53). Quiet and discreet, in the heart of the old town.
Hôtel de la Porte de Paris, 5 rue St Germain, near the abbey (Tel. 86 46 90 09). Attractive, clean hotel with bar.
☆☆ *Parc des Maréchaux*, 6 ave Foch (Tel. 86 51 43 77). Handsome Napoleon III mansion set

in a park. No restaurant.
☆☆ *Seignelay*, 2 rue Pont (Tel. 86 52 03 48). A delightful old timber-framed building with shady courtyard for summer eating. Very good Burgundian cuisine.
Camping (Tel. 86 52 11 15). On route de Vaux (D163); shady location beside the Yonne.
Restaurants ☆ *Jardin Gourmand*, 56 blvd Vauban (Tel. 86 51 53 52). Good-value set menus offering a wide range of interesting dishes.
☆☆ *Jean-Luc Barnabet*, 14 quai de la République (Tel. 86 51 68 88). Excellent regional cooking in a lovely 17th-century riverside building.

Avallon

Trains *8 trains daily from* **Auxerre** *(1 hour), connecting at Laroche-Migennes for* Paris *(3 hours); 6 daily from* **Autun** *(2 hours).*

South from Auxerre, the train passes **Cravant** where in 1423 the English and Burgundian soldiers of the Marshal of Chastellux defeated the French forces commanded by the Constable James Stuart. Little remains of the once extensive fortifications of the town. Beyond lies **Vermenton**, its 13th-century church fronted by 2 towers, and **Arcy** where stalactite grottoes have been uncovered. To the west lie the rising hills of the mountainous and sparsely populated country of the Morvan, now a regional park.

Originally a Gallo-Roman town, close to the Via Agrippa, the Roman road that ran from Lyon to Boulogne, in the Middle Ages Avallon was the seat of a count and an important commercial centre. The town occupies a strategic site on a spur overlooking the River Cousin and preserves some interesting old houses and part of its medieval fortifications, the oldest parts of which date back to the 9th and 10th centuries.

What to see

Medieval Walls

The fortified inner 'city' is compact and fascinating and can be walked round with ease. Parts of the walled *enceinte* and remains of the defensive towers can be seen from beyond the Promenade de la Petite Porte, from where there are precipitous views across the plunging valley of the Cousin, and at the east end of the Promenade des Terreaux. Access to the old quarter, with its narrow and cobbled streets, is gained through the fortified 15th-century Clock Gate, the Porte de l'Horloge, which is surmounted by a sturdy bell-tower and spire.

Eglise St-Lazare

The church of St-Lazare, standing above a deep ravine, has a somewhat battered Romanesque façade, having suffered extensive damage during the Wars of Religion and during the Revolution. It was built on the site of an earlier church that had been constructed around the relic believed to be the head of the patron saint of lepers, St Lazarus. The church had to be extended twice to accommodate the number of pilgrims that came in search of a cure for leprosy, the nave being extended by 60 feet in the 12th century. The attractive stonework of the western façade incorporates the signs of the zodiac and figures from the Apocalypse.

West of Avallon, in the beautiful wooded hills of Morvan, lies Vézelay, one of the most remarkable and beautiful medieval villages of France. Not easily accessible, it is nevertheless a site almost without equal in Burgundy, on whose western border it lies.

Practicalities in Avallon

Tourist Office 4 rue Bocquillot, next to Eglise Collégiale St-Lazare (Tel. 86 34 14 19); accommodation service. Open daily 9:30am–7:30pm in summer.
Railway Station (Tel. 80 43 52 56 for reservations) (Tel. 86 46 50 50 for information)
Buses TRANSCO buses (Tel. 80 42 11 39); from station to Dijon (2½ hours), Semur-en-Auxois, and other local destinations.
Markets Thurs and Sat.
Festivals Fair-Exposition: early May.
Bicycles Cycle hire from station.
Hotels *Hôtel du Parc*, 3 Place de la Gare, right next to station (Tel. 86 34 17 00).
☆ *Au Bon Accueil*, 4 rue de l'Hopital, at

entrance to old town. (Tel. 86 34 09 33).
Hostels *Foyer des Jeunes Travailleurs*, 10 ave de Victor Hugo (Tel. 86 34 01 88).
☆☆ *Capucins*, 6 ave P. Doumer (Tel. 86 34 06 52). Delightful countryhouse-style hotel; excellent restaurant offering traditional Burgundian cuisine.
☆☆☆ *Hôtel Poste*, 13 Place Vauban (Tel. 86 34 06 12). Where Napoleon spent the night just before the Battle of Waterloo; attractive rooms but pricey restaurant.
Camping *Camping Municipal de Sous-Roche* (Tel. 86 34 10 39); 2km towards Lourmes, nearby restaurant. Open March-15th Oct.

Vézelay

Trains/Buses No direct trains. The nearest station is **Sermizelles** on the Avallon–Auxerre line; 7 trains daily from **Auxerre** to **Sermizelles** (45 mins); 2 connecting SNCF buses to Vézelay: 10am and 3pm; also bus at 8am from place Vauban in Avallon (10 mins).

Only 15 kilometres and a lovely bicycle ride from Avallon in a superb position on a high, grassy hill rising above the Yonne and the Cure, is one of the finest Romanesque churches in France, the Basilica of Vézelay. On one side a small village straggles up to the summit of the hill; from the others only the basilica is to be seen, set like a jewelled crown in magnificent, verdant countryside.

What to see

Basilique Ste-Madeleine

The history of the basilica is as fascinating as its setting is beautiful. In the 2nd century AD it was widely believed in France that a small band of Christian exiles had fled Judaea after the Crucifixion and landed at a point on the southern coast of France that is now known as Stes-Maries-de-la-Mer. Among the group were Mary Magdalen, as well as the sister of the Virgin, Mary Salome, Martha, Lazarus and Maximin. The group soon dispersed, Mary Magdalen wandering through Provence until she came to rest in a cave in the hills now known as the Chaine de la Ste-Baume. Here she rested until her death when, by divine intervention, she was transported to a church built nearby by St Maximin. Her tomb quickly became one of the most important pilgrimage centres of southern France and attracted the faithful from all over southern Europe.

It came therefore as a thunderbolt when, in the 11th century, the monks of the little abbey at Vézelay suddenly announced that they had the bones of Mary Magdalen in their possession. Little could have been more calculated to create an impression on the medieval mind than such an extraordinary and spectacular claim. Pilgrims quickly began to abandon the church of St-Maximin in Provence and turned their weary feet northwards to Vézelay, despite vehement protests and denunciations by the guardians of Mary Magdalen's relics at St-Maximin. The vast influx of pilgrims to Vézelay generated a handsome income which was used to build the Romanesque basilica, and for several centuries Vézelay prospered while St-Maximin sunk into jealous obscurity. Later, in 1280, the monks of St-Maximin had their revenge, if revenge it was, when they claimed that they had uncovered the real bones of Mary Magdalen at St-Maximin and that those purloined by the monks of Vézelay were the false ones. A bitter and somewhat unholy dispute ensued with Vézelay losing the day when the Church ruled in favour of St-Maximin. The ruling spelt the end of Vézelay's prosperity as pilgrims quietly abandoned it. In its heyday the town was famous throughout western Europe and it was the scene of a number of important meetings and events: St-Bernard preached the Second Crusade here in 1146; Richard I met Philippe Auguste in the town before setting off on the Third Crusade; and Thomas à Becket was a visitor to the basilica in 1168.

The 600 years following the fateful Church ruling saw a consistent decline in the wealth of the town. In the 16th century the basilica suffered at the hands of the Huguenots and the behaviour of the abbots, with the exception of Berthier in the 1760s, alienated the population to such an extent that they did nothing to help them at the time of the Revolution. Damaged during the Revolution, and by lightning which struck the building in 1819, the basilica was falling into ruin when Prosper Merimée recommended that steps should be taken to prevent its complete disintegration. Restoration work was begun by Viollet-le-Duc when the building was little more than a shell. Certain parts however were still in excellent condition, notably the breathtaking narthex doorway with its central tympanum, portraying Christ with his hands extended filling the Twelve Apostles with the Holy Spirit. This is a masterpiece of 12th-century Burgundian sculpture that reflects the certainties and spirit of medieval faith.

Disputes between the monks and the local populace had led to an abbot being murdered and the monastery set alight in 1105. Work began on the new basilica in the 1120s, starting with the Romanesque nave, built with alternating white and pinky-brown stone, its columns decorated with striking historiated capitals representing the lives of the saints, scenes from the Old and New Testaments and pagan legends such as the education of Achilles.

In the late 12th and early 13th century work began on the Gothic choir; one of its columns in the right transept was reputed to enclose the relics of Mary Magdalen. Beneath the choir is an ancient crypt with 12 columns supporting square capitals, 4 of which probably date back to the 9th century. Just beyond the southern transept is the 13th-century chapter-house, above which is a vaulted hall which once served as a granary, and beyond which is a restored cloister walk.

The village of Vézelay itself is small and quiet when not besieged by the 20th century's substitute for the medieval pilgrim – the tourist, a no less gullible or edifying species. Most tourists can be avoided by skirting the medieval city walls which still encircle part of the hill. From time to time a genuine pilgrim is still to be found setting out from the basilica to the shrine of St James at Santiago da Compostella in north-western Spain. A lyrical and fascinating account of such a modern-day pilgrimage is *La ballade des pélérins* by Edith de la Héronnière, published in French by Mercure de France.

Porte Neuve and Porte Ste-Croix

Following the walls of Vézelay brings one to the massive 15th-century Porte Neuve and Porte Ste-Croix which were once the main gates to the village. Straggling up the steep hillside are numerous old houses while at the foot of Vézelay, in an idyllic location, lies another tiny village, **St Pierre-sous-Vézelay**. It is overshadowed by its beautiful church, Notre-Dame, the presbytery of which houses flints, burial urns, ex-votos, pottery and other archaeological finds discovered at the site of Les Fontaines-Salées, some 2 kilometres from the village, where salt water springs have been exploited since the 6th millennium BC.

Practicalities in Vézelay

Tourist Office Rue St-Pierre, up towards the church (Tel. 86 33 23 69); map, accommodation service, currency exchange. Open daily 10 am–1 pm and 2–6 pm.

Festivals Feast of Ste-Madeleine and pilgrimages: 22nd July

Hotels ☆ Relais du Morvan Place du Champ-de-Foire (Tel. 86 33 25 33). Simple, clean, bright rooms in Logis hotel; restaurant serves good wholesome auberge dishes.

☆☆☆ Poste et Lion d'Or, Place Champ de Foire (Tel. 86 33 21 23). Comfortable and handsome accommodation in the old post inn; restaurant serves good, traditional Burgundian cuisine.

☆☆☆ Hôtel Le Pontot, Place de Pontot (Tel. 86 33 24 40). Delightful 15th-century house with lovely views and tranquil garden. No restaurant.

Hostel Auberge de Jeunesse (HI), route de l'Etang, beyond Gendarmerie. Camping possible (Tel. 86 33 24 18).

Autun

Trains 3 – 5 trains daily from **Avallon** (1 – 2 hours); from **Auxerre** (3 hours 5 mins); 3 from **Paris** (5 hours); 6 from **Chalons-sur-Saône** (2 hours); one bus daily from Vézelay.

At the southern end of the Morvan, on the slopes of the Signal de Montjeu, stands an ancient town, important in Roman times, with one of the most beautiful cathedrals in France.

The Romans established a regional capital at Autun above the river Arroux, naming it Augustodunum, after the Emperor Augustus. One of the most important Gallic tribes of the region was the Eduens whose capital was a short distance to the west on the summit of Mont Beuvray. Although they originally backed Vercingetorix against the Romans, they were pardoned by Caesar and became allies of Rome. The remains of their acropolis, Bibracte, once enclosed by stone ramparts 6 kilometres long, has been partly excavated, revealing the foundations of Gallic houses. Bibracte was abandoned at the beginning of the Christian era for Roman Augustodunum which gained the reputation of being the most learned city in Gaul. So extensive was the Roman settlement that it is only recently that the town has extended beyond the Roman walls which were 4 miles in length and buttressed by 55 towers. Beyond the river is another Roman ruin, the **Temple of Janus**, that might have been an isolated part of the Roman fortifications. In the Middle Ages the town thrived as part of the Duchy of Burgundy before declining almost without interruption until the

20th century. Talleyrand became bishop of the city just before the Revolution.

What to see

Roman Gateways

Only the Rue de Paris and Rue de la Jambe de Bois are still based on the Roman town plan but 2 gateways remain of the extensive Roman walls: the **Porte d'Arroux** and the **Porte de St-André**. The Porte d'Arroux, down near the river of the same name, has 2 main arches for traffic and 2 smaller ones for pedestrians, and an upper gallery supported by Corinthian pilasters. Porte St-André lies to the north of the Roman theatre. It is not quite so impressive as the Porte d'Arroux but it is of similar design and ornamented with Ionic pilasters.

Cathédrale St-Lazare

In the southern corner of the town is the cathedral, one of the few churches in Burgundy whose tympanum escaped unscathed from the Revolution having been completely plastered over in 1766 and hidden from view. It appears that Voltaire's remarks about the style of the sculpture were so disparaging that the bishop agreed to it being covered up. The only part that had been lost, most probably during the Wars of Religion, the head of Christ, was eventually found in the Musée Rolin and replaced in 1948.

The central tympanum therefore represents a remarkable and near-perfect ensemble of Romanesque sculpture. It is unusual too in the fact that the work is signed as being that of Gislebertus and dated to 1135. André Malraux described him in terms of being the 'Romanesque Cézanne' and his work is full of anguish, human frailty and divine splendour. The tympanum, carved of hard limestone that must have come from elsewhere in the region, is framed by medallions illustrating the seasons, the signs of the zodiac and daily and seasonal labours.

Like Vézelay, Autun was a pilgrimage destination in the Middle Ages for the cathedral contained the relics of St Lazarus, the patron saint of lepers, which had been brought north from Marseille. They are contained in a small enamelled reliquary under the high altar. The barrel-vaulted nave, some 23-metres-high, is a beautiful example of the Burgundian Romanesque. Inspiration for the fluted pilasters probably came from similar Roman decoration on the Porte d'Arroux but they are also similar in style to the design followed at Cluny, the vast Benedictine abbey built in the 11th century some 64 kilometre to the south. In the nave the capitals are superb, reflecting not only the dexterity and faith of medieval stone-masons but also their humanity, awareness of the beauty of the natural world and impish sense of humour. A number of capitals whose place has been taken by copies are gathered in the 16th-century chapter-house.

Musée Rolin

A stone's-throw away from the cathedral is the Musée Rolin, an excellent museum of Roman and Gallo-Roman artefacts, including many objects from the excavations of the Eduen capital of Mont Bibracte. Of these the most remarkable are Roman bronzes and a gilt bronze parade helmet. Of medieval objects the finest is undoubtedly a highly unusual carving of Eve, almost certainly the work of Gislebertus, which once appeared above one of the side doors of the cathedral. A very sensual Eve, in a reclining pose, is in the act of turning away from the apple, her hand raised to her cheek and her long hair flowing over her shoulder. Eric Gill's lithe and sensual figures spring immediately to mind.

The museum also has a number of fine paintings that include a *Nativity* of 1480 by the Master of Moulins, in which appears the kneeling figure of Cardinal Rolin. (Open Apr–Sept, Wed–Mon 9.30 am–noon and 1.30–6 pm, Sun 10 am–noon and 2.30–5 pm; Oct–Mar, Wed–Mon 10 am–noon and 2–4 pm, Sun 10 am–noon and 2.30–5 pm.)

Roman Ruins

Rue St-Antoine leads in the direction of the site of the Roman theatre, of which little remains but which was once the largest theatre in Gaul. North of the theatre lies the second Roman gate, the Porte St-André. A short walk to the south-east of the Porte de Breuil, near the village of Couhard, stands a tall partly-ruined pyramid that was most probably a Roman tomb.

Practicalities in Autun

Tourist office 3 ave Charles de Gaulle (Tel. 85 52 20 34); accommodation service.
Markets Wed and Fri.
Festivals *Son-et-Lumière*: daily, except Sun and Mon in July, Aug and Sept; Fri and Sat only mid-May to end-June. *Morvan music*: Fridays and Saturdays mid-July to mid-August.
Hotels *Hôtel de France*, Place de la Gare (Tel. 85 52 14 00). Convenient and cheerful, close to railway station.
☆☆ *Vieux Moulin*, Porte d'Arroux (Tel. 85 52 10 90). Cool and shady watermill in lovely location beside the river; good restaurant.

☆☆ *St-Louis*, 6 rue l'Arbalète (Tel. 85 52 21 03). Near the Hôtel de Ville in a 17th-century *post-relais* with terrace. Good range of interesting menus.
☆☆ *Hôtel Tête Noire*, 1–3 rue Arabesque (Tel. 85 52 25 39). Pleasant and comfortable near Place du Champ de Mars.
Camping *Camping Municipal de la Porte d'Arroux*, past the Porte d'Arroux, on banks of River Ternin (Tel. 88 52 10 82).
Restaurants ☆ *Chalet Bleu*, 3 rue Jeannin (Tel. 85 86 27 30). Very good classic cooking; good value for money.

Beaune

Trains *2–3 trains daily from* **Autun** *south to Etang and then east to Chagny (1 hour 20 mins): change for Beaune; 8 trains daily to Beaune from* **Chalon-sur-Saône** *(20 mins); 12 from Dijon (½ hour); 6 from Lyon (2½ hours); 2 TGVs from Paris (2 hours).*

Only very few trains run daily from Autun to Etang and then east to Chagny and Beaune; the alternative to this route is to back-track to Laroche-Migenne and then take a train south to Dijon and Beaune. The journey from Autun to Beaune however is attractive, as the line skirts the

Côte d'Or, a swathe of gentle hills covered with a patchwork of vineyards, to Chagny a few kilometres south of Beaune.

Beaune is a beautiful town, crammed with treasures and fine old buildings in narrow, cobbled streets and delightful squares. The life of the city still revolves around wine-making and selling, and many of the most beautiful buildings belong to the wine merchants of the city. Fine old stone houses and mansions testify to the wealth and importance of the city, which was the capital of the Dukedom of Burgundy until the Dukes moved to Dijon in the 14th century.

The most rewarding approach to the town is, in fact, from the railway station along the Avenue du 8 Septembre, which leads to two 15th-century towers, all that survives of the castle held by the Dukes of Burgundy until it was dismantled on the orders of Henri IV in 1602.

What to see

Hospice de Beaune

The hospice, or the Hôtel Dieu, is a splendid building that has hardly been altered since its foundation in the 15th century. It was still in use as a hospital for the ill and dying until the Second World War. The Hôtel Dieu, which is instantly recognisable by its brightly-coloured and chequered tile roof, was founded in 1433 as a charity hospital by Nicolas Rollin, Chancellor to the Dukes of Burgundy, John the Fearless and Philip the Good.

Entrance to the Hôtel is gained through a graceful arcaded lodge, beyond which lies a handsome and picturesque courtyard, surrounded by buildings dating from 1443. Their steep roofs are punctured by numerous high, timbered gables above which rise slender and ornate lead pinnacles in Flamboyant Flemish style. A gallery runs right round the building under the eaves while inside is a tall spacious hall, the Grande Salles des Malades, in which the poor and sick were gathered and tended to. This magnificent hall, with its 130 feet long vaulted chestnut roof, has hardly altered in appearance since the Middle Ages. At one end of the hall the chapel, the Chambre des Pauvres, is separated from the main ward by a grille, with its polychrome figure of Christ in chains, a wooden statue dating from the 15th century. Around the walls can be found inscribed the motto 'Seulle', or 'lone star', a reference to Nicolas Rollin's second wife, Guigone de Salins, who represented the star of his life.

Off a second, minor, courtyard is the pharmacy, with an unrivalled collection of faience, pots and pewter from Nevers. The superb polyptych of the *Last Judgement*, one of the finest primitive Flemish paintings by Roger van der Weyden, used to hang above the altar in the Chambre des Pauvres until removed in 1793. It portrays Chancellor Rollin and the half-hidden figure of his wife, Pope Eugenius IV and Philip the Good on either side of Christ and St Michael who is shown weighing souls in a balance. Above, angels carry the instruments of the Passion; below, the small pitiable figures of the Saved on the left are separated from the Damned on the right. (Open daily 9 am–6.30 pm; 18th Nov–March daily 9–11.30 am and 2–5.30 pm.)

Eglise Notre-Dame

During the Wars of Religion the Dukes of Burgundy took the part of the League, despite opposition from the townspeople, but the church of Notre-Dame suffered more from the Revolution than from the religious conflicts of the 16th century. The 14th-century porch takes up most of the western façade but its rich sculpture was severely mutilated and most of the figures to be seen today date from Viollet-le-Duc's restoration in the 1860s.

The interior of Notre-Dame is similar in many respects to that of the Cathedral of St-Lazare at Autun, both having been inspired by the abbey of Cluny. The story of Lazarus inspired the frescoes painted in 1470–73 by the Flemish painter, Pierre Spicre, in the Chapelle St-Léger. Around the choir are a series of fine 15th-century tapestries, depicting the life of the Virgin from her birth to her Coronation.

Hôtel des Ducs de Bourgogne

From the collegiate church of Notre-Dame the Rue de l'Enfer leads to the Hôtel des Ducs, a ducal residence until the Dukes of Burgundy were crushed by the Kings of France at the end of the 15th century. This attractive building, arranged around a courtyard, now contains the **Musée du Vin**, a museum dedicated to the history of wine from antiquity to the 20th century with some huge wine-presses dating back to the 18th century. (Open 9.30 am–6 pm.)

Renaissance Town Houses

Many of Beaune's finest houses are to be found in the Rue de Lorraine that leads north from Place Monge which occupies the site of the former Hôtel de Ville, burnt down during the Revolution. Facing the square is the **Hôtel de la Rochepot**, whose Gothic façade hides an attractive Renaissance courtyard; it was built in the 1520s by a wealthy draper, Jean Pétral. Nearby stands a tall belfry built at the end of the 14th century which was part of the Hôtel de Ville before its destruction.

The Rue de Lorraine can be followed north through the city walls which can then be skirted east, following the ramparts past a Jardin anglais, to the 15th-century castle towers that once guarded the eastern gateway to the city.

Practicalities in Beaune

Tourist Office Rue de l'Hôtel Dieu (Tel. 80 22 24 51) accommodation service; maps, emergency currency exchange; free guided tours of town in French (July–Aug). Open 9 am–midnight; March–May and Oct–Nov 9 am–10 pm; Dec–Feb 9 am–7 pm.
Railway Station Ave du 8 Septembre (Tel. 80 44 50 50) For town centre, follow Ave du 8 Septembre into Rue du château, then left onto rempart St-Jean and cross rue d'Alsace to rempart Madeleine; then right onto rue de l'Hôtel-Dieu and tourist office.
Markets Thurs and Sat.
Festivals Son-et-Lumière at the Hospice: April–Oct; Fair: early June: Classical Music Festival end of June; Folk Festival: September.
Hotels Hôtel Rousseau, 11 Place de la Madeleine (Tel. 80 22 13 59). Quiet and attractive with courtyard and lovely garden, near rue Faubourg Madeleine.
Hôtel Foch, 24 blvd Foch (Tel. 80 24 05 65). Clean and simple; outside town walls.

☆ *Auberge Bourguignonne*, 4 Place Madeleine, near station (Tel. 80 22 23 53). Very pleasant hotel with excellent little restaurant.
☆☆ *Hotel la Paix*, 47 rue faubourg Madeleine (Tel. 80 22 33 33). Set back across courtyard in central location; good restaurant attached.
☆☆ *Central*, 2 rue Victor Millot (Tel. 80 24 77 24). Lovely hotel just round the corner from Hotel Dieu and the tourist office; superb Burgundian dishes from restaurant that's crowded with locals.
Camping *Les Cent-Vignes*, 1 km from town

centre in rue Dubois, off rue du Faubourg St-Nicholas (Tel. 80 22 03 91).
Restaurant ☆ *Maxime*, 3 Place Madeleine (Tel. 80 22 17 82). Good regional cooking and excellent value for money in this popular restaurant with its own shady terrace.
☆☆ *Auberge St-Vincent*, Place Halle (Tel. 80 22 42 34). Excellent location opposite the Hospice in a handsome 17th-century house.
☆☆☆ *Relais de Saulx*, 6 *rue Very (Tel. 80 22 01 35)*. Superb Burgundian cuisine; a wide range of menus and wines.

Chalon-sur-Saône

Trains *8 – 10 trains daily from* **Beaune** *(20 mins);* **Dijon** *(45 mins);* **Lyon** *(2 hours);* *3 – 5 from* **Chagny** *(15 mins).*

A short distance away from Beaune lies Chalons-sur-Saône, an important town ever since Julius Caesar's conquest of Gaul. Despite being an industrial town, Chalon-sur-Saône has retained its old centre, most notably some ancient half-timbered houses in Place St-Vincent and Rue St-Vincent. Situated on 2 islands, Roman Cabillonum was an important junction between Boulogne, Trier and Strasbourg. The central square is the Place de l'Obélisque beyond which lies a circular market, with an elegant 18th-century Neptune Fountain and the Place de l'Hôtel de Ville.

What to see

Musée Denon

On the north of the Place de l'Hôtel de Ville is the Musée Denon, named after Vivant Denon, the French archaeologist and diplomat. Amongst the eclectic collections is a Merovingian sarcophagus, Gallo-Roman bronze figurines, a splendid bronze helmet and a 1st century sculpture of a gladiator and lion. The museum has paintings as well, including works by Géricault and Philippe de Champaigne. (Open Wed–Mon 9.30 am–noon and 2 – 5.30 pm.)

Musée Niepce

The Rue du Port Villiers leads to the Musée Niepce, the museum founded around the collections of Joseph Niepce, a native of the city. Housed in the 18th-century Hôtel des Messageries on the banks of the Saône, the museum is dedicated to the experiments of the French pioneer of photography who was experimenting with photography at the time the Battle of Waterloo. The museum contains all his early photographic apparatus and examples of his work. (Open Wed–Mon 10 am–6 pm.)

Nearby is the Pont St-Laurent which joins the 2 river islands to Chalon. On the first island over the Pont St-Laurent, with its obelisks, is the **Tour du Doyenne**, a

15th-century tower which was moved here from its original site near the cathedral in 1928. Adjacent to it is a Hospital which was founded in the 16th century.

Roseraie St-Nicolas

Beyond the second island a left turn takes you into Rue Julien-Lenouveu where the spectacular rose trail begins. A path winds for 5 kilometres through the Roseraie St-Nicolas, one of the largest rose displays anywhere in the world where thousands of rose trees blossom in a spectacular kaleidoscope of colour from June to September on huge lawns shaded by conifers and apple trees. (Open June-early October.)

Cathédrale St-Vincent

The former cathedral is not a distinguished building, having a 19th-century mock-Gothic western façade, but it has a 13th-century Burgundian-style choir and apse and an attractive Gothic cloister.

Practicalities in Chalon-sur-Saône

Tourist Office Place Chabas on blvd de la République (Tel. 85 48 39 97). (Open Mon–Sat 9 am–12.30 and 1.30–7 pm).
Railway Station Ave Victor Hugo; (Information: Tel. 85 93 50 50; Reservations: Tel. 80 43 52 56). For town centre Ave J. Jaurès leads directly down to square Chabas & tourist office.
Buses Bus station opposite railway station (Tel. 85 48 79 04).
Markets Wed, Fri and Sun.
Festivals *Mardi Gras Carnival*: Shrove Tuesday; 8 days of parades, music and festivities. *Foires Sauvagines* (pelt and fur fairs): end Febr and late June; *National Festival of Street Artists*: July; *Fair*: October.
Hotels *Hôtel Gloriette*, 27 rue Gloriette (Tel. 85 48 23 35). Good, clean, simple rooms.

☆☆☆ *St-Régis*, 22 blvd République (Tel. 85 48 07 28). A traditional family-run and comfortable town hotel. Good restaurant attached.
☆☆☆ *St-Georges*, 32 ave J. Jaurès (Tel. 85 48 27 05). Probably the best hotel in town, with excellent restaurant.
Restaurants ☆ *La Réale*, 8 Place Général de Gaulle (Tel. 85 48 07 21). Delicious Burgundian cuisine.
☆ *Huchette*, 33 rue Lyon (Tel. 85 48 37 25). Good food and wide range of menus, all of which are good value.
☆☆ *Bourgogne*, 28 rue Strasbourg (Tel. 85 48 89 18), 17th century house with converted cellar; good local and regional dishes, excellent value.

Dijon

Trains *14 trains daily from* **Beaune** *(30 mins);* **Chalon-sur-Saône** *(1 hour); every hour from* **Lyon** *(2 hours); 6 stopping trains from* **Paris** *(3 hours); 9 direct* TGVs *from* **Paris** *Gare de Lyon (1 hour 40 mins).*

For a provincial city, Dijon seems to have everything in its favour – graceful and elegant buildings, a thriving cultural and political life, superb restaurants and cafés in which to loiter and access to some of the most beautiful countryside in France.

It is also prosperous, its fortunes having stemmed from the not inconsiderable wine trade of Burgundy, of which it is the centre. Its other specialities – mustard, gingerbread and cassis, a blackcurrant liqueur – may not appear to amount to much but they have formed the basis of many a local fortune.

The history, culture and magnificence of Dijon are all closely tied to its role as the capital of the Duchy of Burgundy since the 11th century. The town was founded by Aurelian in 273 and developed quickly into a powerful duchy in the 12th century. It was under Philip the Bold, John the Fearless and Philip the Good however that the Burgundian duchy reached the height of its power and magnificence in the late 14th and 15th centuries. But the death of Charles the Bold in 1476 at the Battle of Nancy left the Valois dukes without a successor, a weakness that Louis XI of France was quick to exploit. Seizing the province, he established a *parlement* sympathetic to his cause at Dijon and set about fortifying the city. A combined force of 30,000 Swiss, Germans and Francs-Comtois failed to take the city in 1513 but it opened its gates to Henri IV in 1595. The 17th and 18th centuries saw a time of ever-increasing prosperity and the foundation of the Academy of Dijon in 1740 and the construction of numerous town houses by bourgeois merchants who benefitted from the peace and the intelligent government of the princes of Condé.

What to see

Palais des Ducs

At the very heart of the city lies the Palace of the Dukes of Burgundy, its imposing but slightly monotonous classical façade concealing the remnants of the castle built by Philip the Bold in 1366. Its main entrance, set back behind a big courtyard, faces the broad semi-circular Place de la Libération, enclosed by arcades surmounted by balustrades, built in 1686 on the designs of Martin de Noinville. The wings enclosing the main courtyard were designed by Hardouin-Mansart long after Burgundy had lost its independence although the west wing was not finished until the Revolution. On the southern side of the Cour de Flore is the grand staircase built by Gabriel in 1736 which ascends to the Salle des Etats, a huge room decorated with panels of stone carving set within Doric pilasters.

Musée des Beaux-Arts

The Palace contains the Musée des Beaux-Arts which must rank as one of the finest provincial museums and art galleries in France. Apart from a number of Old Masters and Rhenish primitives, the museum also houses the tombs of 2 of the greatest Dukes of Burgundy – Philip the Bold and John the Fearless.

On the ground floor of the Palace is the great vaulted kitchen, a vast room with massive chimneys, and above it the Salle des Gardes, a richly panelled hall ornamented with tapestries and faced by a minstrel's gallery, where feasts were held. Here lies the painted effigy of Philip the Bold, one of the finest examples of Burgundian Gothic sculpture which was brought to the Palace from the Abbey of Champmol after being damaged during the Revolution. The tomb of John the Fearless and his wife Margeret of Bavaria is of a slightly later date. It was commissioned in 1470 by Juan de la Huerta and completed 30 years later by Antoine de Moiturier. Both figures lie outstretched, their feet touching the backs of 2 reclining lions, hands joined in prayer, while angels hold coats-of-arms behind their heads. Beneath them stand a line of hooded mourners. Philip the Bold's tomb is similar in style but simpler and more effective in execution. (Open Wed–Sat and Mon 10 am–6 pm; Sun 10 am–12.30 and 2–6 pm; free on Sunday.)

Maison Milsand

Almost more impressive than the Palace of the Dukes of Burgundy are the town houses of the bourgeoisie. One of the very finest, which reveals the remarkable variety of surface effects and high relief sculpture achieved by provincial architects at this period, is the Maison Milsand. This house, designed by Hugues Sambin between 1515 and 1520, shows the way in which free rein was given to fanciful sculpture even on the constricted façade of a town house. The Musée des Beaux-Arts has one room devoted to Sambin's work, with examples of his elaborate woodcarving, doorways and furniture. Sambin's work is often characterised by the carving of a face wearing a loose neckscarf below the chin or what he referred to as a Burgundy cabbage, although there is no such thing and it resembles no known vegetable.

Many of the wealthy merchants' town houses are built on a similiar plan with a tall archway, closed by elaborately carved doors, which leads from the street to an inner courtyard. The main apartments of the house lie on the far side of the courtyard, while those next to the street were occupied by servants and porters and the sides were devoted to coach-houses and stables.

Hôtel Lantin

One such mansion is the 17th-century Hôtel Lantin, at 4 rue des Bons-Enfants, which now houses the **Musée Magnin**. Decorated and furnished with contemporary furniture and effects, it presents an interior as it would have appeared in the 17th century. Apart from beautiful contemporary furnishings it has paintings by Tiepolo, Vouet, Le Sueur and Poussin collected by Maurice Magnin. Open Sept–May, Tues–Sun 10 am–noon and 2–6 pm; June–Aug, 10 am–6 pm.)

A much earlier mansion, dating from the 15th century, is the **Hôtel Chambellan** at 34 rue des Forges. Galleries open onto the courtyard on the 1st and 2nd floor which are reached by a spiral staircase in a corner of the yard. Of the many 18th-century houses, the finest is the **Hôtel Bouhier** de Lantenay, which now houses the Préfecture.

Eglise Notre-Dame

Near the Palace is the unusual and beautiful church of Notre-Dame, its light but monumental western façade richly decorated with human and animal grotesques rarely found grouped as they are here in 3 broad friezes. One of the corner-turrets supports a Jaquemart clock with mechanical figures that come out to strike the hours and the quarters. It was built by Jacques Marques, a craftsman captured in 1383 by Philip the Bold at Courtrai, who was brought as prisoner to the city. The delicate nave is lit by fine 13th-century stained glass and contains a 12th-century Black Virgin which was once venerated as the Protectress of Dijon.

West of the Ducal Palace stands the **Church of St-Michel** with an ornate Renaissance façade which hides a Gothic nave. One of the western portals has sculptures arranged concentrically in the traditional Gothic fashion; the 2 others are divided into panels.

Cathédrale St-Bénigne

Dijon's cathedral, dedicated to St-Bénigne, lies due west of St-Michel and is a large, somewhat severe Gothic building, erected after 1280. Its multi-coloured roof of glazed tiles is characteristic of the region but the cathedral is of interest chiefly for its crypt which dates from the 6th century. An abbey once existed next to the cathedral, of which little remains except for a magnificent Dormitory with a fine vaulted ceiling. This is now occupied by the **Musée Archaeologique** which displays archaeological finds from the region, including Romanesque, Gothic and Renaissance sculptures, bronze Gallo-Roman statuettes, a gold Merovingian bracelet found in 1970 and other prehistoric items. The crypt contains stelae, bronze and wooden ex-votos found at the source of the Seine. One represents the goddess Sequana on a duck-billed boat; another is a model of a boat in bronze. The Seine – Roman Sequana – was probably worshipped until the 2nd or 3rd century AD. (Open Sept–May, Wed–Mon 9 am–noon and 2–6 pm.)

Practicalities in Dijon

Tourist Office Place Darcy (Tel. 80 43 42 12); accommodation service; currency exchange. Open daily 9 am–9 pm; 15th April–June and Sept–15th Nov 9 am–noon and 2–9 pm. Also branch office at 34 rue Forges (Tel. 80 30 35 39).

Railway Station Ave Maréchal Foch, (Info: Tel. 80 41 50 50; reservations: Tel. 80 43 52 56), for town centre from station, walk up Ave Maréchal Foch to Place Darcy and tourist office.

Buses Ave Mar. Foch next to station (Tel. 80 42 11 00). Buses follow the *route de vin* to Beaune via Nuits-St-George.

Markets Every morning; larger markets on Tues, Thurs and Fri mornings.

Festivals (flower and plant show): mid-March, every 3 years (1996, 1999): *Florissmo*; *Music Festival*: July; *Bell-ringing festival*: Aug; *Wine Festival and International Folkore Festival*: early Sept; *Flea Market*: Sept; *Gastronomic Fair*: 2 weeks, early Nov; *Paulée Wine Celebration and Dinner*: early Dec.

Post Office Place Grangier, close to Place Darcy. Open Mon–Fri 8 am–7 pm, Sat 8 am–noon.

Hôtels *Hôtel Confort*, 12 rue Jules Mercier (Tel. 80 30 37 47). Pleasant and in a quiet alley. *Hôtel Monge*, 20 rue Monge (Tel. 80 30 55 41). Clean rooms overlooking courtyard. *Hôtel Montchapet*, 26–8 rue Jacques Cellerier (Tel. 80 55 33 31). Quiet family-run hotel 10 mins from station.

☆ *Jacquemart*, 32 rue Verrerie (Tel. 80 73 39 74). In a beautiful street close to the Palais des Ducs. No restaurant.

☆☆ *Nord*, Place Darcy (Tel. 80 30 58 58). A beautiful and friendly family-run hotel; with superb restaurant Porte Guillaume serving delicious Burgundian dishes and excellent wine list.

☆☆☆ *Chapeau Rouge*, 5 rue Michelet (Tel. 80 30 28 10). Comfortable old hotel in excellent location.

☆☆☆ *La Cloche*, 14 Place Darcy (Tel. 80 30 12 32). Traditional old-style hotel, luxurious and

very smart; excellent cuisine.
Hostels *Auberge de Jeunesse* (HI), 1 blvd
Champollion (Tel. 80 71 32 12), 4km from
station on bus 5 from **Place Grangier**, direction
Epirey. *Foyer International d'Etudiants*, Ave
Maréchal-Leclerc, noisy but cheap student
hostel (Tel. 80 75 51 01).
Camping *Camping Municipal du Lac*, in superb
location beside lake 1km behind station, bus 12
to **Chartreux** (Tel. 80 43 54 72).
Restaurants ☆ *Petit Vatel*, 73 rue Auxonne
(Tel. 80 65 80 64). Excellent value for money

and delicious cooking.
☆☆ *Toison d'Or*, 18 rue Ste-Anne, near Place
Wilson (Tel. 80 30 73 52). Authentic
Burgundian dishes in magnificent 15th-century
Mayor's house which doubles up as the HQ
of the Company of Burgundian wine-lovers.
Delightful shady courtyard.
☆☆☆ *J. P. Billoux*, Hôtel la Cloche, 14 Place
Darcy (Tel. 80 30 11 00). Outstanding cuisine;
one of the best restaurants in Burgundy offering
lighter and refined versions of traditional
Burgundian dishes.

Excursions from Dijon

Les Laumes-Alésia, The Abbaye de
Fontenay and Ancy-le-Franc are accessible
by train from Dijon but they are only

very minor sites which are best avoided
unless you have plenty of time. Only a
few trains a day stop at either station.

Les Laumes-Alésia

Trains *3 – 4 trains daily from* **Dijon** *(25
mins).*

Les Laumes-Alésia is no more than a
village but it marks the site of the battle
of Alésia where Vercingetorix and his
Gauls were finally defeated by the
Romans in 52 BC. The site of the Gallic

oppidum on the slopes of Mont Auxois
reputed to have been the scene of the
siege and final defeat of Vercingetorix is
marked by a massive statue that was
erected in 1863. Vercingetorix was taken
in chains to Rome where he died six years
later.

Montbard and the Abbaye de Fontenay

Trains *3 – 4 trains daily from* **Les Laumes**
(10 mins) and **Dijon** *(35 mins).*

Montbard is of little interest, apart from
having been the birthplace of the great
naturalist Buffon, but 6 kilometres away
stands the enchanting **Abbaye de
Fontenay**, a Cistercian foundation
established in 1119 by Evrard, the Bishop
of Norwich. It is not easily reached except
on foot through delightful woods and
countryside along a Grand Randonnée
track, GR 213, from Montbard.
   The church is in a Transitional style
while the cloisters and beautiful chapter-
house are Romanesque. The abbey is in
private hands but open for rather cursory
tours. Set in a secluded valley, Fontenay
met the Cistercian requirement that it
should be far removed from the bustle
and distraction of town life. The monks
lived a life of almost complete seclusion
and independence. They not only had
their own farm, gardens and orchards but
also a forge, in which they used poor

quality local iron ore, a bakery and a
prison in which they could detain petty
criminals. At its height there were
probably as many as 300 monks in
residence but numbers had already
declined by the time of the religious wars.
During the Revolution the abbey was sold
by the State and it was converted into a
paper mill before being restored at the
beginning of the 20th century.
   On either side of the gatehouse are
hostels where pilgrims and visitors stayed
on arrival at the abbey. Beyond lies the
abbey church which was begun in 1139
and finished by 1147. The pure lines of
the broken arches, the bareness and
architectural simplicity of church and
cloister alike accord with St Bernard's
rejection of decoration and detail as a
distraction that interfered with prayer.
Château de Bussy-Rabutin A few
kilometres from Fontenay, and again a
little problematic to reach, is the superb
Château de Bussy-Rabutin. It was rebuilt
in 1649 by a cousin of Madame de

Sevigné, Roger, Count of Bussy-Rabutin who was banished from court for his scandalous but amusing *Histoire amoureuse des Gaules*. He softened his years of exile by commissioning portraits from Mignard, Juste and Le Brun, many of them of royal mistresses, including those of Madame de la Sablière and Madame de Maintenon. One allegorical painting even satirises the inconstancy of his own mistress, Madame de Monglat.

Ancy-le-Franc

Trains *3–4 trains daily from* **Montbard** *(20 mins);* **Les Laumes** *(30 mins); and* **Dijon** *(1 hour 10 mins).*

From Ancy-le-Franc *trains lead north to Sens, Fontainebleau and Paris. Five direct trains (TGVs) from* **Besaçon** *(2½ hours), another 6 requiring change at* **Dijon-Ville** *(3 hours) or* **Dôle-ville** *(4½ hours), 6 trains to* **Strasbourg** *(3 hours).*

Burgundy vies with the valley of the Loire in the splendour of its châteaux which are scattered through a superb landscape of forest, fields and vineyards. Some lie inaccessible at the heart of what were once extensive estates; others such as the Château of Ancy-le-Franc, the home of the Clermont-Tonnerre family, could not be more easily reached by train.

Ancy-le-Franc, begun in 1546, was designed by the Italian architect Sebastiano Serlio who had been called to France by Francis i in 1540 or 1541, just at the same time as Primaticcio returned from Rome, bringing with him Vignola. These 2 years are crucial in the history of French architecture for they mark the first time that French architects had become aware of the achievements of the High Renaissance in Italy. Editions of *Vitruvius* were becoming widely available in France at the same time, further influencing a move towards classicism.

After sending a copy of his book on architecture to Francis i, Serlio had dedicated the third book of his treatise on architecture to the French King and shortly afterwards Francis i summoned him to France and put him in charge of the building operations at Fontainebleau, although none of the buildings executed there at that time are directly attributable to him.

Serlio's treatise was unusual in that it was the first illustrated handbook that had been designed specifically for architects to use practically rather than being an academic treatise. Part of Serlio's success was due to his adaptability, a quality lacking in most Italian architects working abroad at the time, and the longer he spent in France the more French he became in his approach to architecture. Serlio only completed 2 buildings while in France, one of which has completely disappeared. Ancy-le-Franc is therefore of particular importance, reflecting an important influence at a critical period of change in French architecture.

When the designs for the Château of Ancy-le-Franc were drawn up in 1546 the building looked almost entirely Italianate with a rusticated ground floor and Doric pilasters on the first floor enclosing an alternating series of niches and windows. Changes took place under Serlio's direction however while the building was being constructed – a high roof with dormers replaced the original shallow one, the niches between the windows were abandoned for windows themselves and the number of bays in the court were reduced – all of which served to increase the feminine qualities of the building at the expense of its masculine ones, in effect becoming increasingly French and losing its initial resemblence to an Italian *castello*.

Although the château is of more

That Bussy-Rabutin was exiled from court at all reflects the extent to which royal susceptibilities had changed over 100 years, since the days of Francis I. The poems penned by Francis I's own sister, Marguerite de Navarre, could well be considered a great deal more scandalous but caused no offence to the king or his court.

historical significance for its architecture than its decoration, it does have a beautiful interior with fine panelling, frescoes in the Salle des Nudités and Chambre de Diane, superb decorated ceilings and contemporary Renaissance furniture. The Galerie de la Pharsale is decorated with frescoes attributed to Niccolo dell'Abbate illustrating the defeat of Pompey by Caesar at Pharsalus while the Chambre des Arts has a brilliant coffered ceiling, with oval paintings by Primaticcio and his pupils.

The plans and designs contained in Serlio's treatise on architecture were to have a wide and lasting influence on French architects, even though his design for Ancy-le-Franc was little imitated in France. The building was commissioned by Antoine III de Clermont-Tonnerre and his wife, Anne-Françoise de Poitiers, the sister of Diane de Poitiers, although he visited it only rarely.

Besançon

Trains 12 *trains daily from* **Dijon** *(1 hour); 8 from* **Lyon** *(2½ hours); 12 from* **Belfort** *(1 hour); 8 from* **Strasbourg** *(2¼ hours).*

Besancon isn't in Burgundy at all, but in neighbouring Franche-Comté of which it was once the capital, but it is more conveniently located on this itinerary. The old city, centred on an ancient fortress, is almost entirely surrounded by an ox-bow meander of the Doubs and thickly wooded hills. A Roman colony under Marcus Aurelius, Besançon enjoyed the status of a free Imperial city under Frederick Barbarossa. In the 17th century the town was taken by Louis XIV after a 27-day seige and the Parlement was transferred here from nearby Dôle. The town's fortunes began to grow when political refugees arriving from Switzerland in 1793 established a watch-making industry which went from strength to strength.

The **Grande Rue** cuts through the city from the Pont de Battant to the cathedral and is the principal axis of the city. Victor Hugo was born at 40 Grand Rue in 1802.

What to see

La Citadelle

Rising in the southern part of the city is the citadel built by Vauban in 1674 following the capture of the town by Louis XIV. Approached via the steep Grande Rue and Rue des Fusillés de la Résistance, the citadel is built on the site of the Roman settlement, guarding the isthmus of the loop within which the city stands. It rises 120 metres above the winding valley of the Doubs and incorporates 18-metre-thick walls designed to repel any possible attacks by the Swiss. Three rows of extended esplanades form impressive defences which made access to the summit of the hill practically impossible. From the sentry walk of the extensive ramparts, there are memorable views out over the old town's brown roofs and the surrounding hills. The Citadel now houses a number of museums including one devoted to the resistance, the **Musée de la Résistance et de la Déportation** (Tel. 81 83 37 14), another to natural history, (both open Wed–Mon 9 am–7 pm; Oct– March 9.30 am–6 pm.)

Porte Noire

Beneath the Citadel stands the Porte Noire, a 2nd-century Roman triumphal arch, believed to date from the Antonine period and covered with allegorical and military sculptures. Beside it is the ornate 18th-century **Cathédrale St-Jean** with its unusual circular marble altar and a masterpiece of Renaissance art, *La Vierge aux Saints* by Fra Bartolomeo. Just behind the church is the massive Horloge Astronomique made in 1860.

Musée des Beaux-Arts

In the Place de la Révolution, occupying the building of a former corn-market, the Musée des Beaux-Arts is a superb and extensive collection including works by Cranach, Rubens, Jordaens, Goya, Tintoretto, Constable Lawrence, Courbet, Ingres, Géricault, David, Daubigny, Bonnard and Renoir as well as tapestries, ceramics and watches. (Open Wed–Mon 9.30 am–noon and 2–5.30 pm.)

Palais Granville

A new museum, the **Musée du Temps**, opens in the magnificent Renaissance Palais Granville in 1995. Constructed for Nicholas Perrenot de Granvelle, Chancellor to Charles V, the Palais Granville is the most splendid, if sometimes severe building in Besançon. Another elegant building is the former **Palais des Intendants** (Administrator's Palace) which now houses the Préfecture. A princely 18th-century mansion, it has an impressive pilatstered façade surmounted by a pediment; the interior has a fine wrought-iron staircase.

Porte Rivotte

Not far from the cathedral is the military Porte Rivotte, a 16th-century gateway to the town flanked by 2 round towers, which was once part of the ramparts that surrounded the town. The projecting part bears the arms of Louis XIV who took the town in 1674.

Practicalities in Besançon

Tourist Office Place de l'Armée Française (Tel. 81 80 92 55); accommodation lists and service, currency exchange (in emergencies). Open Mon–Fri 9 am–noon and 1.30–7 pm, Sat 9 am–noon and 1.45–6 pm, rest of year Mon–Fri 9 am–noon and 1.30–6.30 pm; annex at Place du 8 Septembre.

Railway Station Ave de la Paix (Tel. 81 53 50 50). For town centre from station follow Rue de Belfort, turn right onto Ave Carnot, cross Place Flore, then turn right and walk down to Pont de la République and tourist office.

Buses Monts-Jura, 9 rue Proudhon (Tel. 81 81 20 67).

Hiking Information Club Alpin Français, 14 rue Luc Breton (Tel. 81 81 02 77).

Markets Place de la Révolution: Tues to Sat.

Festivals *Festival des Idées*: late June concerts, exhibitions, plays. June and July: *Jazz en Franche-Comté*: June and July, free jazz concerts; *Festival de Musique de Besançon*: 1st 2 week Sept, young orchestra conductors international competition.

Hotels Hôtel Florel, 6 rue de la Viotte (Tel. 81 80 41 08). Very close to station and good clean bright rooms.

☆*Hôtel Regina*, 91 Grande Rue (Tel. 81 81 50

22). On the central street, all with showers; comfortable and attractive.

☆☆*Paris*, 33 rue des Granges (Tel. 81 81 36 56). Good old-fashioned hotel; quiet and efficient, with delightful shady garden courtyard.

Restaurants *Du Levant*, 9 rue des Boucheries (Tel. 81 81 07 88). Crowded and animated, with good range of cheap menus.

☆*Le Poker d'As*, 14 rue du Clos St-Amour (Tel. 81 81 42 49). Superb little restaurant with outstanding local cuisine, especially fish.

☆☆*Mungo Park*, 11 rue Jean-Petit (Tel. 81 81 28 01). An exciting gastronomic experience in bright new converted warehouse on the River Doubs; delicious cuisine from leading female chef Jocelyne Lotz.

6 Corsica

The largest island in the Mediterranean after Sicily and Sardinia, Corsica is perhaps the loveliest of them all; its lower slopes are covered with the sweet-scented *maquis*, an almost impenetrable thicket of arbutus, cistus, myrtle, lentisk and heather, mingled with thyme, rosemary and honeysuckle. Higher up are forests of beech, oak and fir, and above them rise the irregular crests of the mountains, snow-capped until summer, the highest of which is Monte Cinto at 2,700 metres. Although only separated from Sardinia by the Strait of Bonifacio and 50 miles west of the Tuscan coast of Italy, Corsica is a world of its own, scrubby, wild, Mediterranean, standing in the same relationship to France as Jersey and Guernsey do to England. Its rough mountainsides fall steeply into a sea often cobalt blue, creating deep inlets and craggy peninsulas which are difficult to reach except on foot or by boat. The landscape is varied and the views across the island often stunning, especially in spring when the island is covered with blossom.

The route *Ajaccio – Corte – Calvi – Bastia*

That there is a railway network on the island of Corsica is little short of miraculous but one does exist and makes for a magnificent way of exploring this beautiful island, with its blend of Italian and Spanish influences. The railway network is extremely simple, consisting of only 3 lines which meet in the centre of the island at **Ponte-Leccia**. *The main line runs from* **Ajaccio**, *the capital, to Ponte-Leccia (3 hours; 4 daily) and then continues to* **Bastia** *on the north-eastern shores of the island (1 hour from Ponte-Leccia; 4 daily), while a side line runs north-west from Ponte Leccia to* **Calvi** *(3 hours, 3 daily). As it zig-zags across the mountains, passing through tunnels and over viaducts, the trains look out over a wild and craggy landscape of rock, gorse and dense forest. In summer the interior is extremely dry and hot, except at higher levels where the heat is tempered by cool breezes; in winter snow falls on the island's peaks. The best times to visit the island are between the end of April and the end of June and from early September to mid-October.*

History

Inhabited since Neolithic times, Corsica was colonised with difficulty by the Romans between 260 and 160 BC. Like the neighbouring island of Sardinia, Corsica long remained under Byzantine rule but in the 9th century it was abandoned before being claimed by the Pope who entrusted its government to Italian *marchesi* – the wardens of the marches. The first of these was Bonifacio, Count of Lucca, who is held to be the founder of the city which still bears his name. The donation of the island to the Archbishop of Pisa by the Pope initiated several centuries of intermittent fighting between Pisa and Genoa, the Genoese blockading the island at one point for a period of 6 years. Despairing of ever gaining any benefit from the island the Genoese sold their rights over Corsica to France in 1768. Needing some military success, following major setbacks in the War of the Austrian Succession and the Seven Years War, the French mounted a small expedition in 1768 to conquer the island in which the local leader, Pasquale Paoli, was defeated. The island was formally united to France on 15th August 1769, the very day of

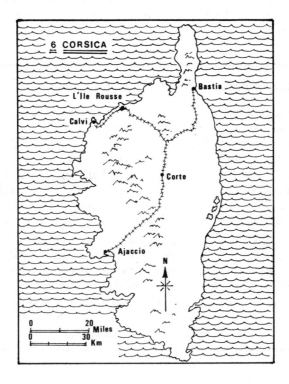

Napoleon's birth. At the Revolution Paoli was given the military governor-ship of the island but when summoned to appear before the Convention in Paris to explain the failure of his expedition to neighbouring Sardinia, he refused and offered the island to George III instead, a move that aroused the bitter hostility of the young Bonaparte. George III was duly declared King and from 1794 to 1796 the English were nominally masters of Corsica, but they were expelled without much trouble and since 1814 Corsica has been an undisputed possession of France. The gain to France was not great – a small population that spoke an Italian dialect and lived under a primitive clan system based on the solidarity of the family and the vendetta.

Ajaccio

Trains *4 trains daily from* **Corte** *(2½ hours)*; *2 from* **Calvi** *(5 hours), change at* **Ponte Leccia**; *4 from* **Bastia** *(4 hours).*

The capital of Corsica, famous as the birthplace of Napoleon Bonaparte, Ajaccio occupies a promontory in a magnificent bay on the western side of the island. Founded, according to legend, by Ajax, the present Citadel was largely built in the 16th century. Italianate in the pink, yellow and ochre wash of its town-houses which cluster round the old port, the old town is laid out on a rectangular plan around the 16th-century cathedral where Napoleon was baptised.

It was in a modest little house in Ajaccio that Napoleon was born in 1769 to a Corsican woman of humble origin, Letizia. The house still stands in place Letizia and is now a **museum** devoted to the Emperor's family with many everyday objects of the period. Napoleon's bedroom has a trap-door through which the future Emperor escaped from the Partisans of Paoli.

What to see

Musée Napoléonien
Napoleon's career is traced in the much larger Musée Napoléonien in the Hôtel de Ville which has a collection of portraits, coins and medals illustrating his achievements and rise to fame. Tombs of members of Napoleon's family lie in the **Chapelle Impériale**, part of the **Musée Fesch**, an art collection donated to the town by Napoleon's uncle who was the French ambassador to the Vatican until falling out with the Emperor over his humiliating treatment of the Pope.

The **cathedral** was built in the Venetian style in the 16th century by Giacomo della Porta; the interior is largely of white marble, notably the font at which Napoleon was baptized, the high altar brought from Lucca and the sumptuous chapel of Notre-Dame-de-la-Miséricorde. Behind the cathedral is the Place du Diamant, a large open space with a monument to Napoleon and his 4 brothers.

Interesting boat journeys can be made from the harbour to the **Iles Sanguinaires**, to Porto in the north past the fantastic ochre rocks of Piana, or to Tizzano in the south.

Practicalities in Ajaccio

Tourist Office Hôtel de Ville, Place Maréchal Foch (Tel. 95 21 66 70).

Railway Station Rue Jean-Jérôme Levie (Tel. 95 23 11 03).

Ferries SNCM Quai l'Herminier. 2 daily to French mainland, alternating between Marseille, Toulon and Nice (6–12 hours, night sailings) (Tel. 95 29 66 99 or 95 29 66 88).

Hôtels *Hôtel Colomba*, 8 ave de Paris (Tel. 95 21 12 66). Small, central hotel and pleasant rooms

Hôtel Kallysté, 51 cours Napoléon (Tel: 95 51 34 45). Comfortable, clean and welcoming.

☆ ☆*Hôtel San Carlu*, 8 blvd Casanova (Tel. 95 21 13 84). Pleasant little hotel in the heart of the old town, close to the Maison Bonaparte.

☆☆☆ *Hôtel Costa*, 2 blvd Colomba (Tel. 95 21 43 02). For sheer comfort, off Cours Grandval.

Corte

Inland from Ajaccio, at an important crossroads on the island, stands the town of Corte, the largest inland town and the home of Corsica's only university. It was the capital of the island during Paoli's provisional government (1762–66). Its 15th-century Citadel, built by Vincentello d'Istrai, an Aragonese viceroy, is set above the little town in an extraordinarily lop-sided position on a craggy rock. It is approached by a steep, cobbled street from Place Gaffori, a square named after the Corsican general whose house was besieged in vain by the Genoese in 1750.

The only buildings of historic interest in Corte are in the upper town. The **Maison Garrori**, opposite the church, was the scene of the heroic stand against the Geneose made in 1750 by Madame Gaffori, who held the house until relieved by her husband. The women of Corte, renowned for their beauty, are descendants of those who refused to marry Genoese invaders during the period of Genoese domination. The town is still a base of the French Foreign Legion who exercise in the wild and rocky forested hills that stretch away on all sides.

Practicalities in Corte

Tourist office Commission Municipal du Tourisme (Tel. 95 64 24 20); at entrance to citadel. To reach centre, turn right, cross bridge and walk up the hill along ave. Jean Nicoli.

Railway station At junction of ave. Jean Nicoli and N193 (Tel. 95 46 00 97). 4 trains daily to Bastia (2 hours), 2 to Calvi (2½ hours, change at Ponte Leccia) 4 to Ajaccio (2½ hours).

Buses *EuroCorse* (Tel. 95 21 06 30). No office. 2 buses daily to Bastia (1 hr 15 mins), 1 to Calvi (2 hr) and 2 to Ajaccio (1 hr 45 mins).

Currency Exchange Numerous banks on Cours Paoli, the main street, and at Post Office: 3 ave. du Baron Mariani.

Hotels *Hôtel Résidence Porette*, 6 ave. du 9 Septembre (Tel 95 61 01 21). Simple, functional and rather basic but clean and cheap.

☆☆ *Hôtel de la Poste*, 2 place du Padoue (Tel 95 46 02 61). Off Cours Paoli, the principal street. Pleasant old-fashioned rooms in attractive old family hotel.

Camping *U Sognu* (Tel. 95 46 09 07). 15 minute walk from town down av. Xavier Luciani, then right down ave. du Président Perucci. Open Mar – Oct.

Restaurant *Le Bips*, 14 Cours Paoli (Tel. 95 46 06 26). Lively and animated café on Corte's principal street with good cheap menus.

Calvi

Trains *3 from* **Ajaccio** *(5 hours); 3 from* **Bastia** *(3 hours); 3 from* **Corte**, *changing at Ponte Leccia (3 hours); 5 from* **Ile Rousse** *(50 mins).*

Calvi, the chief of the Genoese strongholds on the island, was founded in 1268 and never taken by assault, despite the united efforts of the French and Turks in 1553, until the bombardment by the English in 1794 when Nelson lost his right eye. It's a pretty little town on the north-western coast of the island and the capital of the hilly and fertile Balagne area. Its powerful fortress, built by the Genoese in the 16th century, looks down onto the port which was first settled by the Phocaeans 2 centuries before the Romans arrived on the island. High above the castle, mountains rise up towards the centre of the island; down below white-washed houses and matt orange roofs create a kaleidoscope of colour against a bright blue sea.

At the top of the citadel is Calvi's church, **St-Jean-Baptiste**, dating from the 16th century when it was elevated to the status of cathedral. It houses an ancient Virgin of the Rosary of Spanish origin which is dressed in different costumes according to the feast day. Much of the style of both church architecture and religious worship on the island is closer to Spain and Italy in spirit than it is to France.

Superb boat journeys around the spectacular rocky coastline, past the isolated village of **Girolata**, can be made from Quai Landry in the harbour, while beaches of white sand stretch for miles around Calvi. Near to Calvi is the **Ile Rousse**, built by Pasquale Paoli, the ruler of Corsica in the early 1760s. Between the delightful enclave on Ile Rousse and Calvi are the most beautiful beaches on Corsica, all accessible by the delightful little train which runs several times daily along the coastline from Calvi.

Practicalities in Calvi

Tourist Office Port de Plaisance (Tel. 95 65 08 09).
Hotels ☆☆*Hôtel Caravelle*, on the beach just south of town (Tel. 95 65 00 03). *Hôtel Belvédère*, ave de l'Uruguay (Tel 95 65 01 25). Excellent location below Citadel; clean, attractive rooms.
Hôtel Laeticia, 5 rue Joffre, off Blvd Wilson (Tel. 95 65 05 55).
Hostels *BVJ Corsotel*, ave de la République; youth hostel (Tel. 95 65 14 15).

Bastia

Trains *2 from* **Calvi** *(3½ hours), 4 from* **Corte** *(2 hours), 4 from* **Ajaccio** *(4 hours).*

Only the heart of Bastia, round the harbour and the church of St-Jean-Baptiste, retains its old atmosphere. Fishing vessels still enter the harbour, surrounded by

17th- and 18th-century houses, many of which were restored in the 1950s. The old port area, packed with bars and small restaurants, is known as the *Terra Vecchia* while the upper town, above the Place du Donjon, is called the *Terra Nova*. This 'new land' is in fact no newer than the 15th century at which date the Genoese established the fort and constructed the **cathedral**, now church, of **Sainte-Marie**. It contains an 18th century statue of the Assumption of the Virgin which was once the object of great veneration. The work of a Sienese silversmith in the 18th century, it is still carried round the town in a procession every 15th August. Another treasured object of veneration is the black wooden figure of the **Christ des Miracles** in the sumptuous **Chapelle Ste-Croix** decorated in Louis XIV style. The little statue was reputedly found by fishermen floating at sea in 1428.

Rebuilt in 1380 by the Genoese governor of Corsica, Leonardo Lomellino, Bastia was one of the first towns to welcome union with France but because of their strong Catholic ties, they rebelled against the anti-clericalism of the Revolution.

The main thoroughfare of Bastia is the **Traverse**, the local name for the Boulevards Paoli and du Palais. The Place St-Nicolas, on the seafront, commands a fine view of Elba flanked by the islets of Monte Cristo and Capraia. Around the narrow little **Vieux Port** is the old town, a network of alleys connected by dark vaulted passageways, overlooked by the classical façade of St-Jean-Baptiste.

Practicalities in Bastia

Tourist Office Place St-Nicolas (Tel. 95 31 00 89).

Railway Station Just off Ave Maréchal Sebastiani, at top of Rue G. Péri (Tel. 95 32 60 06); luggage storage.

Hotels *Hôtel de l'Univers*, 3 ave Maréchal Sebastiani, a stone's-throw from the station (Tel. 95 31 03 38). Pleasant rooms, clean and central.

☆*Central Hôtel*, 3 rue Miot, central location between Blvd Paoli and Rue Campinchi (Tel. 95 31 03 08).

☆☆*Hôtel Bonaparte*, 45 blvd Gén. Graziani, a little beyond the tourist office on Place St-Nicolas (Tel. 95 34 07 10).

☆☆*Hôtel Posta Vecchia*, Rue Posta Vecchia, close to the quay in the Terra Vecchia (Tel. 95 32 32 38).

7 Languedoc-Roussillon

The ancient province of **Languedoc** corresponds to the vast geographical region that was once ruled over by the powerful counts of Toulouse. It stretches across a wide sweep of southern France, from Toulouse in the west to the frontiers of Provence in the east. Literally speaking, it is the land of the *langue d'oc* (where 'yes' was pronounced as *oc* in the Middle Ages), as opposed to the *langue d'oil* of northern France (where 'yes' was pronounced as *oil* or *oui*.) The later term, Occitania, probably derives from Aquitania – (land of water – the Roman name for the province they conquered between the Garonne and the Pyrenees.

Languedoc became the Roman province of Narbonensis Prima in 381, was overrun by the Moors in 714 and ruled by the powerful counts of Toulouse from the 10th century. In the Middle Ages, under Raymond v, the counts of Toulouse extended their domains eastwards as far as the Rhône but the alliance of Raymond VI with the Albigensian heretics led to a mighty coalition of forces from the north against them and their allies. United in a ferocious crusade against the south, the onslaught by the nobles of northern France led to the crushing defeat of the counts of Toulouse and their ally, the Count of Foix. King Philippe Auguste secured the blessing of the church and Pope Innocent III for this merciless crusade against the Albigensian or Cathar heretics, which was led by Simon de Montfort. Shortly afterwards the province passed to the French crown but north – south tensions came to the surface again during the Religious Wars of the 16th century, the South largely fighting for reform against the official religion of the court. The Edict of Nantes created peace but religious fighting broke out again with the persecution of the Camisards in 1702.

After the crushing of the south in the 13th century, the *langue d'oc* fell gradually into decline, reinforced by the Edict of Villiers-Cotterets in 1539 which imposed the language of the north on the south. Nevertheless, many of the local *patois* spoken by the peasants of the south today are very strongly linked to the *langue d'oc* of medieval southern France.

Roussillon, so named from the red colour of its earth, is the southern-most province of France and corresponds roughly with the département of the Pyrénées-Orientales. In the 13th century it belonged to the House of Aragon before becoming part of the kingdom of Majorca and being occupied briefly by Louis XI in the 15th century. Returned to Spain by Charles VIII, it remained in Spanish hands until invaded and seized by Louis XIII in the 17th century. More Spanish in temperament than French, the Catalans have adapted to the political realities of union with France while keeping alive their distinct culture and language.

Roussillon has a wide variety of landscape, ranging from the high mountains of the eastern Pyrenees to the superb coastline of the Côte Vermeille, the rugged inland hills of the Corbières and the slopes of the Côtes du Roussillon from where come deep full-bodied wines, their taste and aroma varying according to whether they come from vines grown on granitic or schist soils.

Roussillon benefits from its proximity to the Mediterranean, from where comes excellent seafood, while Languedoc is famous for its *cassoulet*, a thick stew of white beans, sausage, pork, and goose, cooked very gently for a long time. *Cargolade*, snails stuffed with bacon, is also a popular dish in Roussillon, one of many with affinities to Spanish *tapas* south of the border. Sweet white wines include Lunel, Mireval and St-Jean de Minervois.

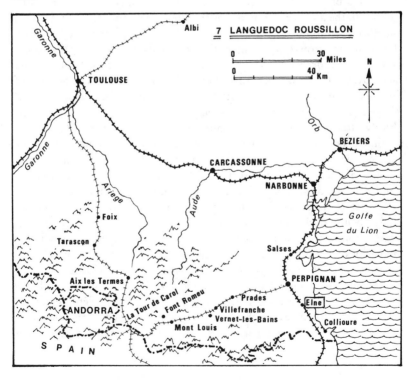

The route *Toulouse – Carcassonne – Narbonne – Salses – Perpignan – Collioure – Prades – Molitg-les Bains – Villefranche-de-Conflent – Mont Louis – Font Romeu – La Tour-de-Carol - Ax-les-Thermes – Foix*

This magnificent circuit takes in some of the greatest delights of the Midi and the eastern Pyrenees, starting at the great capital of the south, **Toulouse.** *A beautiful old city, built for almost a millennia of red brick it has, in the basilica of St-Sernin, the finest Romanesque building in the south of France. With its magnificent museums and Renaissance houses, Toulouse is surpassed in interest amongst the cities of France only by Paris itself.*

Some distance west of Toulouse, above the River Aude, stands one of Europe's most impressive medieval cities – **Carcassonne,** *entirely enclosed by rings of towers and ramparts, and surrounded by the spectacular landscape of the eastern Pyrenees in whose valleys are to be found some of France's most beautiful Romanesque churches and monasteries.*

Narbonne, *once an important Roman seaport on the Mediterranean is overshadowed by the 3 grim towers of the Archbishop's Palace. South of it lies the mighty castle of* **Salses,** *the most perfectly preserved example of medieval Spanish military architecture outside of Spain. A little distance south is* **Perpignan,** *the capital of Roussillon, an enchanting town known for its relaxed southern way of life and the beauty of its women. In the early 20th century Matisse, Derain, Dufy, Dali and Picasso settled in the exquisite fishing village of* **Collioure** *to capture on canvas the brilliant colours of the port, with the azure sea and gaily painted fishing smacks drawn up on the beach. Inland lies Prades, with the nearby Romanesque abbey of St-Michel-de-Cuxa and further up the enchanting valley of the Têt,* **Villefranche-de-Conflent,** *its fort guarding the narrow valley. At* **Mont Louis,** *fortified by Vauban, the Têt swerves north-west but the railway line pushes upwards into the Cerdagne, a high mountain valley very unlike other Pyrenean regions. The Spanish influence is strong and here, surrounded with alpine meadows, forests, lakes and peaks, is* **Font Romeu,** *a resort ideally sited for trekking in summer and skiing in winter. At* **La Tour des Carols** *the Spanish border is reached at the highest railway station in France. Descending through the Pyrenees the spa of* **Ax-les-Thermes**

is reached, beyond which lies **Foix**, *in the Ariège, dominated by its powerful castle. Slipping out of the Pyrenees the broad valley of the Garonne is then followed before arriving at* **Toulouse**, *from where there are fast and frequent connections to Paris.* (**Approximately 5 – 8 days.**)

The spread of the Albigensian heresy and the suppression of the Cathars in the 13th century deeply affected the history of the Languedoc, literally the area of the Oc language. The inspiration of the Cathar movement originated from the beliefs of a Bulgarian Christian sect whose fundamental principle was the rigid separation of Good and Evil. The Cathars central belief was that against the spiritual world ruled over by God stood the material world governed by Satan. Men and women, being material beings themselves, were therefore inextricably linked with Evil by the mere fact of existence. Haunted by the inescapability of Evil, they passionately sought to free themselves of earthly connections to attain a divine purity. Interpreting biblical texts in their own way led them to deny the divinity of Christ even though he represented for them the ultimate model of perfection.

The Cathars made an important distinction between the 'Perfected' and the 'Believers'. The 'Perfected' were expected to lead an austere life, faithful to the principles of poverty, chastity, patience and humility. They were supposed to have already found the light of God and were venerated and ministered to by the 'Believers'.

The Cathars also adopted their own form of Communion, abandonned the traditional sacraments of baptism and marriage and tended to be liberal and unorthodox in their customs and attitudes to such matters as trade and money.

The Cathar church had been established in 1167 by Nicetas, Bishop of Constantinople and spread rapidly through Languedoc. Initially it was embraced by townspeople but then spread to the countryside. Many of the most powerful nobles such as Roger Trencavel, Viscount of Béziers and Carcassonne and Raymond Roger, Count of Foix, were attracted to the Cathar church.

It was the assassination of the Pope's envoy, Pierre de Castelnau, that led the Papacy to launch a crusade against the Albigensian heretics. The crusade, from 1209 to 1218, was led by nobles from the north of France, the most notable being Simon de Montfort, whose son was to become Earl of Leicester. The crusade was marked by extreme cruelty, little quarter being given to the Cathars, who increasingly retreated to their inaccesible mountain fortresses – Queribus, Montsegur, Peyrepertuse. In order to suppress the heresy, the Dominicans moved to Toulouse in 1216, only one year after St Dominic's foundation of the order that bears his name.

Toulouse

Trains *6 – 8 daily from* **Paris** *Austerlitz via Brive (6½ – 7 hours); 4 – 6* TGVS *daily from* **Paris** *Montparnasse with change at Bordeaux (5 hours); 10 – 12 from* **Bordeaux** *(2¼ – 2¾ hours); 6 from* **Lyon** *(6 hours); 8 – 10 from* **Nice** *(6½ hours); 11 from* **Marseille** *(4½ hours); 9 – 11 from* **Nîmes** *(2 hours 40 mins).*

Toulouse, the natural capital of the south of France, straddles the route between Bordeaux and the Mediterranean and retains one outstanding example of its wealth and eminence in the Middle Ages in the magnificent basilica of St-Sernin, the largest and most perfect Romanesque building in France.

Easily accesible from Paris and linked directly to Bordeaux, the Mediteranean coast and Provence, Toulouse is the ideal place to begin a rail journey of the south of France. The centre of the city is a 10-minute walk from the station down Allées Jean Jaurès.

Not only does Toulouse have a fascinating history, reflected in its buildings and museums, but it is still a vibrant and dynamic city, very much in the forefront of technological development and contemporary art and culture.

By the 5th century Toulouse was already the capital city of the Visigoths and under Raymond IV the Kingdom of Toulouse reached as far east as Savoy. Raymond V successfully defended Toulouse from the predatory designs of Henry II of England who had acquired Aquitaine by his marriage to Eleanor but the growing anarchy in the east of his domains encouraged the spread of the Albigensian heresy.

During the Albigensean crusade Simon de Montfort besieged the city in 1212 and was killed in another attempt 6 years later. By the Treaty of Paris in 1229 Raymond VII abandoned attempts to maintain the independence of his 'county' from the Kingdom of France. He married his daughter to the brother of the French King, Louis IX, the treaty specifying that on her death, the county would become the royal province of Languedoc.

What to see

Eglise des Jacobins

The church that the Dominicans built in 1216 to help combat the Albigensian heresy, the Eglise des Jacobins, is one of the most remarkable buildings in Toulouse and a masterpiece of Gothic architecture in the south of France. This enormous building, the mother-church of the Dominican order, is a gigantic construction of thin red brick, extremely severe and austere. By the time it was finished in 1340 the Albigensian heresy had been largely eradicated, the Inquisition having been suspended some 60 years earlier. The interior, bare of all decoration, is impressive and unusual for its division by a single row of 7 columns into 2 naves of equal dimensions. The crypt of the church contains the remains of one of the church's greatest philosophers and theologians, St Thomas Aquinas. The calm, adjacent cloisters are used in summer for piano recitals. (Church open Mon–Sat 10 am–noon and 2–6 pm, Sun 2.30–6 pm.)

Basilique de Saint-Sernin

The vast basilica of St-Sernin is the largest Romanesque building in France, built to receive the tens of thousands of pilgrims who once made their way from northern France to the shrine of St James at Santiago da Compostella in north-west Spain. The best view of the exterior is from behind the choir, where the semi-circle of apsidal chapels leads the eye up to the beautiful octagonal tower. It is built largely of red brick, clay being the most easily available local building material. The basilica has hardly been altered architecturally since 1271 and even today it impresses the visitor by its strength, simplicity of design and majestic beauty. The interior is extremely spacious but dark and severe. As with most pilgrimage churches, there is an ambulatory which allowed pilgrims to circulate round the altar during mass, and a large number of side chapels, particularly in the apse. The ambulatory and crypt contain the tomb of St-Sernin and 7 exquisite marble bas-reliefs of Christ in Majesty and the Evangelists surrounded by angels and apostles. (Open Mon–Sat 8–11.45 am and 2–5.45 pm, Sun 2–5.45 pm; crypt open daily 10–11.30 am and 2.30–5.30 pm.)

Musée St-Raymond

Just outside St-Sernin, on the southern side of the basilica, is the **Porte Miègeville** with a finely carved tympanum representing the Ascension. In the adjacent square is an arresting 16th-century red brick building, the Musée St-Raymond which houses the finest archaeological museum in southern France. Its outstanding collections include a vast number of archaeological finds, including Romanesque sculpture, bronze figures, ancient and medieval coins, lamps, vases and jewellery. One of the highlights of the collections is the finest collection of Imperial Roman portraits outside Italy, with busts of Caesar, Augustus and Tiberius. (Open Wed–Mon 10 am–6 pm; off-season Wed–Mon 10 am–5 pm.)

Notre-Dame-du-Taur

Rue du Taur leads from the museum to the 14th-century church of Notre-Dame-du-Taur. It replaces an earlier church built on the spot where St-Sernin was martyred in 257 after being tied to a wild bull which trampled him to death. It has an impressive façade or *cloche mur*, with 6 innovative angular arches made possible by the use of brick as a building material.

The Capitôle

Beyond Notre-Dame-du-Taur lies the main square dominated by the Hôtel de Ville, the **Capitôle**, an 18th-century building of brick and white stone, with the coats of arms of the Capitouls, the former rulers of Toulouse, in the central coutyard. Stendhal thought it 'the ugliest building you could imagine'. Within this very interior courtyard, part of an earlier Renaissance palace, the Duc de Montmorency, Governor of the Languedoc, was executed in 1632 for having led the rebellion against Louis XIII's omnipotent Minister of State, Cardinal Richelieu. (Open periodically when not in use for official functions.) On the Grand Escalier hangs a painting of the *Jeux Floraux*, the Floral Games organised by the Compagnie du Gai-Savoir – a literary society founded in 1324 to promote the local language, Langue d'Oc.

Renaissance Houses

The other highlights of the city are the fine redbrick *hôtels* or Renaissance houses to be found scattered in the Rue des Changes, Rue Malcousinat and Rue de la Bourse between the Place du Capitole and Church of Notre-Dame-de-la-Daurade on the banks of the Garonne. The **Hôtel de Bernuy**, on Rue Gambetta, was built in the 16th-century by Jean de Bernuy, a merchant whose wealth derived from the production and export of pastel, a blue dye used in the dying of cloth. The use of stone, as opposed to brick, was an extremely costly measure, no building stone being available in the vicinity of the city.

Hôtel d'Assezat

The Hôtel D'Assezat, just off the Rue de Metz, is the finest Renaissance house in the city, the home of a wealthy merchant, and the best work of the leading Toulousain architect of the day, Nicolas Bachelier. The façade incorporates superimposed classical orders which frame arcades and rectangular windows above ornately carved doorways. A superb view over the city is to be had from the top of the tower. The building now houses the ancient literary society, l'Académie des Jeux Floraux. (Open daily 10 am–noon and 2–6 pm.) Almost opposite the Hôtel are the green and shady precincts of the **Jardin Royal** and **Jardin des Plantes**.

Cathédrale St-Etienne

The city's cathedral, St-Etienne, is something of a curiosity for it was never finished and its choir and Romanesque nave are wholly out of alignment, for the intention was to knock the latter down and build a finer one to replace it. Nevertheless the choir represents the first example of Gothic building in the south of France and the austerity of the interior is softened by 16th-century tapestries depicting the life of St-Etienne.

Musée des Augustins

The Musée des Augustins at 21 rue de Metz is partly contained within the remains of an Augustinian priory and has important collections of Romanesque and later medieval sculpture and early Christian sarcophagi. (Open Thurs–Mon 10 am–6 pm, Wed 10 am–10 pm; Oct–May, Thurs–Mon 10 am–5 pm, Wed 10 am–9 pm.) Today Toulouse is one of the most dynamic and exciting towns of France, thriving from its position at the centre of the French aeronautical industry and the high technology firms attracted to the town by its excellent infrastructure, ideal geographical location and business incentives. Very much of part of the Midi, Toulouse has a definite 'southern' feel, accentuated by its large student population, animated bars and cafes, and long hot summers.

Practicalities in Toulouse

Tourist Office Donjon du Capitôle, Rue Lafayette (Tel. 61 23 32 00); accommodation service; walking tours; currency exchange; bus excursions to nearby sights. Open 9 am–7 pm daily, Sat–Sun and holidays 11 am–1 pm and 2–4.30 pm May–Sept; Oct–April open Mon–Sat 9 am–6 pm.
Railway Station *Toulouse-Matabiau* on blvd Pierre Sémard; open 24 hours. (Info: Tel. 61 62 50 50; Reservations: Tel. 61 62 85 44). For town centre from station, cross canal in front of station, head down Rue de Bayard, cross Blvd de Strasbourg and continue down rue de Remusat.
Buses 68 blvd Pierre Sémard (Tel. 61 48 71 84), next to station; buses to Paris, Bordeaux, Lyon, Marseille and other local destinations.
Markets Tues–Sun mornings in Place des Carmes and Blvd Victor Hugo. Also on blvd de Strasbourg: daily; Place du Capitôle: Wed and Sat; Place de Basilique St-Sernin holds a *marché aux puces* (flea market) on Sun mornings.
Festivals *Musique d'Eté*: July–September, classical, jazz and ballet outdoors, in churches and concert halls. Tickets from tourist office; *Fête de la Musique*: 21st June; live music throughout the city.

Hotels Best cheap accommodation beyond Place Wilson in *centre ville*.
☆ *Hôtel Taur*, 2 rue du Taur (Tel. 62 21 17 54). Cheap and basic but right in the heart of the city, just off the main square.
☆ *Nouvel Hôtel*, 13 rue du Taur, off Place du Capitôle (Tel. 61 21 13 93). Central location & pleasant rooms.
☆ *Hôtel du Grand Balcon*, 8 rue Romiquières, on corner of Place du Capitôle (Tel. 61 21 48 08). In the heart of old Toulouse.
☆☆ *Hôtel St-Sernin*, Place St-Sernin, 2 rue Saint Bernard, right next to basilica. (Tel. 61 21 73 08) Clean and comfortable.
☆ *Hôtel St-Antoine*, 21 rue St-Antoine, near Place Wilson. (Tel. 61 21 40 66) Simple but pleasant.
Restaurants ☆ *Chez Emile*, 13 Place St-Georges (Tel. 62 21 05 56). Elegant ground floor restaurant with imaginative fish dishes; traditional Midi dishes on the floor above.
☆☆ *La Belle Epoque*, 3 rue Pargaminières (Tel. 61 23 22 12). Superb, inventive dishes from Pierre Roudgé, chef and proprietor.
Le Café des Allées, 64 allée Charles de Fitte: lively jazz bar.

Carcassonne

Trains *11 trains daily from Toulouse (50 mins); 10 from* **Montpellier** *(2 hours); 7 from* **Nîmes** *(2½ hours); 10 from* **Narbonne** *(50 mins); 2 from Paris d'Austerlitz and 2 night trains (8 hours).*

The enormous walled and fortified medieval city of Carcassonne, the largest medieval fortress in Europe, is one of the most impressive and memorable sights of the

Languedoc. From the station the best approach is down the Boulevard Jean Jaurès, over the Pont Vieux, turning sharply to the right and following the Rue de la Barbecane. This way you follow a path dominated by the château and enter the *cité* through the fortified **Porte d'Aude.**

From a distance the crenellated and battlemented walls, the towers and Keeps, gateways, dry moats and complex fortifications create the illusion of having stumbled across a medieval city in all its splendour. No matter that the walled city has been meticulously restored. If it had not been for the vision and fascination with medieval history enjoyed by the 19th-century French Romantic poet and Inspector of Historic Monuments, Prosper Merimée, little would remain today.

The medieval city is a steep climb from the pleasant but undistinguished town of modern-day Carcassonne. Located stragegically on the banks of the River Aude mid-way on the route between Toulouse and the Mediterranean, Carcassonne played an important role in the Cathar resistance to the crusade that began in 1209. Count Raymond VI of Toulouse and his nephew Raymond-Roger Trencavel, Viscount of Carcassonne, spear-headed the resistance of the Cathars, organising the defence of Carcassonne when it was besieged by Arnaud-Amaury and Simon de Montfort in August 1209, shortly after they had laid waste to Béziers. Betraying his word, Simon de Montfort seized Trencavel when he came out of the citadel to negotiate and shortly after the city capitulated. From this moment, until his death besieging Toulouse 9 years later, the viscountcy was held by Simon de Montfort. In the 14th century the town at the foot of the fortified city was burnt to the ground by the Black Prince who had failed to take the citadel. Later, when Roussillon was annexed to France in 1659, Carcassonne lost its importance as a frontier fortress with Spain and slowly its ramparts and walls began to fall into disrepair. Prosper Merimée began to take an interest in the city in the course of a journey through the south of France in 1835 and restoration work began in 1844 under the supervision of Viollet-le-Duc.

What to see

Château Comtal

Within the double ring of fortified and crenellated walls lies the Château Comtal which is separated from the rest of the city by a dry moat. Originally constructed in the 12th century as the Palace of the Viscounts of Carcassonne, it was the final defensive bastion of the city. One of its towers, the **Tour de la Justice,** was designed as a trap for assailants who managed to penetrate the heart of the castle. The castle now contains a **museum of sculpture** (Open daily 9 am-6 pm; Oct-May 9 am-noon and 2–5 pm; English tours in July and August, starting from just within the château gates.)

Between the outer and inner walls lie the *lices* – an open grass-filled space. A walk around the *cité* between the walls gives an excellent idea of the size of the walls and their impressive defensive features. Viollet-le-Duc's restoration has been criticised for not always remaining true to the original medieval appearance; his worst errors were to make the roofs of the towers too conical and to roof them with grey slate instead of the reddish tiles of the south. These mistakes are slowly being rectified.

Eglise St-Nazaire

Within the medieval walls of the *cité* lies the beautiful church of St-Nazaire, one of the finest churches in the Midi, with an 11th century Romanesque nave and west tower and delicate Gothic choir. The radiant stained glass windows, dating from the 14th to 16th centuries, are of exceptional beauty. On the south side a stone relief depicts one of the 13th-century sieges of Carcassonne. (Open daily 9 am–noon and 2–6 pm.)

Pacticalities in Carcassonne

Tourists Office 15 blvd Camille-Pelletan (Tel. 68 25 07 04); currency exchange (weekends). Open Mon–Sat 9 am–7 pm; annex in Porte Narbonnaise (Tel. 68 25 68 81), the gateway into the *cité*.

Railway Station Ave du Maréchal Joffre, behind Jardin St-Chenier, in *ville basse*. (Info: Tel. 68 47 50 50; Reservations: Tel: 68 25 60 80); bus 4 leaves from station for the *Cité*.

Buses Blvd de Varsovie (Tel. 68 25 12 74); buses to Toulouse, Narbonne, Foix.

Markets Place Carnot/Place aux Herbes: Tues, Thurs and Sat mornings; daily covered market in Place d'Efggenfelden in *Ville basse*, Mon-Sat mornings.

Festivals Festival de Carcassonne: July, centred on Château Comtal, with music, dance, theatre and opera, (Tel. 68 25 33 13 for details); *Médiévales*: Aug, recreation of the medieval city, with period costume and crafts.

Hotels *Hôtel Astoria*, Rue Montpellier (Tel. 68 25 31 38), Quiet hotel with clean, bright rooms, just over bridge in front of station.

☆ *Le Cathare*, 53 rue Bringer (Tel. 68 25 65 92). Good, bright rooms in little hotel near post office; unpretentious restaurant downstairs.

☆ *Bonnefaux*, 40 rue de la Liberté (Tel. 68 25 01 45). Small hotel near the station in the *ville basse*.

☆☆ *Le Bristol*, 7 ave Foch. (Tel. 68 25 07 24); By the river just over the bridge in front of station.

☆☆☆ *Hôtel Montségur*, 27 allée d'Iéna (Tel. 68 25 31 41). Delightful little hotel with period furniture; located just outside the old walls.

Restaurants *Le Baladin*, Place du Château (Tel. 68 47 91 90). Simple, hearty fare and good value; with shady terrace.

L'Ostal des Troubadours, Rue Viollet-le-Duc (Tel. 68 47 88 80). Lively and popular.

☆☆ *Auberge du Pont Levis*, Porte Narbonnaise (Tel. 68 25 55 23). Beside the medieval gateway into the city; exquisite food, served on terrace or in garden during summer.

☆☆ *La Marquière*, 13 rue St Jean (Tel. 68 71 52 00). Excellent mid-priced restaurant in the *cité*; reservation recommended.

Narbonne

Trains *13 trains daily from* **Carcassonne** *(30–40 mins); from* **Toulouse** *(1½ hours); 12 from* **Montpellier** *(55 mins); 14 from* **Perpignan** *(45 mins).*

Founded by the Romans around 600 BC Narbonne was a thriving port rivalling Marseille in importance until the late Middle Ages, but the silting up of its port in the 14th century, and the expulsion of the Jews from the city in 1306, led to a decline in prosperity. Relics of the Roman era are to be found in the former Archbishop's Palace, a fortified building, and in the *horreum* in rue Rouget de l'Isle.

What to see

Cathédrale de St-Just

On a hill above the Canal du Midi, which intersects the town stands the astonishing Cathedral of St-Just. It was begun in 1272 in northern Gothic style and on a majestic scale but construction got no further than the Chancel. The interior, however, is striking for the harmony of its proportions and only Amiens and Beauvais cathedral have higher vaulting. The treasures of the cathedral include a magnificent *Flemish tapestry* depicting the Creation, woven with golden and silken thread. The extreme delicacy of the colours, the elegance of the composition and the physiognomy of the 3 persons of the Trinity combine to make it a work of rare beauty. (Open Mon–Sat 9.30 am–5.30 pm.)

Steps lead up to the cathedral's **Tour Nord**, from where there are panoramic views over the Corbières hills and red roofs of the old town. The centre of the medieval city lies around the cathedral and the Place de l'Hôtel de Ville. The rich and sprawling Archbishop's Palace beside the cathedral, consisting of a number of closely connected religious, military and civil buildings, testifies to the power and wealth of the former archbishops of Narbonne.

Archbishop's Palace

The façade of the Archbishop's Palace looks onto the Place de l'Hôtel de Ville, in which stand 3 square medieval towers – on the right, the oldest, the **Donjon de la Madeleine**, in the centre the **Donjon St-Martial**; on the left the **Donjon Gilles Aycelin**. From the top of the latter there is a fine panorama over the surrounding countryside. The Archbishop's Palace now houses the **Musée Archéologique**, with a collection of prehistoric and Gallo-Roman objects. (Open daily 10 – 11.45 am and 2 – 6 pm).

One of the most enchanting streets lies between the Old and New Archbishop's Palace, the **Passage de l'Ancre**, which runs into the main square. One of the most interesting buildings to be excavated in the city is a Roman grain house, or **Horreum** in Rue Rouget de l'Isle.

To the south and west of Narbonne lies barren country of low rocky hills, scattered with wild rosemary, mint and thyme but the valleys and nearby plain are covered with vines that produce the local Corbières wines. The town is also famous for its white honey.

Practicalities in Narbonne

Tourist Office Place Roger Salengro, 10 mins from station off Rue Chennebier (Tel. 68 65 17 52); currency exchange; guided walking tours. Open daily 8 am–7 pm 15th Sept – 15th June Mon – Sat 8.30 am–12 and 2–6 pm, Sun 9.30 am–12.30 pm.

Railway Station Blvd Frédéric Mistral, close to centre (Tel. 67 62 50 50). For town centre from station, turn right out of station and follow Blvd F. Mistral to Palais de Travail, then left into rue Chennebier which leads to Place Salengro.

Buses Bus station at Quai Victor Hugo, 5 mins walk in direction of **Parc des Expositions** from Mairie, along canal. 2 bus companies: *Michau* (Tel. 68 42 06 28); *Trans-Aude* (Tel. 68 41 40 02).

Markets Daily covered market in *Halles Centrales*, by canal on Cours Mirabeau; Thurs: Plan St-Paul, vegetable market; Sun: Place des

Pyrenees, junk for the asking.

Hotels *Hôtel de la Gare*, 7 ave Pierre Sémard (Tel. 68 32 10 54). Adjacent to station; clean and spacious.

Hôtel Novelty, 33 ave des Pyrénées (Tel. 68 42 24 28). West across the canal, friendly and cheerful; restaurant downstairs.

☆ *L'Alsace*, 2 blvd Carnot (Tel. 63 32 01 86). Near the station.

☆☆ *Le Terminus*, 2 ave Pierre Sémard (Tel. 68 32 02 75). Pleasant, simple rooms, near station.

☆☆ *Hôtel Languedoc*, 3 blvd Gambetta (Tel. 68 65 13 74). Good old-fashioned hotel;

inexpensive regional cuisine in *La Coupole* restaurant.

Camping *Le Languedoc*, 1 km south-east of the town (Tel. 68 85 24 65).

Restaurants *Le Gout-en-Train*, 15 rue Gustave Fabre (Tel. 68 90 61 29). Classic wine-bar behind cathedral.

La Paillote, passage de l'Ancien Courier (Tel. 68 32 25 21). Delicious lamb and beef dishes, with enchanting outdoor terrace.

☆☆☆ *L'Alsace*, 2 ave P. Sémard (Tel. 68 65 10 24). The best restaurant in town, facing the station, with superb classic French dishes.

Salses

Trains *4 trains a day from* **Narbonne** *(30 mins); 4 trains a day from* **Perpignan**. *(15 mins). Check the time of the next onward train before leaving the station.*

Salses makes an interesting optional stop and for anyone interested in military architecture it is a highlight of southern France. For the fortress at Salses, designed by Francisco Ramirez and built between 1497 and 1503, is the most perfect surviving examples of medieval Spanish military architecture in France. Altered slightly by the leading French military architect of the 17th century, Vauban, it is also one of the earliest castles specifically designed to withstand artillery fire. It consists of an immense quadrilateral with towers at each corner, entirely built of red brick, with a Keep on the western side overlooking a vast internal courtyard. Its impressive, rounded towers and walls, some 9-metres-thick, are surrounded by a dry moat which could be filled at a moment's notice with sea water from the Mediterranean, at the edge of which the castle is built.

The fortress was erected on the site of the ancient Roman road to Spain, the Via Domitia, a strategic point where the waters of the lagoon almost reach to the hills of the Corbières. It was built on the orders of King Ferdinand II of Spain, following the restitution of Roussillon to Spain in 1493, to protect the region. Once Richelieu had decided to conquer Roussillon again for France, the fortress of Salses became an important military target. The fort was seized by French forces in 1639, only to be lost again to the Spanish the following year. A combined assault by sea and land was being planned by French forces when the Spanish governor, learning of the capitulation of Perpignan to the south, decided to surrender without a fight having recognised that the Spanish cause was lost. At the end of the 17th century Vauban reduced the height of the Keep and altered the walls to make them less susceptible to artillery bombardment but with the new frontier 50 kilometres further south, the fortress lost its military significance. (Open daily June–Sept, 9.30 am–6.30 pm; off-season closed at lunchtime.)

Practicalities in Salses

Tourist Office 13 rue Gaston-Clos (Tel 68 38 66 13).
Hotels ☆☆*Le Relais del Castel, Ancienne Route*

Nationale (Tel. 68 38 60 26)☆☆*Hotel de la Loge*, Avenue Xavier Lloberes (Tel. 68 38 60 24)

As Perpignan is approached, the view of the eastern end of the Pyrenees becomes more apparent, the Massif du Canigou dominating the landscape inland.

Perpignan

Trains 15 *trains daily from* **Narbonne** *(40–50 mins)*; 4 *from* **Salses** *(15 mins)*; 8 *from* **Toulouse** – *some direct (2 hours), others require you to change at Narbonne (2½ – 3 hours)*; 6 *from* **Paris** *(10 hours)*; 12 *from* **Marseille** *(4 hours)*.

One of the most delightful and relaxed towns of southern France, Perpignan shimmers with heat in summer, its innumerable fronded palms and tall leafy plane trees providing welcome shade from the merciless rays of the sun.

The town rose to prominence in the thirteenth century when in 1276, it became the capital of Roussillon under the Kings of Majorca. The palace of the Majorcan kings became the centre of a brilliant and dynamic court until it was crushed in 1344 by the Kings of Aragon, centred on Barcelona. Under the Aragonese the two provinces of Cerdagne and Roussillon were united in a quasi-autonomous federation, a gesture which did not prevent the Catalans rising against their rulers in Barcelona. In 1463 Louis XI of France lent King John of Aragon 700 mounted calvary to help him subdue the Catalans. No sooner had John of Aragon won the Catalonians over and entered the city than Louis XIII turned on his erstwhile ally and besieged the town. After a desperate resistance, during which the population was reduced to eating rats to avoid famine (for which the Perpignanois were long referred to in France as 'mangeurs de rats'), Perpignan capitulated to French forces in 1473. In 1493 Charles VIII, wishing to have his hands free in Italy, began to court the Spanish. In a generous gesture, designed to demonstrate his friendship, he returned Roussillon to the catholic kings, Ferdinand and Isabella. For the next two hundred years, Perpignan became a Spanish possession.

At the heart of the city rises the rose-coloured fortress, the **Castillet**, a powerful medieval fortress-gate which once formed part of the city's walls. Its impressive crenellations and machicolations overlook the enchanting and animated place de la Victoire and shady Café de la Poste. A narrow twisting back street leads to the graceful Gothic **Loge de Mar** (sadly now a 'Quick' hamburger joint) and the Cathédrale St-Jean, beside which stretches the Campo Santo, the largest medieval cloister-cemetery, its marble arcades recently restored to their former glory but the gravestones now sadly removed. (rue Amiral Ribeil; open daily 10 am–noon and 2:30–5:30 pm).

Ten minutes walk from the Castillet and the Loge de Mar on a slight rise to the south spreads the vast bulk of the red brick fortress built by Vauban to defend the city after its acquisition by France in 1659. Hidden within its three concentric defensive walls, extensively restored in 1845, lies the charming **palace of the Catalan kings of Majorca** which with its palm trees, rectangular shapes and internal courtyard has the feel of a Moorish citadel. The palace was the residence of the kings of Majorca until their illustrious but short-lived kingdom was crushed by the Aragonese in 1344. (Le Palais des Rois de Majorque, 2 rue des Archers. Tel 68 34 48 29. Open daily 10 am–6 pm from June–Sept and 9 am–5 pm Oct–May.

What to see

Promenade des Platanes

Perhaps the most charming aspect of the city is the Promenade des Platanes, planted in 1809, which follows a tributary of the River Têt that cuts through the centre of the town. On long summer evenings, the inhabitants of Perpignan meet under the plane trees to stroll up and down its cool and leafy avenue, animated in conversation. There are a number of hidden delights to be discovered by the unrushed visitor in the old centre on the south bank of the little river Basse. Like Narbonne, Perpignan was once a flourishing port but now finds itself some 3 kilometres from the sea.

Palais des Rois de Majorque

The once magnificent Palace of the Kings of Majorca is now a shadow of its former self, situated within the massive fortress, known as the Citadel, built by Vauban following the capture of the city in 1642. Stepped ramps lead up to the fortified palace which was begun in the 14th century by James II of Majorca. Within its walls lies a beautifully proportioned internal arcaded courtyard, le Cour d'Honneur, and elegant Romanesque and Gothic galleries. On one side of the courtyard are 2 Flamboyant Gothic chapels, one directly above the other, faced with mottled stone and marble while on the first floor is a fine vaulted hall, the Grande Salle. (Open daily 9 am–5 pm.)

Cathédrale St-Jean

Construction of the Cathédrale St-Jean, facing Place Gambetta, was begun under the second King of Majorca in 1321 but only finished at the beginning of the 16th century. The interior is undistinguished except for the width of the nave and the magnificently sculpted retable of the high altar, by Soler of Barcelona, which is a masterpiece of Spanish 17th-century ecclesiastical art. Just outside the south door of the cathedral is a small chapel containing a poignant wooden Crucifixion of the early 14th century, most probably originating from the Rhineland.

On Good Friday the *Procéssion de la Sanch* ('blood'), takes place from the Eglise St-Jacques in which hooded penitents belonging to a medieval brotherhood (dating from 1416) parade through the city carrying a *misteris*, a highly realistic effigy of Christ. The brotherhood used to help to prepare those condemned to death for their fate.

Place Arago

The focus of the city is the Place Arago, a pleasant square planted with palm and magnolias trees and lined with cafés. The **Musée Rigaud** contains portraits by Hyacinthe Rigaud, a native of the town who was court artist for Louis XIV and the leading portrait artist of his day, as well as works by Catalan artists, the most remarkable being the *Retable of the Trinity* by the Master of Canapost. François Arago was another distinguished native of the city; physician and astronomer, he was made a member of the Academy of Science at the age of 23. In summer 2 welcome areas of cool foliage are to be found in the **Promenade des Platanes**, with its fountains, palms and mimosa trees and the little garden of **La Miranda** behind the church of St-Jacques.

Practicalities in Perpignan

Tourist Office In the Palais des Congrès, Place Armand Lanoux (Tel. 68 66 30 30); maps, guided walking tours June–Sept: Open Mon–Sat 9 am–7 pm, Sun, 9 am–1 pm and 3–7 pm; Oct–May Mon–Sat 8.30 am–noon and 2–6.30 pm. A more helpful regional tourist office at 7 quai de Lattre de Tassigny at the far end of town from the station: maps, information on hiking, excursions, hotels, festivals, bus schedules (Tel. 68 34 29 94).
Railway Station Rue Courteline (Tel. 68 35 75 13); automatic lockers; bicycle hire. For town centre from station, follow Ave du Général de Gaulle, turn right onto Cours Escarguel, continue until Ave Brutus, then left to Palace of the Kings of Majorca.
Buses *Gare Routière*, 17 ave Gén. Leclerc, near Place de la Résistance (Tel. 68 35 29 02); buses to Narbonne, Béziers, airport, beaches to the east; CTP town bus line 1 departs regularly from Promenade des Platanes for the beach at Canet, at the mouth of the Têt.
Markets Tues–Sat, Place de la République.
Festivals *Fête de St-Jean*: 23rd June, sacred fire brought from Mt Canigou, *Procéssion de la Sanch*: Good Friday, Easter procession dating back to medieval times.

Hotels ☆*Hôtel Metropole*, 3 rue des Cardeurs, off Place de la Loge (Tel. 68 34 43 34). Quiet, spacious and in the heart of the old town.
☆*Hôtel le Bristol*, 5 rue Grande des Fabriques, off Place de Verdun (Tel. 68 34 32 68). Spacious central and tranquil.
☆☆*Hôtel du Centre*, 26 rue des Augustins (Tel. 68 34 39 69). A pleasant 2-star hotel in the town centre.
☆☆*Hôtel Poste et Perdrix*, 6 rue Fabriques d'en Nabot (Tel. 68 34 42 53). A delightful 2-star hotel in Perpignan's best preserved medieval street; with restaurant.
☆☆☆*Hôtel Park*, 18 blvd Jean-Bourrat (Tel. 68 35 14 14). Large, smart family-run hotel with luxurious accommodation; Claude Petry in the *Chapon Fin* restaurant produces superb, subtle Mediterranean dishes; excellent shellfish.
Hostels *Auberge de Jeunesse* (HI), La Pépinière, off ave de la Grande Bretagne, 10 mins from station, dormitory accommodation (Tel. 68 34 63 32). **Camping** *Le Catalan*, route de Bompass (Tel. 68 63 16 92); Bompas bus from station.
Restaurants *Le Perroquet*, 1 ave Général de Gaulle (Tel. 68 34 34 36). Close to station, good value menus offering interesting dishes. *Le Palarium*, Place Arago, the focus of the town

(Tel. 68 34 51 31). Self-service cafeteria, cheap *plats du jour* with busy popular terrace facing the canal.

☆☆*La Serre*, 2 bis rue Dagobert (Tel. 68 84 34 02). Good cuisine, with many regional dishes in this attractive friendly venue in the heart of the old town.

☆*Le Bistro du Park* 18 bd. Jean Bourrat (Tel. 68 35 14 14). Opposite the Palais du Congrès, for the taste of fresh seafood, grilled fish but also *confits* (duck and goose cooked in their own fat) and *andouillettes*. Good prices in a new setting; closed Sun.

☆☆*Casa Santa*, 2 rue Fabrique d'en Nadal, 3 rue Fabrique Couverte (Tel. 68 34 21 84). Excellent Catalan cuisine, in a cosy and crowded restaurant, always thronged with food lovers.

☆☆*Le Festin de Pierre*, 7 rue du théatre (Tel. 68 51 28 74). Classic French cuisine in traditional surroundings. One of the best restaurants in Perpignan; closed Tues. evening and Wed. Specialities include fish and puff pastry.

☆☆☆*Le Chapon Fin*, 8 bd. Jean Bourrat. Gastronomy with a Mediterranean flavour from famed chef Eric Leferc. Cooking of a very high order in a very elegant and refined setting and excellent attentive service. One of the four best restaurants of the Pyrenées Orientales. Closed Sun and Mon lunchtime. Catalan specialities include *boules de picalottes* – delicate balls of pork and beef cooked with fresh mushrooms and green olives. Menus from 180FF upwards.

Excursion from Perpignan

Elne

En route from Perpignan to Collioure, a few of the trains stop at the little town of Elne which takes its name from Helen, the mother of the Emperor Constantine, Elne having been the capital of Roman Roussillon.

Surrounded by orchards of apricot and peach trees the village hides a magnificent church and cloisters. The **Cathédrale de St-Eulalia** is a beautiful fortified church built in the 11th century and crowned by 2 curiously contrasting towers, one in austere Romanesque style and the other in the more fanciful manner of the 15th century. The Romanesque cloister, a little above the cathedral, is considered one of the finest of its period in France. Its roof is supported by an arcade of double columns exquisitely carved in an extraordinarily realistic manner with scenes from the Old and New Testaments. The slender columns are carved in a wide variety of styles, some decorated with the most delicate foliage, others in spirals. Open daily July–Aug 9.30 am–6.45 pm; June and Sept: 9.30 am–12.15 pm and 2 pm–6.45 pm; April–May: 9.30 am–12.15 pm and 2 pm–5.45 pm; Oct–Mar: telephone first as it only opens on demand (Tel. 68 22 70 90.)

Practicalities in Elne

Tourist office Place de la Republique (Tel. 68 22 05 07).
Hotels ☆*Le Week-End*, 29 ave. Paul Reig (Tel. 68 22 06 68).
Le Carrefour, 1 ave. Paul Reig (Tel. 68 22 06 08).

Collioure

Trains *9–14 trains daily from* **Perpignan** *(30 mins) and* **Narbonne** *(1½ hours); 5 trains daily south to* **Port Bou** *and* **Barcelona** *in Spain.*

Not for nothing did the Fauvists chose Collioure in which to settle and paint. The bright colours of the Mediterranean sky and sea, the vibrant primary colours of the fishing barques and the intense luminosity of the light admirably suited the bright palettes favoured by Derain, Matisse, Braque, and Othon Friesz. The setting of Collioure too is little short of idyllic and at the turn of century, before the advent of tourists and motorised transport, the little fishing town must have been a haven of tranquility and beauty. A handful of fishing barques remain though they are no longer launched from the gentle beach of white sand that sweeps up to the house fronts in the harbour.

In the Middle Ages Collioure was the principal port of Roussillon, from where cloth made in Perpignan was exported all over the Levant. The square Keep of the massive **castle** on a rocky promontory that separates the 2 natural sandy bays was erected by the kings of Majorca in the 12th century and later extended by Charles v and Philip ii. (Open Mar–Oct daily 10 am–noon and 2–5 pm).

Once Roussillon had been acquired by France in 1659 the old town of Collioure was razed to the ground on the orders of Vauban and the church of **Notre-Dame-des-Anges** was built to replace the church just demolished. Recently re-roofed in bright red tiles that would have delighted the Fauvists, the church – which appears almost to rise out of the sea – contains 9 fine gilded and sculpted altar-pieces, the work of the Catalan artist, Joseph Sunyer. From just behind the church a track, the *Sentier de la Moulade*, leads up between the cliff and the sea, affording superb views north along the coast to **Argeles-sur-Mer** and **St-Cyprien**. A number of paintings executed by some of the artists who adopted Collioure at the beginning of the century are to be found in the **Hôtel les Templiers** near the harbour.

Practicalities in Collioure

Tourist Office Place du 18 Juin (Tel. 68 82 15 47); maps, brochures. Open daily 9 am–8 pm in summer.
Railway Station At end of Ave. Aristide Maillol (Tel. 68 82 05 89).
Buses Cars Inter 66 (Tel. 68 82 15 47); buses along the coast and inland.
Markets Wed and Sun mornings, Place de Général Leclerc.
Festivals *Féria de Collioure*: 14th–18th, August, with Portugese-style bullfighting, firworks.
Hôtels ☆*Hôtel le Majorque*, 16 ave Général de Gaulle (Tel. 68 82 29 22). Good, clean, simple rooms.
☆*Hôtel Triton*, 1 rue Jean Bart (Tel. 68 82 06 52). Simple, spotless rooms in superb waterfront location.
☆☆*Hôtel des Templiers*, (Tel. 68 98 31 10); Every oil painting finds a place on the wall in this unusual and welcoming hotel.
☆☆*Hôtel Les Caranques*, Route de Port-Vendres (Tel. 68 82 06 68). Simple and friendly; great seaviews from some of the rooms.
Camping *Les Amandiers*, 20 mins walk north from station, close to beach (Tel. 68 81 14 69).
Restaurant *Le Welsh*, 5 rue Edgar Quinet, Good traditional Catalan fare.
☆☆*La Balette*, Route de Port-Vendres (Tel. 68 82 05 07). Superb local dishes cooked by chef-patron Jean-Pierre de Gelder. Terrace with extensive view for eating outside. (With rooms too, but expensive.)

Prades – Molitg-les-Bains

Trains *4–7 trains daily from* **Perpignan** *(40 mins).*

One of the most delightful and scenic train journeys in southern France follows the charming river valley of the Têt from Perpignan upstream high into the Pyrenees.

At its highest point the train reaches the Spanish border at **La-Tour-de-Carol** and the enchanting upland valley of the Cerdagne which has the benefit of more days of sunshine than any other place in France. From **Villefranche-Vernet les Bains** a special narrow-gauge train – *le petit train jaune* – climbs up through spectacular landscape, traversing the valley on huge viaducts high above the river.

The sheltered valley of the Têt favours the growth of peaches and apricots which grow in profusion around **Ile-sur-Têt**, a small town where the former hospice of St-Jacques is now a small **museum** of sacred art. A little distance to the north of the town, between the rivers Têt and Boules, is the fascinating landscape of weathered sedimentary stone in fantastic shapes known as Les Orgues. A little further north again lies **Bélesta**, a tiny hilltop village completely surrounded by vines, now home to a new **archaeological museum** under the direction of one of the country's talented young archaeologists, Mademoiselle Valérie Porra. The museum contains an unrivalled collection of burial urns found in a nearby cave, the largest neolithic burial site discovered in southern France.

Prades, built at the foot of Mont Canigou, a mountain close to the hearts of all Catalans, was for several decades the adopted home of the violinist Pablo Casals (1876–1973). Casals spent 23 years in Prades as a political exile from Franco's Spain and it was here that he chose to organise a musical festival, which now takes place annually from 25th July to 13th August. Distinguished musicians from all over Europe take part in 3 weeks of concerts and workshops which are held in the 1,000-year-old abbey.

The little church of St-Pierre does not catch the eye from the outside but it hides a gorgeous altar-piece by the Catalan sculptor Joseph Sunyer, dating from 1699. Carved in wood and sumptuously decorated, it is a masterpiece of Catalan Baroque sculpture.

Abbaye St-Michel-De-Cuxa Another reason for descending at Prades is to visit the superb Romanesque abbey of St-Michel-de-Cuxa, a 2-kilometre walk from Prades station through peach and apricot orchards.

The abbey was founded around 900 for Benedictine monks and one of the builders of St Mark's in Venice, Doge Pietro Orseolo I, died here in 987. The steady decline of the monastery's fortunes culminated in the abbey being burnt during the Revolution and in the 20th century many of the capitals of its 12th-century cloister were sold and now adorn The Cloisters Museum in New York. Now occupied by Cistercians, the abbey is being restored. The most interesting aspect of its architecture are the horseshoe-shaped arches, reminiscent of Moorish architecture and rarely found in Europe outside Spain. (Open Mon–Sat 9.30 am–11.45 am and 2–6 pm; Oct–April 2–5 pm.)

Practicalities in Prades

Tourist Office 4 rue Victor Hugo (Tel. 68 96 27 58); information on local hikes with map to get to abbey; above tourist office is the **Musée Pablo Casals**, with collection of Casals' cellos.

Festival Pablo Casals *Association Pablo Casals*, rue Victor Hugo (Tel. 68 96 33 07); tickets and information.

Markets Tues mornings, in front of Eglise St-

Pierre.
Hotels ☆*Hostalrich*, 156 ave Général de Gaulle (Tel. 68 96 05 38). Simple, clean rooms.
☆☆*Hôtel Hexagone*, pt de Molitg, just outside

town (Tel. 68 05 31 31). Modern, functional but lacking in charm.
Camping *Camping Municipal* (Tel. 68 96 29 83). In valley below tourist office.

Villefranche-de-Conflent

Trains 4–7 *trains daily from* Prades *(7 mins) and* Perpignan *(47 mins).*

Villefranche-de-Conflent is a small but impressive fortified village at the confluence of 2 mountain rivers, the Têt and the Cady, a short walk upstream from the station. The town was founded by Count William Ramon in 1092 but its massive ramparts date from 16th century and were consolidated by Vauban following the accession of Roussillon to France in 1659. Some of the fort is built of pink marble hewn from local quarries and it still retains its *chemin de ronde* or covered sentry walk from which the defenders could return fire while still being protected.

Above the town stands the 17th-century Fort Liberia, constructed by Vauban after the Treaty of the Pyrenees to protect Villefranche-de-Conflent from the Spanish; its fortifications form a complex web on 3 levels. (Open daily 10 am–6 pm.)

In the town itself, the little **church of St-Jacques** has a deep Catalan font of pink marble for until the mid-14th century the Catalans practised total immersion at baptism. Since 1980 the town has regained a new lease of life with the arrival of a number of artisans and artists who have established their workshops and studios in the old town.

A short walk from the town are the fascinating **Grottes des Canalettes**, 3 large caves with impressive stalagmites, which were only discovered in 1951. (Open Mon–Sat 10 am–6.30 pm, Sun 2–6 pm; Sept–June daily 10 am–noon and 2–6.30 pm).

Practicalities in Villefranche-de-Conflent

Tourist Office Place de l'Eglise (Tel. 68 96 22 96); hiking information, accommodation assistance; arranges guided tours of town and Fort Liberia.
Festivals *Fête des Feux de St-Jean*: 23rd June,

Catalonian celebration with sardane dancing.
Hotels *Hôtel le Terminus*; next to station (Tel. 68 05 20 24). With restaurant.
Restaurant ☆*Au Grill*, rue St-Jean (Tel. 68 96 17 65).

Mont-Louis

Train 4–7 *trains daily from* Villefranche-de-Conflent *(1½ hours) and* Perpignan *(approx 2 hours 50 mins) – change at Villefranche-de-Conflent; 4–7 from* La-Tour-de-Carol *(1 hour).*

The magnificent narrow-gauge railway begins its journey from Villefranche-de-Conflent high up into the Pyrenees. This line, on its metre-wide track, was established to end the isolation of the upper valley of the Tet and the Cerdagne and was inaugurated in 1911. The line navigates 19 tunnels and 20 bridges and viaducts, including the suspension bridge at Gisclard, the impressive viaduct at Sejourne. The train is painted yellow and red, symbolising gold and blood, the colours of Catalonia. The beauty and majesty of the Pyrenean landscape can be appreciated from the train to a far greater degree than would be possible if travelling by car. In summer open compartments are used which allow breath-taking views in all directions. A much reduced service continues through the winter, a snow plough being used to clear the track after heavy snowfalls, so that it is now very rare for the train to be blocked by snow. There are 22 minor stops en route but if you want to get off the train make sure you tell the conductor or the driver, usually Monsieur Bernard Coudris.

As the train heads up the little valley of the River Têt, it winds from one side of the valley to the other, giving spectacular views of the Pyrenees, mountain streams, waterfalls and tiny hillside villages. Passing ochre coloured cliffs, the hills reveal the ruins of castles that once dominated the valley, an important military route to Spain. At the villages of **Serdinya** and **Joncet** iron and manganese were once mined while **Canaveilles-les-Bains** and **Thuès-les-Bains** are renowned for the therapeutic value of their thermal waters.

The village of **Thuès** lies at a height of 789 metres at the confluence of the Têt and Caranca rivers. The latter emerges from a picturesque and wild gorge which can be explored on foot, in a day's walk, as far as the lakes of Caranca which lie at a height of 2,366 metres.

Beyond Thuès lies the spectacular viaduct of **Séjourné**, consisting of 16 arches that span the valley of the Têt 200 feet above the river. At just over 1,000 metres is **Fontpedrouse-St-Thomas-les-Bains** with, on the left, the ruins of the Château de Prats Balanguer and the thermal spa of St-Thomas-les-Bains. Above Fontpedrouse the train enters a series of tunnels before re-crossing the Têt on another viaduct, the Gisclard bridge that towers 250 feet above the valley bottom. This viaduct represents the first application in France of the principles of suspension bridge engineering to the railway system.

The train passes through **Mont Louis**, the highest garrison town in France, surrounded by impressive defensive ramparts similiar to those at Villefranche, and reaches its highest point at 1,592 metres just beyond Mont Louis at **Bolquère-Eyne**, the highest railway station in France. During the Middle Ages the nearby pass, the Col de la Perche, was the meeting point of pilgrims and merchants who were led by local guides down to the lower valleys.

After Bolquère-Eyne the line skirts the slopes of the Forest of Font Romeu towards the valley of the Cerdagne, closed in to the north by the Massif du Carlit and to the south by Mount Puigmal. It emerges eventually in the Cerdagne, the broadest valley in the Pyrenees which was once the bed of an ancient lake. Under the Treaty of the Pyrenees, the Spanish ceded not only Roussillon to France but also half of the Cerdagne, a small territorial division on the frontier. Llivia, the tiny portion of the Cerdagne which Spain retained under the 1659 treaty, continues to exist – a tiny enclave of Spanish territory surrounded by French soil. The nearest station to Llivia is **Estavar** but there is little to see, although once the favourite haunt of smugglers, apart from its balconied streets which are Spanish in character. From Mont Louis a number of interesting excursions can be made on foot to the Lac des Bouillouses, the Forests of Barres, and Font Romeu and to the 2000 metre high mountain refuge of Combeleran.

Excursions from Mont Louis
Font Romeu

The small town of Font Romeu, 300 metres above the railway station is both a ski and summer resort and a delightful base from which to explore the wooded valleys and hills to the north in summer. The valley of the Cerdagne receives more hours of sunshine than any other place in France and at Odeillo stands a massive solar-energy mirror, part of a solar energy research institution. Sheltered from northerly winds, exceptionally dry and sunny, Font Romeu has become a popular resort and is entirely new but still retains its beauty and tranquility. There are many hotels of all classes to choose from.
Tourist Office Ave E. Brousse (Tel. 68 30 02 74).

La-Tour-de-Carol

Trains *4–7 trains a day from* **Font Romeu** *(1 hour); from* **Perpignan** *(around 4 hours; change at Villefranche-de-Conflent);* 5 *trains daily from* **Ax-les-Termes** *(45 mins) and* **Toulouse** *(2 hours 55 mins). Font Romeu is located 300 m above its own railway station (due to gradients).*

Beyond Font Romeu lie the little villages of Llivia, **Saillagouse**, the starting point for a number of sign-posted local walks, and **Bourg-Madame** which straddles the Spanish border. Rowans and willows grow at the lower altitudes while pines grow higher up on the hillsides. La-Tour-de-Carol is merely the end of the line. Change here for Ax-les-Termes, Foix and Toulouse or Barcelona. A simple but decent railway restaurant and hotel caters for anyone who arrives too late to catch an onward train.

Ax-les-Thermes

Trains 5 *trains daily from* **La-Tour-de-Carol** *(45 mins);* 6 *daily from* **Foix** *(45 mins).*

From La-Tour-de-Carol the train passes the Pic Carlet, the highest of the eastern Pyrenean peaks at 2,921 metres, and drops down after the Col de Puymorens into the valley of the Ariège, the powerful mountain torrent that flows ultimately into the Garonne just south of Toulouse. The landscape is wild and mountainous, becoming less so as the train descends through forests of pine and then silver birch trees towards Ax-les-Thermes. The train meanders slowly south through superb Pyrenean scenery, through tunnels and steep gorges with glimpses of waterfalls and abandoned hill terracing.

Ax-les-Thermes is a small and ancient spa town at a height of 718 metres and can be used as a useful base for walking in the surrounding mountains. Located at the confluence of 3 rivers, the Ascou, the Orlu and the Merens, it is situated in a strategic position on an early route through the Pyrenees from France to Spain and has as a result been sacked over the centuries by Visigoths, Moors, the Spanish and the Catalans. In the Middle Ages it was in addition destroyed 4 times by fire and on another occasion its populace was decimated by plague.

What to see

Place du Breilh

The main focus of the town now is the Promenade du Couloubret but the most intriguing vestige of times past is to be found in the Place du Breilh. Here stands a pool of thermal water, the **Bassin des Ladres**, which is still open to the public; orignally discovered and exploited by the Romans its thermal waters are reputed to help a number of ailments. In the 13th century Louis IX instructed the Count of Foix to establish a leprosy hospital here for soldiers who had fallen ill or been wounded in the course of the Crusades so that they could benefit from the thermal waters. In 1758 the beneficial properties of the waters were scientifically established by Abraham Sicre and since then there has been a steady flow of visitors, many of them using the town as a base from which to explore the hilly Pyrénées Ariégois. Two Grandes Randonnées routes (10 and 7) pass close by; others such as the sentier Cathar and Tour des Vallés d'Ax are less demanding.

Praticalities in Ax-les-Termes

Tourist Office Place du Breilh (Tel. 61 64 20 64); information on ski areas and hiking tours.
Railway Station (Info: Tel. 61 65 50 50; Reservations: Tel: 61 64 20 72); For town centre from station, turn left and keep walking until you come to Place du Breilh.
Hotels☆ *Hôtel de la Paix*, Place du Breilh (Tel. 61 64 22 61). Simple and clean.

☆*Hôtel la Terasse*, 7 rue Marcaillou (Tel. 61 64 20 33). Helpful, friendly Spanish owners.
☆☆*Hôtel le Breilh*, Place du Breilh (Tel. 61 64 24 29). Attractive rooms with balconies.
☆☆*Terminus* (Tel. 61 64 24 31); with restaurant.
Restaurants *Martudo*, 6 rue Rigal, near Place Breich. Hearty provincial cuisine.

Foix

Trains 6 *trains daily from* **Toulouse** *(1 hour); 5 daily from* **Ax-les-Thermes** *(45 mins) and* **La-Tour-de-Carol** *(1½ hours).*

Foix, which lies at the confluence of the Ariège and the Arget, is a sleepy and romantic town, dominated by a massive rock on which stand 3 isolated medieval towers, all that remain of the once impregnable fortress of the Counts of Foix.

In the 12th century Foix was one of the chief centres of the Albigensian heresy and for a long time it held out against the Crusaders led by Simon de Montfort. Eventually however it surrendered to Philippe le Hardi who had threatened to bring the castle down by blowing up its foundations. By the time that Count Roger Bernard of Foix finally submitted to the superior forces of orthodoxy, in 1240, the rich and fertile country belonging to the counts of Foix had been devastated by the Albigensian crusade.

Foix had initially grown up around an abbey built over the grave of St-Volusian, the exiled Archbishop of Tours who was martyred nearby in the 5th century. The abbey was abandoned after the Wars of Religion and taken over by the state after the Revolution. The former abbey buildings, much altered in the 18th century, now house the town hall and civic administration.

What to see

Château

A steep cobbled track zig-zags up to the château, originally built by Bernard Roger, Viscount of Carcassonne, in 1012. It now houses a **museum** with a small collection of 16th-century armour and chain mail and a few Romanesque capitals from the cloisters of the abbey, of which only the church remains below in the town. The views from the 15th-century circular tower, once used as a prison, are superb. Below the castle, in the **Rue du Mercadel**, is a striking 15th-century timber-framed house with protruding eaves, while opposite the Church of St-Volusien stands an outstanding 17th-century house, the **Maison des Cariatides**, a striking building that seems curiously out of place in the medieval setting of Foix. (Château open daily 9:45am–6:30pm; Oct–April 10am–noon and 2.30–6:30pm.)

Praticalities in Foix

Tourist Office Ave Gabriel Fauré (Tel 61 65 12 12); organises tours to grottoes. Open Mon–Sat 9 am–noon and 2:30–7 pm.
Railway Station Just north of town off N20, on opposite side of river (Tel. 61 65 27 00). For town centre from station,
Markets Place St-Volusien, Fri mornings.
Festivals *Médiévales Gaston-Phébus*: July–August, jousting, concerts, banquets and *son-et-*

lumière commemorating Foix's medieval history.
Hotel ☆ *Hôtel Eychenne*, 11 rue Peyrevidal (Tel. 61 65 00 04). Interesting wooden interior and warm welcome.
☆☆*Hôtel Echaugette*, rue Paul Laffont, opposite post office (Tel. 61 02 88 88).
☆☆☆*Hôtel Lons*, Place George Dutihl (Tel. 61 65 52 44). In pretty square in heart of old town.

Hostels *Foyer Leo Lagrange*, 16 rue Peyrevidal (Tel. 61 65 09 04). Modern and efficient student hostel.
Restaurants *Le Médiéval*, 42 rue des Chapeliers (Tel. 61 02 81 50); Ariégois specialities, including trout and crayfish from local rivers. *Camp du Drap d'Or*, 21 rue N. Peyrevidal (Tel. 61 02 87 87). Delicious simple meals, good value menus.

Excursion from Foix
Grottes de Niaux

Sixteen kilometres south of Foix are the **Grottes de Niaux** containing remarkably well-preserved prehistoric paintings depicting horses, wild goat, stags and bison dating from the Magdalenian period, around 20,000 BC.

From Foix the train heads north directly to Toulouse (1 hour), from where there are fast and direct connections to Paris, Bordeaux, Lyon and Avignon.

8 The Loire Valley

No other region of France is so quintessentially French as the Loire valley. No region of France combines grandeur and magnificence in such an elegant and restrained manner. Aesthetically and architecturally, the Loire valley has few rivals. The river itself has a natural majesty that even the Seine cannot pretend to. The Rhône is primarily an industrial river, a waterway; the Dordogne is picturesque; the Garonne is functional. Only the Loire valley can claim to be the playground of kings and princes.

The Loire valley is intimately associated with the formation of the French kingdom. Orléans was the site of the Coronation of Charles the Bald in 842 and virtually became the French capital under the first Capetians. It was the relief of Orléans by Joan of Arc in 1429 that turned the tide against the English and led to the consolidation of the French kingdom.

Ironically it was the English who were in part responsible for the connection of the Loire with the French monarchy. For when the English expelled Charles VII from Paris in the 15th century, he spent most of his exile in Tours and in the châteaux of the surrounding region. He grew to love the Touraine – and this love was shared by most of his successors during the following 2 centuries. Freed from the paramount concerns of defence, the nobles of the 15th and 16th century French court were able to commission magnificent Renaissance creations which ranged from elegant mansions to the most extravagant palaces ever built in France – the greatest of which must surely be the **Château de Chambord**. Hundreds of these châteaux still stand today, remnants of the great wealth and patronage that came to this region in the 15th century.

The River Loire presents a very different aspect in summer and winter. In summer the water slows almost to a trickle, small streams are divided by wide sandbanks on which grow olive-green willows; in winter a grey torrent of swirling water can burst its banks, spreading water far and wide over the flat water-meadows between Tours and Nantes. Westwards, on the gentle slopes bordering the Loire valley, are the small vineyards which produce a number of delectable light wines. Few wines are to be found much further north than the Loire – at least to the west of Paris – for the Loire valley also marks an invisible border – that of climate. To the south, the climate is determined by the climatic patterns of the Midi; to the north by the Gulf Stream and easterly winds blowing in over the flat landscape of north-eastern France from eastern Europe and Russia.

Gastronomically, the Loire valley is famous for its fish and game. From the Loire come pike, salmon and shad, served with a butter sauce, and stuffed bream and eels simmered in wine with mushrooms, onions and prunes. The vast forests and royal hunting grounds have always been a source of game. Boar with prunes, veal cooked in a cream sauce made with white wine and brandy and chicken casseroled in a red wine sauce are all specialities of the region. So too are *rillettes*, a rich pork paté, mushrooms marinated in wine, *coq au vin* and *escalopes*. Asparagus, stuffed-mushrooms and green cabbage with butter accompany the rich game dishes of Sologne. Cheese of the Loire region include St-Benoit, Vendôme and St-Paulin, made from cows milk, and the goats cheeses of Chavignol, Selles-Sur-Cher, Ste-Maure, crémets d'Anjou and Valençay.

The best known white wines are those of Vouvray, a dry, mellow wine, rich and ripe, and Montlouis, which has a delicate fruity flavour. Both are made from the Chenin Blanc grape, known locally as the Pineau de la Loire. Of the red wines, the best known is Breton, made from the Cabernet Franc grape, followed by the stronger, richer Chinon wines. From Anjou come the Rouge de Cabernet and the Saumur-Champigny, both wines with a rich ruby glow. From the eastern end of the valley come the wines of

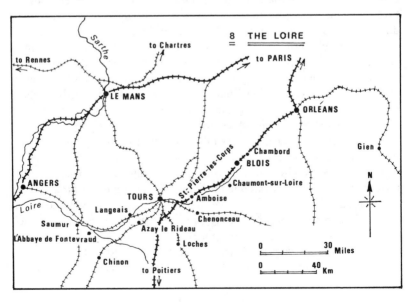

Sancerre, made from the Sauvignon grape. Most of the wine produced in the Loire valley is kept in the old quarries and caves hollowed out of the soft limestone rock at road level which can be visited all year round.

The Route Orleans – Blois – Château de Chambord – Château de Cheverny – Chaumont-sur-Loire – Amboise – Tours – Azay-le-Rideau – Chinon – Langeais – L'abbaye de Fontevraud – Saumur – Angers

The Loire is one of the longest rivers in France, its source a long way south in the Massif Central. The succession of châteaux for which the Loire is famous begin at Orleans and easily accessible from Paris, **Orléans** *makes an ideal starting point for a journey along the Loire by train. Closely associated with Joan of Arc, who liberated the town from the English in 1429, Orléans is a lively town with a beautiful cathedral, lovely parks and pleasant atmosphere. To the west lies* **Blois**, *its old town clustered around the huge and fanciful Renaissance palace built by Louis XII and François I. Henri III's Catholic rival for the throne, the Duc de Guise, was assassinated here in 1588.*

Hidden in woods outside Orléans is the Loire's largest and most extravagant château, that of **Chambord**, *a spectacular Renaissance palace commissioned by François I and set amongst the king's favourite hunting grounds.* **Cheverney**, *stately and reserved in comparison, is one of the few Loire châteaux to have remained in the same hands since the late Middle Ages.* **Chaumont-sur-Loire**, *built at the end of the Middle Ages, is a feudal fortress, still defended by towers, a moat and drawbridge. Catherine de Médici lived in the château until she forced Henry II's mistress, Diane de Poitiers, out of the nearby château of Chenonceaux, which she took for herself. A little to the east lies the château of* **Amboise**, *set on a steep hillside over the Loire, which Charles VIII embellished in Italian Renaissance style after returning from an unsuccessful campaigning in Italy.* **Tours** *is a graceful and lively city situated between the rivers Loire and Cher, and the best spot from which to reach those châteaux which are not so easily accessible by train.* **Langeais** *contains one of the most perfect medieval castles of France, and one of the last to be built with only defence in mind. Beyond it lies the* **Abbaye de Fontevraud**, *a vast Romanesque royal abbey where 2 of England's most illustrious Angevin kings and queens lie buried.* **Saumur**, *reflected quietly in the waters of the Loire, was* *immortalised in Balzac's novel* Eugénie Grandet, *and is home to the* Cadre Noir *equestrian corps.* **Angers** *is dominated by the massive walls of the château which was once the residence of the Dukes of Anjou. It now possesses 2 extraordinary 14th-century tapestries woven from wool and gold thread which are masterpieces of European medieval art.* (**Approximately** 7 – 10 days.)

Orléans

Trains *20 trains daily from* **Paris Austerlitz** *(1¼ hours); 15 from* **Tours** *(1¼ hours); 12 from* **Blois** *(40 mins); 10 from* **Amboise** *(1 hour), most requiring a change at Orléans-Les Aubrais, a station 5km away.*

Orléans is still a beautiful and fascinating town, despite the severe damage it suffered during the course of the Second World War. The city has been connected with the Orléans family since 1344 when it was made the capital of a duchy and given to a younger son of Philip VI. Although originally a Gallic town, the name of Orléans comes from the Roman city of Aurelianis. After the Coronation of Charles the Bald in 842, the town became the capital of the French kingdom. It was, as a result, besieged by the English in 1428, although not for long for the following year the town was relieved by Joan of Arc. This event marked the turning point in the Hundred Years War and within 25 years the English crown had lost all its French possessions, with the exception of Calais. Since 1430 celebrations have been held each year in the city on 8th May to celebrate the ejection of the English from France and to pay tribute to Joan of Arc.

What to see

Place du Martroi

Not surprisingly a statue of *la pucelle d'Orléans* – the maid of Orléans – graces the main square, the Place du Martroi, in the heart of the old town. The western part of Place du Martroi was totally flattened during the war but it has been rebuilt to match the old buildings perfectly. This includes the 18th-century Chancellory and its 19th-century copy, the Chamber of Commerce, which form part of the Rue Royale, the carefully and sympathetically restored thoroughfare which forms the central axis of the city. Of the nearby quarter only 2 buildings survived: the adjacent houses of the Porte Renard which date from the 16th-century.

Maison de Jeanne d'Arc

The Maison de Jeanne d'Arc, in Place Charles de Gaulle, where Joan of Arc stayed in 1429, has been destroyed and rebuilt two times in its history. The museum has superb period costumes and an effective audio-visual presentation of the siege of Orléans. (Open Tues–Sun 10 am–noon and 2–6 pm.)

Hôtel Grosslot

The rue d'Escure is one of Orléans most attractive streets, flanked by handsome 17th-century houses, it leads to the Hôtel Grosslot, now the town hall – a superb mid-16th century Renaissance building with sumptuous rooms and delightful garden which are open to the public. (Open Sun–Fri 10 am–noon and 2–5 pm.) Numerous French kings, including François II, Henri III and IV, stayed in the mansion while in the city. The statue of Joan of Arc at prayer on the steps is the work of Marie d'Orléans, the daughter of Louis-Philippe. Running north from the Rue d'Escure is the Rue Sainte-Anne where the late-16th-century **Maison des Oves** is to be found, its façade curiously decorated with rounded stones.

Cathédrale Ste-Croix

Orleans Cathedral is something of an anomaly. Built in Gothic style in the 17th and 18th centuries, Proust described St-Croix as France's ugliest church. That a new cathedral was needed at all was due to the ravages of the Prince de Condé, whose men desecrated and destroyed the earlier cathedral during the religious wars in 1568. Until 1978 one of the last great medieval cemeteries of Europe, the Campo-Santo, extended around the cathedral. In an unfortunate decision, the town council ordered it to be turned-over by bulldozers to clear the ground for a municipal car and coach park, despite the protest of eminent historians.

Musée des Beaux-Arts

Just across from the cathedral is the modern museum of fine art with a collection of paintings by Tintoretto, Velasquez, Watteau, Boucher, Gauguin and others. (Open Wed–Mon 10 am–noon and 2–6 pm.) Not far away is one of the finest Renaissance mansions in Orléans, the **Hôtel des Créneaux**, on the Place de la République. Rue Jeanne d'Arc leads back to Place Abbé Desnoyers and the 16th-century Hôtel Cabu which houses the **Musée Archéologique et Historique de l'Orléannais**, a superb collection of beautiful Gallo-Roman bronze figurines and votive offerings, medieval objects and antiquities. (Open Tues–Sun 10 am–noon and 2–6pm; Nov–April Tues–Sun 2–6 pm.)

Practicalities in Orléans

Tourist Office Place Albert 1er, close to station (Tel. 38 53 05 95); accommodation service; guided walking tours. Open Mon–Sat 9 am–7 pm, Sun 9.30 am–12.30 pm and 5.30–6.30 pm; Sept–June Mon–Sat 9 am–7 pm.

Railway Station Place Albert 1er (Tel. 38 53 50 50); information office. For town centre follow Rue de la République south to Place du Martroi.

Markets Nouvelle Halle, daily covered market.

Festivals Celebration of Joan of Arc's victory, 7th–8th May; *Jazz Festival*: around 1st weekend in July.

Hotels Budget hotels mainly situated around Rue du Faubourg Bonnier.

Hôtel de Paris, 29 rue Faubourg Bonnier, near station and Place Gambetta (Tel. 38 53 39 58).

Hôtel Cohigny, 80 rue de la Gare (Tel. 38 53 61 60). Simple and clean, short walk from station off Ave de Paris.

☆☆ *Hôtel Urbis*, 17 rue de Paris (Tel. 38 62 40 40). Modern and functional, but efficient and convenient for station.

☆☆ *Hôtel d'Arc*, 37 rue République (Tel. 38 53

10 94). Between the station and the central Place du Martroi.

☆☆ *Hôtel Orléans*, 6 rue A. Crespin, off Rue de la République and close to Place du Martroi (Tel. 38 53 35 34).

Hostels *Auberge de Jeunesse* (HI) 14 rue du faubourg Madeleine, Bus **B** from station (direction **Paul-Bert**).

Camping *St Jean-de-la-Ruelle*, rue de la Roche (Tel. 38 88 39 39). Pleasant wooded ground near Loire, 3 km from city centre. Bus **D** from station to **Roche aux Fées**.

Restaurant *L'Assiette*, 12 Place du Martroi (Tel. 38 53 46 69). Excellent grilled meat and a wide selection of *hors d'oeuvres* and salads.

Blois

Trains *18 trains daily from* Orléans *and* Paris Austerlitz *(1½ hours);* 15 *from* Tours *(1 hour);* 12 *from* Amboise *(20 mins).*

Blois is situated on the steeply rising ground which slopes up from the north bank of the Loire, its brick and stone houses climbing to the great castle which dominates the town and which played such an important role in the early history of France.

From the end of the 9th century the House of Blois was one of the most powerful feudal dynasties of France but with the extinction of the family in the 13th century, Blois was acquired by Louis d'Orléans, the brother of Charles VI.

What to see

Château Royal

After the death of Charles VIII, Louis XII established his court at Blois, followed by François I who enlarged and completed the royal château. Dating from different periods the château is not harmonious in style but it is still magnificent. The oldest part of the château – the state rooms and one wing consisting of a low Louis XII building of brick and stone through which access is gained to a central courtyard – dates from the 13th century. To the left is a 15th-century gallery and to the right the royal building which François I created around the earlier medieval fortress between 1515 – 24. On the far side lies the outstanding classical façade designed by Mansart for Gaston d'Orléans in 1635. Almost all these different buildings, however, are unfurnished, and most of the rooms appear empty and cold. Part of the Queen's apartments in the François I wing are fitted up; they include the dressing-room, bedroom, oratory and beautifully panelled study of Catherine de Médici.

The château of Blois is associated with the murder of the Duc de Guise in the presence of Henri III in 1558. In 1536 Henri III opened a session of the States General in the château, which came out in favour of the League and issued orders favourable to the Protestants, a move which further inflamed religious fighting in the country. In 1558, at the second meeting of the States General, Henri III had the leader of the Catholic party, the Duc de Guise assassinated together with his brother, the Cardinal of Lorraine. 40 of the king's followers were selected to murder the Duc de Guise in Henri III's personal apartments on the second floor of the exuberant Renaissance wing designed for François I.

The most original and eye-catching feature of the François I wing is the massive staircase in the open octagonal tower which was used for balcony appearances at royal receptions and where François's soldiers assembled to greet the king on his return to the château. Despite being the site of his father's murder, Gaston d'Orléans was compelled to live in the château after the assassination of the Duc de Guise. Gaston's intention was to pull the château down and build a finer one in its place but, short of money, he had to be content with building the southwest wing. In order to make room for this, Mansart had to demolish part of François I's palace, which is why the magnificent Renaissance staircase now appears curiously off-centre. After the death of Gaston d'Orléans in 1660 the château lay largely forgotten until the Revolution, when it was pillaged and vandalised. After being restored in the mid-19th century it was badly damaged again in June 1940, since when it has been meticulously restored.

Musée des Beaux-Arts
The first floor of the Louis XII wing, a long gallery and 2 spiral staircases, houses the Musée des Beaux-Arts, a miscellaneous collection of French paintings from the 16th to 19th centuries. Louis XII's emblem, the porcupine, is to be found in niches above many of the doorways, while a magnificent larger-than-life equestrian statue of him occupies a recess above the main door (Open mid – Mar – Oct 9 am – 6 pm; Nov – mid-Mar. 9 am – noon and 2 – 5 pm.)

Cathédrale de St-Louis
Apart from the castle, there are a number of beautiful buildings and many handsome streets to be seen elsewhere in Blois. The Cathedral of Saint-Louis is a 17th-century Gothic reconstruction; with the apse dating from the 16th century. Behind the cathedral is the former Bishop's Palace, a charming classical building designed by Gabriel in the 18th century. From the terraces of the bishop's garden there is a fine view over a pleasing roofscape to the gleaming waters of the Loire and the woods beyond.

Old Quarter
The old town which lies between the Cathedral de St-Louis and the Loire, contains an abundance of picturesque houses, many of them Renaissance in style, especially in Rue des Papegaults, Rue du Puy-Chatel and Fontaine-des-Elus.

The **Hôtel d'Alluye**, built around a courtyard with Italianate galleries decorated with medallions of the Caesars and Aristotle, is particularly fine, as too is the 15th-century **Maison de Denis Papin**.

Practicalities in Blois

Tourist Office 3 ave Jean Laigret (Tel. 54 74 06 49). Located in a Renaissance pavillion designed for Anne de Bretagne; currency exchange; tickets for tours.
Railway Station On top of hill on Blvd Daniel Dupris (Tel. 54 78 50 50); information office. 5 mins from centre down Ave Jean-Laigret to château.
Hotels *Hôtel St-Jacques*, 7 rue Ducoux (Tel. 54 78 04 15). Bright, clean and convenient for station.
Etoile d'Or 7–9 Bourg Neuf (Tel. 54 78 46 93). Bright rooms and lively café downstairs, not far from château.
☆☆ *Hôtel Savoie*, 6 rue Ducoux, very close to the station (Tel. 54 74 32 21).
☆☆ *Anne de Bretagne*, 31 ave du Dr Jean Laigret (Tel. 54 78 05 38). On street leading from station to centre; delightful simple rooms, quiet and comfortable.
☆☆☆ *Hôtel Monarque*, 61 porte Chartraine (Tel. 54 78 02 35). Very comfortable hotel off rue de Bourg-Neuf.
Hostels *Auberge de Jeunesse* (HI), 18 rue de l'Hôtel Pasquier (Tel. 54 78 27 21). 5km outside Blois. Take bus no 4 to **Eglise des Grouets**.
Camping *La Boire*, 2km from town, across Loire, towards Blois; open Mar – Nov (Tel. 54 74 22 78).
Restaurants ☆ *Noë*, 10 bis ave de Vendôme (Tel. 54 74 22 26). Delicious, simple cooking. Local duck and carp cooked gently in white wine are especially fine.
☆☆ *La Bocca d'Or*, 15 rue Haute (Tel. 54 78 04 74). cool, vaulted medieval cellar is the setting for local game dishes beautifully cooked by chef Patrice Galland.

Excursions from Blois
Chambord and Cheverney

Buses *Although Chambord and Cheverney cannot be reached by railway, they are accessible easily from* **Blois** *by bus: Point Bus, 2 Place Victor Hugo (Tel. 54 78 15 66); close to tourist office; Transport Loir-et-Cher (TLC) run buses to the châteaux of Chambord, Cheverny, Chaumont, Chenonceau and Amboise. Passes include admission to château; tickets bought at bus station, tourist office or on bus. Bus departures from train station. Information from tourist office or bus station.*
Only a few miles south of the Loire, hidden by forest, are the 2 famous châteaux of Chambord and Cheverney. Built exactly a century apart, they represent the changing taste in French architecture of the period.

Château de Chambord Chambord was begun in 1523 in a marshy clearing in the huge Forest of Boulogne, and it is the largest château in the Loire valley. Laid out on a precise symmetrical plan, the massive façade is focussed on a central block flanked by 2 vast cylindrical towers, above which jostle a soaring profusion of gables, dormers, chimneys, pinnacles and cupolas. To come across Chambord, without knowing of its existence, is to stumble upon a dream castle of almost unbelievable proportions. Its size creates a feeling of awe, even to a generation accustomed to skyscrapers and giant tower blocks, partly perhaps because of the isolation in which it stands and partly because of its dignity and regularity.

The château was originally designed by an Italian, Domenico da Cortona, but the final design was the work of Jacques and Denis Sourdeau and Pierre Trinqueau. Astonishingly, the main walls were completed between 1519–33. Work continued under Henri ii, Charles ix and Henri iii and François i often stayed here while work was still in progress. After his death French kings from Henri ii to Louis xiv continued to live here.

Chambord has never failed to impress. Châteaubriand remarked of it 'from a distance, the building is like an Arabesque. It is like a woman with her hair blowing in the wind.' Victor Hugo was struck too, commenting that 'magic, poetry, even madness are here in the wonderful strangeness of this palace of fairies and knights'. Its stone is astonishingly white and conveys an almost unreal lightness to what is a massive edifice, 152 metres wide and 116 metres deep. Inside there are 440 rooms and over 80 staircases while the roof is crowned with 800 capitals and 365 chimneys. No wonder it took an astonishing 1,800 workmen to build the palace.

Even Louis xiv sometimes left his beloved Versailles for Chambord and it was here that Molière first played *Monsieur de Pourceaugnac* and the *Bourgeois Gentilhomme* in the Salles des Gardes. During the 18th century the ex-King of Poland, Stanislas Leszczynski, lived at Chambord when he was not at Nancy. The château then passed to Marshall de Saxe, as a reward from Louis xv for defeating the English and Dutch at Fontenoy in 1745, and was later sold to the Duc de Bordeaux, the last survivor of the older branch of the Bourbon family who took the title Comte de Chambord. Later it was acquired by the French state.

The vast edifice is largely empty of furniture, the original furniture having been destroyed or stolen during the Revolution, but there are a number of tapestries, paintings and state coaches which once belonged to the Comte de Chambord, the last legitimate Pretender to the French throne. Although a Renaissance building *par excellence*, the plan of the château remains faithful to the structures of the Middle Ages. It consists of a huge rectangle flanked by large round towers at each angle and completed, in the middle of one side by a monumental Keep, which is itself flanked by round towers. In the centre of the Keep the spirals of the Grand Escalier twist upwards in dizzying fashion to a 100-foot-high lantern. The château is placed at the cross-roads of architectural influences. Its gigantic proportions and lack of harmony may lay it open to criticism but

nevertheless no one can deny that it is a work of extraordinary originality and grandeur of conception.
(Open daily June–15th Sept 9.30 am–6.45 pm; 15th Sept – June 9.30 am–11.45 am and 2–4.45 pm: *Son-et-lumière* show: several times a week, in evening, May–October.)

Château de Cheverny Cheverney is altogether different. Surrounded by a delightful park, it is far more attractive and less ostentatious than the Château de Chambord. Begun in 1634 for Henri Hurault, son of the Chancellor of France, it is still lived in by one of his descendents, the Marquis de Vibraye. The layout of the château is simple, its ornamentation restrained to simple window pediments and 12 niches sheltering busts between the first floor windows. The main central section, which is 3 floors high, is flanked by less elevated wings which end with 2 pavilions roofed by quadrangular domes, themselves crowned by modest lanterns. The entrance doorway is modest in the extreme and the exterior is restrained almost to the point of severity.

The interior however has retained its period furniture and contemporary furnishings, making it the most complete collection of its epoch in France. In the king's room elegant woodwork is adorned by little painted panels with allegorical scenes by the Blois artist Jean Mosnier who also painted the adventures of Don Quixote in an adjacent room. One of Cheverny's undoubted charms is the magnificent park which surrounds the château. This park, where woods and sheets of water merge to create an admirable composition, has undergone a few changes over the centuries but now the formal 17th-century flowerbeds have been recreated anew. (Open daily 9.15 am–6.30 pm; mid-Sept – May 9.30 am-noon and 2.15–5 pm.)

Chaumont-sur-Loire

Trains/Bus *Transports Loir-et-Cher (TLC) bus 'Circuit 2' from* **Blois** *railway station; 6 trains daily from* **Blois** *(10 mins) and* **Tours** *(35 mins): alight at tiny station of* **Onzain**, *2 km north of Chaumont.*

The grim and sombre château of Chaumont-sur-Loire guards the valley of the Loire just as the château of Amboise does a little further down-river. The château was built by Charles d'Amboise in the second half of the 15th century before being acquired by Queen Catherine de Médici who forced her husband's mistress, Diane de Poitiers, to take it in exchange for the Château of Chenonceaux. Diane de Poitiers never took to the fortress-like Chaumont and visited it rarely, her only addition being to have her initial 'D' carved under the parapet walk.

The building, partly shrouded behind a thick screen of foliage, consists of 3 wings and an inner courtyard which opens out onto a terrace overlooking the Loire. The château is primarily a strongly fortified feudal fortress, its entrance flanked by 2 fat round pepperpot towers that are girdled by a covered sentry-walk and machicolations. Nevertheless the windows are large and numerous and in the sculptured decoration of doorways and window surrounds one can detect the coming of the Renaissance. A frieze on the façade is decorated with images of a mountain in flames – the *Chaud mont*, from which the name derives. Charles II of Amboise was one of Louis XII's better and wiser councillors and prudently placed the arms of France and the initials of the king and Anne of Brittany on the 2 main buildings.

Only a small number of rooms can be visited but they have been decorated and have furniture dating from the 16th century. These rooms include the guard room with its beautiful Beauvais tapestries, the bedrooms of Diane de Poitiers and Catherine de Médici and the Council Room hung with 16th-century Flemish tapestries and paved with fine Italian tiles. Even the stables have to be seen to be believed for here, in the 19th century, the Broglie family added what must be the most sumptuous stables to be found anywhere in France.

(Open daily 9.15 am–5.30 pm; April–June and Sept 9.15 am–11.30 am and 1.45 – 5.30 pm; Oct–March 9.15 – 11.30 am and 1.45 – 3.50 pm.)

Amboise

Trains *10 – 12 trains daily from* **Blois** *(15 mins) and* **Orléans** *(1 hour); 12 daily from* **Tours** *(20 mins); 13 from* **Paris** *(2½ hours).*

Only a few kilometres west, on the same ridge overlooking the Loire, stands Amboise, the little town overlooked by its magnificent château whose superb façade rises from 15th-century towers and bastions. The château is of particular architectural interest for it represents some of the earliest Renaissance architecture in France.

The Renaissance came to France through Charles VII who returned from Italy in 1493 to found what became known as the School of Amboise. While still in Italy Charles sent instructions and plans for his new château which was well advanced in construction by the time he returned to France with a group of Italian masons and artists in train. The architectural structure of the château is therefore almost completely French but the decoration and ornamentation is almost wholly Italian. However, before work had finished, Charles VII fractured his skull and died after hitting his head against a stone lintel as he was passing through a low doorway of the Hacquelebac Gallery. Work was continued by Louis II, and François I finished the half-built wing.

François II moved to the château with his wife, Mary Stuart, and mother, Catherine de Médicis in 1560. In the same year Amboise was the scene of a bungled conspiracy against François II by the Huguenot party who intended to remove the king from what they deemed to be the pernicious influence of the Catholic Guises. The conspiracy was discovered before being put into effect and several hundred of the conspirators were hung from the iron balconies on the façade overlooking the river. After this event the château was rarely used as a place of residence by the kings of France, and when Gaston d'Orléans rebelled against his brother Louis XIII, the château ramparts were largely dismantled. In the 17th and 18th centuries the château was used as a state prison, the last prisoner being Abd-el-Kader who was held here from 1848 to 1852.

What to see

Château d'Amboise
The main structure consists of the royal apartments, the Logis du Roi, which date from Charles VIII's reign and extend parallel to the Loire, and the Louis XII wing. The state room, on the first floor, is formed by 2 naves with ogival vaults resting on delicate columns decorated alternately with fleur-de-lys and the ermine of Anne of Brittany. Altogether the impression of this room is one of exceptional elegance and lightness.

The Louis XII wing, with an additional floor, belongs to the Renaissance period whereas the Chapel of Saint-Hubert, once part of the main building, is a jewel of Flamboyant Gothic and was built by Charles VIII at the very end of the 15th century. Its sculptured tympanum shows the Madonna and Child between Charles VIII and Anne of Brittany, while the lintel of the portal represents St Hubert kneeling before a deer and St Christopher carrying the Infant Jesus. Leonardo da

Vinci, who died nearby in 1519, is believed to be buried under a flagstone in the north transept.

Tour des Minimes

The triangular wall that surrounds the château is pierced by 2 towers, the Tour des Minimes and the Hurtault Tower. The former betrays the architectural evolution of the age: Gothic at the base and Italianate at the top. It contains a marvellous spiral ramp on which François I and Charles V rode on horseback when the French king entertained the Holy Roman Emperor at the château in 1539. From the roof there is a stupendous view of the Loire, of the towers of Tours cathedral in the distance, and of the Balcon des Conjurés, on the which La Renaudie's Huguenot followers were hung in 1560. Across the gardens to the south lies the Hurtault Tower, a Gothic structure, but reflecting some Renaissance influence, which was finished by the time Charles VIII left for Italy around 1495. (Château open daily Jan–mid–Apr 9 am–noon and 2 – 5 pm; mid–Apr–June 9 am–noon and 2 – 6:30pm; July and Aug 9 am–6.30 pm.)

Le Clos Lucé

Apart from its monarchs, Amboise's most famous resident was Leonardo da Vinci who was invited to Amboise by François I in 1515. Leonardo spent the last 4 years of his life a little to the east of the town in the 15th-century manor house of Le Close Lucé, which had been lent to him by François I. The manor, now open to the public, contains a collection of astonishing models which have recently been constructed from the sketches Leonardo made of his inventions, among them water elevators, ventilations systems, jacks and prototype paddle-boats. Leonardo almost certainly played some role in outlining the plans for the Château de Chambord which was then in the process of being built and he is known to have put to the King a scheme for regulating the flow of the untamed river Loire. (Open daily mid-Mar – mid-Nov 9 am–7 pm; Feb–mid Mar and mid–Nov–Dec 9 am–6 pm)

Eglise St-Denis

The town of Amboise occupies a delightful position at the base of the château, stretching across to an island in the middle of the Loire. The 12th-century church of St-Denis was once part of a Dominican priory and although Romanesque in date it possesses the fine ribs and curved vaulting associated with the Angevin style. The 16th-century funerary statue of a drowned woman frozen by death, found in a recess inside the church, is reputed to have the features of one of François I's mistresses, Marie Gaudin.

On the quay beside the delightful shaded avenue, the Promenade du Mail, are the early 16th century **Hôtel de Ville** and **Church of St-Florentin**, which has an attractive Renaissance belfry. Behind Amboise stretches a vast tract of beech forest, much of which was once royal hunting grounds. 3 kilometres south of Amboise, on the edge of the forest that bears its name, is the curious sight of the **Pagode de Chanteloup**, which blends Chinese and Louis XVI styles. This bizarre combination was built in the 18th century at the behest of one of Louis XVI's ministers, Choiseul, who had been inspired by Chambers' pagoda at Kew Gardens.

Practicalities in Amboise

Tourist Office Quai Général de Gaulle, beside the Loire (Tel. 47 57 01 37); accommodation service. Open mid-June–Sept Mon.–Sat 9 am–12.30 pm and 1.30–8.30 pm.
Railway Station Blvd Gambetta min walk north of town. For town centre, take Rue Jules Ferry, over Ile St-Jean and the Loire. (Tel 47 23 18 23)
Hôtels ☆ *Hôtel les Platanes* blvd des Platanes, near station (Tel. 47 57 08 60). Spacious and clean
☆ *Hôtel à la Tour*, 32 rue Victor Hugo. (Tel. 47 57 14 46). Close to château, old-world and spotless with polished wooden floors.
☆ *Hôtel de France et du Cheval Blanc*, 6–7 quai Général de Gaulle, opposite tourist office (Tel. 47 57 92 44).
☆☆☆☆ *Choiseul*, 36 quai Charles-Guinot (Tel. 47 30 45 45). Spectacular, luxury hotel on the banks of the river, beneath the château. Pool, garden and superb restaurant.
Hostels *Auberge de Jeunesse*, Ile d'Or, on island in middle of the Loire; 10 mins from station (Tel. 47 57 06 36).
Camping *Ile d'Or*, near the *Auberge de Jeunesse*, facing the château (Tel. 47 57 23 37).
Restaurants ☆*Auberge du Mail*, 32 quai Général de Gaulle (Tel. 47 57 60 39). Regional specialities include fish stew with locally caught eels.

Tours

Trains *Most journeys require you to change at* **St-Pierre-des-Corps**, *a railway junction 5 mins outside Tours: check timetables carefully. 12 trains daily from* **Amboise** *(20 mins) and* **Saumur** *(35 mins); 6 from* **Langeais** *(20 mins); 8 from* **Angers** *(1 hour); 16 TGVs from* **Paris** *Montparnasse, change at St-Pierre-des-Corps (1 hour); 13 from* **Bordeaux**, *change at St-Pierre-des-Corps (2½ hours); 9 from* **Poitiers** *(30–60 mins).*

Just to the north of the Loire, on the gentle south-facing slopes that lie between Amboise and Tours, are the vineyards of Vouvray. They only cover a small area but they produce one of the most delightful light wines of the Touraine, which are matured in the caves and tunnels so easily carved out of the soft calcareous stone of the region. Here and there troglodytic homes can be spotted sunk back into the white cliff-sides and although most are now used for storage rather than habitation, the tell-tale sign of rising smoke or drawn curtains indicates that not all have yet been abandoned. Such homes are reputed to be warm and dry and must certainly be more cosy than some of the châteaux, with which they contrast so startlingly.

The peaceful landscape of Touraine melts naturally into the dignified and peaceful charm of Tours, the capital of the province. Perhaps more than any other town in the Loire valley, **Tours** breathes an air of safety and quiet domesticity, marred only in the height of summer by the number of visitors who come in search of its calm and beauty.

Tours was an important city long before the Middle Ages. St Gatien brought Christianity to Tours in the 3rd century and it was preached vigorously by the third bishop of Tours, St-Martin. A 6th-century bishop, Gregory of Tours, wrote one of the earliest histories of France and Charlemagne's advisor, Alcuin, turned the town into a centre of learning in the early Middle Ages. From the 8th century the town was a great religious centre and place of pilgrimage, visited by every king of France, Louis XI dying nearby on 30th August 1483 in his favourite residence, the Château of Plessis-les-Tours.

Although Tours prospered as a centre of silk production, its prosperity was ruined by the Religious Wars which ravaged the city a number of times and it was only with the accession of Henri IV in 1589 that its fortunes began to recover. In the 18th century Tours saw another revival which was helped by the arrival of the railway in 1846. It was briefly bombed and occupied by the Germans in the Franco-Prussian war, and much more severely damaged in the Second World War, when its bridges were destroyed by the retreating German army.

What so see

Place Plumereau
The haphazard web of narrow medieval streets which grew up along the banks of the Loire was arbitrarily bisected in the 18th century by a fine straight road, the Rue Nationale, which strikes through the town and down to the Loire. To the west of it lies the heart of old Tours, centred around Place Plumereau which retains several beautiful 15th-century gabled houses. Many of the streets of picturesque 16th and 17th century house were destroyed during the Second World War and have since been tastefully restored. Among those that survived are the **Hôtel Gouin**, with its superb early Renaissance façade and the 15th century mansions with their internal courtyards in Rue Paul-Louis-Courier. In rue du Mûrier, close to place Plumereau, is a little museum, the **Musée de Gemmail**, devoted entirely to coloured glass. (Open Tues–Sun 10 – 11.30 am and 2 – 6 pm.)

Musée des Beaux-Arts
To the east of the Rue Nationale is the cathedral and the former Archbishop's Palace, a charming 18th-century building next to delightful gardens in which stands a magnificent Cedar of Lebanon. The palace now houses an excellent **Musée des Beaux-Arts**, with paintings by Mantegna, Niccolo de Tommaso, Rembrandt and Jean Fouquet, amongst others. (Open Wed–Mon 9 am–12.45 pm and 2 – 6 pm.)

Cathédrale St-Gatien
The cathedral is one of the finest in France, despite being a mixture of styles from the 13th to 16th centuries. The façade, which was the last part to be built, is a

magnificent and exuberant example of the early Renaissance style, when Gothic tradition still prevailed over the classical innovations. The façade is built of the local calcareous tufa, a stone easy to carve but also just as easily eroded by wind, rain and frost. Despite this, and the removal of almost all the original statues in the 16th century and during the Revolution, the façade is still a marvel of delicate stone tracery. Both the northern and southern towers are surmounted by elegant Renaissance-style domed lanterns.

Although the nave is of later date than the choir they form a harmonious whole of perfect proportions and the choir has glorious 13th-century stained glass. The transepts likewise have fine rose windows of exceptional beauty dating from the 14th century. In a chapel off the south transept is the tomb of the children of Charles VIII and Anne of Brittany with its figures of kneeling angels. (Cathedral open Mon–Wed 9 am–12.45 pm and 2–6 pm.)

Hôtel Babou de la Bourdaisière

From the cathedral the Rue Lavoisier leads to the bank of the Loire, passing the Tour de Guise, all that remains of Henry II's castle which once defended the nearby bridge across the Loire. Nearby, in Place Foire-le-Roi, stands a delightful building, the Hôtel Babou de la Bourdaisière, the mansion of Philibert Babou, finance minister to François I. Other interesting buildings east of the Rue Nationale include the 13th-century abbey church of St-Julien and a 12th-century Chapter-house where the Parlement de Paris met in 1589.

Although the Loire flows at the foot of the hill, it does not feature prominently in the life of the city for in summer a great part of the river bottom is left dry. One of the most important bridges, the Pont Wilson, was partially destroyed when the Loire flooded in 1978, after which it was resolved to rebuild a bridge identical to the original of 1765–79.

Practicalities in Tours

Tourist Office Place du Maréchal Leclerc, opposite station (Tel. 47 05 58 08); accommodation service; arranges bus tours to local châteaux – Blois, Chambord and Cheverny (Tues); Chenonceau, Chaumont and Amboise (Mon); Azay-le-Rideau, Ussé and Villandry (Sun). *Touraine Evasion*: depart from tourist office; branch tourist office in Place de la Gare, next to Palais du Congres.

Railway Station 3 rue Edouard Vaillant (Tel. 47 20 50 50); currency exchange. To reach centre, cross Place du Marechal Lederc (where the tourist office is located), and the wide Boulevard heurteloup and walk down rue Buffon to the theatre. Turn left down Rue de la Scellerie, cross the central street of the city – rue Nationale – and continue down rue des Halles, to the old quarter to the north of Tour Charlemagne.

Hotels Cheapest hotels are to be found between the station and Ave. Grammont.

Hôtel Vendome, 24 rue Roger Salengro (Tel. 47 64 33 54). Comfortable and spacious rooms.

Mon Hôtel, 40 rue de la Préfecture, off rue Bernard Palissy (Tel. 47 05 67 53). Quiet, clean and spacious rooms; friendly proprietor.

Hôtel Regina, 2 rue Pimbert, behind Grand Theatre (Tel. 47 05 25 36).

☆☆ *Hôtel du Cygne*, 6 rue du Cygne (Tel. 47 66 66 41). Classic, pretty flower-decked old hotel; friendly welcome.

Auberge de Jeunesse (HI), Ave d'Arsonval, Parc de Grandmont (Tel. 47 25 14 45). 4 km from station; bus no 1 (direction Joue Blotterie).

Hostels *Auberge de Jeunesse* (HI), Ave d'Arsonval, Parc de Grandmont (Tel. 47 25 14 45). 4 km from station; bus no 1 (direction Joue Blotterie).

Restaurants *Patisserie Poirault*, 31 rue Nationale. Excellent pastries and teas.

☆ *Hôtel-Restaurant Moderne*, 1 rue Victor-

Laloux (Tel. 47 05 32 81). Good, traditional French cooking and good value.
☆☆ *Les Truffeaux*, 18 rue Lavoisier (Tel. 47 47

19 89). Calm, restrained decoration; delicious cooking; beautifully presented meals.

Heading west out of Tours the train passes through the attractive village of **Luynes** which was once an important feudal centre, as is attested by its sturdy medieval fortress which dominates the Loire. In the late 15th century the château was transformed by Hardouin de Maillé who constructed the brick and stone wing – the classical wing was added to the north of the château in the 17th century. The 4 massive towers, crowning a gentle rise, overlook some of the most beautiful scenery of the Loire valley. The château and village take their name from Albret de Luynes, Louis XIII's faithful minister whose estates were made a duchy by the king in return for the services he had rendered the French crown.

Below the château are a number of attractive 16th-century wooden buildings and troglodyte houses hollowed out from the rock. 2 kilometres north-east are the remains of a Roman aqueduct.

Azay-le-Rideau

Trains *7 trains daily from* **Chinon** *(30 mins); 2 km walk from station to château.*

Two kilometres from the station overlooking the River Indre is the **château of Azay-le-Rideau**, which rivals Chenonceaux in beauty and setting. Commissioned by François I's minister Gilles Berthelot, who used the royal purse to pay for his dreams, Azay-le-Rideau symbolises the grace and new-found beauty of the Renaissance. Much of the interior decoration and furnishings are poor copies of period examples but the whole ensemble is entrancing. Balzac, who lived nearby, describes seeing the château for the first time: 'Climbing a ridge, I admired for the first time this cut diamond set on the Indre and mounted on piles masked by flowers.'

The château was confiscated by François I, seized by Louis XIII and probably visited by Louis XIV. It reflects the transition from the medieval fortress building to the Renaissance palace; the machicolations have become no more than decorative motifs, the towers are reduced to turrets and the moat has become more an ornament than a defensive feature; its symmetrical balance is Italian in influence. Its finest feature of the façade is the grand staircase, which was very much an innovation at the time of its construction. Beneath the windows are the emblems of Claude of France, the ermine, and François I, the Salamander. A beautiful private park surrounds the château. (Open 9 am–6.30 pm; Sept and April–June 9.30 am–5.30 pm; Oct–March 10 am–noon and 2–4.30 pm.)

Practicalities in Azay-le-Rideau

Tourist Office 26 rue Gambetta, 1 km from station on Ave de la Gare (Tel. 46 45 44 10); accommodation assistance.
Hotels ☆☆☆ *Grand Monarque*, 3 Place de la République (Tel. 47 45 40 08). Delightful, beautifully decorated rooms; excellent cuisine and shady tables for outside eating.
Camping *Camping Parc du Sabot* on banks of the Indre; open Easter–mid Nov; canoe and kayak hire (Tel. 47 45 42 72).

Chinon

Trains *5 trains daily from* **Tours** *(1 hour); 7 trains from* **Azay-le-Rideau.**

A few miles west of Tours lie 3 important châteaux, of which the vast ruin of Chinon is the most romantic and impressive. Standing on the level top of a wide hill above the Vienne, the ruined walls and towers of the castle, built by Henry Plantagenet in the 12th century, are silhouetted against the sky. Henry became king of England in 1154 but Chinon, at the centre of his contintental possessions, remained his favourite residence. When he died here on 6th July 1189, the castle passed to his son Richard the Lionheart who is also reputed to have died in the castle after being wounded besieging Chalus in Limousin.

On Richard's death John Lackland, the youngest son of Henry II, inherited the Plantagenet Empire but in 1205 Chinon was lost to the French crown and in 1214 John was defeated in battle by the future Louis VIII at the Battle of La-Roche-aux-Monies near Angers. The Treaty of Chinon of the same year confirmed the French victory and John was reduced to being no more than the King of England. Chinon came to prominence again 2 centuries later when Charles VII was ousted from Paris by the English King Henry VI and moved his court to the town in 1427.

It was at Chinon that Joan of Arc first met Charles VII on 6th March 1429, having travelled unharmed through war-torn country from Lorraine. At this famous meeting the King deliberately tried to confuse Joan of Arc about his identity as a test of her powers. Persuaded by the authenticity of her mission – Charles also had some doubts about his legitimacy which Joan of Arc allayed – they set off together for Orléans, then being besieged by the English, but not before summoning the Estates General to meet here to vote for the funds needed for the war to eject the English from France.

What to see

Le Château

The castle lies high up on a spur at the junction of the regions of Touraine, Anjou and Poitou, and overlooks on one side the vines so beloved of François Rabelais, the satirical and comic genius of 16th-century France. Fond of feasting and drinking, Rabelais' 2 fictional characters, Gargantua and Pantagruel, had a special fondness for the rich ruby-red wine of Chinon. Rabelais was born near

Chinon at La Devinière but grew up in the town, living in Rue de la Lamproie. Once surrounded by high walls, the steep streets leading up to the castle are full of interesting old houses with pointed roofs, carved beams and doorways, mullioned windows and corner turrets.

Abandoned by the court after the 15th-century, the castle has been partly dismantled, mostly on the order of Richelieu who used the stone to build a nearby château. The most impressive part of the castle was St-George's fort in the east, a massive fortress which defended the most vulnerable side of the castle looking onto the plateau. The central part of the castle is entered across the moat and through the 14th-century **Tour de l'Horloge**, in which there is now a small **museum** devoted to Joan of Arc.

From the ruined towers and south wall there is a lovely view over the grey slate roofs of Chinon and the valley of the Vienne. West of the gardens another moat leads to the **Coudray Fort**, built by Philippe Auguste in the 13th century; Templars imprisoned in the Keep by Philip the Fair in 1308 carved the graffiti on the north wall before being taken to Paris to be tried and burnt at the stake. Only the fireplace remains of the great hall in the royal apartments where Joan of Arc was received by Charles VII. The kitchen contains an Aubusson tapestry depicting the moment when Joan of Arc recognised the Dauphin.

Le Grand Carroi

Below the castle in the old town, at the junction of Rue Haute St-Maurice and the Rue du Grand Carroi, are the crossroads, known as the *Grand Carroi*, which was the centre of the town in the Middle Ages. Today it is the focal point of a medieval market recreated on the first weekend of August each year. On one corner of the Grand Carroi is the **Museum of Old Chinon** in the States-General house where Richard the Lionheart is reputed to have died in 1199 and where the States-General met in 1428. Nearby are other picturesque houses, some with courtyards open to the public. The **Maison Rouge** is a pretty, 14th century, half-timbered house, with an overhanging upper storey. Number 45 is decorated with statues which serve as columns; the wide stone doorway of number 48 is the entrance to the **Hôtel du Gouvernement**, which opens into an attractive courtyard surrounded by graceful arcades.

Rue Haute St-Maurice leads west to the **Maison de Bodard de la Jacopière**, a delightful 15th- and 16th-century building; at number 82 is the 16th-century **Hôtel des Eaux et Forêts**, with a little corner turret and handsome dormer windows. At the foot of the town paths lead along the banks of the Vienne to the lovely **Jardin Anglais**, opposite the Ile de Tours.

In the vaulted cellars of the tourist office is a fascinating little **museum** devoted to vine-growing and the wine of the region. (Open May–Sept Fri–Wed 10 am–noon and 2–6 pm.)

Practicalities in Chinon

Tourist Office 12 rue Voltaire, off Place Général de Gaulle (Tel. 47 93 17 85); info. on visits to neighbouring châteaux and wine caves; emergency currency exchange.

Railway Station Ave-Gambetta at junction with Ave du Docteur Labussière (Tel. 47 93 11 04).

Festivals *Marché Médiéval*: 1st weekend in Aug, recreation of medieval Chinon, with music, costume, dance and artisans.

Marché à l'Ancienne: 3rd weekend in Aug, celebrating peasant traditions and agricultural produce.

Hotels *Hôtel le Jeanne d'Arc*, 11 rue Voltaire (Tel. 47 93 07 20) Excellent location, opposite tourist office.

☆☆ *Hôtel Diderot*, 4 rue Buffon, at eastern end of town near St-Mexme (Tel. 47 93 18 87).

☆☆ *Chris' Hôtel*, 12 Place Jeanne d'Arc, a short walk from the Jardin Anglais (Tel. 47 93 36 92).

☆☆ *Hôtel France*, 47 place Général de Gaulle, close to steps leading up to Fort St-Georges (Tel. 47 93 33 91).

☆☆ *Hostellerie Gargantua*, 73 rue Haute-St-Maurice (Tel. 47 93 04 71). A delightful, quiet hotel-restaurant serving local specialities; outside eating in summer.

Hostels Auberge de Jeunesse (HI) Rue Descartes (Tel. 47 93 10 48). 5 mins from station; good facilities and location.

Camping *Camping d'Ile Auger* (Tel. 47 93 08 55), across the vienne at the Ile Auger; superb view of Chinon and close to centre.

Restaurants *Jeanne de France*, 12 Place Géneral de Gaulle (Tel. 47 93 20 12). Popular pizzeria in the main square.

☆☆ *Au Plaisir Gourmand*, Quai Charles VII (Tel. 47 93 20 48). Chef Jean-Claude Rigollet's reputation has spread far and wide; delicate and imaginative dishes, cooking at its best.

Langeais

Trains *5 trains daily from* **Saumur** *(20 mins) and* **Tours** *(15 mins).*

Passing a curious square tower of brick masonry, known as the **Pile de Cinq-Mars**, of unknown purpose but resting on a Gallo-Roman base, the flat valley plain is crossed to **Langeais**, a pleasant old town with a fabulous **castle**, originally a stronghold of Fulk Nerra. After the marriage of Eleanor of Aquitaine to Henry II until 1216 the château was a Plantagenet fortress, occupied by Richard Lionheart before being lost to Philippe Auguste. Much later, in 1427, it was briefly retaken by the English.

Its present appearance dates from soon after the expulsion of the English from France although its Keep – which lies a little way from the 15th-century château dates from around the year 900 and is the oldest in France.

The castle was in a pitiful state when Louis XI gave it to his minister of Finance, Jean Bourré, who set about its complete reconstruction in 1469. At the time, the powerful and independent Dukedom of Brittany was threatening to to form an alliance with the Dukes of Burgundy and by encouraging Bourré to construct a new castle, Louis XI was protecting his western border. The castle never lived to be besieged, however, for with Charles VIII's marriage to Anne of Brittany in 1491, the threat of an attack evaporated. This historic wedding, which severed a thousand years of Brittany's independence from France, was celebrated in this fabulous château on 16th December 1491.

Even if the château never saw action, it retains the forbidding aspect of a feudal stronghold and is a perfect example of late-15th century French military architecture: the windows are narrow and placed high up; the walls are high and thick; the drawbridge is flanked by 2 huge cyclindrical towers; the moats – now filled in – completely surrounded the château; and the Keep, built into the main façade, is only linked via a sentry walk to the main apartments. The internal courtyard is far less daunting than the exterior of the fort: large mullioned windows and gables give a hint of the arrival of the Renaissance.

Acquired and restored with immaculate taste and scholarship by Jacques Siegfried in the 19th century it was bequeathed to the Institut de France in 1904. The interior benefits from magnificent furnishings and furniture dating from the 15th and 16th centuries, including superb Aubusson tapestries representing heroes in the Grand Salon. (Open daily 9 am–noon and 3 – 6 pm; Tel. 47 96 72 60.)

Practicalities in Langeais

Tourist Office 2 Place de la Mairie, opposite the château (Tel. 47 96 58 22).

Railway Station 10 mins from château (Tel. 47 96 82 19).

Cycles *Station Glorex*, 24 rue de Tours (Tel. 47 96 81 17).

Hotels ☆☆ *Duchesse Anne*, 10 rue de Tours (Tel. 47 96 82 03). Small hotel, modest simple rooms; good traditional French cooking in the restaurant.

Camping *Camping Municipal*, 1 km from château; open June-mid Sept (Tel. 47 96 85 80).

Saumur

Trains *11 trains daily from* **Tours** *(35 mins),* **Angers** *(20 mins); 5 daily from* **Nantes** *(1 hour 10 mins).*

Saumur lies on the eastern edge of Maine-et-Loire, a *département* that broadly corresponds to the ancient province of Anjou, the rich and fertile heritage of the Plantagenet Kings of England. Anjou is a richer territory than the neighbouring land of Touraine; gentler in aspect and very fertile, it is devoted almost entirely to corn, artichokes, and wine.

Saumur is an impressive town, with its low, handsome buildings stretching out horizontally in an elegant succession along the southern bank of the Loire. Above, sitting full-square on a raised dias and looking down over the town and river, is its castle with its octagonal corner-towers and high façades crowned with dormer-windows in steeply pitched slate roofs.

What to see

Le Château

The 15th-century château at Saumur commands the junction of the Thouet and the Loire, and from its extensive terrace there is an unparalleled view up and down a majestic stretch of river and across the silver band of water to the low-lying flood plains of Maine-et-Loire.

The château was built in the 11th century to defend the eastern border of Anjou against the encroachments of the Counts of Blois and played an important role during the early struggles between the Plantagenets and the Capetians. After its capture by Philippe Auguste at the turn of the 12th century it remained in French hands, successfully resisting English attempts to capture it during the Hundred Years War. The existing château began to be rebuilt by Louis I of Anjou at the end of the 14th century and was completed by Louis II, his son. Its appearance at that time is faithfully reproduced in the *Tres Riches Heures* of the Duc de Berry, where it appears as a dazzlingly white castle, rising above the town, the steeple of the church of St-Pierre and the belfry of the town hall. Since then the castle has undergone many modifications. King René embellished it in the 15th century and Duplessis-Mornay strenghtened its defences in the 16th century, but as a Huguenot stronghold its defences were no protection against the revocation of the Edict of Nantes in 1685, after which it was turned into a state prison. During the Vendéan rebellion it was held successively by the rebels and Republican forces. At the beginning of the 20th century, when restoration work was put in hand, the north-west wing that had long been in a ruinous state was pulled down and replaced by a terrace and the fanciful jumble of turrets, chimneys, weathervanes and pinnacles that were the work of King René were replaced by pepperpot and conical roofs.

Place de la Bilange

The main activity in the town can be found in the Place de la Bilange, just south of the Pont Cessart. On the quay is the turreted Renaissance **Hôtel de Ville** which defended a former crossing point of the river. On an island opposite is the **Maison de la Reine de Sicile**, a manor-house that was once the home of Yolande of Aragon, Queen of Louis II of Anjou and the Two Sicilies and mother of King René. Set back behind the quay is the part-Romanesque, part-Renaissance **Church of St Pierre** with its sharp, pointed spire soaring above the roofs of a number of early Renaissance houses and the 16th century **Tour Grainetière** which once formed part of the town ramparts. Another hybrid church is that of **Notre-Dame-de-Nantilly**, a fine 12th-century building with a Flamboyant right aisle added by Louis XI and an interesting Renaissance relief of St John preaching in the desert.

In 1763 a riding school was established in Saumur which developed into the **French Cavalry School**, a move that brought a small measure of prosperity to the stagnating town. Its buildings are to be found in Rue Beaurepaire. In 1940 cadets from the school temporarily held up a German force 10 times their number, before heavy casualties and shelling of the town compelled them to surrender. A **museum** devoted to the Cavalry School and riding in general is located in the château, along with the **Musée des Arts Decoratifs**, exhibiting medieval and Renaissance furniture, tapestries and objects. (Open June–Sept, daily 9 am–7 pm; Oct–May Mon–Sat 9.15 am–13.30 pm and 2–6 pm.)

One of Saumur's less attractive natives was the banker Joseph Foullon whose remark during the Revolution 'if the people cannot find bread, let them eat hay' incited a Paris mob to hang him with a handful of hay stuffed into his mouth.

Practicalities in Saumur

Tourist Office Place Bilange, next to Pont
Cessart, on the south bank of the Loir (Tel. 41
51 03 06). 15 mins walk from station on north
bank of the loire; accommodation service;
currency exchange.
Railway Station *Saumur Rive-Droite*, Rue
Volney, on north bank of Loire. (Info: Tel. 41
67 50 50; Reservations: Tel. 41 88 43 18).
Buses *Gare routière*, Place St-Nicholas, on
south bank of Loire (Tel. 41 51 27 29).
Markets Place St-Pierre, Sat mornings.
Post office Rue Volney, same street as station
(Tel. 41 51 22 77).
Bicycle hire SNCF station and *Brison*, 49 ave
Maréchal Leclerc (Tel. 41 51 02 09).
Festivals *National showjumping*: early July;
National Riding School Carousel: end
September; *Fête de la Musique*: June
Hotels *Hôtel de la Croix de Guerre*, 9 rue de la
Petite Bilance, off Place Bilange (Tel. 41 51 05
88). Quiet and welcoming.
Hôtel le Cristal, 10 Place de la République (Tel.
41 51 09 54). Clean and spacious; some rooms

with views.
☆ *Hôtel Nouveau Terminus*, 15 ave David
d'Angers (Tel. 41 67 31 01). Clean, comfortable
hotel opposite the station.
☆☆ *Hôtel Roi Réné*, 94 ave Général de Gaulle,
on the Ile d'Offard (Tel. 41 67 45 30).
☆☆ *Hôtel Anne d'Anjou*, 32 quai Mayaud (Tel.
41 67 30 30). In a delightful 18th-century town
mansion.
Auberge de Jeunesse (HI), Rue de Verden on
Ile d'Offard (Tel. 41 67 45 00). Excellent
location and facilities.
Camping *Camping Municipal* de l'Ile d'Offard,
on island in the Loire, between station and
centre ville; 4☆ campsite with good facilities
(Tel. 41 67 45 00).
Restaurants *Auberge St-Pierre*, 6 rue Place St-
Pierre, beside church. Standard French dishes,
simple and cheap.
La Pierre Chaude, 41 ave Général de Gaulle.
On island in Loire.
☆☆ *La Gambetta*, 12 rue Gambetta (Tel. 41 67
66 66). Gastronomic dishes at affordable prices.

Excursion from Saumur
L'Abbaye de Fontevraud

Buses *3 buses daily from Saumur: bus* 16
(30 mins).

The little village of Fontevraud, at the
junction of Anjou, Touraine and Poitou,
is overshadowed by its great royal abbey
with its extensive Romanesque remains.
For centuries, the Abbaye de Fontevraud
was one of the most magnificent
monasteries in northern France. Founded
in the 12th century, it became the resting
place for some of the most famous
Plantagenet Kings of England who were,
at the same time, Dukes of Anjou. (Henry
II and Eleanor of Aquitaine, Richard the
Lionheart and Isabelle of Angoulême, the
unfortunate wife of King John, were all
buried in the abbey.) Land and financial
donations were given to the abbey by the
Counts of Anjou and other noblemen.
The community at Fontevraud was
unusual in that men and women were not
segregated and were ruled over by an
Abbess, the monks acting as chaplains
and being responsible for the daily

running of the abbey. In the 16th and
17th centuries, much of the abbey was
rebuilt, and part of it was used as a
prison in the 19th and 20th centuries.
The royal tombs were pillaged and
destroyed during the Revolution, but
attempts by the British Government to
have the remains of the English kings
transferred to Westminster in the 19th
century were turned down by the French
Government. The tombs were
subsequently restored; the abbey church
also contains funerary statues of Henry II
and Eleanor of Aquitaine and Richard the
Lionheart.
One of the most intriguing parts of the
abbey is the vast octagonal kitchen in the
Tour Evraud which has 20 chimneys. In
July the abbey makes a superb setting for
a whole host of exhibitions, concerts and
plays. (Open daily 9 am–7 pm; Sept–Oct
9.30 am–12.30 pm and 2–6 pm; Nov–
Easter 9.30am–12.30pm and 2–5.30 pm;
Easter–May 9.30 am–12.30 pm and 2–
6.30 pm.)

Practicalities in Fontevraud

Tourist Office Chapelle Ste-Catherine, June–Sept, (Tel. 41 51 79 45).
Hotels ☆☆ *Hôtel Croix Blanche* (Tel. 41 51 71 11).
☆☆ *Domaine de Mestré* (Tel. 41 51 75 87).

Delightful rooms and excellent home cooking at farm.
☆☆☆ *Hôtellerie Prieuré St-Lazare* (Tel. 41 51 73 16). In a former priory of the abbey.

Angers

Trains *11 trains daily from* **Saumur** *(25 mins),* **Tours** *(1 hour 10 mins),* **Orléans** *(2¼ hours) 16 from* **Paris** *Montparnasse (3 hours 45 mins or 1½ hours by* TGV*); 17 from* **Nantes** *(1 hour or 25 mins by* TGV.

Angers is the capital of the ancient province of Anjou, situated not on the Loire but on the Maine, close to the confluence of the Loire and the Mayenne. Despite its dramatic growth over the last century, the medieval town seems curiously unaffected by the developments that have turned Angers from a market town into a thriving modern city. Angers is immediately distinguished by 2 remarkable buildings – the cathedral, which occupies a commanding position on high ground above the town, and its castle, a stunningly powerful example of a mighty 13th-century fortress.

What to see

Cathédrale St-Maurice

A splendid example of 12th and 13th century Gothic architecture, the cathedral stands at the top of an impressive set of steps which lead up from the river. It is built on the site of earlier churches and has a beautiful, sculpted portal with an exquisite tympanum depicting Christ in Majesty surrounded by symbols of the Evangelists, angels and the elders of the Apocalypse. The interior of the cathedral is awe-inspiring; the large nave lit by remarkable 12th-century stained glass, the choir by iridescent mid-13th century coloured glass and the transepts by 15th-century stained glass. The stained glass was removed during the Second World War, a wise precaution since the RAF attacked the nearby château which was being used as an arsenal by the Germans.

Logis Pincé

There are some fascinating houses around the cathedral in the old part of town: the logis Pincé with its handsome stone façade in the Renaissance style, the **Maison d'Adam** adjacent to the cathedral – a picturesque 15th-century house with finely sculpted corbels, and just one of many timbered merchant's houses in Old Angers. There are many more to be found in neighbouring streets, particularly Rue Saint-Laud, Rue des Poeliers and Rue du Mail.

Musée des Beaux-Arts

Just south of the cathedral is the Logis Barrault where Catherine de Médici and the governors of Anjou stayed. Today it houses the Musée des Beaux Arts, a very fine collection of paintings and sculpture with works by Raphael, Fragonard, Boucher, Delacroix and Géricault. (Open mid-Sept–May Tues–Sun 10 am–noon and 2–6 pm.) Nearby is the Préfecture, housed in former abbey buildings, and the Tour Saint-Aubin which once served as a belfry and Keep for the abbey. Opposite the Préfecture stands the Church of Saint Martin. Close to the Musée des Beaux Arts at 10 rue du Musée is another museum, the **Musée David d'Angers**, with a collection of sculptures by Jean-Pierre David, a native of the city. (Same opening times as the Musée des Beaux-Arts).

Château d'Angers

Henry ii of England inherited the County of Anjou on the death of his father Geoffrey of Anjou in 1151. Only half a century later, however, King John lost this rich possession to Philippe Auguste of France. The massive castle walls which can be seen today were built at great speed between 1230–38 on the orders of Saint Louis who, at the time, was engaged in war with the Duke of Brittany, Pierre Mauclerc. 17 massive towers of quarry-stone or slate interspersed with courses of white sandstone were thrown up and joined by strong ramparts. Massive as they are, the walls and towers were originally twice their present height and crowned with watch-towers while a deep moat linked with the Maine separated the fortress from the town. Not surprisingly, Angers was one of the most powerful Citadels in the Kingdom and proved impregnable, never being taken by assault.

In the 15th century, Yolande d'Anjou had the fortifications strengthened further, to defend the County against the English, and built the elegant Flamboyant Gothic chapel in the internal courtyard. The last Angevin prince to live in the castle was King René, who had formal gardens laid out and remodelled the royal apartments in the northern gallery, which carry his coat of arms on the keystone. When Réné bequeathed Anjou to France on his death in 1480, the independent history of the County of Anjou came to an end.

In the 16th century a Huguenot, du Hallot, succeeded in taking over the château by dint of a trick, and it was only with great difficulty that he was eventually ejected. To prevent any such reoccurrence, Henri iii ordered the walls and towers to be razed to the ground but the demolition went slowly. 10 years later, the château had only lost one and a half floors and with the return of peace the work was suspended with the agreement of the king. The château served as a prison, in the 17th century – it is where Fouquet was incarcerated – and it was used to hold monarchist rebels captured by Republican troops during the Vendean rebellion in the 18th century. (Château open Palm Sunday to 31st May 9 am–12.30 pm and 2–6.30 pm; 1st June to 15th September 9 am–7 pm; from 16th September 9.30 am–12.30 and 2–6 pm.)

Tapestry Museum

Within the thick curtain walls lie a large outer and smaller inner courtyard, within which a part subterranean gallery has been built to exhibit a remarkable series of tapestries commissioned by Louis I d'Anjou. This astonishing series, known as the *Apocalypse Tapestries*, was woven between 1375 and 1380 by the Parisian weaver Nicolas Bataille, from the cartoons of Jean de Bruges and, in spite of having been cut up during the Revolution, measure 104 metres in length. On alternating backgrounds of red and blue, the tapestries illustrate scenes drawn from the Apocalypse of St John.

Woven for Louis I, then Duke of Anjou, they were housed in the cathedral until the 1750s when the canons demanded that they should be removed as they deadened the sound of the daily service. After lying in basements for decades they were finally thrown onto the streets during the Revolution and were partly cut up. In 1843 the Bishop of Angers managed to salvage about two-thirds of the tapestries from the homes of the inhabitants. They are considered by many to be the most sumptuous of all French tapestries. (Open daily, mid-Sept–May, Tues–Sun 10 am–noon and 2–6 pm; June-mid-Sept, daily 9.30 am–12.30 pm and 2–7 pm.)

Other tapestries, no less remarkable but of later date, hang in the beautifully vaulted chapel of **Sainte-Genevieve**. A modern tapestry, designed by Jean Lurcat and finished in 1966 hangs in the Hopital de St Jean across the river from the château. Some 109 metres long and hung around the airy Grande Salle, the tapestry is a riot of brilliant colours against a sombre black background.

Practicalities in Angers

Tourist Office Opposite the château on place Kennedy (Tel. 41 88 69 93); arranges trips to châteaux; currency exchange.

Railway Station *Angers-St-Laud*, Rue de la Gare; (Info. Tel. 41 88 50 50; Reservations Tel 41 88 43 18); buffet; for town centre, walk up Rue de la Gare, turn left onto rue Hoche, then first right at Place de l'Académie and the castle is before you.

Post Office 1 rue Franklin Roosevelt, in centre.

Markets Covered market in *les Halles*, Place de la République; daily except Mon and Sat afternoon.

Hotels *Hôtel des Lices*, 25 rue des Lices, near château (Tel. 41 87 44 10). Small but spotlessly clean rooms.

Hôtel la Coupe d'Or, 5 rue de la Gare (Tel. 41 88 45 02). Smallish rooms but close to station.

☆*Hôtel Royal*, 8 bis Place Visitation, close to station (Tel. 41 88 30 25).

☆☆*Hôtel Champagne*, 34 rue D. Papin, almost opposite the station (Tel. 41 88 78 06).

☆☆*Hôtel Continental*, 12 rue L. de Romain, close to the cathedral (Tel. 41 86 94 94).

☆☆☆*Anjou*, 1 blvd Foch (Tel. 41 88 24 82). Recently renovated in 18th-century style; spacious, handsome rooms and good restaurant.

Hostels *Foyer des Jeunes Travailleurs* (HI), Rue Darwin; bus 8 (direction **Beaucouzé**) to CFA. Largest youth hostel in Europe; good facilities (Tel. 41 72 00 20).

Restaurants *Jean Foucher*, Les Halles, Place Mondain (Tel. 41 86 06 32); *fruits-de-mer*; dishes straight from the market itself.

Maître Kanter, Les Halles, Place Mondain (Tel. 41 87 93 30); another market eating place; many good dishes, served quickly and very good value.

☆☆*Toussaint*, 7 Place Kennedy (Tel. 41 87 46 20). Michel Bignon serves regional specialities, especially Loire River fish, with fine local wines.

West of Angers, the railway line follows the northern bank of the Loire, skirting the edge of the flood-plain, through rich water-meadows and plantations of poplars. From time to time in winter the Loire bursts its banks, sending a sheet of grey flood-water across the valley as far as the eye can see, the slender trunks of the poplars emerging from flat expanse of water.

Heading west down the valley of the Loire, the most westerly and the latest of the Renaissance châteaux of the Loire, the **Château de Serrant**, is passed. This elegant building, surrounded by a magnificent moat, was begun in the 16th century but not finished until the 18th century. Before the Revolution it belonged to Anthony Walsh, Compte de Serrant, an Irishman who supplied Prince Charles Edward with ships for his Scottish expedition of 1745.

Further west still the superb ruins of the castle of **Champtocé** are visible to the north. Beyond here lies **Ancenis**, strategically situated at the eastern border of the former Duchy of Brittany, a castle was built here in the 10th century. The ruins that exists today date from the 15th to 17th centuries, and consists of a postern flanked by powerful round towers, ornamented with gargoyles, a vaulted gallery and a Renaissance wing. Skirting water-meadows enclosed by hedges of pollarded willow and poplar, the railway line passes **Varades**, recognisable by the large church crowning the summit of the hill, and arrives at the ancient city of **Nantes**, from where there are fast TGVs direct to Paris and trains into Brittany. (For a description of Nantes, see page 393.)

9 Lyon and Savoie and Dauphiné (The Alps)

The French Alps form a broad sweep of mountains that extend south from Lac Léman until they merge into the blue hills of Haute Provence. This large area, bordered by the Rhône in the west, the Jura and Lac Léman (Lake Geneva) in the north, Provence in the south and Switzerland and Italy in the east, was for many centuries divided into the 2 important kingdoms of Savoie and Dauphiné. Savoie, which comprises the northern part of the French Alps is one of the most beautiful regions of France with Lakes Annecy and Bourget, rich pastoral valleys of Swiss character and the high Alps culminating in Mont Blanc. It is an ancient duchy and province which was united to France only in 1860.

From the 11th century the 2 regions of Savoie and Dauphiné, though similar in many respects, had quite separate histories. Humbert 'of the White Hands' became Comte de Savoie while Giuges I, 'the Old', took control of the domains of the Dauphiné. The 13th and 14th centuries saw the steady rise in power of the rulers of Savoie, a rise which was checked in 1477 when Louis XI established a protectorate over the country. In 1536 François I invaded Savoie, forcing the Comte de Savoie to remove his capital east of the Alps to Turin. Henri IV's invasion in 1601 compelled the rulers of Savoie to make further territorial concessions to France, which were exploited by Richelieu and Louis XIV who occupied Savoie twice in the 17th century. After a period in which Savoie was occupied by the Spanish and ruled by Charles Emmanuel III, French revolutionary troops occupied the province in 1792, forcing Charles Emmanuel's abdication. Napoleon's defeat at Waterloo led to Savoie being restored briefly to the Italian King Victor Emmanuel I but in 1858 France received Savoie and Nice in return for helping to drive the Austrians out of Italy. A plebiscite 2 years later confirmed the decision to unite with France.

The Alps contain some of the most breath-taking scenery in Europe and culminate in the continent's highest peak, Mont Blanc. Savoie, to the north of Dauphiné, contains the peaks of the Haute Savoie, a series of lakes as beautiful as those of northern Italy, and the beautiful Vanoise National Park. Due to its stormy history the towns of Savoie preserve relatively few medieval monuments but ruined castles and villages with their typical belfries are a frequent feature of the landscape.

The Dauphiné Alps are more forbidding than those of Savoie, their deep wide valleys merging into great stony slopes which rise up to craggy peaks, to create a curiously lonely and deserted atmosphere. The scenery is full of grandeur but somewhat desolate, especially in the upper valleys. The Vale of Grésivaudan near Grenoble is one of the most attractive parts of the province. In the south the Durance river forms the boundary between the *départements* of Basses-Alpes and Hautes-Alpes, and so between Provence and the mountainous province of Dauphiné.

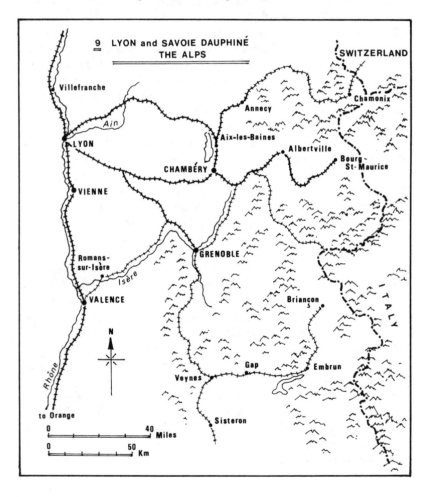

The greatest sights of the Alps are reserved for those prepared to climb; trails and hikes through the mountains are possible on marked paths and guides and hiking maps widely available. Travelling by train however affords superb views of the Alps, especially as the train climbs steadily in height towards Chamonix, where skiing first began in the Alps, Bourg St-Maurice and Briançon. Cable-cars enable visitors to reach a number of high places in the mountains from where there are superb panoramas of neighbouring peaks and surrounding Alpine valleys.

The Route Lyon – Chambéry – Aix-les-Bains – Annecy – Chamonix – Albertville – Bourg-St-Maurice – Grenoble – Briançon – Sisteron

Easily accessible by direct train from Paris, **Lyon** *or* **Chambéry** *both make an ideal starting point for train journeys around the French Alps. The former capital of Savoie, Chambéry is a typical old French provincial capital in a delightful valley between the Grande Chartreuse and the Bauges mountains.* **Aix-les-Bains**, *once one of the most fashionable spas of Europe, lies just north of the Lac du Bourget at the foot of Mont Renard. A little to the north lies* **Annecy** *on the blue Lac d'Annecy, its old town intersected by canals and lined with arcaded streets.* **Chamonix**, *virtually on the Swiss border, is dwarfed by the peak of nearby Mont Blanc which rises to a height of 4,800 metres. From the town journeys by cable-car can take visitors high into the mountains for the most spectacular panoramic views of the neighbouring mountains of Le Brévent and L'Aiguille du Midi. Adjacent to Albertville, home to the 1992 Winter Olympics, is the little old town of* **Conflans**, *whose fortifications were dismantled by François I in 1536 and from where there are breath-taking views down the Isère valley towards the Grande-Chartreuse mountains. At the very end of the line,* **Bourg St-Maurice** *is a little fortified town, rather prettily situated in a broad valley full of poplars, beneath pine forests that slope down from Mont-Pourri.* **Grenoble,** *to the south, is the old capital of Dauphiné, on the banks of the Isère in the Vallée du Grésivaudan, at the foot of the mountains of the the Grande-Chartreuse. A large, bustling, dynamic city, it claims with justice to be the most beautifully situated town in France.* **Briançon**, *an ancient walled town, occupies a strategic position guarding the passage from Italy into France on the slopes of a height overlooking the confluence of the Durance and the Guisane. Lower down on the Durance,* **Sisteron** *dominates a narrow defile in the valley* *and marks the transition from the stony slopes of Dauphiné to the softer landscape and clearer light of Provence to the south.*

Lyon

Trains *12–15* TGVs *daily from* **Paris** *(2 hours);* 8 *from* **Dijon** *(2½ hours);* 12–15 *from* **Grenoble** *(2 hours);* 6 *from* **Strasbourg** *(5–7 hours);* 13 *from* **Marseille** *(3–4 hours).*

Lyon is France's second greatest city, not just in terms of size and population but also in terms of sophistication, grandeur and self-assurance. The city is situated on 2 great rivers, the Rhône and the Saône, just above their confluence and can be divided into 3 parts. **Central Lyon** lies on the narrow peninsula between the 2 rivers, **Vieux Lyon** occupies the west bank of the Saône beneath the steep hill of Fourvière, an area of medieval and Renaissance houses, while **East of the Rhône** is a residential district, a large shopping area and the huge Part-Dieu commercial centre and train station.

What to see

Central Lyon: La Presqu'île
The peninsula *(presqu'île)* which lies between the Saône and Rhône rivers is the central part of Lyon although not the first to be settled.

Place Bellecour
In the middle of the peninsula is the magnificent Place Bellecour, a huge shaded square laid out in 1617. Henri IV urged the town council to lay out the square and Louis XIV forbade building on it. One of the largest squares in France, it is surrounded by elegant Louis XVI houses but the east and west sides were destroyed in 1793 and rebuilt by Napoleon in 1800. The equestrian statue of Louis XIV in the centre of the square was melted down during the Revolution; the current one is a replacement by Lemot. Near the south-east corner is **Place Antoine-Poncet** with a tower which is all that remains of a 17th-century Hospice de la Charité.

Musée des Arts Decoratifs
The Rue de la Charité leads south to the Hôtel de Lacrois-Laval in which is the Musée des Arts Decoratifs, notable for its fine collection of 18th-century French furniture, silver and tapestries (Open Tues–Sun 10 am–noon and 2–5.30 pm; joint ticket to Musée Historique des Tissus.)

Musée Historique des Tissus
Silk-making was the primary industry of the city for centuries, silk being produced

by the *canuts* or silk workers who were concentrated in the Croix-Rousse district of central Lyon in the north of the *presqu'île*. At the end of the 18th century over 20,000 looms were at work in the city, producing silk which was exported all over Europe.

Almost adjacent to the museum of decorative arts is the Musée Historique des Tissus, with one of the best European collections of silk and embroidery, not only from the looms on which Lyon grew rich, but also from all over the world. The collections include examples of Coptic, Greco-Roman and Byzantine textiles, Seljuk tapestries, Persian and Turkish carpets, oriental silks and brocades, ecclesiastical vestments and early costumes. There are beautiful Genoese velvets, Gobelins and Brussels tapestries as well as the most superb collection of Lyonnais silks of all periods. Costumes on display include clothes embroidered for Louis xv and Napoleon amongst others. (Open Tues–Sun 9.30 am–noon and 2 – 6 pm; joint ticket to Musée des Arts Décoratifs.) A little to the west of the museums is the little Romanesque church of St-Martin-d'Ainay, the oldest church of Lyon, and all that remains of the Benedictine abbey established here in the 5th century. Beneath the dome are 4 Roman columns from an altar of Augustus found at Croix-Rousse.

Hôtel Dieu
From the Place Bellecour Rue du Président Herriot and Rue de la République lead north, the latter passing the Hôtel Dieu, a large hospital with a long façade created by Soufflot in 1741, surmounted by an imposing dome where Rabelais worked as a doctor in the 1530s.

Musée de l'Imprimerie
Further north, down the Rue de la Poulaillerie, is the late 15th century Hôtel de la Couronne, in which is a fascinating museum devoted to printing, with a recent reconstruction of the kind of hand printing press used by Gutenberg. A page of the Gutenberg Bible and other *incunabula* are displayed, together with some of the earliest books printed in the city. One section is devoted to the techniques of reproduction of woodcut and copper-engraved illustrations.

Place des Terreaux
A little to the north the ornate Renaissance Hôtel de Ville faces the Musée des Beaux-Arts on the Place des Terreaux. In the square the Marquis de Cinq-Mars and François de Thous were beheaded in 1642 for their conspiracy against Richelieu. In the centre of the square 4 majestic horses rise up, gracing a gorgeous fountain designed by Frédéric Bartholdi, the creator of New York's Statue of Liberty.

Musée des Beaux-Arts
Probably the greatest art collection in provincial France, the Musée des Beaux-Arts occupies the splendid abbey building of St-Pierre. Italianate in style, it was built in 1659 for the Benedictine convent of St-Pierre. The cloister of the former monastery is now devoted to sculpture, with several works by Rodin as well as ancient

Egyptian and Etruscan statues, while the vast museum in the Palais St-Pierre contains an extensive collection of painting and sculpture spread through some 80 rooms. The collections are particularly rich in 19th and 20th-century paintings, especially by Courbet, Géricault, Delacroix, Ingres, Manet, Daubigny, Corot, Van Gogh, Renoir, Gauguin, Derain, Vlaminck, Dufy, Ernst and Masson, as well as a number of Spanish and Dutch old masters. (Open Wed–Sun 10.30 am–6 pm.)

Hôtel de Ville

The east side of the Place des Terreaux is dominated by the façade of the Hôtel de Ville which is ornamented with an equestrian statue of Henri IV. Restored by Jules Hardouin-Mansart in 1702 after a fire, the Hôtel de Ville is approached via 2 attractive courtyards separated by an arcade. Behind the town hall is the Grand-Théatre rebuilt in the 19th-century after Soufflot's original theatre was burnt down.

Les Traboules

A little to the north of the Place des Terreaux is the hill of Croix-Rousse which was once the centre of the silk-weaving industry. The most fascinating quarter of the hill is that known as Les Traboules, where the narrow lanes are connected in a labyrinth of tiny inter-connecting passages and alleyways. At number 10 rue d'Ivry is the **Maison des Canuts** where silk-looms are still in action. One oddity of the area is to be found on the Blvd de la Croix-Rousse where a massive boulder was deposited by an ice-age glacier. Another interesting site is the **Roman ampitheatre** excavated in the Jardin des Plantes, dating from the year 19 AD.

Vieux Lyon

West of place Bellecour the Pont du Maréchal Juin leads to the old town at the foot of Fourvière Hill, capped by the silhouette of Notre-Dame. Situated on the right bank of the Saône, old Lyon extends through a labyrinth of streets and alleyways. A little alley leads to Place de la Baleine, a small square lined with 17th-century houses. **Rue St-Jean** leading from the square is lined with elegant houses built for the bankers and silk merchants during the 16th century; foremost amongst them are the Gothic **Hôtel du Chamerrier** at number 37 and the lavish **Demeure des Vistes** at number 29. In the courtyard of number 16 is the **Tour Rose** which gives access to the splendid Rue Boeuf. Many of the houses have a feature unique to Lyon – the *traboule*, or vaulted passage, which allowed the precious silk to be transported around the city without being spoiled.

The **Rue de Trois-Maries**, also exiting from Place de la Baleine is full of interesting houses, and at number 2 a *traboule* leads through to Rue St-Jean, the main street of the area. At number 24 is the Maison du Grand Palais, with a marvellous courtyard with an octagonal staircase tower. Rue St-Jean leads to the Place du Change, where the finest house is the **Maison Thomassin**, a 14th-century building with spiral staircase and painted beams.

In **Rue Lainerie**, number 14 has a richly sculptured Gothic façade while many of the other picturesque houses date from the 15th or 16th centuries. It leads to Place St-Paul where the creator of the puppets Guignol and Gnafron lived.

Maison Henri IV

The 16th-century galleried mansion also known as Hôtel Paterin has its entrance at 4 rue Juiverie, south of which is the Hôtel Bullious, a galleried house built by Philibert de l'Orme in 1536. Other interesting Renaissance houses are to be found in Rue de Gadagne.

Musée du Vieux Lyon

At number 14 rue de Gadagne in a hôtel built between the 14th and 16th centuries is the Musée du Vieux Lyon with collections of medieval sculpture, local furniture, pottery, paintings and ceramics. The 2nd floor contains the **Musée de la Marionette**, an unusual puppet museum which traces the history of Guignol and Madelon, Lyon's equivalent to Punch and Judy, created by Laurent Mourguet in 1795. (Open Wed–Mon 10 am–6 pm.)

Cathédrale Saint-Jean

Next to the **Jardin Archéologique** is the cathedral of St-Jean. A mixture of styles, the cathedral was started in the mid-12th century, finished in the 15th century and embellished in the 16th, just before the onslaught of the Religious Wars. Work on the nave continued for a century but the choir and apse show Provençal influence. In the northern transept is the cathedral's **astronomical clock**, one of the oldest in France which dates back to the 14th century. Some 10 metres-high, it shows the feast days from 1400 to the year 2000.

Fourvière Hill
Basilique de Fourvière

Above the district of old Lyon rises the Fourvière Hill, crowned by the important basilica of Notre-Dame. Approached by steps or funicular, the **Fourvière Esplanade** looks down over Lyon and the valleys of the Saône and Rhône. A path leads uphill to the extravagant 19th-century basilica, built like Sacré-Coeur to symbolise the nation's Catholicism after the birth of the secular Third Republic. Begun in 1872 by Pierre Bossan and finished by 1896, the basilica is a heady mixture of neo-Romanesque and Byzantine styles, profusely decorated with marble, mosaic, bronze and gold which prompted Huysmans to describe it as 'Asiatic and barbaric'. (Open daily 8 am–noon and 2–6 pm.)

Roman Lyon

The Fourvière hill was the site of the original Roman settlement. Julius Caesar made Roman Lyon, Lugdunum – the hill of the crows – the commercial and military centre of Gaul. The larger of the 2 semi-circular theatres, the **Grand Théatre**, is the oldest Roman theatre in France; able to hold 10,000 spectators, it dates back to 15 BC. With a width of 108.5 metres it is marginally larger than those of Orange and Arles, having been doubled in size by Hadrian in the 2nd century. The smaller **Odéon** has an attractive geometric-patterned tile floor; both are used for theatrical performances in the Lyon International Arts Festival in September. Nearby are the remains of a **Temple of Cybele** and a Roman aqueduct. (Open Easter–Oct 8 am–noon and 2–6 pm; Sat 9 am–noon and 3–6 pm; Sun 3–6 pm.)

Musée de la Civilisation Gallo-Romaine

Just above the theatres at number 17 rue Cléberg lies the exciting Gallo-Roman museum, with an impressive collection of statues, coins, swords and fine mosaics decorated with fish and chariot-racing from excavated sites all over the city. It is housed in a part-subterranean building, built into the hillside, designed by Bernard Zehrfuss. The finest items include a ritual chariot from the 8th century BC and the Claudian Tables, a record on bronze of the concessions made by the Emperor Claudius in AD 48 during a speech in which he gave the Roman citizens of Gaul senatorial rights. (Open Wed–Sun 9.30 am–noon and 2–6 pm.)

Modern Lyon: Part-Dieu

On the eastern bank of the Rhône is the modern quarter of Lyon developed in the 1970s, to include a new railway station, administrative quarter, concert halls, city library and commercial and business district. Looking down on this vast new development is the **Tour de la Part-Dieu**, a cylindrical building capped by a pyramidal roof. One museum in the Part Dieu district of particular interest is the **Musée de la Résistance**, at 5 rue Boileau, which documents the activities of the Resistance during the war, for whom Lyon was an important centre.

Practicalities in Lyon

Tourist Office Place Bellecour (Tel. 78 42 25 75); city guide, comprehensive list of shows and events; accommodation service; guided tours to city; sells 1 day ticket that covers all museums. Open Mon–Sat 9 am–6 pm, Sun 10 am–6 pm; 16th Sept–14th June Mon–Fri 9 am–7 pm, Sat 9 am–5 pm, Sun 10 am–5 pm. Branch office in the Centre d'Echange at Perrache station (Tel. 78 42 22 07).

Railway Stations Lyon has 2 stations and trains to the same destinations leave from both, but the majority arrive at **Lyon Part-Dieu**. Check timetables carefully to see which station your train leaves from.

(1) Lyon Perrache (Tel. 78 92 50 50) is located in Central Lyon, between the Saône and Rhône rivers and is the more central of the 2 stations: shops; bars; currency exchange; SOS Voyageurs facilities for handicapped people and babies; Information office open Mon–Sat 8 am–7.30 pm.

(2) Lyon Part-Dieu, in business district on the east bank of Rhône (Tel. 78 92 50 50). Information desk open Mon–Sat 8 am–7.30 pm.

Buses Departures from bottom floor of Perrache station (Tel. 78 71 70 00); buses to Vienne, Annecy, Grenoble.

Public transport TCL, from outside Part-Dieu station; Metro open 5 am–midnight, Funicular railway from Place St-Jean to Roman theatres and Musée Gallo-Romain on Fourvière Hill (open 8 am–8 pm).

Post Office Place Antonin Poncet, next to Place Bellecour (Tel. 78 42 60 50).

Police Place Antonin Poncet, next to Place Bellecour and post office (Tel. 78 28 92 93); Emergency: Tel. 17.

Boat tours Along the Saône and Rhône, departures from Quai des Célestins (4 departures daily, 1 hour trip), Tel. 78 42 96 81.

Markets Covered market daily at *La Halle*, 102 cours Lafayette; open-air markets: *Quai St-Antoine*, Tues–Sun mornings; *Blvd de la Croix Rousse* beside the Rhône: Tues–Sat mornings.

Festivals *Fête de la Vierge*: 8th Dec, celebrating the delivery of the city from the Black plague, candle-lit processions and masses. *Festival des Musiques Européennes*: May, musical bonanza; *Festival de Théâtre Amateur*: May; amateur performances throughout the city.

Hotels *Hôtel Croix-Paquet*, 11 Place Croix-Paquet (Tel. 78 25 51 49). Metro station **Croix-Paquet** or walk from Place des Terreaux. Clean, simple rooms.

☆*Hôtel Vaubecour*, 28 rue Vaubecour (Tel. 78 37 44 91), Mid-way between Perrache and Bellecour. Good, cheap, clean rooms.

☆*Hôtel Alexandra*, 49 rue Victor Hugo (Tel. 7837 75 79). Superb location in Central Lyon, between Perrache station and Place Bellecour. Pleasant rooms.

☆*Celestins*, 4 rue des Archers (Tel. 78 37 63 62), Near Place Bellecour in centre.

☆*Montesquieu*, 36 rue Montesquieu (Tel. 78 72 47 47). Near Place Bellecour in centre.

☆☆*Azur*, 64 rue Victor Hugo (Tel. 78 37 10

44). Near Perrache station.

☆☆*Bellecordière*, 18 rue Bellecordière (Tel. 78 42 27 28). Clean, simple and functional rooms in the heart of the city.

☆☆☆*Bristol*, 28 cours de Verdun (Tel. 78 37 56 55). Large, modernised comfortable hotel between Lyon Perrache and centre.

Hostel *Auberge de Jeunesse* (HI), 51 rue Roger Salengro, Vénissieux (Tel. 78 01 04 35; after 5 pm: Tel. 78 76 39 23); bus 35 from Place Bellecour to George Levy (30 mins) or bus 53 from Perrache to Etats-Unis-Viviani, then 500 metres along railway line.

Restaurants ☆*Chez Mounier*, 3 rue des Marroniers (Tel. 78 37 79 26). Just north of Place Antonin Poncet; mouth-watering dishes include *gnafron*, local sausage in fresh cream sauce.

☆*Brasserie Georges*, 30 cours de Verdun (Tel. 78 37 15 78). One of the oldest and largest 1920s brasseries with fine panelled ceiling and good, hearty French cooking.

☆*Café des Fédérations*, 8 rue du Major Martin (Tel. 78 28 26 00). Bustling and animated café with good Lyonnaise fare.

☆*Chez Sylvain*, 4 rue Tupin (Tel. 78 42 11 98); Lyonnaise cuisine including such specialities as tripe and andouillettes in one of the *bouchons*, the old hostelleries of Lyon.

☆*Le Garet*, 7 rue Garet (Tel. 78 28 16 94); Traditional *bouchon* serving *cochonailles* (hot pork dishes) and andouillettes with strong local wines.

☆*Le Vivarais*, 1 Place Gailleton (Tel. 78 37 85 15). A delightful restaurant, serving classic French and Lyonnaise cuisine.

☆☆*Garioud*, 14 rue du Palais-Grillet, off rue Ferrandère (Tel. 78 37 04 71). Exquisite Lyonnaise dishes prepared by chef Paul Griard.

☆☆*La Tassée*, 20 rue Charité (Tel. 78 37 02 35), Good value for the excellent standard of traditional Lyonnaise dishes.

Chambéry

Trains *Frequent trains daily from* **Lyon** *(1 hours); and* **Grenoble** *(1–2 hours;); 12 from* **Annecy** *(45 mins); 8 from* **Geneva** *(1½ hours); 8 from* **Paris** *via Lyon (5½ hours); 6* TGVs *daily direct from Paris (3½ hours); 8 from* **Aix-les-Bains** *(10 mins).*

The capital of a sovereign state until the 16th century, Chambéry lies at the heart of Savoie. Originally a Roman city, the town was still little more than a village when it became the capital of the Counts of Savoy in 1232. Three Counts, each with the name of Amadeus, contributed to the rise of the House of Savoy, the first dying of plague after successfully extending the limits of his domains into Switzerland, the Jura and Italy. Amadeus VII joined Charles VI in his fight against the English and added the County of Nice to Savoy. Amadeus VII was made a Duke by the Emperor before becoming Pope but from the mid-15th century the fortunes of Savoy dwindled and France slowly gained the ascendancy, occupying parts of Savoy which forced the Conte de Savoie to move the capital to Turin.

What to see

Château des Ducs de Savoie

High above the centre of town towers the castle of the Dukes of Savoy, which was completely rebuilt in the 14th and 15th centuries and partly burnt down in the 18th century. It is an impressive and picturesque stronghold, still retaining in the **Tour Ronde**, the Keep of the medieval castle built by the first Lords of Chambéry.

At the end of the castle's north wing is **Sainte-Chapelle**, its 18th-century façade hiding a 15th-century Gothic nave which has some fine stained glass windows. The

famous Holy Shroud of Turin was kept here between 1502 and 1578 where it was
nearly destroyed by fire in 1532. (1 hour guided tours, 2-5 daily.)

The Alleyways

Although badly bombed in the Second World War there is still a labyrinthine web
of alleyways and secret passages that connect the arcades in the Rue Boigne to the
château. These passageways, known as *allées* were used by the town's defenders to
reach parts of the town that were being besieged without exposing themselves to
enemy fire. Rue Basse-du-Château was the principal street that led from the town
to the château. Off it runs the Rue de Boigne, a prostitute's haunt in medieval
times, but now an attractive street with its cafés and patisseries behind Italianate
porticoes.

Fontaine des Elephants

At the bottom of Rue de Boigne stands the most famous feature of the town, the
enchanting Fontaine des Elephants which was erected to the memory of General
Comte de Boigne, who had made a fortune in the service of the Rajah Scindia in
India, and which he left to the town in his Will.

The 15th-century church of **St-François** has a fine Flamboyant portal but the
interior was decorated with *trompe-l'oeil* by Vicario in the 19th century. Adjacent
is the former Archbishop's Palace which now houses the **Musée Savoisien**. South of
the cathedral runs the **Rue de la Croix d'Or** with some of the oldest and finest
houses in the city; Rousseau served as the music-master at number 14, the Hôtel
Costa, before moving to the villa of Les Charmettes where he lived between 1735
and 1740 with Madame de Warens.

Musée des Beaux-Arts

North of the Fontaine des Eléphants, in the Place du Palais de Justice is the Musée
des Beaux-Arts with an outstanding collection of Italian paintings, with works by
Uccello, Titian and Tintoretto, as well as French pictures by Guérin and Watteau.
(Open Wed–Mon 10 am–noon and 2-6 pm.)

On a hill on the other side of the town stands the 15th-century church of **St-
Pierre**, its crypt containing a 6th-century baptistry built using Roman columns.

Practicalities in Chambéry

Tourist Office 24 blvd de la Colonne (Tel. 79 33
42 47).
Railway Station Place de la R. Sommeiller,
(Info: Tel. 79 85 50 50; Reservations: Tel. 79 62
35 26); information office open Mon–Sat 8 am–
12:15 pm and 1:30–6:15 pm. To reach town
centre, walk left from station, cross Place du
Centenaire and follow Blvd de la Colonne to
number 24.
Festivals Play *Confession d'un Chambérian*,
enacted in Château des Duc de Savoie, last
week of July and 1st 2 weeks of Aug, Sat 9 pm;
tickets from tourist office. *Foire de Savoie*,
September: annual celebration of the region's

traditions, cuisine, culture and folklore.
Markets *Les Halles*, Place de Geneve: Tues,
Thurs, Sat mornings.
Hotels *Hôtel de la Blanche*, 10 Place de l'Hôtel
de Ville (Tel. 79 33 15 62). Cheap rooms in
half-timbered house in the old quarter.
Hôtel du Château, 37 rue J-P Veyrat (Tel. 79
69 48 78). Very simple but clean and close to
the castle.
☆☆*Hôtel Princes*, 4 rue Boigne, at junction
with rue Favre (Tel. 79 33 45 36). Close to the
Musée Savoisien.
☆☆☆*Hôtel Le France*, 22 fg Reclus (Tel. 79
233 45 36). Smart, comfortable and close to

station.
Restaurants *Grill aux Piétons*, 30 Place Monge. Steaks and good low-priced menus. *La Bodega*, 18 rue Jean-Pierre Veyrat (Tel. 79 96 10 65). Excellent fish dishes. ✰*La Poterne*, 3 Place du Marché (Tel. 79 96 23 70), at entrance to château. Good local dishes including *fondue savoyarde*. ✰*Trois Voutes*, 110 rue de la Croix d'Or (Tel. 79 33 38 56). Large, lively restaurant near cathedral, regional specialities include *fondues*. ✰✰ *La Vanoise*, 44 ave P. Lanfrey (Tel. 79 69 02 78). Opposite the Parc du Verney, south-west of the station; excellent regional cuisine.

Aix-les-Bains

Trains *8–12 trains daily from* **Chambéry** *(10 mins); from* **Annecy** *(45 mins);* **Grenoble** *(1¼ hours); 6–8 from* **Geneva** *(1 hours).*

The Roman name for Aix was Aquae Gratianae: the waters of the Emperor Gratian. Traces of the Roman town indicate that the waters were already well exploited by the 1st Century AD. The thermal baths have been used without a break since then although after the Barbarian invasions and for much of the Middle Ages, the only pool available was one 12 metres square and in the open-air – a far cry from the Roman establishment with its baths, showers, gymnasiums, massage parlours, hot and cold pools and promenades.

What to see
Les Thermes Nationaux
What remains of the Roman baths, which were built in many different coloured marbles, are contained in the huge New Baths, built between 1857 and 1934, the Thermes Nationaux, which dominate the town centre. They are supplied by 2 hot springs, the sulphur spring and the alum spring, and are best known for a treatment called a 'shower massage', which was reputedly first discovered by Napoleonic troops in Egypt and adopted enthusiastically at Aix on their return (Tours of baths leave from opposite tourist office on Place Maurice Mollard; Tel. 79 35 38 50.)

Arc de Campanus
Other Roman remains include a triumphal arch, the Arc de Campanus, which stands in what was the centre of the Roman spa. It is dedicated to members of the Pompeia clan, and was erected by a member of the family, Lucius Pompeius Campanus. Close to it stands another important Roman building, the **Temple of Diana**, a superbly built square stone structure; its stonework is so well cut that no cement or other bonding material was used in its construction.

Musée d'Archeologie et de Préhistoire
A whole host of fascinating Roman objects, unearthed in excavations in the city, have been collected in the Musée d'Archeologie et de Préhistoire (entrance via tourist office on Place Mollard).

It was only in the 16th century that the springs at Aix came back into fashion, but it was not until the 19th century that they received any other than local visitors.

One of the most famous was the poet Alphonse de Lamartine, who arrived at the age of 26 in 1816. Ostensibly Lamartine had a liver complaint but in reality, like so many other visitors to the baths then and since, he came largely because he had nothing better to do. He took lodgings, went for listless walks along the lake shore and boated on the lake where, during a sudden storm, he saved a woman from drowning. She fell ill and Lamartine nursed her back to health; suddenly he found his life had some purpose after all. After a brief period of exceptional happiness they were compelled to separate: Madame Charles Julie returned to Paris and Lamartine to Mâçon. They met once again but her health worsened and she died the following year, after inspiring Lamartine's poem 'The Lake', one of the greatest French Romantic poems.

Le Château

The former Château des Marquis d'Aix, the most interesting part of which dates from the early 16th century, houses the town hall and has a magnificent staircase built in the early Renaissance with stones taken from old Roman buildings in the vicinity.

Abbaye Royale de Hautecombe

The Lac du Bourget itself can be explored by boat – by far the most attractive way of seeing the lake – and the only way, for the train traveller, of getting to the magnificent Abbaye Royale de Hautecombe where the princes and princesses of Savoy are buried. Boats leave from the Grand Port, some 2 kilometres north-west of the city centre.

The romantic and fascinating Abbaye de Hautcombe stands on the west side of the lake backed by high wooded hills which descend to the water's edge. The abbey was founded 800 years ago by St-Bernard and Count Amadeus II of Savoie but the main buildings were rebuilt in the 18th century in a grand classical style. The church itself was largely rebuilt in the 1830s by Charles-Felix, King of Sardinia and Count of Savoie, in a wild Italian neo-Gothic style widely adopted at the time. The interior contains the tombs of no less than 41 princes and princesses, including that of Humbert III the Good, Beatrix of Savoie whose 2 daughters went on to become Queens of France, England, the Two Sicilies and Empress of Germany respectively, as well as the early rulers, Amadeus VI and VII, known as the Green and Red counts. Boats to the abbey leave twice daily from Aix's Grand Port (4 hour round trip); on Sundays a special trip leaves at 8.30 am. Tel. 79 88 92 09 for information. From the Grand Port, it is also possible to make a delightful 4-hour boat journey around the lake.

Practicalities in Aix-les-Bains

Tourist Office Place Mollard (Tel. 79 35 05 92); maps; automatic city map giving hotel vacancy information; occasional guided tours.
Railway Station *Aix-les-Bains-le-Revaud*. (Information: Tel. 79 85 50 50; Reservations: Tel. 79 62 40 60). For town centre, follow Ave Général de Gaulle, turn left before Thermes Nationaux.
Hotels *Hôtel Angleterre*, 22 ave Victoria (Tel.

79 35 03 59). Clean, cheap and close to the station.
☆*Hôtel Dauphinois*, 14 ave de Tresserve (Tel. 79 61 22 56). Good rooms, lovely garden and delightful long dining-room in welcoming hotel-restaurant.
Hostels *Auberge de Jeunesse* (HI), promenade de Sierroz (Tel 79 88 32 88); bus 2 to 'Camping' stop.

Annecy

Trains *10 – 13 trains daily from* **Aix-les-Bains** *(15 mins)*; **Chambéry** *(45 mins)*; **Chamonix** *(2 – 2½ hours)*; *8 from* **Lyon** *(2 hours)*; *8* TGVs *from* **Paris** *(4½ hours)*; *4 from* **Nice** *(6 hours)*.

Although on a smaller scale than the Italian lakes, the **Lac du Bourget** and **Lac d'Annecy** are as beautiful as any of those of northern Italy. The countryside between them too is enchanting, a patchwork of undulating fields and fertile valleys, in which are grown maize, vegetables and vines, while the great majority of slopes are devoted to meadows, emerald green in spring and early summer and scattered with mauve-flowering crocus in autumn.

Annecy's setting at the head of the lake is enchanting: dark green hills are reflected in the surface of the lake while the snow-capped mountains of the Bauges, Beaufortins and Massif du Mont Blanc form a superb panorama to the south and east. On the south side of the town stands the medieval castle on a precipitous rock at the base of which cluster a maze of narrow streets and canals which connect the Thiou with the bright waters of the lake. The riot of colour in summer, the half-timbered and stuccoed houses with their profusions of geraniums, the rushing water of the river Thiou and clear blue skies combine in summer to make Annecy one of the most delightful towns of the French Aps.

What to see

Ile des Cygnes

The earliest settlement on the lakeside at Annecy, on the Island of Swans, was abandoned during the barbarian invasions and a new site was created on the hillside. Under the Counts of Geneva in the 13th and 14th centuries Annecy became the capital of an important region before being absorbed into the County of Savoy in the 15th century.

With the expulsion of Catholics from Geneva during the Reformation, the town saw an influx of theologians and priests, the most important of whom was St-Francis de Sales who became bishop in 1602 and is buried in the Basilica of the Visitation. It was in the town that Jean-Jacques Rousseau, then aged 16, met Madame de Warens with whom he lived at Chambéry before moving to Les Charmettes.

Château d'Annecy

The château dominating the town has architectural features of all ages. The oldest part is the massive square **Tour de la Reine** dating from the 13th century. The Tour St-Paul and the main gateway are 14th century; the Tour St-Pierre and Tour Perrière 15th-century; the Logis de Nemours and New Residences 16th century. Recently restored, the château now houses the **Musée du Château**, with a miscellaneous and varied collection relating to history and archaeology. (Open daily 10 am–noon and 2–6 pm.) There are superb views over the lake from the towers of the castle.

The town below is centred on the **Thiou**, a canalised river, bordered with fine old houses, passageways and arcades, which flows out of the lake. The Canal du Thiou leads past the baroque locks to the imposing **Palais de l'Ile**, a 12th-century prison which rises on a tiny island.

Hôtel de Sales

In Rue Paquier stands the 17th-century Hôtel de Sales, once a residence of the Kings of Sardinia, originally built by a nephew of François de Sales. It is attractively decorated with figures representing the seasons. A small bridge leads from the huge Champ-de-Mars across a canal to the **Jardin Public**, off the eastern end of which is the little **Ile des Cygnes**. Another bridge on the south of these gardens leads over the Canal de Thiou, from where there is a view of the **Palais** de l'Ile, an ancient building that has seen service as a mint, law-court, council chamber and chancellory. The nearby church of St-Francis, built in the 15th-century, has a fresco executed the following century by Pourbus the Elder.

Along the public garden of the **Champ de Mars** boats, canoes and kayaks can be hired while swimming is possible from the Plage des Marquisats or private Impérial Plage. Cruises depart from Quai Napoléon III around the lake (5–6 daily, 1 hour).

Practicalities in Annecy

Tourist Office 1 rue Jean Jaurès, at Place de la Libération (Tel. 50 45 00 33); free maps; information on hiking, hotels, festivals, campgrounds. Open daily 9 am–6.30 pm.
Railway Station Place de la Gare (Tel. 50 66 50 50); information office open Mon–Sat 8.30 am–7 pm. To reach town centre, follow Rue Sommeiller, turn right, then left onto Rue Vaugelas.
Buses *Voyages Crolard*, adjacent to train station (Tel. 50 45 08 12); buses to Chamonix and other local destinations.
Markets *Place Ste-Claire*: Tues, Fri and Sun mornings.
Festivals *Fête du Lac*: 1st Sat in August; *Festival de la Vielle Ville*: mid-July; outdoor music and concerts.
Hotel *Hôtel des Alpes*, 12 rue de la Poste, near station (Tel. 50 45 04 56). Small, comfortable; some rooms are noisy.
Hôtel Savoyard, 41 ave de Cran, behind station (Tel. 50 57 08 08). Clean, comfortable and friendly.

Rive du Lac, 6 rue des Marquisats (Tel. 50 51 32 85). Attractive hotel in excellent location near lake and town centre.
☆ *Hôtel Nord*, 24 rue Sommeiller (Tel. 50 45 08 78). Clean, bright rooms near station.
☆ *Hôtel d'Aléry*, 15 ave d'Aléry (Tel. 50 45 24 75). Close to station off Rue de la Gare.
Hostels *Maison des Jeunes et de la Culture*, 52 rue des Marquisats (Tel. 50 45 08 80). Attractive modern hostel on the lake; comfortable and popular.
Restaurants *Au Lilas Rose*, passage de l'Evêché (Tel. 50 45 37 08). Excellent location in the old town, with superb *fondue savoyarde*.
Taverne du Freti, 12 rue Ste-Claire (Tel. 50 51 29 52). Delicious, inexpensive, fondues.
☆ *Le Petit Zinc*, 11 rue de Mont-Porens (Tel. 50 51 12 93). Delicious traditional French cooking in popular, timbered dining-room.
☆ *Le Boutaé*, 1 Place St-François (Tel. 50 45 03 05). Excellent mid-priced restaurant, close to Eglise St-Maurice.

Chamonix

Trains *6 – 8 trains daily from* **Annecy** *to St Gervais-les-Bains (1¼ – 2 hours), from where train connection to Chamonix-Mont-Blanc; 5 from* **Paris** *Gare-de-Lyon (7 hours); 6 from* **Lyon** *(4 – 5 hours).*

From Annecy the railway line heads in a large curve to the north-east, following the Arve valley to **Bonneville**, a small town identified by a column erected close to the river in honour of Charles Félix of Sardinia who was responsible for the canalisation of the Arve. To the north-east of the town rises the peak of Le Mole. Ascending all the time, the railway heads south up the valley of the Arve entering, after **Cluses**, the narrowest ravine in the valley. To the east is the massive waterfall of the **Cascade d'Arpenas**, some 216-metres-high, shooting forth from a rocky channel. Further south rise the peaks of Mont Joly and the massif of Mont Blanc.

St-Gervais-les-Bains is a small resort with hot springs in a sheltered position overlooked by Mont d'Arbois, Prarion and Mont Blanc to the west. The town occupies a superb open site, sheltered and sunny, clustered round its church on the gentle slopes of the Val Montjoie. A special train service operates from the town to Chamonix-Mont-Blanc which was not much more than an Alpine village, visited by a handful of visitors, until the middle of the present century.

Chamonix is the oldest and most prestigious French winter-sports resort and even if the town of Chamonix itself is of little interest, the surrounding alpine scenery is breath-taking and can be visited either on foot or by cable-car.

What to see

Le Brévent

Cable-cars and ski-lifts ascend to several of the surrounding peaks. Le Brévent, to the north, is a famous belvedere in the Aiguilles Rouges range from where there is an outstanding view of Mont Blanc, its glaciers and the Aiguilles de Chamonix. It can be reached by cable-car that leaves from the heart of the town, just up the hill from the tourist office.

Aiguille du Midi

The most impressive view of the Alps and the highest point that can be reached by cable-car is the Aiguille du Midi at a height of 3,842 metres. (Open daily, May–Sept 8 am–4.45 pm; Oct–Apr 8 am–3.45 pm; departing from South Chamonix; 120FF round trip.) The view from the Aiguille is breath-taking, with the Col du Midi beneath one and a panoramic view of the glaciers of the Vallée Blanche and Géant. The Col du Géant was probably used by smugglers and hunters for centuries but the first recorded crossing was made in June 1787 by 2 guides from Chamonix.

Mer de Glace

A third journey requiring no effort is that from the Gare de Montveners, from where a rack-railway climbs to the Mer de Glace, the most impressive glacier than can be reached with ease. (May–Sept 8 am–6 pm.)

Mont Blanc

Mont Blanc is, at 4,807 metres, the highest Alpine peak and the highest mountain in Europe, part of a chain that forms the watershed between the Rhine and Po drainage systems, and a barrier between France and Italy. Until the middle of the 18th century the Chamonix valley was little known. Its early history is connected with 2 Englishmen, Windham and Pocock who explored the valley in 1741 and were probably the first to climb up to the Mer de Glace.

The impetus to climb Mont Blanc however was largely the work of Horace Benedict de Saussure, a Swiss, who offered a reward to the first person to climb to the summit. This prompted a number of attempts by local men, some of which reached ridges below the summit, until the very peak was reached on 8th August 1786 by Jacques Balmat, on his second attempt, with his friend Dr Paccard. De Saussure who had attempted to get to the summit himself 10 times without success eventually reached the summit on 3rd August the following year and a week later Colonel Beaufoy made the first successful ascent by an Englishman. It wasn't until 1838 that it was successfully climbed by a woman, a claim by a local woman from Chamonix, Marie Paradis, being discounted on the grounds that her companions had carried her much of the way. Only 13 ascents are recorded from 1786 to 1829, but the numbers steadily grew, Chamonix expanding to cater for the growth of visitors which culminated in the opening of a skating rink in 1893 and the winter sports of the 1923 Olympic Games being held in the town. The ascent of Mont Blanc normally takes 2 days and is usually made from Chamonix; guides are essential, as is fitness even if extensive mountain climbing experience is not. Every year an average of 3 or 4 climbers die on the ascent – or more dangerous descent – due to inexperience or attempting to do without the services of a qualified guide.

Practicalities in Chamonix

Tourist Office Place du Triangle (Tel. 50 53 00 24); efficient accommodation service; maps; list of cable-cars; computerised information system; currency exchange. Open daily 8.30 am–7.30 pm.

Railway Station Ave de la Gare (Tel. 50 53 00 44); Information office open daily 9 am–noon and 2–6 pm. For town centre from station, follow Ave Michel Croz to Rue Dr Paccard, then left down Rue Dr Paccard and first right to Place de l'Eglise and tourist office.

Buses *Société Alpes Transports*, at train station (Tel. 50 53 01 15); buses to Annecy, Grenoble, Geneva, and summer excursions.

Markets *Place du Mont Blanc*: Sat mornings; and at foot of *Aiguille du Midi cable-car* in Chamonix sud: Tues mornings.

Hiking Information *Maison de la Montagne*, Place de l'Eglise, next to the church. Weather monitor, maps, guides at *Office de Haute Montagne*; *Compagnie des Guides* (Tel. 50 53 00 88) organises skiing and climbing lessons and leads guided hikes. *Club Alpin Français*, 136 ave Michel-Croz (Tel. 50 53 16 03); information on climbing, mountain refuges, conditions.

Weather conditions Issued 3 times daily by meterorological office in the Maison de Montagne. (Tel. 36 65 02 74) for recording of weather conditions.

Hotels *Les Grands Charmoz*, 468 Chemin de Cristalliers (Tel. 50 53 45 57). Cheap but comfortable rooms in a large house. ☆ *Arve*, 60 impasse Anémones (Tel. 50 53 02 21). Down a quiet cul-de-sac, off Rue J. Vallot. ☆☆ *Au Bon Coin*, 80 ave Aiguille-du-Midi (Tel. 50 53 15 67). Off Ave Ravanel-le-Rouge; pleasant and comfortable. No restaurant. ☆☆ *International*, 255 ave M Croz (Tel. 50 53 00 60). Convenient for station. Modernised, comfortable and spick and span. ☆☆☆ *Le Prieuré*, allée Recteur Payot (Tel. 50 53 20 72). A comfortable and stylish hotel in an excellent central location. ☆☆☆☆ *Hôtel Albert Ier et Milan*, 119 impasse du Montveners, 74400 Chamonix (Tel. 50 53 05

09). Chalet-style hôtel, luxurious, many rooms with balconies. Superb food and views of Mont Blanc from restaurant. *Auberge de Jeunesse* (HI), 127 montée Jacques Balmata, in Les Pélerins (Tel. 50 53 14 52). Take bus from Place de l'Eglise (direction **Les Houches**) and get off at **Pélerins Ecole**, then uphill.

Restaurants *Brasserie des Sports*, 82 rue Joseph Vallot. Simple, cheap dishes. ☆ *Atmosphere*, 123 Place Balmat (Tel. 50 55 90 09). A popular restaurant, crowded with locals, offering a wide range of well-cooked dishes.

Albertville

Trains *8 trains daily from* **Chambéry** *(35 mins) and* **Bourg-St-Maurice** *(1 hour).*

From Chambéry another superb mountain journey can be made by train, this one up the valley of the Isère to Albertville, the scene of the 1992 Winter Olympics, **Moutiers** and **Bourg-St-Maurice**, just west of the Italian border. The railway skirts round the Bauges mountains east of the Chambéry until it meets the Combe de Savoie which it then follows north-east as far as Albertville before snaking south and then east to Bourg St-Maurice.

Albertville lies at the eastern end of the Combe de Savoie, the name given to this stretch of the Isère valley. It is a rich agricultural area, its orchards, vineyards and fields of tobacco protected from the possibility of flooding by embankments built early in the 19th century by Sardinian engineers. The vines, on south-facing slopes of the Bauges, produce some of the finest wines of Savoy. Vineyards surround the picturesque villages of Montmélian, St-Pierre d'Albigny and Mercury-Gemilly.

What to see

Old Conflans

Albertville itself is not ancient but above it on a steep hillside is the old town of Conflans looking down onto the confluence of the Isère with the Arly. It is a dramatically situated town, its old houses and Baroque church hidden behind its Gothic town gates and massive walls. When the route of the Tarantaise road was altered in the 18th century, Conflans suddenly found itself cut off from all passing traffic and sank into a steady decline.

The climb to Conflans from Albertville is extremely steep but short, the town is entered through the **Porte de Savoie**, close to which stands a graceful little tower and a delightful fountain dating from the French occupation of the town in 1703. Most interesting are the **Château de Manuel de Locatel** and the **Musée Municipal** which has amongst its collections cannonballs used in the 1600 siege of Conflans by Henry IV. Above the 18th-century church is the **Grand Place** and the

Maison Rouge, a 14th-century brick building which was once a monastery before being turned into military barracks. The steps beside it lead up to a terrace planted with ancient limes some 120 metres above the valley bottom. From the terrace there is a superb view looking back down the straight and narrow valley of the Combe de Savoie.

It was at Albertville, then known as l'Hopital, that 10 days after Waterloo the French Colonel Bugeaud confronted and routed a massive army of 10,000 Austro-Sardinian soldiers which was attempting to descend from the Beaufortin and Tarentaise valleys into France.

Practicalities in Albertville

Tourist Office 1 rue Bugeaud (Tel. 79 32 04 22). **Railway Station** Ave Général de Gaulle; (Information: Tel. 79 85 50 50; Reservations: Tel. 79 62 40 60). **Hotels** ☆☆☆ *Hôtel Albert 1er*, 38 ave Victor Hugo (Tel. 79 37 77 33). Right next to station; expensive but virtually the only place to stay. **Restaurants** *L'Etrivier*, 17 ave Général de Gaulle (Tel. 79 37 14 70).

Bourg-St-Maurice

Trains *8 trains daily from* **Albertville** *(1 hour) and* **Chambéry** *(1 hour 35 mins); 5 daily from* **Paris** *Gare-de-Lyon, with change at Aix-les-Bains or Chambéry (5 hours 25 mins).*

The valley of the Isère makes an abrupt dog-leg to the south-east at Albertville; on the slopes above are the ruins of the castle of **Chantemerle** and beyond lies **Moutiers**, the old capital of the Tarentaise. It owes its name to a monastery in the See of Darentasia that was founded in the 5th century. To the east of the town rises the Massif de la Vanoise. At Moutiers the valley of the Isère changes direction abruptly a second time and heads north-east to the little village of **Aime** which has, in the Basilica St-Martin, one of the earliest Romanesque buildings in Savoy. Its squat tower and simple apse feature rough but attractive, antique herring-bone patterned stone-work. Excavations have revealed the existence of a Roman temple and a Carolingian church below the present building.

This part of the Isère valley, known as the **Haute-Tarentaise**, is famous for its apples and honey, as well as for its curious breed of small cattle called *tarines*. On the eastern side of the valley the jagged peaks of Mont Jovet, Aiguille Grive and Pointe du Four rise up and dominate the scene as far as the busy garrison town of **Bourg-St-Maurice**. The town is the main market-town of the upper valley and enjoys a delightful site in a wide valley full of poplars and surrounded by orchards. *Bourg-St-Maurice* is the final railway station in France; over the Italian border the line continues to **Aosta**. Apart from the magnificent scenery the town is famed above all for its Beaufort cheese.

Practicalities in Bourg-St-Maurice

Tourist Office Place de la Gare (Tel. 79 07 04 92).

Railway Station (Information: Tel. 79 85 50 50; Reservations: Tel. 79 62 40 60).

Hotels ☆ *Hôtel Bon Repos*, Ave Centenaire (Tel. 79 07 01 78). An attractive little hotel. No restaurant.

☆☆ *Hostellerie Petit St-Bernard*, ave Stade (Tel. 79 07 04 32).

Hostels *Auberge de Jeunesse Seez-les-Arcs* (HI) in secluded forest 5km from town. Bus towards Val d'Isère, alight at **Longefoy** stop. Very popular hostel with good facilities in superb location.

Grenoble

Trains *12–15 trains daily from* **Chambéry** *(1 hour); 3–6 from* **Annecy**, *with connection at Aix-les-Bains (2 hours), 7 from* **Avignon** *(3 hours) and* **Lyon** *(2 hours); 7–11 from* **Paris** *(3 hours by* TGV; *6–8 hours by other trains); 3–6 from* **Strasbourg** *(7 hours 40 mins).*

Skirting the mountain mass of the Bauges, the railway heads east along the same route it followed to Bourg-St-Maurice and then turns abruptly south, following the Isère downstream to Grenoble. This stretch of the Isère valley, known as Le Grésivaudan, consists of a broad, deep corridor eroded by former glaciers. Superbly sheltered by the mountains on either side of it in spring and autumn, it is suffocatingly hot in summer and funnels bitter easterly winds in winter. It is however a rich agricultural valley, its northern bank exposed to the sun and planted densely with vineyards and orchards.

Just outside **Pontcharra** stand the ruins of Château Bayard, one of whose rulers, Pierre Terrail, became a page to the Duke of Savoy after impressing him with his horsemanship and handling of arms, before being sent to the court of Charles VIII. His outstanding military career came to an abrupt end in 1524 when a stone hurled by an early catapult broke his back while campaigning with François I in Italy.

At the bottom of the valley the Isère cuts west through a gap between the Massif de la Chartreuse to the north and the Massif du Vercors to the south. Between the 2, occupying a strategic location in a massive meander cut by Isère, lies the great city of **Grenoble**, the economic and intellectual capital of the French Alps.

Standing on both banks of the Isère, in the Vallée du Grésivaudan, at the foot of the mountains of the Grande Chartreuse, Grenoble is one of the most beautifully situated towns in France.

History

The early rulers of Dauphiné did not live in Grenoble but in the Château de Beauvoir west of the mountainous Vercors district – now a romantic ruin. One of the early counts, Guiges III, married an Englishwoman, a descendant of the last claimant to the English throne before the Norman invasion. Her son was christened with the name Dolphin, a common name in 12th-century England. Corrupted as Dauphin in French, the name quickly came to signify the dynasty of counts which had been known hitherto as the Comtes de Viennois, and by extension, the domains they ruled. When the impoverished Humbert II, Comte de Viennois, sold his domains to King Philip VI of France in 1349, they were referred to as the Dauphiné. Under the Treaty of Romans by which the lands were transferred, it was decided that Dauphiné should be the personal fief of the oldest son of the Kings of France who would thenceforward bear the title of Dauphin. A very similar system existed in England, where the eldest son of the ruling monarch automatically received the title of Prince of Wales. The first Dauphin of France was Charles, the future Charles V.

The town was captured for Henri IV in 1590 and grew enormously in power and wealth under the rule of the Connetable de Lesdiguières, a dynamic administrator and leader of the Protestant reform movement in the second half of the 16th century. Appointed Lieutenant-General of Dauphiny by Henri IV, he reorganised the town, commissioning new buildings, paving the streets, enlarging the forts above the town, promoted the fairs for which Grenoble was famous and instituted a mail service between Grenoble and Lyon.

What to see

Place Grenette

The heart of the city lies around Place Grenette, to the north of which lies the beautiful **Jardin de Ville**, once part of the gardens of the château of the Duc de Lesdiguières. Part of the château has now been restored, and serves as the Hôtel de Ville, which also houses the **Musée Stendhal**. The Grande Rue, which leads to Place St-André, is lined with fine town houses. There are many other equally delightful squares with fountains, gardens, flower-beds and window-boxes cascading with geraniums so that even though a large city, Grenoble has the feel of a mountain town. The mountains are never far away; their white peaks rise above and are constantly glimpsed from the avenues and boulevards that criss-cross the city.

Fort de la Bastille

Lesdiguières was responsible for part of the Fort de la Bastille which can be reached by a funicular railway, the *téléphérique*, that makes a dramatic ascent from Quai

Stéphane-Jay on the banks of the Isère to the rocky spur north of the river. From here there are panoramic views of the town, the confluence of the Isère and the Drac, and the peaks of Belledonne, Taillefer, Objou, Vercors and Mont Blanc, far away to the east. (Open April–Oct, 9 am–midnight; Nov–Dec and Feb–Mar 10 am–7.30 pm.)

A walk down the hill past gardens, cafés and old houses brings one to the **Musée Dauphinois**, a dynamic regional museum in a former 17th-century convent. (Open Wed–Mon 9 am–noon and 2–6 pm.)

Palais de Justice

Close to the river below the Fort de la Bastille, near the little church of St-André, is the Palais de Justice, the most interesting building in the town. It occupies the site of the ancient palace of the Dauphins. Built on one side in white stone and the other in blueish-grey it was originally the meeting place of the Estates of the Dauphiné. The oldest part, the left wing, was built under Charles VIII in a Flamboyant Gothic style and then largely rebuilt in the 19th century. The right wing was built under Francis I in the 16 century and contains superb wood carvings by the German artist Paul Jude and impressive painted ceilings. Opposite it, on the other side of **Place St-André**, is a brick **chapel** built in 1220–36 which was the private chapel of the Dauphins, whose palace rose on the site now occupied by the Palais de Justice. The Chevalier Pierre Terrail de Bayard, who died while campaigning with François I in Italy, was interred in the north transept of the chapel.

Cathédrale Notre-Dame

In Place Notre-Dame, to the east of Place St-André, is the Cathedral of Notre-Dame, with a beautiful interior. The choir possesses a tabernacle of 1455–57 more than 14 metres high which has been robbed of its statues.

Stendhal, one of the most famous French novelists of the early 19th century, was born in the town in 1783 at number 14 rue J. J. Rousseau; a museum devoted to him has been created in the **old Hôtel de Ville**, a mansion once the residence of the Connetable de Lesdiguières. The vast majority of Stendhal's manuscripts are possessed by the municipal library.

Musée des Beaux-Arts

Another distinguished native of Grenoble is Henri Fantin-Latour, many of whose paintings are to be found in the Musée des Beaux-Arts on Place de Verdun, one of the finest provincial art galleries and museums of France. Apart from Fantin-Latour, the museum contains paintings by Veronese, Canaletto, Guardi, Bonnard, Derain, Monet, Sisley, Renoir, Signac, Vlaminck, Matisse, Mirò, Ernst and Tanguy. (Open Wed–Mon 10 am–noon and 2–6 pm.)

North of the Isère, beneath the hill crowned by the fortress of La Bastille, lies the little Romanesque **church of St-Laurent** with a Merovingian crypt of the 6th century.

Grenoble is indelibly associated with the Hundred Days that followed Napoleon's escape from captivity on Elba. It was at the little town of **Laffrey**, just to the south of Grenoble, that Napoleon was confronted in 1815 by the army sent by the Bourbons to arrest him. After a moment of prevarication the troops went over to his side and he entered Grenoble on 7th March 1815 to receive a rapturous welcome. The significance of the defections to his side before Grenoble was not lost on Napoleon. Of this episode he wrote in his memoirs: 'As far as Grenoble I was an adventurer; at Grenoble I was a prince.'

Practicalities in Grenoble

Tourist Office 14 rue de la République, in centre (Tel. 76 54 34 36); maps; information on guided tours; accommodation service. Open Mon–Fri 9 am–6.30 pm; Sat 9 am–12.30 pm and 1.30–6.30 pm; branch office at the station (Tel. 76 56 90 94).

Railway Station Place de la Gare; (Information: Tel. 76 47 50 50; Reservations: Tel. 76 47 54 27). Information office open Mon–Fri 8.30 am–7.30 pm, Sat 9 am–6 pm. For city centre follow Rue Alsace-Lorraine, bear left along Place Victor Hugo, continue up Rue Molière and Rue F. Poulat, then turn right down Rue Raoul Blanchard.

Buses *Gare routière*, to left of train station; excursions in summer to nearby towns.

Markets *Place St-Bruno*, near station: Mon-Sat mornings; also *Place Ste-Claire*, near tourist office: covered market every morning.

Festivals *Feast of the Assumption celebrations*: 15th Aug; *Large Bastille Day celebrations*: 14th July, fireworks over Bastille Fort.

Hotels *Hôtel de la Poste*, 25 rue de la Poste, in pedestrianised zone (Tel. 76 46 67 25). Friendly managers, spacious, clean rooms.

Hôtel Victoria, 17 rue Thiers, mid-way between station and tourist office. (Tel. 76 46 06 36). Good, simple, clean rooms.

☆ *Hôtel Acacia*, 13 rue Belgrade, near Jardin de Ville (Tel. 76 87 29 90). Spotless modern hotel; all rooms with showers.

☆☆ *Alpes*, 45 ave F. Viallet (Tel. 76 87 00 71). On the main street leading from station to Jardin de Ville.

☆☆ *Institut*, 10 rue Barbillon (Tel. 76 46 36 44). comfortable hotel close to station off ave F. Viallet; clean, spacious rooms.

☆☆ *Ibis*, 5 rue Miribel, Centre Commercial les Trois Dauphins (Tel. 76 47 48 49). Large, characterless modern hotel which often has rooms when others are full.

Restaurants *Brasserie Bavaroise*, 2 rue Vicat, near tourist office. Delicious cuisine in small restaurant crowded with locals.

Le Tonneau de Diogene, 6 Place Notre-Dame. Simple tasty dishes, sometimes served at outdoor tables.

Bleu Nuit, 9 Place de Metz, 1 block south of place de Verdun. Attractive blue and white decor with a good range of delicious, inventive dishes.

☆ *Berlioz*, 4 rue de Strasbourg (Tel. 76 56 22 39). Delicious, light cooking in this bright and airy restaurant; always packed at lunchtime.

☆ *Le Pot au Feu*, 6 Place Lavalette (Tel. 76 42 27 66). Interesting and lively bistrot with a modern twist.

☆☆ *Auberge Napoléon*, 7 rue Montorge (Tel. 76 87 53 64). Excellent regional cuisine and delicate cooking opposite a corner of the Jardin de Ville.

Briançon

Trains *2–4 trains daily from* **Grenoble**, *changing at Veynes-Devoluy (4½ hours).*

The journey to Briançon from Grenoble is one of the most scenic and delightful train journeys to be made in eastern France, passing through superb mountain scenery and ending high up in the delightful alpine town of Briançon, a strategic town commanding an ancient crossing of the Alps between France and Italy.

South of Grenoble lies the **Trièves district**, a great, verdant depression through which the rivers Drac and Ebron have cut deep gorges. The Drac is followed south to **Monestier de Clermont**, south-west of which rises an extraordinary, isolated, flat-topped mountain, Mont Aiguille, known as the Olympus of Dauphiné. This vast and curiously shaped mountain attracted the attention of the youthful King Charles VIII in 1489 who was then on his way to the pilgrimage site of Notre-Dame-d'Embrun. Intrigued by the curious stories he was told of its summit, where angels' robes had supposed to be seen to float, he gave orders for the mountain to be climbed – perhaps the first royal patronage of a mountain climbing expedition. In the summer of 1492 some of the King's men found a way up its vertical cliffs to the top where they found a delightful meadow covered with wild flowers on which chamois were contentedly grazing. They spent a week on the top where they celebrated mass and erected several crosses. No further attempt to climb the mountain was made for 340 years.

Behind the white cliffs of Mont Aiguille the Vercors mountains stretch away west; to the south lie the dark fir woods and pastures of the Col de la Croix Haute which marks the watershed dividing the north flowing river Drac and the Buech and Durance which flow south to the Rhône at Avignon. The village and railway junction of **Veynes-Devoluy** is reached from where the southerly line descends to **Manosque** and **Marseilles** and the easterly line heads up the valley of the Durance as far as the delightful Alpine town of **Briançon**.

The first town heading east is **Gap**, a half Alpine, half Provençal town on the route Napoleon, the first French town to welcome Napoleon on his march north during the Hundred Days. Historically it belongs to Dauphiné but it has something of the feel of the Midi – an encouraging sign to anyone with a weakness for Provence. There is little to see of antiquity however, the town having been burnt to the ground by the Duke of Savoy in 1692.

Further east up the Durance valley, **Embrun** has a fascinating history and was once one of the most important pilgrimage sites in Dauphiny. The little town occupies a superb position at an altitude of 870 metres on a crag 70 metres above the Durance river. Both Charles VIII and Louis XI came to pray at the miraculous image of the Virgin in the little church of Notre-Dame. Louis XI, who as Dauphin resided long in Dauphiny, was a devotee of the Virgin of Notre-Dame and was rarely to be seen without a copy of her image on his hat; he displayed his attachment to the church by making it a gift of an organ, the oldest in France. The church, once a cathedral, is the most beautiful Romanesque church in Dauphiné – a graceful building of black and white chequered stone built at the end of the 12th century. It has the most beautiful example of Lombard art in its delicate vaulted porch which rests on pink marble columns which are supported by lions and seated male figures. Beneath it stood the image of the Black Virgin whose cult was so much encouraged by Louis XI. Italian influences are to be seen in the imaginative use of marbles of varying colour. Few people, let alone kings, now make the journey to Notre-Dame, set on its rock 70 metres above the Durance. The seat of a bishop since the 4th century, the town still has a Franciscan convent and the remains of its 12th-century Keep, the **Tour Brune**.

East of Embrun the Durance valley narrows between ravines of yellowish chalky stone streaked here and there with reddish strata. Almost at the head of the valley, in a remarkable strategic position, lies **Briançon**, the highest town in Europe, some 1,325 metres above sea level. It lies at the foot of the Croix-de-Toulouse on the slopes of a height overlooking the confluence of the Durance and the Guisane. The appearance of the town is almost entirely due to the great military engineer of Louis XIV, Vauban, who built a complex web of fortifications to create an impregnable defensive system on the new eastern border of France. The town is completely enclosed by this extensive defensive system and overlooked by further outlying defensive forts which dominate the surrounding valleys while the deep gorges of the Guisane and the Clarée serve as natural entrenchments flanking the fortress.

To create the fortifications Vauban razed the old church to the ground and built a new one in its place; a cold, severe building it is unusual in being one of the few buildings designed by Vauban that was not for defensive purposes. The most endearing part of the church, 2 exhausted-looking lions outside the main doorway, were part of the earlier church demolished by Vauban.

The success of Vauban's fortifications was later demonstrated but not in the way that Vauban could have anticipated. After Napoleon's defeat at Waterloo, an Austro-Sardinian army invaded Dauphiné and captured Grenoble, Gap and Embrun. Briançon was not important strategically but it blocked the pass to the east with Italy. Ignoring France's defeat at Waterloo, and the terms of the Treaty of Paris, the local garrison under General Eberlé held out for months, keeping at bay an Allied force that outnumbered them by a ratio of 20:1. In 1940 the town also held out against Italian attacks.

Within the walls the streets are steep and narrow, many houses have open balconies on the 1st and 2nd floors, arcades on the ground floor, and wide overhanging eaves. Italian influence is visible in many of the 17th-century houses that climb up to the Citadel. The main street, the **Grand Rue**, has the delightful local name of La Grande Gargouille. Like its sister, La Petite Gargouille, it was laid out in the Middle Ages and takes its name from the rivulet that runs permanently down its centre – something that must have played a much needed function in medieval times. From the top of the Grande Rue, the winding Chemin de Ronde descends to the **Pont d'Asfeld**, a bold single-arch bridge built over the Durance by Marshal d'Asfeld in 1734, from where there are superb views.

Close by is the superb **Parc National des Ecrins**, usually approached from the train station at Argentières-la-Bessée (15 mins by train from Briançon in direction of Gap). From there a small road leads to Mont-Dauphin from where a road follows the valley towards **Vallouise** and the peak of Mont-Pelvoux which rises to a height of 3,946 metres. The Grand Randonné route 54 makes a circuit through the national park passing through Vallouise; the best stretch of the walk is probably from the town to Le Monetier and the Lac de l'Eychauda. Hiking and climbing information, hotels, camping and gite d'étape, are all to be found in Vallouise.

Practicalities in Briançon

Tourist Office Parte de Pignerol (Tel. 92 21 08 50). Located at entrance to the Ville Haute or Upper town.
Railway Station (Tel. 92 51 50 50).
Hôtels *Hôtel de la Paix*, 3 rue Port Méane, off Grande Rue (Tel. 92 21 37 43).
Hôtel Edelweiss, 32 ave de la République (Tel. 92 21 02 74). Pleasant hotel on main street

opposite cultural centre.
☆☆*Mont Brison*, 3 ave Général de Gaulle (Tel. 92 21 02 94). Just north of Durance river on way into Citadel from station.
Restaurants ☆☆*Le Peché Gourmand*, 2 route Gap, at junction with av. M. Petsche, just over the river Guisane (Tel. 92 20 11 02). Excellent Dauphinoise cuisine.

Sisteron

Trains *5 – 7 trains daily from* **Veynes-Devoluy** *(40 mins); 3 from* **Briançon**, *may require change at Veynes-Devoluy (2 hours 50 mins); 6 from* **Manosque** *(55 mins).*

South of Veynes-Devoluy the landscape begins to change, opening out, losing height, and steadily becoming less Alpine. The River Buech flows south, passing a ruined 14th-century castle, beyond which lies the small of town of **Serres** on a ridge above the Buech. Almond orchards can be glimpsed in the valley around Le Bersac and **Savournon**, a small village with a ruined castle and 11th-century Keep. The valley then narrows as it approaches the town of **Sisteron**, its castle guarding the ravine south of the confluence of the Buech and Durance rivers.

Sisteron marks the borders of Dauphiné and Provence, the defile carved here by the Durance river being known as the 'gate of Provence'. The historical connection with Provence is also strong: the See once belonged to the kingdom of Arles and was only joined to France in the 15th-century.

Sisteron is in fact more typical of a Provençal town than a Dauphinoise one, with narrow, steep streets irregularly built around a rocky height. Settled by the Romans, and known by them as Segustera, the town was the seat of a bishopric from the 4th century until the Revolution.

What to see

Notre-Dame-des-Pommiers

Within the 14th-century ramparts, pierced by 3 towers, is the Provençal Romanesque church of Notre-Dame-des-Pommiers, with an obvious influence from Lombardy in its columns and sculptured capitals. One characteristic feature of Provençal architecture is the dome supported by columns at the entrance to the chancel.

Above the former cathedral is 13th-century Citadel, altered and extended in the late 16th century by Jean Erard, an engineer in the service of Henri IV. It occupies a prominent rock that dominates the river below and from which there are outstanding views of the surrounding countryside, the vertical strata of the Rochers de la Baume on the opposite side of the Durance, and the Laup and

Aujour mountains to the north. Due to its strategic location in the Durance valley the fortress was bitterly fought over in the Wars of Religion. The Rue de Provence leads to the Porte de Dauphiné at the foot of a rock crowned by the Guérite du Diable, one of the outworks of the Citadel.

Château-Arnoux-St-Auban

South of Sisteron lies Château-Arnoux-St-Auban, an important railway junction. There is a magnificent train journey to be made through the spectacular landscape of inland Provence from nearby Digne to Nice and Château-Arnoux-St-Auban is the place to get off the train to make this journey. This line is run by a private company, *Chemins de Fer de Provence*, which lays on 4 trains a day for the 3½-hour journey. The connection between St-Auban, on the main SNCF network, and Digne, where the private line begins, is made by SNCF buses in a 35-minute journey. A description of the landscape and route between Nice and Digne is given in the chapter on Provence on pages 412–442.

The main SNCF line continues south to Manosque, Aix-en-Provence and the great port of Marseilles, from where there are fast connections to Paris.

Practicalities in Sisteron

Tourist Office Hôtel de Ville, (Tel. 92 61 12 03).
Railway Station Ave. de la Libération (Tel. 92 51 50 50).

Hotels ☆*Hotel Touring Napoléon*, 22 ave. de la Libération. (Tel. 92 61 00 06). Convenient for station, with restaurant offering choice of good inexpensive menus.

☆☆☆*Grand Hôtel du Cours*, Allée de Verdun (Tel 92 61 04 51). Large comfortable hotel, without restaurant, close to the tourist office and the church of Notre-Dame.

10 Normandy and Maine

Although closely united geographically to its western neighbour, Normandy differs greatly from Brittany in character. It is not just a richer relation, agriculturally and commercially, but its people spring from quite different cultural and linguistic roots. The Bretons are primarily a Celtic people who began to arrive from Britain in the 6th century BC, fleeing before the Picts, Scots, Saxons and Angles. Although for centuries the Bretons remained divided into groups of colonies, they held in common British princes, institutions and speech that formed the basis of a cultural and national identity. The Normans were late arrivals in comparison, descending on to the northern coast of France from Scandinavia during the 9th century. In 911 the Viking leader of the Norsemen, Rollo, secured a treaty that legitimised his rule over the area he had overrun, converted to Christianity and made Rouen his capital. Once the Norsemen had established a footing in their new land, there followed an influx of Vikings and Danes, some from England and Ireland, others from Scandinavia. Not all consisted of raiding parties bent on pillage; some were expressly invited in to help colonise the land. In 1013 Duke Richard III, the Norse ruler, invited Olaf the Norwegian and Lacman the Swede to assist him in his war against Odo of Chartres. His descendent, Duke Robert the Magnificent, died while on pilgrimage to Jerusalem, leaving an illegitimate heir, William, who was destined to play a seminal role in English history.

The small province of Maine, though less spectacular than Normandy, has a fine capital in the town of Le Mans and a gentle countryside which is quintessentially French in character. Hugues Capet created Maine as a hereditary countship as a buffer state between his domains and the kingdom of the Normans to the north. Eventually it was united to Anjou by the marriage of its heiress to Fulk of Anjou and then passed to Phillippe Auguste in the 13th century.

Lying so close to the English coast, Normandy has often seen English naval activity along its coasts and periodic incursions and invasions. English troops, led by the Duke of Bedford, captured Joan of Arc after a victory in September 1430. Taken to Rouen and confined in what is now known as the Tour Jeanne d'Arc, she was burnt at the stake on 30th May 1431 at the age of 19. Maine was the scene of innumerable battles during the Hundred Years War, the English only being expelled from Le Mans in 1447. Shortly afterwards Maine was joined to the royal domains of the Kings of France.

As one of the richest agricultural areas, devoted in particular to dairy farming, Normandy and Maine are famous for their butter and cheeses, of which Camembert is the best known abroad. The speckled brown and white Normandy cows soon become a familiar sight in the landscape, grazing in orchards laden with apple blossom or fruit. Apples have been used to produce cider since time immemorial while the Cognac of Normandy is Calvados, an apple brandy which should be aged for 12 to 15 years. *Galettes* – whole wheat pancakes stuffed with concoctions of meat, cheese or vegetables – and *crêpes* are as close to fast-food as Normandy cuisine is prepared to go.

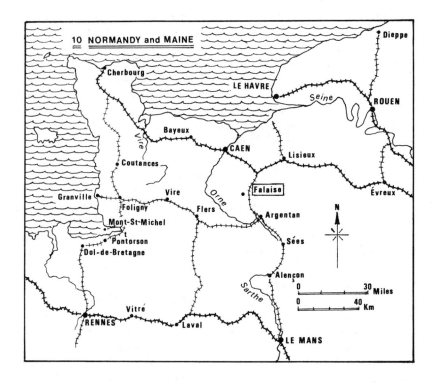

The route *Rouen – Lisieux – Evreux – Caen – Bayeux – Cherbourg – Coutances – Granville – Pontorson/ Mont-St-Michel – Vitré – Laval – Le Mans – Alençon – Sées – Argentan – Falaise*

This journey, through beautiful Normandy countryside, begins in the provincial capital, Rouen, easily reached by direct train from the Channel ports of Dieppe, Le Havre, Caen and Cherbourg and direct train from Paris. Instead of heading first of all for Rouen, travellers arriving by ferry at Cherbourg or Caen can, just as easily, join this circular route at their port of entry and visit Rouen at the end of their visit. This route takes in the best of Normandy and the neighbouring province of Maine, making a big loop west of Rouen through the Normandy departements of Seine-Maritime, Eure, Orne, Calvados and Manche and the Maine departments of Mayenne, Sarthe and Maine-et-Loire.

Rouen, where Joan of Arc was burnt at the stake, Gustave Flaubert roamed the streets as a boy and Claude Monet captured the cathedral façade in immortal paintings, makes a fitting starting point for a journey through Normandy. To the north lies the old port of Dieppe, to the west Lisieux, a modern pilgrimage town with the oldest Gothic church in Normandy, to the south Evreux, a typical Norman cathedral town situated on the pretty River Iton. Caen is one of the most interesting towns in Normandy and still boasts the castle and 2 fabulous abbeys, founded by William the Conqueror and his wife Matilda, which miraculously escaped the severe bombing of the Second World War. Bayeux not only contains Bishop Odo's famous tapestry depicting the invasion of England but is a beautifully preserved and ancient town with delightful streets and many medieval timbered houses. Like many towns in lower Normandy, Coutances is located on the summit of a tall hill and crowned by a beautiful cathedral, this one built by Tancred de Hauteville and consecrated in 1056 in the presence of William the Conqueror. At Granville the Normandy coastline is approached again; this fortified port was used by the English to make forays against the French who were firmly ensconced in the jewel-like fortress-abbey of Mont-St-Michel. Madame de Sévigné described the latter as 'the eighth wonder of the world' while Victor Hugo claimed it stood in the same relation to France as the Pyramids did to Egypt. The journey then briefly enters Brittany (with **Rennes** *covered in chapter 4 on Brittany) and heads east through the old province of Maine to* **Vitré** *with its superb castle and* **Laval** *with its rambling medieval quarters. Le Mans' majestic Romanesque and Gothic cathedral is surrounded by streets of very early houses where stone doorways, carved friezes and high projecting gables remain little altered since the 15th century. Leaving Maine the route then heads north into Normandy for the second time, reaching* **Alençon,** *a pretty Norman town known as the 'capital of lace'. The charming, quiet and ancient cathedral city of* Sées *is reached before arriving at* **Argentan,** *a quiet little town on the Orne from where there are direct trains to Paris. (7 – 10 days)*

Rouen

Trains *Trains hourly from* **Paris** *(1 hour 10 mins); 12 daily from* **Caen** *(2 hours); 3 from* **Lille** *(3 hours); 12 from* **Le Havre** *(1 hour).*

The ancient capital of the duchy of Normandy is now a vast city surrounded by enormous docks and suburbs. Fortunately however the old town forms a compact area on the northern bank of the Seine reached via the wide boulevard, rue Jeanne d'Arc, that runs south from the *art nouveau* railway station. Even though several bombs fell on the cathedral during the Second World War and the majority of old houses between the cathedral and the river were completely destroyed, Rouen remains a fascinating and rewarding city.

Rouen's pre-eminence as the city of Normandy dates from 911 when Rollo made it the capital of his Norse dukedom. Throughout the Middle Ages and the Renaissance it was the focal point of Norman politics and trade, benefitting from its strategic position on the Seine between Paris and the Channel. Richard the Lion heart was crowned king there in 1189 as was his brother John 10 years later. King John lost the town during the Hundred Years War to Philippe Auguste but it was recaptured in 1419 by Henry V after a long siege. Joan of Arc was tried here and was burnt to death in a square near the town centre in 1431. Of the castle built by Philippe-Auguste where Joan of Arc was tried before an ecclesiastical court nothing remains except for a solitary tower, now named the Tour Jeanne-d'Arc, between the railway station and the Musée des Beaux-Arts. Almost inevitably the city was ravaged by Catholics and Huguenots in turn during the Wars of Religion in the 16th century.

What to see

Cathédrale Notre-Dame

Much of the old town was destroyed in the Second World War but 3 important Gothic churches survived, the finest of which is the glorious cathedral of Notre-Dame, built between 1201 and 1504. It is, without doubt, one of the greatest Gothic buildings in existence. The chevet is of quite outstanding beauty, so too is the ambulatory which has an unusual feel of space and elegance. The choir is also exceptional, being a pure example of the *rayonnant* style and containing magnificent woodwork dating from 15th century. Within the cathedral are a number of impressive tombs including that of **Richard Coeur de Lion**, whose heart is buried there.

In the Lady Chapel are 2 outstanding examples of French Renaissance sculpture – the tomb of the Cardinals of Amboise by Roulland le Roux in which the cardinals, although on their knees, seem not to be deeply engaged in prayer – and that of Louis de Brèze. This exuberant tomb, dating from 1530, has a sculpture of his kneeling widow, Diane de Poitiers, who was later to employ her charms on Henri II, becoming his mistress and confidante for many years until retreating to the magnificent Château d'Anet which Henri had had built for her. In the ambulatory is buried the heart of Duc Rollo, the ancestor of William, Duke of Normandy, who made Rouen his capital in the 10th century. The elaborate western front, painted so often by Monet, is a brilliant profusion of beautiful sculptural decoration completed in 1530. The main western doorway, ornamented with a Tree of Jesse and various statues, some decapitated during the Revolution, is flanked by 2 irregular towers whose contrasting styles never fail to astonish. The tower of St-Romain on the left, which dates from the end of the 12th century, has an ethereal and almost brittle appearance and rises in superb contrast to the Flamboyant 15th to 16th century tower of Le Beurre, with its sloping roof. The latter derives its name not from any resemblance to butter but from the fact that its construction was paid for by the sale of indulgences granted by the church for the eating of butter during Lent. A little staircase leads up to a small balcony to the left of the transept; known as the **Escalier de la Librairie**, it is attributed to the 15th-century stone-mason Guillaume Pontifs.

The Old Quarter

The most interesting and picturesque old quarter of Rouen lies immediately to the north of the cathedral around Rue St-Romain. Here the narrow streets are crammed with half-timbered houses, some with gables and faced with tiles, many of them painstakingly restored since the war. In 1525 it was forbidden to build houses with projecting storeys that would overhang the street, making them dark and unhealthy; virtually all of those with overhanging storeys precede this date.

St-Ouen

The 2 other churches of significance in Rouen are St-Ouen and St-Maclou. The former abbey church of St-Ouen was built between the 14th and 15th centuries and although of great architectural purity and with 14th-16th century stained glass, is unable to rival the cathedral for beauty. Adjacent to St-Ouen lies the **Hôtel de Ville** in 18th-century former abbey buildings and beyond it the **Lycée**, once a Jesuit college, that counts Corneille, Flaubert, Corot, Delacroix and Maupassant amongst its pupils.

St-Maclou

The other great church of Rouen is St-Maclou, a striking Gothic church with richly carved Renaissance sculpture decorating its central doorway. Close to the church, at 184 rue Martainville, is the **Aître St Maclou**, a former ossuary used to house the bodies of Plague victims, its massive frieze decorated with skulls, bones and gravediggers' tools. It is now home to **Rouen's School of Art and Architecture**. (Open daily 9.30 am–8 pm.)

Rue Damiette, the narrow street which runs north from St-Maclou contains a number of interesting mansions, including the Hôtel d'Etancourt and the Hôtel de Senneville where Lord Clarendon lived in exile and finished his *True History* before his death in 1674.

Musée des Beaux-Arts

North-west of the Cathedral, in rue Thiers, is the Musée des Beaux-Arts with a fine collection of 16th–19th-century French paintings, including works by Monet, Sisley, Renoir and Théodore Gericault, a native of the city. The museum's collection of Norman ceramics, one of the best in France, has recently been moved to its own premises in the **Musée de la Céramique**, just down the road.

Another museum, just behind the Musée des Beaux-Arts, is the **Musée de Ferronerie Le Secq des Tournelles** with a huge collection of functional and decorative wrought-ironwork, from surgeon's instruments to balconies and grilles. (All museums open Thurs–Mon 10 am–noon and 2–6 pm; combined ticket.)

Palais de Justice

One of the finest buildings of pre-war Rouen was the Palais de Justice, a late-Gothic structure that suffered a direct hit during the Second World War. Little remains of the original building except the fine Flamboyant façade on the Rue aux Juifs. The parallel street, the **rue de l'Horloge**, preserves its enchanting Renaissance gatehouse with its giant and elaborate clock-face. The special arch spanning the street was built for the Gros Horloge in 1527; steps lead up to the ornate belfry. Rue du Gros Horloge leads down to the **Place du Vieux-Marché**, an animated quarter of town where a chapel marks the spot where Joan of Arc perished on 30th May 1431. Old cobbled streets thread through the old town, many with picturesque half-timbered houses.

Practicalities in Rouen

Tourist Office 25 Place de la Cathédrale, opposite the cathedral (Tel. 35 71 41 77). Accommodation service. Open Mon–Sat 9 am–7 pm, Sun 9.30 am–12.30 pm and 2.30–6 pm; Oct.–Mar Mon–Sat 9 am–12.30 pm and 2–6.30 pm.

Railway Station Rue Jeanne d'Arc, at the northern end of a major street which cuts through the city to the Seine; poste restante; currency exchange. (Tel 35 98 50 50). For town centre from station, walk down Rue Jeanne d'Arc to Rue du Gros Horloge, then left to cathedral and tourist office.

Market days Tues, Wed, Fri, Sat at market halls, Place Vieux Marché.

Festivals Fêtes de Jeanne d'Arc on last Sunday in May; Nov: St Romain's Fair.

Hotels Hostellerie du Vieux Logis, 5 rue de Joyeuse (Tel. 35 71 55 30). Simple, slightly faded and worn but quiet and cheap. Hôtel St-Ouen, 43 rue des Faulx. (Tel. 35 71 46 44). Close to the church of the same name; cheap, spacious and central.

Hôtel du Palais, 12 rue Tambour, off rue du Gors Horloge (Tel. 35 71 41 40). Good, clean, cheap and central.

☆ Hôtel Vieille Tour, 42 Place Haute Vieille Tour (Tel. 35 70 03 27).

☆ Hôtel Lisieux, 4 rue Savonnerie, between the cathedral and the Seine (Tel 35 71 87 83).

☆ Hôtel Astrid, Place de la Gare, right next to the station, at top of rue Jeanne d'Arc (Tel 35 71 75 88).

☆☆ Québec, 18 rue de Québec (Tel. 35 70 09 38). Small rooms but comfortable and central.

☆☆☆ Hôtel Dieppe, place Bernard Tissot (Tel. 35 71 96 00). Attractive, quiet rooms in a lovely hotel in central location. Attached is an excellent restaurant Les Quatre Saisons, which serves classic Norman dishes.

Hostels Auberge de la Jeunesse (HI) 118 blvd de l'Europe, 5km from station on bus 12, south of the Seine down rue Jeanne d'Arc and Ave de Bretagne (Tel. 35 72 96 45).

Restaurants Vieux Logis, 5 rue Joyeuse (Tel. 35 71 55 30). Tiny elegant restaurant near Hôtel de Ville; excellent value and good classic French cooking.

☆ La Petite Auberge, 164 rue Martainville (Tel. 35 70 80 18). Popular with locals for its good home-cooking and low prices.

☆ La Cache-Ribaud, 10 rue du Tambour (Tel. 35 71 04 82). Good Normandy fare at good prices.

☆ Les Halles du Vieux Marché, 41 place du Vieux Marché (Tel. 35 71 03 58). Traditional Norman food in cheap bistro on central square.

☆☆ Le Beffroy, 15 rue Beffroy (Tel. 35 71 55 27). Strong on local dishes, especially marmite Dieppoise and lotte vallée d'Auge; and good range of local Normandy cheeses.

☆☆☆ Gill, 60 rue St Nicolas (Tel. 35 71 16 14). Excellent and expensive; one of the best restaurants in Rouen.

☆☆☆ Bertraind Warin, 7–9 rue de la Pie (Tel. 35 89 26 69). Excellent Norman cuisine in a beautiful Norman building; best at lunchtime.

Lisieux

Trains 6 trains daily from **Evreux** (50 mins), **Paris** St Lazare (2 hours) and 6–7 from **Caen** (30 mins).

Lisieux lies just within the eastern limits of the département of Calvados where the Normandy landscape is at its most classic – small broken hills divided by high hedges into patches of bright green meadows thickly planted with apple trees. Beneath them graze the brown and white speckled Normandy cows. Without doubt the best time to see Normandy is in the spring when the apple trees are in blossom and the otherwise unspectacular landscape takes on a short-lived but breath-taking beauty. In many respects the landscape is reminiscent of pre-war England before farmers began to remove hedges to save time and accommodate large agricultural machinery. For centuries apple trees and cows were the primary concern of the Normandy peasants, from which they produced excellent cider, Calvados and cheeses such as Pont l'Evêque, Livarot and Camembert. The latter was invented in a little village to the south of Lisieux by Marie Harel in 1761 whose celebrity is commemorated by a statue to her in the main square.

Until the final years of the 19th century Lisieux was a quiet and typical Normandy market-town with a fine Gothic cathedral, a handsome Archbishop's Palace and a large number of picturesque timbered houses that were among the finest in France. Two events however combined to alter the appearance of the town more in 50 years than in the preceding 500 – the death of a nun in 1897 and the Second World War. Shortly after the death of the Carmelite nun, Sister Theresa, it was reported that miraculous cures had been effected on those that came to pray by her grave and the town began to attract visitors, both curious and pious. As her fame increased, so too did the influx of pilgrims and her canonisation in 1923 led to the construction of a vast basilica in what has been described as 'French casino style.' Lisieux now ranks as one of the important pilgrimage centres of France.

What to see

Eglise St-Pierre

The Second World War was equally cataclysmic and more devastating in its consequences but somehow the Cathedral of St-Pierre survived the bombing of June 1944. Virtually completed by the end of the 12th century, it is the oldest Gothic church in Normandy, with a simple nave in the purest early Gothic style. The majestic western façade, surmounted by 2 dissimilar towers, was slightly damaged but the interior of milk-white stone was untouched by the war. The stained-glass windows, removed for the duration of the war – as with all the cathedrals in France – has given back the cathedral its former glory. The Lady Chapel was erected as a sign of repentance by Bishop Pierre Cauchon who had presided over the trial of Joan of Arc.

Archbishop's Palace

Adjacent to the cathedral is the Archbishop's Palace with a delightful brick and stone façade and the Law Courts with a 17th-century painted ceiling. Behind them lie charming gardens that were once the precincts of the bishop. Few of the old timbered houses for which Lisieux was once famous remain but an impression of the appearance of the old town before the war can be gained from **Rue Henri-Cheron**.

Practicalities in Lisieux

Tourist Office 11 Rue d'Alençon, on way to *centre ville* via rue de la Gare (Tel. 31 62 08 41).
Railway Station Info: Tel. 31 83 50 50; Reservations: Tel. 31 52 14 14.
Festivals Sunday closest to 15th July, celebrating consecration of the Basilica of Ste-Thérèse. *Procession of the Smiling Virgin*: mid-

Aug. *Festival of Ste-Thérèse*: last Sun in Sept, with processions carrying shrine of Ste-Thérèse.
Hotels *Hôtel Régina*, 14 rue de la Gare, very close to station (Tel. 31 31 71 83).
Hôtel St-Louis, 4 rue St-Jacques, just opposite the church of St Jacques (Tel. 31 31 15 43).

☆☆ *Hôtel La Coupe d'Or*, 49 rue Pont-Mortain (Tel. 31 31 16 84). Attractive, comfortable hotel in the *Logis de France* network, with restaurant serving good regional food at attractive prices. **Restaurants** ☆ *France*, 5 rue au Char (Tel. 31 62 03 37). A pleasant little old-fashioned restaurant close to the cathedral.

☆☆ *Parc*, 21 blvd Herbert-Fournet (Tel. 31 62 08 11). An interesting little restaurant located in the old music room of a château. ☆☆ *Ferme du Roy*, 122 blvd Herbert-Fournet (Tel. 31 31 33 98), another option in the same street. Good traditional Normandy cooking in a restaurant evoking an old Norman farm.

Evreux

Trains *6 – 7 trains daily from* Paris *St Lazare (1¼ hours) and* Lisieux *(50 mins).*

Surrounded by some of the finest beach forests in France lies Evreux, a pleasant old Norman town that has somehow survived despite repeated catastrophes. Burnt to the ground in 1119 by Henry I, its city elders massacred by Prince John of England in 1193, burnt again in 1365 and captured by Thomas Duke of Exeter in 1418, Evreux has had a long history of misfortune which culminated in successive German and Allied bombing raids during the Second World War. Much of the town has therefore been rebuilt but nevertheless it is still an attractive place, through which flow several gurgling branches of the river Iton.

What to see

Cathédrale de Notre-Dame

The town's Flamboyant Gothic cathedral, with its late Norman nave and soaring Perpendicular Gothic chancel, survived the war largely unscathed, and still has some magnificent carved woodwork and beautiful stained glass. The present cathedral replaces the one burnt down by Henry I in 1119. In a curious procedure that reflects the religious sensibilities of the day, Henry I sought permission from the Bishop of Evreux before setting light to the cathedral – which the obliging bishop gave on condition that Henry replaced it. With the **Bishop's Palace**, a Flamboyant building dating from 1481, it forms an attractive and harmonious whole, grouped round a beautiful courtyard.

Archbishop's Palace

The palace now houses a delightful **museum** of which the highlights are 2 1st century bronze statues of Jupiter and Apollo that came to light locally. From the gardens behind the cathedral it is possible to follow the river beneath the ramparts to the picturesque **Tour de l'Horloge**. The former abbey **Church of St-Taurin** is also of interest, in particular for its exceptional 13th-century silver and enamel reliquary in the form of a miniature chapel showing St Taurin, the 5th-century bishop of Evreux, holding his crosier. The 18th-century classical façade hides an interior which is a riotous mixture of Norman, Decorated Gothic and Renaissance styles which makes it one of the most intriguing churches in Normandy.

Practicalities in Evreux

Tourist Office 1 Place Général de Gaulle (Tel 32 24 04 43).
Railway Station Place de la Gare (Info: Tel. 32 38 50 50; Reservations: Tel. 35 15 30 30); to tourist office, turn right out of station, then first left down rue J Jaurès, continue down rue de la Harpe, turn right down rue C Corbeau and left down rue de l'Horloge.
Hotels ☆☆ *Hôtel Gambetta*, 61 blvd Gambetta, a stone's throw from the station. (Tel. 32 28 16 36).

☆☆ *Hôtel Grenoble*, 17 rue St Pierre, very close to tourist office, off Ave rue Dr Oursel (Tel. 32 33 07 31).
☆☆☆ *Hôtel Normandy*, 37 rue Edouard Feray (Tel. 32 33 14 40). Comfortable old Normandy hotel with restaurant serving classic Norman dishes.
☆☆ *Hôtel France*, 29 rue St-Thomas. (Tel. 32 39 09 25) Attractive, simple and comfortable rooms and excellent restaurant serving good modern cuisine.

Caen

Trains *6 – 7 trains daily from* **Lisieux** *(30 mins); 5 from* **Bayeux** *(20 mins); 2 from* **Rennes** *(3 hour); 6 from* **Tours** *(3 ½ hours); 12 – 15 from* **Paris** *St-Lazare (2 hours); 8 from* **Cherbourg** *(1 ½ hours).*

West of Lisieux in magnificent open country lies Caen, the ancient capital of the Normans, from where William of Normandy set out to conquer an unruly and divided kingdom to the north – England. William was born at the Château de Falaise near the southern border of Calvados but it was Caen that he made his principal place of residence. With his wife Matilda he began construction of the castle which still overlooks the town and founded the 2 abbeys, the Abbaye aux Hommes and the Abbaye aux Dames, where they are respectively buried. By some miracle both abbeys survived the destruction that tore the city apart during the fierce 2-month battle for the city in June 1944. Both abbeys were built at the instigation of Pope Leo IX who refused to recognise the marriage of William to Matilda, daughter of the Count of Flanders, until both she and her husband promised to undertake some great work on behalf of the Church. By marrying William, Duke of Normandy, Matilda had married a close cousin – a marriage prohibited by the church unless granted a Papal dispensation. Only by performing some great and pious penance was her excommunication lifted.

The Abbaye aux Hommes is particularly fine, being one of the most complete and important Romanesque churches in France.

What to see

The Castle

A long walk down the Avenue du 6 Juin from the station leads one to the heart of the city, clustered now as it has been for 900 years around the enormous castle begun by William the Conqueror. It occupies a large, flat area of high ground dominating the north of the town and is still surrounded by its massive 12th-century walls – astonishingly high and punctured regularly by square defensive towers. Until the Second World War the castle was so hemmed in by ancient buildings that it was almost hidden from view. The destruction of the entire area has opened the area up and has become once again the visible focus of the town. In the southern and eastern castle walls 2 fortified gateways, once accessible only over a drawbridge, lead into the castle grounds.

Although covering an extensive area, the castle precincts come as something of a disappointment for they are remarkably empty, little remaining of the Keep or castle buildings other than the walls and the Treasury. This, a simple Romanesque hall, is one of the earliest secular buildings in Normandy. The castle grounds also contain a small chapel besides which stands a cross of white Normandy stone marking the 900th anniversary of the Norman invasion of England and the **Musée de Normandie**, an excellent museum tracing Norman history. (Open Wed – Mon 10 am–1 pm and 2–5 pm.)

Musée des Beaux-Arts

Nearby in a modern but unobtrusive building is the city's art museum which possesses a distinguished collection of paintings, a large proportion of which were looted from foreign collections by French soldiers during the Napoleonic campaigns. The fine collections of Dutch, Flemish and Italian paintings thus acquired were complemented by others looted by Napoleon's uncle, Cardinal Flesch, and by Bernard Mancel's collection with its magnificent prints by Durer, Mantegna, Rembrandt, Callot and Goya. One of the finest paintings looted by Napoleon's troops is Perugino's *Marriage of the Virgin*. Other fine works include ones by Breughel and Veronese and 17th-century paintings by Rubens and Poussin, whose *Death of Adonis* hangs in the gallery. (Open in summer Wed–Mon 10 am–noon and 2–6 pm; winter 2–5 pm.)

Eglise St-Pierre

Immediately opposite the southern gateway stands the Gothic church of St-Pierre whose nave and spire were destroyed in 1944. The most remarkable part of the church, its Renaissance apse, decorated in the most exuberant style at the beginning of the 16 century, did just survive however, as did most of its Flamboyant western porch. After the war the church seemed so ruined as to be almost beyond repair; only photographs taken in 1945 revealing the extent of the devastation can bring home the size of the task facing the restorers of the church. Close by is **Place Courtonne** which retains a single tower now looking somewhat lonely and forlorn surrounded by modern buildings; it is all that survives of the old town walls.

Abbaye aux Dames

Some distance to the west lies the Abbaye aux Dames, founded as a convent for noble ladies in 1062. The western façade was somewhat brutally restored in the

19th century as a result of which it has little feel of being nearly a thousand years old, but the interior is utterly magnificent – a model of Norman architecture with tall arcades of romanesque arches, grotesque capitals and bold, pure lines. The building is almost exclusively Romanesque in style except for the chancel which was rebuilt in Gothic style and the tall spires of its western towers which were added in the early 18th century. (Guided tours daily at 2.30 and 4pm.)

Abbaye aux Hommes

At the far end of town lies the Abbaye aux Hommes otherwise known as the Church of St Etienne, built by William the Conqueror to serve as his resting-place and completed 10 years before his death. It is striking for its austerity and noble proportions, its western façade being almost completely devoid of decoration of any sort. The tomb of William the Conqueror was violated by the Huguenots during the Wars of Religion and destroyed at the Revolution, and all trace of his remains has disappeared. A plain marble slab near the altar marks his grave. (Guided tours of the abbey, daily at 9.30 am, 11 am, 12.30 and 4 pm.)

Old Caen

Very few of the hundreds of medieval buildings existing in Caen before the war survived the bombing of June 1944 but what remains of old Caen is to be found round and about **Rue Ecuyère** and the delightful **square of St Sauveur**. Here the beautiful Renaissance apse of the church of St Sauveur is being carefully restored. The handsome local limestone being used in the restoration is the same as that exported to England, for the construction of English cathedrals such as Norwich in the late 11th century. Opposite the statue of Louis XIV stands the *Hostellerie Löwenbrau*, one of the many restaurants in Caen noted for the excellence of its seafood, and a desirable place in which to observe the inhabitants of Caen enjoying all that the nearby sea has to offer.

The growing prosperity of the city in the 12th and 13th centuries led Edward III to invade and pillage the town in 1346. It was captured again in 1417 by Henry V and held by the English until 1450 when Dunois compelled the Duke of Somerset and his garrison of 4,000 men to surrender the castle, since which time the town has been in French hands. It suffered the usual depredations during the Wars of Religion and became a stronghold of the Girondins during the Revolution. Charlotte Corday set out from Caen to murder Marat, a leading opponent of the Girondin party and instigator of the September Massacres, in an attempt to put an end to them. After stabbing Marat to death in his bath, she was seized herself and guillotined. On the site of her house now stands a *chocolatier* of the first order.

Practicalities in Caen

Tourist Office Place St-Pierre, beside the Eglise St Pierre (Tel. 31 86 27 65); accommodation service; guided tours; currency exchange.
Railway Station Place de la Gare; lockers; information office; buses 3, 4, 10, and 11 from SNCF station to *centre ville*.

Ferries From Oustreheim, 13km north of Caen, to Portsmouth; 3 daily April–Dec. (6 hours). 6 *Bus verts* daily from the railway station and Place Courtonne to the port of Oustreheim (20 mins) from where ferries leave for Portsmouth.
Markets Place Courtonne, Tues-Sat mornings;

Place St Sauveur, Fri mornings.
Hôtels *Hôtel de la Paix*, 14 rue Neuve-St-Jean, off ave du 6 Juin (Tel. 31 86 18 99). Central and comfortable.
Hôtel St-Jean, 20 rue des Martyrs; next to Eglise St-Jean (Tel. 31 86 23 35). Quiet and modern.
☆ *Hôtel Quatrens*, 17 rue Gemare (Tel. 31 86 25 57). Quiet and secluded but right in the heart of town.
☆ *Hôtel de France*, 10 rue de la Gare (Tel. 31 52 16 99).
☆ *Hôtel Le Dauphin*, 29 rue Gémare (Tel. 31 86 22 26). Cosy little rooms in this lovely old priory near the castle. Restaurant downstairs serves excellent Normandy fare at fair prices.
☆☆ *Hôtel Moderne*, 116 blvd Maréchal Leclerc (Tel. 31 86 04 23). Mapotel with attractive restaurant *Les Quatre Vents* attached serving good food, especially fish, at very reasonable prices.
☆☆ *Hôtel Mercure*, 1 rue de Courtonne (Tel. 31 93 07 62).

☆☆☆ *Hôtel and Restaurant Relais des Gourmets*, 15 rue de Geôle (Tel. 31 86 06 01). Lovely, comfortable rooms with superb service; charming hotel with pricey restaurant serving excellent Normandy cuisine.
Hostels *Auberge de Jeunesse* (HI), Foyer Robert Reme, 68bis, rue Eustache-Restout; 25 min walk from station to bus 5 or 7 to Lycée Fresnel. (Tel. 31 52 19 96).
Camping Terrain Municipal, route de Louvigny; bus 13 (direction **Louvigny** to **Camping**. Lovely riverside site, open May-Oct (Tel. 31 73 60 92).
Restaurants ☆☆ *Relais Normandy*, Place de la Gare, remarkably good regional cuisine, right next to the station.
☆☆ *L'Ecaille*, 13 rue de Geôle (Tel. 31 86 49 10). Superb seafood restaurant serving the best shellfish in Caen.
☆☆☆ *La Bourride*, 15 rue Vaugueux (Tel. 31 93 50 76). A superb 17th-century house in the old quarter. Outstanding cuisine, expensive but worth it, especially for *bourride*, the thick white fish stew made with garlic mayonnaise.

Bayeux

Trains *10 – 12 trains daily from* **Caen** *(20 mins); 5 – 6 trains daily from* **Cherbourg** *(1¼ hours); 5 from* **Paris** *(2 hours).*

The beautiful old Normandy cathedral town of Bayeux was the first French town to be liberated during the Battle of Normandy in June 1944 and almost the only one to survive unscathed from the destruction that devastated much of Normandy in the bitter fighting that followed the Allied invasion. It still retains the atmosphere of a quiet country town, with its magnificent cathedral, part-Romanesque, part-Gothic, old stone houses and steep cobbled streets.

It is doubly lucky that Bayeux escaped the war for it is not only typical of pre-war Normandy but it was even then one of its most beautiful towns with its narrow streets lined with picturesque old houses.

What to see

The Bayeux Tapestry

Bayeux's fame however is naturally due to its tapestry, one of the most famous works of art to have survived from the Middle Ages. Its fascination arises partly from the fact that nothing similar exists elsewhere and partly from its strong visual representation of one of the most important events in English history. In fact it is not a tapestry in the usually accepted sense of the term but a woollen embroidery on a white linen background. It was almost certainly made in a Saxon workshop soon after the Conquest, having been commissioned by Bishop Odo of Bayeux, half-brother of the Conqueror, to adorn the cathedral. It consists of 58 animated scenes, 231 – feet in length, taking the story from the moment when Edward the Confessor decided to bequeath the crown of England to the Duke of Normandy until the victory of William over the English army at Hastings. The figures are depicted in the liveliest colours with little attempt at realism, as many horses being green or purple as chestnut, grey or brown. Although most of the scenes are self-evident each is captioned in dog-Latin with symbols in the upper and lower borders.

During the Revolution the tapestry was saved from being used as wagon-covers after having been looted from the cathedral. Under the directorate Napoleon recognised its propaganda value and had it taken a round France and exhibited in prominent places to drum up support for his projected invasion of England. (**Musée de la Tapisserie**, Centre Guillaume le Conquerant, rue de Nesmond. Open mid-May–mid-Sept, daily 9 am–7 pm; mid-Sept–mid-Oct. and mid-Mar–mid-May, 9 am–12.30 pm and 2–6.30 pm; mid-Oct–mid-Mar, 9.30 am–12.30 pm and 2–6 pm.)

If Bayeux is world famous today for its tapestry, for most of the last five hundred years it was famed above all for its lace, a fine collection of which can be seen in the **Musée Baron Gérard** in the old Bishop's Palace. (Open daily 9 am–7 pm; Sept–15 Oct 16 March – May 9.30 am–12.30 pm and 2–6.30 pm; 16 Oct – 15 Mar 10 am–12.30 pm and 2–6 pm)

Bayeux Cathedral

Although somewhat austere due to the use of sombre grey local stone, the cathedral is one of the finest Norman Gothic churches existing. The western towers and nave are Romanesque but the vast bulk of the building dates from the 13th century, as do the spires above the towers. The nave is distinguished by its irregularly spaced Romanesque piers and the exquisite 13th-century trefoiled arcade above which runs a clerestory of narrow lofty windows. Of particular beauty is the apse with its graceful blind arcading and deep-set chapel windows. In stark contrast to the Romanesque nave is the Baroque pulpit, a wild 18th-century extravaganza. The portal on the south side of the transept depicts the assassination of Thomas à Beckett in Canterbury Cathedral in 1179. (Open July–Aug, Mon–Sat 8 am–7 pm, Sun 9 am–7 pm; Sept–June, Mon–Sat 8.30 am–noon and 2.30–7 pm, Sun 9 am–12.15 pm and 2.30–7 pm.)

With its quiet hidden squares and peaceful streets, Bayeux repays gentle unhurried wandering. In the **Cour des Tribunaux** stands a giant plane tree planted in 1797 outside the former Bishop's Palace, a harmonious miscellany of late-medieval and early-Renaissance buildings. A very modern museum devoted to the Battle of Normandy, with tanks guarding the entrance, traces the invasion and battles of the British and American forces. (**Musée de la Bataille** de Normandie, blvd Général Fabian-Ware; open daily 9 am–7 pm except November and Febuary, when it opens Sat and Sun only.)

Practicalities in Bayeux

Tourist Office 1 rue des Cuisiniers, in a medieval timbered building Tel. 31 92 16 26; accommodation service; emergency currency exchange.

Railway Station Place de la Gare (Info: Tel. 31 83 50 50; Reservations: Tel. 31 52 14 14); open 6 am–8 pm. To town centre from station, turn left onto Blvd Sadi-Carnot and bear right into Rue Larcher, then down Rue St-Martin to Rue des Cuisiniers for *centre ville*.

Buses *Bus Verts*, Place de la Gare (Tel. 31 92 80 50); buses 70 and 74 to Normandy landing beaches.

Festivals 1st week-end of July: *Marché Médievales* – dance, street musicians, artisans and actors recreate the spirit of medieval Bayeux.

Hotels ☆ Hôtel Notre Dame, 44 rue des Cuisiniers (Tel. 31 92 87 24). Simple accommodation but remarkably good value for the location.

☆☆ *Hôtel Reine Mathilde*, 23 rue Larcher (Tel. 31 92 08 13). Opposite post office and close to cathedral and tapestry.

☆☆ *Hôtel du Lion d'Or*, 71 rue St-Jean, (Tel. 31 92 06 90). A delightful hotel, once a coaching inn, in a quiet location on its own courtyard right in the heart of the town.

☆☆☆ *Hôtel Argouges*, 21 rue St-Patrice (Tel. 31 92 88 86). Occupying a handsome 18th-century town house; beautiful rooms. No restaurant.

☆☆☆ *Hôtel Luxembourg et Quatre Saisons*, 25 rue des Bouchers (Tel. 31 92 00 04). Very comfortable accommodation in an old Relais de Poste building.

Hostels *Auberge de Jeunesse* (HI) – Family Home, 39 rue Général de Dais, off rue de la Juridiction (Tel. 31 92 15 22). 16th-century mansion with restaurant.

Camping *Municipal Camping*, blvd Eindhoven (Tel. 31 92 08 43). Rue Genas Duhomme leads to ave de la Vallée des Pres and blvd Eindhoven.

Restaurants ☆ *Le Petit Normand*, 35 rue Larcher (Tel. 31 22 88 66). 16th-century premises overlooking the cathedral, with wide range of menus.

☆ *Taverne des Ducs*, 4 place St Patrice (Tel. 31 92 09 88), a popular and pleasant little brasserie on a square in the centre of town.

Cherbourg

Trains *7 trains daily from* **Paris** *(3½ hours); 3 from* **Rouen** *(3 hours); 6 from* **Caen** *(1½ hours); 9 from* **Bayeux** *(1 hour); 3 from* **Rennes** *changing at Lison (4 hours).*

For those coming from Bayeux, Cherbourg does not warrant the long deviation north up the Cotentin peninsula since it is more rewarding to head south for the old cathedral town of Coutances but for those arriving from Portsmouth it is the jumping off point for train journeys through Normandy. Although Cherbourg is known as one of the major ports of France, it only came into its own in the late 19th century in the era of great transatlantic liners. With their decline, however, the city lost something of its romance and elegance that cross-Channel ferries have not been able to substitute.

If Cherbourg appears to have little in the way of ancient buildings it is largely due to the English who attacked and burnt the town with tiresome frequency throughout its history. One of the last such visits was in 1758 when an English fleet destroyed the town's arsenal and burnt every ship in the harbour. Perhaps the nature of English visits for most of the previous 6 centuries explains why English visitors have not always received the warmest of welcomes here. Arthur Young, travelling throughout France immediately prior to the Revolution, complained bitterly that it was at Cherbourg that he was 'fleeced more infamously than at any other town in France'.

The best of Cherbourg is to be found in its museum, the **Musée Thomas Henry**, which possesses a number of excellent paintings, especially by Jean-François Millet who was born in the nearby hamlet of Gruchy and painted in Cherbourg until moving to Barbizon near Paris.

Practicalities in Cherbourg

Tourist office 2 quai Alexandre III, near Pont Tournant, facing the water in the harbour (Tel. 33 93 52 02).

Railway Station Bassin du Commerce, 15 mins walk from ferry terminal (Tel. 33 57 50 50).

Ferries Gare Maritime, to north of Bassin du Commerce, off quai de l'Ancien Terminal; *Irish Ferries* (Tel. 33 44 28 96) to Rosslare, Ireland. *P & O European Ferries* (Tel. 33 44 20 13) to Portsmouth. 4 daily midsummer; 1 daily winter. Day trip 4 hours. Night trip 7 hours. *Brittany Ferries* (Tel. 31 96 80 80) to Poole; 1–2 daily (4 hours). *Sealink* (Tel. 33 20 43 38) to Southampton. 1–2 in summer (4–7 hours), depending on the time of year.

Markets Fish market daily except Sunday. General market in Place Général de Gaulle:

Tues, Thurs, Sat mornings.

Hotels Cherbourg is not famous for its sights, nor for its hotels. Try to reach Bayeux if possible. Otherwise try:

Hôtel Le Vauban, 22 quai Caligny (Tel. 33 44 28 45). Close to tourist office, facing the harbour.

Hôtel Moderna, 28 rue Marine, quiet backstreet, (Tel. 33 43 05 30).

☆☆ *Hôtel Louvre*, 2 rue Henri-Dunant (Tel. 33 53 02 28). Modernised and quiet despite being in noisy street.

Restaurants *Chez Pain (Le Plouc)*, 59 rue au Blé (Tel. 33 53 67 64). Good value, small family-run restaurant.

Grandgoussier, 21 rue l'Abbaye (Tel. 33 53 19 43); small bistro serving good fare at low prices.

Coutances

Trains *4–5 trains daily from* **Bayeux***; most require a change at Lisons (1¼ hours); 5–6 trains daily from* **Cherbourg***; most require changing at Lison (40 mins); 2 from* **Rennes** *(1 hour); 5 from* **Caen** *(1½ hours); 2 from* **Paris** *(4 hours); 3 from* **Granville** *(1 hour); 3 from* **Avranches** *(45 mins).*

South of Bayeux the delightful white Normandy stone is left behind, the land becomes open and flatter, devoted in equal measure to pasture and cereals, and hedges become less apparent as you travel south to the great right angle of coastline which is formed by the junction of Normandy and Brittany.

St-Lô was the scene of fierce fighting in the second World War and little beyond the ramparts remain of the old town that once occupied a naturally strong defensive site on a promontory above the Vire. In a similar hilltop position a short distance west lies Coutances dominated by its magnificent 13th-century cathedral, one of the most beautiful in France. From the town and the surrounding region came many of William the Conqueror's most noble supporters whose descendents were to create illustrious pedigrees in England – the Percys, Nevilles, Bohuns, Pierponts, Grevilles, Carterets and Hautvilles or Havells. Granville belonged for centuried to the Argouges family, who lived in the château de

Gratot, north-west of the town. In 1439 an indigent member of the family sold Granville to the English, a move which gave the English a strategic base from which to attack Mont-St-Michel and prey on French shipping along the coast. Coutances is a pretty and somewhat forgotten small provincial town set high on a hill and completely overshadowed by its huge 11–13th century **cathedral**. Steep stone and cobbled streets lead up to the **Jardin des Plantes**, beautiful and carefully-tended public gardens planted with ancient cedar trees which resist the strong westerly winds which often blow in from the coast. Coutances reached the height of its fortunes under the Hautevilles in the 13th-century, since when it has slumbered peacefully in the shadow of its **cathedral**, which Victor Hugo deemed to be the most beautiful in France after Chartres.

What to see

Cathedral

Standing proudly at the highest point of the town, the cathedral's delicate western façade is flanked by 2 soaring towers around which cluster miniature towers as if for protection. One distinguishing feature of the cathedral is its large but graceful lantern tower that rises above the crossing. Another is the purity of line and proportion: the absence of detailed decorative work and sculpture give the interior an unusual grace and simplicity. Gorgeous delicate screens of mullioned tracery separate the chapels in the aisles. The stained glass, which was removed during the war, produces a rich kaleidoscope of brilliant reds, greens and blues which create pools of colour on the white stone. 15 windows are 13th-century, the oldest showing St George, St Thomas à Beckett (of Canterbury) and St-Blaise. The central chapel contains a much-venerated statue of Notre-Dame de Coutances.

Hôtel Poupinel

The focus of the town is the **Place du Parvis** in front of the cathedral, close to which are the delightful gardens of the Hôtel Morinière. At the entrance to these is the town's museum, the **Musée Quesnel Morinière**, in an 18th-century mansion, the Hôtel Poupinel, the highlight of which is a magnificent bronze bust of the Emperor Hadrian. (Open Wed–Mon 10 am–noon and 2–6 pm.) Further south down the hill lies a second cathedral, that of St Pierre, rebuilt at the turn of the 15th century in Renaissance style. Its design is very similiar to the cathedral, with 2 western towers and a massive central one, but is on a much smaller scale and is not so striking as its larger sister.

Practicalities in Coutances

Tourist Office Place Georges Leclerc off Rue G. de Montbray, not far from cathedral (Tel. 33 45 17 79); organises guided tours.
Railway Station At foot of hill from cathedral and hill-top town; 20 min walk. (Tel. 33 07 50 77).
Buses (Tel. 33 05 65 25). Departures from train station to Cherbourg, Granville and St Lô.

Market Mon.
Festivals Jazz festival held in late May; organ and classical music concerts in Cathédrale Notre-Dame in July and August.
Hôtels *Hôtel des Trois Pilliers*, 11 rue des Halles (Tel. 33 45 01 31). A little cramped but right in the heart of things, close to cathedral.
☆ *Hôtel de Normandie*, Place du Général de

Gaulle. Attractive little hotel with good Norman food downstairs. (Tel. 33 45 01 40) *Relais du Viaduct*, 25 ave Verdun (Tel. 33 45

02 68). Simple rooms, some noisy, with good *Relais Routiers* restaurant downstairs.

Granville

Trains *2 trains daily from* **Coutances** *to* **Foligny** *(20 mins); change required at Foligny for Granville; 4 trains daily from* **Argentan** *and* **Paris,** *Montparnasse (3 hours 35 mins); 2 from* **Cherbourg** *(3 hours); 2–3 from* **Bayeux** *(1½ hours).*

Granville is little more than a small fishing port on a rugged headland but it is one of the few towns on the western coast of Normandy accessible by train and from here journeys can be made by boat in summer to the offshore islands of Chausey and Jersey.

Situated at the southern end of the Cotentin's Atlantic coast, Granville was an important port when French fishing vessels took off for the Newfoundland fisheries in the 16th century. Granville is of particular interest to the English however for it was they who founded the town about 1438. Unable to take Mont-St-Michel, the English decided to build themselves a fortress on the rocky promontory that juts out at Granville into the sea. They hadn't even finished the work however before they were taken by surprise by the French and compelled to surrender. For a long time the town claimed to be 'le Monaco du Nord' on the strength of its esplanade and a lone casino but such pretensions have now been quietly dropped.

The town consists of 2 distinct parts, the old town or *Haute Ville* on its high peninsula and the new town around the harbour. The **Rue des Juifs** leads through the old gateway to the *Haute Ville* with its charming narrow streets and granite church. The whole of the old town is surrounded by **ramparts** built in the early 18th century to replace earlier ones demolished only a little earlier. They came into their own in 1793 when the town successfully resisted a siege by a Vendean army of 20,000 men. The old town has only a few sights of interest but there are delightful walks to the **lighthouse** at the Pointe du Roc from where there are magnificent views south across to the Iles Chausey and Cancale on the Brittany coast.

Practicalities in Granville

Tourist Office 4 cours Jonville, midway between station and the *Haute Ville* (Tel 33. 50 02 67).
Railway Station Rue Général Leclerc; lockers (Info: Tel. 33 57 50 50; Reservations: Tel. 31 52 14 14). For town centre from station, turn left and follow Ave Maréchal Leclerc to *centre ville*, turning right at square onto Cours Joinville.
Festivals February, one of the most splendid Mardi Gras carnivals of northern France held from the Saturday before Mardi Gras until the following Tuesday; last Sunday in July: *Pardon*

of blessing the sea, with open-air mass, processions and street celebrations.
Ferries 1–3 departures daily in summer to Chausey Islands; vedette *Jolie France* (Tel. 33 50 31 81) or *Emeraude Lines*, 1 rue Lecampion. (Tel. 33 50 16 36); Ferries to Jersey: 1 daily, *Emeraude Lines* or vedettes *Armoricaines*. (Tel. 33 50 77 45); information also from Gare Maritime, in harbour.
Hotels *Hôtel Hérel*, Port de Plaisance (Tel. 33 90 48 08). Good views from this position on the

peninsula.
Hôtel Michelet, 5 rue J. Michelet (Tel. 33 50 06 55). Close to beach and public gardens.

☆☆ *Hôtel Les Bains*, 19 rue Clémenceau (Tel. 33 50 17 31). Grand old seafront hotel, recently renovated. Own restaurant serves excellent seafood.

☆☆ *Normandy-Chaumière*, 20 rue Paul Poirier (Tel. 33 50 01 71). Pleasant hotel in central shopping area. With restaurant serving excellent seafood and fish at reasonable prices.

Hostels *Auberge de Jeunesse* (Tel. 33 50 18 95) Bd. des Am. aux Granvillais, Sharing the precincks of the Centre Régional de Nautisme. Excellent watersport facilities and close to centre.

Restaurants ☆☆ *Phare*, 11 rue Port (Tel. 33 50 12 94). An excellent seafood restaurant, with fantastic sea views.

Pontorson – Mont-St-Michel

Trains *2/3 trains daily from* **Foligny** *(55 mins);* **Bayeux** *(1 hour 50 mins) and* **Dol-de-Bretagne** *(15 mins).*

Immediately south of Foligny lies the village of **La Haye-Pesnel**, the centre of the Normandy horse-trade and the site of important yearly horse-races. A little further south still, on a rock high above the surrounding plain, lies Avranches, a delightful hilltop town before it was almost completely destroyed in 1944.

Pontorson – Mont-St-Michel is as close as one can get by train to Mont-St-Michel which lies some 8 kilometres to the north. **Mont-St-Michel** is one of the wonders of the western world: a breath-taking abbey perched high on a pinnacle of granite in the middle of a vast expanse of sand. The distant view is spellbinding and even as one approaches it is difficult to take one's eye off the magical and romantic silhouette of this little, lonely island out at sea. Rare is the visitor who is left unawed by the beauty of this improbable pinnacle of rock crowned by its delicate architecture, rising so dramatically from the absolute flatness of the surrounding wastes.

At low tide the sea recedes 16 kilometres and when it returns it does so at the speed of a galloping horse, racing back over the flat sand in just 90 minutes to wash up against the base of the rock and lap against the causeway. Some of the sands around Mont-St-Michel are treacherous too, being quicksands from which there is no means of escape. Unwary pilgrims making their way across the bay to the Mount at low tide were regularly sucked beneath the sands, giving Mont-St-Michel another name – 'St-Michel-au-Péril-de-la-Mer'.

Whether surrounded by sea or sand, the Mount is a remarkable sight, its thick walls and towers pierced by a single gateway defending the approach to the citadel. Within these defences little houses cling like limpets to the steep slopes, their clustered roofs dwarfed by the huge buttressed walls which support the platform on which the abbey buildings are built. The history of the abbey dates back to the 8th century when the Archangel Michael appeared to St Aubert, Bishop of Avranches. Prompted by the vision he built an oratory which was replaced by a Carolingian abbey and this in turn was built over in the 11th century, the old abbey then becoming the crypt of the new church. From the 13th to the 16th centuries a whole series of Gothic buildings were erected as the abbey grew in fame and wealth. Almost all the stone was imported from Brittany or the Chausey islands, there being little granite available on the Mount itself. The magnificent buildings on the north side of **La Merveille** were built to accommodate monks and pilgrims at the beginning of the 13th century. On the south side a series of abbey buildings were built between the 13th and 15th centuries to serve as administrative quarters, the residence of the Abbot and the garrison who protected the abbey from bandits and the English. The little castle, the Châtelet, and the fortifications guarding the entrance to the Citadel on the east side of the island were built in the 14th century. So impregnable was the site, and so strong the fortifications, that the abbey was never taken by storm. During the Hundred Years War pilgrims continued to come to the abbey, buying safe-conducts from the English who then controlled most of the surrounding country.

What to see

Grande Rue

The fortifications are impressive. Only one entrance, the **Porte de l'Avancée**, leads through the ramparts and this is only into a fortified courtyard. Beyond this lies a 2nd gateway and a 2nd fortified courtyard, and beyond that yet another gateway, the **Porte du Roi**, with its machicolations and portcullis. Only beyond these is the Citadel itself entered, the Grande Rue rising steeply up the hill to which cling houses dating from the 15th and 16th centuries. This street, congested in summer with dense throngs of people and souvenir shops, is probably closer today to the way it appeared in the Middle Ages than at any time since the 16th century. The tourist has replaced the pilgrim, but the ebb and flow of people around the streets and terraces is much as it must have been in medieval times. Even then the trade in souvenirs was brisk: pilgrims bought token with images of St Michael and leaden flasks filled with sand from the sea-shore to take home with them.

Abbaye de La Merveille

While still an important pilgrimage destination, the Romanesque chancel of the church collapsed and was rebuilt, between 1446 and 1521, in a magnificent Flamboyant Gothic style. As a result the contrast between the chancel and the severe and sombre Romanesque nave is very striking.

La Merveille is in fact a number of different buildings on different levels – Almonry, Guest's Hall and Refectory, Cellar, Knight's Hall and Cloisters – but from the outside it has the appearance of a fortress. The cloisters are exquisite with delicate carving and perfectly proportioned. The Guest's Hall, an elegant vaulted hall over – 30 metres long, was used by Abbots to receive distinguished visitors, among which can be counted 3 Kings of France, St Louis, Louis XI and Francis I. Impressed by his visit to the abbey in 1469 Louis XI founded a military order devoted to St Michael. It had its headquarters in the abbey and met in the Knight's Hall, a majestic room divided by 3 rows of massive columns.

Another superb room is the **refectory**, flooded with soft opaque light that comes from tiny slits deep in the embrasures.

The 15th century saw perhaps the peak of the abbey's fortunes; with the Religious Wars in the 16th century the abbey witnessed something of a stagnation and numbers of pilgrims began to fall. In the 17th century the fortunes of the abbey went into a steep and irreversible decline: the abbots were laymen who pocketed the revenue of the abbey but exercised no religious function. Eventually the abbey became a prison, the fabric steadily deteriorating until taken over by the department of Historic Monuments in 1874. Fortunately for posterity Viollet-le-Duc, the architect and restorer who had been consulted in the early stages, died before work had started. As a result the restoration was directed by Courvoyer in a much more sensitive manner: immense care was taken to reproduce the original stonework as carefully as possible; stone was brought over from the same island where it had been quarried in the Middle Ages; and the tools used were identical to those that had been used by the medieval stone-masons. The result is a testament to his care and painstaking methods.

Practicalities in Mont-St-Michel

Tourist Office Corps de Garde des Bourgeois, as one passes through the entrance into the walled city (Tel. 33 60 14 30).
Railway Station At Pontorson (Tel. 33 60 00 35); luggage storage.
Buses Departures from the Porte du Roy. STN buses to Pontorson and other local destinations; last bus to Pontorson leaves at 6.40 pm. SCETA buses connect Pontorson with Dol-de-Bretagne, St-Malo, Granville and Rennes.
Cycle Hire Pontorson train station.
Hotels Hotels in Mont-St-Michel are prohibitively expensive. Hotels in **Pontorson**: ☆ *Relais Clemenceau*, Blvd Clemenceau (Tel. 33 60 10 96). Simple but clean and comfortable.
☆ *Hôtel Bretagne*, Rue Couesnon (Tel. 33 60 10 55). Small and attractive timber-framed medieval building, handsomely decorated and furnished.
☆☆ *Le Montgomery*, 13 rue Couesnon (Tel. 33 60 00 09). A superb *France Acceuil* hotel in a 16th-century mansion of the Counts of Montgomery, with a delightful garden. Good Normandy fare in the restaurant.

For onward travel *west to* **Dol-de-Bretagne, St-Malo** *and* **Rennes** *see pages 143– 171 under Brittany: 2–3 trains daily from* **Pontorson-Mont St Michel** *to* **Dol-de-Bretagne** *(15 mins) and* **Rennes** *(50 mins).* **Other option:** bus *from Mont St Michel to St-Malo*

Vitré

Trains *6–9 trains daily from* **Rennes** *(20–30 mins) and* **Laval** *(40–55 mins).*

East of Rennes, in Brittany, lies the superb medieval fortified town of Vitré, on a spur overlooking the deep valley of the Vilaine. Surrounded by impressive walls pierced by great machicolated gateways, it is dominated by a vast 14th-century castle, one of the most formidable in northern France. For ease of travel it is included in this itinerary and not under Brittany.

What to see

Le Château

Vitré was a fortress town on the eastern-most border of Brittany, its castle built to defend the kingdom against the ambitions of French monarchs to the east. It is a remarkable building, dramatic and impressive, heavily fortified, with massive walls, numerous towers, a portcullis and a drawbridge over a deep, wide moat. One of the finest examples of a fortified building of the 14th and 15th centuries to be found anywhere in France, its massive stone structure rises from precipitous granite rocks. Built for the La Trémouille family, who occupied it until 1820, it was bought by the town for 8,500 francs and then deteriorated steadily so that by the time Prosper Merimée visited it in the 1860s it was half-ruined, only the Renaissance loggia on the Tour de l'Oratoire in the inner courtyard remaining intact. The restoration work that was put in hand was done however with the utmost care and as a result its present appearance is faithful to the original. (Open Apr–June, Wed–Mon 10 am–noon and 2.30–5.30 pm; July–Sept, daily 10 am–noon and 1.30–6 pm; Oct–Mar, Wed–Fri 10 am–noon and 2–5.30 pm, Mon 2–5.30 pm).

East of the castle, but within the ramparts, stands the **church of Notre-Dame**, a 15th-century building decorated with pinnacled gables and a pulpit from which Catholic preachers disputed publicly with Protestant speakers standing on a tribune in the house opposite. Vitré was one of the chief centres of Calvinism in Brittany, and the home town of the Protestant Coligny family.

Not only does the castle resemble how it would have looked 400 years ago, but so does the town and to a greater extent than almost any in France. The narrow streets are lined with ancient timber-framed houses, the upper floors of which nearly meet each other across the cobbled streets. For centuries the prosperity of the town depended on the manufacture of hemp, woollen cloth and cotton stockings which were sold all over Europe and exported as far as America and the French West Indies.

During the Hundred Years War the English tried to seize the castle a number of times but without success. Nevertheless they must have been an unsettling factor and eventually the citizens of Vitré, tired of the irritation, bought the English off by giving them land on the far bank of the Vilaine. 'Rachapt' or 'repurchase' became attached to the spot where the English settled and the area still goes by the name **Faubourg du Rachapt**. Above it lies a hill known as the Tertres Noirs from which there is a fine view of the town and castle.

Practicalities in Vitré

Tourist Office Places St-Yves; close to station (Tel 99 75 04 46).
Railway Station (Tel. 95 65 50 50).
Hôtel ☆ *Hôtel Chêne Vert*, place Général de Gaulle (Tel. 99 75 24 09). Classic French provincial hotel, welcoming, slightly faded and clean. Virtually opposite station; reliable traditional cooking in restaurant.
☆ *Hôtel Minotel*, 47 rue Poterie, off rue Beaudrairie (Tel. 99 75 11 11). Modern and convenient for station, château and tourist office.

Laval

Trains *6 – 9 trains daily from* **Vitré** *(40 – 55 mins) and* **Le Mans** *(45 mins).*

A little east of Vitré lie a number of small lakes and beyond them the thick woods of Misedon on the edge of which stand the remains of the **Abbaye de Clermont**, founded by St Bernard in 1150 as a daughter house of Clairvaux. Laval itself straddles the Mayenne river which flows south to meet the Loire at Angers. The town was a Royalist stronghold in the Revolution and the birthplace of Henri Rousseau, the primitive painter. Only one of his paintings however is preserved in the **Musée Henri Rousseau** in the Vieux Château.

What to see

Vieux Château

A long, wide street cuts through the centre of the town and over the medieval hump backed-bridge. Standing on high ground near the river is the majestic castle, the main object of interest in the town. The Vieux Château has a massive cylindrical Keep 49-metres-high which, with the crypt, is the only surviving part of the original castle. Built in the 12th and partly rebuilt in the 16th century, it almost certainly saw action against the English who ruled almost all of Maine at the beginning of the 15th century. The Vieux Château has some Renaissance sculpture in its gables but the best Renaissance work is to be found on the façade of the adjoining Nouveau Château which now houses the Law-Courts. On the first floor of the Vieux Château is a fine Salle d'Honneur with a wooden vaulted ceiling, in which have been collected medieval carvings and tombs.

Notre-Dame d'Avénières

The cathedral itself is a medley of styles and ages and of less interest than the Basilica of Notre-Dame d'Avénières, which is a little downstream from the Pont Vieux. Reflected in the waters of the Mayenne, the church has a Romanesque apse and a wooden triptych which was a gift of Jeanne de Laval, the wife of 'Good' King René, Duke of Anjou and Count of Provence. Towards the end of his life the amiable René allowed Louis XI to annex Anjou, and withdrew to the warmer kingdom in the south, dying at Aix in 1480.

Practicalities in Laval

Tourist Office Place du 11 Novembre, in the large square over the bridge Pont A. Briand (Tel. 43 53 09 39).
Railway Station (Info. and Reservations, Tel: 43 53 50 50); at bottom of Ave R. Buron which leads to Rue de la Paix.

Hotels ☆ *Hôtel de la Terrasse*, ave R. Buron (Tel. 43 24 91 00); on main street leading to centre from station (Tel. 43 53 55 02).
☆ *Hôtel Marin*, 102 ave R. Buron, stone's throw from station (Tel. 43 53 09 68).

Le Mans

Trains *10–15 trains daily from* **Paris** *Montparnasse (55 mins); 7 daily from* **Alençon** *(30–40 mins);* **Laval** *(40 mins–1¼ hours);* **Vitré** *(1 hour 10 mins) and* **Rennes** *(1¼ hours).*

Le Mans, lying in the wide valley of the Sarthe, is the capital of the old province of Maine, a quiet agricultural district that lies to the south of Normandy. Famous above all for its motor-race in late June and September, Le Mans is a large, busy town and somewhat industrial. It does however have an interesting old quarter and an unusual cathedral.

What to see

Cathédrale de Saint-Julien

The superb cathedral is dedicated to the evangelist who became the first bishop of Le Mans in the 3rd century. Its extreme architectural lightness stem from the Romanesque and Gothic styles which are curiously combined due to a fire in the 12th century which partly destroyed the earlier building. Rather than start from scratch, Gothic arches and arcades were built on top of what survived of the Romanesque cathedral; the result is a *pot-pourri* of styles. The magnificent paired Gothic buttresses of the apse, placed at an acute angle, are unique in France. In 1562 Huguenots broke most of the stained-glass windows but luckily for posterity seemed to have tired before reaching the great west window and the choir, which contain some of the oldest and most beautiful stained glass in France.

Old Quarter

Not a great deal remains of the medieval quarter where Henry ii, the first Plantagenet King of England, was born in 1133. The town is largely modern and uninteresting except for a tight nucleus of 15th-century houses situated around the cathedral. These, with their Renaissance stone doorways, carved friezes and projecting gables, form a picturesque cluster between the cathedral and the little church of St-Benoit. The finest is misleadingly known as the **Maison de la Reine Berangère**, after the wife of Richard the Lionheart, but in fact was built some 2 centuries after her death. The queen's remains are buried in the nearby cathedral. The other most attractive 15th-century mansions are the Maison du Pilier Rouge and the Maison d'Adam et Eve, both to be found in the **Grand Rue** running south from the cathedral.

Half way between the old quarter and the railway station is the part Romanesque, part Gothic church of **Notre-Dame-de-la-Couture**, identifiable by its 2 unfinished towers. Car enthusiasts are more likely to be interested in the **Musée de l'Automobile**, in the middle of the Bugatti and 24-hours circuits, which has a superb collection of racing cars.

Practicalities in Le Mans

Tourist Office Hôtel des Ursulines, at junction of rue Etoile and ave de la Préfecture (Tel. 43 28 17 22).
Railway Station Blvd de la Gare (Info: Tel. 43 24 50 50); Reservations: Tel. 43 24 59 50), at bottom of Ave Général Leclerc.
Hotels ☆ Hôtel Elysée, 7 rue Lechesne, close to station off ave Général Leclerc. (Tel. 43 28 83 66).
☆ Hôtel Emeraude, 18 rue Gastelier, close to station off ave Général Leclerc (Tel. 43 24 87 46).
☆ Hôtel de la Terasse, 15 blvd de la Gare.
☆☆ Hôtel Anjou, 27 blvd de la Gare, close to station (Tel. 43 24 90 45).

Alençon

Trains 5 trains daily from **Le Mans** (30 mins); 5 from **Sées** (15 mins) and 6 from **Argentan** (35 mins).

North of Le Mans the railway follows the valley of the Sarthe through open country before reaching Alençon, a delightful town combining handsome town mansions, a picturesque castle, beautiful churches and excellent food. Straddling the border of Normandy and Maine, the historic heart of the city preserves picturesque streets and a wealth of houses dating from the 15th to 18th centuries.

A market town on the Sarthe river, whose old buildings and medieval streets largely survived the fierce fighting of 1944, Alençon makes an excellent place from which to set off walking, lying as it does on the edge of the **Normandy – Maine National Park**. To the north is the Écouves Forest – a huge area of ancient beach and oak forest where wild deer and boar roam and which is criss-crossed by walking paths. In Écouves Forest, Général Leclerc's Free French forces defeated a German Panzer division before liberating the city, the first to be liberated after D-Day by French forces. To the south-east of the town is the Perseigne Forest, another fine forest of beach, oak and fir while to the south-west lie what are knowns as the **Mancelles Alps** – an area of steep, heather-covered granite hills which enclose the Sarthe valley.

Close to the Briante, a tributary of the Sarthe which flows through the lower part of the town, stands the formidable medieval castle of the Ducs d'Alençon, with its robust towers. In the **Château** Marguerite d'Angoulême, sister of Francis I and grandmother of Henri IV, held court in the company of distinguished writers, theologians and poets. Opposite is the arcaded **Palais de Justice** and the **Hôtel de Ville**, an elegant and curved 18th-century building which houses a **museum** with some fine paintings by Restout, Philippe de Champaigne, Géricault, Courbet and Boudin.

The fortunes of the town were greatly boosted in the 17th century by Colbert, Louis XIV's ambitious Minister of State, who promoted and financed the manufacture of lace in the town. Point d'Alençon became famous throughout France and brought long-lasting prosperity to the town. A fine collection of lace is displayed in the **Musée-Ecole Dentellière** in the Hôtel de Ville. (Open Mon – Fri 15th May-15th Sept.)

What to see

Cathédrale de Notre-Dame

It was in the cathedral of Notre-Dame that Thérèse Martin, later to become St Theresa of Lisieux, was baptised. The cathedral is a curious mixture of 15th-century Flamboyant Gothic and 18th-century Classical architecture. At its west end is a 3-sided porch, built between 1506 and 1508, extremely rich and delicate in its design, appropriately for Alençon conjuring up the image of fine lace-work.

Notre-Dame stands in the lower part of the main street, the **Grande Rue**, which passes through the heart of the town. Close by are attractive timber-framed houses; higher up, in rue St-Blaise is the **Préfecture**, a superb 17th-century town-house of brick and granite dating from the reign of Louis XIII. The *oeil de boeuf* windows, stone quoins and steep roof are characteristic features of the architecture of the period. St Theresa was born in the building opposite, the **Hôtel des Intendants**. One of the most beautiful mansions in the town is the **Hôtel Libert** in the narrow and enchantingly-named Rue de Cygne.

Practicalities in Alençon

Tourist Office 15th-century Maison d'Ozé, close to Cathedral of Notre-Dame in Place Lamagdelaine (Tel. 33 26 11 36).
Railway Station (Info: Tel. 31 83 50 50; Reservations: Tel. 31 52 14 14); ave Wilson and Rue St-Blaise lead to *centre ville*.
Markets Fri, Sun
Festivals *Music Festival*: Sept.
Hotels *Grand Hôtel Gare*, 50 ave Wilson (Tel. 33 29 03 93). Virtually opposite the station; clean, comfortable and convenient.

Hôtel Ibis, 13 Place Poulet-Malassis (Tel. 33 26 55 55). Modern, in quiet street off Cours Clemenceau.
☆ *Chapeau Rouge*, 1 blvd Duchamp (Tel. 33 26 20 23). An attractive white building with quiet rooms although on a busy road.
Restaurants ☆☆ *Petit Vatel*, 72 Place Cdt Demeulles. A superb restaurant serving traditional and inventive Norman cuisine at its best.

Sées

Trains *5 trains daily from* **Argentan** *(20 mins); 5 from* **Alençon** *(15 mins); 5 from* **Le Mans** *(1¼ hours).*

A little to the north of Alençon the great **forest of Écouves** extends over a huge area of hilly country, rising to a high point of 396 metres. The largest forest in Normandy, it stretches 24 kilometres from west to east, traversed by long straight rides which make for delightful walking. Just to the north-east of the forest is the little town of Sées, once an extremely wealthy See, now a tranquil and charming cathedral city, unhurried, unspoilt and largely unvisited.

What to see

Cathédrale de Notre-Dame

The cathedral at Sées, on a pleasant market square, is one of the most beautiful religious buildings in Normandy and replaces one burnt to the ground by Henry II in 1174. Begun in the early 13th century, Notre-Dame is the epitome of soaring Gothic architecture. The western façade has been much altered but the interior is striking for the elegance and purity of its design which is further enhanced by some glorious 14th- and 15th-century stained glass. At the east end of the cathedral is the Old Bishop's Palace, a huge and splendid building (closed to the public) which reflects the religious importance of the See which had become an important ecclesiastical centre with its own bishop by the 4th century. Designed by Joseph Brousseau in 1778, the palace was ransacked of its treasures during the Revolution at which time the west front of the cathedral was also badly mutilated. The **Hôtel de Ville**, at the top of the cathedral square, is a good example of the classical style of the 18th century.

Practicalities in Sées

Tourist Office Place Général de Gaulle (Tel. 33 28 74 79)
Railway Station (Info: Tel. 31 83 50 50; Reservations: Tel. 31 52 14 14.)
Markets Sat morning.
Hotels *Hôtel Cheval Blanc*, 1 Place St-Pierre (Tel. 33 27 80 48). A charming and simple country inn, with restaurant serving good classic fare.
Hôtel The Garden, 12 rue Ardrilliers (Tel. 22 37 98 27).

Argentan

Trains *5 trains daily from* Sées *(20 mins); 3 – 6 daily from* Alençon *(45 mins) and Le Mans (1 hour).*

Immediately north of Sées lies the small railway junction of Surdon. This unprepossesing little place is in fact only a 2½ kilometre walk from one of the most curious châteaux of France, the oddly named **Chateau d'O**. Surrounded by a moat which broadens onto a lake, its pale-rose brick and white stone walls rise into a plethora of mad-cap roofs, high, conical and witch-like. The east side of the château that faces the approaching visitor is a delightful example of early 15th-century Renaissance work, while the south wing dates from the 16th century and the west the 18th. Only a little distance to the north, on the river Orne, stands the town of Argentan where Henry II made the fateful remark that he would like to be rid of a 'turbulent priest', whereupon 4 of his knights set off to assassinate Becket before the high altar at Canterbury.

What to see

Tour Marguerite

Of the once extensive ramparts only the Tour Marguerite remains and a small part of the 14th-century castle, later incorporated into the Palais de Justice. James II of England took refuge in number 17 rue Pierre-Onzane after the defeat of the French fleet at La Hogue in 1692 while Charles X, of whom it was said that the Bourbons could 'learn nothing and forget nothing', stayed in the Hôtel de Raveton on his way to exile in England following his overthrow in the July Revolution of 1830.

Argentan found itself at the centre of intense fighting in August 1944 for it is located at the centre of an important transport network and as a result suffered extensive damage. The most severe destruction occurred on 19th August when British, Canadian and Polish forces coming from the north-west met up with American and French forces advancing from the south in a pincer movement which cut off and surrounded the retreating German 7th Army, thus effectively ending the Battle of Normandy.

Eglise St-Germain

Like much of the town, the church of St-Germain had to be largely rebuilt after the war but its restorers managed to preserve its rather lovely Flamboyant porch. Princess Marguerite of Lorraine is commemorated by an inscription in a chapel close to the north porch; her tomb was melted down at the Revolution, as with others, the lead being used to produce bullets for the revoltionary armies. A little to its south stands a severe 14th-century château, the Chapelle St-Nicolas, and the romantic ruins of a 12th-century Keep.

From Argentan trains can be caught north to **Lisieux** *and* **Rouen** *(with change at Mézidon), to* **Caen** *(45 mins), west to* **Granville** *(1¼ hours) and east to* **Dreux** *(1 hour 20 mins) and* **Paris** *Montparnasse (2¼ hours).*

Practicalities in Argentan

Tourist Office 1 Place du Marché, close to Cathedral and post office (Tel 33 67 12 48).
Market Tues
Railway Station (Info: Tel. 31 83 50 50; Reservations: Tel. 31 52 14 14). For town centre from station, cross Blvd Carnot, follow Ave de la Fôret Normande across the River Orne, bear left onto Rue du Beigle, then first right to tourist office in square.
Hotels ☆ *Hôtel France*, 8 blvd Carnot (Tel. 33

67 03 65). Renovated, virtually opposite the station; with restaurant offering good-value, classic, Normandy cooking.
☆☆ *Hôtel La Renaissance*, 20 ave 2ème Division Blindée (Tel. 33 36 14 20). An attractive, comfortable hotel; with the advantage of superb cooking from a distinguished chef, Michel Moulin, in a beautiful restaurant.

Excursion from Argentan and Caen

Falaise

Like Argentan, Falaise suffered badly in the climax of the Battle of Normandy in August 1944, in a battle fought in the area known as the Falaise 'Gap'. Falaise is nevertheless of special interest to the English for it was in the massive castle here that, in 1027, a bastard son was born to a tanner's daughter and Robert le

Diable, one of the earliest Dukes of Normandy. Long known as William le Bâtard, to identify him from other offspring, this duke was to have a resounding success when, at the age of 39, he defeated Harold and was proclaimed King of England.

It was from the castle of Falaise that he organised his expedition to England, after which he became known by another title that has endured history: William the Conqueror. The appearance of the castle today is mostly due to the work of one of William's sons. Fortified by the first Dukes of Normandy, it was used as a prison by King John for his unfortunate nephew Arthur. The castle was captured in 1417 during the Hundred Years War by Henry IV, who placed his cannon on the steep cliff of Mont Mirat which overlooks the castle on one side. It was lost again to the French in 1450 and then further damaged in the religious wars when it was taken by Henri IV; the breaches made by his guns are visible by the side of the Tour de la Reine. The donjon built on the very edge of the cliff is a square stone building of massive strength. It communicates by a passage with the Tour Talbot, supposed to have been added during the English occupation (1418–50) when Sir John Talbot was left here by Henry V as warden of the Norman marches.

Today the castle is a magnificent ruin with its 13th-century ramparts and main gateway flanked by towers. During the Second World War, the Germans used the 30-metre-high Tour de Talbot as an observation post, but even a shell which penetrated the 4-metre thick walls failed to knock it down. The 12th-century Norman Keep has huge solid walls and small Romanesque windows; according to local legend it was here that William the Conqueror was born.

Below the castle, in the Place Guillaume le Conquérant, is a fine bronze statue of William on horseback by the sculptor, Louis Rochet. William is depicted in full armour with open vizor, as shown in the Bayeux Tapestry, with uplifted lance, as if urging his soldiers into battle.

Practicalities in Falaise

Tourist Office 32 rue Georges Clemenceau (Tel. 31 90 17 26).

Hotels ☆ *Hôtel Normandie*, 4 rue Amiral Courbet (Tel. 31 90 18 26). Modern but comfortable, in a side-street running to château from rue G Clemenceau; with excellent good-value restaurant.

☆☆ *Hôtel Poste*, 38 rue G Clemenceau (Tel. 31 90 13 14). Virtually adjacent to tourist office and opposite the Château de la Fresnaye; can be noisy, but attached restaurant serves good and cheap Norman cooking.

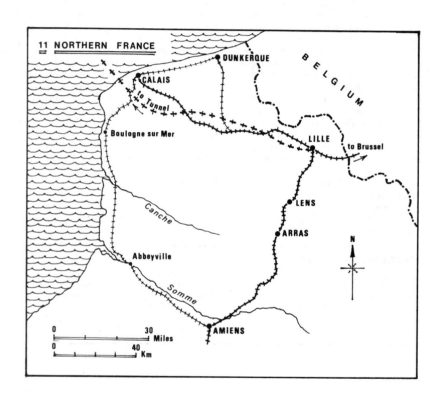

11 NORTHERN FRANCE

BELGIUM

DUNKERQUE

CALAIS

to Tunnel

Boulogne sur Mer

LILLE

to Brussel

Canche

LENS

ARRAS

N

Abbeyville

Somme

0   30
        Miles
0   40
        Km

AMIENS

11 Northern France

Although the scene of devastating fighting during the First World War and sporadic bombing during the Second, the north of France is somewhat neglected by English visitors, with the exception of the Channel ports. In their rush to get to the Alps, the Dordogne or the beaches of the Mediterranean, the charms of the some of the northern towns are often overlooked by visitors travelling south. Some of the towns were the site of heavy industries which meant that in the past they were not the cleanest cities to visit, but as many of these have changed to lighter industries and services, the towns have become cleaner and much more attractive. Old town centres have been restored, parks laid out, cultural centres opened and a whole host of cultural events organised so that many of these once decaying towns are now dynamic and attractive.

Architecturally the area has much in common with Flanders, of which it was once a possession. Gastronomically too, the area shares much with Flemish cuisine; *crêpes* and mussels are consumed in vast quantities and both come with an astonishing variety of accompaniments and sauces. Beers are excellent and drunk as enthusiastically as in Britain, Belgium or Holland.

The major battlefields of the First World War are sometimes difficult to get to by train, but can often be glimpsed as the train passes through the undulating wheatfields of Picardy. Here the landscape is one often of rising and falling fields, bright green with shoots in spring, the colour of golden limestone in late summer, a beautiful landscape which makes it difficult to conjure up today the horrors of the First World War battlefields.

The Route *Calais – Lille – Arras – Boulogne-sur-Mer – Dunkerque*

Two routes will be followed, both leading from the Channel ports to Paris, the route that most English visitors arriving by ferry are likely to follow. The first route heads for Paris in a sweep to the east via **Lille**, **Arras** *and* **Amiens**; *the second via* **Boulogne-sur-Mer**.

Calais

Trains *14 daily to* **Paris** *(2½ hours)*; *14 to* **Lille** *(1½ hours)*, **Boulogne** *(30 mins)*; *4 daily to* **Dunkerque** *(40 mins).*

Calais is more a cross-roads than a destination and as such benefits commercially more than aesthetically from the arrival of 15 million passengers from Britain each year. Rebuilt after the Second World War, Calais nevertheless has some interesting buildings. One such is the flamboyant **Hôtel de Ville**, a reconstruction in Flemish Renaissance style. In front of it stands one of Rodin's most poignant group of sculptures, the *Burghers of Calais*, which recalls a dramatic episode in the closing moments of the Hundred Years War after the city surrendered to the English King Edward III after an 8-month siege. Edward III was on the point of taking reprisals on the city's inhabitants when the burghers stepped forward with the request that they should be sacrificed and the population spared. Edward agreed and was then persuaded by his French wife, Philippine, that such a noble gesture should allow them to go free too. Edward conceded and the city was spared.

The town was to remain an English domain for another 100 years until François de Guise won it back for the French crown in 1558.

What to see

Musée des Beaux-Arts et de la Dentelle

The busy boulevard Jacquard leads through the city and off it down a side street is the Musée des Beaux-Arts et de la Dentelle. (Open Wed–Mon 10 am–noon and 2–5.30 pm.) which is mainly of interest for the examples of elegant and intricate lace-work once produced in the city.

During the Second World War, the German navy used a bunker opposite the town hall in the Parc St-Pierre as a telephone exchange; it has now been converted into an impressive *War Museum* with fine collections of artillery and military uniforms. (Open Mar–Nov daily 10 am–5 pm.)

Practicalities in Calais

Tourist Office 12 blvd Clemenceau, close to *Calais-Ville* station (Tel. 21 96 62 40); ferry information; accommodation list; currency exchange.

Railway Station Calais is served by 2 train stations: *Calais-Ville* and *Calais-Maritime*, the latter next to the ferry and hovercraft ports. Free buses connect the hoverport and ferry terminals with Gare Calais Ville in the town centre: blvd Jacquard (Tel. 21 80 50 50); from station walk directly up blvd Jacquard to *centre ville*.

Ferries Hoverspeed, 20 departures daily in summer to Dover (35 mins) (Tel. 21 96 67 10). Sealink, Car Ferry Terminal; 10 departures daily in summer to Dover (1½ hours) (Tel. 21 96 70 70); **P & O Ferries**, Car Ferry Terminal; 7 departures daily in summer to Dover (1½ hours) (Tel. 21 97 21 21).

Hôtels *Hôtel le Littoral*, 71 rue Aristide Briand. (Tel. 21 34 47 28). Cheap and cheerful. *Hôtel Liberté*, blvd Jacquard (Tel. 21 96 10 10). Close to station, large rooms, clean and simple. *Hôtel Windsor*, 2 rue Cdt Bonningue, not far from the lighthouse (Tel 21 34 59 40).

☆ *Hôtel Richelieu*, 17 rue Richelieu (Tel. 21 34

61 60). Pleasant little hotel with window-boxes filled with geraniums, opposite the parc Richelieu. One of the town's most attractive hotels. ☆☆ *George v*, 36 rue Royale (Tel. 21 97 68 00). Comfortable, pleasant hotel on the main street; food does not quite live up to its pretensions. ☆☆☆ *Hôtel Meurice*, rue Edmond Roche (Tel.), Comfortably furnished, if rather an austere building. **Restaurants** *Au Coq d'Or*, Place d'Armes (Tel. 21 34 79 05). Popular and cheap restaurant on the central square. ☆ *Au Cote d'Argent*, 1 digue G Berthe (Tel. 21 34 68 07). A good little seafood restaurant in an excellent seafront location. ☆ *Le Channel*, 3 blvd de la Résistance (Tel. 21 34 42 30). Crowded with locals at lunchtime; good value for money. ☆☆ *Sole Meunière*, 1 blvd de la Résistance (Tel. 21 34 43 01). Excellent fish and seafood restaurant next to the harbour. Good value menus.

Lille

Trains *310 trains daily from* **Calais** *(1 hour), 10 ordinary trains to* **Paris** *(2½ hours), 10* TGVs *daily to* **Paris** *(1 hour); 4−8 direct trains from* **London** *Waterloo International (2 hours), 10 trains daily from* **Arras** *(35 mins)*

One of the largest cities of France, dynamic and thriving on commerce and industry, Lille has a proud history and a tradition of good living and eating which makes it a pleasure to visit. Keeping up with the times, it has a modern métro system which is clean, efficient and entirely computerised. So modern in fact that the trains don't even have a conductor. Until a few years ago Lille was one of the most depressed industrial cities in the north, but under the direction of ex-Prime Minister Pierre Mauroy − the town's mayor − there has been a transformation of the city with new industries, a new cultural role and a new civic pride. The commercial centre of the north since the 14th century, when the town was presented to Philip the Bold of Burgundy as the dowry of Maragaret of Flanders, the city has seen endless sieges and wars. There are no real gems of religious architecture but the blackened church of **Saint-Maurice** near the station is a typical example of north French church architecture with its 5 equal aisles, tall columns and finely ribbed vaulting. Owned first by the Counts of Flanders and then by the Dukes of Burgundy, Lille was annexed by Spain before becoming part of France. The **Roubaix** and **de Gand** gates, built in the early 17th century, survive as testimonials to the impressive defences which were reinforced by Louis xiv when he took the town in 1667.

What to see

Vauban's Citadel

It was Louis xiv who commissioned Vauban to create the massive *Citadelle* on a pentagram plan, complete with bastions. Access to the star-shaped Citadel on the north side of the city can only be arranged via the tourist office, but a good view of it can be gained from the **Jardin Vauban** opposite. The Citadel is in effect a town within a town and was entered through impressive entrance ways, of which the most monumental is the **Porte Royale**. Another is the magnificent **Porte de Paris**, a triumphal arch erected to the glory of Louis XIV by Simon Vollant in the late 17th century. Among the many mythological figures represented above the semi-circular arches is a figure of Victory about to crown Louis XIV. The Citadel is still used as a barracks. (Open for visits only on Sunday during summer.)

Musée des Beaux-Arts

Perhaps the chief attraction of this busy city is its Musée des Beaux-Arts which has masterpieces by Rubens, Goya, David, Delacroix, El Greco and Renoir in a magnificent building on Place de la République. Re-opened in June 1993, it is superbly arranged, with the paintings displayed to best effect. It also houses an excellent collection of Flemish paintings including superbly eccentric works by Hieronymus Bosch and classic Flemish landscape paintings by Bruegel the Elder.

Musée de l'Hospice Comtesse

Another superb museum is the Musée de l'Hospice Comtesse, 32 rue de la Monnaie, in the heart of the old town. This magnificent building was founded in 1237 by the Comtesse de Flandre and used as a hospital. A fire destroyed part of the building in the 15th century after which it was rebuilt in late medieval style. The Hospice is considered to be one of the most perfect and enchanting buildings in Lille with its magnificent arcaded *Salles des Malades* (Sick Room). It now houses some superb pieces of furniture but the most interesting feature are the exquisite 15th-century Flemish tiles, used in the original interior decoration, which are still in place. (Open Wed–Mon 10 am–12.30 pm and 2–6 pm.)

Of the massive palace of the Dukes of Burgundy, the **Palais Rihour**, little is left except for a spiral staircase turret in red brick. From the 17th century there are a number of houses such as the **Maison des Vieux Hommes**, built using a mixture of materials in 1624, and the **Maison de Gilles de la Boe** which was decorated profusely with carving in 1636.

Ancienne Bourse

For sheer fecundity of carving and imagination, however, the Ancienne Bourse is without equal. It consists of 28 houses built as a commercial exchange, side by side with an arcaded gallery, enclosing a central courtyard, by Julien Destrée in the 1650s. The carved decoration is unashamed Flamboyant: caryatids, garlands and medallions jostle for space, creating the rich tapestry of colour so characteristic of Flemish art.

Elsewhere in the town are merchants houses whose façades were treated as sculpture; some were conceived and executed in isolation; others as part of a grander design, as was the case with the **Hôtel Beauregard**. In the 18th century French influence becomes more marked in the façades of such buildings as the **Hôtel d'Avelin**, executed in 1777 and the **Hôtel de Wambrechies**. Charles de Gaulle was born at 9 rue Princesse, his house now serving as a small museum. (Open 10 am – noon and 2 – 5 pm.) He was married in the Gothic church of St-Maurice in rue de Paris.

Practicalities in Lille

Tourist Office Place Rihour, in what remains of the old palace of the Dukes of Burgundy (Tel. 20 30 81 00). Accommodation service; guided tours in English.
Railway Station Place de la Gare (*Info*: Tel. 20 74 50 50; *Reservations*: Tel. 20 06 26 99). Information centre; currency exchange (poor rates). The new TGV station is located ½km to the north-east of the old station; from principal station follow rue Faidherbe to place de Gaulle beyond which lies place Rihour.
Festivals The first weekend of September sees the largest junk fair in Europe – *la braderie* – as anyone can come and set up stall for a week. Stalls stretch for miles around the city and eager buyers search all night for treasures, using torches, before retreating to the restaurants which stay open all night selling heaped bowl-fulls of *moules frites*.
Markets Marché de Wazemmes, Place de la Nouvelle. Sun, Tues and Thurs mornings.
Hotels Cheap hotels are not very attractive in Lille and the areas around the train station and the Wazemmes market are best avoided at night. *Hôtel Chopin*, 4 rue de Tournai (Tel. 20 06 35 80). Small, friendly proprietor and cheap.

☆ Hôtel Ibis, 21 rue Lepelletier (Tel. 20 06 21 95). Modern but not far from the *ancienne bourse*.
☆☆ *Hôtel Paix*, 46 bis rue Paris (Tel. 20 54 63 93). Comfortable large rooms, between *ancienne bourse* and Eglise St-Maurice, close to station.
☆☆ *Hôtel Treille*, 7 Place L de Bettigneis (Tel. 20 55 45 46). Comfortable hotel near the Hospice Comtesse.
Hostels *Auberge de Jeunesse* (HI) 1 ave Julien Destrée (Tel. 20 52 98 94). Next to Foire Internationale; newly renovated, dormitory accommodation.
Restaurants *Aux Moules*, 34 rue de Béthune: famous for its mussels.
Grand Café, 1 Place Rihour. A classic café in the heart of the city, with good snack food and a wide range of beers.
☆ *La Coquille*, 60 rue St Etienne (Tel. 20 54 29 82). Delicious dishes in an elegant 18th century house in a street parallel to Rue Nationale.
☆☆ *La Devinière*, 61 blvd Louis XIV (Tel. 20 52 74 64). Superb *nouvelle cuisine* from chef Willy Waterlot in small, flower-filled restaurant. Reservation advised.

Arras

Trains 10 *trains daily from* Lille *(35 – 45 mins);* 15 *from* Paris *(1½ hours)* TGVs *(50 mins);* 10 *from* Dunkerque *(1½ hours),* 7 – 9 *from* Amiens *(45 mins–1 hour 10 mins).*

The capital of the historic Artois region between Flanders and Picardy, Arras may have gained its name from the rats which once were legion in the city. Whatever the truth, homage is payed to the rodent every year on Whit Sunday in the **Fête des Rats.**

What to see

Grand Place and Petit Place

The great treasures of Arras are its 2 magnificent squares, both Flemish in character, the Grande Place and Petit Place or Place des Héros, which have been painstakingly restored to their former appearance.

It was outside the city that the Battle of Arras began on 9th April 1917, in the course of which Vimy Ridge was seized and 13,000 German prisoners and 200 guns captured. A German counter-attack in March 1918 failed to break through the Allied lines and an Allied counter-attack along the Cambrai road freed Arras from danger and led to a hurried German retreat.

In September 1914 French and German forces held different parts of the city and so much of the city was subsequently reduced to rubble by shelling that after the First World War, it seemed impossible that Arras could ever be brought to life again. Most of the buildings in the centre were painstakingly rebuilt in the 1920s, only to be severely damaged again in Second World War, yet now the Grande Place, surrounded by its uniform red-brick 15th-century Flemish townhouses, looks as if it has hardly been touched by war.

The **Hôtel de Ville** dominates the smaller arcaded Petit Place. Rebuilt with a superb 16th-century façade which hides a series of interesting rooms, it is attached to a lofty belfry from which there are panoramic views over the city and surrounding country. Beneath the town hall and much of the city stretch a labyrinthe of tunnels or *boves* which were excavated in medieval times and which were used to protect wounded British soldiers during the First World War. Visits are arranged daily via the tourist office.

Musée des Beaux-Arts

Not far away, in the 18th-century **Abbaye St-Vaast** is the Musée des Beaux-Arts with an outstanding collection of 18th- and 19th-century French and Dutch porcelain. (Open Wed–Fri and Mon, 10 am–noon and 2–5 pm, Sat 10 am–noon and 2–6 pm, Sun 2–5 pm.) Beyond the museum is the 19th-century **cathedral**, St-Vaast, which was built to replace one destroyed during the Revolution. Half razed to the ground by shelling during the First World War, it has been painstakingly restored.

From the station, blvd Carnot leads to the Basse-Ville beyond which the Promenade des Allées leads to the huge **military Citadel** constructed by Vauban in 1674. To the north of it is the **British military cemetery** and the **Arras Memorial** dedicated to the 36,000 men missing in the Battle of Arras.

Practicalities in Arras

Tourist Office Place des Héros, in the Hôtel de Ville (Tel. 21 51 26 95); map with accommodations list.

Railway Station Place Maréchal Foch (Tel. 21 71 00 42); open 7 am–7 pm. To reach town centre, cross Place Foch, pass fountain, follow Rue Gambetta. Turn right onto rue Ronville and left onto Rue de la Housse as far as the square.

Markets Place des Héros, every Wed and Sat.

Hotels *Grand Hôtel Raoul*, 29 ave Michonneau (Tel. 21 55 45 17). Small and simple, close to station.

Hôtel le Commerce, Place du Maréchal Foch (Tel. 21 71 10 07). Simple, clean and close to the station.

☆ *Hôtel Moderne*, 12 blvd Faidherbe (Tel. 21 23 39 57). Comfortable old bed-and-breakfast hotel, very close to station.

☆☆ *Les Trois Luppars*, 49 Grande Place (Tel. 21 07 41 41). Right in the heart of things, on the main square.

☆☆ *Hôtel-Restaurant Chanzy*, 8 rue Chanzy (Tel. 21 71 02 02). Simple but comfortable hotel with superb Flemish cooking and one of the best wine cellars in northern France.

Hostel *Auberge de Jeunesse*, 59 Grande Place (Tel. 21 23 54 53). Superb location on central square.

Restaurants *Les Grandes Arcades*, 23 Grande

Place, superb old restaurant, serving good, classic French cuisine.
Ambassadeur, place Foch (Tel. 21 23 29 80). Cheap good food in the station restaurant.
☆ *L'Antoniolus*, 2 rue Eugène-Pottier (Tel. 21 51 66 99). Excellent cooking in delightful verdant setting. Cheapest menu at lunchtime is good value.

☆☆ *Univers*, 3 Place Croix-Rouge (Tel. 21 71 34 01). Good value meals in a very attractive 18th-century monastery.
☆☆ *La Faisanderie*, 45 Grand Place (Tel. 21 48 20 76). Superb restaurant in Flemish building on the main square; old wood fireplace on ground floor and cool dining in cellar among attractive stone columns.

Boulogne-sur-Mer

Trains 7 *trains daily from* **Calais** *(30–45 mins); 7 daily from* **Amiens** *(1½ hours); 12 daily from* **Paris** *(3 hours); 13 from* **Lille** *(1½ hours).*

Boulogne is one of only 3 French towns to be completely enclosed within its original medieval ramparts, within which are a maze of tortuous streets and alleyways. The ramparts were built in 1231 on Gallo-Roman foundations by Count Philippe Hurepel and reinforced in the 16th and 17th centuries. It is probable that Roman troops set out from here in AD 43 to conquer England; certainly the Romans had a settlement here by the name of Gesoriacum. Some 6 centuries later, according to tradition, a boat was washed up on the beach at Boulogne containing a statue of the Virgin Mary around which a pilgrimage tradition grew.

Today Boulogne is a major transit point for British travellers to France but despite the advent of tourism, fishing is the most important activity, and Boulogne remains the largest fishing port in France. Its marine activity lends it a special salty atmosphere which Calais seems to have lost. Lovers of sea-food still flock to Boulogne between 12th–28th July when the *Fête du Poisson* takes place to sample the best that the northern fishermen can catch.

Boulogne consists of a lower town on the right bank of the Liane, rebuilt and rather ugly, and a more interesting *Haute Ville*, enclosed by ancient ramparts, which stands high up on the eastern side of the town.

What to see

Eglise Notre-Dame
The *Haute Ville* is dominated by the bulk of the Notre-Dame basilica, a 19th-century church built to replace the 12th-century one burnt down during the Revolution which housed one of the most venerated Madonnas in Europe – the black wooden figure of the Virgin which was supposed to have miraculously arrived by boat in the 7th century. Only the enormous Romanesque crypt survives of what was once one of the largest pilgrimage churches of northern France.

Ramparts
The most striking part of the upper town, which contains the **Hôtel de Ville** and an 11th–13th century belfry, is the rectangle of 13th-century fortified walls, with their

gates and château and bastion nesting inside one corner. There are superb views from the parapet walk which is punctuated with delightful, shade-filled gardens. Henry VIII captured the town in 1544 but sold it to Charles IX only 6 years later. At the beginning of the 19th century, extensive preparations were made by Napoleon at Boulogne for his planned invasion of Great Britain, which came to nothing with the defeat of the French navy at Trafalgar on 21st October 1805.

Colonne de la Grande Armée

One mile north of the city is the column of the Grande Armée which commemmorates Napoleon's great dream of conquering Britain. Work on the 49-metre high marble column began in 1804 but was only finished under Louis Philippe. Steps lead up for a panoramic view which on a fine day extends as far as Dover. (Free, open daily 10 am–noon and 2–5 pm.)

Practicalities in Boulogne-sur-Mer

Tourist office Pont Marquet (by the port), Place Frédéric Sauvage (Tel. 21 31 68 38); accommodation service; ferry information.
Railway Station 2 train stations: Gare Boulogne-Ville, blvd Voltaire (Tel. 21 80 50 50), from where most trains leave; lockers, information office.
Gare-Maritime, Car Ferry Terminal, service only to Paris. From Gare Boulogne-Ville, cross Blvd Voltaire and follow Blvd Daunou, tourist office is near Pont Marquet.
Ferries Hoverspeed, Sea-Cat, 6 depatures daily in summer for Folkestone (55 mins) late May–end September, and 4 departures daily Oct–late May. (Tel. 21 30 27 26).
Markets Wed and Sat am, Place Dalton.
Hotels Hôtel Hamiot, 1 rue Faidherbe (Tel. 21 31 44 20). Facing beach; large, plain rooms with simple restaurant downstairs offering good cheap food.
Hôtel le Mirador, 2 rue de la Lampe (Tel 21 31 38 08). Pleasant and reasonable.

☆ Hôtel Climat de France, Place Rouget de Lisle (Tel. 21 80 14 50). Ivy-covered hotel, clean and convenient, opposite station, with quiet back garden.
☆☆ Hôtel Métropole, 51 rue Thiers, off Rue Faidherbe (Tel. 21 30 45 72). Uninteresting functional hotel but convenient for ferry passengers. No restaurant.
Hostels Auberge de Jeunesse (HI), 36 rue de la Port Gayole (Tel. 21 31 48 22). Just outside the vieille ville.
Camping Moulin Wibert, Blvd Ste-Beuve, 2km west of tourist office, along Quai Gambetta and its continuation (Tel. 21 31 40 29).
Restaurants ☆☆ La Liégoise, 10 rue A Monsigny (Tel. 21 33 76 30). One of Boulogne's smartest restaurants; cool, elegant, modernistic restaurant with imaginative cuisine.
☆☆☆ La Matelote, 80 blvd Ste-Beuve, a superb restaurant offering a huge range of exquisitely cooked fish and shellfish.

Dunkerque

Trains 7–10 trains daily from Calais (35 mins); 5 daily from Paris (3 hours); 7 from Arras (1½ hours); 9 from Lille (1 hour).

Before the Second World War Dunkerque was essentially a 17th and 18th-century Flemish city. 1944 however left it in ruins and today it is a bustling modern city, with a large, dynamic port. Of the old town just one of the 28 towers of the old 14th-century fortifications remains – the octagonal **Tour de Leughenaer**. It can be found in the old port near the Minck, the former fish market.

What to see

St-Eloi

Although restored, the late Gothic church of Saint-Eloi is interesting with its old free-standing bell tower and the adjacent square brick tower which also doubles up as a belfry. The 500-year-old belfry houses 58 bells, the largest of which weighs 7 tons. At the heart of the town stands a statue of Jean Bart, the corsair, who was born in the town in 1650; somehow it escaped the general destruction of 1944. Jean Bart, and his fellow corsair the Chevalier de Forbin took part in the abortive atttempt by the Old Pretender to land in Scotland in 1706.

It was to Dunkirk that British and French troops withdrew in late May 1940 in the face of an unstoppable German advance. Despite being encircled and continuously strafed by enemy planes, around 350,000 men were evacuated by an armada of craft, large and small, which had crossed the Channel in an attempt to bring away as many troops as possible. 4 years were to pass before the Normandy invasions brought British troops back to France in what was the largest sea invasion ever mounted.

Musée des Beaux-Arts

The Musée des Beaux-Arts, near the theatre on place Général de Gaulle, has an exhibition devoted to the Evacuation of 1940, while most of the building is devoted to paintings of the 17th-century Dutch and Flemish schools. (Open Wed–Mon 10 am–noon and 2–6 pm.) Located close to the youth hostel is the extraordinary building which houses the **Musée d'Art Contemporain** in rue des Bains. (Open Wed–Mon 10 am–7 pm.)

Practicalities in Dunkerque

Tourist Office 4 place du Beffroi, on the ground floor of the belfry (Tel. 28 66 79 21); accommodation lists; map; currency exchange (cash only).

Railway Station Place de la Gare; information office open daily 8 am–7 pm (Tel. 20 78 50 50). To town centre from station, follow Ave Guynemer and its continuation Rue Thiers and Rue du Sud, then turn left into Rue Nationale and walk towards belfry.

Ferries Sallyline, Place Emile Bollaert (Tel. 28 21 43 44). 8–10 sailings daily to Ramsgate.

Festivals March: *Mardi Gras Carnival*, one of the largest in northern France; July–Sept: *Contemporary Art Festival*; 1st week of Sept: *Fête des Moissons* – harvest home celebrations with music and dancing.

Hotels *Hôtel le XIX siècle*, Place de la Gare (Tel 28 66 79 28). Substantial old station hotel, occupying an entire corner of the Place de la Gare, with flowers at every window. Good restaurant offering interesting dishes at good prices.

☆ *Hôtel du Tigre*, 8 rue Clemenceau (Tel 28 66 75 17). Pleasant, spotless rooms with in town centre.

☆☆ *Hôtel Welcome*, 37 rue Poincaré, close to St-Eloi and the Musée des Beaux Arts (Tel. 28 59 20 70).

Hostels Auberge de Jeunesse (HI), Place Paul Asseman, 15 minutes from station (Tel. 28 63 36 34).

Camping *Dunqerque-Malo-les-Bains*, Blvd de l'Europe (Tel. 28 69 26 68). Bus 3 to 'Malo CES Camping' stop; open March–Nov; swimming pool.

Restaurants ☆ *Aux Ducs de Bourgogne*, 29 rue Bourgogne (Tel. 28 66 78 69).

☆ *Richelieu*, Place de la Gare (Tel. 28 66 52 13). Outstanding station buffet, with superb seafood and wine-list.

☆☆ *Au Bon Coin*, ave Kléber, Malo-les-Bains (Tel. 28 69 12 63). Some way from centre but with excellent, old seafood restaurant.

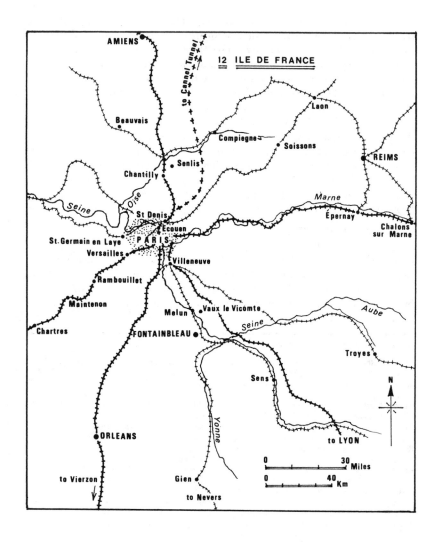

AMIENS

to Cannel Tunnel

12 ≡ ILE DE FRANCE

Laon

Beauvais

Compiegne

Soissons

REIMS

Senlis

Chantilly

Oise

Marne

Seine

Épernay

St Denis

Ecouen

Chalons
sur Marne

St. Germain en Laye

PARIS

Versailles

Villeneuve

Rambouillet

Aube

Maintenon

Melun

Vaux le Vicomte

Chartres

FONTAINBLEAU

Seine

Troyes

Sens

N

Yonne

to LYON

ORLEANS

0   30 Miles

0   40 Km

to Vierzon

Gien

to Nevers

12 Paris and Ile de France

Paris

The capital of France and a département in itself, Paris has the reputation of being one of the most beautiful cities of Europe. This distinction is in fact less due to the number of ancient buildings surviving in the city than to its overall elegance and grandeur in conception. Kings, Napoleon Bonaparte and successive governments and Presidents have all viewed the beauty and embellishments of the city as a reflection of the majesty and power of the French nation, so that the city has always been the object of much more conscious and deliberate town planning than, for instance, London has ever been. In their efforts they have been greatly aided by the natural beauty of the Seine which divides to create the two islands at the heart of the city. Vistas from one bank of the Seine to the other were deliberately planned for effect and they are one of the most memorable aspects of the city.

Nowhere is the grandeur of the scale more evident than from the Place de la Concorde, from where the majestic Champs-Elysées leads away west to the Arc de Triomphe. In the opposite direction, beyond the formal gardens of the Tuileries, lies the vast palace of the Louvre, to the north of which the runs the elegant Rue de Rivoli. This particularly French gift for civic planning, which is inevitably of a formal nature, continues to this day, the Grande Arche forming a natural progression of this concern for grand architectural design. Running west to east across the city in a virtually unbroken line the Rue de Rivoli leads eventually, via its continuation, the Rue St-Antoine, to the Place de la Bastille. This road, as much as the river itself, cuts Paris into two equal parts.

Another striking feature of the city, in marked contrast to London, is the way in which Paris is focused on the Seine. The Seine is much more a feature of the city than the Thames is of London, partly because of the islands lying in it midstream which were a natural defensive site, but also because of an early awareness of the way in which the river could be used to enhance the beauty and majesty of the capital.

The whole face of the city was changed in the 19th century by the

Baron Georges Eugène Haussmann prefect of the Seine département, who widened some of the streets, developed the sewage system and laid out new thoroughfares and streets to allow troops to move faster through the city in case of a popular uprising. Much of the old city was destroyed in the process but at the same time some beautiful streets were created, notably Boulevard St-Michel on the Left Bank which turns into the Boulevard Sébastopol on the Right Bank, Boulevard St-Germain and the Rue de Rivoli, running north of the Louvre and the Jardin des Tuileries, which must be one of the most beautiful streets in the city. Baudelaire and others lamented the passing of the city: '*Le vieux Paris n'est plus,*' he wrote, '*la forme d'une ville change plus vite que le coeur d'un mortel.*' (Old Paris exists no longer. The form of a city changes faster than the heart of a mortal.) The best way to get to know the city is to explore it on foot, taking one area at a time, and not to try and see too much. The parks and cafés, quite apart from the restaurants, are there to be enjoyed; remorseless sight-seeing is no joy at all. One excellent way to get a feel for the layout of the city is to take a *bateau mouche*, one of the sight-seeing boats that ply up and down the Seine with commentaries in English and other languages. Another is to climb up high – to the top of Notre-Dame, the Panthéon or Montmartre. It was the first thing Goethe did wherever he went, to get a picture of the layout of any new city he arrived at.

History

Historically, the focus of Paris is the **Ile de la Cité**, the earliest inhabited part of the capital, and the royal, legal and ecclesiastical centre of the city for some 1,700 years. The Ile de la Cité is a natural defensive site and was occupied and fortified by the Romans following Julius Caesar's defeat of Vercingetorix at Alésia in 52 BC. The Romans made Lutetia – the capital of the Parisii (then an insignificant Gallic tribe) – their capital and it was here that the deputies of the Gallic tribes conquered by Rome were required to meet. The Franks had been partially Christianised by the time of the Barbarian invasions in the 3rd to 5th centuries. With the defeat of the Roman governor of Soissons in 486, Clovis I adopted Christianity, was baptised at Reims and established his capital at Paris in 508. From this date the history of the city was inextricably linked to that of France, which emerged as a nation as its kings succeeded in centralising their power. Philippe Auguste contributed enormously to the growth in power of the French monarchy and in the importance of Paris. He surrounded the town with walls between 1180 and 1210 and the city prospered in the 13th century when the University of the Sorbonne was established and the Sainte Chapelle built. Further ramparts were built by Charles v but neither they, nor the fortress of the Bastille, could withstand the attacks by the English who took the city in 1420 and held it for 40 years. It was in the cathedral of Notre Dame that Henry vi of England was crowned King of France in 1431 at the age of 10. English domination was however short-lived and after their expulsion the city saw a period of tremendous development under François i and Henri iv who extended the town's defences. In the 17th and 18th centuries Paris expanded rapidly into the surrounding countryside – north into the Marais and the areas now occupied by the Palais-Royal and the Place Vendôme, and west to the Invalides, and Gobelins. Louis xiv ordered the construction of new city walls, some 24 kilometres in length, known as 'des Fermiers Généraux', which were broken by toll gates.

At the Revolution Paris was the centre of the revolutionary developments and witnessed both bloodshed and extensive damage, especially to its religious monuments. In the 19th century, the city expanded again very rapidly while the appearance of the heart of the city was dramatically altered by Baron Haussmann who drove great thoroughfares through many of the oldest quarters of the city, destroying much that was ancient, if unhealthy, in the process. At the end of the 19th century the outlying areas of Auteuil, Passy, Montmartre, Belleville, La Villette, Grenelle and Vaugirard were joined to Paris. The inter-war years saw further industrialisation and modernisation, the 1960s and 1970s saw the large-scale building of tower blocks in the suburbs and by the creation of the Boulevard Périphérique around Paris, the Centre Pompidou and the redevelopment of the old market site of Les Halles. The 1980s saw further modernisation with the creation of the new business and financial district of La Défense to the west of Paris and the construction of the monumental Grande Arche, a late 20th-century version of Napoleon's Arc de Triomphe. Work currently continues on a new Bibliothèque Nationale, being constructed next to the Gare d'Austerlitz railway station. As with all other recent 'grands projets', it has been severely criticised on aesthetic, practical and political grounds.

What to see

Ile de la Cité

The heart of Paris, now as in the very earliest times, is the Ile de la Cité, a small elliptical island standing in the middle of the Seine. The earliest inhabited part of the capital, the Ile de la Cité contains 3 buildings of outstanding interest and beauty, all closely connected with the early history of France – Notre-Dame, the Conciergerie and the Sainte-Chapelle.

Notre-Dame

The façade of the cathedral of Notre-Dame is unusual for its extraordinary homogeneity and was almost certainly the work of a single architect. Begun in c. 1160 but not completed until the end of the 13th century, it is one of the great Gothic cathedrals of France, vying with Chartres, Bourges, Reims and Beauvais for the highest place in the mantle of French Gothic architecture. One of its greatest treasures is its western façade, designed as a picture book of the Bible, largely for the illiterate but devout congregation. The central portal represents the Last Judgement, with the weighing of souls, the wise and foolish virgins and the celestial court. The southern portal represents the scenes from the life of Virgin Mary and that of St Anne; the northern one portrays the Coronation of the Virgin. Above these is ranged a gallery of kings which were decapitated by the Paris mob during the French Revolution under the delusion that they were the kings of France. They were in fact patriarchal kings from the Old Testament. Most of the original heads were found in 1977 and have been gathered in the Musée de Cluny, south of the river; replicas of the heads were reattached during the restoration work of Viollet-le-Duc in the late 19th century. The side façades and the apse of Notre-Dame have a similar uniformity of style while the flying buttresses of the apse are outstanding for their boldness and beauty. Although much restored, Notre-Dame is the best example of Transitional Gothic architecture in France: the 13th century nave could not be excelled in grandeur or purity of style. An unusual feature of Notre-Dame, common only to cathedrals in the Ile de France, are the circular windows between the triforium and clerestory which were designed to give extra light to the nave. The most spectacular feature of the interior are the 3 great rose windows which still contain their original 13th-century glass, the finest being that in the north transept. Free guided tours of the cathedral give one a good understanding of the history and architecture; information about tours from information booth on right as one enters. (Tours in English Wed noon; tours in French Mon–Fri at noon, Sat–Sun 2 pm.)

The twin towers, reached by a hair-raising climb up 386 steps, bring one out on to a narrow balcony, level with the dozens of bizarre and extravagant gargoyles. The home of the Hunchback of Notre-Dame, Victor Hugo's fictional character, the south tower contains the massive 13-ton bell, on which Quasimodo used to swing high up out over the cathedral façade. The views from the base of the towers, looking out over the Ile de la Cité, the cathedral and the roofscapes of Paris are stupendous. (Open daily Aug 10 am–6.30 pm; Sept and April–July (9.30–11.30 am and 2–5.30 pm; Oct–March 10 am–4.30 pm.)

In front of the cathedral lies the cathedral 'parvis', below which lies the **Archaeological Museum**, with an archaeological dig which has laid bare the remains of part of the Roman village which once covered the Ile de la Cité. The site was discovered in 1965, when an underground parking site was being built. Displays and dioramas guide visitors through the early history of the city after the Roman conquest of 52 BC. (Open daily 10 am–6 pm.)

Sainte-Chapelle

Near by, just off the Cour du Mai, stands the Sainte-Chapelle, one of the most exquisite examples in Paris of 13th-century French Gothic architecture. Built in 1243 – 48 by Louis IX, probably on designs by Pierre de Montreuil, as a shrine to house a number of religious relics which have since been dispersed, it once contained the most precious relic of all – the crown of thorns from Christ's passion (now to be found in Notre-Dame). Now somewhat hidden amongst the 19th-century Palais de Justice, except for its tall slender spire, the Sainte-Chapelle in fact consists of 2 superimposed chapels, the lower one dark and serene, decorated with 13th-century murals in royal reds, blues and golds, the upper one dazzling with light and colour through its walls of stained glass. Sainte Chapelle has been the scene of many royal marriages and Richard II of England was betrothed to Isabelle of France here in 1396. The huge windows of brilliant stained glass vie with those of Chartres cathedral in magnificence. Those portraying scenes from the Apocalypse in the large rose window were a gift of Charles VIII; the others portray scenes from the Old and New Testaments. Occasional concerts are held in this magnificent setting; details from information booth at entrance. (Open daily (9.30 am–6.30 pm; combined ticket for Sainte-Chapelle and the Conciergerie.)

Palais de Justice

On the western side of the island, and almost adjacent to the Sainte-Chapelle, is the Palais de Justice, which developed around a medieval palace where in 1431 the coronation banquet of Henry VI of England took place. Since the 13th century the district courts of Paris have been gathered here and today it's possible for a visitor to enter the courtroom and watch the proceedings for all trials are open to the public. Amongst the many trials held here has been that of Marshal Pétain who was convicted of collaboration after the collapse of the Vichy Government with the end of World War Two. One of the finest rooms open to the public is the Chambre Dorée which was the bedroom of Louis IX and later used by the Parlement. The Revolutionary Tribunal occupied the building during the Terror of 1793. (Open Mon–Fri 1.30 – c.5.00 pm.)

Conciergerie Immediately south of the Pont au Change and occupying the lower floor of the Palais de Justice, the Conciergerie has a neo-Gothic façade and towers facing the Quai de l'Horloge. The northern façade, best viewed from the Right Bank, has the appearance of a medieval fortress. Originally the residence of the Royal Concierge, the building was used as a prison under the *ancien régime*, and during the Revolution became a prison of notoriety. Its 14th century Gothic halls served as a state prison during the Terror, prisoners being detained here before being sent to be guillotined in the Place de la Bastille. Amongst those held here can be numbered Queen Marie-Antoinette – who spent 2½ months here – Charlotte

Corday, the poet André de Chénier, Mme du Barry, Danton, Robespierre and the public prosecutor, Fouquier-Tinville. More than 2,200 prisoners held in the Conciergerie were guillotined within the space of 18 months between 1793 and 1794. The *Salle des pas perdus* derived its name from the fact that prisoners destined for execution had to pass through the Gothic hall on their way to the guillotine. Beyond the enormous Great Hall, stairs lead to the cells, Robespierre's now containing some of his letters while Marie-Antoinette's cell has been turned into a chapel. The Conciergerie is still used to hold prisoners awaiting trial in the nearby Palais de Justice. Several souvenirs, including the blade of a guillotine, are preserved in the chapel which prisoners could attend in the gallery. (Open daily 9.30 am–6 pm; Oct–March 10 am–5 pm; combined ticket for Sainte-Chapelle also available.)

Linking the Ile de la Cité, at the western end of the island, to the north and south bank of the Seine, is the oldest bridge in Paris, ironically named **Pont-Neuf**.

Ile St-Louis

At the eastern extremity of the Ile de la Cité the Pont St-Louis leads to the tiny and exclusive little island of Ile St-Louis which seems to be moored to its larger western neighbour. Until the 17th century the Ile St-Louis was 2 separate islands; less crowded than the Ile de la Cité, it is quiet and peaceful, especially in the early mornings and out of season, a world of its own in the heart of Paris. A walk around the little island affords superb views of the banks of the Seine, the apse of Notre-Dame, the delightful mansions lining the quays and the long barges slipping through the heart of the city.

Down the Quai de Bourbon are some elegant 17th-and 18th-century mansions and at 17 Quai d'Anjou stands the **Hôtel de Lauzun**, built by Le Vau between 1650 and 1658, which has magnificent interior decoration. Théophile Gautier and Baudelaire stayed here in the 19th century while Voltaire stayed at the **Hôtel Lambert**, designed by Le Vau and decorated by Le Brun and Le Sueur, at number 2, rue St-Louis-en-l'Ile. The unremarkable exterior of the **Eglise St-Louis-en-l'Ile** hides a superb rococo interior, with gilded *putti*, and elaborate marble and woodwork. (Open 9 am–noon and 3–7 pm.)

The Left Bank

5th Arrondissement: The Latin Quarter

Immediately south of the Ile de la Cité is the *Quartier Latin*, the Latin Quarter, traditionally the student quarter of Paris, seedy and chic in turns, full of character, narrow streets, bustling bars and restaurants. It is still the home of the Sorbonne, and crowded with students as it has been since 1253 when Robert de Sorbon opened a school of theology for poor students which became the administrative and teaching quarters of the University of Paris. Its central artery is Boulevard St-Michel, with its thronged cafés spilling out into the streets, second-hand book-shops, restaurants and cinemas. Central to Boulevard St-Michel, and a popular meeting place, is Place St-Michel, with its beautiful fountain. A little to the south, on Boulevard St-Michel, is the Place de la Sorbonne, a small square lined with cafés around a central space usually devoted to contemporary sculpture. The Sorbonne stands on the eastern side of the square. The medieval buildings have been replaced a number of times, most recently in the 19th century, except for Ste-Ursule-de-la-Sorbonne, the main building, which was commissioned by Cardinal Richelieu in 1642. The Cardinal lies buried inside, his hat suspended above him by threads hanging from the ceiling. (Public admitted to chapel only; open Mon–Fri 9 am–5 pm.)

Musée de Cluny

One of the great museums of Paris, the Musée de Cluny, 6 place Paul-Painlevé, 5ème, is not only an outstanding museum of medieval art, jewellery and tapestries but is located in one of only 3 medieval homes in Paris, once the Paris residence of the abbots of Cluny. The collections are diverse and superbly displayed, ranging from art, sculpture, chests, tapestries, to medieval games, household objects belonging to the houses of the nobility, costume, stained glass and medieval goblets and jewellery. The greatest treasures are perhaps the extraordinary tapestries, particularly the 5 brilliant and beautiful ones known as the *Dame à la Licorne* (Woman with a Unicorn) series which were woven in the Netherlands for Jean le Viste in the 1490s. Five are believed to depict the senses; the sixth, *Mon Seul Désir*, shows the Lady giving up her jewellery, or overcoming her worldly senses, for her lover. Other superb exhibits include one room devoted entirely to medieval royal jewellery and crowns (room 16), and magnificent medieval altar-pieces of gold and silver, works of exquisite and minute craftsmanship.

Amongst the museum's 23,000 items are the great sculpted heads of the Old Testament kings which were knocked off the figures on the west façade of Notre-Dame in the Revolution. The Galerie des Rois (room 7) displays the 21 heads of Judaean and Israelite kings, carved between 1210 and 1230. They were only discovered in 1977 during construction work in the 7th arrondissement.

The medieval manor house, the Hôtel de Cluny, in which the museum is located is sited on the foundations of a Roman building; steps descend from the ground floor to the Frigidarium of the Gallo-Roman baths which still possess their original vaulting. One of the earliest Roman items is the Autel des Nautes, a 1st-century monument dedicated to the God Jupiter by the boatmen ferrying passengers across the Seine. Concerts of early chamber music are held frequently in the Hôtel on Friday afternoons; admission free with museum entry ticket. (Tel. 43 25 62 00; Open Wed–Sun 9.45 am to 5.15 pm.)

Panthéon

The majestic dome of the Panthéon towers over the Latin Quarter from the highest point of the Left Bank. A church has occupied this strategic site since a shrine was built by Clovis in 508 to celebrate his victory over Alaric at the Battle of Vouillé. Louis XV was responsible for the present building, ordering its construction in thanksgiving for recovering from a serious illness. Externally imposing, it is built in the shape of a Greek cross with a massive pediment by David d'Angers depicting France between the figures of Liberty and History. Begun in 1754, work was not completed until the year of the outbreak of the Revolution 1789, as a result of which the building hardly saw use as a church, the Revolutionary Convention decreeing that it should instead be the burial place for distinguished citizens. The interior is coldly classical and spartan with austere Corinthian columns and a few monuments to Diderot and the Encyclopaedists. To transform the Panthéon from a church into a mausoleum, the 42 tall windows were walled up and all symbols of Christian worship were removed. After extensive restorations, the Panthéon reopened to visitors in 1994. In the crypt are to be found the remains of such notables as Voltaire, Rousseau, Victor Hugo, Zola, Braille, Bougainville, and Jean Jaurès, amongst others, their tombs located in niches behind iron grilles. A stairway leads from the crypt to the top of the dome, from where there are good views over the roof-tops of the Latin Quarter. (Open daily 10 am–5.45 pm. METRO: Luxembourg.)

A short walk from the Panthéon is the restful **Jardin des Plantes**, a large area of welcome greenery, opened by Guy de Brosse, Louis XIII's doctor, in 1640. Originally a medicinal garden established to grow the herbs needed for medicinal purposes, the garden now incorporates a natural history museum, a geological museum, a maze, tropical hot-houses and a zoo.

6th Arrondissement: St-Germain-des-Prés

More sophisticated than the 5th, less aristocratic than the 7th, the 6th arrondissement combines the animation of the *Quartier Latin* with the lively and artistic characteristics of the 6th. Fashionable cafés, innumerable art galleries and small restaurants characterise this intimate and interesting quarter which stretches from the boulevard St-Germain to the south bank of the Seine and south as far as Montparnasse with its cinemas and theatres. Once the literary focus of Paris, where people such as Sartre and Apollinaire, met with their contemporaries to talk at length in cafés and restaurants, St-Germain-des-Prés has so much to offer that some of its residents have never found reason to cross to the north bank of the Seine. At its heart lies the **Eglise St-Germain-des-Prés**, which retains much of its Romanesque work despite being much mutilated over the centuries. The church, facing the little cobbled square, is all that remains of a Benedictine abbey founded in 558 by Childebert I, who is buried in the crypt. Although battered, it is the oldest church still standing in Paris, and its choir reveals early attempts to combine Gothic with earlier Romanesque style.

Jardin and Palais du Luxembourg

A short walk up from Boulevard St-Germain is the delightful Jardin du Luxembourg, a beautiful garden with promenades, a round pond on which float toy boats with gaily coloured sails, shaded gravelled paths and rose gardens, an oasis of greenery and tranquillity in the heart of St-Germain-des-Prés. Attempts by the 19th-century prefect Haussmann to build a street through the gardens were thwarted by the vigorous campaign against the idea by local residents. The gardens face the

Palais du Luxembourg, a heavily rusticated palace built by Salomon de Brosse for Marie de Médicis in 1615–27, who desired an Italianate palace reminiscent of her native Tuscany. In the 19th-century it was enlarged, becoming the home in 1852 of the French Senate, the President of which lived in the smaller Petit Luxembourg, itself a gift from Marie de Médicis to Cardinal Richelieu. Occasionally open to the public, the most attractive room of the palace is the Cabinet Doré, but the magnificent series of paintings by Rubens which once hung in the palace, depicting the life of Marie de Médicis, is now in the Louvre.

The other side of Boulevard St-Germain from the Jardin du Luxembourg, on the bank of the Seine facing the Louvre, is the handsome semi-circular façade of the **Palais de l'Institut de France.** Surmounted by its brilliant gilded dome, it was designed by Le Vau and erected in 1662–4 as a college in accordance with Cardinal Mazarin's Will. Originally a college in the 17th century, then a prison during the Revolution, the building is now the home of the prestigious Académie Française, founded by Richelieu in 1635, the guardian of the purity of the French language. A little to the east lies the neo-classical **Hôtel de la Monnaie,** built by Jacques-Denis Antoine in 1771, which contains superb collections and exhibits relating to the minting of French coinage. To the west on Quai Malaquais is the **Ecole des Beaux Arts** with its large courtyard, one of the best art colleges in France, which has occasional exhibitions of students' work.

7th Arrondissement

Grander and more elegant than the 6th, the 7th arrondissement was the most fashionable part of Paris to live in during the 18th century. Stretched between the Rue des Saints-Pères and the Invalides, the 7th arrondissement contains innumerable grand *hôtels particuliers*, set back from the street with large handsome courtyards behind noble stone walls and elegant gates. Many of these buildings are now government ministries and foreign embassies.

Musée d'Orsay

Heading west along the southern bank of the Seine from the Pont du Carrousel, which crosses the river to the Palais du Louvre, one reaches the Musée d'Orsay, one of the newer museums in Paris, located in the massive former railway station, the Gare d'Orsay, once the station serving south-western France. The collections are mainly devoted to French 19th-century painting and are arranged chronologically, contrasting the different styles and approaches, particularly between the Impressionists and the formal Academic tradition from which the Impressionists were trying to escape. Cabanel's *Naissance de Vénus*, with its formal approach, heavy symbolism and mythological subject matter is a perfect example of the rigid technique and restricted subject-range the Impressionists intended to dispense with.

Amongst the many outstanding paintings are Manet's *Olympia* which caused uproar and scandal when first exhibited at the 1865 salon. Basing his painting of Titian's *Venus of Urbino*, Manet's *Olympia* portrayed the female nude in a modern way for the first time – as a natural and physical being, aware and conscious of her own physicality and force, as opposed to the ethereal, unreal and vulnerable female figures of traditional Academic painting. Another of Manet's masterpieces is his *Déjeuner sur l'herbe* which created an equal furore when first exhibited. Impressionist paintings are largely gathered on the top floor, benefiting from the light from the station roof. Here are paintings by Monet and Renoir which reflect the new interest in daily life and the immediate world around them. Some of the paintings reveal parts of Paris as they appeared in the late 19th century – *Gare St-Lazare* by Monet or *Le Bal du Moulin de la Galette* by Renoir. Monet's paintings of Rouen cathedral should not be overlooked.

Diversifying from the early concerns of the Impressionists, the Post-Impressionists took experimentation further in terms of colour, form, space and perspective. Van Gogh and Cézanne represent 2 very different paths pursued by the Post-Impressionists, Cézanne increasingly preoccupied by the inter-relation of form, space and colour, Van Gogh by expressive drawing and colour.

The final section of the museum is devoted to Belle Epoque sculpture, painting and Art Nouveau decorative art produced prior to the First World War. (Open Tues–Wed and Fri–Sun 9 am–6 pm; Thurs 9 am–9.30 pm; Sept 21st–June 19th Tues–Wed and Fri–Sat 10 am–6 pm; Thurs 10 am–9.45 pm; Sun 9 am–6 pm. METRO: Solferino.)

Palais Bourbon

Further west along the south bank of the Seine lies the large classical façade of the Palais Bourbon, accommodating the Assemblée Nationale, the French legislature. Directly opposite the Madeleine across the river on place de la Concorde, the Palais Bourbon was originally a palace built in 1722 for the Duchess of Bourbon, the daughter of Louis XIV and Madame de Montespan. The heavy classical façade, with its Corinthian columns and pediment adorned with allegorical figures, was the work of Napoleon in 1807. Its more elegant extension, the Hôtel de Lassay, was built from 1722.

Hôtel des Invalides

A little beyond the Palais Bourbon a large area of open grass, the Esplanade des Invalides, opens up, beyond which is the majestic Hôtel des Invalides, a vast Grand Siècle masterpiece covering an area of 127,000 square metres. Founded in 1671 as a home for disabled soldiers, the Hôtel once housed 4,000 pensioners. The building opened its doors to the first wounded soldiers in October 1674 and pensioners still live in the magnificent building designed by Libéral Bruant and completed by J. Hardouin-Mansart. The dormer windows of the imposing 200-metre-long façade take the form of trophies. Entrance to the main large courtyard is gained through a splendid gateway above which is an equestrian bas-relief of Louis XIV by Pierre Cartellier. Opposite the entrance to the Cour d'Honneur is the **Eglise St-Louis**, the 'soldiers' church' of the hospital.

Musée de l'armée Within the extensive buildings is the Musée de l'Armée, an outstanding collection of arms, armour and military souvenirs and the **Musée des**

Plans-Reliefs in the attics, with dozens of extraordinary models of fortified cities. (Open daily 10 am–6 pm.) Of greater interest is Napoleon's tomb, located under the magnificent dome, covered with gilded lead, designed by Hardouin-Mansart. Originally a church, the Eglise du Dôme became a temple to Mars during the Revolution and was used to house the flags of defeated enemies. Turned into a mausoleum during the Consulate, it now houses the Emperor's tomb. Napoleon rests within 6 concentric coffins, some of lead, the last of red porphyry on top of a pedestal of green granite, in the epicentre of the Dôme des Invalides. The tomb was designed by Visconti but Napoleon was only placed in it in 1840, 40 years after his death at St-Helena. The surrounding chapels contain the tombs of Joseph Bonaparte, the great military architect Vauban, Marshal Foch, Lyautey and Turenne. (Open daily 10 am–7 pm; Sept and April–May 10 am–6 pm; Oct–March 10 am–5 pm. METRO: Invalides.)

St-Louis des Invalides Adjacent to the tomb is the church of St-Louis des Invalides where Berlioz's *Requiem* was played for the first time. The church is decorated with military standards although it now contains only a fraction of the number it used to have; the governor of the Invalides burned 1,400 of them as enemy troops arrived in Paris on 30th March 1814.

Musée Rodin

At 77, rue de Varenne the Musée Rodin lies close to the Hôtel des Invalides, in the Hôtel Biron, an elegant building designed by Aubert and Gabriel, typical of the aristocratic houses erected in the Faubourg St-Germain in the 18th century. Auguste Rodin, a close friend of Monet's, is probably France's most famous sculptor and is acknowledged as a father of modern sculpture. Within the gardens are some of Rodin's most famous statues, including *Le Penseur*, possibly meant to represent Dante contemplating *Inferno*. The figure is both taut and absorbed, epitomising energy and concentration. Elsewhere is the group known as *Les Bourgeois de Calais* (the Burghers of Calais), based on a moment during the Hundred Years War when King Edward III agreed to hang the Mayor of Calais and several prominent residents rather than kill all the town's inhabitants. At the last moment the burghers were spared at the intercession of Edward's wife, Philippine, who had been moved by their bravery. One of Rodin's largest statues stands beyond the Burghers – *La Porte d'Enfer*, directly inspired by Dante's *Divine Comedy*.

The smaller statues are to be found inside the Hôtel. *Le Baiser*, based on the lovers Paolo and Francesca, is one of several similar sculptures carved from white marble. Suffering is portrayed with agonising reality in such sculptures as *La Douleur* (Suffering), *Le Cri* (The Cry), *La Pleureuse* (The Weeper) and *Le Désespoir* (Despair.) In summer the rose-filled gardens are cool and fresh, offering a welcoming and shady resting place from the nearby streets.

The Hôtel Biron had been made a residence for artists in 1904 and Rodin arrived in 1908, renting a studio on the ground floor. When the Ministry of Education and Fine Arts wished to close the building in 1910, Rodin offered to leave all his sculptures for the creation of the museum on condition that he could stay there until his death. The proposal was accepted and the Musée Rodin was born. (Open Tues–Sun 10 am–5.45 pm; Oct–March Tues–Sun 10 am–5 pm. METRO: Varenne or Invalides.)

Faubourg Saint-Germain

The Hôtel Biron is located in the grand and aristocratic Faubourg St-Germain, the great 18th-century residential quarter, now home to many of the city's embassies and ministries. The area, which was woodland and meadow until the 16th century, was only developed in the 17th century with the construction of a vast mansion in the area by Marguerite de Valois, first wife of Henri IV. A little east of the Rodin Museum down the Rue de Varenne, at 57, is the Hôtel de Matignon, the official residence of the French Prime Minister. Begun in 1721 by Jean Courtonne, it is named after one its early owners. In the pretty street Rue de Grenelle is a delightful 18th-century fountain, the Fontaine des Quatre Saisons. In Rue St-Dominique, the Ministry of Defence now occupies the convent to which Madame de Montespan, one of Louis XIV's many mistresses, withdrew. Another handsome aristocratic house is the Hôtel de Brienne, at number 14.

Eiffel Tower

West of the Hôtel des Invalides, on the Left Bank of the Seine, the Tour Eiffel rises 300 metres into the sky, a rocket of ironwork, the 19th-century symbol of Paris, better known than the Sacré-Coeur of Montmartre, taller than Notre-Dame, more revolutionary in its day than the glass pyramid of the Louvre or the Grande Arche at La Défense. Castigated and vilified by almost everyone when it was built by Gustave Eiffel for the Exposition Universelle of 1889, it has since become a symbol not just of Paris but of France itself. At 300 metres, in 1889 it was the tallest structure in the world and a testament to French engineering ability, the centre-piece of the world fair held to celebrate the centennial of the French Revolution. Guillaume Apollinaire called it 'the shepherdess of the clouds', but Guy de Maupassant and Alexandre Dumas fils campaigned vigorously against what they saw as a useless monstrosity. Their reaction was not that surprising – composed purely of metal girders, the tower at that time must have appeared gargantuan and dominated the Paris skyline to a far greater extent than it does today. Built in record time, its 7,000 tons incorporate 18,000 pieces of iron held together by 2,500,000 rivets. Despite its size it has an unexpected elegance, especially at night when its lace-like metal tracery is illuminated. The tower has three floors, the first 2 accessible by stairs, the third only by lift (the 1,652 steps to the 3rd floor being considered too many.) From the highest level there are superb views north over the river to the vast Palais de Chaillot, built for the exhibition of 1937, and south over the vast Champ de Mars, a parade ground created in the 18th century. (Open daily 4th July 4–6th Sept, 9 am–midnight; 7th Sept – 20th March, 9.30 am–11 pm; 21st March – 3rd July, 9 am–11 pm. METRO: BirHakeim.)

Champ de Mars and Ecole Militaire

Immediately below the Eiffel tower, stretching away to the south-east is the vast Champ de Mars, a huge expanse of grass. In the 18th century the area was the drill ground for the soldiers from the neighbouring Ecole Militaire; here Napoleon reviewed his troops and the Allied armies of Great Britain, Prussia and Russia celebrated the defeat of Napoleon and the capture of Paris in 1815. Napoleon III chose the field for the Great Exhibition of 1867, the French equivalent to the Crystal Palace exhibition in England. Glass pavilions covering the Champ de Mars were visited by millions of people as well as by almost every reigning monarch in Europe. Similar exhibitions were held on the Champ de Mars in 1878, 1889, 1900 and 1937. At the southern end is the Ecole Militaire, created by Louis XV at the request of his mistress, Madame de Pompadour, who was keen to allow poor gentlemen the chance to become educated officers. In 1784 a young cadet from Corsica, Napoleon Bonaparte, arrived at the age of 15 to take up his place in the imposing building designed in 1751 by Jacques Ange Gabriel. On the Place de Fontenoy, the courtyard is dominated by the elegant main façade.

In complete contrast is the UNESCO (**United Nations Educational, Scientific and Cultural Organisation**) building opposite, the work of the American architect Marcel Breuer, the Frenchman Zehrfuss and the Italian Nervi. Built in the shape of the letter 'Y', this large pre-stressed concrete building was decorated by a team of international artists, with ceramics by Miró, a painting by Picasso, mosaics by Bazaine and a Japanese garden. (Open Mon–Sat 9 am–6.30 pm.)

14th and 15th Arrondissements

Montparnasse

The 14th and 15th arrondissements are located to the South and South-East of the only major eye sore central Paris possesses – the massive **Tour Montparnasse**, a steel and plate glass monstrosity built by American architects in 1973, which looks as if it would be more at home in downtown New York than Paris. Still, the lesson was learnt and only one such building disfigures central Paris; in its wake the wise decision was made that a whole area should be set aside for modern, hi-rise and hi-tech development. Thus La Défense, the new banking and business quarter in the east of Paris, was born.

From the end of the 19th century Montparnasse was known for its night-life and as the meeting place of artists and intellectuals in the Belle Epoque and the 1920s. Modigliani, Kandinsky, Picasso, Klee, Matisse, Chagall, Rouault, Miller and Hemingway frequented the bars and cafés of Montparnasse. Balzac lived in Montparnasse for a period, his statue by Rodin stands at the junction of the Boulevard du Montparnasse and the Boulevard Raspail, and Picasso, Gauguin and Whistler rented ateliers in the 14th arrondissement.

The Cimetière Montparnasse is an overgrown and neglected part of Montparnasse but here, at 3, blvd Edgar Quinet, are buried many distinguished writers and artists, including Baudelaire, Maupassant, Beckett, Sartre and de Beauvoir (in a shared grave), Saint-Saens and Man Ray, amongst others. (Open Mon–Fri 7.30 am–6 pm, Sat 8.30 am–6 pm; Sun 9 am–6 pm. METRO: Edgar Quinet.)

The Catacombs

Another curiosity of the 14th arrondissement connected with the dead is Les Catacombs at 1, place Denfert-Rochereau. Originally excavated to provide building stone for the city, the quarries were converted into catacombs because of overcrowding in Parisian cemeteries. During the Paris Commune of 1871 fleeing 'Communards' took refuge in the passageways until hunted down and shot; during the Second World War the passages came into their own again, giving the Resistance the perfect hiding place. (Open Tues–Fri 2–4 pm, Sat–Sun 9–11 am and 2–4 pm. METRO: *Denfert-Rochereau*.) **Parc Montsouris** makes a pleasant change from the dark and gloomy passageways of the Catacombs. Arboretum and park, Montsouris is planted with hundreds of rare and unusual trees, both native and foreign to France. The park also has a delightful artifical lake, home to myriads of duck and geese, and a 'jardin anglais', which seeks to imitate the informality and naturalness of an English garden.

Rive Droite (The Right Bank)

1st Arrondissement
The Louvre

The Palais du Louvre is not only one of the greatest art galleries in the world but for a long time was a magnificent royal palace. In 1527 François I, dissatisfied with the medieval palace originally built by King Philippe Auguste, announced his intention of rebuilding it in the new style of the Renaissance and commissioned Lescot, the leading architect of the day, to design it. The oldest part of the Louvre is Lescot's Square Court which was begun in 1546, a building of ornamental beauty which represents an early example of French classicism. Further work on the Square Court was initiated by Lemercier and continued by Le Vau in the 1650s. In the 1660s Colbert did his utmost to persuade Louis XIV not to desert Paris for Versailles, devoting his energies to completing the Louvre in the hope that it would remain the king's principal royal palace. Louis XIV however increasingly lost interest in the Louvre as his involvement with his new palace at Versailles increased. Work continued however until 1670, the Colonnade of the eastern front being completed under the direction of Le Vau, Le Brun and Perrault. With the departure of the court for Versailles, work was discontinued and the building fell slowly into disrepair until Louis XV commissioned Gabriel to renovate the building in 1754. The building was turned into a museum during the Revolution and Napoleon added the **Arc de Triomphe du Carrousel** to commemorate his victories of 1805.

The main entrance is now through a glass **pyramid** in the middle of the courtyard, the Cour Napoléon. The subject of intense controversy as to its aesthetic merits and appropriateness for its setting, the pyramid was designed by the architect I. M. Pei. The evacuation of the Ministry of Finance from the northern wing of the Louvre to make further room for exhibits has turned the

Louvre into the largest museum in the world. The western wing of the palace, the Tuileries, was demolished in 1871 after being burnt out during the Paris Commune.

Recently reorganised, the Louvre contains magnificent and extensive collections, including the royal collections formerly belonging to the kings of France, as well as thousands of works of art looted from royal and aristocratic collections throughout Europe by French troops during the Napoleonic wars.

Famous above all for paintings, the Louvre contains a vast collection of objects exhibited in miles of rooms and galleries. With over 400,000 works, weeks would be required to see everything, even briefly. Naturally the Louvre is particularly rich in French paintings and Old Masters, especially in works by Poussin, Claude Lorrain, Georges de la Tour, Louis le Nain, Chardin, Watteau, Boucher, David, Gros, Ingres, Géricault and Delacroix.

French paintings range from the Portrait de Jean le Bon, executed around 1360, to Delacroix, Corot and Courbet (later 19th-century French paintings being in the Musée d'Orsay and Centre Georges Pompidou.) Amongst foreign artists there are extensive collections of Rembrandt, Memling, Van Dyck, and Rubens (including his series on the life of Marie de Médicis once in the Palais du Luxembourg); Zurbarán, Ribera and Murillo; Cranach the Elder and Holbein the Younger. Italian paintings are very well represented, especially those by Cimabue, Giotto, Simone Martini, Fra Angelico, Paolo Uccello, Sandro Botticelli, Tintoretto, Raphael, Mantegna, Perugino, Veronese, Titian, Francesco Guardi, Giovanni Battista Tiepolo, and Domenico Tiepolo. Leonardo da Vinci's *Mona Lisa* was bought by François I and is supposed to represent Mona Lisa di Gherardini, the young wife of a Florentine doctor. The two other paintings by Leonardo da Vinci in the Louvre include the *Madonna and Child with St-Anne* and the *Virgin of the Rocks*.

Apart from paintings there are also magnificent Greek, Roman and Etruscan collections of sculptures, friezes, mosaics, monumental vases, bronzes, jewellery, arms, figurines and utensils. Foremost amongst them are the *Winged Victory* or Nike of Samothrace, a Greek masterpiece from the 3rd or 2nd century BC, the *Vénus de Milo* from the 2nd century BC and fragments of the frieze of the Parthenon.

The Egyptology collection has a number of outstanding sculptures, of which the most remarkable are a colossal granite Sphinx, probably from the Old Empire and the *Scribe accroupi*, a small limestone figure of a scribe sitting cross-legged which dates back 3 millennia. There are countless other funeral steles, effigies, statuettes and rooms devoted to household objects such as mirrors, scarabs and jewellery.

Among the Oriental antiquities are the *Codex of Hammurabi*, a block of basalt with inscriptions dating from 1800 BC, and the *Moabite Stone* (842 BC), Samarian and other Babylonian antiquities, including reliefs from the palace of Darius.

Objets d'art include rooms devoted to medieval and Renaissance goldsmiths' work, ivories, enamels, bronzes, medals and ceramics. There are also tapestries and furniture, largely of the 18th century, by such crafstmen as Charles-André Boule, Cressent, Cramer, Riesener and the Jacob family. The famous diamond, Le

Régent, and the crown jewels are displayed in the Galerie Apollon on the 1st floor of the Petite Gallerie. Amongst the collections of Romanesque, Gothic and Renaissance sculpture are Michelangelo's Slaves.
(Open Mon and Wed 9 am–10 pm; Thurs–Sun. 9 am–6 pm; tours in English Wed–Sat every 30 mins 10–11.30 am and 2–3.30 pm, departing from *Accueil Groupes* area. Automatic ticket dispensors. METRO: Louvre or Palais-Royal.)

Jardin des Tuileries

The gardens of the Tuileries, originally laid out beside the Seine for Catherine de Médicis in 1564, extend from the western edge of the Louvre to the Place de la Concorde. From the elevated terrace running along beside the Seine, there are superb views over the river to the Left Bank. In 1649 Le Nôtre, the architect of the gardens at Versailles, redesigned them on a formal pattern with long vistas, geometrical hedges and flower beds and pollarded trees, which were then made open to the public. At the same time as the gardens were laid out for Catherine de Médicis a palace was built for her which enclosed the vast Louvre complex to the east and looked out over the Jardin des Tuileries to the west. After the Revolution the Louvre was turned into a museum but the Palais des Tuileries remained the royal residence until Napoleon III, the last French monarch, was forced out in 1870. During the violent fighting of the Paris Commune, the palace was blown up by the Communards in a symbolic move. Today, peaceful and beautiful, ornamented with two large circular ponds, fountains and statues, the Jardin des Tuileries extends as far as the Jeu de Paume, the Orangerie and the place de la Concorde. Along the northern edge of the gardens runs the Rue de Rivoli, lined with early 19th-century buildings fronted by elegant arcades. (Gardens open daily 7 am–10 pm April – Sept; 7 am–8 pm Oct – Mar. METRO: Tuileries or Concorde.)

Musée du Jeu de Paume One of the 2 buildings in the Jardin des Tuileries overlooking the Place de la Concorde, the Musée du Jeu de Paume was originally constructed by Napoleon III as a court on which to play 'jeu de paume', a forerunner of today's game of tennis. Converted into an art exhibition hall, it used to house Impressionist paintings which have now been transferred to the Musée d'Orsay. Since 1991 the Jeu de Paume has been a gallery of contemporary art. (Open Tues noon–9.30 pm; Wed–Fri noon-7 pm; Sat–Sun 10 am–7 pm. METRO: Concorde.)

Musée de l'orangerie The Musée de l'Orangerie is the other small building in the Jardin des Tuileries overlooking the Place de la Concorde, in the corner close to the Seine. This small and delightful building has a small collection of Impressionist paintings by Cézanne, Matisse, Renoir, and Picasso but the main focus is on the 2 huge compositions by Monet, entitled *Nymphéas* (Water Lilies), inspired by his water garden at Giverny between Paris and Rouen. (Open Wed–Mon 9.45 am–5.15 pm. METRO: Concorde.)

Place Vendôme

North of the Rue de Rivoli and the Tuileries gardens the Rue de Castiglione runs north to the magnificent Place Vendôme, begun in 1687 by Jules Hardouin-

Mansart with backing from Louis xiv and 5 wealthy financiers. Funds ran out and the uniform mansions stayed empty until 1720. Originally the centre of the square was occupied by a 21-foot-high statue of Louis xiv in Roman costume. This was destroyed during the Revolution and replaced by the present column, completed in 1810 in the style of Trajan's column in Rome. Cast from 1,250 Austrian and Russian bronze columns captured by French soldiers during the Napoleonic campaigns, the column was toppled during the 1871 Commune at the instigation of the radical artist Gustave Courbet. Outside the entrance to the Ministry of Justice at number 13 is 'the metre', which was taken as the official standard unit of measurement, all other metres having to conform to this one.

Palais Royal

Further east, across Rue de Rivoli from the Louvre is the Palais Royal. The palace was constructed for Cardinal Richelieu in 1634–9. Originally known as the Palais Cardinal, Richelieu bequeathed the building to Louis xiii and it became a royal palace when Anne of Austria, regent for Louis xiv, moved there. Designed by J. Lemercier, it was modified during succeeding centuries, Louis-Philippe d'Orléans building and renting out the ground floor that encloses the palace's formal garden as a commercial enterprise. During the Revolution the Palais Royal was the scene of much revolutionary activity and early clashes with royal cavalry in the Palais Royal gardens. In the 9th century, the arcades regained their reputation as a focus for luxury goods which they still maintain while the floors above the arcades are occupied by government offices. Today the restful gardens and arcades are a delightful backwater but they have recently been partly disfigured by the tasteless addition of truncated columns. At the south-western corner of the Palais Royal, facing the Louvre, the Comédie Française occupies an elegant theatre built in 1790 by the architect Victor Louis.

Les Halles

Further east from the Palais Royal is the large open space known as Les Halles, the site of a huge food market described by Victor Hugo as 'le ventre de Paris' (Paris's stomach). In the 19th century a huge iron and glass pavilion was built on the site which became a feature of central Paris, busy day and night with market stalls. In the 1970s, the market was moved to a site outside Paris at Rungis and the pavilions demolished to make way for a subterranean shopping mall, the **Forum des Halles**, designed by Claude Vasconi and Georges Penreach, which has nothing to recommend it, except for some desultory gardens above. To the north lies the circular **Stock Exchange** building dominated by a slim fluted 16th-century tower. Beyond it lies **St-Eustache**, the large Gothic-Renaissance church begun in 1532 and consecrated in 1632. Its neo-Classical façade was only finished in 1754 and is curiously out of step with the rest of the building. The organ is one of the best in Paris and organ concerts are held in the church during June and July. (Metro: Les Halles/Châtelet-Les Halles.)

2nd Arrondissement

Two galleries near the Palais Royal, the **Galerie Vivienne** and **Galerie Colbert**, are the finest examples of 19th-century Parisian arcades, with their cafés, restaurants and smart boutiques. In the Rue de Richelieu, the **Bibliothèque Nationale**, is France's foremost library with a collection of some 15 million books. Since 1642 the Bibliothèque Nationale has been a copyright library, receiving a copy of every book published in France. The nearby **Cabinet des Médailles et des Antiques**, at 58, rue de Richelieu, contains numerous objects from the royal collections including the throne of the medieval king Dagobert, Greek and Etruscan jewellery and items confiscated from the houses of the aristocracy during the course of the Revolution. (Open 1–5 pm.) North-east from the Bibliothèque Nationale is the Place de la Bourse, number 4 housing the Bourse, or French stock exchange. Founded in 1724, the present building dates from 1808. (Open 11 am–1 pm for guided tours only. METRO: Bourse.)

3rd and 4th Arrondissements: The Marais

The 3rd and 4th arrondissements have been called Le Marais (the swamp) since the early Middle Ages, when the area was still undrained and unsuitable for building. Cut in two by Rue St-Antoine, which follows the route of a Roman road, the Marais extends from the **Hôtel de Ville** to the **Bastille** and from the banks of the Seine north to Boulevard Beaumarchais. Extensively restored in the 1970s the Marais is a veritable treasure trove of 17th-century French domestic architecture.

In medieval times the marshy land of the Marais was occupied by a few religious orders and settlement extended only very slowly from the banks of the Seine towards the Hôtel Saint-Paul, a former royal residence which has long been demolished. Jews were prevented from living within the city by Philippe-Auguste and the Marais became established as Jewish quarter of Paris from the 13th century. The area around Rue des Rosiers and Rue des Ecouffes is still the heart of a thriving Jewish community. The area witnessed a major transformation at the beginning of the 17th century when Henri IV established the Place Royale, now the Place des Vosges. Suddenly the area became the fashionable district of Paris and nobles bought land, building elegant mansions sheltered from the street by walls and with spacious internal courtyards in front and gardens behind. Throughout the 17th century the Marais was the most fashionable residential district of Paris, until supplanted by the Faubourg St-Germain in the early 18th century.

Place des Vosges

The most beautiful part of the Marais, the Place des Vosges is a spacious square surrounded by 39 handsome houses of red brick with stone facings built on a uniform plan over arcades on the ground floor. It stands on the site of a residence of the Duke of Bedford and in 1559 was the scene of the fatal tournament in which Henri II was accidentally killed by Montgomery. Place des Vosges is one of the oldest public squares in Paris after Henri IV specified that the buildings lining it were to be built 'according to the same symmetry'. The arcaded, 2-storey brick houses with their steep slate roofs today face a delightful shady garden enclosed by delicate wrought-iron railings. Madame de Sévigné was born at number 1 bis, Cardinal Richelieu lived at number 21, Victor Hugo lived at number 6 and Mozart played a concert here on his tour of Europe at the age of 7. Even when the nobility moved to the Faubourg St-Germain, writers in particular continued to live in the area, notably Victor Hugo, the romantic poet Théophile Gautier and Alphonse Daudet. An excellent little museum devoted to Victor Hugo, housing letters and daily objects belonging to the writer, is to be found in his old house at number 6.

The southern half of the Marais, with its narrow streets, between rue St-Antoine and the Seine, reveals the medieval layout of the first part of the Marais to be built upon.

Hôtel de Sens

The Hôtel de Sens, at 1, rue du Figuier, was built in the late 15th century for Tristan de Salazar, the archbishop of Sens; the building is notable for its military features, the turrets at the corners serving as observation posts while the square tower in the corner of the internal courtyard was built as a dungeon. It now contains the Forney library. At the eastern end of the quai is the **Hôtel Fieubet**, designed by Hardouin-Mansart in the 17th century. In the neighbouring streets are some very old **houses**, those in Rue François-Miron being half-timbered while the 17th-century **Hôtel de Beauvais** was built by Antoine le Pautre.

At the junction of Rue de Jouy and Rue Nonains-d'Hyères is a plain building designed by Louis Le Vau in 1648 and subsequently altered by François Mansart. The central street of the Marais, Rue St-Antoine, is flanked by the **Temple Sainte-Marie**, also by François Mansart, the church of **Saint-Paul–Saint-Louis** and a number of interesting *hôtels*. The **Hôtel de Sully**, at number 62, extends up to the Place des Vosges and dates from 1634; it now houses the office of the Caisse des Monuments Historiques. The Rue des Francs-Bourgeois and the Quartier Carnavalet is one of the most fascinating parts of the Marais.

Hôtel Lamoignon

At the junction of the Rue des Francs-Bourgeois and the Rue Pavée is the Hôtel Lamoignon, one of the oldest and most beautiful houses in the Marais. Built in 1584 for Diane de France, daughter of Henri II, it now houses the historic library of the city of Paris, the Bibliothèque Historique de Paris (Open Mon–Sat 9.30 am–6 pm.) The impressive façade, with its two-storey Corinthian columns, is an early example in Paris of the 'colossal' style of decoration. Charles de Valois added the left-hand wing.

Hôtel Carnavalet

The nearby street, Rue de Sévigné, contains the Hôtel Carnavalet, a 16th-century Renaissance mansion enlarged and decorated in the 17th century by François Mansart. The architect Lescot was the architect of the Hôtel Carnavalet, the only example of a Paris house which survives from the middle of the century. Once occupied by the Marquise de Sévigné, it now houses the Musée Historique de la

Ville de Paris which traces the history of the city from prehistory to the present day. The statues and bas-reliefs ornamenting the Hôtel are by Antoine Coysevox and Jean Goujon and in the centre of the courtyard is a statue of Louis XIV which once stood before the Hôtel de Ville. (Open Tues–Sun 10 am–5.45 pm. METRO: Rivoli or Carnavalet.) Further down the street, at number 26, is another superb building, the Hôtel de Peletier, built in 1686. Other fine 17th-century mansions line the short Rue du Parc-Royal and the Rue Vieille-du-Temple to the west of the Hôtel Carnavalet. A short distance north of the Hôtel Carnavalet, in the Hôtel Salé, is the Musée Picasso, 5 rue de Thorigny, with a large collection of Picasso's less famous works which are grouped chronologically tracing his artistic development. (Open Thurs–Mon 9.15 am–5.15 pm, Wed 9.15 am–10 pm. METRO: Chemin Vert.)

Hôtel Soubise

The Hôtel Soubise, at 58 rue des Archives (and 60 rue des Francs-Bourgeois), is a fine example of 18th-century aristocratic architecture. Built between 1705 and 1709, the Hôtel Soubise has superb contemporary interior decoration. Its gateway is all that survives of a medieval mansion built in 1380, the angle of the entrance designed to allow the easy access of carriages from the narrow street. Entered through 60 rue des Francs-Bourgeois, the Hôtel Soubise houses the Musée de l'histoire de France, with a large collection of highly important French historical documents, which include a letter written by Jeanne d'Arc, the wills of Napoleon and Louis XIV, Louis XVI's diary, the Declaration of the Rights of Man and the Edict of Nantes. (Open Wed–Mon 1.45–5.45 pm. METRO: Hôtel de Ville or Rambuteau.)

Another important *hôtel particulier* is the Hôtel de Rohan, at 87 rue Vieille-du-Temple, which was built between 1705–8 for the Bishop of Strasbourg. It was saved from destruction by Napoleon who made it the site of the Imperial printing press. Above the former stables in the courtyard is a magnificent relief of the horses of the sun by Robert le Lorrain. The interior of the palace, which is richly decorated, is now used for temporary exhibitions.

At the eastern extremity of the Marais is the Place de la Bastille, the site of the former fortress prison demolished by the Revolutionary mob after falling into their hands on 14th July 1789.

Hôtel de Ville

The Hôtel de Ville, Paris's city hall, faces a large square ornamented with fountains just off the Rue de Rivoli. The Hôtel de Ville has been the centre of Paris government since the 14th century but the present building is a replica of the original one designed by Boccadoro in 1533. During the Paris Commune of 1871 the elaborate Renaissance Hôtel de Ville was torched and burnt out. The square facing it, the Place de l'Hôtel de Ville, has been the scene of political protest throughout French history and was once used for executions. (Open Mon–Sat 9 am–6pm; guided tours only, in French, from Information office, at 29 rue de Rivoli.) Towards the Seine stands the isolated Tour St-Jacques, a flamboyant

Gothic tower which is all that remains of the 16th-century Eglise St-Jacques-la-Boucherie which was destroyed in 1802.

Centre Georges Pompidou

Now nearly 20 years old, the Centre National d'Art et de Culture, or Palais Beaubourg unleashed great controversy when first proposed and built. The huge square glass and metal building contrasts strongly with its surroundings and the nearby church of Saint-Merri. The old houses around have been renovated and the area is thronged with cafés, art galleries and restaurants. The architectural solution chosen for the small square in the Marais by architects Richard Rogers and Renzo Piano was to turn the proposed building inside out, placing all the piping and ventilation ducts on the outside, thus freeing up the interior for uncluttered exhibition space. Colour-coded for effect and practicality, blue tubes conduct air, green conduct water, yellow conduct electricity and red conduct heat vertically and horizontally on the outside of the building. Advanced for its time, the thousands of exterior pipes are now somewhat dusty and grimy, providing the ideal nesting spot for thousands of birds. More popular than the Louvre, Versailles or the Eiffel tower, the Pompidou Centre is a focus for visitors and Parisians alike. The main feature of the multi-purpose building is the **Musée National d'Art Moderne**, which is home to a superb collection of 20th-century art. Entrance to the museum, on the 4th floor, leads to superb collections of paintings by Matisse, Picasso, Derain, Magritte, Braque and Kandinsky, amongst others. More contemporary works, executed after 1960, are located on the lower level. (Open Mon and Wed–Fri noon–10 pm, Sat–Sun 10 am–10 pm. METRO: Rambuteau, Hôtel de Ville or Châtelet-Les Halles.)

Apart from its excellent collection of modern paintings, the Centre Pompidou also contains an excellent public **library**, the **Centre de Création Industrielle**, devoted to the study of the relationships between humanity, architecture and technology, and an institute for musical research. From the restaurant and café on the fifth floor there are excellent views looking out over the Marais, to Notre-Dame and the Seine. Outside, the square in front of the Centre Pompidou has become the focus for actors, musicians, pick-pockets, buskers, mime- and street-artists.

8th Arrondissement

The Champs-Elysées and Arc de Triomphe

One of the grandest and most elegant districts of Paris, the 8th arrondissement is home to the Palais de l'Elysée, the official residence of the French President, around which crowd embassies and luxurious *haute couture* shops. Leading from the Place de la Concorde to the Arc de Triomphe, the Avenue des Champs-Elysées cuts through the 8th arrondissement, flanked by smart cafés and luxury shops. Le Nôtre laid out avenues of trees in the 17th century as part of the plans of the Palais des Tuileries but it was only during the Second Empire that the area acquired its fashionable reputation. Running dead straight for two kilometres, part of it is now lined with modern blocks and the majority only dates to the 19th century.

Arc de Triomphe

At the western end of the Champs-Elysées, the Arc de Triomphe dominates Place Charles-de-Gaulle, or the Etoile as it's called by Parisians with its 12 radiating avenues. Underneath this gargantuan construction is the Tomb of the Unknown Soldier of the 1914–18 war. Commissioned by Napoleon as a memorial to his victories, work began on the arch in 1806 but was not finished until 1836. Designed by Chalgrin, the arch is decorated with some interesting sculptures, the most impressive being that facing the Champs-Elysées by Rude, known as the *Départ des volontaires en 1792*. Above the groups commemorating France's victories is a frieze by Rude.

Close to the bottom of the Champs-Elysées, the **Petit Palais** and the Grand Palais, both utilising the possibilities of glass and steel, are examples of late 19th-centuries architectural taste. The **Musée du Petit-Palais**, 8 av. Winston Churchill, possesses beautiful and varied collections, mostly devoted to French 19th-century painters, especially Ingres, Géricault, Courbet, Bonnard, Vuillard and Renoir. There are also a number of sculptures from the same period plus temporary exhibitions. (Open Tues–Sun 10 am–5:30 pm.) The **Grand Palais** is now used for temporary exhibitions only. Just south-west of it the **Pont Alexandre III** crosses to the Invalides.

Place de la Concorde

The Place de la Concorde lies at the eastern extremity of the Champs-Elysées, covering a huge space next to the Jardin des Tuileries. The elegant square, now somewhat dominated by traffic, was designed by Jacques-Ange Gabriel during the reign of Louis XV. On the side of the square which leads into the Champs-Elysées stands a group of statues by Coustou of the Chevaux de Marly; other fine statues of Renommée and Mercure by Coysevox stand on the opposite side at the entrance to the Tuileries gardens. The square, originally dedicated to Louis XV, was renamed Place de la Révolution in 1789. In its centre a guillotine was set up on which 1300 people met their ends, including Louis XVI (on 21st January 1793), Marie-Antoinette, Philippe-Egalité, Danton, Charlotte Corday, Lavoisier and Robespierre. Severed heads rolled into baskets before being held up to the eager crowds who invariably attended such spectacles. The square was renamed Place de la Concorde after the end of the Terror. In the centre of the square now stands the granite *Obélisque de Louqsor*, inscribed with the deeds of Ramses II and dating from the 13th century BC, which once stood at Thebes in Upper Egypt. The rose-coloured obelisk, towering 21 metres above 2 large 19th-century fountains, was a gift of Mehèmet Ali, Viceroy of Egypt, to Charles X in 1829.

The Madeleine

North of the Place de la Concorde, at the end of the rue Royale, stands the classical building known as the Madeleine, built in 1764 at the instigation of Louis XV and modelled on a Greek temple. Construction of the building, originally intended as a church, was halted during the Revolution and in 1806 Napoleon instructed that it should be opened as a Temple of Glory. Converted back into a church in 1842, it is an impressive building, its exterior graced by 52 large Corinthian columns while the interior is lit by four ceiling domes rather than by windows. (Open daily 8 am–6.15 pm.)

Chapelle Expiatoire

Place Louis XVI, on Rue Pasquier close to Boulevard Haussmann, contains the Chapelle Expiatoire where victims of the guillotine were buried. Louis XVI and Marie-Antoinette were later taken to Saint-Denis in 1815, but the remains of Charlotte Corday and Philippe-Egalité (Louis XVI's cousin who voted for the king's death and was later beheaded himself) are still buried in the chapel. The chapel still contains the statues of Louis XVI and Marie-Antoinette, their crowns lying on the ground at their feet. (Open daily April–Sept 10 am–6 pm; Oct and Feb–Mar 10 am–5 pm; Nov–Jan 10 am–4 pm.)

9th Arrondissement: L'Opéra

At the end of the Avenue de l'Opéra stands the majestic **Opera** building built in 1862–75 by Charles Garnier and until recently the home of the National Academy of Music and Dance. Commissioned by Napoleon III, the Opéra is the largest theatre in the world, elaborately decorated inside and out, a symbol of 19th-century bourgeois social life. The sculpted group on the right of the main façade is the famous *Groupe de la Danse* by Paul Belmondo, a copy of the original by Carpeaux. The interior is equally fabulously decorated with a magnificent ceiling by Chagall, gilded mosaics and Gobelin tapestries. The magnificent 6-ton chandelier fell on to the audience in 1896. With the opening of the new Bastille opera house in 1989, the old opera house has been used almost solely for ballet performances. (Open for guided tours: Mon–Sat 10 am–4.30 pm; for performances, Tel. 47 42 53 71, pm only.)

From the Place de l'Opéra wide boulevards lead towards the east to 2 17th-century triumphal arches erected to the glory of Louis XIV and his armies: the **Porte St-Denis** and the **Porte St-Martin**. Almost adjacent to the Opéra is the Café de la Paix, a stylish café, thronged with crowds from the Opera house. To the north, bordering the 18th arrondissement, is Pigalle, home to cabaret and the Moulin Rouge, but now a dangerous place for women to walk around alone at night.

18th Arrondissement: Montmartre and Sacré-Coeur

High above the city of Paris stands **Montmartre**, a very lively and distinctive quarter which still retains something of a village atmosphere, dominated by the unusual silhouette of **Sacré-Coeur**. On this hill St-Denis was decapitated by the Romans in 272. According to legend St-Denis and 2 other martyrs picked up their severed heads and walked north to where the Eglise St-Denis still stands. The name of their place of execution, Montmartre, 'the hill of the martyrs', has remained unchanged since the 3rd century. Around the place of their martyrdom a Merovingian sanctuary was built which was later turned into an abbey of which the 12th-century church of St-Pierre-de-Montmartre still stands to the west of Sacre Coeur.

Until as recently as the 19th century Montmartre was still an agricultural area, with vines growing on the south-facing slopes. Even today a few small vinyards are still tended on the steep hillsides. Of the windmills that once took advantage of the high windswept position only 2 remain of which the most famous are the Moulin Rouge and Moulin de la Galette.

In the 19th and early 20th centuries, Montmartre was full of artists: Renoir, Suzanne Valadon, Utrillo, Emile Bernard, Gauguin, Dufy, Pulbot and Toulouse-Lautrec lived in the area. Parts of Montmartre still have a bohemian feel, and many of the old haunts and cafés which gave it its reputation are remarkably unchanged.

The Rue des Saules leads from the end of Rue Ravignan to Rue Cortot, where the **Musée de Montmartre** evokes the history of the area. (Open Tues–Sat 2.30–6 pm; Sun 11 am–6 pm.) Rue des Saules also leads to the remaining Montmartre vineyards, the grapes of which are usually harvested around the first weekend in October. At the corner of Rue des Saules and Rue St-Vincent is the *Lapin Agile* cabaret which became popular in the period leading up to the First World War when it was one of the favourite haunts frequented by the artists of Montmartre.

Sacré-Coeur Right at the top of the hill of Montmartre stands the Basilique du Sacré-Coeur, one of the most extraordinary buildings in Paris, its white onion-shaped domes visible from all over the city. An eclectic mixture of neo-Roman-esque and Byzantine styles, the basilica was begun in 1876 and consecrated in 1919. A climb to the top of its 91 metres bell tower affords wonderful views south over Montmartre and Paris. (Open daily 9 am–7 pm. METRO: **Anvers, Abbesses** or **Château-Rouge**.)

Behind the basilica is the Place du Tertre, a focal point for tourists, around which spread the narrow, winding streets of Montmartre with their shops, galleries and little cafés and restaurants. One of the most attractive areas is the area west of Place du Tertre, especially the little streets, Rue des Abbesses, Rue des Trois Frères and Rue Lepic, with their cafés and boulangeries. Cobblestone roads give glimpses of houses and delightful gardens partly hidden behind walls and wrought-iron gates. The *Moulin Rouge*, on Boulevard Rochechouart, immortalised by the paintings of Toulouse-Lautrec, does not look its best by day but springs to life by night.

Practicalities in Paris

Where to Stay

Due to the many international fairs which take place in Paris from September to December and from February to May, it is wise to book your hotel room in advance during these months. Surprisingly it is often easier to find a room in Paris during July and August than at other times of year. Hotels listed are chosen for their convenience, moderate price and comfort.

There are many budget hotels in the centre of Paris and some of these have been listed. Do not expect large spacious rooms, however; rooms in the cheaper hotels in the centre will be perfectly clean, and sometimes very attractive, but do not expect to have space and comfort and a view if paying budget prices. The vast majority of the hotels listed in the Paris section are 1, 2 or 3-star hotels.

Hôtels The Left Bank
5th Arrondissement: The Latin Quarter
☆ *Hôtel Dhély's*, 22 rue de l'Hirondelle (Tel. 43 26 58 25); simple little hotel tucked down a tiny street close to the animated place St-Michel.

☆ *Hôtel d'Esmeralda*, 4 rue St-Julien le Pauvre (Tel. 43 54 19 20). METRO: St-Michel. Simple, unpretentious rooms, in tiny side-street next to the English language bookshop Shakespeare and Co, 1 minute's walk from Notre-Dame.

☆☆ *Hôtel des Carmes*, 5 rue des Carmes, off Blvd St-Germain (Tel. 43 29 78 40). METRO: Maubert-Mutualité. Quiet street and clean, attractive rooms.

Hôtel de Médicis, 214 rue St-Jacques (Tel. 43 29 53 64). METRO: Luxembourg. Very cheap but the rooms are clean, if basic.

☆☆ *Hôtel Sorbonne*, 6 rue Victor-Cousin (Tel. 43 54 58 08). METRO: Luxembourg; a beautiful 18th-century building adjacent to the Sorbonne. No restaurant.

☆☆☆ *Hôtel des Grandes Ecoles*, 75 rue Cardinal Lemoine (Tel. 43 26 79 23). METRO: Cardinal Lemoine. A delightful ivy-clad hotel with spotless rooms and enchanting peaceful garden.

☆☆☆ *Grand Hôtel du Progrès*, 50 rue Gay Lussac (Tel. 43 54 53 19). METRO: Luxembourg. Clean, spacious and light rooms, some looking out over the rooftops to the Panthéon.

☆☆☆ *Collège de France*, 7 rue Thénard, 5ème (Tel. 43 26 78 36); delightful quiet hotel with simply decorated rooms in the heart of the Latin quarter. METRO: Maubert-Mutualité.

6th Arrondissement: St-Germain-des-Prés
☆ *Hôtel Nesle*, 7 rue Nesle, off Rue Dauphine (Tel. 43 54 47 02). METRO: Odéon. Clean, attractive and welcoming hotel with unusual decoration, in the heart of St-Germain.

☆☆ *Hôtel St-Michel*, 17 rue Gît-le-Coeur, near place St-Michel, very close to the Seine (Tel. 43 26 98 70). METRO: St-Michel. Friendly, clean and comfortable.

☆ *Hôtel Stella*, 41 rue Monsieur le Prince (Tel. 43 26 43 49). METRO: Odéon or Luxembourg. Pleasant, cool, clean bedrooms.

7th Arrondissement: The Eiffel Tower
☆ *Hôtel de la Paix*, 19 rue du Gros Caillou, off Rue de Grenelle (Tel. 45 51 86 17). METRO: Ecole Militaire. Somewhat faded and worn interior but one of the few 'cheap' hotels in the 7th.

☆☆ *Hôtel Kensington*, 79 ave de la Bourdonnais (Tel. 47 05 74 00). METRO: Ecole Militaire; tiny but lovely, clean rooms, with superb views out over the Eiffel Tower from top floors.

☆☆ *Hôtel Muguet*, 11 rue Chevert, off ave de Tourville (Tel. 47 05 05 93). METRO: Ecole Militaire or Latour-Maubourg. Spacious, clean and comfortable.

☆☆☆ *Hôtel Pavillon*, 54 rue St-Dominique (Tel. 45 51 42 87). METRO: Latour-Maubourg; peaceful oasis in converted convent with enchanting courtyard for breakfast. Rooms tastefully decorated, some a little small.

☆☆ *Hôtel Solférino*, 91 rue de Lille (Tel. 47 05 85 54). METRO: Châtelet or Hôtel de Ville. A superb location opposite the Musée d'Orsay, attractive with nice, spacious and comfortable rooms.

14th Arrondissement: Montparnasse
☆ *Hôtel Plaisance*, 53 rue Gergovie, off Rue Raymond Losserand (Tel. 45 42 11 39). METRO: Pernety. Basic and functional, but cheap and in quiet street.

☆☆ *Hôtel Midi*, 4 ave René-Coty (Tel. 43 27 23 25). METRO: Denfert-Rochereau; unattractive reception lobby but good, spacious, quiet rooms.

☆☆ *Hôtel du Parc*, 6 rue Jolivet (Tel. 43 20 95 54). METRO: Montparnasse-Bienvenue. Large and modern, comfortable and clean.

☆☆ *Hôtel du Midi*, 4 ave René-Coty (Tel. 43 27 23 25). METRO: Denfert-Rochereau. Large hotel with clean rooms, all with their own bathroom.

☆☆ *Hôtel de Blois*, 5 rue des Plantes, off Rue Sablière (Tel. 45 40 99 48). METRO: Mouton-Duvernet. Friendly proprietress, a comfortable and attractive hotel.

☆☆ *Hôtel Ariane Montparnasse*, 35 rue Sablière (Tel. 45 45 67 13). Comfortable and spacious accommodation in handsome hotel.

The Right Bank
1st Arrondissement
☆☆ *Hôtel de Lille*, 8 rue du Pélican, off Rue Croix des Petits Champs (Tel. 42 33 33 42). METRO: Palais Royal. Slightly shabby but clean, simple rooms right in the heart of Paris, close to the Louvre.

☆ *Hôtel Lion d'Or*, 5 rue de la Sourdière (Tel. 42 60 79 04). METRO: Tuileries or Pyramides. A little worn but clean.

☆☆ *Hôtel de Rouen*, 42 rue Croix des Petits Champs, off Rue St Honoré (Tel. 42 61 38 21). METRO: Louvre or Palais Royal. Newly renovated, clean and pleasant.

☆☆ *Hôtel du Palais*, 2 quai de la Mégisserie (Tel. 42 61 38 21). METRO: Châtelet. Beside the Seine, at corner of Place de Châtelet, with views over Ile de la Cité. Clean and comfortable rooms.

☆☆ *Hôtel St-Honoré*, 85 rue St-Honoré, off Rue du Louvre (Tel. 42 36 20 38). METRO: Louvre or Châtelet-Les Halles. Recently renovated, pleasant, friendly and popular.

☆☆ *Hôtel Family*, 35 rue Cambon, 1er (Tel. 42 61 54 84). METRO: Madeleine; small family hotel near the Madeleine and close walk away from the Tuileries garden.

☆☆ *Hôtel Ducs d'Anjou*, 1 rue Ste-Opportune (Tel. 42 36 92 34). METRO: Châtelet. Superb comfort in an attractive hotel in an excellent location.

☆☆☆ *Hôtel Montpensier*, 12 rue de Richelieu (Tel. 42 96 28 50). METRO: Palais Royal; handsome and comfortable 17th-century *hôtel particulier*, lovely rooms and excellent location close to Palais Royal.

☆☆☆☆ *Hôtels Ducs de Bourgogne*, 19 rue du Pont Neuf (Tel. 42 33 95 64). METRO: Pont-Neuf. Delightful, comfortable rooms in handsome hotel in superb location next to the Pont Neuf.

2nd Arrondissement

Not many sights are to be found in the 2nd arrondissement but it is within easy walking distance of the Marais, the Louvre, the Palais Royal and the Ile de la Cité. There are many small and pleasant but cheap hotels but the area also has a few unattractive streets, such as the Rue St-Denis, a centre of prostitution, which are better avoided.

Hôtel Tiquetonne, 6 rue Tiquetonne, near junction of Rue St-Denis and Rue de Turbigo (Tel. 42 36 94 58). Fairly basic but clean and cheap. METRO: Etienne-Marcel.

☆ *Hôtel Sainte-Marie*, 6 rue de la Ville Neuve, simple but pleasant and clean (Tel. 42 33 21 61). METRO: Bonne Nouvelle.

☆ *Hôtel La Marmotte*, 6 rue Léopold Bellan (Tel. 40 26 26 51). METRO: Sentier. Clean, friendly and comfortable.

☆☆ *Hôtel Choiseul-Opéra*, 1 rue Daunou (Tel. 42 61 70 41). METRO: Opéra; imposing façade hides simple, clean rooms.

☆☆ *Hôtel Bonne Nouvelle*, 17 rue Beauregard (Tel. 40 08 42 42). METRO: Strasbourg-St-Denis or Bonne Nouvelle. Clean rooms, with bath or shower.

☆☆ *Hôtel Chénier*, 1 rue Chénier (Tel. 42 33 92 32). METRO: Strasbourg-St-Denis. Clean, bright and recently renovated.

☆☆☆ *Hôtel Vivienne*, 40 rue Vivienne (Tel. 42 33 13 26). METRO: Bourse, Richelieu-Drouot or Montmartre. Friendly, comfortable and smart.

3rd and 4th Arrondissements: The Marais

☆ *Grand Hôtel des Arts et Métiers*, 4 rue Borda, 3ème (Tel. 48 87 77 00). METRO: Arts et Métiers. Central location, slightly worn.

☆ *Hôtel Andréa*, 3 rue St-Bon, 4ème (Tel. 42 78 43 93). METRO: Châtelet or Hôtel de Ville. Clean, bright rooms; simple and comfortable.

☆ *Hôtel Sévigné*, 2 rue Malher, 4ème (Tel. 42 72 76 17). METRO: St-Paul-le-Marais; clean, simple rooms, lovely breakfast room, and excellent location close to Place des Vosges.

☆☆ *Hôtel Bretagne*, 87 rue des Archives (Tel. 48 87 83 14). METRO: République or Temples.

Clean and pleasant little hotel off Rue des Archives.

☆☆ *Hôtel Picard*, 26 rue de Picardie, off Rue de Franche-Comté (Tel. 48 87 53 82). METRO: République or Filles du Calvaire. Friendly, charming and clean; popular with American students.

☆☆ *Hôtel Henri IV*, 25 place Dauphine, on Ile de la Cité (Tel. 43 54 44 53). METRO: Cité. One of the few cheap hotels left on the Ile de la Cité.

☆☆ *Grand Hôtel du Loiret*, 8 rue des Mauvais Garçons, 4ème (Tel. 48 87 84 09). METRO: Bastille or St Paul. Simple hotel with unexceptional, clean rooms close to the Hôtel de Ville.

☆☆ *Hôtel de Nice*, 42 bis, rue de Rivoli, 4ème (Tel. 42 78 55 29). METRO: Hôtel de Ville. Pleasant room in good location, clean and attractive.

☆☆ *Place des Vosges*, 12 rue Birague, 4ème (Tel. 42 72 60 46). METRO: St-Paul-le-Marais. Pleasant little hotel, just off the historic Place des Vosges, in the heart of the Marais.

☆☆☆ *Hôtel Vieux Marais*, 8 rue du Plâtre, 4ème (Tel. 42 78 47 22). METRO: Temple. Comfort and style in this attractive 16th-century *hôtel particulier* in the heart of the Marais.

☆☆☆ *Hôtel St-Louis-Marais*, 1 rue Charles V (Tel. 48 87 87 04). METRO: Sully-Morland; lovely rooms, each decorated differently in 17th-century mansion between the Marais and the Seine.

☆☆☆ *Hôtel St-Merry*, 78 rue de la Verrerie (Tel. 42 78 14 15). METRO: Châlet or Hôtel de Ville. A tiny hotel in the former presbytery of Eglise St Merri. Small but luxurious hotel in superb location.

9th Arrondissement

☆☆ *Hôtel London Palace*, 32 blvd des Italiens (Tel. 48 24 54 64). METRO: Opéra; excellent location close to the Opéra; simple, functional rooms.

11th Arrondissment: The Bastille

East of the Marais, and the site of the new Opera house, the 11th arrondissement offers some reasonably-priced accommodation not too far from the sights of interest. Hotels here may still have vacancies when other areas are booked solid.

☆ *Résidence Alhambra*, 13 rue de Malte (Tel. 47 00 35 52). METRO: Oberkampf; pleasant pastel-coloured rooms if a little small; comfortable, homely lobby with big leather armchairs.

☆ *Hôtel Baudin*, 113 ave Ledru-Rollin (Tel. 47 00 18 91). METRO: Ledru-Rollin. Large, clean rooms not far from the Bastille.

☆☆ *Hôtel de Vienne*, 43 rue de Malte (Tel. 48

05 44 42). METRO: Oberkampf or République. Peaceful, clean and comfortable.
☆☆ *Hôtel Rhetia*, 3 rue du Gén. Blaise, not far from Bastille (Tel. 47 00 47 18). METRO: St-Ambroise or St-Maur. Attractive, bright rooms overlooking park, and not far from the Bastille.

18th Arrondissement: Montmartre
☆ *Timhotel Montmartre*, 11 rue Ravignan (Tel. 42 55 74 79). METRO: Abbesses. Cheap, functional rooms but lovely location in leafy square in heart of Montmartre.
☆☆ *Hôtel Régyn Montmartre*, 18 place des Abbesses (Tel. 42 54 45 21). METRO: Abbesses. Small but lovely rooms, some with wonderful views over Paris.
☆☆ *Hôtel Utrillo*, 7 rue Aristide Briant (Tel. 42 58 13 44). METRO: Blanche. Delightful, renovated hotel in quiet street at foot of Montmartre.

Youth Hostels and Foyers

For the vast majority of youth hostels and *foyers* for young people in Paris there is no need to have HI membership and in the two HI youth hostels one night membership can be bought for 19FF.

Foyers are mainly dormitory residences during the academic year which rent out places during the holidays. Others are for young people working or training away from home. It is advisable to arrive or telephone early in the morning to check out availability of places; alternatively, visit or call the *Accueil des Jeunes en France* (AJF).

Accueil des Jeunes en France (AJF) The main office of this non-profit-making organisation is at 119 rue St-Martin, 5ème, close to the Pompidou Centre. (Open Mon–Sat 9.30 am–6 pm; Tel. 42 77 87 80; METRO: Rambuteau.) Other offices are at 139 blvd. St-Michel in the 5th arrondissement (open Tues–Sat. 10 am–12.30 pm and 1.30–6.15 pm; Tel. 43 54 95 86; METRO: Port Royal) and at the Gare du Nord in the 10th arrondissement (open 1st June–4th Sept only; 10.30 am–10 pm; Tel. 42 85 86 19). Even in mid-summer the AJF guarantees you decent and low-cost accommodation with immediate reservations for the same day only. You have to pay the full price of the *foyer* room when you make your reservation, even before seeing the room. It does however mean that you can always be sure of finding somewhere to stay.

Fédération Unie des Auberges de Jeunesse (FUAJ), the Headquarters of Hostelling International (HI) in France. Offices within their own hostel at 8 blvd Jules Ferry (Tel. 43 57 02 60). Membership possible, also organises sightseeing trips. They have 2 main hostels in central Paris:
(1) *Auberge de Jeunesse Jules Ferry* (HI), 8 blvd Jules Ferry, 11ème, near Place de la République

(Tel. 43 57 55 60). METRO: République or Porte de Bagnolet. 400 beds, large clean rooms in excellent location, 4-day maximum stay. Reception open 6 am–2 am; most spaces taken by 9 am. 72FF per person, breakfast and showers included. Sheets: 15FF.
(2) *Auberge de Jeunesse Le d'Artagnan* (HI), 80 rue Vitruve, 20ème (Tel. 43 61 08 75). METRO: Porte de Bagnolet. Vast 7-floor hostel, with 400 beds, 3–8 beds per room. 3–day maximum stay. Reception closed noon-2pm; rooms closed 10 am–2:30 pm. 82FF, sheets extra. Call or arrive early.

Maisons des Jeunes Rufz de l'Avison, 18 rue Jean-Jacques Rousseau, 1er (Tel. 45 08 02 10). METRO: Louvre or Palais Royal. Excellent location off Rue St-Honoré; university residence with places only available during holidays. 3-day minimum stay. Reception open 7 am–7 pm. 95FF per person, shower and breakfast included. Doubles, triples and quads. Arrive early.

Centre International de Paris (BYJ), run a series of very comfortable youth hostels: all except Paris Louvre have singles, all open 6am–2pm; rooms available from 2:30pm. 100FF per person, including breakfast and showers:
Paris Louvre, 20 rue Jean-Jacques Rousseau, 1er (Tel. 42 36 88 18). METRO: Louvre. 200 places in large dormitory-style accommodation.
Paris Opéra, 11 rue Thérèse, 1er (Tel. 42 60 77 23). METRO: Pyramides; excellent hostel with larger rooms and fewer beds than at Paris Louvre.
Paris Les Halles, 5 rue du Pélican (Tel. 40 26 92 45). METRO: Palais Royal. Rather small rooms with less good facilities than the others.
Paris Quartier Latin, 44 rue des Bernardins, 5ème (Tel. 43 29 34 80). METRO: Maubert-Mutualité. BVJ hostel with 140 spacious modern rooms. 100FF per person for doubles, triples or quads; 110FF for singles, breakfast and showers included. No reservations, arrive early, around 8 am.

Hôtel des Jeunes hostels (MIJE)
Le Fauconnier, 11 rue du Fauconnier (Tel. 42 74 23 45). METRO: St-Paul.
Le Fourcy, 6 rue de Fourcy (Tel. 42 74 23 45). METRO: St-Paul or Pont-Marie.
Maubisson, 12 rue des Barres (Tel. 42 72 72 09). METRO: Hôtel de Ville or Pont Marie.

All these hostels are located in elegant old aristocratic mansions in the Marais district of the 4th arrondissement. All are close to the sights of the Marais and to each other. Open to 18–30 year olds, maximum stay 7 days; no reservations; lock-out noon–4 pm. 105FF per person, including breakfast and showers.

Young and Happy Hostel, 80 rue Mouffetard, 5ème (Tel. 43 29 34 80). METRO:

Censier-Daubenton. Clean rooms in the heart of the student quarter. Lockout 11 am–5 pm. 2–4 beds per room. 85FF, shower included. Reservations accepted with deposit. Foyer International des Etudiants 93 blvd St-Michel, 6ème (Tel. 43 54 49 63). METRO: Luxembourg. A stone's-throw from the Jardin du Luxembourg. Superb facilities and prime location. July–Sept, men and women for minimum of 5 days; Oct–June women only for long stays. Reception open Sun–Fri 6 am–1.30 am, Sat all night. Singles 140FF, doubles 95FF per person; showers and breakfast included. Reserve 2 months ahead. Arrive early to check for cancellations. Centre International du Séjour de Paris hostels (CISP) Ravel, 6 ave Maurice Ravel, 12ème (Tel. 43 43 19 01). METRO: Porte de Vincennes. Primarily for groups, 2–4 beds per room. Reception open 6.30 am–1.30 am, singles 135FF, doubles–5 bed rooms 116FF, other dorms 93FF, breakfast included. Bar, restaurant, access to swimming pool. Another at 17 blvd Kellermann (Tel. 45 80 70 76). METRO: Porte d'Italie.

Women-only hostels 234 rue de Tolbiac, 13ème (Tel. 45 89 06 42). METRO: Tolbiac, short stays only July–Aug.; rest of year 1 month minimum stay. UCJF (Union Chrétienne de Jeunes Filles) 22 rue Naples, 8ème (Tel. 45 22 23 49). METRO: Europe or Villiers. For women aged 18–24 for 3-day minimum stay between June and Sept; rest of year for women 18–24, long stay only, with half-pension. 30FF membership fee and 100FF processing fee mandatory for all. Singles 105FF, doubles 85FF per person. Also *Foyer International des Etudiants* (details above).

Others
CIS Léo Lagrange, 107 rue Martre Clichy (Tel. 42 70 03 22). METRO: Marie de Clichy. *Maison des Clubs* UNESCO, 43 rue de la Glacière, 13ème (Tel. 43 36 00 63). METRO: Glacière. *Foyer International d'Accueil de Paris*, 30 rue Cabanis (Tel. 45 89 89 15). METRO: Glacière. *Hôtel Ste-Marguerite*, 10 rue Trousseau, 11ème (Tel. 47 00 62 00) METRO: Ledru Rollin. 250 small beds, in rooms of 2–6 beds. 90FF per person. Arrive early or reserve through FUAJ, the Fédération Unie des Auberges de Frances, the HQ of Hostelling International (HI) in France at 8 bd. Jules Ferry, 11ème. (Tel. 43 57 02 60).

Useful addresses of hostelling organisations
Union des Centres de Rencontres Internationales de France (UCRIF), 4 Jean-Jacques Rousseau, near their hostel (Tel. 42 60 42 40). *Fédération Unie des Auberges de Jeunesse* (FUAJ), the Headquarters of Hostelling International (HI) in France: 8 blvd Jules Ferry (Tel. 43 57 02 60).

Camping
Camping outside Paris is an alternative to finding hostel accommodation in central Paris but campsites are extremely crowded in summer. There is also the disadvantage and cost of travelling into the centre and back each day. Detailed information on campsites from *Camping Club International de France*, 14 rue Bourdonnais, 1er (Tel. 42 36 12 40). METRO: Châtelet-Les Halles or from tourist office at 127 Ave des Champs-Elysées, 8ème (Tel. 47 23 61 72). METRO: Charles de Gaulle-Etoile. *Camping du Bois de Boulogne*, allée du Bord de l'Eau (Tel. 45 24 30 00). METRO: Porte Maillot, then bus 244. Around 40FF, per person and tent, arrive early in summer. *Camping du Tremblay* (TCF), blvd des Alliés, 945 Champigny-sur-Marne (Tel. 43 97 43 97); RER line A2 (direction Boissy-St-Léger) from Gare d'Austerlitz to Joinville-Le-Pont station (10 mins), then bus 108N to campsite on riverbank. Around 30FF, per person and tent.

Restaurants and Food
Eating is one of the great pleasures of being in Paris. Most Parisians eat out every day as a matter of course, usually at lunchtime which is when menus are cheaper. Even though Parisians will quickly abandon a restaurant not up to their standards, not every Parisian restaurant offers gastronomic delights. Most restaurants offer at least 2 types of menu: à la carte and fixed price. The fixed-price menu (known as *le menu*) will always offer the best value and will usually consist of between 3 and 6 or 7 courses depending on the price. Eating à la carte offers you the choice of anything on the menu and is usually quite a bit more expensive. An invaluable number that can be called for information on all restaurants in Paris (as well as to book tables) is 43 59 12 12.

The Left Bank
5th Arrondissement: The Latin Quarter
Perraudin, 157 rue St-Jacques, 5ème (Tel. 46 33 15 75). METRO: Luxembourg. Good little family-run restaurant serving timeless dishes. Arrive early. *L'Apostrophe*, 34 rue de la Montagne Ste Geneviève, 5ème (Tel. 43 25 14 77). METRO: Maubert-Mutualité. Tiny premises

on street below the Panthéon. Good simply fare.

☆ *Saumoneraie*, 6 rue Descartes, 5ème (Tel. 46 34 08 76). METRO: Cardinal-Lemoine; excellent fixed-price menu offering superb salmon specialities in delightfully cool stone bistro.

☆☆ *Vagénande*, 142 blvd St-Germain (Tel. 43 26 68 18). METRO: St-Germain-des-Prés; classic *Belle Epoque*-style, busy and popular, delicious classic French cuisine.

☆☆ *Chez Toutoune*, 5 rue de Pontoise, 5ème (Tel. 43 26 56 81). METRO: Maubert-Mutualité. Classic bourgeois cooking, slightly heavy for some, but hearty, tasty and filling.

☆☆ *Au Pactole*, 44 blvd St-Germain (Tel. 43 26 92 28). METRO: Maubert-Mutualité. Successful combination of nouvelle and traditional cuisine; bold orange and yellow designed interior.

☆☆☆ *Auberge des Deux Signes*, 46 rue Galande (Tel. 43 25 46 56). METRO: St-Michel. Excellent traditional cuisine, in 13th-century chapel opposite Notre-Dame.

6th Arrondissement: St-Germain-des-Prés

Restaurant des Beaux Arts, 11 rue Bonaparte, opposite the Ecole des Beaux Arts (Tel. 43 26 92 64). METRO: St-Germain-des-Prés. Well-cooked traditional dishes, such as *lapin à la moutarde* and *entrecôte Bordelaise* make this popular with locals.

Orestias, 4 rue Grégoire de Tours, 6ème (Tel. 43 54 62 01). METRO: Odéon. Good hearty dishes, simple but very cheap.

☆ *Bistro de la Gare*, 59 blvd Montparnasse, 6ème (Tel. 45 48 38 01). METRO: Montparnasse-Bienvenue. Worth the detour for the outstanding Art Nouveau décor and magnificent stained-glass window.

☆ *Polidor*, 41 rue Monsieur-le-Prince, 6ème (Tel. 43 26 95 34). METRO: Odéon. Classic old bistro, with indoor and outdoor eating in the heart of St-Germain. Straightforward simple dishes.

☆ *Petit St-Benoît*, 4 rue St-Benoît, 6ème (No reservations). METRO: St-Germain-des-Prés. Simple but good fare, always lively and crowded, with diners sharing tables.

☆☆ *Echaudé St-Germain*, 21 rue de l'Echaudé, 6ème (Tel. 46 33 62 09) METRO: St-Germain-des-Prés. Delightful little restaurant serving good classic French fare and good-value set menus.

☆☆ *Le Petit Zinc*, 11 rue St-Benoît, 6ème (Tel. 46 33 51 66). METRO: St-Germain-des-Prés. Superb seafood and excellent intimate atmosphere crowded with diners and bustling waiters. Reservation essential.

☆☆ *Le Muniche*, 22 rue Guillaume-Apollinaire, 6ème (Tel. 46 33 62 09). METRO: St-Germain-des-Prés. Traiditional St-Germain brasserie, classic French cuisine, excellent seafood, good

fixed-price menus. Open till late. Reservation advised.

☆☆☆ *Chez Papa*, 3 rue St-Benoît, 6ème (Tel. 42 86 99 63). METRO: St-Germain-des-Prés. A streak above the other St-Germain restaurants, *Chez Papa* offers a stylish interior, and light versions of classic French dishes. Reservation advised.

7th Arrondissement: The Eiffel Tower

Au Babylone, 13 rue de Babylone (Tel. 45 48 72 13). METRO: Sèvres-Babylone. Classic French quartier restaurant, serving good standard dishes.

La Pie Gourmande, 30 rue de Bourgogne. METRO: Varenne. A wide range of delicious pancakes (crêpes) make this an excellent lunch-stop.

☆ *Fontaine de Mars*, 129 rue St-Dominique, 7ème (Tel. 47 05 46 44). METRO: Ecole Militaire. Unobstrusive family-run restaurant in the chic Eiffel Tower area. Good value lunch-time menu, eating outside beside fountain in summer.

☆ *Thoumieux*, 79 rue St-Dominique, 7ème (Tel. 47 05 49 75). METRO: Latour-Maubourg. Delicious Périgourdin dishes, notably duck, in this classic 1920s-style restaurant close to the Eiffel Tower.

☆☆ *La Petite Chaise*, 36 rue de Grenelle, 7ème (Tel. 42 22 13 35). METRO: Rue du Bac. A classic unchanged neighbourhood restaurant, catering to local residents. Simple, good value dishes, especially seafood crêpes.

13th Arrondissement

☆ *Chez Grand-Mère*, 92 rue Broca, 13ème (Tel. 47 07 13 65). METRO: Gobelins. Classic home cooking of rabbit and duck in thick rich sauces; intriguing décor evoking the youth of 'grand-mère'.

14th and 15th Arrondissements: South Paris and Montparnasse

☆ *Le Jeroboam* 72 rue Didot (Tel. 45 39 39 13). METRO: Plaisance. Delicious cooking at excellent prices. Mouthwatering dishes include fish stew prepared with marinated lemons and olives.

☆ *Le Berbère*, 53 rue Gergovie. METRO: Pernety. Above-average Moroccan restaurant offering good range of couscous dishes.

☆☆ *Bistrot d'André*, 232 rue St-Charles, 15ème (Tel. 45 57 89 14). METRO: Balard. Classic bistro evoking life in pre-war Paris, next to the old Citroën factory. Snails, *boeuf bourguignon* and *confit de canard* are among the best dishes.

☆☆ *Au Boeuf Gros Sel*, 299 rue Lecourbe, 15ème (Tel. 45 57 36 53). METRO: Lourmel. Specialising in salt beef dishes; traditional cooking and simple décor.

☆☆☆ *Aux Senteurs de Provence*, 295 rue

Lecourbe, 15ème (Tel. 45 57 11 98). METRO:
Lourmel. Superb Provençal specialities, evoking
the cusine and flavour of the south of France.

The Right Bank
1st Arrondissement: The Louvre and Châtelet-Les Halles

La Trappiste, 3 rue St-Denis, 1er (Tel. 42 21 37
96) METRO: Châtelet. A little north of place du
Châtelet. Quick French dishes, such as *moules
frites*, washed down with one of over 200
international beers. Tables on pavement and 1st
floor.
Au Petit Ramoneur, 74 rue St-Denis, 1er.
METRO: Les Halles. Hearty, cheap food.
Situated on the edge of the red-light district.
☆ *Willi's*, 13 rue des Petits Champs (Tel. 42 61
05 09). METRO: Bourse. Delicate, light food
accompanies excellent wines chosen by British
wine expert, Mark Williamson.
☆ *L'Epi d'Or*, 25 rue Jean-Jacques Rousseau
(Tel. 42 36 38 12) METRO: Les Halles.
Excellent service, elegant interior and fine
cooking, notably superb steaks.
☆☆ *Chez Paul*, 15 place Dauphine (Tel. 43 54
21 48). METRO: Pont Neuf. Fine traditional
cooking, including calf's brains in shallot sauce,
in superb location on the Ile de la Cité.
Reservation advised.
☆☆ *Louis XIV*, 1 bis pl. des Victoires, 1er (Tel.
40 26 20 81). METRO: Sentier. Superb location
on Place des Victoires; traditional décor and
beautifully prepared and cooked dishes.
Reservations advised for lunch.
☆☆☆ *L'Escargot Montorgueil*, 38 rue
Montorgueil, 1er (Tel. 42 36 83 51). METRO:
Etienne-Marcel. One of the best restaurants in
Paris but affordable at lunchtime with fixed-
price menu. One of the best places to try snails.
Reservations advised in evening.
2nd Arrondissement: Around the Bibliothèque Nationale
Ma Normandie, 11 rue Rameau (Tel. 42 96 87
17). Metro: Pyramides, close to the Bibliothèque
Nationale. Crowded and animated restaurant,
an excellent lunchtime stop. *Crémerie Louvois*,
5 rue Louvois. METRO: Quatre-Septembre.
Simple food, quick service and rock-bottom
prices. Closed in August.
☆ *Au Petit Coin de la Bourse*, 16 rue Feydeau,
2ème (Tel. 45 08 00 08). METRO: Bourse.
Unusually much cheaper in the evening than at
midday. Attractive 1920s interior and
traditional French cuisine.
3rd and 4th Arrondissements: the Marais
Trumilou, 84 quai de l'Hôtel de Ville, 4ème
(Tel. 42 77 63 98). METRO: Pont Marie. Bright
and animated little bistro opposite the Ile St-
Louis. Earthy, friendly atmosphere and good,
classic, fare.

L'Arbre aux Sabots, 3 rue Simon Leclerc, 4ème.
METRO: Rambuteau. Artistic clientèle; close to
the Pompidou Centre. Open till late.
☆ *Grizzli*, 7 rue St-Martin, 4ème (Tel. 48 87 77
56). METRO: Châtelet. Excellent Pyrenean
dishes from Bernard Arény. Reservations
advised.
☆☆ *Coconnas*, 2 bis place des Vosges, 4ème
(Tel. 42 78 58 15). METRO: St-Paul-Le Marais.
Enchanting Italian interior and choice of
nouvelle cuisine or classic French dishes. Very
popular, reservation essential.
☆ *Jo Goldenberg*, 7 rue des Rosiers, 4ème (Tel.
48 87 20 16). METRO: St-Germain-des-Prés.
Atmospheric restaurant in heart of Jewish
quarter of the Marais, specialising in Jewish,
Hungarian and Russian dishes.
☆☆ *Brasserie Bofinger*, 3 rue de la Bastille,
4ème (Tel. 42 72 87 82). METRO: Bastille. One
of the oldest brasseries in Paris, with dark
atmospheric interior and black-jacketed, white-
aproned waiters. Good brasserie fare, especially
seafood and sausages with sauerkraut.
Reservations advised.
☆☆ *La Colombe*, 4 rue de la Colombe, 4ème
(Tel. 46 33 37 08). METRO: Cité. Delightful
location beside Seine close to Notre-Dame.
Good value, traditional cuisine with some
lighter touches; shady terrace with tables for
summer eating.
9th Arrondissement: Between the Opera and Montmartre
Le Chartier, 7 rue du Faubourg Montmartre,
9ème (Tel. 47 70 86 29). METRO: Rue
Montmartre. Simple, tasty classic French fare at
prices difficult to beat.
Le Pupillin, 19 rue Notre Dame de Lorette,
9ème (Tel. 42 85 45 06). METRO: St Georges.
Simple bistro between Montmartre and the
centre. Good snacks at the bar or dining-room
upstairs with good value set menu.
Casa Miguel, 48 rue St-Georges, 9ème (Tel. 42
81 09 61). METRO: St-Georges. Marxist
principles apply in this eclectic restaurant: you
pay according to your means. Lively exotic
clientele makes up for the unexciting food.
☆ *Taverne Kronenbourg*, 24 blvd des Italiens
(Tel. 47 70 16 64). METRO: Richelieu-Drouot.
Excellent Alsatian dishes and convivial,
animated atmosphere.
☆ *Le Paradis*, 21 rue de Douai, 9ème (Tel. 42
82 08 79). METRO: Pigalle. Classic French
quartier restaurant with traditional checked
tablecloths and movie theme.
11th Arrondissement: the Bastille
Occitanie, 96 rue Oberkampf (Tel. 48 06 46 98).
METRO: St-Maur. Specialising in dishes from
southern France. Very good value.
Au Trou Normand, 9 rue Jean-Pierre
Normand. METRO: Oberkampf. Very good

straighforward cooking at low prices. Closed in August.

☆ *Mansouria*, 11 rue Faidherbe (Tel. 43 71 00 16). METRO: Faidherbe-Chaligny. Excellent Moroccan dishes, especially the spicy Moroccan stews known as *tagines*. Reservations required.

18th Arrondissement: Montmartre

La Villa des Poulbots, 10 rue Dancourt. METRO: Anvers. Elegant interior and a wide range of delicious menus offering such delicacies as *magret de canard*.

Au Grain de Folie, 24 rue la Vienville (Tel. 42 58 15 57). METRO: Abbesses. Vegetarian restaurant with huge range of salads, couscous and cheeses. Choice of set menus.

☆ *Le Refuge des Fondues*, 19 rue des Trois Frères (Tel. 42 55 22 65). METRO: Abbesses. A superb range of meat and cheese fondues at affordable prices.

☆ *Le Maquis*, 69 rue Caulaincourt, 18ème (Tel. 42 59 76 07). METRO: Lamarck-Caulaincourt. Small but excellent little restaurant; traditional dishes served by chef Claude Lesage. Very good value at lunchtime. Reservations advised.

☆☆ *De Graziano*, 83 rue Lepic, 18ème (Tel. 46 06 84 77). METRO: Blanche. Italian specialities beside one of the last windmills of Montmartre. Excellent cooking and inexpensive lunchtime set menu.

☆☆☆ *L'Assommoir*, 12 rue Girardon, 18ème (Tel. 42 64 55 01). METRO: Lamarck-Caulaincourt. Outstanding cuisine from chef Philippe Laure in delightful little bistro down quiet side-street of Montmartre. Exquisite fish dishes.

Cafés, Brasseries and Wine Bars

Paris would simply not be the same without its cafés and brasseries. They are the places to rest and enjoy an excellent coffee, iced drink or beer and watch life go by. Cafés, brasseries and bistros all offer simple, tasty meals which can be ordered at any time of day. Bistros are normally small and usually cheap with a limited selection of dishes available. Brasseries are much larger affairs, often with huge menus and are usually animated and busy. Some of the most famous are magnificently decorated in Belle Epoque style with long zinc bars, huge mirrors and exotic tiles walls or floors. *Bofinger* near the Bastille, *Le Dôme*, *Le Sélect* and *La Coupole* in Montparnasse and *Brasserie Lipp* on Boulevard St-Germain are among the most famous examples. Many brasseries were established in the nineteenth-century by Alsatians and still have an Alsatian character, serving excellent Alsatian wines, and sausage and sauerkraut dishes. Others specialise in seafood and are instantly recognisable from the magnificent displays of fresh oysters, mussels and crabs stacked up on ice in the street. Many stay open late into, the night, making them a useful destination after an evening's nightclubbing or visit to the theatre.

Cafés on the other hand open early and tend to close around 9 pm unless catering primarily to tourists. Snacks, such as salads and sandwiches, can be ordered at any time and many cafés will also offer a few hot dishes at lunch time. The speciality of the day (*le plat du jour*) is often the best one to opt for. One of the most delicious little snacks is *chèvre chaud* – lightly grilled goats cheeses served on toast with a light salad. The smartest and most famous cafés, such as *Les Deux Magots* and *Café Costes* serve food until late at night, and some until 3 in the morning.

A café is the best place for breakfast, allowing one to watch Paris come to life. Parisians often drop in to cafés on their way to work for a quick black coffee (*un café* or simply *un noir*) at the bar, usually drunk standing at the bar. Breakfast might consist of a small white coffee (*un petit crème*), a large white coffee (*un grand crème*) and a fresh croissant or *un pain au chocolat*, similar to a croissant but filled with chocolate.

Wine bars are usually small intimate places, frequented loyally by people in the neighbourhood. They often have a simple and inexpensive lunch menu and serve wine by the glass and will be crowded by one o'clock. They are excellent places to try out and get to know French wines; the patrons are enthusiastic and knowledgeable and usually have good stocks of very carefully selected wines. Snacks, often delicious, are served throughout the day until around 9 pm.

Paris has two different places for drinking beer: pubs, which are simply for drinking, and beer bars which have a wide range of imported beers and are much larger. They often serve simple but classic French or Belgian dishes, such as *moules frites* (a huge bowl of mussels and chips), *tarte aux poireaux* (leek tart) or *tarte aux oignons* (onion tart). Salons de thé open either for breakfast or mid-morning and stay open until early evening, offering excellent coffees, hot chocolate and teas, and a wide selection of mouthwatering pastries. *Angélina* on the Rue de Rivoli is famous for its hot chocolate.

The Left Bank

5th Arrondissement: The Latin Quarter

Café Mouffetard, 116 rue Mouffetard, an old café in a quaint old street 5 minutes walk south-east of the Panthéon.

Wine bar: *Les Pipos*, 2 rue de l'Ecole

Polytechnique, north of the Pantheon and east of the Sorbonne.

Beer bar: *La Gueuze*, 19 rue Soufflot, an excellent beer bar, specialising in heavy Belgian malted beers, on the street leading from the Jardin du Luxembourg to the Panthéon.

Beer bar: *L'Académie de la Bière*, 88 blvd de Port-Royal. Popular and thriving, the Beer Academy is located on a broad boulevard south of the Jardin du Luxembourg.

Pub: *Finnegan's Wake*, 9 rue des Boulangers, a short walk from Metros Jussieu and Cardinal Lemoine.

Ice-Cream Parlour: *Häagen-Dazs*, 3 place de la Contrescarpe; behind the Panthéon at beginning of rue Mouffetard.

6th Arrondissement: St-Germain-des-Prés

Bar de la Croix Rouge, 2 Carrefour de la Croix Rouge, an excellent place for salads, sandwiches and delicious snacks. 2 mins walk south of blvd St-Germain down rue du Dragon.

Café de Flore, blvd St Germain. A beautiful flower-bedecked café in the most animated and fashionable section of blvd. St-Germain, with striking Art Deco interior, hardly changed since Jean-Paul Sartre and Simone de Beauvoir met over pastis to debate existentialism. Next door to Les Deux Magots. Open until 1.30 am.

Brasserie Lipp, 151 blvd St-Germain. One of the great brasseries of St Germain, all of which are within a few yards of each other. Excellent Alsatian beer, sauerkraut and sausages and some of the best coffee in Paris in a lively tiled interior. A feature of the Left Bank, still popular with politicians, literati and models of the fashion world.

Les Deux Magots, 170 blvd St-Germain. Perhaps the most famous café in the world, les Deux Magots was the favourite meeting place of Hemingway in the 1920's, and Sartre, André Maurois and the French 'Family' of existentialists in the 1950s. Strategically situated at the corner of blvd. St-Germain and rue Bonaparte, it's ideally located for watching the *va et vient* of the Left Bank. Open daily 8 am – 2 am.

Cafés: *Le Rostand*, 6 pl. Edmond Rostand; opposite the Jardin du Luxembourg, halfway up blvd St-Germain.

Le Sélect, 98 blvd du Montparnasse, 6ème, patronised by Lenin, Stravinsky, Picasso and Hemingway amongst others.

La Closerie des Lilas, 171 blvd de Montparnasse. Another Hemingway haunt, a mass of flowers in summer. Open daily 10.30 am – 2 am.

Wine bar: *Bistro des Augustins*, 39 quai des Grands-Augustins. Excellent selection of wines in bar facing the Ile de la Cité, close to Metro St-Michel.

7th Arrondissement: The Eiffel Tower

Wine bar: *Le Sauvignon*, 80 rue des Saints-Pères, 7ème. Atmospheric bar lined with caricatures dedicated to the patron and wines, between Seine and blvd St-Germain. Beaujolais tastings in early November and excellent light dishes to accompany an extensive wine list.

Salon de thé: *Christian Constant*, 26 rue du Bac. Smart modern decor and mouthwatering pastries and chocolates.

14th and 15th Arrondissement: South Paris and Montparnasse

Cafés: *Le Dôme*, 108 blvd du Montparnasse, 14ème. One of the stylish Belle Epoque brasseries of Montparnasse, with long gleaming bar and fast-moving black tail-coated, white-aproned, bar-tenders.

La Rotonde, 105 blvd du Montparnasse, 14ème; a rival to Le Dôme.

Wine bar: *Le Rallye*, 6 rue Daguerre, 14ème.

Salon de thé: Max Poilâne, 29 rue de l'Ouest, 14ème. Poilâne's bread is famous all over Paris.

Café Bar: *Le Coupole*, 102 blvd du Montparnasse, 14ème; stylish 1920's café, with columns decorated by Chagall, Brancusi and others, recently restored to its former glory. Open till 2 am.

The right bank
1st Arrondissement: The Louvre and Châtelet-Les Halles

Wine bar: *La Cloche des Halles*, 28 rue Coquillière, off the rue du Louvre, behind the circular Bourse de Commerce.

Juvenile's, 47 rue de Richelieu, in narrow street leading north from the Louvre and Comédie Française.

Le Bar du Caveau, place Dauphine. Popular lunchtime rendez-vous for elegant Parisians, vast selection of wines available by the glass, accompanied by tasty little dishes, such as grilled goats cheese on toast.

Salon de Thé: *Angélina*, 226 rue de Rivoli; pricey but elegant and famous for its hot chocolate.

Café Costes, 4–6 rue Berger, place des Innocents. Post-modern café designed by Philippe Starck, between Les Halles and the Beaubourg centre. Young, stylish and fashionable clientele.

Pub: *Flann O'Brien*, 6 rue Bailleul, in tiny little street just off the rue de Rivoli where it intersects with the rue du Louvre.

2nd Arrondissement: Around the Bibliothèque Nationale

Café de la Paix, elegant and sophisticated (and pricey) café at the corner of av. de l'Opéra and rue de la Paix, the stamping ground of the rich and famous. Open daily 10 am-1 am.

Salon de thé: *A Priori Thé*, 35–37 Galerie

Vivienne. Delicious teas and snacks in one of the most elegant arcades in Paris. Open Mon–Sat noon–7 pm, Sun 1–6 pm.

Wine bar: *Jeroboam*, 8 rue Monsigny. One of the most expensive and fashionable wine bars in Paris. Delicious tartines and meals to accompany your choice of wine.

3rd and 4th Arrondissements: The Marais

Cafés: *Ma Bourgogne*, 19 place des Vosges; classic Parisian café in the heart of the Marais. Very attractive but pricey due to location.

Café Beaubourg, 100 rue St-Martin, 4ème. Close to the Pompidou Centre.

Brasserie Bofinger, 5–7 rue de la Bastille. The oldest brasserie in Paris with gleaming brass, mirror and stained glass interior. Oysters and seafood platters, Alsatian sauerkraut dishes, simple *plats du jour* accompanied by simple local wines (*vin de pays*) or fine wines (*grands crus*). Open until 2am, last orders at 1am.

Wine bar: *La Tartine*, 24 rue de Rivoli, at eastern end of rue de Rivoli, close to Métro St-Paul.

Beer bar: *Café des Musées*, 49 rue de Turenne, 3ème.

Salon de thé: *Le Loir dans la Théière*, 2 rue des Rosiers, 4ème, just south of the Hôtel de Lamoignan in the Marais. Delicious teas and pastries (*patisseries*). Open noon–11 pm, Sun 11 am–11 pm.

Salon de thé: *Marais Plus*, 20 rue des Francs Bourgeois, 3ème. A delightful, relaxed tea house attached to a bookshop in the picturesque setting of the Marais. Open 10 am–7 pm.

Ile de la Cité and Ile St-Louis

Wine bars: *Au Franc Pinot*, 1 Quai de Bourbon, on the northern side of the Ile St-Louis, facing the Seine.

Taverne Henri IV, 13 pl. du Pont Neuf, 1ème. Strategically located at the western tip of the Ile de la Cité.

Salon de thé: *La Crêpe-en-l'Ille*, 13 rue des Deux-Ponts; on the central north-south axis traversing the Ile St-Louis.

Ice-Cream Parlour: *Maison Berthillon*, 31 rue St Louis-en-l'Ille, for the best ice-cream in Paris.

8th and 9th Arrondissements: Between the Opera and Montmartre

Wine bars: *L'Ecluse*, 64 rue François Ier, 8ème, south of the Champs-Elysées, off rue Pierre Charron.

Ma Bourgogne: 133 blvd. Haussman, stylish wine bar off rue de Miromesnil which runs north from the Elysée Palace.

Le Val d'Or, 28 av. Franklin D Roosevelt. Just off the Champs-Elysées. Huge selection of wines and excellent Beaujolais in November. Open until 9pm, 6pm on Saturday.

Salon de thé: *René St-Ouen's salon de thé*, 111 blvd Haussmann, at the corner of rue d'Argenson. Bread here comes in all forms and shapes, from dogs to the Eiffel Tower.

Café: *Le Grand Café des Capucines*, 4 blvd des Capucines. Delicious cold meats and cheeses served with 'pain Poilâne' or 'pain de campagne.'

10th Arrondissement

Brasserie Flo, 7 Cour des Petites-Ecuries; excellent Alsatian brasserie in slightly down at heel district but superb stained-glass décor and good Alsatian wines and dishes.

11th and 12th Arrondissement: The Bastille

Bar: *Fouquet's Bastille*, 130 rue de Lyon, 12ème. Very close to the new Bastille opera house.

Wine bar: *Jacques Mélac*, 42 rue Léon Frot. Outstanding wine list, the choice of Jacques Melac. Friendly and popular with delicious meals. Open until 7 pm on Mon, Wed and Fri, until 10pm on Tues and Thurs.

Salon de thé: *Thé-Troc*, at the junction of rue de Nemours and rue de Jean-Pierre Timbaud. Idiosyncratic, lively and bohemian. Open Mon–Fri 9 am–noon and 2–8 pm, Sat 10 am–1 pm and 4–8 pm.

Markets

Every 'quartier' of Paris has its own open-air food market, with a vast selection of cheeses, fruit and vegetables, fish and seafood, fresh and smoked meats and sausages, wine, and country-style breads. The quality of the food on offer is quickly apparent and it is considered perfectly normal to ask if you can taste something to see if you like it before you decide to buy any. Among the many food markets, some of the best are those in the Rue de Buci in the 6th arrondissement (open daily), Rue Mouffetard in the 5th (best at the weekend), Rue du Château d'Eau in the 10th (open Tues-Sat) and Rue Lepic in the 18th (best at the weekend).

☆ *Marché aux Puces de St-Ouen*, or flea market. One of the biggest in the world with 6 kilometres of shops selling second-hand goods, junk, antiques and curios, some in covered markets, some piled up in the streets. Every Sat, Sun and Mon, from 8 am to 6 pm. METRO: Porte de Clignancourt.

☆ Antiques and second-hand goods in the open air: *Porte de Montreuil and Porte de Vanves*, weekends from 7 am to 7.30 pm. METRO: Porte de Vanves.

☆ Fabrics and cloth market: the *Saint-Pierre* market at the foot of Montmartre. METRO: Anvers.

☆ *Marché du Temple*, Carreau du Temple,

3ème, Tues – Sun. 9 am–noon; new clothes at wholesale prices. METRO: Hôtel de Ville.

☆ *Marché St-Martin*, 33 rue du Château d'Eau, 10ème; Tues-Sat. 8.30 am–1 pm and 4–7.30 pm, Sun 8 am–1 pm; one of the best of the many excellent covered food markets.

☆*Marché aux fleurs*, place Louis Lépine, Ile de la Cité, 4ème; Mon – Sat 8 am–7 pm; superb colourful flower market. METRO: Cité.

☆ Market for stamps: at the lower end of the Champs-Elysées, at the corner of Avenue Marigny and Avenue Gabriel, on Thursdays, Saturdays and Sundays, from 10 am. METRO: Champs-Elysées-Clémenceau.

☆ Algerian market, rue de la Goutte d'Or; Mon – Sat. Algerian and North African spices and ingredients.

☆ The *Nouveau Drouot* auction rooms. Every day except Sunday, from 1 am to 6 pm. 9 rue Drouot, 9ème (Tel. 48 00 20 20). METRO: Richelieu-Drouot.

☆ *Louvre des Antiquaires*, 2 place du Palais-Royal, 1er, from 11 am–7 pm, except Mondays (Tel 42 97 27 00). METRO: Palais-Royal.

Paris's Airports

Roissy-Charles de Gaulle

Virtually all flights from the United Kingdom and the United States land at Aéroport Roissy-Charles de Gaulle, 22 kilometres north of Paris. Broadly speaking Terminal 2 serves *Air France* (Tel. 43 20 14 55 for general information, 43 20 12 55 for arrivals details, 43 20 13 55 for departures details), while Terminal 1 serves all other airlines. To reach central Paris, the cheapest route is by **Roissy Rail**. A free shuttle bus takes passengers to the **Roissy** train station, from where the RER line B3 heads directly to central Paris, stopping at **Gare du Nord** and **Châtelet-Les Halles**. When buying your ticket to central Paris, specify the metro station that you want to go to. A single ticket will then take you all the way to your destination. Heading from central Paris, take the RER line B3 to **Roissy** and then transfer to the shuttle bus for the 10-minute ride to the terminal building.

RATP also run **buses** from Roissy-Charles de Gaulle to central Paris. Bus 350 leaves for the **Gare du Nord** and **Gare de l'Est** every 15 minutes from 5.30 am to 11 pm; bus 351 leaves for **Place de la Nation** every 30 minutes between 6 am and 8.30 pm. **Taxis** to central Paris take at least 50 minutes and cost approximately 250FF–300FF.

A tourist office at Roissy-Charles de Gaulle can be found near gate 36 arrival level (Tel. 48 62 22 81). Open daily 7 am–11.30 pm.

Paris-Orly

A few planes arrive at Paris Orly airport, 10 miles to the south of Paris. From Orly, the quickest and easiest way to central Paris is on the RER C line. A free shuttle bus leaves every 15 minutes from the airport terminal building to the train station and the journey to central Paris takes 30 minutes. Buses also leave for the Air France terminal at **Les Invalides**, the journey taking between 30 and 60 minutes.

Tourist offices at Paris-Orly airport can be found near gate H at Orly-Sud, and near gate F at Orly-Ouest. Both open 6 am–11.45 pm.

Train Stations

Paris has 6 main stations with lines to the *banlieues* (suburbs) and *grandes lignes* which depart for distant cities in France. Some ticket windows (*guichets*) only issue tickets for the *banlieues*, others only for *grandes lignes*. Make sure you join the right queue. Despite computerisation, and automated ticket machines, queues for tickets sometimes move agonisingly slowly. Allow plenty of time for queuing when buying your ticket or making a reservation.

Gare d'Austerlitz

Trains to the Loire Valley (Blois, Orléans, Saumur), the Midi (Toulouse), Roussillon (Perpignan) and south-western France (Bordeaux, Pyrénées).
Train Information Tel. 45 82 50 50, Mon–Sun, 24 hours a day.
Reservations Tel. 45 65 60 60, Mon–Sun 8 am–7 pm.
Tourist Information Tel. 45 84 91 70, Mon–Sat 8 am–10 pm; Nov–April Mon–Sat 8 am–3 pm.
Post Office Mon–Fri 8 am–7 pm; Sat 8 am–noon.
Currency exchange Mon–Fri 8.30 am–5 pm.
Bar-Brasserie Mon–Sun 6 am–midnight.
Showers 5.30 am–8.30 pm.
Left-luggage lockers accessible up to 0.30 am and after 5.30 am.
Left-luggage office Open 6 am–0.30 am.
Waiting-room and wcS Open up to 0.30 am and after 5.30 am.
Station closed 0.30 am–5.30 am.
Connections with other stations: SNCF bus to most other train station. Metro line 5 (direction Bobigny) to **Gare de l'Est** and **Gare du Nord**. Bus 61 to 65 to **Gare de Lyon**.

Gare du Nord

Trains to northern France (Lille, Amiens), the Channel ports (Calais, Boulogne), Britain (via the Channel Tunnel), Belgium, the Netherlands and N. Germany.
Train information Tel. 45 82 50 50, Mon–Sun, 24 hours a day; office open 6 am–10 pm.
Reservations Tel. 45 65 60 60, Mon–Sun 8 am–7 pm.
Tourist information: Tel. 45 26 94 82, Mon–Sat 8 am–10 pm, Sun 1–8 pm; Nov–Easter daily 8 am–8 pm.
Post office Mon–Fri 8 am–7 pm, Sat 8 am–noon.
Currency exchange Mon–Sat 6.30 am–10 pm.
Bar-Brasserie Mon–Sun 6 am–11 pm.
Restaurant Mon–Sun 11.30 am–2 pm and 6.30 pm–9.45 pm.
Showers 6 am–8.30 pm
Left-luggage lockers Accessible 24 hours a day.
Left-luggage office Open 6 am–midnight.
Waiting-room and WCs Open up to 2 am and from 5.45 am.
Station closed 2 am–5.45 am.
Connections with other stations: SNCF bus to most other train stations. Métro line 5 (direction 'Place d'Italie) to Gare de l'Est, Gare de Lyon (changing at Bastille onto Metro line 1) and Gare d'Austerlitz. Fast alternative to the metro to Gare d'Austerlitz is RER line B to Châtelet-Les Halles, changing there onto RER line A.

Gare de L'Est

Trains to eastern France (Strasbourg, Metz, Nancy, Belfort), to Switzerland, Austria and southern Germany.
Train information Tel. 45 82 50 50, Mon–Sun, 24 hours a day.
Reservations Tel. 45 65 60 60, Mon–Sun 8 am–7 pm.
Tourist information Tel. 46 07 17 73; Mon–Sat 8 am–10 pm; Nov–April Mon–Sat 8 am–1 pm and 5–8 pm.
Currency exchange Mon–Fri 7.30 am–8 pm.
Bar-Brasserie Mon–Sun 7 am–11 pm.
Showers Mon–Sun 6.15 am–10 pm.
Left-luggage lockers Accessible up to 1.15 am and after 5.45 am.
Left-luggage office Open 6 am–midnight.
Waiting-room and WCs Open up to 1.15 am and after 5.45 am.
Station closed 1.15 am–5.45 am.
Connections with other stations: SNCF bus to most other train stations. Metro line 5 (direction Bobigny) to Gare du Nord; line 5 (direction Place d'Italie) to Gare d'Austerlitz.
Bus 65 to Gare de Lyon.

Gare de Lyon

Trains to southern and south-eastern France (Lyon, Chambéry, Chamonix-Mont-Blanc), Provence (Arles, Nîmes), the Riviera (Marseille, Nice, Menton, Cannes); and to Italy and Greece.
Train information Tel. 45 82 50 50, Mon–Sun, 24 hours a day.
Reservations Tel. 45 65 60 60, Mon–Sun 8 am–7 pm.
Tourist information Tel. 43 43 33 24, Mon–Sat 8 am–10 pm; Nov–April Mon–Sat 8 am–1 pm and 5–8 pm.
Post Office Rue Diderot, Mon–Fri 8 am–7 pm, Sat 8 am–noon.
Currency exchange 6.30 am–10 pm.
Bar-Brasserie Mon–Sun 5.45 am–11.30 pm.
Restaurant Ground floor, Mon–Sun 5.45 am–11.30 pm; first floor: 11 am–2 pm and 6 pm–9.15 pm.
Showers Mon–Sun 6 am–8.30 pm.
Left-luggage lockers Accessible up to 1 am and after 4 am.
Left-luggage office Mon–Sun, 24 hours a day.
Waiting-room and WCs Open up to 1 am and after 4 am.
Station closed 1 am–4 pm.
Connections with other stations: SNCF bus to most other train stations. Metro line 1 (direction Grande Arche de la Défense) to Bastille, then change to line 5 (direction Bobigny) for Gare de l'Est and Gare du Nord; or line 5 (direction Place d'Italie) for Gare d'Austerlitz. Another (faster) way of getting to the Gare du Nord is to take RER line A to Châtelet-Les Halles, changing there onto RER line B to Gare du Nord.

Gare St-Lazare

Trains to Le Havre for Portsmouth ferries (2 hours); to Dieppe for Newhaven ferries (2 hours 20 mins); to Caen for Portsmouth ferries (2½–3 hours) and to Cherbourg for ferries to Portsmouth and Southampton (4 hours).
Train information Tel. 45 82 50 50. Mon–Sun, 24 hours a day.
Reservations Tel. 45 65 60 60. Mon–Sun, 8 am–7 pm.
Connections with other stations: Metro line 3 (direction Galliéni) to Réamur-Sebastapol; then line 4 (direction Porte de Clignancourt) for Gare du Nord. Or line 13 (direction Châtillon-Montrouge) to Les Invalides; then RER line C to Gare d'Austerlitz.

Gare Montparnasse

Trains to Britanny (Rennes) and TGVs to Loire Valley (Tours, Nantes) and TGVs to south-western France (Bordeaux, Pau, Lourdes).

Train Information Tel. 45 82 50 50, Mon–Sun, 24 hours a day.
Reservations Tel. 45 65 60 60, Mon–Sun 8 am–7 pm.
Tourist Information Tel. 43 22 19 19, Mon–Sat 8 am–9 pm.

Tourist Information

Paris's main tourist information office: 127 Avenue des Champs-Elysées, (Tel. 49 52 53 54); METRO: Charles de Gaulle-Etoile. Open Mon–Sun 9 am–8 pm; vast quantities of information on Paris and the Ile de France; accommodation service for small fee as usual. Recorded tourist information is available in English on Tel. 49 52 53 56. Branch offices at all train stations except Gare St-Lazare. All tourist offices sell the *Carte Musées et Monuments*, allowing unrestricted access to 65 museums and monuments.

Post Office

Main Post Office and Poste Restante 52 rue du Louvre, 1er (Tel. 40 28 20 00); open 24 hours a day; METRO: Louvre.
American Express Office 11 rue Scribe (Tel. 47 77 77 07); open Mon–Fri 9 am–5.30 pm, Sat 9 am–5 pm; METRO: Opéra.

Embassies

British Embassy 35 rue du Faubourg St-Honoré, 1er (Tel. 42 66 91 42); emergency consulate at 9 ave Hoche (Tel. 42 66 91 42); METRO: Charles de Gaulle-Etoile.
US Embassy 2 ave Gabriel (Tel. 42 96 12 02); open Mon–Fri 9am–6pm; METRO: Concorde.
Australian Embassy: 4 rue Jean Rey (Tel. 45 75 62 00); METRO: Bir-Hakeim.
Canadian Embassy: 35 ave Montaigne (Tel. 47 23 01 01); METRO: Franklin-Roosevelt.

Emergencies

Police: Tel. **17**; **ambulance**: Tel. **15** or 45 67 50 50; **doctor**: Tel. 43 37 77 77; **fire service**: Tel. **18**. Each arrondissement has its own gendarmerie to which non-urgent enquiries should be taken. Get the local number from the operator (Tel. **12**).
   SOS help line: English-speakers able to help with personal problems (Tel. 47 23 80 80).

Hospitals

Hospitals are numerous and give high-quality service. Usually they will treat you irrespective of whether you can pay for their services in advance.
The Hertford British Hospital, 3 rue Barbès, Levallois-Perret (Tel. 47 58 13 12) has a 24 hour emergency service. METRO: Anatole-France.
The American Hospital, 63 blvd. Victor Hugo,

Neuilly. (Tel. 46 41 25 25 or 47 45 71 00) has a 24-hour emergency service.

Chemists

Pharmacie des Champs-Elysées, Galerie des Champs, 84 ave des Champs-Elysées, 8ème (Tel. 45 62 02 41). METRO: George V, open 24 hours a day.
Drugstore St-Germain, 149 blvd St-Germain, 6ème (Tel. 42 22 80 80). METRO: St-Germain-des-Prés. Open until 2 am.
Pharmacie des Arts, 106 blvd Montparnasse, 14ème (Tel. 42 22 80 80). Open until midnight.
Every arrondissement has a *pharmacie de garde* which is either open 24 hours a day or will open in emergencies. The locations change but every local pharmacy will be able to tell you which is the nearest one.

Lost Property

Bureau des Objets Trouvés, 36 rue des Morillons, 15ème (Tel. 45 31 14 80). Metro: Convention. Open Mon–Fri. 8.30 am–5 pm; Sept–June Mon, Wed and Fri 8.30 am–5 pm, Tues and Thurs 8.30 am–8 pm.

English Language Bookshops

W. H. Smith, 248 rue de Rivoli (Tel. 42 60 37 97), has the largest stock in Paris of books in English, closely followed by *Galignani*, nearby at 224 rue de Rivoli, 1er (Tel. 42 60 76 07) and *Brentano's*, 37 ave de l'Opéra, 2ème (Tel. 42 61 52 50). The chaotic and much-loved *Shakespeare and Co*, in rue de la Bûcherie, 5ème, has a changing selection of second-hand books.

Travel Agencies

American Express, 11 rue Scribe, 9ème (Tel. 47 77 70 00). METRO: Auber. No commission on American Express travellers' cheques. Average exchange rates.
Air France, 119 av. des Champs-Elysées, 8ème (Tel. 42 99 23 64).

Exchange Offices

Exchange offices in the main train stations are open usually from 7 am to 8 pm but usually offer poor rates. Better rates are to be had from the banks in central Paris, who usually charge a fixed commission. There is also a 'Change Automatique' at 66 ave des Champs-Elysées, 8ème, which is operational 24 hours a day and will give change for British, US, German, Swiss and Italian banknotes.

Buses

City buses are marked on their sides with the bus number, destination and the names of the major stopping places. Most routes begin operating at 6 am and continue to 8.30 pm, while some continue to midnight. There are a few night buses, most of which originate from Châtelet and lead to various suburbs. The route of every bus is clearly marked on large legible maps to be found in every bus stop. A journey of any length will probably require two tickets; one ticket is valid only for a journey within a single zone. Look at the zones marked on a panel in the bus when you get on to work out if you need to punch (composter) more than one ticket. Failure to punch two tickets if required means an on the spot fine (une amende).

Paris does not have a central bus station but the main bus station for **long-distance and international** buses is the **Gare Routière Internationale**, 3 ave Porte de la Villette, 19ème. (Tel. 40 38 93 93); City Sprint Bus from England stops at the Hoverspeed office near the Gare du Nord at 135 rue Lafayette (METRO: Gare du Nord). Eurolines, the largest Paris-based bus company, have their office at 3 ave de la Porte de la Villette, 19ème. (Tel. 40 38 93 93).

Taxis

Paris taxis do not have the best of reputations. Unfortunately it is largely deserved. In general Parisian taxi drivers will not lift a finger to help you with your luggage, and often seem to take pride in being offhand or downright rude. There is little you can do about this. All cabs have meters and the rate should be 2.80FF per kilometre between 7 am and 7.30 pm and 4.20FF per kilometre thereafter. There is a standard charge of 10FF for all rides and taxi drivers will also charge for every piece of luggage. Cabs are far less numerous than in London and it is extremely difficult to hail a taxi in the street. It is far better to call one from your hotel (or ask your hotel to do so) or make your way to a taxi stand (une station de taxis).

The Metro

The metro is the fastest and easiest way to get around Paris; it is remarkably cheap, especially if tickets are bought in carnets or wadges of ten from the metro ticket office or tabacs (ordinary tobacconists recognisable in the street from their distinctive red double-ended cones). Un carnet costs about 35 FF and a single ticket is valid for a journey of any length. The metro system operates from 5 am to around 1 am. Metro stations are recognisable in the street either from a large yellow 'M' within a circle or from the elegant art nouveau wrought-iron railings inscribed with the full title: Métropolitain.

Lines are designated both by number and by the name of the last station on the line. Metro tickets are also valid on the buses, but two tickets are required if you travel into a second zone.

Late at night the metro is no safer than other underground systems in Western Europe; take care, especially if female and travelling alone. The Gare du Nord has the worst reputation of the Paris stations.

The metro system connects with the RER system, a network of high speed trains which criss-cross Paris stopping only at major locations within central Paris and the suburbs. Metro tickets are valid for the RER.

Tourist passes, known as Paris Visite are available which allow unrestricted travel in 3 or 4 zones for either 3 or 5 days. They can be bought at the ticket office of most central metro stations, in tourist offices, at airports and at all the Paris railway stations. A 3-day pass costs 80FF and the 5-day pass 130FF.

If staying in Paris for any length of time consider buying a 2-zone coupon orange which allows unlimited travel for a calendar month. There are also 1-day passes (formule 1 coupon) and week-long ones, valid from Monday–Sunday (coupon jaune). For the weekly and monthly pass you also need an ID card (carte orange) with your photograph. These can be obtained at any metro or RER station. Your carte orange comes with a useful map of the bus, metro and RER networks.

Museums

Details of the opening times of museums and galleries are given in the text; it is worthwhile noting however that all state-owned museums in Paris close on Tuesdays while those owned by the city close on Mondays. Those intending to visit a number of museums and monuments would be well advised to buy the Carte Musées et Monuments (Museums and Monuments Card) which allows unrestricted, direct and unlimited access to 65 monuments and museums in Paris and the Ile de France. Having a card saves you from waiting in line; with the pass you head straight pass the queue to the entrance. It can be bought at museums and monuments, at the main metro (underground) stations and at the principal tourist office at 127 ave des Champs-Elysées, 8ème.

Recent **architectural projects** include the Grand Louvre with its great glass Pyramid, the new Foreign Ministry extending over the Seine, the Arab World Institute and the Great Arch at La Défense. **New museums** include the Picasso Museum (1985); the Sciences and Industry Centre (1986); the Arab World Institute (1987); the Carnavalet Museum (1989); the Cognac-Jay Museum (1991); the Gallery of the Buddhist Pantheon of China and Japan (1991); the Drawings and Reliefs Museum (1992); the opening of the Richelieu wing of the Louvre (1993) and the National Technology Museum (1994). 1997 will see the completion of the Grand Louvre, the world's largest museum.

Museums in Paris and the Ile de France, with opening times.

All these museums can be visited with the Museums card.

Arab World Institute 1 rue des Fossés St-Bernard, 5ème (Tel. 40 51 38 38). METRO: Jussieu or Cardinal Lemoine. Open 1 pm–6 pm Tues–Sat Closed Mondays. Contemporary art of Arab countries.

Arc de Triomphe Place Charles de Gaulle, 8ème (Tel. 43 80 31 31). METRO or RER: Charles de Gaulle/Etoile. (Open 1st April–30th Sept 10am–5.30 pm; 1st Oct–11 Nov 10 am–5 pm; 1st Feb–31 st Mar 10 am–2.30 pm.) Symbolic of Napoleon's achievements, the Arc de Triomphe offers an exceptional panorama over the Champs-Elysées and the whole of Paris.

Army Museum Tomb of Emperor Napoleon, Drawings and Reliefs, Hôtel des Invalides, Esplanade des Invalides. METRO: Latour Maubourg. Open 10 am–5 pm in winter, 10 am–6 pm in summer. A rich collection illustrating military history from prehistoric times to the present day. The Eglise du Dôme houses the tomb of the Emperor Napoleon.

Balzac's House 47 rue Reynouard, 16ème (Tel. 42 24 56 38). METRO: Passy. Open Tues–Sun 10 am–5.40 pm. Closed on Mondays. Literary documents and souvenirs of the writer in the house where he lived from 1840 to 1847.

Cluny Museum of the Middle Ages and Roman Baths 6 place Paul Painlevé, 5ème. (Tel. 42 25 62 00). METRO: Cluny or La Sorbonne. Open Wed–Mon 9.45 am–12.30 pm and 2–5.15 pm. Closed on Tuesdays. The Gallo-Roman baths house antique sculptures while the fifteenth-century Hôtel des Abbés de Cluny displays one of the richest medieval collections in the world.

Bourdelle Museum 16 rue Antoine Bourdelle, 15ème (Tel. 45 46 67 77). METRO: Falguière or Montparnasse-Bienvenüe. Open Wed–Mon 10 am–5.45 pm. Plasters, bronzes, marbles, drawings, paintings . . . in the workshop where the sculptor Antoine Bourdelle lived and worked all his life. The recent extension of the museum has made it possible to house the

artist's personal collection, donated by his daughter to the city of Paris.

Carnavalet Museum 23 rue de Sévigné, 3ème (Tel. 42 72 21 13). METRO: St-Paul or Chemin Vert. Open Tues–Sun. 10 am–5.40 pm. Closed on Mondays. Installed in the sixteenth-century Hôtel Carnavalet, this museum traces the history of Paris through objets d'art, paintings, drawings and models.

Catacombs 1 Place Denfert-Rochereau, 14ème (Tel. 43 22 47 63). METRO and RER: Denfert-Rochereau. Open Tues–Fri 2–4 pm; Sat, Sun and public holidays: 9 am–11 am and 2–4 pm. Closed on Mondays. The general charnel house for Parisian cemeteries installed in disused quarries beneath Paris.

Centre Georges Pompidou (including The National Museum of Modern Art) Rue Rambuteau, 4ème (Tel. 42 77 12 33). METRO: Rambuteau or Hôtel de Ville. Open Mon, Wed, Fri 12 noon–10 pm; Sat, Sun and public holidays 10 am–10 pm. Closed on Tuesdays. Located in the Pompidou Centre, this museum boasts one of the best collections in modern art in the world, combining all forms of plastic arts since the turn of the century.

Ceramics Museum Place de la Manufacture, 10ème (Tel. 45 34 99 05). METRO: Pont de Sèvres. Open Wed–Mon 10 am–7.15 pm. European china, porcelain and pottery from the Middle Ages to the 19th century.

Cernuschi Museum 7 avenue Velasquez, 8ème (Tel. 45 63 50 75). METRO: Villiers or Monceau. Open Wed–Mon 10 am–5.30 pm. Closed on Tuesdays. Ancient Chinese art: potteries, bronzes, funerary statuettes and contemporary Chinese paintings.

Chapelle Expiatoire/Monument to Louis XVI Place Louis XVI, 29 rue Pasquier, 8ème (Tel. 46 65 35 80). METRO: St-Lazare. Open Feb–Oct 10 am–5 pm, Nov–Jan 10 am–4 pm. This chapel was built in neo-Classical style during the Restoration to commemorate Louis XVI and the victims of the Revolution.

Cognacq-Jay Museum Hôtel du Donon, 8 rue Elzévir, 3ème (Tel. 40 27 07 21). METRO: Saint-Paul, Chemin-Vert or Rambuteau. Open Wed–Sun. 10 am–5.30 pm. Closed on Tuesdays. Magnificent collection of 18th-century paintings, with works by Fragonard, Chardin, Boucher and others bequeathed to the city of Paris by Ernest Cognacq.

Château de Compiègne Place du Général de Gaulle, 60200 Compiègne (Tel. 16 44 40 02 02) Open Wed–Mon 9.30 am–5 pm. Closed on Tuesdays. The Château houses three museums: the Musée des Grands-Appartements (in which Louis XVI, Napoleon I and Napoleon III stayed), the Musée du Second Empire and the Musée de la voiture et du tourisme.

Conciergerie 1 quai de l'Horloge (Tel. 43 54 30 06). METRO: Cité and Châtelet. Open 1st April–30th September 9.30 am–6 pm, 1st October–31st March 10 am–6.30 pm. This important vestige of the Capetian palace is a remarkable example of 14th century civil architecture; guardroom, arms room, kitchens, and Marie-Antoinette's cell.

Crypte Archéologique de Notre-Dame Place du Parvis de Notre-Dame (Tel. 43 29 83 51). METRO: Cité. Open 1st April–30th September 10 am–5.30 pm; 1st October–31st March 10 am–4.30 pm. The largest archaeological crypt in Europe: the history of Paris discovered during recent excavations.

Decorative Arts Museum 107/109 rue de Rivoli, 1er (Tel. 42 60 32 14). METRO: Palais Royal. Open Wed–Sun. 12.30–6 pm. Closed Mondays and Tuesdays. Outstanding collection of decorative arts from the Middle Ages to the present day: furniture, porcelain, jewellery, toys, glass.

Delacroix Museum 6 Place de Furstenberg, 6ème (Tel. 43 54 04 97). METRO: St-Germain-des-Prés. Open 9 45 am–12.30 pm and 2–5 15 pm. Closed on Tuesdays. The last home of the artist Eugène Delacroix (1798–1863) with works by the artist and documents relating to him and his relations.

Château d'Ecouen (incorporating the National Renaissance Museum), 95400 Ecouen (Tel. 39 90 64 04) Open Wed–Mon 9.45 am–12.30 pm and 2–5. 15 pm. Closed on Tuesdays. METRO to St-Denis Porte de Paris and then bus 268C in direction of Ezanville. An imposing Renaissance château housing a fabulous museum of the same period: tapestries, furniture, objets d'art . . .

Ennery Museum of Chinese and Japanese Art 59 avenue Foch, 16ème (Tel. 45 53 57 96) METRO: Porte Dauphine. Open Thursday and Sunday afternoons only, 2–5 pm. Closed in August. 7,000 objets d'art from China and Japan in a Second Empire setting.

Château de Fontainebleau 77300 Fontainebleau (Tel. 64 22 27 40). Open Wed–Mon. 9.30 am–12.30 pm and 2–5 pm. Closed on Tuesdays. Train from Gare de Lyon to Fontainebleau-Avon station. The royal residence of sovereigns from François I to Napoleon III. Outstanding collections of paintings, furniture and objets d'art . . . and a museum devoted to Napoleon I.

French Monuments Museum Palais de Chaillot, Place du Trocadéro, 16ème (Tel. 42 27 35 74). METRO: Trocadéro. Open Wed–Mon 9 am–6 pm. Closed on Tuesdays. Original and copies of major works by French sculptors from the 11th to the 19th centuries. French mural paintings of the 11th to the 16th centuries.

Gallery of the Buddhist Pantheon of China and

Japan 18 ave d'Iéna (Tel. 47 20 11 54) METRO: Iéna. Open Tues–Sun 9.45 am–5.30 pm. Closed on Tuesdays.

Guimet Museum (National Museum of Asian Art), 6 place d'Iéna, 16ème (Tel. 47 23 61 65). Open Wed–Mon 9.45 am–7 pm; closed on Tuesdays. METRO: Iéna or Boissière. Masterpieces from Afghanistan, Pakistan, India, South-East Asia, Central Asia, China, Korea, Japan . . . One of the largest museums of Asian Art in the world.

Hébert Museum Hôtel de Montmorency-Bours, 85 rue du Cherche-Midi, 6ème (Tel. 42 22 23 282). METRO: Sèvres-Babylone. Open Tues–Fri 12.30–6 pm; Sat, Sun and holidays 2–6 pm. Closed on Tuesdays. Oil paintings, watercolours and drawings by Ernest Hébert (1817–1908).

Henri Langlois Cinema Museum (Tel. 45 53 74 39). METRO: Malesherbes. Open Wed–Mon guided tours at 10 am, 11 am, 2 pm, 3 pm and 4 pm. Closed on Tuesdays. Décors, costumes, objects, posters and manuscripts relating to the cinema from its beginnings to the present day.

Louvre Museum, Palais du Louvre (Tel. 40 20 50 50). METRO: Palais Royal or Louvre. Open Wed–Mon 9 am–6 pm, staying open until 9.45 pm on Mondays and Wednesdays. Closed on Tuesdays. One of the greatest and most complete museums in the world: Oriental, Egyptian, Greek, Etruscan and Roman antiquities, paintings, sculpture, furniture and objets d'art. With the Museums Pass, enter through the passage Richelieu on the rue de Rivoli.

Château de Malmaison Avenue du Château, 92500 Rueil Malmaison (Tel. 47 49 20 07). Open Wed–Mon 10 am–noon and 1.30–5 pm. Take RER line A to La Défense and then bus 158A as far as Bois-Préau or Château stop. The apartments of Napoleon Bonaparte and his wife, Empress Josephine.

Modern Art Museum of the City of Paris Ave du Président Wilson, 16ème (Tel. 47 23 61 27). Open Tues–Sun 10 am–5.30 pm, Wed to 8.30 pm. METRO: Iéna or Alma Marceau. Closed on Mondays. Paintings by Cubists, Fauvists and members of the Paris school. Mural decorations by Sonia and Robert Delaunay, Matisse and Dufy.

Museum of African and Oceanic Art 293 ave Daumesnil, 12ème (Tel. 43 43 14 54). METRO: Porte Dorée. Open Wed–Mon 10 am–noon and 1.30–5.30 pm. Closed on Tuesdays. Collections of African art (North Africa and sub-Saharan Africa) and Oceanic Art. Tropical aquarium.

Museum of Gustave Moreau 14 rue La Rochefoucauld, 9ème (Tel. 48 74 38 50). METRO: Trinité. Open 10 am–12.45 pm and 2–5.15 pm, Mon and Wed 11 am–5.15 pm.

Closed on Tuesdays. Gustave Moreau's workshop (1826–1898): 1,200 paintings, watercolours and 5,000 drawings.
Museum of Popular Arts and Traditions 6 ave du Mahatma Gandhi, 16ème (Tel. 40 67 90 00). METRO Sablons. Open Wed–Mon 9.45 am–5.30 pm. Closed on Tuesdays. The French ethnological heritage: objets d'art, archives, audiovisual presentations.
Museum of Romantic Life/Renan-Scheffer Atelier 16 rue Chaptal (Tel. 48 74 95 38). Open Tues–Sun 10 am–5.40 pm. Closed on Mondays.
Naval Museum Palais de Chaillot, Place du Trocadéro, 16ème (Tel. 45 63 31 70) METRO: Trocadéro. Open 10 am–6 pm. Closed on Tuesdays. An extremely rich collection bringing alive the history of the French navy from the 17th century to the present day.
Nissim de Camondo Museum 63 rue de Monceau, 8ème (Tel. 45 63 26 32). Open Tues–Sun 10 am–noon and 2–5 pm. Closed on Mondays. METRO: Villiers or Monceau. The atmosphere of the 18th century is recreated here by an exceptional collection of furniture, paintings, tapestries, porcelain and silver.
Notre-Dame Towers Place du Parvis de Notre-Dame (Tel. 43 54 22 63). METRO: Cité. Open 1st April–30th Sept 9.30 am–12.15 pm and 2–8 pm; from 1st Oct to 31st Mar 9.30 am–12.15 pm and 2–5 pm. Outstanding view from the towers of the cathedral and the surrounding city.
Open Air Sculpture Museum Quai St-Bernard, 5ème. METRO or RER: Austerlitz or METRO: Sully-Morland. A vast garden, created in 1980 on the banks of the Seine, to house sculptures from the 2nd half of the 20th century (César, Ipousteguy . . .)
Orsay Museum 1 rue de Bellechasse, 7ème (Tel. 45 49 48 14) METRO: Solférino or RER Orsay. Open Wed–Sun 10 am–5.30 pm. Closed on Mondays. An extensive collection illustrating artistic creation from 1848 to 1914, on show in the former Orsay railway station.
Panthéon Place du Panthéon, 5ème (Tel. 43 54 34 51) METRO or RER Luxembourg or MÉTRO: St-Michel. Open 1st April–30th Sept 10 am–5.30 pm; 1st Oct–31st March 10 am–noon and 2–5 pm). Soufflot's masterpiece, formerly Ste-Geneviève's church, was transformed during the Revolution into the Panthéon for the burial of national heroes.
Petit Palais Museum ave Winston Churchill, 8ème (Tel. 43 65 12 73). METRO: Champs-Elysées Clémenceau. Open Tues–Sun 10 am–5.40 pm. A rich collection of paintings, sculptures, furniture, tapestries and objets d'art representing the main artistic developments from antiquity to the beginning of the 20th century.

Picasso Museum 5 rue de Thorigny, 3ème (Tel. 42 71 25 21). METRO: St-Paul or Chemin Vert. Open Wed–Mon 9.15 am–5.15 pm, open on Wednesdays until 10 pm. Closed on Tuesdays. Works by Picasso displayed in an 18th-century mansion.
Priory Departmental Museum (Symbolists and Nabis), 7 bis rue Maurice Denis, 78100 St-Germain-en-Laye (Tel. 39 73 77 87). RER A line to St-Germain-en-Laye. Open Wed–Fri 10 am–5.30 pm, Sat and Sun 10 am–6.30 pm. Closed on Mondays and Tuesdays. The home of the artist Maurice Denis, the Musée du Prieuré houses an important collection of works by Denis and his friends: Gauguin, Bonnard, Vuillard . . .
Château de Rambouillet Place de la Libération, Rambouillet (Tel. 34 83 00 25). Open 1st Oct–30th March 10–11.30 am and 2–4.30 pm; 1st April–30th Sept 10 am–11.30 am and 2–5.30 pm. Closed on Tuesdays. Train from Gare-Montparnasse to Rambouillet station. Formerly a royal residence (from the 14th to 18th centuries), the château is now one of the French President's official residences.
Rodin Museum 77 rue de Varenne, 7ème (Tel. 47 05 01 34). METRO: Varenne. Open Tues–Sun 10 am–6 pm in summer, 10 am–5 pm in winter. Closed on Mondays. Bronzes and marbles sculpted by Auguste Rodin (1840–1917), exhibited in an 18th-century mansion.
St-Denis Basilica Place de l'Hôtel de Ville, 93200 St-Denis (Tel. 48 09 83 54). Open 1st April–30th Sept 10 am–7 pm, Sundays from noon–7 pm; 1st Oct–31st Mar 10 am–5 pm. METRO: St-Denis-Basilique. One of the earliest examples of Gothic art in France. Tombs of Kings of France.
Château de St-Germain Place du Château, 78130 St-Germain-en-Laye. (Tel. 34 51 53 65). RER: St-Germain-en-Laye. Open Wed–Mon 9 am–7.30 pm. Closed on Tuesdays.
Sainte-Chapelle Boulevard du Palais, 1er (Tel. 43 54 30 09). METRO: Cité. Open 1st April–30th Sept 10 am–5.30 pm; 1st Oct–31st Mar 10 am–noon and 2–5 pm. A jewel of Gothic architecture, the Sainte-Chapelle was built on the orders of Saint-Louis in the middle of the 13th century and possesses one of the most complete and perfect series of medieval stained glass in France.
Top of the Great Arch, La Défense 1 Pavis de la Défense, 1ere (Tel. 49 07 27 27). METRO: La Défense. Open 1st July–31st Aug Sun–Thurs 10am–7 pm; Fri, Sat and public holidays 10 am–9 pm; 1st Sept–30th June 9 am–7 pm from Mon–Fri, and 10 am–7 pm on Sat, Sun and public holidays. Opened in 1989 the Grande Arche is the newest Parisian monument. Panoramic view and exhibitions.

Tuileries Orangerie Museum Place de la Concorde, 1er (Tel. 42 97 48 16) METRO: Concorde or Tuileries. Open Wed–Mon 9.45 am–5.15 pm. Closed on Tuesdays. Exhibition of the Walter Guillaume collection (Cézanne, Renoir, Matisse, Picasso . . .) with Claude Monet's *Water Lilies*.
Versailles (Tel. 30 54 74 00). RER: Versailles Rive Gauche. Open 9.45 am–5.30 pm, entrance by A2 door with Museum pass, supplement payable for King's bedroom. Train from Gare Montparnasse to Versailles-Chantiers station or from Gare St-Lazare to Versailles-Rive Droite station, or RER line C to Versailles Rive Gauche station. Home of the Kings of France from 1678 to 1789.
Victor Hugo's House 6 place des Vosges (Tel. 42 72 10 16). METRO: Bastille. Open Tues–Sun 10 am–5.30 pm. Closed on Mondays. Victor Hugo lived in this house from 1832 to 1848. More than 400 drawings by the writer, who was also a painter and interior decorator, are on show.

For details of temporary exhibitions, theatre and cinema, see *Pariscope*, the main weekly magazine detailing current events in the city.

Ile-De-France

The area around Paris is known generally as the *Ile-de-France*, for it is the historic heart of the French kingdom. The term 'France' was first used to designate the small area around Paris subjugated by the early kings of the House of Capet during the 10th and 11th centuries. And in medieval times the word *île* meant not only an island in the current sense of the word but also much larger areas wholly or partially surrounded by rivers. Such an appellation was wholly appropriate for the province ruled by the early French kings, for their territory was almost completely enclosed by the rivers Seine, Oise, Aisne, Ourcq and Marne. The extent of the domains actually ruled by the French kings fluctuated wildly throughout the Middle Ages, largely as a result of wars and treaties with the Plantagenet kings of England. Phillipe-Auguste succeeded in adding Normandy, Anjou, Maine and Touraine to the dominions of the French crown, but much of these were lost by the French during the Hundred Years War before being regained in the mid-15th century. At its lowest ebb, the French monarchy lost control of the Ile-de-France altogether when, in 1421, Henry V occupied the province in its entirety and his son was declared King of France in Paris the following year. But the English, under the regency of the Duke of Bedford, only held the Ile for 15 years, after which they were permanently ejected by Joan of Arc. In 1437 Charles le Victorieux was finally able to regain his capital.

The Ile-de-France was only to enjoy a century of peace before becoming embroiled again in fighting that resulted from religious controversy. Jean Calvin, who was born in the Ile at Noyan in 1509, played a prominent part in the reform movement but on the whole the inhabitants of the Ile remained loyal to the Catholic church, as did Paris. Henri IV's 'conversion' to Catholicism in 1593 put an end to the religious conflict that had wracked the region for the best part of a century.

The route Beauvais – Amiens – Chantilly – Compiègne – Senlis – Écouen – St-Denis cathedral – Reims – Châlons-sur-Marne – Rambouillet – Gien– Vaux-le-Vicomte – Fontainebleau – Troyes – St-Germain-en-Laye – Chartres

Within 100 kilometres of Paris lie dozens of fascinating towns and villages, magnificent châteaux and abbeys, and some of the most beautiful Gothic cathedrals of France. Because of the centralised nature of the French railway network, with everything focussing on Paris, the vast majority of these sights are easily accessible from **Paris** *by train. Depending on their direction – north, south, east and west – these destinations are served by different railway stations in Paris. The principal ones are the* **Gare d'Austerlitz** *serving the south-west, the* **Gare de L'Est** *serving the east, the* **Gare de Lyon** *serving the south-east, the* **Gare Montparnasse** *serving Brittany and southern Normandy, the* **Gare du Nord** *serving the north-east and the ferry ports of Boulogne, Calais and Dunkerque, and the* **Gare St Lazare** *serving Normandy and the ferry ports of Dieppe, Le Havre and Cherbourg.*

Beauvais

Trains *3 – 7 trains daily from* **Paris** *Gare du Nord (1 hour–1½ hours).*

It was one of the Bishops of Beauvais, Pierre Cauchon, who was responsible for sending Joan of Arc to the stake in the 15th century, Beauvais at that time siding with the English and the Burgundians against the kings of France. From the late 17th century the town had an important tapestry factory which was destroyed by the German incendiary bombardment of June 1940 which razed most of the city to the ground, destroying over 1,500 15th and 16th century houses. The cathedral and adjacent Bishop's Palace miraculously escaped the conflagration.

What to see

Cathédrale St-Pierre

One of the glories of northern France is Beauvais cathedral, one of the most heavenly and perfect Gothic cathedrals in existence. Dominating the centre of the town by virtue of its vast height, the **Cathedral of St-Pierre**, is a masterpiece of French Gothic architecture, even though it was never completed. Work on the cathedral began in 1227 and continued for 3 ½ centuries, completion being delayed by the roof caving in twice and the tower above the crossing on another occasion. Had it been completed, it would have been the largest Gothic cathedral in the world; as it is its choir and transepts alone represent one of the most ambitious masterpieces of medieval architecture.

Work on the nave was never even begun and the western end was abruptly finished with a covering of slates. It is the façades of the transepts that reveal the craftsmanship and beauty of vision of the medieval stone-masons and craftsmen. The impression of height in the interior is overwhelming and accentuated, of course, by the absence of any nave. The choir, the highest in existence, is no less than 49-metres-high while the cathedral in its entirety is only 70 metres long. Where the nave was to have been built still stand 3 bays of the old Carolingian nave of an earlier church, the Basse-Oeuvre. This ungainly building stands in stark contrast to the towering Gothic structure abutting it to the east.

When the 152-metre-high spire collapsed in 1573 it destroyed the tower and damaged the transepts. Money to carry out all the rebuilding work and add the nave was not forthcoming and work effectively came to an end.

Galérie nationale de la Tapisserie

The looms of the Beauvais' tapestry works were evacuated from the town in 1939 and have now been amalgamated with the Gobelins tapestry workshops in Paris, where they continue to make 'low' warp tapestries for the French state. Unfortunately the magnificent Beauvais tapestries which used to hang on the cathedral walls are no longer on show, having been removed to Soissons. The Galerie Nationale de la Tapisserie, next to the cathedral, does however have a fascinating collection of Beauvais' most famous tapestry artist, Jean-Baptiste Oudry. (Open Mar–Oct, Tues–Sun 9.30 – 11.30 am and 2 – 6 pm; Nov–Feb, Tues–Sun 10 – 11.30 am and 2.40 – 4.30 pm.)

Conical towers west of the cathedral mark the entrance to the courtyard of the **Old Bishop's Palace**, a 14th to 16th-century building, one of the few to survive the bombing of 1940. It now houses a small but interesting **museum** devoted to local history, archaeology and art. (Open Wed–Mon 10 am–noon and 2 – 6 pm.) Some distance south-east of the cathedral stands one of the few other buildings to escape the fire of 1940, the **Church of St-Etienne** which marries 2 strikingly different architectural styles, combining a Romanesque nave with a late Gothic choir.

Practicalities in Beauvais

Tourist Office 1 rue Beauregard, close to cathedral of St-Pierre (Tel. 44 45 08 18).
Railway Station Ave de la République (Tel. 44 21 50 50).
Hotels ☆ *Hôtel Palais*, 9 rue St Nicholas (Tel 44 45 12 58). Small family-run hôtel in quiet side-street down from the old archbishop's palace.
☆ *Hôtel Bristol*, 60 rue Madeleine (Tel. 44 45

01 31). Short walk from station off blvd J Brière.
☆☆ *Hôtel Chenal*, 63 blvd Général de Gaulle; adjacent to station (Tel 44 45 03 55).
Restaurants ☆ *Marignan*, 1 rue Malherbe (Tel. 44 48 15 15). Traditional dishes in pleasant restaurant near St-Etienne church, just off Place Hachette.

Amiens

Trains *8 – 10 trains daily from* **Paris** *Gare du Nord (1 hour 10 mins–2 hours); 7 daily from* **Calais** *via Boulogne (2 hours); 3 from* **Rouen** *(1 ½ hours); 8 from* **Arras** *(20 mins) and* **Lille** *(1 hour 5 mins).*

In the Middle Ages, Amiens prospered as the centre of an important textile and velvet industry. At that time the old town, mostly built of brick, was located well within the ramparts that existed until destroyed in the Second World War. At the beginning of the 19th century the population of the town was only 40,000, a quarter of its present size. The city suffered severely from German bombardment that formed part of its offensive of March 1918, after having been only 30 kilometres west of the front for much of the war. The cathedral was protected by sandbags during the war, escaping serious damage despite being hit by shells 9 times.

What to see

The Cathedral

The Cathedral of Amiens vies with that of Beauvais as one of the wonders of the medieval world. As at Beauvais the cathedral survived virtually unscathed from the destruction that flattened much of the town. The most northerly of the great cathedrals, Amiens is the largest cathedral in France and a jewel of Gothic art.

It represents the zenith of 13th-century Gothic and reveals in some of its details the beginning of the transition towards the Flamboyant style. The sheer size is overwhelming but so too are the perfection and harmony of the proportions. Unlike Beauvais, work on the cathedral progressed rapidly: the foundations were laid in 1220, the nave completed in 1236, the choir in 1268. It is laid out on the plan of a Latin cross and is 145 metres long, 70 metres wide at the transept and has a vault 140 feet high.

The magnificent western façade, encrusted with myriads of statues, was completed in 1236. Above the 3 massive western portals stand 22 huge statues of the kings of France clutching swords and sceptres, each with their own idiosyncratic pose and gaze. Higher still, between the bays of the towers, is a large rose window with elegant tracery, and above this the Bellringer's Gallery.

The immensity and homogeneity of the interior are very impressive and are enhanced by the great height of the nave in proportion to its width and the general architectural purity. The most remarkable part of the interior is the choir, raised some 6 inches above the level of the nave, from which it is separated by elegant 18th-century wrought-iron railings. The choir is also distinguished by its 16th-century stalls, richly carved in a Flamboyant Gothic style, and the finest to be found anywhere in France. More than 3,600 figures represent 400 scenes from the

Old Testament and the *Life of the Virgin*, as well as portraying medieval trades and crafts. Another gem is the choir screen in the ambulatory, with its gilded stone reliefs which contain a wealth of information on early Renaissance costume.

Marché sur l'Eau

One curious and interesting quarter is to be found in the low-lying part of town down by the Somme, where the *Marché sur l'Eau* or Water Market, still receives long, black flat-bottomed boats laden with fruit and vegetables from the *Hortillonnages*, a strange area of market-gardens and orchards divided by canals and streams.

Not a great deal remains of old Amiens, but in rue Victor-Hugo stands the 17th-century **Hôtel des Trésoriers de France** and a little further west the **Lois du Roi** and Renaissance **Maison du Sagittaire**. The **Hôtel de Berny**, an elegant 1634 mansion, is furnished with period furniture and houses a small local museum. (Open Tues–Sun 10 am–noon and 2–6 pm.) The 19th-century law courts stand on the site of an abbey dedicated to St-Martin, said to mark the spot where St Martin divided his cloak and shared it with a beggar.

South of the little church of St-Remi is the **Musée de Picardie** with excellent art collections containing 16th-century examples of the Amiens School, as well as good 18th-century and contemporary French paintings.

Between the old town and the railway station stands the **Tour Perret**, a dominating feature of the town, a 26-floor concrete construction by the French architect Auguste Perret, whose dreary concrete apartment blocks disfigure Le Havre.

Practicalities in Amiens

Tourist Office 12 rue du Chapeau des Violettes (Tel. 22 91 79 28); branch office at station. (Tel. 22 92 65 04) and on place Notre-Dame in front of cathedral (Tel. 22 91 16 16).

Railway Station Gare du Nord, place Alphonse Fiquet (Tel 22 92 50 50); lockers; information office.

Buses 6 rue de l'Oratoire (Tel. 22 91 46 82). Buses leave for surrounding towns from blvd Alsace-Lorraine, next to the train station.

Festival May; *Jazz Festival*, in clubs, squares and streets. June, *Fête d'Amiens*: a joyful weekend of celebrations.

Hotels *Hôtel Normandie*, 1 bis rue Lamartine, in side street off rue de Noyon (Tel. 22 91 74 99). ☆☆ *Grand Hôtel Univers*, 2 rue Noyon, on corner of rue Noyon and place Réné Goblet,

heading towards centre (Tel. 22 91 52 51). *Hôtel Ibis*, 4 rue Mar de Lattre de Tassigny (Tel. 22 92 57 33). Short walk from the Musée de Picardie. *Hôtel Victor Hugo*, 2 rue l'Oratoire, between cathedral and station (Tel. 22 91 57 91). Handsome and welcoming. *Les Touristes*, place Notre-Dame (Tel. 22 91 33 45). Small rooms but facing cathedral right in heart of old town.

Restaurants *Joséphine*, 20 rue Sire-Firmin-Leroux (Tel. 22 91 47 38). Simple, straightforward meals in pleasant good-value restaurant. ☆ *Mermoz*, 7 rue Jean-Mermoz (Tel. 22 91 47 63). Nouvelle and traditional cuisine, wide range of interesting dishes; close to station.

Chantilly

Trains *10 – 12 trains daily from* Paris *Gare du Nord (30 mins).*

The château of Chantilly is an extraordinary jewel set in the crown of the Ile-de-France. Set within a magnificent park laid out in the 17th century and surrounded by ancient forests, the château is one of the most splendid in France, with the most magnificent art collections and treasures to be found outside Paris. The château, surrounded by sheets of water and ornamental gardens, is reached on foot from the station via ave du Maréchal Joffre and rue du Connétable which leads past the stables and then veers to the right.

The little town of Chantilly itself is the Newmarket of France and has been famous for its race meetings since 1836. Long before these had become a regular event, however, palatial stables – with places for 240 mounts – had been built by Jean Aubert in 1719 – 40 for the Prince de Condé. The famous races held here every year are run behind these magnificent stables which Gérard de Nerval once compared to a basilica.

What to see

Château de Chantilly

Standing on an island in a lake formed by the Nonette, the Château de Chantilly consists of 2 buildings, the **Petit Château** on the south-west which was designed about 1560 by Bullant for the Constable Anne de Montmorency, and the **Grand Château** to the north, a late 19th-century building which replaces a much finer one built by Mansart for Louis II de Condé, one of Louis XIV's most brilliant generals. Of the original Grand Château Lord Herbert of Cherbury remarked that 'it was an incomparable residence, admired by the greatest Princes of Europe'. Its enchanting setting of water and parkland was planned for de Condé by Le Nôtre, Louis XIV's preferred landscape-gardener. A fine statue of Le Nôtre, looking elegant and relaxed and in the act of directing operations, can be found near the Terrasse du Connétable.

The Petit Château, also known as the Capitainerie, was designed by French architect Jean Bullant who was a great admirer of the Italian style. From the outside it consists of a long, rather low building linking 2 higher pavilions at right angles to it. The way in which the upper windows cut through the entablature, setting up a sort of syncopation between the 2 small storeys and the single large Order, is characteristic of Ballant's style and can be seen as a French form of Mannerism. Bullant was one of the 2 dominating figures of French architecture during the period of the Wars of Religion and his name is closely associated with that of Constable

Anne de Montmorency, for whom he worked at Écouen and Fère-en-Tardenois, as well as at Chantilly. At some point in his career he visited Rome where he made drawings of ancient buildings and later he published 2 works relating to architecture, one of which was dedicated to his patron, Montmorency. In the early 16th century the Constable Anne de Montmorency was, after the king, the most important nobleman of northern France. Companion-in-arms to François I and close advisor to Henri II, he owned over 130 castles and estates and 600 fiefs. Also, through his 5 sons and the husbands of his 7 daughters, he controlled many of the state's most important offices. It was Montmorency who ordered the construction of a new château on an island separated from the Grand Château by a moat – now filled in – and summoned the greatest artists of the day to decorate it. He was to die fighting against the Protestants in 1567 at the age of 75. Despite his age, it allegedly took 5 blows with a sword and 2 with a bludgeon to his face before he died, but not before breaking his opponent's jaw with the pommel of his sword.

The Petit Château is joined by a wing to the Grand Château which was rebuilt in 1875–81 by the Duc d'Aumale, a son of Louis-Philippe, the old château having been largely destroyed during the Revolution of 1799. After the 1848 Revolution the duke had been banished to exile in Twickenham and the property was confiscated by the French state. Allowed to return to France at the end of the Second Empire the duke commissioned Daumet to rebuild the Grand Château in the Renaissance style. Shortly before his death he generously bequeathed it, together with his outstanding art collection, to the Institut de France.

It was in the original Grand Château that Molière's *Les Précieuses Ridicules* was performed for the first time in 1659. Louis XIV was a frequent visitor to the château, and it was during one of his visits that the head chef Vatel was so distraught at the thought that the fish would arrive too late for the King's meal that he committed suicide. One century later, some 12 years before the Revolution, the English traveller Philip Thicknesse was invited to attend supper. He observed that 25 servants were called upon to attend on the Prince de Condé when he sat down to an 'informal' meal with 7 friends. The Duc d'Aumale's art collection forms the basis of the vast **Musée Condé**, the most important collection of paintings in northern France. It is a vast, heterogeneous and unique collection, ranging from Old Masters to exquisite gems and illuminated manuscripts which are spread through 2 châteaux.

The museum was put together in a somewhat idiosyncratic way, the duke being more interested in creating an impressive collection than an educational museum. One stipulation of his legacy was that no changes could be made to the interior or exterior of the château. The entire collection deserves attention but the highlights include a magnificent collection of 16th and 17th century portrait drawings of important French historical figures; works by Raphael, Filippino Lippi, Memling, Botticelli, Piero di Cosimo and miniatures by Jean Fouquet; and the *Très Riches Heures* of the Duc de Berri with illuminated pages of the months of the year, although the original is rarely on view. The Prince's suite in the Petit Château is superbly furnished and decorated with Regency and rococo wainscoting. It contains a marvellous collection of illuminated manuscripts, a long painted gallery, and a magnificent little chapel with elegant wainscoting and superb stained glass. The vast majority of works of art however are housed in the Grand Château where paintings of different periods and styles are hung side by side. Here can be found paintings which once adorned the dining-room of Louis XIV's private apartments at Versailles – such as De Troy's *Oyster Lunch*. There are paintings by Poussin and Corot and the *Loreto Madonna* by Raphael, together with Piero de Cosimo's portrait of Simonetta Vespucci who was almost certainly Botticelli's model for his masterpiece, the *Birth of Venus*.

The Orléans chamber contains an unrivalled collection of soft-paste Chantilly porcelain manufactured in workshops set up by the Duc de Condé in the early 18th century and the Cabinet des Clouet has a superb collection of historical portraits of French kings and queens. Other outstanding treasures are Raphael's painting of the *Three Graces* and his *Orléans Madonna*, both of which are to be found in the Sanctuary. Here too are to be found 40 miniatures by Jean Fouquet, once part of Estienne Chevalier's book of hours.

The impressive park was laid out for the Grand Condé by Le Nôtre who diverted part of the river Nonette through the formal and geometric parterres. The park is ornamented with sculptures and hides a Louis XVI style hamlet, used for *fêtes champetres* which was to be copied by Louis in Le Petit Trianon at Versailles, and a pretty little house, the **Maison de Sylvie**. In the 17th century, the fountains of Chantilly were without equal; only Louis XIV at Versailles succeeded in excelling them in magnificence. The parterres are framed by 2 avenues of lofty lime trees which lead to the Grand Canal and flanked by stretches of water and landscaped gardens. Behind the superb park stretches the forest of Chantilly, 5,000 acres of oak, lime and birch woodland, intersected by tracks and sandy paths used by horses from the training-stables of the neighbourhood. (Château and museums open Easter–Oct, Wed–Mon 10 am–6 pm; Nov–Easter 10.30 am–12.30 am and 2–5 pm.) The vast forests can also be explored on foot: the oak, hornbeam and lime forests of Coye, Orry and Pontarmé are for foot-walkers only.

Practicalities in Chantilly

Tourist Office 23 ave Maréchal Joffre, opposite post office on main street at diagonal from station (Tel. 44 57 08 58).
Railway Station Chantilly-Gouvieux, (Info: Tel. 44 21 50 50; Reservations Tel. 22 91 95 30).
Hotels ☆☆Hôtel Campanile, route Creil, some 2 km north of the station, beyond the Nonette river (Tel. 44 57 39 24).
☆Etoile, 3 ave du Maréchal Joffre (Tel. 44 57 05 75). Small, cheap, located on avenue leading from station to château.
Restaurants Capitainerie, in the château's medieval basement; simple self-service meals.
☆Relais du Coq Chantant, 21 route de Creil (Tel. 44 57 01 28). Reasonably priced menus offering good traditional French dishes but expensive à la carte.
☆☆Relais Condé, 42 ave Maréchal Joffre (Tel. 44 57 05 75). Smart restaurant, good wine list, expensive à la carte and in evening.

Senlis

Trains *10–12 trains daily from* Paris *Gare du Nord to* Chantilly *(30 mins);* *virtually all trains are met by bus to Senlis (25 mins).*

The quiet and attractive little town of Senlis, set amongst the rich cornfields and woods of Valois, played an important role in the early history of France. Here, in 987, a meeting was summoned by the Archbishop of Reims to decide on the future king of France after Louis V had died while out hunting. The choice was for Hugh Capet – the Duc des Francs – the first of 15 Capetian kings.

Château Royal

The royal castle at Senlis was gradually abandoned by the French kings, first for Compiègne and then for Fontainebleau, although it was used as a resting place during the journey to Paris after the coronation of the kings at Reims. Not a great deal remains of the Château royal apart from a stolid square 'praetorium' tower with walls 4½-metres thick. In the 13th century St Louis ordered the construction of a priory in the castle grounds; 2 of these buildings still stand: the Canon's building and the Prior's Lodge which houses a **Hunting Museum** with paintings by Desportes, Oudry, Vernet, Bonheur and Hallo. Hunting was the principal attraction of Senlis for the early French kings – indeed it was a hunting accident which brought the end of the Carolingian dynasty. (Open for guided visits. Mon 10 am–noon, Tues and Wed 2–5 pm, Thurs–Sun 10 am–noon and 2–5 pm.)

Senlis had been occupied and strongly fortified by the Romans and the Royal Gardens occupy what was once the moat of the Gallo-Roman ramparts. 28 towers defended the Roman city; 16 survive, some partly hidden in private properties and others still visible. Close by lies the cathedral and the old market square onto which it faces, the Place du Parvis.

What to see

Cathédrale Notre Dame

The cathedral is modest in size in comparison with others which were being built at the time, but it is extremely beautiful. Work began in 1153, 10 years before Notre-Dame in Paris, but progressed slowly and the cathedral was only consecrated in 1191. In the 16th century it was struck by lightning and the transepts had to be rebuilt; at the same time new side aisles were added. From outside the eye is quickly drawn to the fine spire above the southern tower. Until the 13th century the towers were identical in appearance; then a magnificent spire was added on one side, giving the cathedral façade an unbalanced but powerful attraction.

The realism and freedom of expression of the sculpture of the central doorway of the western façade was to serve as the model for religious architecture in the

Valois area. The doorway is dedicated to the Virgin and portrays her Dormition and Assumption in 2 low reliefs on the lintel and her Coronation on the tympanum. The 8 *Old Testament* figures in the embrasures were mutilated during the Revolution; the heads are 19th-century copies while the torsos are 13th-century. While the western façade is an example of austere Gothic architecture, a very different feel is to be found in the work of Pierre Chambiges in the south transept. Chambiges was responsible for most of the rebuilding following the cathedral being struck by lightning in 1504. In his work can be seen the combination of late Flamboyant with Renaissance style, then making its appearance in France as a result of French involvement in the Italian wars. Fleurs-de-lys grace the gallery of the south transept, while on the north can be found the sculpture of the salamander – the motif of Francis I who contributed generously to the 16th-century rebuilding programme.

The nave is long, tall and narrow and remarkable particularly for the triforium galleries above the aisles which are exceptionally beautiful. The best stained glass is to be found in a side chapel which houses a 14th-century stone sculpture of the Virgin.

Adjacent to the cathedral is the **Old Bishop's Palace**, a much altered 13th-century building, which now houses a museum of art and archaeology. Immediately behind it is St-Pierre, a deconsecrated church with a damaged but still fine and elaborate façade – an attractive example of Gothic Flamboyant style.

The oldest and **most picturesque streets** are to be found between the cathedral and the Chancellory in rue de la Treille which is flanked by 2 towers which defended the original city gates. The rue du Chatel was the main street of the medieval town; here and in the nearby rue de la Treille stand the oldest and most interesting houses. At the southern end of Rue du Chatel, just beyond the Gallo-Roman enceinte, lies the **Hôtel de Ville**, rebuilt in 1495 and ornamented with a bust of Henri IV. Half-way between the Hôtel de Ville and the bishop's palace lies a royal chapel, founded by the wife of the first Capetian king, and rebuilt by Louis VII in 1177. The **Chapelle Royale St Frambourg** is a simple Gothic building with a single nave which was built to house the relics of a 10th-century recluse, St Frambourg. It fell into disrepair and has recently been restored due to the efforts of the pianist Georges Cziffra. It is now the Franz Liszt Auditorium and an important venue for classical music.

Practicalities in Senlis

Tourist Office Place Parvis Notre-Dame, opposite the cathedral (Tel. 44 53 06 40).
Hotels ☆ *Hostellerie de la Porte Bellon*, 35 rue Bellon, simple but attractive hotel just within the ramparts north of the Abbaye St-Vincent

(Tel. 44 53 03 05).
Restaurants ☆ *Les Gourmandins*, 3 Place de la Halle (Tel. 44 60 94 01). Intimate restaurant on 2 floors. Good cooking, wine list and interesting dishes.

Compiègne

Trains *10–15 trains daily from* **Paris** *Gare du Nord (50 mins); 6 daily from* **Beauvais,** *with change at Creil (45 mins).*

Although the landscape of Compiègne cannot be said to be of great beauty in itself, its forests are magnificent and cover a huge area of more than 80 square kilometres. This great forest is dissected by more than a 1,600 kilometres of avenues and hunting paths cleared by the kings of France to allow them to hunt far and wide through the forests. Since the 9th century Compiègne has been a residence of French kings when Charles the Bald built a modest palace and founded an abbey on the banks of the Seine close to its junction with the Aisne.

The Capetian kings frequently stopped off at Compiègne on their way back from their coronation at Reims, as did Charles VII in the company of Joan of Arc in 1429. The following year she was captured by the Burgundians as she tried to come to the rescue of the garrison of Compiègne, who sold her to the English.

Louis XIV was a frequent visitor although he complained of the accommodation the palace provided. 'At Versailles I am housed like a king,' he remarked, 'at Fontainebleau like a gentleman, at Compiègne like a peasant.' Louis XV set out to rectify the position, knocking down the old, much altered château of Charles V and ordering Jacques Gabriel senior and junior to design a new castle. The new château was completed by Louis XVI who opted for a more sumptuous palace than was originally envisaged by his predecessor and this was made even more magnificent by Napoleon I.

What to see

Palais de Compiègne

The palace has often been described as an example of French neo-classic decadence: imposing in its mass-effect but ultimately unappealing because of its cold sterility and sobriety. The main façade however is relieved by a graceful portico and the columns on to the main palace courtyard. From the terrace there is a superb view of the great forest behind which is traversed by a single broad avenue, the work of Napoleon I for whom the palace was a favourite place of residence. To one side lies the **Petit Parc** designed by Napoleon to remind Marie-Louise, the daughter of Francis I of Austria, of the Schönbrunn Gardens in Vienna. Napoleon celebrated his marriage to Marie-Louise in the palace, the ceiling of the vast Galerie du Bal being painted for the occasion with scenes depicting Imperial victories.

The interior of the palace contains a number of handsomely decorated apartments with their original Empire furniture and Gobelin and Beauvais tapestries. Marie-Antoinette's Games Room has been restored to its pre-Revolution appearance with exquisite silk curtains and hangings from workshops at Lyon. The most impressive apartment is the Galerie des Fêtes, decorated in white and gold, in which are to be found rather grandiose statues of Napoleon and his swarthy Corsican mother in Roman costume. (Château open Wed–Mon 9.30 am–5 pm; Tel. 44 40 02 02.)

Hôtel de Ville

The royal château inevitably overshadows the rest of the town. The Hôtel de Ville is a Franco-Flemish Flamboyant building in style dating from 1502–10 but has been restored so many times that one would hardly know it was built by Louis XII, were it not for the equestrian statue of him placed in a niche. Its belfry contains the charming figures of 3 gaily dressed *Picantins* who strike the bells at their feet at every quarter and hour. The Hôtel contains an intriguing and priceless museum, the **Musée de la Figurine**, devoted to toy soldiers that are believed to number nearly 100,000 (Open April–Oct, Tues–Sun 9 am–noon and 2–6 pm.) Another unusual museum, this one devoted to that 20th-century symbol of affluence and agent of destruction, the car, is to be found in the **Kitchen Courtyard** of the royal palace. For those who tire of endless royal apartments, palaces, and museums, a short walk will take one into the delightful and shady forests where it is easy to forget quickly the existence of the nearby town.

Practicalities in Compiègne

Tourist Office Place Hôtel de Ville, in the square at bottom of rue Solferino over bridge of same name (Tel. 44 40 01 00); currency exchange; accommodation service.
Hotels *Hôtel du Nord*, Place de la Gare; adjacent to station (Tel. 44 83 22 30).
☆ *Hôtel de France*, 17 rue E Floquet (Tel. 44 40 48 37). 17th-century house in quiet

backstreet in the heart of the city.
☆☆ *Hôtel de Harlay*, 3 rue Harlay (Tel. 44 23 01 50). Down sidestreet just over Pont Solferino.
Restaurants *Picotin*, 22 Place de l'Hôtel de Ville (Tel. 44 40 04 06). Inexpensive but unexciting menus in a convenient location close to château.

Ecouen

Trains RER *line D1 from* **Châtelet-les-Halles** *or* *Gare du Nord station in central Paris to* **Villiers-le-Bel** *(20–25 mins)*.

Set in a beautiful park, some 2 kilometres from the RER station, lies the splendid Renaissance château of Écouen. Built in the middle of the 16th century for Constable Anne de Montmorency, it now houses the **Musée de la Renaissance**, the finest collection of Renaissance treasures in northern France.

What to see

Château d'Ecouen

Partly designed by Jean Bullant, Ecouen château reflects the transition in French architecture from the Early Renaissance of the châteaux of the Loire to the High Renaissance of Henri II's era. Bullant was probably responsible for the north wing with its façade decorated with 2 superimposed Orders, Tuscan and Doric. Building was carried out in the middle 1550s by which time the west and south wings had already been completed. But the most original part of Bullant's work at Ecouen is the pavilion added to the courtyard side of the south wing. The massive columns used here instead of 2 superimposed Orders represent the first example of such an architectural innovation in France,   created a little earlier in Italy by Michelangelo. Bullant's inspiration for this feature almost certainly came from the portico of the Pantheon which he had drawn while in Rome. The niches were designed to receive perhaps the greatest sculptures by Michelangelo in France – the *Slaves*, now in the Louvre – which had been a present to Anne de Montmorency from Henri II.

Musée National de la Rénaissance The elegant Renaissance château makes the ideal setting for the magnificent collection of 16th and early 17th-century furniture, tapestries, ceramics, enamels, paintings and wainscoting, most of which come from the Renaissance collections of the Cluny Museum in Paris. Some original interior decoration exists, as in the painted friezes, but the painted fireplaces are the highlight of the château's interior. The work of French artists in the reign of Henri II, they reflect the Italian inspiration of the Fontainebleau School. Combining biblical scenes with allegorical and invented classical images and motifs of arms and armour, they reflect the influence of Rosso and Niccolo dell'Abate.

The decoration of the chapel incorporates the monograms A and M of Anne de Montmorency and his wife, Madeleine of Savoy. After a magnificent collection of arms come a series of rooms devoted in turn to a particular trade, which include a recreation of a goldsmith's workshop.

The first floor contains the Constable's and Madeleine of Savoy's suites, both superbly furnished with period furniture, and the west wing is hung with one of the greatest Renaissance tapestries to be found in France. Woven from wool, silk and silver braid, the tapestry of David and Bathsheba consists of 10 panels some 250 feet in length. It was produced in Brussels in the mid-16th century and tells the story of the romance between King David and Bathsheba. For beauty of design and quality of execution it is only rivalled by the tapestry of *The Hunts of Maximilian* in the Louvre.

The king's suite is also remarkable for the floor tiles made expressly for the château in 1542 and those with unusual heraldic motifs. On the second floor are gathered the household objects which would have been used by Anne de Montmorency and nobles of his wealth and stature – imported Isnik pottery, superb French ceramics, painted marriage chests, furniture, embroideries, majolicas, enamels, goblets belonging to Catherine de Médicis, jewellery and silverware. (Open Wed–Mon 9.45am–12.30pm and 2 – 5.15pm; Tel: 39 90 64 04.)

St-Denis Cathedral

Trains *Frequent* RER *trains on line D1 from* Châtelet-Les Halles **and Paris Gare du Nord to St-Denis Basilique** *(15 mins).*

Set in the rather grubby northern suburbs of Paris stands the cathedral of St-Denis, the magnificent mausoleum of the Kings of France. Initially a Roman city, Catoloacus, by the 5th century it was an important Christian settlement, clustered around the burial place of the evangelist St-Denis, the beheaded first bishop of Lutetia. By the 8th century the abbey had become the most celebrated in France and under Abbot Suger, in the 12th century, the present cathedral was built. Suger had become a close friend and advisor of Louis VII and when Louis left to take part in the Second Crusade, the King appointed him Regent of France in his absence.

Suger's design for the church was revolutionary in many ways – it was the first to feature the new 'Gothic' style in the choir and chapels around it, with pointed arches on slender columns – and was copied at Chartres, Senlis and Meaux and the choir of Notre Dame in Paris is a longer version of it. Work progressed rapidly after 1136, Suger inspiring widespread local support and Louis VII contributing heavily to its construction costs. In the 13th century a spectacular spire was added to the north tower and the central part of the choir, transepts and nave refashioned in a new 'Rayonnant' style which inspired later Gothic cathedrals such as Beauvais and Troyes. After being ineptly restored after the Revolution, the tower collapsed in 1846 so that the harmony of the west front was destroyed. The 3 doorways of the west front, depicting the Death of St Denis, the Last Judgement and the Last Communion of St Denis, were restored by Viollet-le-Duc between 1858 and 1879.

What to see

Royal Tombs

The great glory of St Denis however are the royal tombs – the resting place of the kings of France for 12 centuries. Almost every French King from Dagobert I to Louis XVIII were buried in the cathedral. At the Revolution the tombs were opened and the remains thrown into a common pit but Alexandre Lenoir moved the tombs to the Petits-Augustins to prevent their destruction and in 1816 they were returned to the basilica.

The finest tombs are those of François I and Claude de France, in the south transept, Henri II and Catherine de Médicis in the north transept, and Louis XII and Anne of Brittany in the north aisle. Apart from the tombs of French kings, queens and royal children are those of some of the most distinguished courtiers, the most notable being that of Bertrand du Guesclin.

The earliest effigies were all commissioned by St Louis in 1260 and have no claim to historical likeness but others are much more striking and have a strong resemblance to the figures they represent – particularly Philippe the Bold, Charles v and Charles vi, whose tombs were carved, in accordance with the practice of the time, while they were still alive. The Renaissance tombs are, naturally, far more monumental and lavish than the medieval ones, portraying the king and queen both in the magnificence of their royal regalia and as merely mortal human figures, subject to the inevitability of death. One of the finest of these tombs, depicting the king and queen in life and in death, is that of Henri ii by Primaticcio and Pilon which was begun in 1563. Another is that of François i by Philibert de l'Orme and Bontemps which takes the form of a Roman triumphal arch.

In the 15th century it became the custom to remove the heart and viscera of the kings before embalming their body; the bodies were buried at St-Denis while the heart and inner organs were buried elsewhere. The monument for the heart of François i, the work of Bontemps, however, is now at St-Denis. It consists of a round urn on a tall rectangular base and is one of the finest examples of the decorative style of the Fontainebleau School. The reliefs depict the arts and sciences which Francis i had so extensively patronised in his lifetime, while the nymphs reveal the influence of Primaticcio and Rosso.

The alarming realism of the dead figure of Catherine de Médici carved for her tomb so horrified Catherine that she is reputed to have fainted on seeing it for the first time. Recoiling from the stark portrayal of her, she ordered a new effigy in which she would appear to be sleeping in death rather than being consumed by it. Both effigies are now found in the cathedral.

Beneath the cathedral is a superb 12th-century crypt, built by Suger in the Romanesque style. It contains the remains of Louis xvi and Marie-Antoinette and a communal grave containing the remains, dispersed at the Revolution, of 800 royal kings, queens, princes and princesses of the Carolingian, Capetian, Valois and Bourbon dynasties. (Open 1st April to 30th Sept 10 am–7 pm; Sun noon–7 pm; Oct–Mar 10 am–5 pm. Tel. 48 09 83 54.)

Practicalities in St Denis Basilique

Tourist Office 2 rue Légion d'Honneur (Tel. 42 43 33 55).

Hotels ☆☆☆*Hôtel Campanile*, 2 quai St Ouen (Tel. 48 20 29 88), with attached restaurant.

Reims

Trains *8–12 trains daily from* **Paris** *Gare de l'Est (1½–2 hours); 4 daily from* **Metz** *(3 hours); 4 from* **Strasbourg** *(6 hours).*

Mid-way between Paris and the German border, Reims has been devastated in 2 world wars. During the first it lay for 4 years in the centre of a battle zone and by 1918 only 2 of its 14,000 houses were still standing.

Another 5,000 were destroyed during the Second World War. Despite the general destruction wrought in the First World War, the cathedral survived surprisingly unscathed and was then carefully restored for nearly 20 years, opening to the public only 2 years before the Second World War broke out.

Reims is intimately associated with the history of France for the Frankish king Clovis was baptised here in 496, and most of the kings of France have been crowned in the cathedral, from Philippe-Auguste in 1180 to Charles X in 1825. Edward III marched on the city with the intention of having himself crowned king of France but it was not until 1420 that Henry IV took the town. The English occupation of the town was to last only 9 years and in 1429 the cathedral was the scene of one of its most famous coronations – that of Charles VII in the presence of Joan of Arc who held a standard over his head during the coronation ceremony.

What to see

Cathédrale Notre-Dame
Architecture and sculpture combine to make Notre-Dame one of the great Gothic cathedrals of France and a testament to 13th-century Christian faith. Work began on the cathedral in 1211 and was all but completed by the end of the following century, although the western towers were not finished until 1430. The western façade is magnificent and perfectly balanced, enriched by a wealth of sculpture, some replicas, some original. The central doorway depicts scenes from the life of the Virgin: the Annunciation, Visitation, Purification and Coronation. The right-hand doorway portrays the Last Judgement, somewhat mutilated, and the left-hand one, the Passion. Here too is to be found a guardian angel with a mischevious smile, known as the *Angel with a smile*, reflecting sensual and serene qualities. The figures of angels proliferate to such an extent all over the building that Reims has been called 'the cathedral of angels'. Above the rose window, which was destroyed by shelling, is the figure of David challenging Goliath, flanked by Old Testament figures and the apostles.

Above this again, between the towers, is a sculpture of the baptism of Clovis, on either side of which extend impressive statues of the kings of France, towering some 49 metres above the ground.

Inside, the western end of the nave is of particular interest, with tier after tier of 13th-century statues, carved in a flowing and naturalistic style, enclosed in niches decorated with realistic foliage. Apart from this, the interior is remarkably plain and notable for the lightness of the construction and pointed arches and ribs which give the vaulting a great sense of grace and movement. Stained-glass windows by Marc Chagall adorn the western and eastern windows.

Palais du Tau
Adjacent to the cathedral is the Palais du Tau, the restored 17th-century Archbishop's Palace used by the kings of France when they journeyed to Reims

for their coronation. In the gothic Salle du Tau royal coronations were celebrated with great pomp and luxury. In the palace are gathered together many statues and casts that were once part of the cathedral, incuding the Coronation of the Virgin that once adorned the central gable of the western façade. Tapestries include 15th-century works from Tournai depicting the Life of Clovis (Open daily 9.30 am–6.30 pm, mid-March to June and Sept–Nov 9.30 am–12.30 pm and 2–6 pm; mid–Nov to mid-March Mon–Fri 10 am–noon and 2–5 pm.)

Musée des Beaux-Arts

In the 18th-century buildings that once belonged to the abbey of St-Denis is the Musée des Beaux-Arts, with one of the finest provincial art collections of northern France. The works of art span a wide period from Cranach, Philippe de Champaigne and Poussin to Fragonard, Delacroix, Corot and Pissarro, Sisley and Renoir. (Open Mon and Wed–Fri 10.30 am–noon and 2–6 pm, Sat–Sun 10 am–6 pm.)

Reims was already an important city in Roman Gaul and had a population of some 80,000 by the beginning of the 3rd century. It is not surprising therefore that the city has a number of Roman remains, some of which were only discovered in the rebuilding following the devastation caused by the First World War.

Porte de Mars

The most impressive Roman remain is the Porte de Mars, a Roman triumphal arch from the early 3rd century. The months of the year are depicted under the central archway and Romulus and Remus being suckled by the she-wolf, and Jupiter and Leda are shown under the side arches. Roman underground galleries used as warehouses have been discovered in the Place du Forum. The Musée du Vieux-Reims, housed in the early Renaissance Hôtel le Vergeur, also contains engravings, notably by Dürer.

Of the medieval era, one of the finest buildings is the Maison des Comtes de Champagne, a 13th-century Gothic mansion. From the Renaissance era, the most interesting building is probably the Hôtel de la Salle with its superb Renaissance façade and courtyard, while the Hôtel de Ville is the best surviving example in Reims of Louis XIII architecture, dating from 1636. Of 18th-century architecture, the Place Royale, begun in 1758, is a handsome and characteristic example.

Champagne Caves

Down in the south of the city, not far from the Basilique St-Remi are to be found the caves of the great champagne companies of Reims – Veuve-Cliquot-Ponsardin, Taittinger, Krugs. For Reims vies with Epernay as being the 'Champagne capital', even though this famous drink is believed to have been invented by a monk of the abbey of Hautvillers, Dom Pérignon. The important champagne firms have miles of subterranean galleries tunnelled beneath the city, some of Gallo-Roman origin, a few of which can be visited. Mumm's caves at 34 rue du Champ de Mars, are amongst the best. (Open Wed–Mon, 10 am–noon and 2–6 pm.)

One of the more curious sights in Reims is the **Chapelle Foujita** in the north of the city, near the caves of Champagne Mumm. The stained glass and frescoes were designed and executed by the Japanese painter Foujita after his conversion to Catholicism. After his death in 1968 he was buried in the chapel named after him.

Practicalities in Reims

Tourist Office 2 rue de Machault, 15 minutes walk from station, next to cathedral, in the remains of the old charterhouse (Tel. 26 47 25 69); currency exchange.

Railway Station Blvd Joffre, across the park from the centre of town (Tel. 26 88 50 50); luggage storage open daily 5:45 am–8:30 pm; lockers; information desk open Mon–Fri 8:30 am–7:30 pm, Sat 9 am–6:15 pm. From station, walk up Rue Thiers, turn right onto cours Langlet which leads to cathedral.

Buses City buses stop in front of station; tourist ticket from *tabacs* and automatic distributors allows unlimited 1 day travel.

Hotels ☆*Hôtel Gambetta*, 9 rue Gambetta (Tel. 26 47 41 64). Smallish, simple rooms but clean, central and inexpensive.

☆☆*Hôtel de la Paix*, 9 rue de Buirette (Tel. 26 40 04 08). Modern, large hotel on 8 floors, with garden, swimming pool; pricey restaurant.

Restaurants ☆ *Les Brisants*, 13 rue de Chativesle, off Place Drouet d'%erlon (Tel. 26 40 60 41). Refreshing, cool interior and courtyard with good simple meals.

☆☆Le Vigneron, Place Paul-Jamot (Tel. 26 47 00 71). Superb little brasserie in 17th-century mansion evocative of the champagne-producing process; excellent hearty meals, with local specialities carefully prepared.

Châlons-sur-Marne

Trains *8 trains daily from* **Paris** *Gare de l'Est (1½ hours); 2 daily from* **Strasbourg** *(3½ hours), 7 from* **Reims** *via Epernay (35 mins), 7 from* **Metz** *(1½ hours).*

Châlons lies in the midst of a vast rolling plain devoted to cereal production, and in the heart of the city lies the cathedral of St-Etienne, a curious and unharmonious building that reflects every era and style of French architecture. Although the cathedral is not the most fascinating building in the city, it is of particular interest to any student of architecture.

What to see

Cathédrale St-Etienne

The main body of the building is late 13th-century Gothic but the northern tower is 12th-century Romanesque, a remnant of the previous cathedral. The western façade is a curious contrast, being in a severe classical style and dating from the reign of Louis XIII. Originally the apse and choir had no aisles but in the 14th century chapels were made by breaking through the walls below the clerestory. The stained-glass windows are stunning for the brilliance of their colour and complexity. The rose window in the southern transept is a glorious fanfare of reds and crimsons, seen to great effect when light streams through the window at midday. The stained glass in the northern transept is also outstanding and dates from the 13th century, while the glass of the aisles, in the great series of windows that dominate the nave, dates from the 16th century.

Notre-Dame-en-Vaux

More interesting than the cathedral is Notre-Dame-en-Vaux which was rebuilt in the 12th century. Despite the depredations committed during the Revolution, Notre-Dame is one of the finest 12th-century buildings in Champagne. The Romanesque façade dates from this period, the rest of the cathedral being built slightly later in an early Gothic style, so that while the columns and capitals are Romanesque, the structure of the nave and the apse reflect the arrival of Gothic architecture. Like St Etienne, the aisles retain superb 16th-century stained glass. The adjacent **museum** contains many fragments of very fine statues, capitals and columns from the destroyed Romanesque cloister unearthed in a series of lengthy excavations.

Châlons was once a centre of the wool trade, Chaucer referring to the woolen cloth of the town as 'Chalouns' while Swift later referred to it as 'Shalloons'. With the decline of the wool trade the town's prosperity came to rely increasingly on wine and then the military, for Châlons is to the French army what Aldershot is to the British.

Two events mark the association of the town with Louis XVI and Marie-Antoinette, one propitious, one inauspicious. For Marie-Antoinette arrived in Châlons on her way to be married to the Dauphin, and a triumphal arch was built just outside the town to mark the event. Her second arrival was not such a happy occasion, for it was to Châlons that she and Louis XVI were escorted after their abortive and ignominious attempt to flee to Varennes in 1791.

Practicalities in Châlons-sur-Marne

Tourist Office 3 quai des Arts, off Rue de la Marne (Tel 26 65 64 69).
Railway Station Place de la Gare (Tel 26 88 50 50); cross river Marne to reach centre ville.
Hotels Hotel de la Cité 12 rue de la Charrière; 15 minute north-west from station (Tel. 26 64 31 20)
☆☆Hôtel Angleterre, 19 Place Monseigneur-Tissier (Tel. 26 68 21 51). Stylish renovated hotel in centre, close to Notre-Dame-en-Vaux; delicious cooking from chef Jacky Michel.
Hostels Auberge de Jeunesse (HI), Rue Kellerman, on far side of town from station close to junction with rue Chevalier (Tel. 26 68 13 56).
Camping Ave des Alliés, just to south of town; open April–Oct (Tel. 26 68 38 00).

Rambouillet

Trains 8 – 12 trains daily from Paris Montparnasse (30 mins)

South-west of Versailles, on the edge of a vast forest, stands the **Château of Rambouillet**, the country residence of the French President which may be visited when he is not in residence (except on Tuesdays and Wednesdays). The château was originally built in the 14th century but only one machicolated tower remains of this building, the present château having been built by the Comte de Toulouse, one of Louis XIV's sons by Madame de Montespan. Louis XVI later bought the château to create an experimental farm to satisfy the whim of Marie-Antoinette.

For her the most extraordinary dairy was built, complete with grotto, chequered pink marble floors and Roman style ceiling. It appears to have done little to endear her to the place however which she referred to as 'la crapaudière' (the toad-hole). Louis also established a sheep farm which developed into the Bergerie Nationale. The first merino sheep were shepherded to Rambouillet from Spain in a journey that took 4 months; after living in the open for a long time special stables were built for them under the Empire.

The château has been altered a number of times and is now a curious medley of styles of sombre red brick with rounded stone towers at the corners, but the interior is handsome with superb panelling and fine tapestries. The park contains a beautiful avenue of Louisana cypresses, formal French gardens in the style of Le Nôtre and a *Jardin anglais*, almost any informal garden being considered by the French to be in the English style. An enchanting pavilion in the grounds decorated with shells and mother of pearl, the Pavillon des Coquillages, was built by the Duc de Penthievre for his daughter-in-law, the Princesse de Lamballe. Francis I died in the château in 1547 and Charles X signed his abdication here in 1830 after the July Revolution confirmed the widely-held belief that the Bourbons were able to 'learn nothing and forget nothing'. It was reported of Charles X that he was so distraught at the prospect of sitting at an oval table, which had no clear place of precedence for a king, that he preferred to remain standing until a rectangular table could be found. (Open Oct–Mar, Wed–Mon 10 – 11.30 am and 2 – 4.30 pm; April–Sept 10 – 11.30 am and 2 – 5.30 pm, when President not in residence.)

Practicalities in Rambouillet

Tourist Office In the Hôtel de Ville, close to château off Place de la Libération (Tel. 34 83 21 21).

Railway Station (Information and Reservation: Tel. 30 64 50 50.)

Restaurants ☆*Cheval Rouge*, 78 rue Général de Gaulle (Tel. 30 88 80 61). A short walk along rue Gén. de Gaulle from the château.

☆*La Poste*, 101 rue Général de Gaulle (Tel. 34 83 03 01). Traditional cooking, good range of menus in old coaching inn in town centre.

Gien

Trains *3 – 6 trains daily from* **Paris** *Gare de Lyon (1½ hours).*

Situated on the borders of the old provinces of Orléanais and Berry, Gien is a delightful little town on the banks of the Loire. The château was badly damaged by the German invasion of June 1940 but has since been superbly restored. It was built at the end of the 15th century by Anne de Beaujeu, a daughter of Louis XI and Regent during the minority of her brother, the future Charles XIII. Anne had received the county of Gien on her marriage to Pierre de Bourbon. The town prospered under her direction, witnessing the construction of new convents, mansions and town houses. It was at Gien that Anne of Austria, Louis XIV and Mazarin took refuge during the Fronde in 1652.

The château is built in an unusual local style of black and red patterned brick within stone frames; these same local bricks were used to unusual effect in the rebuilding of the local church directly opposite the château after the war. Although built in 1494 the château presents the appearence less of a military stronghold than of a pleasure-house. It's composed of 2 parts set at right angles; towards the Loire the main building is flanked by a small square tower; on the other side by a round one. From the château there are magnificent views of the valley of the Loire while from the restored 16th-century bridge there is an equally fine view looking back of this attractive river-side town. In the 18th century Gien prospered from its manufacture of earthenware, for which it was widely famed.

What to see

Musée de la Chasse

The château is of particular fascination for anyone with an interest in hunting for since 1952 it has contained an unusual museum devoted to exclusively to the sport; it now possesses the most comprehensive collection of hunting trophies, arms, powder flasks, falconry objects and works of art inspired by hunting to be found anywhere in Europe. Apart from engravings, ceramics and sculptures, there are fine paintings by Jean-Baptiste Oudry and Francois Desportes.

Practicalities in Gien

Tourist Office Centre Anne-de-Beaujeau, on Place Jean Jaurès (Tel. 38 67 25 28).
Railway Station (Info: Tel. 38 53 50 50; Reservations: Tel. 38 62 56 65.)

Hotels ☆☆*Hôtel Rivage*, 1 quai Nice (Tel 38 37 79 90). Superb view over the Loire.
Restaurants *Le Poularde*, 13 quai Nice (Tel. 38 67 36 05); adjacent to Hôtel Rivage.

Vaux-le-Vicomte

Trains *Frequent trains daily to Melun from* **Paris** *Gare de Lyon (40 mins), thence direct buses from* **Melun** SNCF *to the château, 5 km away.*

At Vaux-le-Vicomte stands the exquisite **château** built by Le Vau for Louis XIV's finance minister, Nicholas Fouquet, in 1656–61. This, Le Vau's first important commission, was at the time the most splendid château and gardens to be found anywhere in France. Work was carried out at breakneck speed: Le Vau was commissioned in 1657, the roof was being put on by the end of 1658 and the decoration of the interior was nearly complete by the time of the famous fête which took place in 1661.

The palace is a superb example of mid-17th century architecture with sumptuous internal decorations by Le Brun and magnificent gardens designed by Le Nôtre in one of his first commissions. It stands in an idyllic and entirely rural location, a haven of peace and quiet in all seasons. Enclosed by a moat, the château is reached via a vast courtyard partly enclosed by ornate brick and stone wings. The château itself is approached via a second, formal courtyard, while the south side, with a projecting central pediment and dome, faces onto the formal gardens. The middle of the building consists of a rectangular vestibule which leads to a highly original oval salon lying across the main axis of the building. The wings on either side contain a splendid 'appartement', – that on the east side for the King and that on the west for the owner of the château. Both look out onto the formal gardens, where a succession of ornamental lakes, fountains and terraces descend gracefully to a small river channelled into a formal stretch of water. The combination of château and gardens is virtually without rival in France, the terraced parterre sloping away slowly from the château for over half a mile until it reaches the canal and the grotto, beyond which rises a long grass stretch flanked by trees. With its fountains, terraces, grottoes, canal and sweeps of greensward, the gardens of Vaux-le-Vicomte prefigured those of Versailles. The perfection was such that it was to arouse the jealousy of Louis XIV, a jealousy carefully played upon to the destruction of Fouquet by the king's astute minister and adviser, Colbert.

The sumptuously furnished apartments are centred around the high oval hall beneath the central dome. The salon is relatively staid in its ornament but other buildings are elaborately decorated, some with painted grotesque panels and others, like the King's bedroom, in a style new to France which Lebrun had brought from Italy. Lebrun's combination of stucco, gilding and painting probably derives from Pietro da Cortona's decoration of the Palazzo Pitti. The style, which was to be copied in the decoration of Louis XIV's first rooms at Versailles, is Baroque, derived from Italian sources, but tempered and restrained by the French classical spirit. The rooms were further embellished with tapestries, woven specifically for a château in a workshop set up locally for the purpose, but these unfortunately are no longer on the property.

The young King Louis was sumptuously entertained at the newly completed château by Fouquet on 17th August 1661. It was a memorable occasion, of unparalleled luxury and grandeur, which was to have disastrous consequences for the host, Nicholas Fouquet. Not only was the King present but the Queen, the King's current mistress Mademoiselle de la Vallière and the whole court. After a feast prepared by Vatel, the court was entertained by a performance of Molière's new play Les Fâcheux, on a stage decorated by Lebrun and with music composed specially for the occasion by Lully. The festivities, which ended with a magnificent firework display, were described by La Fontaine who, as Fouquet's poet, was present at the occasion. Only 19 days after this extravagant fête Fouquet was abruptly arrested and sent to gaol on charges of embezzlement and his property confiscated. Rarely can a fall from favour have been so spectacular. His rival and destroyer, Colbert, then commanded all the artists, architects, sculptors, painters, composers and poets who had worked for Fouquet to work thenceforward for the King. At a stroke, Colbert thereby acquired a team that could be called upon to satisfy the King's taste for splendour. Quite apart from taking over all the artists responsible for the success of Vaux-le-Vicomte, Colbert ordered the best statues and rarest trees in the park to be transported to Versailles, where work began under Le Vau in 1667. (Château open April–Oct Mon–Sat 10 am–12.30 pm and 2 – 5.30 pm, Sun and holidays 10 am–6 pm; Feb–March, 1st–29th Nov and 19th Dec– 4th Jan Mon–Sat 11 am–12.30 pm and 2–4.30 pm, Sun and holidays 11 am–5 pm. Tel. 60 66 97 09.) The gardens are open for the same hours as the house but stay open at lunch time. The fountains in Le Nôtre's gardens are turned on April– October every second and last Saturday of the month from 3–6 pm.

Practicalities in Vaux-le-Vicomte/Melun

Tourist Office In Melun is just across from station at 2 ave Gallieni (Tel. 64 37 11 31). **Railway Station** Melun station is 6 km from the

Château of Vaux-le-Vicomte. **Taxi Service** 64 52 51 50.

Fontainebleau

Trains 10 – 12 trains daily from Paris Gare de Lyon (45 mins); thence direct bus service to the château 1½ kms away.

On his return from captivity in Madrid François I made Paris his head-quarters, so that whereas before 1525 the Loire valley had been the most advanced region of France, after 1528 the lead passed to the Ile-de-France. All the new royal palaces built in this period, in which French architecture began to free itself from Gothic influences, are to be found within a relatively short distance of Paris.

The earliest Capetian kings had originally been drawn to Fontainebleau on account of its magnificent and stately forests that made ideal hunting country. A vast expanse of mature oak, birch, beech, holly, juniper and hornbeam, the forêts de Fontainebleau are no less beautiful a sight today than they were 800 years ago, when they were first referred to as a royal hunting ground.

On his return to France in 1528 François I decided to make a number of improvements to the medieval castle of Fontainebleau which was little more than a hunting lodge, then in a state of disrepair. It had been abandoned by Charles VII and his successors who had deserted it for Amboise, Blois and other châteaux on the Loire. But François I did not sweep away the derelict château and start afresh; additions were made and wings built on to earlier buildings so that, although attractive, the château is a composite building, lacking the harmony and symmetry one might expect of a new royal residence.

What to see

After Versailles the **Château of Fontainebleau** is one the most famous and historically important royal palaces in France. Here François I marshalled the artists, masons, architects, musicians and scholars he had enticed to France from Italy, a group that was later to become known as the School of Fontainebleau. The painters Giovanni Rosso from Florence and Primaticcio, a native of Bologna, were foremost among them. The overall architectural manner of Fontainebleau is definitely French, most of the early work having been carried out under the direction of the master-mason Gilles Le Breton. The new entrance to the court of the old castle, the **Porte Dorée**, betrays the influence of Italian sources on Le Breton, but the asymmetricality is typically French, as is the way in which the pediment of one window cuts into the support of the one above or the entablature of the main order. Although medieval elements remain – such as the high-pitched roof – French architectural style changed in the 1530s and 1540s, absorbing Italian influences and no longer merely applying them to the surface of what were still fundamentally late Gothic buildings.

The actual interior decoration of the château however is more Italian than French, for the work there was largely carried out by 2 Italian artists of distinction, Giovanni Battista Rosso and Francesco Primaticcio. Much of their work has been destroyed by subsequent alteration but the **Galerie François I** and the **Chambre de la Duchesse d'Etampes** retain the brilliant combination of painted panels with stucco sculpture in relief which is the characteristic of Fontainebleau decoration. Rosso's main work, the Galerie François I, survives whereas the decoration executed by Primaticcio has disappeared over time, except for the upper part of the fireplace in the Chambre de la Reine. Primaticcio had worked on the Castello of the Gonzagas at Mantua before coming to France and this experience is clearly evident in the fruit swags, sphinxes and elongated figures of the mantlepiece.

In the Galerie François I, Rosso created a gallery of unparalleled richness, variety and ingenuity. The lower part of the walls were panelled while the upper part is decorated with stucco and painting, in which Rosso displayed an unflagging ability to produce new motives, much of it fantastic and entirely original. This decoration is purely Italian but the form of the gallery, which was to become such a feature of French châteaux, as it was too of English country houses, is not at all Italian in origin.

Further important changes were made by later monarchs. Henri II and Catherine de Médicis made various additions on the designs of Jean Bullant and Philibert Delorme. Henri IV embellished the palace further at great cost, adding greatly to the size of the château with the Cour des Offices, the Cour des Princes and the Jeu de Paume, and here in 1601 his son, the future Louis XIII, was born. Louis XIV however preferred Versailles to Fontainebleau which he referred to disparagingly as a 'new Rome'. Nevertheless, he still commissioned Le Nôtre to improve the gardens and had some of the rooms redecorated for his mistress, Madame de Maintenon.

Amongst the distinguished visitors received here were Christina of Sweden, James II of England, Peter the Great, Christian VII of Denmark and Pius VII who was made to renounce his temporal sovereignty while held prisoner by Napoleon. Louis XV and Marie Leszczyńska were married here and Jean-Jacques Rousseau was a guest in 1754. It was the palace of Fontainebleau that Napoleon made his principal residence, spending 12 million francs on its restoration. It was here too that he was compelled to sign his abdication in 1814, before leaving for Elba from the Cour du Cheval Blanc. The palace was later restored in somewhat questionable taste by Louis-Philippe.

The vast palace is composed around 5 courtyards, the largest being the Cour du Cheval Blanc, flanked to the north by the François I wing and to the south by the Louis XV wing. The eastern façade has a superb horseshoe staircase designed by Jean du Cerceau. The second courtyard, the Cour de la Fontaine, is dominated by the François I gallery which looks out onto a formal lake inhabited by carp which are reputed to live to the ripe old age of a hundred. The Porte Dorée leads to the Cour Ovale with its sumptuous **Salle de Bal**, one of the most splendid rooms in the palace which was decorated under Henri II by Philibert de l'Orme, and the apartments of Marie-Antoinette which lead in turn to the final courtyard, the Cour des Offices, dating from Henri IV's reign.

The extraordinarily sumptuous decorations of the royal apartments are immensely varied, reflecting the long time-scale over which the palace was built and extended. Italian influence is at its strongest in the Galerie François I with its frescoes representing allegorical and mythological scenes while the Salle de Bal, the most splendid room in the palace, displays the greatest artistic achievement of Henri II's reign. His monograms are everywhere interlaced with those of Diane de Poitiers and her emblems, bows and arrows and crescents. Napoleon's apartments are superbly ornamented with Empire-style furniture and decoration, and are scattered with his personal belongings and effects. Just before Marie Antoinette's apartments is the King's bedroom, later turned into the throne room by Napoleon, which has a Louis XIII ceiling and Louis XIV and Louis XV wall decoration. Another magnificent room is the **Salon Louis XIII**, or Grand Cabinet du Roi, which was decorated by Paul Bril under Henri IV. Here Marie de Médicis gave birth to Louis XIII in 1613. Three of the panels painted by Ambroise Dubois for this room had to be removed in the reign of Louis XV to allow the passage of the new voluminous dresses of the period through the doors. The **Salle des Tapisseries** contain a series of fine Gobelin tapestries depicting the life of Constantine made for Louis XIV. (Château open Wed–Mon 9.30 am–12.30 pm and 2–5 pm; Gardens open 9 am–dusk.)

Practicalities in Fontainebleau

Tourist Office On rue de France, close to the luxury hotel, *Aigle Noir*, in centre.

Railway Station 1½ km north-east of the château along rue Aristide Briand.

Hotels ☆☆ *Hôtel de Londres*, Place Général de Gaulle, (Tel. 64 22 20 21). 19th-century hotel overlooking château, pleasant rooms, most with baths.

☆☆ *Hôtel Toulouse*, 183 rue Grande (Tel. 64 22 22 73). Delightful balconied hotel in a side-street parallel to rue Aristide Briand; some rooms overlooking château.

☆☆ *Ile de France*, 128 rue de France (Tel. 64 22 17 25). Renovated old mansion; some quiet modernised rooms looking on to garden.

Restaurants *Le Dauphin*, 24 rue Grande (Tel. 64 22 27 04). Rustic, welcoming restaurant near the Hôtel de Ville. Specialities include *confit de canard* and snails.

Troyes

Trains *6–9 trains daily from* **Paris** *Gare de l'Est (1½ hours); 8 daily from* **Chaumont** *(1 hour); 5 from* **Mulhouse** *(3 hours).*

In the Middle Ages and Renaissance, the regional fairs of the Champagne area turned Troyes into one of the great commercial centres of Europe situated on an important trade route between the North Sea and the Mediterranean. The Counts of Champagne, benefitting from the prosperity this created, contributed to the magnificence of their city, commissioning work throughout the 16th century from the leading architects, stonemasons, artists, wood-carvers and glass workers of the day. It was only with the revocation of the Edict of Nantes that the fortunes of the town began to fade; fearful of persecution its industrious Huguenot population began to flee abroad and the population steadily fell from a high of 60,000 in the reign of Henri IV to 23,000 at the end of the 18th century. King Henry V of England came to the city in 1420 to marry Catherine of France in the church of St-Jean. Known as the 'city of a hundred towers' Troyes is famous above all for its superb Gothic churches.

What to see

Cathédrale St-Pierre et St-Paul

The cathedral, built over 4 centuries, is somewhat lacking in unity but it is nevertheless one of the finest religious buildings of the Champagne region, with a huge, lofty nave and superb stained glass. From outside, the western façade is curiously imbalanced for there is no southern tower and the northern tower, not finished until 1640, displays a variety of styles. The style of the façade is Flamboyant but almost all its statues were destroyed at the Revolution. Fortunately most of the stained glass escaped the same fate for it is exceptionally beautiful. The great western rose window is a superb example of the feathery elegance and grace of Flamboyant tracery at its most accomplished. The earliest stained glass represents the *Tree of Jesse* and is to be found in the ambulatory; the latest, portraying the mystic wine-press, is in a chapel off the nave. While still unfinished the cathedral was consecrated in the presence of Charles VII and Joan of Arc in 1429. (Open daily 8 am–6 pm in summer, 9 am-noon and 2–5 pm in winter.)

Musée d'Art Moderne

Close to the cathedral is the Musée d'Art Moderne, an impressive collection of 20th-century French art. The museum is housed in the 17th-century Bishop's Palace, graced with a rich Renaissance interior. The museum is based on the Pierre and Denise Levy collection of modern art which is strong on paintings and sketches by Cézanne, Degas, Dufy, Braque, Matisse, Modigliani and Picasso. (Open Wed–Mon 11 am–6 pm.) Nearby is the **Musée St-Loup**, in the old Abbaye St-Loup at 21 rue Chrétien-de-Troyes, with an eclectic collection of Merovingian, Gallo-Roman and medieval objects; attached to the museum is the **library** of the abbey with one of the largest library halls in France, housing a superb collection of illuminated manuscripts and incunables. The rue de la Cité leads past the Hôtel Dieu to the quai Dampierre and the entrance to the **Musée de la Pharmacie** in the only part of the 18th-century hospital open to the public. (Open Wed–Mon 10 am–noon and 2–6 pm.)

St Urbain

Another fine church is that of St Urbain, in rue Clemençeau, which was built in the mid-13th century in an elaborate Rayonnant Gothic style by Pope Urban IV who was a native of the city. Huge windows contain delicate stained glass, much of it 13th-century. The stained glass in the choir depicts Christ and the prophets and in the side chapel is an exquisite statue, the *Virgin with a Grape*, a masterpiece of local 16th-century sculpture.

Ste Madeleine

The oldest church in Troyes, Ste-Madeleine also has an exceptional statue; close to the south-west pillar of the crossing is a statue of *St Martha* which is a moving portrayal of humility and grace. Ste-Madeleine also has a remarkable **rood screen** carved by Jean Gailde between 1508 and 1517. Another church, that of **St Pantaleon**, contains sculptures by the Florentine-born artist known in France as Domenique Florentin. He had worked on stuccos at Fontainebleau under the direction of Rosso and Primaticcio but settled in Troyes in 1541. His sculptures, notably of *Charity* and the seated Virgin in the church of St Pantaleon, imply a knowledge of the work of Michelangelo and reflect the influence of Sansovino and Rosso.

Apart from its numerous superb churches, which gave rise to Troyes' reputation as 'the city of the hundred towers', there are many ancient half-timbered houses with projecting upper storeys and corner turrets. **Rue Champeaux** and the narrow **rue des Chats** are especially evocative of the medieval city.

Hôtel de Mauroy

One of the most impressive Renaissance mansions is the Hôtel de Mauroy at 7 rue de la Trinité. Dating from 1560, this is a superb chequered stone and brick half-timbered building characteristic of the region. It now contains a fascinating and unusual collection of tools used by wood-carvers, stone-masons and other crafts-men throughout the centuries, gathered together in a **Museum of Implements**. (Open daily 9 am–noon and 2–6 pm.)

Hôtel de Vauluisant

Rue Bordet leads to the church of **St Pantaléon** in rue de Turenne and another fine Renaissance mansion – the Hôtel de Vauluisant, flanked by turrets, and housing an excellent museum of local history, the **Musée Historique**, and a museum devoted to one of the traditional trades of the city – the manufacture of bonnets, the **Musée de la Bonneterie**. (Open Wed–Mon 10 am–noon and 2–6 pm.)

Practicalities in Troyes

Tourist Office 16 blvd Carnot, almost opposite the station (Tel. 25 73 00 36); accommodation list; guided tours of the city. **Railway Station** (Tel. 25 73 50 50); from station, follow blvd Gambetta until end, then right into quai Dampierre; information office; lockers. **Hotels** *Hôtel du Théatre*, 35 rue Lebocey, close to station, on street parallel to rue Gén de Gaulle (Tel. 25 73 18 47). *Hôtel de Paris*, 54 rue Roger Salengro (Tel. 25 73 11 70). Superb and modestly priced 2 star hotel in 12th century building, once a mint belonging to the counts of France. *Hôtel le Marigny*, 3 rue Charbonnet (Tel. 25 73 10 67). Attractive old hotel close to centre.

St-Germain-en-Laye

Trains RER *trains every 15 mins daily to* RER *station St Germain-en-Laye, the final stop west on* RER *line A1, from* **Châtelet-les-Halles** *(30 mins).*

A very short distance west of Paris lies St Germain-en-Laye with its former royal château now housing the **Musée des Antiquités Nationales**. Unfortunately frequent restorations have not added to the architectural interest of this building which was originally constructed by Louis VI, known as Louis the Fat, in the 12th century to defend Paris from the west.

The Black Prince burnt the earliest château to the ground and in its place a new one rose under Charles V and Francis I. Under the Empire the château was used as a cavalry school and then as a prison under Louis-Philippe before becoming a museum under Napoleon III.

What to see

Château Royal

The royal palace of St Germain-en-Laye once consisted of 2 buildings – the Château Vieux which was rebuilt in the 16th century and the Château Neuf, a country house begun by Henri II and finished by Henri IV. The latter no longer survives, except for the tiny fragments known as the Pavillon Henri IV and Pavillon Sully, and it is the Château Vieux that Louis XIV made alterations to before abandoning the Château altogether for grander projects at Versailles.

The Château Vieux had been rebuilt by François I who knocked down the earlier castle except for the large Keep built by Charles V and the beautiful Sainte Chapelle erected by St Louis in 1230. This little chapel, older than the Sainte Chapelle in Paris, is a jewel of Gothic art but its beauty and interest has been impaired by the loss of its stained glass.

Louis XIV commissioned Hardouin-Mansart to replace the feudal corner turrets with rounded pavilions and Le Nôtre to lay out the gardens and terraces and replant the forest behind the château. Part of these gardens were destroyed with the arrival of the railway line in the 1870s but the parterres are still laid out much as they were at the time of Louis XIV. One of the most original features of the château at the time it was built was the flat Italianate roof terrace. The balustrades and urns with which it is decorated are carved with the letter 'F' and the salamander – the emblem of King François I.

St Germain-en-Laye has many connections with England for it was the residence of the widowed queen Henrietta Maria during the Protectorate and James II lived there in the 17th century, with his queen Mary of Modena, until his death in 1701. James II's tomb, containing only his heart, lies in the church opposite the château. The extensive view from the terrace of the château – on the Seine with Paris in the distance was likened by James II in his exile to the view of the Thames that could be enjoyed from the terrace at Richmond.

Musée des Antiquités Nationales The Musée des Antiquités Nationales housed in the château is one of the great archaeological museums of Europe and was established by Napoleon III in the château after the building had been restored to its Renaissance appearance. The collections are extensive and range from prehistory to the Carolingian era with fine collections of Stone Age tools and Gallo-Roman statues, brooches, weapons, funerary stele, jewellery and everyday objects. (Open Wed–Mon 9 am–7.30 pm; Tel. 34 51 53 65.)

Musée du Prieuré

The town of St Germain-en-Laye itself is chiefly of interest for its Musée du Prieuré with its collection of paintings by the Symbolists Maurice Denis and Nabis who opposed the naturalism of the Impressionists. The museum is housed in the tranquil precincts of a former Jesuit priory. (Open Tues–Fri 10 am–5.30 pm, Sat–Sun 10 am–6.30 pm; Tel. 39 73 77 87.) The town is also of interest for the church of **Saint Louis Saint Germain** which contains the tomb of James II, and its pleasant old quarter which still retains many fine 17th- and 18th-century houses. Claude Debussy was born here in 1862. The extensive forests of St Germain still stretch away to the north, beyond the **Grand Terasse**, a delightful 2,286-metre-long terrace above the Seine laid out by Le Nôtre in the early 1670s for Louis XIV.

Practicalities in St Germain-en-Laye

Tourist Office 38 rue Au Pain (Tel. 34 51 05 12).

Railway Station Very close to château opposite the church of St Germain.

Restaurants *La Feuillantine*, 10 rue des Louviers (Tel. 34 51 04 24). A delightful, friendly restaurant with delicious low-priced set menu.

Chartres

Trains *Frequent trains daily from* **Paris** *Gare Montparnasse (1 hour); and* **Versailles** *(55 mins).*

Apart from arriving by foot across the fields, there is no more evocative way of approaching Chartres than by train. Coming across the flat rich wheatfields of La Beauce, the great mass of the cathedral appears much as it would have done to kings and pilgrims for centuries. On a fine day it can be seen for 20 or 30 miles, its 2 pointed spires stretching high above its copper-green roof.

The donation of what was believed to be the Virgin's robe to the church by Charles the Bald in the 9th century instantly made Chartres an important pilgrimage centre. When the church was burnt down in 1194 and the tunic survived the fire, a vast cathedral was built in the record space of just 25 years to celebrate the miracle.

What to see

Cathédrale Notre-Dame

The **Portail Royal**, sculptured in the mid-12th century of the western front is one of the great sights of the Christian world. The stylised figures in and around the tympana are perhaps the most beautiful early Gothic statuary in France, combining a tranquility and ethereal spirituality that has rarely been surpassed. The tympanum of the right-hand doorway portrays the Virgin and the childhood of Christ; the central one Christ in Glory with the Evangelists and the Apostles, and the left-hand one the Ascension. The magnificent rose window and, above it, the gallery of the Kings of Judah date from the 13th century. The northern tower is surmounted by a 16th-century Flamboyant spire while the southern one, Romanesque in style, is late 12th-century.

The north and south transepts both have 3 doorways carved with complete schemes of High Gothic sculpture in the early 13th century, 50 years after the *Portail Royal*. On the north transept, the central tympanum shows the Coronation of the Virgin; the left one the adoration of the Magi and on the right the story of Job. The south Transept has the Last Judgement on the central tympanum; the martydom of Christ and other saints on the left tympanum; the martyrdom of Christ and other saints on the left tympanum and on the right the stones of St Martan and St Nicholas, two saints particularly venerated in the Middle Ages.

On entering the cathedral, the overwhelming sensation is one of space and colour, the latter coming from the brilliant hues of medieval glass which fill more than 160 windows. The **stained glass** of Chartres is a marvel in its own right, being some of the earliest and richest stained glass in Europe, and ideally should be seen against bright sunlight, different windows being inspected at different times of day. The glass is not only of exceptional luminosity and brilliance, quite exceptional for its age, but each window tells a story that would have made a deep and lasting impression on the medieval mind. Most of the glass dates from the 13th century but that in the 3 western lancets, of which one depicts the *Tree of Jesse*, survived the fire in 1194.

25 years ago an English art-student arrived to see the glass for himself; he never left and is now acknowledged to be the world authority on the stained glass of Chartres cathedral. He still frequently takes visitors on guided tours – one of the most fascinating and worthwhile to be found anywhere in France. Most of the windows depict the lifes and legends of saints; of less significance but no less fascinating are the pictures of the craftsmen whose guilds and corporations sponsored the different windows. In all the glass covers some 21,000 square feet.

The large rose-window of the western façade depicts the *Last Judgement*; that in the north transept which was a gift from St Louis portrays the Virgin, while that in the south transept glorifies Christ. Another outstanding window, the second in the south ambulatory, represents the Virgin and is known as Notre-Dame-de-la-Belle Verrière.

The theatrical and lively sculptures of the stone choir screen make a strong contrast with the almost Byzantine Gothic figures on the exterior of the cathedral. These late Gothic sculptures, depicting the life of Christ and the Virgin, were begun in 1514 on the designs of Jehan de Beauce and worked on slowly throughout the Renaissance. The vast majority of the building however dates from the 13th century, work having progressed very rapidly on the new cathedral built to replace the one burnt down in 1194. Alone of almost all the great cathedrals of France, Chartres survived unscathed from the ravages of the Religious Wars, the Revolution and the Second World War. 'It is at Chartres that the encyclopaedic nature of medieval art is best seen,' wrote Emile Mâle. 'The cathedral is the visible expression of medieval thought: nothing important has been left out. Its 10,000 painted or sculpted figures form an assemblage that is unique in Europe.'

The **crypt**, dating from the beginning of the 11th century, is the largest in France, with traces of 13th-century frescoes. The cathedral is the justification of any visit to Chartres but there are a number of narrow streets with interesting wooden and gabled houses to be seen, a fine early 17th-century mansion, the **Hôtel Montescot** and a 13th-century tithe barn, the **Cellier de Loens**.

Musée des Beaux-Arts

Just behind the cathedral, at 29 rue Cloître Notre-Dame, in a beautiful 18th-century building which was once the Archbishop's Palace, is the museum of fine arts. The Musée des Beaux-Arts contains a series of Flemish tapestries depicting the life of Moses which once hung in the choir of the cathedral, Renaissance enamels, armour, some fine French paintings including a collection by Maurice de Vlaminck who lived in the area. (Open Wed–Mon 10 – 11.45 am and 2 – 5.45 pm.)

Next to the museum are some delightful gardens which look down over the old streets that descend to the River Eure.

In the rue des Ecuyers a turret is to be found which hides a 16th-century oak spiral staircase, the **Escalier de la Reine-Berthe**; a little later this road turns into the rue St-Pierre which contains an interesting Renaissance house, the **Maison des Trois-Pigeons**. The most delightful corner of the old town is perhaps the **Place de la Poissonnerie** with its 15th-century wooden houses, the Maison de la Truite-qui-File and Maison du Saumon.

The longer one spends in Chartres, the more difficult it is to leave. Charles Peguy, the poet, fell under the spell of Chartres the moment he saw it and twice made the journey there from Paris on foot, mesmerised by what for him was a symbol both of faith and of France itself.

Practicalities in Chartres

Tourist Office Opposite cathedral entrance (Tel. 37 21 50 00); accomodation service.
Railway Station (Tel. 37 28 50 50).
Hotels ☆ Hôtel Poste, 3 rue Général Koenig, just off place des Epars and close to post office (Tel 37 21 04 27). Smallish rooms but comfortable and central; pleasant modest restaurant with good-value menus.

Hostels *Auberge de Jeunesse* (HI), 23 ave Neigre, 2km north of station; over river close to Eglise St-André.
Restaurants *Le Buisson Ardent*, 10 rue au Lait (Tel. 37 34 94 66), timbered restaurant on 2nd floor; delicious, generous and affordable nouvelle cuisine.

13 Poitou–Charente

Poitou–Charente covers a vast sway of western France, from the great port of Nantes at the mouth of the Loire to another of the most important ports of France 300 miles further south on the Atlantic coast – Bordeaux. This vast area contains an extraordinary diversity of landscape and soil, from the marshes and waterways of *Marais Poitevin* to the huge area further south covered by oak forest or devoted to sheep husbandry.

The ancient province of Poitou stretched westwards from the picturesque valley of the Anglin, which lies east of Poitiers, to the Atlantic seabord of the Vendée. Poitou, as part of Aquitaine, became an English domain through the marriage of Eleanor of Aquitaine to Henry Plantagenet, the new King of England in 1154 and it remained in English hands for more than 100 years until du Guesclin secured it for the French crown in 1429. During English rule wine was exported in great quantities to England from Bordeaux and Poitou served as a base from which the English kings mounted their campaigns, often short-lived, against the domains of the French kings to the east.

In later years the Atlantic ports traded with French possessions in North America, particularly Canada and Newfoundland, and the wealth generated from this trade led to the construction of the fine merchants houses and public buildings still to be seen today.

Gastronomically, the area benefits from the extensive coastline and lush pastures of the Charente. Hauls of fish have been brought back to its Atlantic ports since time immemorial, while today a third of the lamb consumed in France is supplied from Poitou. Along the coast, the oysters of Marennes and Oléron, some greeny-blue from the *navicule bleue* seaweed in which they thrive, are world-famous. Mussels are also plentiful and served in vast quantities, often as a first course, either in the simplest of forms, cooked in white wine as *moules marinières* or in a wine, cream and egg sauce known as a *mouclade*.

In the Marais Poitevin, eels are caught and eaten with a red wine sauce, known as *fricassée d'anguilles*; but lampreys are only found for a few weeks a year. King John died of a surfeit of them – their appearance in a thick black sauce is anything but inviting but they are delicious. To accompany the fare of Poitou–Charentes come the light red, white and

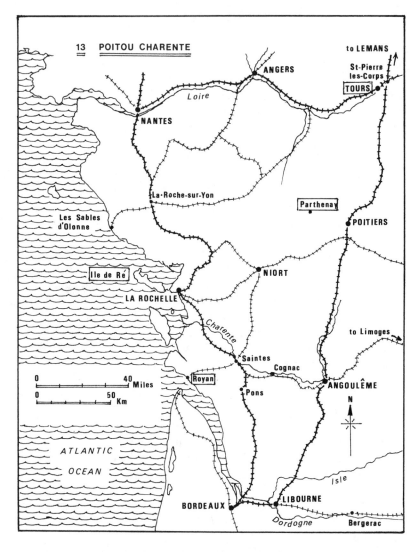

rosé wines of Haut-Poitou. Light white wines, *blanc marine*, come from the Charente region, which is perhaps better known for its sweet apéritif *Pineau de Charente*, made from a mixture of Cognac and grape or pear juice, and the drink for which the area is best known – Cognac, named after the town which lies between Saintes and Angoulême.

Architecturally the area is distinguished by its superb Romanesque churches and hostels built to accommodate the flow of pilgrims who began to make the long journey by foot from Canterbury and the abbeys and churches of France to Santiago de Compostela during the 11th century. Nantes has a fine cathedral and one of the most impressive ducal château of the region; in Notre-Dame-la-Grande, Poitiers has one of the most remarkable Romanesque façades of western France; Angoulême still lives perched high within its castle walls, as if the modern world has passed it by and left it undisturbed. The small towns too have their treasures – La Rochelle with its 14th-century towers guarding the port, Cognac with its labyrinths of lanes hiding ancient brandy warehouses and Parthenay still enclosed by medieval walls and towers.

The Route Nantes – La Rochelle – Saintes – Royan – Cognac – Pons – Angoulême – Poitiers – Niort – Parthenay – [Tours]

Starting from Nantes, *the great port of the north at the mouth of the Loire and once the capital of Brittany, the route heads south to the romantic fishing port of* La Rochelle, *once a bastion of Protestantism in France. Further south lies the quiet town of* Saintes, *sprinkled with beautiful churches, and* Cognac *which seems steeped in history and devoted with almost reverential dedication to its vocation as the pilgrimage site for brandy connoisseurs. Inland lies 2 towns intimately connected with the history of France:* Poitiers *and* Angoulême; *both have kept magnificent buildings from their medieval past, with exquisite 13th-century Romanesque sculpture. The route then leads back to the Loire at* Tours, *from where there are fast connections to Paris and Nantes. (Approximately 5–7 days.)*

Nantes

Trains *3–4 slow trains from* Paris Montparnasse *(3½ hours); also 12–14* TGVs *from Paris (2 hours); 5–8 from* Bordeaux *(4 hours); from* Rennes *(2 hours); 3 from* Vannes *(1½ hours) and* Quimper *(3 hours).*

Around Nantes lies lovely countryside of shallow rolling hills covered with arable fields and large sweeping woods scattered with fine châteaux, many surrounded by fine parks and the vineyards of Muscadet. Although severely bombed during the Second World War and the scene of rapid expansion since then, the historic old port of Nantes still retains some superb medieval and 18th-century architecture.

What to see

Château des Ducs de Bretagne

The massive Château of Nantes stands close to the docks and was originally surrounded by a moat fed by the waters of the Loire; the moat is now dry and the hexagonal curtain wall and towers rise instead from a lawn of grass. Today, the castle appears as it did when rebuilt in 1466 by Mathelin Rodier for Francis II, Duke of Britanny. The courtyard contains several imposing towers built in the early Renaissance style and covered with a mixture of Gothic and classical ornamentation characteristic of the epoch. The tower in the northern corner of the courtyards is the one in which Gilles de Rais, the infamous Bluebeard, was incarcerated prior to his execution in 1440. Virtually every French king since Louis XI has been a visitor to the castle, and the Duchess of Berri was imprisoned here in 1832 after attempting to stir up another rebellion against Louis-Philippe in the Vendée. Also in the Château are the **Musée des Salorges**, devoted to the naval history of Nantes, and the **Musée d'Art Populaire Régional**, a good collection of folk art from the Vendée. (Castle and museums open Sept–June, Wed–Mon 10 am–noon and 2–6 pm; July–August, daily 10 am–noon and 2–6 pm.)

Cathédrale St-Pierre

Mathelin Rodier also designed the nearby cathedral of St-Pierre, one of France's latest Gothic cathedrals. Although begun in 1434 the building was not completed until the 19th century since when the choir has been bombed and burnt by fire. The 16th-century nave however is imposing and the fine tomb of Duke François II, who died in 1488, and his second wife, Marguerite de Foix, (in the south transept) is a masterpiece of French Renaissance sculpture.

Close to the cathedral is the handsome Place Maréchal Foch which, unlike most of this part of the town, is purely 18th-century in character. To the east stretches a maze of narrow streets with a number of delightful old houses. The late Gothic **Porte St-Pierre** was once part of the bishop's palace and the adjacent gardens contain the remains of the Gallo–Roman wall.

Place Graslin

Eighteenth-century Nantes is centred on the Place Graslin, from which the streets radiate in a formal plan. The elegant **theatre** adorned with statues of the 8 Muses and a handsome Corinthian portico is reminiscent of Victor Louis' theatre in Bordeaux. It was inaugurated in 1788 just as Arthur Young arrived in the city; he was very impressed, reckoning it to be twice as large as Drury Lane and 5 times as magnificent. A short walk away is the impressive **Cours Cambronne**, an elegant street lined with 18th-century houses, designed by Mathurin Crucy in the 1780s.

Nantes is famous in French history for being associated with the Edict of 1598 by which Henry IV guaranteed religious liberty to Protestants in France after 35 years of disastrous civil war. The religious wars between Catholic and Protestant, known as the Wars of the League, had been sparked off in 1560 by the accession of Charles IX to the French crown. At the instigation of his bigoted mother, Catherine de Médicis, Charles IX signed the order for the massacre of Protestant Huguenots on the Eve of St Bartholomew, the 23rd August 1572. This abominable act divided the country and led to bitter fighting in every city and region of France, culminating in the assassination of the ultra Catholic, Henry, Duke of Guise by Henry III in 1589 and the latter's assassination the following year.

Henry IV, a Protestant, eventually succeeded in defeating the Catholic forces in 1590 but he was unable to enter Paris until 1594 after he had foresworn his faith with the cynical remark that 'Paris is well worth a mass'. Nevertheless, the Edict of Nantes ushered in a period of peace that lasted until the rise to power of the bigoted and powerful cardinal Richelieu in the 1620s. Despite growing oppression from Richelieu, the Edict of Nantes gave the Protestants a measure of legitimacy and security until it was revoked 87 years later by Louis XIV, an act that provoked a tide of emigration to Protestant Germany and England.

One of the most dramatic episodes of the history of Nantes occurred in the 1882 when the Duchesse de Berri attempted to rally the loyal people of the Vendée in favour of her son, the Comte de Chambord, in opposition to the claims of Louis-Philippe of Orléans. Meeting with little success, she was forced to take refuge in the house of a friend, at No. 3 rue Mathelin-Rodier, where she hid herself in a secret space behind the chimney on the third floor, before being smoked out when the soldiers searching for her lit a fire in the hearth.

Musée des Beaux-Arts

The Musée des Beaux-Arts in rue Georges Clemenceau, offers a fine collection of art from the 14th and 20th centuries, including some excellent early Renaissance panels (Open Wed–Mon 10 am–noon and 1–5.15 pm.) The **Musée Dobrée** in Place Jean V, an eclectic collection containing medieval and ecclesiastical objects, is housed in a mock Romanesque building which belonged to the art collector Thomas Dobrée.

Practicalities in Nantes

Tourist Office Place du Commerce, in the old stock exchange Tel.; organises guided tours; open Mon–Fri 9 am–7 pm, Sat 10 am–6 pm; branch office at Place March Elder, in front of entrance to château.
Railway Station 27 blvd Stalingrad. (Info: Tel. 40 08 50 50; Reservations: Tel. 40 04 60 60): to château, turn left out of station onto cours J. F. Kennedy which leads to the château.
Hotels ☆*Hôtel Astoria*, 11 rue Richebourg (Tel. 40 74 39 90). Close to station, clean and comfortable.
☆ *Hôtel Vendée*, 8 allée Cdt Charcot (Tel. 40 74 14 54). Well situated half way between the station and château.

Hôtel Renova, 11 rue Beauregard, off cours des 50 Otages (Tel. 40 47 57 03). Slightly faded but cheap, central and peaceful.
Hôtel Calypso, 16 rue Strasbourg, off cours J. F. Kennedy, on one of the principal thoroughfares (Tel. 40 47 54 47).
Hostels *Auberge de Jeunesse* (HI) 2 place de la Manufacture, 10 mins from station down blvd de Stalingrad and rue Manille (Tel. 40 40 57 25).
Camping 3 km from town. *Camping du Val de Cens*, 21 blvd du Petit Port. Bus no 51 or 53 from Place du Commerce to **Marhonnière** stop (Tel. 40 74 47 94).
Restaurants *La Cigale*, 4 Place Graslin (Tel. 40

69 76 41). Delightful, elegant Belle Epoque café, complete with palm trees, bright enamel tiles and painted ceilings.

☆☆ *Colvert*, 14 rue Armand Brossard (Tel. 40

48 20 02). Chef Didier Macoin prepares seafood and game depending on what is in season; inventive sauces, delicate cooking; good value lunchtime menu.

La Rochelle

Trains *4 – 5 trains daily from* **Nantes** *(1 hour 50 mins); 6 – 8 daily from* **Bordeaux** *(2 – 4 hours); 3 from* **Paris** **Austerlitz** *(5 hours); 7 – 9* TGVs *from* **Paris** **Montparnasse;** *some require a change at* **Poitiers** *(2 hour 50 mins); 8 – 10 from* **Poitiers** *(1 hours).*

La Vendée South of Nantes is the Vendée, the most westerly portion of the old province of Poitou, which was renowned for its devotion to the royal family during the French Revolution. The risings against the Paris revolutionaries by the peasants of Brittany and the Vendée were crushed with great cruelty by General Hoche in 1795 and the first place the train passes through on leaving Nantes is Rocheservière, scene of the last Vendean uprising which was crushed by General Lamarque in 1815.

The countryside of this part of the Vendée is known by the name of *Bocage*, a term implying a country rich in small copses. This domesticated landscape, full of hedges, bridlepaths and small woods, was ideal country for the supporters of the crown, the *Chouans*, who could fight a guerrilla-type action against the much larger conscripted armies controlled by the revolutionary committees based in the towns and cities.

Although the capital of the Vendée, **La-Roche-sur-Yon** is a disappointing town lying on a plateau dominating the valley of the Yon. It was virtually destroyed by Republican troops in 1794 and a decade later Napoleon laid out a new town on a regular plan, modestly naming it Napoléon in an attempt to ingratiate himself with the royalist inhabitants of the Vendée. At the Restoration the town was renamed Bourbon-Vendée, Napoléon III changing its name once again to Napoléon-Vendée before the long-suffering town was allowed to return to its original medieval name in 1871. One suspects that such directives from Paris only served to confirm the Vendeans' worst fears about State interference from Paris. The vast Place Napoléon with its bronze equestrian statue of the Emperor in the middle only adds to the town's bleak and uninviting appearance.

A train can be caught west from La-Roche-sur-Yon however to **Les Sables d'Olonne**, once a quiet bathing resort and now a highly popular and modern resort, renowned for its long curving beach of fine white sand. Until the Second World War the fisherwomen still wore their *sabots* as well as short black stiff skirts and white-winged caps known as *papillons*. The old fishing quarter, known as Les Chaumes, is overlooked by the remains of an old English fort dating from the 14th century. John James Audubon, the famous North American naturalist and ornithologist was born here in 1785, his father, a ship's captain was a native of the town. The church of Notre-Dame-du-Bon-Port dates from the 17th century, a time of great prosperity for the town.

Marais Poitevin Between La-Roche-sur-Yon and La Rochelle lies the Marais Poitevin, an enchanting tract of fen-like country much of it reclaimed from the sea in the 17th century by Dutch engineers called to France by Henry IV. Its dense maze of tranquil waterways, shaded by overhanging willows and poplars, is transformed in summer into a verdant paradise known as the *Venise verte*. A little to the south lies La Rochelle, the heart of the city a short walk straight down the avenue de Gaulle.

La Rochelle is one of the most picturesque and interesting of the smaller cities of France. During the Middle Ages it was held for long periods by the English, who called it the White City on account of the reflection of the light on its sands and rocks. In 1372 the English fleet under the Earl of Pembroke was virtually destroyed in the harbour by Castilian galleys and the English left La Rochelle for good. In the 16th and 17th centuries the city flourished, through trade with the New World and the West Indies, and La Rochelle became one of the richest maritime towns in France. The Wars of Religion, the revocation of the Edict of Nantes and the cession of Canada to England in 1763 however effectively destroyed the city's commercial prosperity. At the same time the harbour slowly silted up, because of the dike Richelieu ordered to be built across the harbour in 1627 to obstruct marine traffic.

La Rochelle was a staunchly Protestant city but despite the protection the Protestants were entitled to by the Edict of Nantes, the Rochelais were repeatedly harassed by Richelieu who attempted to starve the town into submission in 1627. Two relief expeditions sent out by the English king, Charles I, failed miserably to help the town, the first due to the incompetence of the Duke of Buckingham and the second due to his assassination at Portsmouth in 1628. Eventually the town, reduced by famine to a pitiful state, was compelled to surrender, whereupon the town's defences were pulled down.

What to see

Old Port

The old port is extremely picturesque, framed by 2 sturdy medieval towers which protect the harbour entrance. Both date from the period immediately after the English loss of La Rochelle, the English castle which stood in what is now the Place de Verdun, being demolished in 1371. The Tour St-Nicholas has a double spiral staircase and vaulted apartments and from its tower is a good panoramic view of the surrounding town and distant vineyards. (Open Wed–Mon 9.30 am–12.30 pm and 2.30 – 6 pm.) In times of war a chain was pulled across the harbour entrance at night, from the Tour Chaine opposite, to prevent hostile ships sailing unchecked into the heart of the city.

The brightly painted fishing smacks which used to crowd the harbour are fewer than before but fresh fish and crustaceans are still landed daily in the town and La

Rochelle still enjoys a well-deserved reputation for the excellence of its seafood, especially the delicious green oysters of the Marennes.

Tour de la Grosse Horloge

From the city, access to the harbour is through the Tour de la Grosse Horloge, an impressive 13th-century gateway crowned with 18th-century armorini bearing the celestial and terrestial globes and a classical cupola in a curious architectural juxtaposition.

Above the port are the delightful arcaded streets of the old city, dating largely from the 16th to 18th centuries. The **Palace of Justice**, a superb classical building completed in the first year of the Revolution is in the Rue du Palais, its perfectly-proportioned façade ornamented with Corinthian columns. In the same arcaded street is the **Hôtel de la Bourse**, another fine 18th-century building.

Hôtel de Ville

In stark contrast to these restrained and elegant buildings is the flamboyant Hôtel de Ville begun in the reign of François I. Its courtyard is entered through a wall with overhanging battlements flanked by tiny turrets. Inside a heavy arcade is surmounted by composite columns framing allegorical figures, surmounted in turn by ornately decorated dormers. To one side is a much more delicate Renaissance pavilion containing a 19th-century statue of Henry IV. To the north-west lies the Cathedral of St-Louis, a classical building of 1784 with an austere façade that was never completed.

Musée du Nouveau Monde

Of the 3 museums in La Rochelle the most rewarding is the Musée du Nouveau Monde in the elegant residence of the rich ship-owning family, the Fleuriaus. Changing exhibitions are staged relating to French maritime commerce with the new world. (Open Wed–Mon 10.30 am–13.30 pm and 1.30–6 pm, Sun 3–6 pm.) The smaller **Musée d'Orbigny-Bernon** has an interesting collection relating to the history of the city.

One of the principal streets of La Rochelle is the **Cours des Dames**, which is lined with mature trees and 18th-century houses; the finest 16th-century house in La Rochelle is the beautiful **Maison Henri-Deux** just off the Rue du Palais, an enchanting loggia on 2 floors with a square tower.

Practicalities in La Rochelle

Tourist Office Quai de Gabut (Tel. 46 41 14 68); currency exchange in summer; accommodation service.
Railway Station Blvd Maréchal Joffre (Tel. 46 41 50 50). For the centre walk down Ave du Géneral de Gaulle towards quai Valin and the centre.
Buses Autoplus run to campgrounds, local hostel (bus no 10) and centre ville (bus no 1); Citram buses (Tel. 46 99 01 36) from Place de Verdun to Bordeaux, Angoulême, Niort
Ferries Bus de Mer (Tel. 46 34 02 22), runs

from old port to port de Plaisance des Minimes.
Markets Place du Marché, daily, mornings; fish market on quais near the harbour.
Festivals *Franco Folies*: early July, 6-day music festival with musicians and bands from all Francophile countries.
Grand Pavois: September, a grand boat-show with 100s of boats open to the public in the Port des Minimes.
Hotels Accommodation in La Rochelle is expensive; a few cheaper hotels are to be found between the station and place du Marché.

l'Auberge, 33 rue Thiers (Tel. 46 41 62 23).

☆ *Hôtel Terminus*, 11 Place Cdt de la Motte Rouge, on the other side of the Place de la Motte Rouge, on way in to *centre ville* (Tel. 46 50 69 69).

☆ *Hôtel La Marine*, 30 quai Duperré (Tel. 46 50 51 63). Modest little hotel right in the centre.

☆ *Hôtel de la Paix*, 14 rue Gargoulleau, near Place de Verdun and the Musée du Nouveau Monde (Tel. 46 41 33 44).

☆☆ *Hôtel Tour de Nestle*, 2 quai L. Durand, almost on the edge of old port (Tel. 46 41 05 86). Smallish rooms but clean, friendly and well located for exploring the harbour and the old town.

☆☆ *Hôtel St Jean d'Acre*, 4 Place Chaine. (Tel. 46 41 71 55). Comfortable, good-sized rooms with modern facilities right in the heart of the old port.

☆☆ *Hôtel Le Manoir*, 8 bis ave Gén. Leclerc (Tel. 46 67 47 47)

Hostels *Centre International de Séjour/Auberge de Jeunesse* (HI), Ave des Minimes, 2 km south of station. Bus no 10 (direction **Port des Minimes**) from Ave de Colmar, or 25 min walk (Tel. 46 44 43 11).

Restaurants *Pré Vert*, 43 rue St-Nicholas (Tel. 46 41 24 43). Cool and tucked away down a quiet side-street. This delightful restaurant offers regional specialities such as eel, duck and shellfish.

☆ *André*, 5 rue St-Jean (Tel. 46 41 28 24). Slightly exaggerated marine decoration but superb local oysters, mussels, crab, langoustines and seafish.

Excursion from La Rochelle
Ile de Ré

Accessible by bus from La Rochelle. *Also Citram buses from Rochefort (Tel. 46 99 01 36). Rébus buses (Tel. 46 09 20 15) leave from the railway station in La Rochelle for* Sablanceaux *(15 daily, 30 mins), the first town on the island, for* St Martin-de-Ré *(7 daily, 1 hour) the most important town of the Ile de Ré and for* Les Portes *(9 daily, 1½ hours) at the far end of the island. Buses stop at every town so it's easy to get around.*

Boats *Boats daily from La Rochelle harbour for* Iles de Ré, Aix *and* Oléron.

The delightful Ile de Ré lies a little distance off the Atlantic coast, an elongated island only 4 miles wide and 16 miles long. The eastern part of the island is devoted to vines, the western to the cultivation of oysters, the most important element in the island's economy, which thrive in the shallow sea-water. The principal village of the island is **St-Martin de Ré** which clusters round a picturesque harbour and is dominated by a citadel built by the military architect Vauban in 1681. Many of the white-washed houses, which date from the same period, are laden with window boxes full of flowers. At the far end of the island is the **Phare de la Baleine lighthouse**, from where there are panoramic views looking back over the island.

Practicalities on Ile de Ré

Restaurants *Café du Phare* (Tel. 46 29 46 66); the lighthouse café has a remarkably good menu.

Beaches *Sablanceaux* or the more deserted *Place de la Conche* des Belaires at the far end of the island.

Practicalities in St-Martin

Tourist office Av. Victor-Bouthillier (Tel. 46 09 20 06). Open Mon–Sat. 10 am–7 pm, Sun 10 am–noon; Oct–May Mon–Sat 10–noon and 3–5 pm.
Hotels ☆ ☆ *Hôtel le Sully*, rue Jean Jaurès, St-Martin (Tel. 46 09 70 00). Just up from the walls of Vauban's fortified port.
☆ ☆ ☆ *Hôtel-Restaurant Les Colonnes*, 19 quai Job-Foran (Tel. 46 09 21 58). Handsome waterside hotel, with very comfortable rooms and good restaurant.
Camping Innumerable campsites; pick up leaflet at tourist office.
Market Daily morning market in covered hall off rue Jean Jaurès, near the port.

Saintes

Trains *6 – 8 trains daily from* **La Rochelle** *(50 – 60 mins); 6 – 8 daily from* **Bordeaux** *(1 hour 15 mins); 6 from* **Angoulême** *(1 hour 10 mins); 6 from* **Cognac** *(20 mins); 2 from* **Paris** *(5 ½ hours) via* **Poitiers** *(2 hours).*

South of La Rochelle the train never moves far away from the coast. Rochefort, a military port and arsenal of rather severe appearance was laid out by Colbert in 1666. Heavily fortified, the arsenal successfully fought off a number of attacks made by English fleets between the end of the 17th and beginning of the 19th centuries. The town has an excellent naval museum which traces the maritime history of this important naval base.

Apart from the naval museum, the only other real attraction of the town is the extraordinary house of the novelist Julien Viaud or Pierre Loti, who was born and spent most of his childhood in Rochefort. An eccentric in dress and behaviour and an inveterate traveller, Loti's exotic novels enjoyed an enormous vogue at the end of the 19th century. Inside what appears to be the most humdrum of exteriors at **141 rue Pierre Loti** is a romantic palace revealing Loti's kaleidoscopic and eclectic taste for the Orient with a series of extravagantly decorated Turkish and Arabian rooms littered with objects collected in the course of his extensive travels. (Open for tours, July–Sept, daily at 10 am, 11 am, 2 pm, 3 pm, 4 pm, and 5 pm; none on Sunday morning; fewer tours off-season.)

As the train heads west from Rochefort it passes **Tonnay-Charente**, the birthplace of Madame de Montespan, one of Louis XIV's most enduring mistresses, who gave birth to 8 of his children. The woman appointed to oversee the education of these children was none other than Madame de Maintenon who in turn became Louis' mistress, before marrying him secretly after the death of his wife Maria-Theresa of Spain. What remains of Madame Montespan's château, of which there is a brief glimpse from the train, is now incorporated into a hospital.

Following the gentle and fertile valley of the Charente, the train passes the ruins of the castle of Taillebourg near where in 808 Charlemagne inflicted a decisive defeat on a Moorish army that had marched north from Spain.

After one or two lazy meanders the Charente river enters **Saintes**, the capital of the ancient province of Saintonge, a delightful and interesting town.

What to see

Arc de Germanicus

When Julius Caesar conquered Gaul Saintes was already a flourishing trading town. The town's affluence under the Romans is attested to by its great crumbling amphitheatre which was built in the 1st century AD and by the beautiful votive arch, l'Arc de Germanicus, erected in honour of the Emperor Tiberius.

Abbaye aux Dames

Rue de l'Arc de Triomphe leads to the Abbaye aux Dames which must have been a noble edifice in medieval times but has since suffered from a number of fires and use of the buildings by the French military. Nevertheless the abbey church still possesses a beautiful Romanesque façade and tower, and some finely carved capitals depicting fantastic beasts and demons. Madame de Montespan received her early education here in the 1650s.

At the far end of the town lies the church of St-Eutrope, with a superb Romanesque choir which now serves as the nave, the original nave having been burnt by the Protestants in 1568, as was the cathedral of St-Pierre on the far bank of the Charente. The surprise of St-Eutrope is its vast 11th-century crypt, the largest of any church in France, save that of Chartres Cathedral, a magnificent subterranean building of great beauty.

Practicalities in Saintes

Tourist Office Villa Musso, 62 cours National in a beautiful 19th-century villa (Tel. 46 74 23 82); accommodation assistance; offers tours of town and cruises on Charente; currency exchange.

Railway Station Ave de la Marne, 15 mins from centre. (Info: Tel. 46 41 50 50; Reservations: Tel. 46 92 04 19); for town centre from station, turn left, follow Ave de la Marne, then right onto Ave Gambetta and continue to river. Cross bridge and continue down Cours National.

Buses 1 cours Reverseaux (Tel. 46 893 21 41); buses to Ile d'Oléron, Royan, La Rochelle, Rochefort, Cognac.

Markets Tues and Fris; Cours Reverseaux; Weds and Sats outside Cathédrale St-Pierre; Thurs and Suns on Ave de la Marne and Ave Gambetta, near station.

Festivals *Jeux Santons*: 2nd week of July, international folk festival. *Fête de Musique Ancienne*: 1st half of July, classical music concerts lasting 10 days.

Hotels *Auberge Terminus*, 2 rue J. Moulin, a stone's-throw from the station (Tel. 46 74 35 03).

Hôtel Parisien, 35 rue Frédéric Mestreau (Tel. 46 74 28 92). Clean, friendly and simple; close to station.

Hôtel St-Palais, 1 Place St-Palais, overlooking the Abbaye-aux-Dames (Tel. 46 92 51 30). Delightful hotel with large, clean, attractive rooms.

☆ ☆ *Hôtel Messageries*, rue Messageries, in a little cluster of backstreets off the cours National (Tel. 46 93 64 99).

Hostels *Auberge de Jeunesse* (HI) 6 rue du Pont Amilion, close to centre and the Abbaye-aux-Dames; open mid-Jan–mid-Dec (Tel. 46 92 14 92).

Restaurants *L'Abbatial*, 7 Place de l'Abbaye (Tel. 46 92 05 25). Delightful brasserie, opposite the abbey.

Excursion from Saintes

Royan

Trains *7 trains daily from* **Saintes** *(30 mins)*. Situated at the mouth of the Gironde estuary, directly opposite the Pointe de Grave, Royan is a post-war purpose-built seaside resort, in a sheltered position surrounded by long beaches of fine sand

and steep cliffs scattered with oak and pine trees. Largely rebuilt after the devastating shelling in 1945, Royan symbolised the determination to commission new forward-looking architects in the 1950's. As a result there are some intriguing buildings designed by Claude Ferret and others which used concrete in a new and imaginative way. Architecturally two of the most interesting buildings are the huge domed concrete market building, at the top of Bd Aristide Briand and the **church of Notre-Dame**, a remarkable eliptical structure made of reinforced concrete which was designed by Guillaume Gillet and Hébrard. (Place Notre-Dame, 3 mins. walk inland from the casino).

A magnificent beach, some two kilometres long, streches along the south-eastern coast of the town as far as the curved facade of the Casino. Just beyond the casino is the port for the fishing vessels which trawl the Atlantic waters for sardines. Only a tiny area of the old town, the Pontaillac quarter, survived the devastating bombardment of 14–15 April 1945 which compelled the Germans to surrender the town. The best way to reach it is via the Corniche de Pontaillac, the scenic coastal road.

Corniche de Pontaillac Best seen at high tide, the Corniche de Pontaillac follows the **Boulevard de la Falaise** from the **Palais des Congrès** round the cliff tops past the old **Chay fort** and racetrack to a small sheltered beach and joins the **Boulevard de la Côte d'Argent** which snakes its way around the cliff-tops with superb views out over the Gironde.

Practicalities in Royan

Tourist Office Palais des Congrès, Façade-de-Foncillon (Tel 46 38 65 11). and Place de la Poste (Tel. 46 05 04 71).

Railway Station Opposite Place du Dr. Gantier. To reach centre cross roundabout and walk down Cours de L'Europe to Place de la Poste, where one of the two tourist offices is located. Then head round the seawall in the direction of the casino and marinas. The **Palais des Congrès** is just round the corner of Bd Thiers.

Hotels ☆☆☆ *Hôtel Bleuets*, 21 façade Foncillon (Tel. 46 38 51 79). Small but comfortable hotel, very close to the tourist office in the Palais des Congrès.

☆☆☆ *Beau Rivage*, 9 façade Foncillon (Tel. 46 39 43 10). Pleasant comfortable hotel virtually adjacent to Palais des Congrès.

Restaurant ☆☆ *Trois Marmites*, 37 ave. Ch. Regazzoni (Tel. 46 38 66 31). Excellent traditional cuisine, 15 minutes walk from centre past the market building, up av. Daniel Hedde and close to the roundabout Rond-Point du Cdt. Thibeaudeau.

Cognac

Trains *Cognac does not lie on the main line between Nantes and Bordeaux but may be visited on a branch line that runs east from Saintes. 6 trains daily from Saintes (25 mins); 5 from Angoulême (1 hour).*

The landscape between Saintes and Cognac is some of the most delightful in France. Vineyards naturally predominate but they are broken up by small woods and pockets of arable land. There is one very good reason for visiting Cognac, a place of pilgrimage for brandy connoisseurs the world over, Cognac having been produced here since the 17th century. A warren of alleyways leading to the *Chais* or brandy warehouses of Messrs Martell, Hennessy and Remy-Martin lie between the church and the river.

The Otard chais is to be found in the Château de Valois where François I was born in 1494, the Otard family having installed themselves in the former royal château in the wake of the Revolution. Tours of the castle and Otard *chais* give a good introduction to the process of distilling Cognac, and there are excellent views of the town and surrounding country from the château windows.

Apart from visiting the different houses, most of which are happy to conduct visitors round their cellars, there is a **museum** devoted to the manufacture of Cognac which is housed in an 18th-century mansion adjoining public gardens. (Musée du Cognac, open Wed–Mon 10 am–noon (in summer) and 2–5.30 pm.)

Practicalities in Cognac

Tourist Office 16 rue du XIV Juillet (Tel. 45 82 10 71); accommodation assistance; emergency currency exchange.

Railway Station At top of rue R. E. Mousnier (Tel. 45 82 03 29). For town centre from station follow Ave du Général Leclerc to rue de Barbezieux, continue to rue Bayard on right, and cross the square to rue du 14 Juillet.

Hennessy warehouse or Chais Rue Richonne (Tel. 45 82 52 22); **Martell Chais:** Place Martell (Tel. 45 82 44 44).

Hotels ☆ *Hôtel du Cheval Blanc*, 6–8 Place Boyard (Tel. 45 82 09 55). Simple but very cheap; good value restaurant.

Hôtel St-Martin, 112 ave Paul-Férino-Martell, with simple but good restaurant downstairs (Tel. 45 85 01 29).

☆☆ *Hôtel François Ier*, 3 Place François Ier (Tel. 45 32 07 18). A handsome and comfortable hotel overlooking the square.

☆☆ *Hôtel Le Valois*, 35 rue 14 Juillet, down rue Bayard, close to tourist office (Tel. 45 82 76 00). Modernised and comfortable.

Restaurants *La Sangria*, 35 rue Grande Tel. In the old quarter; Spanish and Portuguese dishes as well as standard French cooking.

☆ *Auberge*, 13 rue Plumejeau (Tel. 45 32 08 70). Good but unexceptional traditional French cuisine.

From Saintes trains run through the rich vineyards of the Saintonge, which produce Bons Bois, a brandy that vies with that made further north between Royan and La Rochelle. To the south of Saintes, beyond swampy ground drained by the Seugne river, lies the interesting little town of Pons.

Pons

Trains *4–5 trains daily from* **Saintes** *(15 mins); and* **Bordeaux** *(1 hour).*

Largely unvisited, this charming town has a large rambling **château** with an impressive 12th-century keep pierced by Romanesque windows. The rest of the fine feudal castle, of 15th–17th century buildings, is now occupied by the town hall. The main square of the town occupies an elevated plateau and is surrounded by delightful public gardens created on the site of a castle pulled down on the orders of Louis XIII in 1622 in reprisal for the town's intransigent espousal of Protestantism.

In the south of the town is the little chapel of St-Vivien with a Romanesque façade and nearby 12th-century bridge crossing the river Seugne. A short walk away are 2 interesting and romantic châteaux: the ruins of the Château de St-Maury and the elegant Renaissance Château d'Usson.

Practicalities in Pons

Tourist Office Donjon de Pons (Tel. 46 96 13 31).

Railway Station (Tel. 46 41 50 50)

Hotels ☆*Hôtel Bordeaux*, 1 rue Gambetta (Tel.

46 91 31 12).

☆☆☆ *Auberge Pontoise*, 23 ave Gambetta. (Tel. 46 94 00 99). Superb château hotel with outstanding cooking.

20 kilometres south of Pons, heading towards Bordeaux, lies **Jonzac** and the superb 13th–14th century castle situated in its main square. The massive twin towers flanking the entrance gateway are connected to the small Keep by a *corps du logis*, the main

residential part of the château. The impressive façade however is somewhat illusory for behind it there is only a disparate group of buildings through which runs a public road. Further south lies the extensive Forest of Bussac which gives way beyond Cavignac to the first of the Bordeaux vineyards. Just beyond St-André-de-Cubzac, the Dordogne can be crossed on a bridge dating from 1889.

The tongue of land between the Dordogne and the Garonne is the wine-growing district of Entre-Deux-Mers. Soon after you will enter the industrial suburbs of Bordeaux and once you have crossed the Garonne the train pulls into the great port of **Bordeaux**. (For a description of Bordeaux, see Aquitaine on page 92)

Angoulême

Trains *12 trains daily, including* TGVs *from* **Bordeaux** *(1 hour) and* **Poitiers** *(45 mins), 3–4 from* **Saintes** *via Cognac (1 hour); 3–4 slow trains from* **Paris** *(4½ hours); 10–12* TGVs *from* **Paris** *(2½ hours).*

The line from Bordeaux to Angoulême heads east through Entre Deux Mers to the ancient wine town of **Libourne**, crosses the Dordogne and heads up the winding valley of the Isle. Beyond the town of **Coutras**, the scene of Henri of Navarre's victory over the Duc de Joyeuse in 1587, the pretty valley of the Dronne is followed north-east to **Chalais**. The château is the home of the Talleyrand family, whose most illustrious member, Henri, was an intimate friend of Louis XIII until, accused of conspiring against Richelieu, he was executed.

The ruined château of Montmoreau is passed and the tiny valley of the Boême followed to **la Couronne**. Here the ruins of a beautiful abbey church dating from 1200 may be glimpsed to the west, unfortunatey greatly overshadowed by a giant cement factory. Built on a steep hill between the valleys of the Charente and the Anguienne, **Angoulême** is of interest chiefly for its unusual Romanesque cathedral and its ramparts which entirely surround the city. Located high up on a hill, there are wonderful views in all directions over the gently rolling landscape. In the Middle Ages the city was the capital of the province of Angoumois, a rich and fertile region that was hotly disputed during the Hundred Years War. King John of England journeyed to the city in 1200 to marry Isabelle d'Angoulême but even though France conceded Aquitaine to England by the Treaty of Brétigny in 1360, the English were expelled from the town a mere 13 years later.

Marguerite de Valois, also known as Marguerite de Navarre and locally as Marguerite d'Angoulême, the distinguished sister of François I and Queen of Navarre, was born in the city in 1494. She was probably born in the ancient castle of the counts of Angoulême which stood in the heart of the city until replaced by Abadie's **Hôtel de Ville** in 1865. A remarkable and talented woman, and author of the *Heptameron*, she was one of the major figures of the French Renaissance. After the death of her first husband, Charles IV, the Duke of Alençon, she married Henri d'Albret, King of Navarre and used her influence with her husband to protect the leading figures of the Protestant reform movement in France.

What to see

Ramparts

A steep walk up from the station leads to the ramparts which should be followed in an anti-clockwise direction. A plaque on the **Tour Larden**, overlooking the valley of the Charente far below, commemorates Angoulême's claim to be the site of man's first flight. In 1806 a local military man, Général Résnier, took off from the ramparts, effectively making the first flight without an engine, using a machine he had made himself. No indication however is given as to whether the general survived his leap from the city walls.

The shady boulevard leads round to a delightful square at the northern end of the old town, the **Place Beaulieu**, which lives up to its name – a tranquil and restful spot where the menfolk of Angoulême gather to play boules on summer evenings. The Rue de Beaulieu, leading off the square, contains a number of interesting buildings including the **Hôtel Dieu**, or hospice, the **Hôtel de Bardines** and the little **Chapelle des Cordeliers**.

Cathedral

By far the most interesting building in Angoulême however is the cathedral which was constructed in the early 12th century. It is a curious combination of Romanesque and Byzantine styles with a western façade of great beauty even though it was damaged during the religious wars and the Revolution. It suffered most of all in the 19th century at the hands of Abadie who liberally 'restored' the building as his fancy took him. He mutilated some of the sculptured groups on the façade in the course of restoration, others he replaced. He added towers to the western façade and rebuilt the northern tower, breaking up its original sculptures in the process while on the inside of the cathedral he planed down all the walls and pillars to a smooth, uniform surface, filling the joints with black mortar. Despite all this, the Romanesque western façade is still remarkably impressive, especially the striking sculpture of the *Last Judgement* and the bold figures of *St George and the Dragon* and *St Martin* dividing his cloak with a beggar.

Behind the cathedral stands the Old Bishop's Palace, a Renaissance building facing a pleasant enclosed courtyard, now housing the local **museum**.

Hôtel de Ville

The Hôtel de Ville represents Abadie's rather narrow and severe interpretation of medieval architecture; 2 of the original castle towers are incorporated rather unsuccessfully into Abadie's design – a massive drum tower and the polygonal Tour Isabelle, named after Isabelle d'Angoulême who married the unfortunate and hapless king of England, John Lackland. Isabelle had been betrothed to Hugh of Lusignan but was compelled to marry King John for reasons of state in 1200. By any yardstick, King John was an unattractive character and no sooner had Isabelle inherited Angoumois in 1213 than King John had her imprisoned prison in Gloucester. With John's death in 1216, she was eventually free to leave England, which she rapidly did, returning to Angoulême and marrying her old lover after an absence of 20 years.

One of the delights of Angoulême are its quiet streets of white stone houses which spread out around the cathedral in the *Ville Haute* or upper town. Down a narrow entrance in the rue de la Cloche-Verte stands an enchanting Renaissance mansion, the **Hôtel St-Simon**, its façade decorated with diamond-shaped and circular motifs, set within a diminuitive courtyard.

Practicalities in Angoulême

Tourist Office 2 place St-Pierre (Tel 45 95 16 84); walking tours of the city; tickets for boat excursions; maps; information kiosk outside station.

Railway Station Place de la Gare (Tel. 56 92 50 50); information office open Mon–Fri 9 am–7 pm. For town centre steep climb up Ave Gambetta and rampe d'Aguesseau, then through Place Marengo to Rue Marengo and Hôtel de Ville; skirt to the left and follow Ave Georges Clemenceau to the right to ramparts and Place St-Pierre.

Buses (Tel. 45 25 42 60), bus departures from Place de Champ de Mars to Cognac, La Rochelle, Bordeaux.

Markets Covered market *Les Halles*, Place des Halles Centrales.

Festivals *Salon International de la Bande-Dessinée:* January, the largest international gathering of artists and cartoon enthusiasts, Festival International de Jazz et Musiques

Métisses: May.

Hotels *Hôtel les Messageries*, Place de la Gare, close to the station (Tel. 45 92 07 62). Clean, simple, unpretentious.

Hôtel le Palma, 4 rampe d'Aguesseau, near the Eglise St-Martial on the climb up to the old town (Tel. 45 95 22 89). Welcoming owner and spotless rooms.

☆☆ *Hôtel du Palais*, 4 Place Francis-Louvel, right next to the Palais de Justice, in heart of old town (Tel. 45 92 01 83).

☆☆ *Hôtel Terminus*, Place de la Gare, probably the best of the hotels close to the station (Tel. 45 92 68 19). Restaurant serves good regional specialities.

Hostels *Auberge de Jeunesse* (HI), on Ile de Bourgines, below town, beside the Charente in idyllic setting. Bus no 7 (direction Le Treuil) from Place du Champ du Mars to St-Antoine stop, cross bridge and follow river (Tel. 45 92 45 80).

Poitiers

Trains 12 *trains daily from* **Angoulême** *(45 mins), and* **Bordeaux** *(1 hour 50 mins); 10–12* TGVs *from Tours via St-Pierre-les-Corps (45 mins); 10–12* TGVs *from* Paris *Montparnasse (1 hour 40 mins); 3–4 slow trains from* Paris Austerlitz *(3 hours); 7 daily from* **La Rochelle** *(2 hours).*

Approaching Poitiers from the south, the train passes close to the village of **Nouaillé** where the battle of Poitiers that re-established English power in Poitou and augumented the reputation of the Black Prince took place in 1356. Poitou had passed to the English crown on the marriage of Henry II to Eleanor of Aquitaine, who often lived at Poitiers, and the province was ruled by the English for most of the 13th and 14th centuries. Poitou finally became French territory when it was retaken by the French under Du Guesclin in 1365.

Much earlier than this the city had seen another battle which was of significance not just for France but for the whole of western Christendom. For it was here in 732 that Charles Martel defeated the Saracens under Abd-er-Rahman, at a moment when they seemed destined to conquer western Europe.

What to see

Baptistry of St-John

Today Poitiers is famous for its ecclesiastical architecture as well as its battles, even if its fine medieval monuments are now somewhat lost amongst recent developments. There are 3 outstanding churches in the city, of which the earliest is the Baptistry of St John, thought to be the oldest Christian monument in France. Originally erected in 356–68, the stone building is sunk into the ground and consists of a rectangular chamber, used for baptisms, and an eastern end added during the 6th and 7th centuries when the practice of baptism by full emersion was abandoned and the *piscina* was filled in and the building enlarged. Part of the floor and some of the arches date from the 4th and 7th centuries and the paintings of the apostles from the 12th century. (Open Mar–Jan daily 10–12.30 and 2–4 pm, Feb, Thurs–Tues 10 am–12.30 pm and 2–4.30 pm.)

Nearby, in bizarre but no doubt deliberate juxtaposition, is the futuristic and none-too-complementary shapes of the technological and scientific industrial centre, **Espace Pierre Mendes-France**. A small but pleasant town **museum** is located close to the baptistery at 61 rue St-Simplicien, displaying objects found in archaeological excavations in the city. (Open Wed–Mon 10 am–noon and 1–5 pm.)

Notre-Dame-la-Grande

Far more beguiling than the simple lines of the baptistery is the breathtaking western façade of Notre-Dame-la-Grande which is adorned with more statues than any Romanesque church in France. The façade is composed of 3 ranges of arcades encrusted with a bewildering number and variety statues and bas-reliefs. Many have been decapitated but those remaining include Christ Triumphant surrounded by the symbols of the Evangelists in the upper storey and scenes from the Scriptures in the lower storeys. Statues of saints and the apostles fill the other arches. (Open daily 7.15 am–7 pm.)

Ste-Radegonde

The Church of Ste-Radegonde has undergone several restorations since the 11th century but it possesses a beautiful choir and nave. The 9th-century crypt contains a marble sarcophagus of Ste-Radegonde, from which the remains of the patron saint of Poitiers were hauled and burnt by Calvinists in 1562. The church of **St-Hilaire le Grand**, although restored with a shortened nave, was one of the grandest French Romanesque churches of the mid-11th century. It has some vigorous early romanesque and decorative wall painting.

Cathédrale de St-Pierre

A short distance away stands the cathedral of St-Pierre, which was commissioned by Eleanor of Aquitaine. Her figure is to be found with that of her husband King Henry II at the foot of the Cross in the magnificent 13th-century stained glass in the apse. The largest church in Poitiers, the cathedral has 2 assymetrical towers, which are always in view from the **Grand Rue**, the long medieval street which runs through the old town.

Palais de Justice

Although not obvious from the outside the Palais de Justice contains a truly magnificent early 13th-century hall, the Salle des Pas-Perdus, which was once part of the Palace of the Dukes of Aquitaine. Charles VII was proclaimed king here in 1422. The Parlement de Paris was transferred to Poitiers soon after his Coronation and here it remained until 1436. Joan of Arc was interrogated on the authenticity of her mission to free France of the English in the hall, which had been rebuilt shortly before by Duc Jean de Berry.

Practicalities in Poitiers

Tourist Office 8 rue des Grandes Ecoles (Tel. 49 41 21 24); guided city tours in July–Aug; accommodation service, regional tourist office at 15 rue Carnot, near Place Maréchal Leclerc (Tel. 49 41 58 22).

Railway Station Blvd du Grand Cerf (Info: Tel. 49 58 50 50; Reservations Tel. 49 63 60 60); to town centre, follow Blvd Solférino which climbs up to the old town, then continue along Rue Boncenne to Notre-Dame-la-Grande.

Buses STP buses provide city transportation; timetable from tourist office.

Markets Les Halles, Place Charles de Gaulle, Mon–Sat; larger regional market on Saturday mornings.

Festivals Poitiers l'Eté: July and August, succession of jazz and classical recitals, operatic performances, firework displays etc. Le Printemps Musical de Poitiers: May, another series of concerts, largely classical. Rencontres Musicales de Poitiers: late Oct–April, bi-weekly concerts; details from tourist office.

Hotels Hôtel Continental, 2 blvd Solférino, on the corner as the road winds up from the station (Tel. 49 37 93 93). Simple and clean.
☆ Hôtel Jules Ferry, 27 rue Jules Ferry, near Eglise St-Hilaire (Tel. 49 37 80 14). In quiet street, with clean, attractive, rooms.
☆☆ Hôtel Central, 35 Place du Maréchal Leclerc (Tel. 49 01 79 79). Comfortable rooms, right on the central square with good roofscape views.
☆☆ Hôtel du Plat d'Etain, 7 rue Plat d'Etain (Tel. 49 41 04 80). Pleasant little hotel in a calm cul-de-sac in the heart of the old town.
☆☆ Hôtel Europe, 39 rue Carnot (Tel. 49 88 12 00). A large, traditional 19th-century hotel right in the town centre. No restaurant.

Hostels Auberge de la Jeunesse, 17 rue de la Jeunesse, 3 km from station. Bus no 3 from station (direction **Pierre Loti** to **Cap Sud** (Tel. 49 58 03 05).

Restaurants ☆ Maxime, 4 rue St-Nicolas (Tel. 49 41 09 55). pleasant 1920s, frescoed interior plus delicious inventive dishes from chef Christian Rougier.

Niort

Trains 6 trains daily from **Poitiers** (45 mins); 6–8 from **La Rochelle** (1 hour).

The capital of Deux Sèvres, at the edge of the district of Poitevin Marais, Niort looks almost Mediterranean with its pale houses capped by red Roman tiles and large sunny central square. Niort was originally a Roman town which benefitted from its strategic position on the bank of the river Sèvre-Niortaise which divides into several branches through the town.

What to see

Donjon des Contes de Poitiers

The massive Donjon dominates Niort, just as it must have done when it was first built 700 years ago. The imposing late 12th century and early 13th century Keep was part of an English fortress founded by Henry ii which fell to France after Du Guesclin's attack in 1372. During the Religious Wars, the keep was fought over by the Catholics and Huguenots before eventually being sacked by the Protestants in 1588. The château consists of 2 enormous square towers with round corner turrets linked by an impressive 15th-century building. The castle buildings now house the **Musée d'Ethnographie Régionale**, a fascinating collection of local peasant costume, head-dresses and weapons. (Open Apr–Oct, Wed 9 am–noon and 2 – 6 pm; Nov–Mar, Wed–Mon 9 am–noon and 2 – 5 pm.)

Musée du Pilori

Off the nearby rue Victor Hugo is the old **Hôtel de Ville**, a curious triangular building completed in 1535. The work of Renaissance architect Mathurin Berthomé, it now houses a miscellaneous collection of archaeological finds and medieval and Renaissance objects, including a complete collection of coins from the Carolingian mint at Melle and a fine ebony chest encrusted with gold and silver. (Open Apr–Oct, Wed–Mon, 9 am–noon and 2 – 6 pm; Nov–Mar Wed–Mon 9 am–noon and 2 – 5 pm.)

The central square in Niort is the **Place de la Brèche**. Napoleon spent his last night on the French mainland here, on 2nd July 1815, in a house on the northern side of the square. Other interesting houses can be seen at 13 rue Victor Hugo where there is the 15th-century **Maison de Candie**; the **Hôtel de Chaumon** at 5 rue du Pont was probably the birth-place of Françoise d'Aubigny whose father was held prisoner in the Donjon.

Nôtre-Dame

Rue Thiers leads to the new Hôtel de Ville, beyond which is Nôtre-Dame, a Gothic construction by Berthomé. Altered in the 18th-century it is still notable for the elegance of its lofty spire. Close by is the **Musée des Beaux-Arts** in the former Collège de l'Oratoire with collections of tapestries and Renaissance works of art including unusual 14th-century painted panels from the nearby Château of La Mothe-St-Héraye. (Open Wed–Mon 9 am–noon and 2 – 6 pm.) The old houses are mainly in and around Rue St-Jean, such as the Maison du Gouverneur with its Gothic arcade and the elegant Hôtel d'Estissac in Rue du Petit-St-Jean.

Praticalities in Niort

Tourist Office Rue Ernest-Pérochon (Tel. 49 24
18 79).
Railway Station (Information and Reservations:
Tel. 49 24 50 50). For town centre from station,
follow rue de la Gare up to rue Ernest-
Pérochon.
Markets Covered daily market in *Les Halles*.

Hotels *Hôtel St-Jean*, 21 ave St-Jean d'Angély
(Tel. 49 79 20 76): Clean, bright rooms and
friendly welcoming proprietor.
Camping Municipal, blvd S. Allende (Tel. 49 79
05 06). Beside the stadium; bus no 2 from Place
de la Breche to **Chabut** stop.

Excursion from Niort
Parthenay

Buses *10 buses a day (50 mins).*

From Poitiers an SNCF bus can be taken
east across the gently undulating rich
fertile soil of Poitou to the picturesque
town of Parthenay, built in a strong
defensive position above the gentle valley
of the River Thouet. The entrance to the
town is guarded by a gaunt machicolated
gateway, the **Porte St-Jacques**, once part
of the 13th-century walls which
surrounded the town. The street ahead is
the ancient thoroughfare, the Rue de la

Vaux St-Jacques, lined with attractive
brick and timber-framed 15th-century
houses. Higher up is the site of an inner
ring of fortifications that formerly
defended the Citadel, to which access is
gained through another superb fortified
gateway, the gothic **Porte de l'Horloge**.
Within the Citadel is to be found a rabbit
warren of lanes and alleyways, the
Romanesque **Church of St-Croix** and 3
13th-century towers, all that survives of
the medieval fortress.

Practicalities in Parthenay

Tourist office Palais des Congrès, square R.
Bigot (Tel. 49 64 24 24).
Buses SNCF (Tel. 49 58 50 50). 10 daily to
Poitiers; leave and arrive at Parthenay Railway
Station.
Festivals *Flip* 2–18 July: Processions, folklore,
music.
Jazz, 9–18 July: In streets and public venues
(details from tourist office).
Market Wed morning. Place du Drapeau and
stretching through the old town.

Hotels ☆☆ *St Jacques*, 13 av. 114e RI (Tel. 49
64 33 33). Just outside the southern limits of
the old city walls.
☆☆ Hôtel du Nord, 86 av. Gén. de Gaulle
(Tel. 49 94 29 11). Small restaurant/hotel facing
the old and now disused railway station, on the
eastern side of the town.
Restaurants ☆ *Le Fin Gourmet*, 28 rue Ganne
(Tel. 49 74 04 53). Traditional French cooking
of a high order.

Tours/St-Pierre-des-Corps

Trains to Tours *10–12 trains from* **Poitiers** *(45 mins); from* **Angoulême** *(1½
hours); 13 daily from* **Bordeaux** *(2½ hours); 16* TGVs *from* **Paris Montparnasse** *(1
hour); 3–4 slow trains from* **Paris Austerlitz** *(2 hours 50 mins).* NB: *Virtually all
trains to Tours require a change at* **St-Pierre-des-Corps,** *a* TGV *station 5 mins by
train-shuttle from the centre of Tours itself.*

North from Poitiers the train travels through the flat landscape of Vienne to
Châtellerault, the Sheffield of France, a duchy once bestowed on James Hamilton,

Duke of Arran and Regent of Scotland, by Henri II for his role in promoting the marriage of his ward, the child Queen Mary, and the French Dauphin.

Skirting and then crossing the River Vienne the train traverses a wide plateau of flat, arable land to **Ste-Maure de Touraine**, a town famous for its goats' milk cheese. Shortly afterwards the train begins to pass through the vineyards of Touraine and crosses the River Indre at **Montbazon**, distinguished by its massive 12th-century square Keep and ruined castle walls. The train then pulls across the wide valley of the Loire, most trains for Tours stopping at the newly built TGV railway station called St-Pierre-les-Corps, from where connecting trains make the 5 minute ride into the centre of Tours.

For Tours and the châteaux of the Loire, see The Loire Valley page 227.

Tours: Railway Station Info. Tel 47 20 50 50.

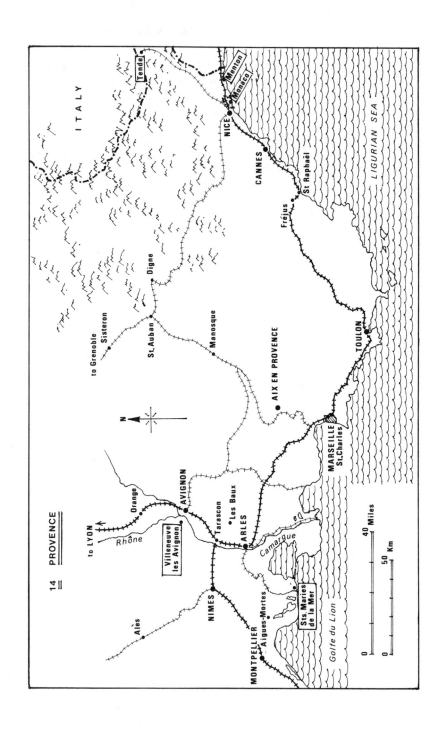

14 PROVENCE

14 Provence

A land of infinite variety, rich in history, Provence is blessed by climate and its proximity to the Mediterranean. Olive groves and vineyards climb the hills which burst into life in spring with mimosa and dazzling fields of lavender in early summer. When the mistral blows, the scent of sage, rosemary and thyme is carried with the wind and the leaves of the olive trees shake and dance.

For centuries Provence's sunny and accessible shores attracted nations from all parts of the Mediterranean. The Phoenicians colonised the coast from the 7th century BC and the Romans entered France here for the first time in 125 BC, calling the area 'Provincia' or 'the province'. Originally Provence stretched from the mouth of the Rhône to the eastern frontier of France; now it is a term applied loosely to include a large part of the hinterland which was part of the land ruled by the counts of Provence.

The landscape of Provence is varied and enchanting, ranging from the mountains in the east to the desolate marshland of the Camargue and the rocky cliffs of the Vaucluse. Mont Ventoux, so often painted by Van Gogh, is one of the highest peaks of Provence, 30 kilometres east of the Roman city of Orange. Petrarch climbed Mont Ventoux and settled in what must have been one of the most beautiful and tranquil spots in Provence, Fontaine de Vaucluse.

It is not all idyllic though. The influx of visitors has wrought lasting damage on the beauty of the coast and what attracted Lord Brougham and other early visitors would surely deter them now. The beaches of the coast are crowded in summer, the idyllic fishing villages of the Côte d'Azur now large cities and much of the coast geared to making money. Inland the damage is less severe and the towns have coped more successfully with the influx of visitors. Best visited in early June and September, when the crowds are thinner, the Côte d'Azur and Provence are always going to be popular.

The Roman cities of Arles and Orange retain impressive monuments from antiquity that are brought to life in summer for plays, concerts and dance, for Provence is famous for its festivals which take place outdoors through the summer months.

This journey includes the greater part of Provence and the Côte d'Azur, the thin stretch of coastline heading east towards Italy, and includes some of the most famous towns in France – Avignon, Arles, Tarascon and, most lovely of all, Aix-en-Provence. The landscape of Provence is ever changing – with altitude, the seasons and the soil, but its face is generally dry, with light or silvery tones predominating. The land ranges from chalky limestone to pebbly fields and clay baked as hard as pottery and upon this land are scattered the distinctive shapes of the olive, the cypress, the maritime pine and mottled plane.

The route *Avignon – Villeneuve-les-Avignon – Tarascon/Beaucaire – Arles – Saintes-Maries-de-la-Mer – Les Baux de Provence – Marseille – Toulon – Saint Raphaêl – Frejus – Cannes – Nice – Monaco – Menton – Digne-les-Bains – Manosque – aix-en-Provence*

Avignon, *one of the most fascinating cities in the south of France, makes a perfect starting point for a tour of Provence. For 100 years it was the Papal capital, the rival of Rome itself, from which time dates the massive Palace of the Popes, a fitting reflection of the power and wealth of the medieval church. Easily accesible from Paris, dynamic, full of life and animation, Avignon is the archetypal symbol of Provence. A few miles west lies* **Tarascon** *with one of the most perfect 15th-century castles of Provence, idyllically reflected in the Rhône. At* **Arles** *are to be found some of the most superb Roman ruins of Provence, with a beautiful Roman theatre and ampitheatre, and a fascinating medieval city full of narrow winding streets. A short ride to the east leads to* **Marseille,** *the 3rd largest port of France, once famous for its beauty, now more for its animation and large immigrant population. Although part of the old town was razed to the ground during the war, Marseille still possesses a certain infectious magic, with its balmy climate, superb seafood restaurants and life lived on the streets. Along the coast lies* **St-Raphaël,** *one of the slightly quieter Riviera towns in a delightful setting on the Bay of Fréjus, at the beginning of the Corniche de l'Esterel. Further east* **Cannes** *was once deemed the most aristocratic of the Riviera winter resorts. Much has changed since then but the old town round Mont Chevalier and the port still evoke Cannes as it was in the 2nd half of the 19th century. The bright and noisy town of* **Nice** *still enjoys the most magnificent location on the Baie des Anges, backed by a crescent of hills, beyond* *which rises a receding ampitheatre of impressive mountains. From Nice an entirely different landscape opens up as a journey begins inland, on a private railway line, through the hills of Provence to* **Digne**, *a good base for walking in the Provençal Alps. South of Manosque lies* **Aix-en-Provence**, *one of the most attractive towns of the south of France, with its superb aristocratic mansions, tree-shaded boulevards and numerous fountains. From Aix-en-Provence, trains lead south to Marseille, from where there are fast connections to Paris and Nice.* (**Approximately 7 to 12 days.**)

Avignon

Trains *10–13* TGVs *daily from* **Paris** *(4 hours); 5–8 from* **Nîmes** *(30 mins); 17 from* **Marseille** *(1 hour 15 mins); 12–18 from* **Montpellier** *(1 hour); 7–8 from* **Toulouse** *(4 hours).*

'Avignon! Avignon with its ramparts and battlements! Avignon, city of joyful bells, city of richly ornamented towers and spires . . . Avignon, like a gracious lady with the Mistral rustling her pinned-up skirts and her windtossed hair, contemplating her glorious past with jaunty indifference.' So sang the Provençal poet, Mistral, of his favourite city.

Avignon thrived under the Romans but very little of Roman Avignon now remains, their theatres, public baths, villas and temples swept away by the invasions of Germanic barbarians, Normans and Saracens. During the Albigensian war, the town supported the Count of Toulouse; as a result it suffered reprisals at the hands of King Louis VIII of France. Nevertheless Avignon soon recovered and became rich and powerful, largely due to its position on the bank of the Rhône where many land routes met. Traffic was greatly encouraged to travel via Avignon on account of its **magnificent bridge** across the Rhône. Saint Bénézet had played a role in its construction in the 12th century; the citizens of the city devoutly named it after him.

From the railway station the town centre is a short walk down a delightful street lined with mature plane trees – the **Cours Jean Jaurès** which turns into the **Rue de la République**. The defensive walls that one passes through were virtually rebuilt in the 19th century by Viollet-le-Duc but they still give a very good idea of the extent of the medieval city.

What to see

The City Walls

The best way to discover Avignon, 'Saint Peter's Godchild', is to walk round it. The ramparts which still entirely surround the city are half buried under the earth and give no idea of the protection which they afforded the town when Innocent VI began to build them in the middle of the 14th century. But by walking round them the dimensions and structure of the town are revealed, as are its profile and mass.

The Doms Rock

After walking round the town outside the ramparts, the next destination should be the Doms Rock, the highest point of the town and its focal point, strategically and spiritually, since the site was first settled in prehistoric times. From its summit there is one of the most wonderful views to be found anywhere in the Midi. Beyond the Rhône with its ruined bridge and the Ile de La Barthelasse, rises the tower of Philippe-le-Bel, behind which are the twin towers of the Fort St-André. Near by, just below are the cliff-like walls of the Palace of the Popes while far away, on the horizon, blue hills and mountains are discernible above the surrounding plains.

Palace of the Popes

The feudal and military side of the history of Provence is seen in the Palace of the Popes in Avignon, the refuge of Popes Clement and Urban and of the Anti-Pope, Benedict. Avignon's fortunes began when Pope Clement V was driven from Rome by political turmoil and decided to establish his court in the city in 1309. At that time the Papacy already possessed the Comtat Venaissin in France, a large area of territory between the rivers Rhône and Durance, although Avignon itself belonged to the Count of Provence. Clement V's successor converted the Archbishop's Palace into the Papal seat but the Cistercian Benedict XII, had this demolished and set about building the austere fortress-like Old Palace. The west and south wings and the Audience Chamber were added by Clement VI who bought Avignon from Joanna, Queen of Naples and Countess of Provence, for 80,000 ducats. The **Tour St-Laurent** was added by Innocent VI and the Great Court with its well was arranged by Urban V.

The shape and size of the palace, modified by all the 7 pontiffs who occupied it, shows the twin preoccupation with majesty and magnificence on the one hand and military security on the other. Opposite the palace of the austere Cistercian Benedict XII, built around a simple cloister, stands the residence of the ostentatious Clement VI. This is the part which faces the 'Place' and contains the great audience chamber and the pontifical chapel, a jewel of southern Gothic architecture. Perhaps the most impressive room of this rambling palace is the vast banqueting hall, the **Grande Tinel**, a gigantic vaulted room with a large fireplace, off which is an enormous kitchen with a huge central chimney.

But more intimate and interesting are the **private apartments** of the popes, in particular his bedroom with its richly coloured tile floor and walls delicately painted with scenes of birds entwined in vines and squirrels climbing oak trees against a background of blue tempera. The adjoining room, the Chambre du Cerf is decorated with 14th-century frescoes of rural pursuits and sports – fishing, stag-hunting, hawking and fruit and flower picking. These were almost certainly the work of Provençal artists, working within the school of French mural and miniature painting and tapestry design.

The best Provençal artists were reinforced by Italians of the Papal retinue, Matteo of Viterbo and Simone Martini of Siena. But despite frescoes in the chapels by the Italian artist Matteo Giovanetti, of John the Baptist and the life of St Martial and on one vault of the Salle de la Grande Audience, there is very little feeling of spirituality in the palace. Nor is it easy to conjure up the magnificence and luxury of the palace in its heyday for today it is almost completely empty and deserted. In the 14th century it would have been luxuriously furnished with tapestries and sumptuously painted and a scene of intense animation, with the constant to-ing and fro-ing of cardinals in red silk and the arrival of endless ambassadors and princes.

Externally it has more the appearance of a fortress than a palace and is in fact a magnificent example of 14th-century military architecture, with enormously tall buttressed walls of great thickness. Clement vi's successor Innocent vi began to build the ramparts and they were completed by Urban i who also designed and laid out the gardens on the eastern side of the palace. Strong though the city walls were, the palace was the line of last resort, built to be impregnable.

In 1376 Gregory xi, the last of the 7 popes resident at Avignon, was persuaded by Saint Catherine of Siena to return to Rome. This event however sparked off the beginning of the Great Schism for the cardinals of the Sacred College, of whom the majority were French, elected another – French – cardinal to be the new Pope, Clement vii, who returned in 1378 to Avignon. The Great Schism divided the Christian world, although the Avignon Pope was recognised mainly in France. Popes and anti-popes mutually excommunicated each other and it was only after a 5-year siege, ending in 1403, that Benedict xiii was forced to flee and the Schism came to an end. By 1410 the Pope of Rome had regained control of the town and it remained the property of the Holy See, administered by a Papal legate, until 1791. Taken over by the State, the wonderful palace was used as a barracks for Napoleon's soldiers, who prised away and sold parts of the magnificent murals.

Cardinals' Palaces

Around the Palace of the Popes sprung up a number of smaller palaces for the cardinals, court dignitaries and ambassadors who attended the Papal court. Among the most exquisite is the **Palais du Roure**, another is the **Petit Palais**, built by Arnaud de Via in the 14th century. The **Hôtel des Monnaies**, the Papal mint, which was in use until the closing decade of the 18th century, is housed in the elaborately carved building facing the Papal palace.

Avignon's many residents include Petrarch who condemned the town as a sink of iniquity and withdrew to nearby Vaucluse; it was in Avignon that he first caught sight of Laura, the object of his poetic passion. Olivier Messiaen, the composer, and Joseph Vernet, the marine artist, are natives of the city and John Stuart Mill retired and was buried here.

The Petit Palais At the other end of the Place du Palais is the Petit Palais, between the Pont d'Avignon and the Rochers des Doms garden. Within this 14th-century archbishop's residence is the **Musée du Petit Palais**, containing the finest collection of early Italian painting in France. Amongst the many Italian Old Masters is Botticelli's *Virgin and Child*. (Open Wed–Mon 9.30 am-noon and 2-6 pm; free Sun.) Just behind the Petit Palais is the famous **Pont d'Avignon** (Pont St-Bénézet) of the nursery rhyme, an elegant and poignant bridge of 4 arches stepping out into the Rhône. The original bridge, built in the 12th century and the first to span the Rhône at Avignon, was destroyed by flood in the 17th-century.

Notre-Dame-des-Doms

The centre of the town is focused on the Place du Palais onto which face not only the Palace of the Popes but the 12th-century cathedral, Notre-Dame-des-Doms, which houses the Gothic tomb of Pope John XI and the Mint, an elegant 17th-century mansion with an ornate façade incorporating the Borghese coat of arms, cherubs, dragons and eagles, carved from golden sandstone.

Some of the finest private mansions are to be found in **Rue Joseph Vernet** while the **Rue des Teinturiers** still retains some of the waterwheels used to drive the machinery in the printed calico works. This picturesque cobbled street shaded with trees follows the course of the River Sorgue; the Franciscan bell tower is all that remains of the convent where Petrarch's Laura may have been buried after dying of the Plague in 1348.

Practicalities in Avignon

Tourist Office 41 cours Jean Jaurès, on main street towards centre on right (Tel. 90 82 65 11); branch office at train station (Tel. 90 82 05 81); accommodation service (Tel. 90 82 05 81).
Railway Station Porte de la République (Information: Tel. 90 82 50 50; Reservations: Tel. 90 82 56 29).
Buses blvd St-Roch, east of train station (Tel. 90 82 07 35); buses to Vaison-la-Romaine, Orange and Châteauneuf-du-Pape.
Post Office Ave du Président Kennedy, just within walls from train station; currency exchange and *poste restante*.
Festivals *Festival d'Avignon*; early July–early Aug, huge festival of theatre, in official locations and on the streets.
Bike Rental *Cycles Peugeot*, 80 rue Guillaume Puy (Tel. 90 86 32 49) or *Transhumance*, at train station (Tel. 90 82 05 81).
Markets Avignon's large covered market, *Les Halles*, is located in Place Pie. Tues-Sun mornings. Another open air market is held near the porte St-Michel just outside the city walls, close to the railway station, on Sat. and Sun.

Hotels ☆*Hôtel Le Parc*, 18 rue Perdiguier, off cours Jean Jaurès, near tourist office (Tel. 90 82 71 55). Attractive, clean and bright.
☆*Hôtel Splendid*, 17 rue Perdiguier, next door to *Le Pa* : (Tel. 90 32 17 30). Good spacious rooms in the centre.
☆*Hôtel Innara*, 100 rue Joseph Vernet, near rue de la République (Tel. 90 82 54 10).
☆☆*Médieval*, 15 rue Petite Saunerie (Tel. 90 86 11 06). Delightful 17th-century hotel down a side-street near the Eglise St-Pierre; rooms on street side a little dark.
☆☆*Hôtel Garlande*, 20 rue Galante (Tel. 90 85 08 85). Near the little church and square of St-Didier.
☆☆☆*Hôtel Blauvac*, 11 rue de la Bancasse (Tel. 90 86 34 11). In a quiet little street parallel to the Rue de la République.
☆☆☆☆*Hôtel la Mirande*, (Tel. 90 85 93 93) Sumptuous accommodation in a cardinal's palace in a tranquil cobbled square at the foot of the Palace of the Popes; recently restored with the utmost elegance and taste.
Hostels *Foyer: Bagatelle*, Ile de la Barthelasse,

across river over Pont Daladier (Tel. 90 86 30 39). Basic but adequate dormitory accommodation.

Camping *Bagatelle*, Ile de la Barthelasse, short walk from station over Pont Daladier, good facilities (Tel. 90 86 30 39).

Restaurants *Le Pain Bis*, 6 rue Armand-de-Ponmartin (Tel. 90 86 46 77). Off a small square with seating outside; mostly vegetarian and healthy organic food.

Restaurant l'Arlequin, 84 rue Bonneterie (Tel. 90 85 79 56). A delightful brightly coloured little restaurant offering good local cuisine.

Cafétéria Flunch, 11 blvd Raspail, off Rue de la République (Tel. 90 86 06 23). One of the cheapest eating places in town.

Le Magnanen, 19 rue St-Michel, off Place des Corps Saints Tel. Tiny, popular restaurant crowded with locals; interesting dishes from Canadian-French chef.

☆*Férigoulo*, 30 rue Joseph-Vernet (Tel. 90 82 10 28). Excellent mix of traditional and *nouvelle cuisine*; fresh and light cooking.

☆*Les Domaines*, 28 place Horloge, right on the central square (Tel. 90 82 58 86).

☆*La Fourchette*, 17 rue Racine (Tel. 90 85 20 43). Delicious dishes including rabbit with mustard – a Provençal speciality.

☆☆*Hiély-Lucullus*, 5 rue de la République (Tel. 90 86 17 07). Outstanding cuisine from chef André Chaussey; probably the most delicious food in Avignon.

☆☆*Jardin de la Tour*, 8 rue Tour (Tel. 90 85 66 50). Excellent food in a superb old building, recently renovated.

Excursion from Avignon
Villeneuve-lès-Avignon

1 hour walk from central Avignon; frequent buses from railway station.

On the right bank of the Rhône stands Villeneuve-lès-Avignon, confronting the majesty of Avignon from the opposite river bank. The hill on which the town stands was fortified at a very early date. Strictly speaking Villeneuve-lès-Avignon is part of Languedoc and not Provence, for the borders of Languedoc stretch up to the banks of the Rhône. Defended by extensive ramparts, including the massive fortifications of the **Saint-André Fort**, which can still be seen today, Villeneuve was also protected by the French king to whom it gave its allegiance.

Louis VIII and Philippe le Bel established a fortress here in the 13th century from where they could keep an eye on Provence over the river. Later the Popes seized the town, fearing the use to which the round towers and great square Keep added by Philippe-le-Bel, which guarded the west end of the Pont St-Bénézet, could be put. When Avignon became too small for the myriads of court officials, gentlemen, cardinals, secretaries and priests attached to the Papal court,

many of them moved across the Rhône and settled around Villeneuve. The palaces built by the cardinals became known as *livrées* or liveries; the remains of some of these are still to be seen.

In the **hospice** is the tomb of Innocent VI while the **museum** contains several paintings by the Mignards and Enguerrand Charonton's *Coronation of the Virgin* – the most complete and expressive painting of the Provençal school. In the Rue de la République is the entrance to the **Charteuse du Val de Bénédiction**, founded by Innocent VI in 1356, who is buried there. Ransacked during the Revolution, it is being restored as a cultural centre.

Away from the bustle and crowds of Avignon, Villeneuve had the feel until a few years ago of a dead town, still slumbering in decay and past splendour. Grass-covered ruins, cobbled streets, and its isolation on the edge of the Rhône, still give it a unique atmosphere. From the top of one of the towers the view of the swiftly moving river, the roofs and towers of Avignon and the outline of Mont Ventoux in the bluish haze of the distance, evoke the pattern of past ages.

Practicalities in Villeneuve-les-Avignon

Tourist Office 1 Place Ch David (Tel. 90 25 61 33).

Hotel ☆☆*Hôtel Atelier*, 5 rue Foire, in a beautiful 16th-century house (Tel. 90 25 01 84).

Tarascon/Beaucaire

Trains *10 trains daily from* **Avignon** *(13 mins); 6 daily from* **Arles** *(20 mins).*

What to see

Le château de Tarascon

Rising dramatically from the banks of the Rhône, in whose waters it is often reflected, lies one of the most spectacular medieval castles in France. Its massive bulk is softened by its proximity to the water and it almost seems to be a natural extension of the smoothed and rounded rock from which it rises. In the 13th-century its forerunner defended Provence's western boundary; the present castle was begun in 1400 and completed by King René, count of Provence and Anjou, in the mid-15th century. Despite its massive bulk, it is not unharmonious and the interior was decorated and furnished with great taste and elegance. The finest vaulted rooms are those overlooking the Rhône.

Festivities and tournaments organised by King René were held in the inner courtyard. He entertained on a grand scale, playing host to the future Louis XI and the troubador duke, Charles of Orléans, but also debated with skill, played musical instruments proficiently, wrote treatises on tournaments and composed music.

In the 16th-century the castle was abandoned and the following century was turned into a prison, which it remained until 1926. It has now been carefully restored and presents once again the appearance it had 500 years ago. The King's living quarters were on the south side, and on the Rhône side the walls rise over 45 metres vertically from the river. The terrace affords an unparalleled panorama of Beaucaire across the Rhône, the town of Tarascon, Arles to the south and the Alpilles chain of hills to the south-east. (Open July and Aug, Wed–Mon 9 am–7 pm, Sept–June guided tours only 9–11 am and 2–6 pm.)

Beaucaire

On the western bank of the Rhône lies Beaucaire, a short walk away over the bridge. For 700 years, from the 13th to the 19th centuries, it was the site of one of the most famous medieval fairs in Europe, merchants coming with their wares from not just all over Europe but from north Africa and the Levant. As many as 300,000 people gathered for the fair which lasted for a week in July; even in the 1840s 100,000 people were still attending it. The arrival of the railway put an end to the fair in a very short space of time.

Le Château de Beaucaire Standing on a hill is a picturesque ruined château, its crenellated towers rising up against a backdrop of pine-covered limestone rock. It had a curious triangular Keep which is now largely in ruins, Cardinal Richelieu having ordered the dismantling of the castle in the 17th century. To the south vineyards and orchards stretch away across the flat plains to Arles.

Practicalities in Tarascon

Tourist office 59 rue Halles (Tel. 90 91 03 52). **Railway station** Bd du Viaduc. (Tel. 90 82 56 29). To reach centre, cross Place Colonel Berrurier, Cours Aristide Briand and Ave de la République to the Château and the Rhône. **Hotels** ☆☆☆*Hôtel Provence* 7 bd Victor Hugo

(Tel. 90 91 06 43). Handsome, comfortable hotel, close to the railway station and the Porte St-Jean.
☆☆*Hôtel Echevins and restaurant Mistral*, 26 Bd Itam (Tel. 90 91 01 70). Just within the old limits of the city.

Practicalities in Beaucaire

Tourist office 24 cours Cambetta (Tel. 66 59 26 57). **Railway Station** Tarascon railway station is the closest to Beaucaire (see Tarascon). To reach Beaucaire from Tarascon, cross bridge over Rhône to south of Château, continue along

Quai Gén. de Gaulle. Cours Gambetta and tourist office are on the right. **Hotels** ☆☆☆☆*Les Doctrinaires*, Quai Gén. de Gaulle (Tel. 66 59 41 32). Luxurious hotel in a splendid 17th-century former college.

Arles

Trains 6 *trains daily from* **Tarascon** *(20 mins); frequent trains from* **Avignon** *(30 mins);* **Nîmes** *(25 mins); 15 from* **Montpellier** *(1 hour 10 mins);* **Marseille** *(1 hour); 10 daily from* **Aix-en-Provence** *(1 hour 45 mins).*

Arles is one of the splendours of Provence, an enchanting and animated town, that never fails to surprise and charm. Foremost amongst its glories are the Roman ampitheatre, one of the most famous necropolises of the western world, and one of the finest Romanesque churches in southern France.

What to see

Roman Arles

Roman ruins lie at every corner for Arles is an ancient city and flourished under the Romans as a naval and commercial port, especially after Caesar's sack of Marseille in 49 BC. Founded by a colony of veterans of the 6th Roman legion, Arles thrived from its location at the southernmost bridge over the Rhône on the Domitian Way, the direct road between Italy and Spain, and by its proximity to the sea. Water was brought to the Roman town by aqueduct from the Alpilles Chain and channelled to local fountains, public baths and private houses. By the 2nd century the Roman town had its own drainage system, public lavatories, shipyards, circus and residential quarters and prospered to such an extent that in 395 AD it became the political capital of the Gauls. It was also an important centre of the early Christian church before being pillaged by the Barbarians and Saracens from the end of the 5th century.

Amphitheatre Arles, in fact, has not just one outstanding Roman building but 2, the amphitheatre and the theatre proper. The amphitheatre is a vast oval building of 2 storeys with seating for 20,000 spectators. Its third storey disappeared during the Middle Ages when it was transformed into a fortress and watchtowers were built on top of the walls. As late as the 18th century, it was crowded with squalid tenements and inhabited by the poor of the city. Restoration work began in 1825 and it is now used for bull-fights during the summer (Open June–Sept daily 9.30 am–noon and 2–4.30 pm, Apr–May and Oct, daily 9 am–12.30 pm and 2–6.30 pm; Rue du Cloître; joint ticket to all monuments and museums.)

Roman Theatre Adjacent to this is the theatre which was built in the reign of Augustus in the 1st century BC. Even in the 5th century it was being used as a quarry to build churches and was eventually built over entirely. It was only much later that it was rediscovered and in 1651, during excavations, the *Venus of Arles* was discovered here. It was presented to Louis XIV and is today in the Louvre. The stepped seating has been restored so that the theatre can be used once more for plays. Unlike the theatre in Orange, however, there was no natural hill for the theatre at Arles to be built into; an artificial structure with 27 arches had to be specially constructed. (Open June–Sept daily 9.30 am–noon and 2–4.30 pm, Apr–May and Oct, daily 9 am–12.30 pm and 2–6.30 pm; Rue du Cloître.)

St-Trophime Apart from its Roman remains Arles possesses perhaps the finest Romanesque church in Provence, St-Trophime, where Frederick Barbarossa was crowned emperor in 1178. In 1190 a magnificently carved western doorway was added to the church: its sculptures of Christ, the Apostles and Angels, the Elect and the Damned, the Adoration of the Magi and the Shepherds, the Magi before Herod and the Massacre of the Innocents, are of exceptional strength and simplicity. The cloisters, reached via a nearby lane, also have outstanding Provençal Romanesque sculptures that reflect the influence of antique bas-reliefs and are quite different in style and feel to northern Romanesque work of the same period. (Open June–Sept., daily 8.30 am–7 pm; Nov–Mar, daily 9 am–noon and 2–4.30 pm; Apr–May and Oct, daily 9 am–12.30 pm and 2–6.30 pm).

Musée Lapidaire Païen and Musée Lapidaire Chrétien

Opposite the church of St-Trophime is the Musée Lapidaire Païen. The huge quantity of archaeological finds found locally are split between the Musée Lapidaire Païen, to be found in the former church of Ste-Anne and the Musée Lapidaire Chrétien that contains the finest collection of early Christian sarcophagi, many dating from the 4th century, outside the Vatican. Most were carved in marble in the 4th century and depict scenes from the Old and New Testaments or typical rural scenes such as an olive harvest in progress. (Both museums open June–

Sept, daily 8.30 am–7 pm; Nov–Mar, daily 9 am–noon and 2–4.30 pm; Apr–May and Oct, daily 9 am–12.30 pm and 2–6 pm).

The Alyscamps

One unique feature of Arles is the Alyscamps or Champs-Elysées, all that remains of the once enormous necropolis of Arles. It consists of an avenue of marble tombs that once stretched down the Aurelian Way to the city. Because St Trophimus had been buried here and miracles had taken place close to his tomb, it became the general wish to be buried near by. Several local princes were interred in the vicinity in the 4th century and citizens from towns higher up the Rhône used to float the coffins of the dead downstream to be buried here. Both Dante in *Inferno* and Ariosto in *Orlando Furioso* make reference to the cemetery.

Museon Arlaten

The museum dedicated to the preservation of the Provençal identity, the Museon Arlaten, was the inspiration and creation of Frédéric Mistral. In the museum he collected and displayed costumes, household furnishings, ceramics and myriads of other household objects, evocative of traditional Provençal life. (Open June–Sept, daily 8.30 am–7 pm; Nov–Mar, Tues–Sun 9 am–noon and 2–4.30 pm; Apr–May and Oct, Tues–Sun 9 am–12.30 pm and 2–6.30 pm).

It was to Arles that Van Gogh came from Paris in 1888. Unfortunately the 2 buildings that he lived in, the Hôtel-Restaurant Carrel in Rue de la Cavalerie and the Yellow House on Place Lamartine were both destroyed during the Second World War. The solid shapes and forms of the Provençal countryside and its luminosity prompted Van Gogh to paint extensively outside, often returning to the same subject again and again. His paintings of Arles include the *House of Vincent*, *Les Alyscamps*, *L'Arlésienne*, *Crau Plain* and *Langlois Bridge*. It was here, however, that his mental health deteriorated and the year after his arrival he left Arles for the asylum at St Rémy-de-Provence. The **Musée Réattu**, in Rue du Grand Prieuré, contains no works by Van Gogh but a few sketches and paintings by Picasso, Léger and Vlaminck. Beside it are the ruins of the Palais Constantin, the site of Provence's largest Roman baths, the Thermes de la Trouille.

Practicalities in Arles

Tourist Office In Esplanade Charles de Gaulle opposite the Jardin d'Eté (Tel. 90 96 28 35); guided tours; accommodation service, branch office in railway station (Tel. 90 49 36 90).
Railway Station P. Talabot (Tel. 90 96 43 94); luggage lockers. Tourist office annex open Mon–Sat 9 am–noon and 2–6 pm. To town centre from station, turn right out of station, continue to Place Lamartine, walk through medieval gate into Rue de la Cavalerie. At Place Voltaire, turn right onto Rue du 4 September, then left down Rue de l'Hôtel de Ville as far as Blvd des Lices and the tourist office.

Hotels *Hôtel La Gallia*, 22 rue de l'Hôtel de Ville (Tel. 90 96 00 03). Spacious and immaculate; in a superb location.
Hôtel Gauguin, 5 Place Voltaire (Tel. 90 96 14 35). Clean and central.
Hôtel de Provence, 12 rue Chiavary, between station and centre with view of arena (Tel. 90 96 03 29).
Hôtel Lamartine, 1 rue Marius-Jouveau (Tel. 90 96 12 32). Tucked inside medieval gateway near pl. Lamartine.
☆☆*St-Trophime*, 16 rue de la Calade (Tel. 90 96 88 38). Old-fashioned and smallish rooms but good value and close to ampitheatre.

Hostels *Auberge de Jeunesse* (HI), Ave. Maréchal Foch, 20 mins from station (Tel. 90 96 18 25). Clean, modern and popular; lockers.
Camping *Camping-City*, 57 route de Crau; bus 2 in direction of **Pont de Crau** from Blvd des Lices; get off at **Greauxeaux** stop (Tel. 90 93 08 86).
Restaurants ☆*Côte d'Adam*, 12 rue de la

Liberté (Tel. 90 49 62 29). Excellent value for money in pleasant popular restaurant in heart of the old city.
☆☆*Le Vaccarès*, 11 rue Favorin (Tel. 90 96 06 17). Traditional Provençal dishes from chef Bernard Dumas; upstairs restaurant looks out over Place du Forum.

Excursions from Arles
Saintes-Maries-de-la-Mer

Buses *SNCF bus departs from the train station; buses leave from opposite the Station Bar on Blvd des Lices; 8 daily (1 hour); information from* Les Cars de Camargue *(Tel. 90 96 36 25).*

According to Provençal legend in the year 40 AD a boat was miraculously washed up on the shore where Stes-Maries is now situated, containing Mary, the mother of James, Mary Magdalene, Martha and her brother Lazarus, together with a number of other disciples. Legend has it that after erecting a simple oratory to the Virgin, the disciples then separated, the 2 Marys and Sarah remaining in the Carmargue where they were buried in the oratory. Their tomb rapidly became a pilgrimage

destination, particularly for Gypsies who developed a special veneration for Sarah, and was replaced in the 9th century by a fortified church. Two celebratory pilgrimages are still held here each year on 24th and 25th May, Gypsies coming from all over the world to participate in the festivities. 26th May is another day of celebration with the women of Arles in traditional costume taking part in the local dance, the *farandole*, horse racing and bull running. The only real sight in this village is the fortified church with its massive crenellated walls, in which are kept the statues and boat carried in the May processions.

Practicalities in Saintes-Maries-de-la Mer

Tourist Office 5 ave van Gogh, next to arena on the seafront (Tel. 90 97 82 55); currency exchange.
Buses Arrive and leave from just north of Place Mireille.
Cycle Hire *Camargue Vélo*, 27 ave Frédéric

Mistral (Tel. 90 97 94 55).
Hotels *Hôtel Le Delta*, Place Mireille (Tel. 90 97 811 12). Clean and close to bus stop.
☆*Hôtel Méditerranée*, 4 blvd Frédéric Mistral, off Rue Victor Hugo (Tel. 90 97 82 09). Clean, comfortable and convenient.

Les-Baux-de-Provence

Buses *4 buses depart daily from office on Boulevard Clémenceau, Arles (30 mins).*

Although not on the railway line, the beauty and magic of Les Baux is such that it is surely worth abandoning the railway line for a short journey east by bus. On a high isolated promontory detached from the Alpilles chain stands the deserted town of Les Baux, now so ruined and decayed that it seems to dissolve into the rocks out of which it was built. In the early Middle Ages it was the residence of

the Counts of Provence and the strongest town in the country. Its ruined houses and grass-grown deserted streets dominated by the remains of a fortified castle lie high up on a bare rock spur with wide vertical ravines plunging steeply down on either side. Here and there an early Renaissance doorway or window is to be found standing boldly out against a cloudless sky. In summer the sun beating down on the treeless ruins turns the village into a furnace but refuge can be taken in the charming **Place St-Vincent** and its adjacent church in the tiny village below. Near to the 12th-century church, to which shepherds herd their flocks for midnight mass at Christmas, is the 16th-century Hôtel des Porcelets, with a small art collection. On the southern side of the town a sheer precipice of several hundred metres drops to a dusty plain of coarse scrub interspersed with vines which stretches away in an unbroken expanse until it melts into the pale blue of the Mediterranean.

Practicalities in Les-Baux-de-Provence

Tourist Office In the Hôtel de Ville, half-way up hill to Cité Morte (Tel. 90 97 34 39). Open Easter-Oct, daily 9 am-noon and 2–6 pm; currency exchange.

Hotels Hôtel Le Mas de la Fontaine, at foot of village, the only budget hotel in Les Baux (Tel. 90 54 34 13).

From Arles the railway line crosses the wild and desolate plain of Crau, a grey-white desert of rocks and stones half covered by resilient tufts of grass known as coussous which grow between the stones. This empty and unfertile plain was once the mouth of the Durance river before its course altered direction to enter the Rhône just south of Avignon. For centuries the Grande Crau has supported sheep raising, tended by shepherds who lived from October to June in 1-roomed stone huts next to the rectangular sheepfolds. At the beginning of June the sheep are taken to summer pastures at a higher altitude. North of the railway is the Petite Crau which has been increasingly cleared of stone to allow cultivation, irrigation channels bringing water from the Durance river.

The train then skirts the Berre lagoon, a vast shallow lake that now serves as France's principal petroleum port to arrive at Marseille, one of the oldest and most bustling French cities.

Marseille

Trains 15 trains daily from Arles (1 hour); 9 daily from Paris Gare de Lyon (9–9½ hours); 10 TGVs from Paris (4 hours 30 mins); 8 from Lyon (3½ hours); frequent trains from Toulon (1 hour).

Despite its large immigrant population, Marseille remains quintessentially French. If the artery of the city is the Canebière, famous throughout France, the heart of the city is the great horsehoe of sunny quays which branches out from the bottom of the Canebière round the old port.

The Greeks arrived in the harbour of what is now the old port as long ago as 600 BC and established a trading port known as Massalia that grew quickly in prosperity and repute. Excavations of the old port have shown that under the Greeks the town was surrounded by ramparts and contained temples to Artemis and Apollo as well as a theatre. During the Second Punic War Massalia had allied herself with Rome and when the Romans first entered Provence in 125 BC, Rome came to her assistance in her wars against the Salian Franks. But during the struggle between Pompey and Caesar for power, Marseille backed Pompey, was besieged by Caesar and lost its trading privileges, treasures and fleet as a result of defeat. Nevertheless, despite this setback, Marseille remained a free city with its own university until pillaged by Saracens and Franks from the 7th century. Roman docks from the 1st century AD, complete with gigantic urns for storing wine, grain and oil and Roman pottery, can be found in the **Musée des Docks romains**, just behind the Quai du Port in Place Vivaux.

In the Middle Ages Marseille's fortunes revived, the city benefiting from its role supplying the Crusades, in recognition of which it was granted ownership of an area of Jerusalem together with its own church. It traded extensively with virtually every country in the Mediterranean basin, its prosperity stemming from the monopoly of trade which it enjoyed with the Levant. When Provence became part of the French kingdom in 1481, so too did Marseille but in 1720 Plague arrived on board a ship coming from Syria and devastated the city, reducing the population from 90,000 to 30,000 within 2 years. It recovered however with astonishing speed, the late 18th century seeing an enormous growth in trade in sugar, coffee and cacao with Latin America and the West Indies that brought untold wealth to the city.

What to see

The Canebière

The Canebière, once one of the most elegant and graceful streets of any city in France, has fallen on hard times and no longer conveys the feeling of prosperity and refinement for which it was once justly renowned. It still has some delightful buildings, however, the most notable being the 17th-century **Hôtel de Montgrand**, with a fine collection of contemporary paintings and sculptures and separate collection of Marseille and Moustiers faience.

The city, however, is known for its bustle, colour and animation rather than its beauty, and its streets are often congested with traffic.

Vieux Port

The most rewarding part of the city is in fact the poorest and lies in the labyrinth of narrow streets north of the harbour. Much of this area of the old town was razed to the ground by the Germans during the Second World War but there are fascinating alleyways and corners still to be explored. This area contains the **Hospice de la Vieille Charité** (5 mins walk NE of the cathedral) a former hospice with a gorgeous Baroque chapel by Puget surrounded by 3 storeys of arcaded galleries in elegant pink and yellow stone. Around the port are innumerable cafés and restaurants. Marseille has a reputation for its seafood, especially *Bouillabaisse* (fish stew) which can be eaten in the expensive restaurants around the port.

The Musée du Vieux Marseille

The history of the city in the 18th and 19th centuries is vividly brought to life in the Museum of Old Marseille in the Renaissance **Maison Diamantée** in the old port. (Open Tues–Sun 10 am–5 pm; rue de la Prison.)

The earliest history up to the Gallo-Roman era is presented in the **Musée de l'histoire de Marseilles**, at the end of the Garden of Ruins in the old Bourse or stock exchange. One of the prize exhibits is an 18-metre-long Roman boat. (Open Tues–Sat 10 am–4.45 pm; Cours Belsunce.)

Notre-Dame de la Garde

Down in the old port, now only used by yachts and private boats, the eye is quickly attracted to the neo-Byzantine basilica of Notre-Dame de la Garde on a tall hill surmounted by a huge gilded statue of the Virgin. The basilica, which dates from 1864, is of little artistic interest but the view from the church of the islands off the coast, the forts guarding the city harbour and the town itself is spectacular. The best time to climb for a view is early morning; by late morning the heat haze hides the view of the mountains and coastline, especially if the mistral is blowing.

The Château d'If

A rewarding boat trip can be made from the **Quai des Belges** to the Château d'If, the castle where Alexandre Dumas had 2 of his fictional heroes in *The Count of Monte Cristo* imprisoned. Originally built to defend the city in 1524, the castle was turned into a prison and it was here that Huguenots and the Man in the Iron Mask were held in the 17th century. (Open June–Sept, daily 8.30 am–noon and 1.30–6.30 pm; Oct–May, daily 8.30 am–noon and 1.30–4 pm; departures hourly (1½ hours.)

Basilique St-Victor

The most interesting church in Marseilles is the Basilique St-Victor, to the south of the port. A heavily fortified church built in the 11th century, it rests on 5th-century crypts which were part of an abbey founded by St-John Cassian in honour of St-Victor, patron saint of sailors and millers. They contain ancient pagan and Christian sarcophagi and a 3rd-century shrine holding the remains of martyrs on which the abbey was built. On 2nd February the church is the site of a Candlemas procession attended by the city's fishmongers.

Practicalities in Marseille

Tourist Office 4 la Canebière, on the main thoroughfare, near the *vieux port* (Tel. 91 54 91 11); accommodation service; maps; cultural events listings; SNCF reservations; daily tours; branch at railway station (Tel. 91 50 59 18).
Railway Station *Gare Marseille St-Charles* (Tel. 91 09 50 50); Information desk open Mon–Sat 8 am–8 pm; also reception desk open daily 4 am–midnight; luggage lockers open 6 am–midnight.
Buses *Gare des Autobus de Marseille* (Tel. 091 08 16 40), Place Victor Hugo, behind station;

buses to Cannes, Nice, Avignon, Aix-en-Provence, Cassis, Arles, Toulon.
Currency Exchange *La Bourse*, Place Général de Gaulle (Tel. 91 54 92 00); open Mon–Fri 8.30 am–noon and 2–6.30 pm; good rates, no commission.
Markets Fish market on Quai des Belges, daily.
Festivals *Festival de Musique*, Abbaye de St-Victoire: Dec.
Beaches *Plage du Prado* and *Plage de la Corniche*, good sandy beaches 3km east of city,

by local bus from train station.
Ferries SNCM, 61 blvd des Dames (Tel. 91 56
62 05); 2 ferries daily to Corsica (10 hours).
Police 2 rue Antoine Becker (Tel. 91 91 90 40);
Emergency: Tel. 17.
Consulates UK: 24 ave du Prado (Tel. 91 53 43
32); US: 12 blvd Paul Peytral (Tel. 91 54 92 00).
Hotels Many cheap hotels, especially in Rue
Breteuil and Rue Aubagne; if possible avoid
cheap accommodation in north African quarter
between train station and La Canebière which
can be dangerous at night.
☆ *Hôtel Azur*, 24 cours Franklin Roosevelt
(Tel. 91 42 74 38). Spacious and quiet
overlooking garden, close to station.
Hôtel Moderne, 11 blvd de la Libération (Tel.
91 62 28 66). Clean, cheap and popular.
☆ *Hôtel Moderne*, 30 rue Breteuil, between
station and the old port (Tel. 91 53 29 93).
☆ *Hôtel Gambetta*, 49 allée Léon Gambetta
(Tel. 91 62 07 88). Central and close to station.
☆☆ *Lutétia*, 38 allée Léon Gambetta (Tel. 91
50 81 78). Small, simple hotel, renovated and
conveniently located between La Canebière and
St-Charles station.
☆☆☆ *Pullman Beauvau*, 4 rue Beauvau (Tel.
91 54 91 00). Large, opulent, and luxurious old
hotel, on Vieux Port at end of La Canebière.
Hostels *Auberge de Jeunesse de Bois-Luzy* (HI),
76 ave de Bois-Luzy, bus 8 from **La Canebière**
by day or bus K from 8–10 pm to **Bois-Luzy**
stop; spacious and clean but far from centre
(Tel. 91 49 06 18).
Auberge de Jeuneusse Bonneveine (HI), 47 ave J
Vidal, metro to **Place Castellane**, bus 19 to **Les
Gatons Place**; large but some distance from
centre (Tel. 91 73 21 81).
Restaurants *Chez Soi*, 5 rue Papère (Tel. 91 54
25 41). Well-cooked simple dishes.
☆ *Chez Angèle*, 50 rue Caisserie (Tel. 91 90 63
35). Pleasant relaxed atmosphere and classic
Provençal dishes.
☆ *La Charpenterie*, 22 rue de la Paix (Tel. 91
54 22 89). Set back a little from the Quai de
Rive Neuve.
☆☆ *Chez Madie*, 138 quai du Port (Tel. 91 90
40 87). The best of the quayside restaurants;
delicious lobster, *bouillabaisse* and fish.
☆☆ *Dar Djerba*, 15 cours Julien (Tel. 91 48 55
36). The best of the many African restaurants
in Marseille; many excellent couscous varieties.
☆☆☆ *Michel-Brasserie des Catalans*, 6 rue des
Catalans (Tel. 91 52 30 63). Excellent seafood
and shellfish.

Toulon

Trains *Frequent trains daily from* **Marseille** *(1 hour);* **St-Raphaël** *(1 hour);* **Nice** *(2 hours); and* **Cannes** *(1 hour 10 mins).*

The journey to Toulon is through a wide range of broken, pine-covered hills.
Although the coast is rocky and steep, some of the hillsides are still terraced for the
cultivation of early spring flowers. High above, concealed amongst the pines and
arbutus, are great forts built to protect Toulon harbour while down below the blue
sea breaks on the savage rocks of the deserted shore.

The town, France's main naval base, was extensively fortified in the 17th-
century, primarily against the English who attacked it during the War of the
Spanish Succession in 1708 and again in 1744 under Sir John Bentley. At the
revolution the local people handed the city over to the British but the capture of
forts overlooking the city by the republicans forced the English fleet under Hood to
flee. During the Second World War the French fleet was scuttled in Toulon
harbour to prevent it falling into German or British hands and the city was heavily
bombed by the Allies before being recaptured by French forces on 25th August
1944.

What to see

The Old Quarter

Unfortunately Toulon suffered extensive damage during the Second World War, the most enchanting part, the Quai Kronstadt and the buildings overlooking the inner harbour, were completely destroyed, ugly concrete buildings being erected in their place. The area of interest is therefore small, clustered between the theatre on **Rue Jean Jaurès** and the Hôtel de Ville, particularly the pedestrianised streets **Rue Hoche** and **Rue d'Alger** that run down to the quay. The **naval museum** at the western end of Quai Stalingrad contains an excellent collection relating to the maritime and naval history of the port.

Practicalities in Toulon

Tourist Office 8 ave Colbert at Rue Victor Clapier (Tel. 94 22 08 22); accommodation service; branch office at train station (Tel. 94 62 73 87).
Railway Station blvd P. Toesca (Tel. 94 93 11 39); information office; baggage storage open daily 7.30 am–8.30 pm; lockers 6 am–10 pm; currency exchange. For town centre from station, turn left out of station and head down as far as Ave Colbert, then turn right.
Buses (Tel. 94 93 11 39); opposite station, frequent departures to St Tropez and other coastal destinations.
Currency Exchange 15quai Stalingrad, in the harbour (Open 9 am–7 pm).
Hotels *Hôtel la Résidence*, 18 rue Gimelli, off Ave Vauban, near station (Tel. 94 92 92 81). *Hôtel des Trois Dauphins*, 9 place des Trois Dauphins, near Place Puget (Tel. 94 92 65 79).

Spacious and newly renovated.
Hôtel Molière, 12 rue Molière, on place Victor Hugo (Tel. 94 92 78 35). Attractive and superb central position.
Hôtel de Provence, 53 rue Jean Jaurès, in pedestrianised zone close to post office (Tel. 94 93 19 00). Clean and simple.
☆ *Dauphiné*, 10 rue Berthelot (Tel. 94 92 20 28). Off Blvd de Strasbourg.
Camping *Beauregard*, 6 km away, close to sea, bus 7 from station to La Terre Promise (Tel. 94 29 56 35).
Restaurants ☆☆ *Pascal 'Chez Mimi'*, 83 ave de la République (Tel. 94 92 79 60). Specialises in Tunisian cuisine.
☆ *Au Sourd*, 10 rue Molière (Tel. 94 92 28 52). Busy and popular restaurant; famous for its seafood.

St-Raphaël and Fréjus

Trains *Frequent trains from* Toulon *(1 hour);* Cannes *(25 mins);* Nice *(1 hour).*

Between St-Tropez and Cannes lie the twin cities of St-Raphaël and Fréjus, now so close together that they almost form a single town. St-Raphaël has all the restaurants and hotels while Fréjus has the sights. Napoleon landed in the harbour here on his return from Egypt in 1799 and left for exile on the Island of Elba from here in 1814. It is a pleasnt resort lying at the foot of the Massif de l'Esterel which was very popular with English visitors at the turn of the century.

What to see

Amphitheatre

St-Raphaël and Fréjus were both founded by the Romans but Fréjus, lying 3 kilometres uphill, has more to show of its past, with a Roman ampitheatre, half the size of that of Arles and Nîmes, and the remains of a ruined Roman theatre and aqueduct. The present-day population is smaller than the population of the Roman City, which was founded by Julius Caesar in 49 BC.

In place Formeige is an early Provençal **cathedral** with an elegant cloister and painted 15th-century wooden ceilings. Its **baptistry**, dating back to the 5th century, is one of the oldest in France.

St-Raphaël itself is the closest railway stop to the beaches of **St-Tropez**, made famous by Brigitte Bardot in the 1950s. Between Fréjus and Cannes, the railway skirts the coast line between the Massif de l'Esterel and the sea. The wild and uninhabited hills inland were the haunt of highwaymen until the 19th century and it was here that William Lithgow was ambushed by 3 footpads 'in a theevish Wood twelve miles long', but he succeeded in convincing them he was no more than a poor pilgrim and was allowed to go unmolested. The Massif is wild and beautiful, offering demanding walking in a dramatic landscape of ragged, volcanic rocks, deep ravines and dense scrub.

Practicalities in St-Raphaël and Fréjus

Tourist Office Across from railway station in St-Raphaël (Tel. 94 19 52 52); also in Fréjus, 325 rue Jean Jaurès, opposite the fountain in Place Paul Vernet (Tel. 94 51 54 14) and Place Calvini (June–Sept; Tel. 94 51 53 87).
Railway Station Place de la Gare; information office; (Information Tel. 93 99 50 50; Reservations: Tel. 94 95 16 87).
Buses *Gare routière*, Ave Victor Hugo, behind station (Tel. 94 65 21 00)
Hotels *Hôtel des Pyramides*, 77 Ave Paul Doumer in St-Raphaël (Tel. 94 95 05 95). Clean, comfortable and close to beach.
☆ *La Bonne Auberge*, 54 rue de la Garonne in St-Raphaël (Tel. 94 95 69 72). Simple, attractive, good location.
☆ *Hôtel Bellevue*, Place Paul Vernet in Fréjus, next to Rue Reynaude (Tel. 94 51 42 41). A

popular hotel-bar in the very heart of Fréjus.
☆☆ *l'Aréna*, 139 blvd Général de Gaulle (Tel. 94 17 09 40). An excellent, modernised hotel in Provençal style, close to the Roman remains in St-Raphaël.
☆☆ *Le Vieux Four*, 57 rue Grisolle (Tel. 94 51 56 38). Restaurant-Hotel, with 8 rooms, offering excellent Provençal food in a delightful rustic dining-room in the centre of old Fréjus.
Restaurants ☆☆ *Lou Calen*, 9 rue Desaugiers (Tel. 94 52 36 87). Attractive restaurant close to the church in Fréjus centre; good food and atmosphere.
Festivals *du Jazz*, 1st weekend of July in St Raphaël, beside the sea.
Camping next to Auberge de Jeunesse (HI) Chemin de Counillier (Tel. 94 82 18 75).

Cannes

Trains *Trains virtually every ½ hour from* St Raphaël *(25 mins);* Nice *(25 mins);* Monaco *(50 mins);* Menton *(1 hour); hourly from* Toulon *(1 hour 15 mins); and* Marseille *(2 hours);* TGVs *to* Paris *via Marseilles.*

Cannes, one of the oldest winter resorts on the Riviera, has changed enormously since it first became a fashionable destination for the idle wealthy in the middle of the last century. Lord Brougham, who first realised it would make the most warm and enchanting spot in which to pass the winter months, would certainly not recognise and probably have little time for the town that exists today.

Lord Brougham was on his way to Nice in 1834 when an epidemic of cholera in Provence delayed him sufficiently to fall under the spell of the beauty of Cannes. He bought land and built himself a villa, dying here in 1868. It was to escape the crowds of Antibes and Nice that he settled here, overlooking the little fishing village and the deep blue sea, with the small amphitheatre of hills behind the village that sheltered the bay from northerly winds. An English community rapidly became established here; an Anglican church was built and croquet lawns marked out. Speculative building began around 1850 but it was with the advent of the railway in 1863, apparently, 'that its fate was sealed'.

What to see

Boulevard de la Croisette

Cannes has lost most of its character since then but the old part of town round Mont Chevalier and the port still retain a certain charm. The main seafront street is the Boulevard de la Croisette, a throbbing palm-lined thoroughfare, overlooking the mile-long beach of white sand where armies of bright parasols are drawn up in neat formations. Here stand the gigantic Edwardian hotels, the Carlton and Majestic, reminders of the former elegance and luxuriance of Cannes in its heyday. At its eastern end is a beautiful rose garden, the Parc de la Roserie, beyond which is the new port.

Offshore from Cannes lie the **Iles de Lérins**, the larger one, **Ste-Marguerite**, covered with eucalyptus and pine forest. Cool paths lead through the dense fragrant hills where thyme and rosemary grow wild. The small island of **St-Honorat** is named after a hermit who came to the island in the 5th century. A 2-hour walk round the island brings one to the fortified monastic buildings enclosing a central cloister. (Open daily 10.30 – noon and 1.30 – 4.30 pm.)

Practicalities in Cannes

Tourist Office 1 blvd de la Croisette in the Palais des Festivals, in the *Vieux Port* (Tel. 93 99 01 01); accommodation service; branch office on 1st floor of railway station (Tel. 93 99 19 77).
Railway Station 1 rue Jean Jaurès (Tel. 93 99 50 50); information desk open 8.30 – 11.30 am and 2 – 6 pm; left-luggage 6 am – 1.30 pm and 2 – 9.30 pm.
Buses *Gare Routière*, next to Hôtel de Ville, in *Vieux Port* (Tel. 93 64 50 17); buses to Antibes, Juan-les-Pins, Nice, Menton, Grasse, etc.
Currency Exchange 17 rue Maréchal Foch, opposite train station. Open daily 8 am – 8 pm
Markets *Place Gambetta*, Tues-Sun mornings.
Festivals *Fête Americaine*: 4th July; *Bastille Day celebrations*: 14th July
Ferries To Ile de Lérins, several times daily from harbour (Tel. 93 39 11 89), departures from near the Palais des Festivals. (15 mins to Ste-Marguerite; 30 mins to St-Honorat.)
Hotels Cheap hotels are few and far between; a

few are close to Rue d'Antibes.
Hôtel du Nord, 6 rue Jean Jaurès (Tel. 93 38 50 80) A stone's-throw from railway station.
☆ *Chalet de l'Isère*, 42 ave. de Grasse (Tel. 93 38 50 80). Steep climb from station but inviting shady garden makes it worthwhile.
☆ *Hôtel Chanteclair*, 12 rue Forville, bright and comfortable (Tel. 93 39 68 88).
☆☆ *La Madone*, 5 ave. Justinia (Tel. 93 43 57 87). Comfortable, in a charming setting in leafy garden planted with palm trees and mimosa, with own swimming pool.
☆☆ *Les Dauphins Verts*, 9 rue Jean-Dollfus (Tel. 93 39 45 82). Simple but with air-conditioning, private bathrooms and pleasant garden.
Camping *Le Grand Saule*, 24 blvd Jean Moulin; bus 610 from place de l'Hôtel de Ville towards Grasse. 3-star site with pool (Tel. 93 47 07 50).
Restaurants ☆ *Au Bec Fin*, 14 rue du 24 Août (Tel. 93 38 35 86). Delicious home cuisine in family restaurant near station.

☆☆☆ *La Poêle d'Or*, 23 rue des Etats-Unis (Tel. 93 39 77 65). Excellent cooking in this popular restaurant just off the Croisette. Superb waffles with unusual sauces.
☆☆ *La Mère Besson*, 13 rue des Frères-Pradignac (Tel. 93 39 59 24). Only evening meals during July and August in this delightful family restaurant; superb Provençal dishes.
☆☆ *L'Orangerie*, Hôtel Martinez (Tel. 93 68 91 91). Good French cuisine with the occasional Provençal speciality.

Beyond Cannes, the train passes through **Juan-les-Pins**, a small resort made fashionable in the 1920s by the American millionaire, Frank Jay Gould. Scott Fitzgerald based the Hôtel des Etrangers in *Tender is the Night* on Eden Roc. There is no longer any discernible countryside left between Juan-les-Pins and **Antibes**, a small resort of consequence mainly because of its Picasso collection in the 16th-century Château Grimaldi. The collection consists of paintings, drawings, ceramics and tapestries, many of them with mythological themes, executed by Picasso when he lived here after the war. From Antibes it is but a short journey to the animated and sophisticated city of Nice.

Nice

Trains *Trains about every 20 mins from* **Cannes** *(35 mins);* **Antibes** *(20 mins);* **Monaco** *(25 mins);* **Menton** *(35 mins); 11 daily connect with the* TGVs *from* **Marseille** *to* **Paris** *(7½ hours).*

Nice, capital of the *département* of Alpes-Maritimes, is situated in a magnificent position of the Baie des Anges, surrounded by the foothills of the maritime Alps, only 30 kilometres from the Italian frontier. With its sheltered situation and mild climate, Nice is one of the oldest established winter resorts on the Côte d'Azur.

Nice has had a turbulent political history, belonging sometimes to the Counts of Provence or Savoy, to Italy or France or being fought over by the Lascaris of Tende or Grimaldis of Monaco. Only in 1860 did it vote finally for union with France. While Cannes was still only a fishing village, Nice was already a flourishing fashionable resort with a casino that opened in 1777. Tobias Smollett had little to say in its favour, however, despite a sojourn of 15 months in 1764, remarking that 'its shopkeepers are greedy and over-reaching and do little but lounge about the ramparts, bask themselves in the sun or play at bowls in the streets from morning till night'.

What to see

The Colline du Château

The oldest settlement of Nice occupied the Colline du Château, a high hill which overlooks the town but the castle which occupied the summit was destroyed in

1706. From the hill steps lead town to the seafront promenade, past the **Tour Bellanda**, built in 1880 on the site of the St-Lambert bastion, which houses the **Musée Naval**. (Open Wed–Mon 10 am-noon and 2–7 pm.) The long tree-lined boulevard, Avenue J. Médecin, leads directly to the **Place Masséna**, attractively laid out in the Genoese style of the 17th century, its buildings picked out in terracotta and pistachio green.

The Old Town
Beyond Place Masséna, and west of the Colline du Château, lies the maze of narrow streets and lanes of old Nice, the *Vieille Ville*, with the **Cours Saleya**, the scene of a morning flower market and the Italianate **Place Pierre-Gautier**.

Palais des Lascaris
One of the finest buildings in Nice is the handsome Palais des Lascaris in Rue Droite, a 17th-century mansion decorated in Genoese Baroque style. This magnificent Baroque building was once the palace of the Counts of Castellar and has an elegant entrance hall and rich stucco decoration with elaborate ceiling paintings and tapestries in the State apartments. Part of the château contains a reconstructed 18th-century pharmacy. (Open Tues–Sun 9.30 am–noon and 2.30–6 pm.)

Chapelle de la Miséricorde
A little north of the flower market on Cours Saleya is the Chapelle de la Miséricorde, built in 1736. It now houses the **Préfecture** and adjoins the 19th-century building of the Palais de Justice.

Promenade des Anglais
From the old town the famous Promenade des Anglais stretches away to the west; it was laid out by the English colony in the 1820s after their return to the Riviera following the end of the Napoleonic wars. It is lined by elegant and luxurious buildings, including the **Palais de la Méditerranée**, the **Casino Ruhl** and the famous **Hôtel Négresco**. On the far side are beaches from which there are panoramic views of the Baie des Anges.

Rue de Rivoli leads up from the Hôtel Négresco to the **Musée Masséna**, largely devoted to Napoleonic themes and the locally born general André Masséna. (Open Tues–Sun 10 am–noon and 2–5 pm.)

Musée des Beaux-Arts
Beyond the Musée Masséna Rue de France and Ave des Baumettes lead to the Musée des Beaux-Arts Jules Chéret, in a palatial mansion built in 1878 for a Russian princess. The collection includes paintings by Dégas, Dufy and Monet, sculptures by Rodin and ceramics by Picasso. Chéret, after whom the museum is named, was a *belle epoque* artist, best remembered for his poster design. (Open May–Sept, Tues–Sun 10 am–noon and 3–6 pm; Oct–Apr, Tues–Sun 10 am–noon and 2–5 pm.)

Musée Chagall

Nice is fortunate in having 2 fine collections of modern paintings. The Musée Chagall, in Ave du Dr Ménard, has a collection of Chagall's paintings and sketches inspired by Hebrew themes. The works are located in a light and spacious building, built specifically to house the collection, a short walk from the railway station. (Open July–Sept, Wed–Mon 10 am–6.30 pm; Oct–July Wed–Mon 10 am–12 noon and 2–5 pm.)

Roman Remains and the Musée Matisse

The Musée Matisse, 2 kilometres north of the *Vieille Ville* at 164 ave des Arènes-de-Cimiez, has a comprehensive collection of paintings, drawings, pottery and sculpture by Matisse that span the whole of his creative life. Matisse died here in 1954 not long after decorating the Chapelle du Rosaire at Vence. Recently reopened after 4 years, the museum has many works by Matisse but none of his very greatest works. (Open June–Aug, Tues–Sat 11 am–6 pm; Apr, May and Sept, Tues–Sat 10 am–noon and 2–6 pm; Oct and Dec–Mar, Tues–Sat 10 am–noon and 2–5 pm.)

Near by in **Cimiez** is the monastery of Notre-Dame-de-Cimiez, a Benedictine foundation taken over by the Franciscans in the 16th-century and enlarged in the 17th, which contains a fine *Crucifixion* by Bréa. Below the church, on a plateau, are the extensive remains of the Roman town of **Cemenelum**. The **Roman amphitheatre**, with seating for over 5,000 spectators, and the baths are both well preserved. The **Musée d'Archéologie**, in the same building as the Musée Matisse, displays finds from the excavated sites. (Same opening times.)

Practicalities in Nice

Tourist Office Ave Thiers, right beside station (Tel. 93 87 07 07); accommodation service; another branch at 5 ave Gustave V (Tel. 93 87 60 60).

Railway Station There are 2 railway stations in Nice: (1) *Gare Nice-Ville*, in centre on Ave Thiers (Tel. 93 87 50 50); information office; showers open 7 am–7 pm; lockers; left-luggage service open daily 5.30 am–midnight. For town centre, turn left out of station, right onto Ave Jean-Médecin, as far as arcaded Place Masséna, the city's main square. (2) *Gare du Sud* (Tel. 93 84 89 71), 33 ave Malausséna, on the continuation of Ave Jean-Médecin: for private trains, belonging to the *Chemins de Fer de Provence*, which leave for Digne through the southern Alps; 4–5 daily (3½ hours).

Buses Promenade du Paillon (Tel. 93 85 61 81), off Jean Jaurès.

Currency Exchange 17 ave Thiers, opposite station. Open daily 7am–midnight.

Post Office 23 ave Thiers. Open Mon–Fri 8am–7pm, Sat 8am–noon.

Hotels *Hôtel Idéal Bristol*, 22 rue Paganini, off Rue Alsace-Lorraine (Tel. 93 88 60 72). Immaculate, spacious and central.

Hôtel Belle Meunière, 21 ave Durante (Tel. 93 88 66 15). Oasis of peace close to station with large garden, small dormitory accommodation.

Hôtel Lyonnais, 20 rue de Russie, near rue d'Italie (Tel. 93 88 70 74). Clean and simple.

☆ *Hôtel Novelty*, 26 rue d'Angleterre (Tel. 03 87 51 73). Near station, simple, clean and welcoming.

☆ *Hôtel Clair Meuble*, 6 rue d'Italie (Tel. 93 87 87 61). Near station, clean and spacious.

☆☆ *La Mer*, 4 Place Masséna (Tel. 93 92 09 10). Small, simple hotel but superb location close to old town and seafront.

☆☆☆ *Hôtel Harvey*, 18 ave Suède (Tel. 93 88 73 73). Large, comfortable hotel very close to tourist office, beach and Promenade des Anglais.

☆☆☆ *Hôtel Victoria*, 33 blvd Victor Hugo (Tel. 93 88 39 60). Victorian in name, Victorian in style; comfortable rooms, some overlooking gardens.

Hostel *Auberge de Jeunesse* (HI), Route Forestière du Mont-Alban, 4km from Nice; on bus 5 from station, friendly and very popular (Tel. 93 89 23 64).

Restaurants Le Faubourg Montmartre, 32 rue Pertinax, off Ave Jean Médecin Tel. Excellent couscous dishes and bouillabaisse.

Chez Annie, 6 rue Delille, near Rue Masséna Superb bistro serving Niçois specialities such as aioli (raw vegetables in a garlic mayonnaise dip).

☆ Chez Davia, 1 bis rue Grimaldi, near Place Masséna. Tel Excellent French and Italian food with wide range of menus.

☆☆ Barale, 39 rue Beaumont (Tel. 93 89 18 94). An unusual proprietress runs this popular restaurant offering good Niçois food.

☆☆ Le St-Laurent, 12 rue Paganini (Tel. 93 87 18 94). Good little restaurant between Eglise Notre-Dame and the station.

☆☆☆ Les Dents de la Mer, 2 rue St-François-de-Paule (Tel. 93 80 99 16). Exotic décor but in fact one of the best seafood restaurants in Nice.

Excursions from Nice

There are extremely frequent trains running to **Menton** and **Monaco** on the Ventimiglia line between Nice and the Italian border.

Monaco

Trains Trains ½-hourly from Nice (25 mins); Antibes (45 mins); Cannes (1 hour 10 mins) and Menton (10 mins).

Monaco is a miniature independent sovereign state that owes owes its continued existence to its status as a tax haven. Officially it consits of 3 districts: Monaco, La Condamine and Monte Carlo but they have long since fused into a single city. There is little to see, however, except the Palace from where the Grimaldi family, who established themselves as lords of Monaco in the 14th century, still reign. The most interesting feature of the palace lies not in the royal apartments but in the interior courtyard with its 16th- and 17th-century frescoes by the Genoese painter Luca Cambiaso.

Practicalities in Monaco

Tourist Office 2a blvd des Moulins, near casino (Tel. 93 50 60 88); accommodation service **Railway Station** Ave Prince Pierre (Tel. 93 87 50 50); information desk open 9 am–7 pm; lockers.

Hotels Accommodation very expensive; cheaper to stay in Nice or Antibes.

☆☆ Hôtel Cosmopolite, 4 rue de la Turbie (Tel. 93 30 16 95). Close to station and clean.

☆☆ Hôtel Helvetia, 1 rue Grimaldi (Tel. 93 30 21 71). Lovely hotel with spotless rooms.

☆☆ Hôtel Balmoral, 12 ave Costa (Tel. 93 50 62 37). A comfortable, very centrally situated hotel with views over the port.

Restaurants ☆☆ Polpetta, Rue Paradis (Tel 93 50 67 94). Authentic Italian food and good value for money (for Monaco!).

Menton

Trains ½-hourly trains from Monaco (10 mins); Nice (35 mins); Cannes (1 hour 10 mins).

Menton, a 10-minute journey to the east, enjoys the mildest climate on the Riviera and is an altogether more attractive place than Monte-Carlo/Monaco. Robert Louis Stevenson and Katherine Mansfield lived here for a while but by 1890 Augustus Hare decried that 'hideous and stuccoed villas in the worst taste and pretentious paved promenades have taken the place of the beautiful walks under tamarisk groves by the sea shore. Artistically, Menton is vulgarised and ruined . . .' Nevertheless, lemon and orange trees still grow in profusion, mimosa blossoms through the winter months and the sun still shines as brightly as it ever did. It is probably the most pleasant and leisurely of the French Mediterranean resorts; it has many grand 19th-century buildings, long and elegant tree-lined avenues and an attractive old quarter with 17th-century streets.

Place St-Michel The most unspoilt and delightful square is the Place St-Michel in the centre of the old town. In this graceful

Italianate square, faced by the Baroque church of St-Michel, concerts of chamber music take place in summer.

The Hôtel de Ville contains a curious Salle des Marriages decorated by Jean Cocteau, and an indifferent series of pastels by him entitled the *Inamorati* are to be found in an old fort on Quai Napoléon III.

Practicalities in Menton

Tourist Office 8 ave Boyer inside the grand Palais de l'Europe (Tel 93 57 57 00); accommodation service; a 24-hour electronic board outside gives availability of hotel rooms **Railway Station** Rue de la Gare; luggage storage; lockers (Tel. 93 35 45 00).
Hotels Hotels in Menton are expensive; Nice and Antibes are cheaper options.
☆ *Le Terminus*, Place de la Gare, opposite station (Tel 93 35 77 00).
☆☆ *Hôtel Le Globe*, 21 ave de Verdun (Tel 93 35 73 03). Opposite the Palais de l'Europe with good, bright rooms.
Hôtels *Auberge de Jeunesse* (HI), Plateau St-Michel; steep climb but clean and modern with superb view (Tel 93 35 93 14).
Restaurants ☆*Le Galion*, Port de Garavan (Tel. 93 35 89 73). Informal and relaxing, with good Italian food at reasonable prices.
☆ *Paris-Palais*, 2 ave Félix Faure (Tel. 93 35 86 66). Good food in a charming restaurant with its own delightful garden and lovely views.

Tende

Trains *3 trains daily from Nice (2 hours).*

This small excursion up into the mountains, via many small villages to Breil-sur-Roya and Tende, is purely for the pleasure of seeing the hinterland of the Côte d'Azur. For summer walkers wishing to explore the Parc National du Mercantour, Tende makes an excellent jumping-off point. The extraordinary Vallée des Merveilles, between Mont Bego and Cime du Diable, contains thousands of Bronze Age carvings cut into the rock face. The ruined castle above the curious old town of Tende itself belonged to the Lascari family; the suffering of Béatrice de Tende at the hands of the Viscontis inspired an opera by Bellini.

Practicalities in Tende

Tourist Office Rue A. Vassalo, near station details of hikes in the Parc National du Mercantour.
Railway Station At top of town, off main street
Hostel *Auberge de Jeunesse*, at end of Rue Ste-Catherine
Hôtel ☆ *Centre*, (Tel. 93 04 62 19). No restaurant.

Nice – Digne-les-Bains

One of the most superb railway journeys in southern France can be made on the private railway through the southern Alps from the Mediterranean coast to Digne on the borders of Dauphiné. It is a fascinating journey that reveals the beauty of Provence and takes the visitor away from the noise, bustle and glamour of the Côte d'Azur.

North of the Côte d'Azur the narrow valleys that run northwards into the hills are famous for their cherries which are the earliest to be harvested in France. But the hills quickly become wild and stony, giving a foretaste of the Alps beyond. Nevertheless the thin soil supports 2 important crops – lavender and truffles. Thriving on stony fields at an elevation of 650 or 1,000 metres, fields of purple lavender grown in neatly aligned rows transform the landscape of the Var and Alpes-de-Haute-Provence in summer into a riotous blaze of colour. As the hills rise towards the Alps, the towns crouch ever lower into the valleys for protection and shelter.

This scenic route leaves Nice heading north up the valley of the Var, overlooked to the left by Gattières, Carros and Le Broc to the station of **La Vésubie** – Plan-du-Var. The valley of the Vésubie, up the valley to the right, is renowned for its scenery, its alpine character earning it the reputation of being 'the Switzerland of Nice'. At **Malaussène** the contorted and tilted strata of the rock can be easily seen and a little further on the train passes through the picturesque village of **Villars-sur-Var**. **Touet-sur-Var**, the next stop, huddled against a high cliff, has a ruined Romanesque chapel and, higher up, a church dramatically sited over a waterfall. **Puget-Théniers** is an old village dominated by a ruined château and was the birthplace of the revolutionary, Auguste Blanqui. A little higher lies **Entrevaux**, an old frontier fortress with Vauban-style fortifications and a 16th-century church.

The hills around **Annot** abound in caverns and eccentrically shaped rocks but these give way around **St-André-les-Alpes** to a gentler landscape of orchards and lavender fields. This is also a good point for walkers to alight to follow the Grande Randonnée route through the **Gorges du Verdon** which runs from **Castellane**, 21 kilometres south, westwards to **Manosque**. Not long after, the train arrives at Digne-les-Bains, the end of the private railway line.

At Digne SNCF buses take passengers either to **St-Auban** [35 mins by bus] for onward trains to Manosque (25 mins); Marseille (1¾ hours); or to Veynes [1¾ hours by bus] for onward trains to Gap (1 hour 25 mins); Briançon (2 hours 40 mins) and Grenoble (4 hours 25 mins).

Digne-les-Bains

Trains *Chemins de Fer de Provence, a private railway company, operates a service from Nice to Digne station via 15 small stations (3 hours 20 mins). 4 – 5 trains daily from* **Nice Gare du Sud** *(Tel. 93 84 89 71), 33 ave Malausséna, on the upper continuation of Ave Jean-Médecin;* SNCF *tickets not valid except Eurodomino pass. Also Alpazur train touristique (1st July-9th Sept only) from* **Grénoble** *and* **Lyon** *(4½ hours).*

The reputation of Digne-les-Bains rests on its therapeutic mineral waters and this pleasant little town is an attractive one in which to pause. It's famous for its lavender, superb honey and dried fruits which come from the foothills of the Alpes de Haute-Provence that surround the town. In spring and early summer blossoming fruit trees cover the valley of the River Bléone. Victor Hugo based the figure of Monseigneur Myriel in *Les Misérables* on Bishop Miollis of Digne.

In the centre of the town is the **Great Fountain**, furred up with calcium deposits. Some distance to the south is the **Alexandra David-Néel Foundation**, dedicated to the study and preservation of Tibetan culture, which was launched by the distinguished French traveller and Tibetan scholar.

Practicalities in Digne-les-Bains

Tourist Office Blvd Gassendi, the main street (Tel. 93 21 42 73).
Festivals *Lavender Festival*: early Aug; *Jazz Festival*: July.
Markets Blvd Gassendi, selling local lavender products, and honey.
Hôtels ☆ *Hôtel Le Petit St Jean*, 14 Cours des Arès (Tel 92 31 30 04). With good little restaurant offering hearty Provençal fare.
☆☆ *Hôtel Central*, 26 blvd Gassendi (Tel. 92 31 31 91). Pleasant hotel on the main street.
☆☆☆ *Hôtel Mistre*, 63 blvd Gassendi (Tel. 92 31 00 16). Comfortable, handsome hotel; attractive rooms and good restaurant.

Manosque

Trains *6 trains daily from* **Digne-les-Bains** *(25 mins).*

St-Auban lies at the confluence of the Durance and Bléone rivers which combine and flow south to the small town of Manosque, the old town lying a little way uphill from the railway station. The old town is entered through a superb battlemented gateway, the **Porte Saunerie**, that was the key element in the 14th-century fortifications. Quiet pedestrianised streets lead up to the tranquil churches of **St-Sauveur** and **Notre-Dame** within which is to be found a 6th-century sarcophagus.

Manosque is the best place to begin the 10-day walk along the magnificent chasm eroded over millennia by the river Verdon – the **Gorges du Verdon**, perhaps the most breath-taking and impressive natural sight in Provence.

Practicalities in Manosque

Tourist Office Place Dr P. Joubert (Tel. 92 72 16 00).
Railway Station (Tel. 92 51 24 84 for reservations) and (Tel. 92 51 50 50 for information).
Hotels ☆☆ *Hotel de la Peyrache*, Place de l'Hotel de Ville (Tel. 92 72 07 43).
☆☆ *Hotel François I*, 18 rue Guilhempierre (Tel. 92 72 07 99).

Aix-en-Provence

Trains *6 trains daily from* **Manosque** *(45 mins); 20 daily from* **Marseille** *(40 mins); 10 daily from* **Nice** *(3 hours); 12 daily from* **Cannes** *(2½ hours).*

Aix-en-Provence typifies all that is best in Provence and must rank as one of the most civilised and elegant small cities not just in France but anywhere in the world. Not for nothing was it for many centuries the capital of an independent Provence and today it maintains the culture and sophistication of a capital city with the tranquil and relaxed pace of a provincial town. The architectural unity of the city is impressive with 200 private mansions of the 17th and 18th centuries, wide avenues, magnificent fountains, a university dating back to the 15th century, and its majestic thoroughfare, the **Cours Mirabeau,** lined with plane trees and cafés. The powerful wind from the north, the Mistral, sometimes blows with an extraordinary ferocity but it ends as quickly as it begins, leaving a clear unpolluted sky of dazzling purity.

Before the arrival of the Romans in the 2nd century BC Aix was already a Celto-Ligurian stronghold. The sacking of Marseille by Caesar in 49 BC greatly boosted the fortunes of Aquae Sextiae, the first Roman settlement in Gaul, but the Lombard invasions led to a decline and the city was even abandoned temporarily in the 6th century. Its fortunes revived when the Catalan counts of Provence made it their capital during the Middle Ages and Aix rose to become the most prominent city of the County of Provence. The patronage and leadership of the nominal king of Naples, *le bon roi René,* in the late 15th century, encouraged a dynamic flourishing of arts and commerce which ensured the continued prosperity of the city for a long time after the County had merged with the Kingdom of France. 'Good King René' was not only a brilliant mathematician and linguist but also a considerable patron of the arts. Under him the university was established, making Aix a foremost seat of learning in southern France. René is also credited with having introduced the famous muscat grape to Provence.

The 17th and 18th centuries saw a proliferation of elegant mansions, the construction of the principal avenue, the Cours Mirabeau, and an increasing number of fashionable visitors to the thermal waters. The many English visitors included the irascible Tobias Smollett, not someone noted for his complimentary comments about the French, who described the citizens as 'well bred, gay and sociable'. Amongst the many distinguished citizens of the town are Paul Cézanne and Emile Zola who were at school together.

What to see

Cours Mirabeau

The focus of the city, now as over the last 3 centuries, is the elegant and dignified Cours Mirabeau, the wide avenue lined with cafés and plane trees that stretches from Place Général de Gaulle to Place Forbin. It is lined with many of the city's most distinguished mansions, many built soon after the wide boulevard was first laid out in 1650. On the avenue are 3 fountains; the middle one, the **Fontaine Chaude,** dispenses water from the thermal springs. In Place du Général de Gaulle, at the western end of the avenue, is the large **Fontaine de la Rotonde**. The Cours Mirabeau is lined with elegant buildings, such as the Hôtel des Villiers (number 2), the Hôtel d'Isoard de Vauvenargues (number 10), the Hôtel d'Arbau-Jouques (number 19), the Hôtel de Forbin (number 20) and the Hôtel de Maurel de Pontevès (number 38). At the east end of the Cours is the **Fontaine du Roi René** by David d'Angers and a chapel, once part of a Carmelite convent, which was restored in 1700. Cours Mirabeau divides the city broadly into 2, with the medieval quarter to the north and the elegant 18th-century district to the south.

Museum of Natural History

From the Cours Mirabeau, rue Clemenceau runs north to the Place St-Honoré. Down a side street is the Musée d'Histoire Naturelle in the 17th-century mansion, Hôtel Boyer d'Eguilles; amongst its collections are a number of dinosaurs' eggs found in Provence.

Place de l'Hôtel de Ville

The Place de l'Hôtel de Ville is the central feature of the old town; around the central 18th-century fountain in the middle of the square the daily flower market is held. On one side of the square is the old **Halle aux Grains**, built in 1759, with its magnificent pediment and sculptural decoration. On the west side of the square is the Hôtel de Ville in Italian Baroque style with a central courtyard and 17th-century wrought-iron balcony. The building contains the **Bibliothèque Méjanes**, an 18th-century library of some 350,000 volumes. Adjoining the Hôtel de Ville is the early 16th-century **Tour de l'Horloge**, one of the old town gates, built on Roman foundations.

No city could be more conducive to meandering around at a leisurely pace than Aix or more rewarding. At every corner, down every street, are to be found beautifully proportioned houses built from warm honey-coloured stone. The earliest aristocratic town house, the **Hôtel de Carces**, is to be found in Rue Lacépède and the most elegant quarter is around Rue Mazarine and the charming **Place des Quatre Dauphins**, cooled in summer by its tinkling fountain. Other old noble mansions are found in Rue Gaston-de-Saporta, running north of the Place de l'Hôtel de Ville, including the 17th-century **Hôtel d'Estienne de St-Jean**, now occupied by the local history museum.

Cathédrale St-Sauveur

In the north of the old town is the cathedral of St-Sauveur, built over 5 centuries from the 12th century. The late Gothic doorway has fine walnut doors carved by Jean Guiramand in the 16th century. The cathedral is entered through a Romanesque doorway; immediately within is the early Christian baptistry dating back to the 6th century. The cathedral possesses some fine tapestries which once adorned the choir of Canterbury Cathedral. During the English Civil War they were looted from Canterbury Cathedral and sold during the Commonwealth to the Canon of Aix. The greatest treasure of the cathedral is a magnificent *Triptych of the Burning Bush*, a delicate and detailed painting executed for King René by his court artist Nicolas Froment. King René is represented on the left-hand panel, his wife on the opposite panel, both surrounded by saints while the central panel portrays the Virgin and child in the flames of the Burning Bush appearing to Moses.

Musée des Tapisseries

Other tapestries of interest are those from Beauvais depicting scenes from *Don Quixote* which are to be found in the Musée des Tapisseries in the adjacent Archbishop's Palace. (Open Wed–Mon, 10 am–noon and 2 – 6 pm.) In summer the courtyard of the Archbishop's Palace is one of many delightful settings used for open-air performances during the July music festival. Beside the elegant palace built for the Duc de Vendôme, the Pavillon de Vendôme, are handsome gardens that make a pleasant retreat on a summer's evening.

Musée de l'Atelier Paul Cézanne

Although Paul Cézanne was born in Aix, at 28 rue de l'Opéra, there is little of his work to be seen in the city. The **Musée Granet** which lies just to the south of the Cours Mirabeau at 13 rue Cardinale has a few minor works including 2 drawings, 3 landscape watercolours and a lithographic self-portrait. His studio, the **Atelier Cézanne** at 9 avenue Paul Cézanne to the north of the old town has been reconstructed as it was at the time of his death and contains a number of personal mementoes and reproductions but no original works. Cézanne spent the greater part of his life in and around Aix and found constant inspiration in the surrounding countryside although not in the town itself. Again and again he painted *La Montagne Ste-Victoire*, the striking mountain to the east of the town, often from the road to Le Tholonet. It was from the ridge of Les Lauves just to the north of his studio that Cézanne painted the lovely landscapes looking towards La Montagne Ste-Victoire, at the end of his life. (Atelier open Wed–Mon 10 am–noon and 2.30 – 6 pm.)

Musée Granet

To the east of the beautiful Fontaine des Quatre Dauphins is the Musée Granet, an attractive provincial art gallery and museum. It not only contains the few works by Cézanne but also early Celto-Ligurian sculpture, Greek reliefs, Roman sculpture, an early Christian sarcophagus, medieval sculpture and works by Jost van Cleve, Hans Holbein the Younger, Rubens, Rembrandt and Pissarro. The collections are housed in the former Palais de Malte, a priory of the Order of Malta, built in 1671. (Open Wed–Mon 10 am–noon and 2 – 6 pm.) Adjoining it is the church of St-Jean-de-Malte, the earliest Gothic building in Aix and once the property of the priory.

Practicalities in Aix-en-Provence

Tourist Office 2 Place du Général de Gaulle (Tel. 42 26 02 93); accommodation service; currency exchange; guided tours; monthly guide to events. Open Mon–Sat 8 am–10 pm, Sun 6–10 pm; mid Sept–June, Mon–Sat 8 am–7 pm, Sun 8.30 am–12.30 pm.)

Railway Station At end of Ave Victor Hugo (Tel. 91 08 50 50). To reach most other destinations in Provence it is necessary to take a train to Marseille (35 mins), from where there are frequent trains to Paris, Avignon, Orange, Arles, Nîmes, Cannes and Nice.

Buses *Gare Routière*, Rue Lapierre (Tel. 42 27 17 19), behind post office. Information office open Mon–Sat 6 am–7 pm, Sun 8 am–noon and 2–6 pm.

Currency Exchange 15 Cours Mirabeau (Tel. 42 38 58 82); no commission and good rates. Open Mon–Sat 9 am–7 pm, Sun 9.30 am–12.30 pm. Also at post office, 2 rue Lapierre; commission 1%; open Mon–Fri 8 am–7 pm, Sat 8 am–noon.

Markets Street markets held in *Place de Verdun*: Tues, Thurs and Sat mornings.

Festivals *International Music Festival*: mid-July to early Aug, international orchestras and musicians converge for performances in the Théâtre de l'Archevêché, the Cathédrale and Cloître St-Louis and Cloître St-Sauveur; *Aix en Musique*: 2nd week in June, festival of jazz, rock and classical music, many concerts free. Locations from tourist office.
International Dance Festival: early July, classical ballet, modern and jazz dance. Information from Comité Officiel des Fêtes, Cours Gambetta (Tel. 42 63 06 75).

Hotels ☆ *Hôtel Vigouroux*, 27 rue Cardinale, between Place des Dauphins and Musée Granet (Tel. 42 38 26 42). Spacious, attractive rooms in central location.
☆ *Splendid Hôtel*, 69 cours Mirabeau, on the most famous street in Aix. (Tel. 42 27 68 69). Bright rooms with own bathrooms.
☆ *Hôtel du Casino*, 38 rue Victor Leydet (Tel.

42 26 06 88). Attractive little hotel with clean rooms, just off Cours Mirabeau.
☆☆ *Caravelle*, 29 blvd du Roi René (Tel. 42 21 53 05). 5 mins from Cours Mirabeau, quieter rooms facing the back more expensive.
☆☆ *Hôtel Quatre Dauphins*, 54 rue Roux Alpheron (Tel. 42 38 16 39). Attractive, comfortable accommodation a short walk from the Musée Granet.
☆☆ *St-Christophe*, 2 ave Victor Hugo (Tel. 42 26 01 24). Very comfortable accommodation very close to tourist office and Cours Mirabeau.

Hostels *Auberge de Jeunesse* (HI) 3 ave Marcel Pagnol, next to the Fondation Vasarely, 30-min walk from town or bus 12 from **La Rotonde** to **Vasarely** stop (Tel. 42 20 15 99). Modern, good facilities, professionally run.

Camping *Arc en Ciel*, Pont des Trois Sautets, Route de Nice (Tel. 42 26 14 28); 3 km from town centre; bus 3 from **La Rotonde** to **Trois Sautets**.

Restaurants *Bistrot Aixois*, 37 cours Sextius (Tel. 42 27 50 10). Attractive and popular restaurant serving delicious regional specialities; good salads and duck dishes.
La Table Provençale, 13 rue Maréchal Joffre, at end of Cours Mirabeau. (Tel. 42 27 36 99). Good local dishes from a range of well-priced menus.
☆ *Brasserie Royale*, 17 cours Mirabeau (Tel. 42 26 01 63). Another bustling, animated venue. Provençal dishes, but come here more for the sights and sounds of Provence than the food.
☆ *Côté Cour*, 19 cours Mirabeau (Tel. 42 26 32 39). Also a pleasant place to take a leisurely lunch and watch life on the famous boulevard.
☆☆ *Les Bacchanales*, 10 rue Couronne (Tel. 42 27 21 06). A popular restaurant offering a wide range of superb French cuisine.
☆☆☆ *Les Frères Lani*, 22 rue Leydet (Tel. 42 27 76 16). Superb regional and national cuisine in this elegant and stylish restaurant.

From Aix-en-Provence, trains lead south to Marseille, from where there are fast connections with Paris, Nice, Avignon and Lyon.

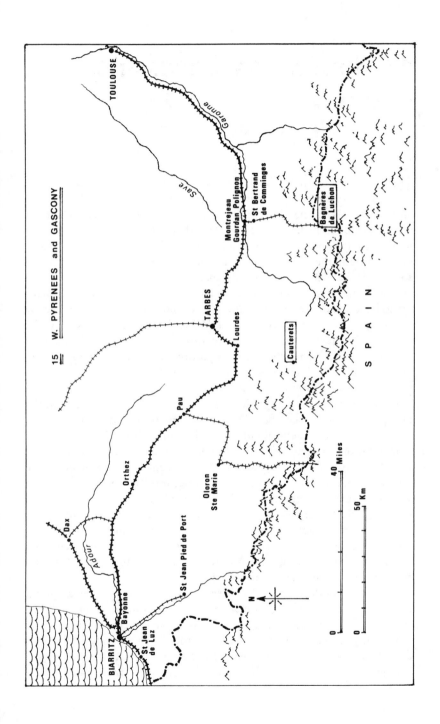

15 W. PYRENEES and GASCONY

15 Western Pyrenees and Gascony

The Pyrenees are usually thought of as a wall of mountains with a single watershed, running east to west from the Mediterranean to the Atlantic and neatly separating the French and Spanish peoples. The reality is somewhat different however for in fact they are formed of 2 chains of mountains, the one slightly out of alignment with the other. These 2 chains do not meet in the centre for there is a gap between them of some 8 miles south of St-Gaudens. Nor do the Pyrenees divide the inhabitants of France and Spain neatly on ethnological grounds for both Basques and Catalans are to be found on either side of the political border. These 2 races occupy the western and eastern extremities of the Pyrenees respectively while in the centre of the chain lie the ancient provinces of Béarn, Bigorre, Comminges and Foix which formed the northern portion of the Kingdom of Navarre until the end of the 15th century. These 3 racial divisions are closely related to the physical nature of the Pyrenees.

Apart from the most accessible valleys, the Pyrenees were practically unexplored until the end of the 19th century and the world was unaware of its largest lake, the Lac de Rieux above the vallée d'Aran, until 1882. The humid European climate to the west facilitated the exploration of the French side but the almost rainless African climate of the Spanish side militated against the settlement and exploration of the maze of long winding chains of barren foothills on the southern slopes. The French side was once heavily forested but deforestation has led to the disappearance of the forest fauna. Lynx and red deer became extinct and wolves are now extremely rare. The noble ibex is only found around Mont Perdu but bears have increased since measures were introduced to protect them and chamois inhabit the more remote valleys.

The history of the Pyrenees has been largely determined by geographical considerations. When the Roman province of Aquitania disintegrated small duchies were founded in the foothills. In the 7th century the Basques crossed the mountains from Spain and settled in the vicinity of Bayonne and Basse-Navarre. One of the most important principalities in the Pyrenees, the viscounty of Béarn, was governed by the princes of the

Centulle family until passing to the throne of France in 1589. French Navarre, or Basse-Navarre, whose capital is St-Jean-Pied-de-Port, was an independent principality which united with Foix and Béarn in 1479 and only became united with France with the accession of Henri of Navarre, le Béarnais. The County of Foix, now roughly represented by the department of the Ariège, was the home of one of the most illustrious families of the Pyrenees which, by intermarriage, extended its sway over Béarn and Navarre. Due to the comparative narrowness of the Pyrenees and the difficulties of intercommunication, the independence of most of the valley-republics did not last, although Andorra remains an isolated survivor.

To the north and east of the Basque country lies the ancient province of Gascony which stretches in a wide sweep east to west over the foothills of the western Pyrenees – an area of forested greenery, superb national parks, mountainous valleys and scattered with towns straddling the rivers flowing north out of the Pyrenean range towards the Garonne. This is outstanding walking country, famous for its magnificent scenery, clean air and sheltered valleys. South of Pau lies the Parc National des Pyrénées, offering walkers and skiers some of the most magnificent Pyrenean landscape and unspoiled nature in southern France. Antelopes, eagles, vultures and the protected Pyrenean brown bear still inhabit the more remote valleys, to which access can be gained only on foot. The long distance footpath, Grand Randonnée 10, traverses the entire length of the Pyrenees, from the Atlantic to the Mediterranean, passing through some of the most beautiful Pyrenean valleys.

East and north of Gascony, up the Atlantic seaboard to Bordeaux, lies one of the wildest and most barren districts of France – the Landes, a vast area of forest which is still very sparsely populated. In the 18th century it appeared that this vast region might become a desert of sand, blown inland by the strong Atlantic gales. That it did not is due to the engineer, Nicholas Bremontier, who came up with the idea of planting huge tracts of pine forest, a move that successfully checked this destructive inroad and transformed the appearance of the most westerly portion of Gascony.

Much of this vast area, stretching from the Spanish border to Bordeaux and west to Toulouse, was under English rule during the 14th and 15th centuries until the English were defeated at Castillon-la-Bataille in 1453 in what was the last great battle of the Hundred Years War.

Gastronomically, the area is interesting as it is the home of France's best ham – jambon de Bayonne – and excellent fish, notably tuna from the Bay of Biscay brought back to land at St-Jean-de-Luz. Other Basque specialities included an omelette called *pipérade*, made with onions, green peppers, tomatoes and thyme – which are the ingredients which often characterise dishes cooked *à la Basquaise*. *Gâteau Basque* is a rich cream-filled cake, a precursor at meal-times to the Basque digestif, Izarra which comes in 2 varieties, yellow and green. The Basque country however produces little in the way of wines, one of the few being the red d'Irouleguy, which makes a good accompaniment to the regional brebis cheese which is found throughout the Basque country.

The Route *St-Jean-de-Luz – Biarritz – Bayonne – St-Jean-Pied-de-Port – Orthez – Pau – Oloron Ste-Marie – The valley of the Aspe – Lourdes Cauterets – Labroquères/St-Bertrand-de-Comminges – Luchon – [Toulouse]*

This journey, exploring the Basque country and western Pyrenees, begins in the extreme south-western corner of France, not far from the Spanish border but easily accessible by train from Paris. Starting from the ancient whaling port of **St-Jean-de-Luz**, *its white-washed houses clustered round the old port, this route works eastwards through the foothills of the Pyrenees to the once fashionable resort of* **Biarritz**, *formerly frequented by European royalty and then to* **Bayonne**, *the capital of the Basque country. In complete contrast to the glitter and razzmatazz of Biarritz is the medieval village of* **St-Jean-Pied-du-Port**, *set like a jewel in a crown high in the Pyrenees just below the Roncevaux Pass that marked the ancient route to Spain. Descending out of the Pyrenees over the foothills the route heads east to* **Orthez** *where the Gave de Pau is crossed by one of the few fortified medieval bridges still standing in France. Beyond it lies* **Pau**, *once a fashionable resort with a large British ex-patriate community, set high on a hill with panoramic views of the Pyrenees and surrounded by magnificent walking country. The route then continues to one of the most famous pilgrimage sites in the world visited by 3 million people every year,* **Lourdes**. *It then follows a valley up into the Pyrenees to the beautifully sited medieval village of* **St-Bertrand-de-Comminges**, *founded by the Romans, its Romanesque cathedral towering over the village on an isolated crag. A few Pyrenean valleys are then explored south to* **Cauterets** *and* **Luchon** *before following the Garonne river to the great capital of the south –* **Toulouse**. **(Approximately 4 – 8 days.)**

St-Jean-de-Luz

Trains *7 – 12 trains daily from* **Bayonne** *(30 mins);* **Biarritz** *(20 mins); 10 daily from* **Paris** *Montparnasse and* **Paris** *Austerlitz (*TGV *5 hours; others 7 hours); 13 from* **Bordeaux** *(1¾ hours); 6 from* **Dax** *(1 hour 10 mins).*

Close to the Spanish border lies the attractive fishing port and resort of St-Jean-de-Luz in the heart of the French Basque country. An important port during the 3 centuries of English occupation, boats set forth from the little harbour in search of whale and cod and reached as far as Newfoundland which Basque mariners claim to have discovered as early as 1372. After its defeat in the War of the Spanish Succession France lost its Newfoundland fishing rights to Britain in 1713 and St-Jean-de-Luz languished until it found a new role fishing for Atlantic tuna, sardine and anchovy.

Ironically, although Louis XIV's ambitions were largely responsible for the catastrophic downturn in the town's fortunes, it was at St-Jean-de-Luz that the French king had married the Spanish Infanta, Maria Theresa, on 9th June 1660. The wedding preparations lasted for over a month and culminated in the marriage in the church of St John the Baptist which was then in the process of being extended. Cardinal Mazarin's wedding gift to Louis XIV was nothing less than princely: 1,200,000 *livres* of diamonds and pearls, a vast dinner service of pure gold and 2 state carriages, one pulled by 6 Russian horses, the other by 6 from India, each decorated in silk trappings of brilliant colours. After the wedding service, the newly married couple dined at the house occupied by Louis XIV in the presence of the court who then escorted them, as royal etiquette required, to the nuptial bed. In a theatrical gesture, intended to impress the populace, the main door of the church was solemnly walled up after the wedding, no mortal being considered worthy enough to stand on the spot where Louis had passed out of the church on his wedding day. It was but one of many actions carefully designed and orchestrated by Mazarin to create an illusion of extraordinary power and magnificence for 'the Sun King'.

Louis' preoccupation with *La Gloire* involved him first in the rapid war of 1667 – 68 by which France obtained several towns in Flanders and then in the Dutch War of 1672 – 8 which resulted in the acquisition of the Franche-Comté. Less successful, however, were the campaigns against the Grand Alliance and the War of the Spanish Succession in which French forces were repeatedly defeated by Marlborough and Prince Eugene, at

Blenheim in 1704, Ramillies in 1706, Oudenaarde in 1708 and Malplaquet in 1709. 'If greatness of soul consists in a love of pageantry, an ostentation of fastidious pomp, a prodigality of expense, an affectation of munificence, an insolence of ambition, and a haughty reserve of deportment, Louis certainly deserved the apellation Great. Qualities which are really heroic, we shall not find one in the composition of his character.' As was often the case, Smollett's assessment, though exaggerated, was not wide of the mark.

What to see

Maison Lohobiague

The house where Louis stayed during the wedding celebrations, the Maison Lohobiague, exists in Place Louis XIV, the heart of the old city. The Infanta stayed close by in a graceful Louis XIII mansion overlooking the harbour built of red brick and white stone with Italianate galeries that belonged to the rich Haraneder family.

Eglise St-Jean Baptiste

St-Jean Baptiste, where the wedding took place, is one of the finest Basque churches with beautiful wooden galleries on 3 levels surrounding the nave. These were reserved for men while the womenfolk occupied the pews below.

The Digue-Promenade or **Boulevard de la Plage** is the centre of the modern town but the principal interest of St-Jean-de-Luz is concentrated around the **Place Louis XIV**, built in 1635.

During the Napoleonic campaign, the Duke of Wellington made the Maison Grangabaita in Rue Mazarin his headquarters in the winter of 1813. Bad weather making the roads impassable, Wellington made the most of the enforced idleness to go fox-hunting in the surrounding countryside. Later in the century, the town was patronised by English visitors who preferred its charms to the more sophisticated atmosphere of nearby Biarritz, George Gissing dying here in 1903 in the company of H. G. Wells.

Practicalities in St-Jean-de-Luz

Tourist Office 1 Place Foch (Tel. 59 26 03 16); maps, Open Mon–Sat 9 am–12.30 pm and 2–7 pm, Sun 10 am–12.30 pm.

Station St-Jean-de-Luz-Ciboure, on Blvd du Commandant Passicot (Tel. 59 26 02 08). For town centre from station, turn left onto Blvd du Commandant Passicot, bear right to Ave de Verdun which leads to Place Foch and tourist office.

Buses Place Foch, close to the tourist office (Tel. 59 26 06 99); buses to Biarritz, Bayonne, Henday, St Sébastien (Spain).

Markets Tues and Fri; daily morning market at Place des Halles.

Festivals *St Jean Fête*: end June, traditional festival celebrating St-Jean; *Tuna Festival*: July, celebrating 1000 years of history as a fishing port; *Ttoro Festival* (Ttora is a Basque fish stew made from seafish, garlic, onions and tomatoes: early Sept;) *Ravel Music Festival*: Sept.

Hotels *Hôtel Verdun*, 13 blvd du Commandant Passicot (Tel. 59 26 02 55). Close to station, clean and simple.

☆ *Hôtel Toki-Ona*, 10 rue Marion Garay, close to station (Tel. 59 26 11 54).

☆ *Lafayette*, 20 rue République (Tel. 59 26 13 20). Delightful Logis hotel in quiet pedestrianised street. Reliable classic cooking in *Kayola* restaurant.

✩ *Hôtel Bolivar*, 18 rue Sopite (Tel 59 26 02
00). Quiet and right in the centre.
✩✩ *Bel Air*, Promenade Jacques-Thibaut (Tel.
59 26 04 86). Villa hotel next to casino;
spacious rooms and delightful terrace with
seaviews.
✩✩ *Hôtel Continental*, 15 ave Verdun (Tel. 59
26 01 23).
Restaurants *Relais de Saint Jacques*, 13 blvd du
Commandant Passicot, opposite station. Good
affordable local food, including local seafood.
✩ *Vieille Auberge*, 22 rue Tourasse (Tel. 59 26
19 61). Beautiful cooking and excellent value;
specialises in Basque dishes.
✩✩ *Le Tourasse*, 25 ave Tourasse (Tel. 59 51
14 25). One of the very best restaurants in St-
Jean-de-Luz, offering superb cuisine.

Biarritz

Trains *11 daily from* **Bayonne** *(10 mins);* **St-Jean-de-Luz** *(15 mins); 10 from* **Paris-Montparnasse** *(5½ hours).*

Visiting the tiny fishing village of Biarritz in the early years of the 19th ceuntury, Victor Hugo marvelled at the beauty of the coastline and the power of the waves crashing down onto the deserted beaches and rocky outcrops: 'On all this coast there is an abundance of noise,' he wrote in his diary. 'I have only one misgiving – it may become fashionable.' Only a few years passed before the fishing village began to change, initially with the influx of Spanish exiles fleeing the first Carlist war in 1838 and later with the arrival of the Spanish countess de Montijo and her daughter Eugénie, who was to become the future Empress of the French, whose annual holidays marked the beginning of the town's patronage by Spanish nobility. Following her marriage with Napoleon III, the Empress constructed the Villa Eugénie on a small promontory above the little town in 1855 which was to become her favourite summer residence. The artist, Eugène Boudin, often depicted members of the imperial court being blown along the sandy seashore.

The growth of the town as a winter residence however was largely due to the British, of whom by 1865 there were around 200 residents. Four years later their number had doubled, an Anglican church had been built, and soon after the British Club was founded and a golf-course laid out. John Murray describes Biarritz in his 1843 Handbook as 'a group of white-washed lodging houses, cafés, inns, traiteurs and cottages, generally of a humble character' where 'French ladies and gentlemen in bathing costume consume hours in aquatic promenades. The ladies may be seen floating about like mermaids, being supported on bladders or corks, and over-shadowed by broad-rimmed hats.' Apart from its sea-bathing, rocks and view, however, he deemed it 'the dullest place on earth'. After the fall of the Second Empire, Biarritz suffered a temporary eclipse. But the arrival of

Queen Victoria in 1889, followed by the virtually annual visits of King Edward VII, established it as the most fashionable resort on the Atlantic coast. The likelihood of being able to fraternise with Edward VII induced many opulent English to make the journey to Biarritz in February and March, the coldest months of the year. By 1946, however, Biarritz was already being described as 'as vulgar and overcrowded as any large seaside resort in France or England,' and the seemingly unchecked growth of houses and villas up and down the coast in the second half of the 20th century has done nothing to improve the situation. Nevertheless the incoming Atlantic waves still hurl themselves with their old fury against the rocky Atlaye promontory and the Rocher de la Vierge, sending white foam seething over the black rock.

What to see

Grande Plage and Plage des Basques

The great attraction of Biarritz is the magnificent promenade which extends along the shore to the Côte des Basques. In the middle is the Atlaye promontory and north and south of this rocky peninsula stretch 2 fine beaches, the **Grande Plage**, overlooked by 2 casinos, and the **Plage des Basques**. Sandwiched between the Atlaye promontory and the Rocher du Basta lies the diminutive **Port des Pêcheurs**, the original focus of the old fishing village.

From the esplanade de la Vierge a bridge leads to the **Rocher de la Vierge** which is a superb viewpoint, especially when the sea is rough, commanding a view which extends from the mouth of the Adour to the Cantabrian mountains. Much of the charm of the town derives from its 3 long beaches of fine sand and its delightful promenades and gardens created at the foot of the cliffs, planted with palms, tamarisk and mimosa.

Musée de l'Automobile Miniature

One of the curiosities of modern day Biarritz is its Musée de l'Automobile Miniature, on the plateau de l'Atlaye. Unique in France, the museum has thousands of miniature vehicles representing virtually every car ever made. (Open Mon–Thurs July–Aug daily 9 am–7 pm; Sept–June Mon, Wed and Fri 2–6 pm, Sat–Sun 10 am–12.30 pm and 3–6 pm.)

Practicalities in Biarritz

Tourist Office Javalquinto, Place d'Ixelles, off Ave Edouard VII (Tel. 59 24 20 24).
Railway Station Biarritz-Negresse, 3km from town centre; bus 2 to centre ville every 20–40 mins, (Tel. 59 55 50 50); office open 24 hours.
Markets Marché Municipal, Rue des Halles, daily, mornings only.
Buses From Rue Joseph Peiti, adjacent to tourist office; to St-Jean-de-Luz, Hendaye, St-

Sébastien in Spain.
Festivals Firework Extravaganza: 15th–16th August Basque dancing and music; Fête de la Mer: 15th–16th August Fête de Biarritz: Nov.
Hotels Hôtel le Dahu, 6 rue Jean Bart, off ave Foch (Tel. 59 24 63 36). Small and immaculate; excellent restaurant with cheap menus.
Hôtel Berhouet, 29 rue Gambetta (Tel. 59 24 63 36).

☆ *Auberge du Relais*, 44 ave Marne (Tel. 59 23 09 36). Pleasant and welcoming; modest but good value.
☆ *Hôtel Atlantic*, 10 rue du Port-Vieux (Tel. 59 24 22 25). Clean and pleasant; good cuisine including local basque dishes such as *poulet Basquaise*.
☆☆ *Windsor*, Grande Plage (Tel. 59 24 08 52). Good value pleasant seafront hotel; pricey restaurant serving traditional cuisine.
☆☆ *Central*, 8 rue Maison Suisse (Tel. 59 22 92

16). Pleasant and central.
Camping *Municipal*, on Ave Kennedy (Tel. 59 54 59 41). Close to station but far from town.
Restaurants *La Belle Epoque*, 10 ave Victor Hugo (Tel. 59 24 66 06). Good local cuisine in establishment popular with locals.
Alambic, 3 place Bellevue (Tel. 59 24 43 84). Good simple home cooking; excellent value.
☆☆ *Chez Albert*, Vieux Port des Pêcheurs (Tel. 59 24 43 84). Extremely popular restaurant offering outstanding fish dishes.

The Basques

The western end of the Pyrenees is the homeland of the **Basques**, an ancient people whose identity was forged well before the Romans arrived in the mountainous valleys of the Nive and Oloron in the first century AD. Their origins are lost in history but they still maintain a strong sense of cultural identity.

The Basques occupy the valleys from the Atlantic coastline to the Pic d'Anie, south of Oloron, separated from the Catalans who spread inland from the Mediterranean as far as the Carlitte mountains and the frontier town of Bourg-Madame by Navarre.

'What are the Basques?' Voltaire once asked, only to answer the question himself with characteristic wit: 'Why, a little people which dances at the foot of the Pyrenees!' A little but not a great deal more is now known of this hardy and ancient race of whom a quarter of a million live on the French slopes of the Pyrenees and one and a quarter million on the Spanish. The exact origins of the Basques are shrouded in history but they were once spread over a much more extensive area than they occupy today that stretched as far as the Loire, western Spain and northern Portugal. Their social and political organisation was traditionally matriarchal, important decisions being taken by the womenfolk who gathered together on Sundays after Mass but this custom has all but evaporated in the space of less than half a century. Of their traditional costume, nothing now remains except for their large red beret or *boina* and rope-soled shoes. On the French side, as on the Spanish, the Basques continue to maintain a sturdy independence towards their government.

The Basque language, Euskara, is so complicated that according to Basque legend even the Devil himself could not master it despite a 7 years' sojourn amongst them. It is, along with Finnish, one of the few European languages not to originate from the Indo-European group of languages. And, like Welsh, the language has been kept alive in the face of the pressures of the 20th century and the integration of French social and economic life. Now taught in schools, it is enjoying a comeback and is a source of great pride to its people. Basque demands for independence from France are muted, partly perhaps because of the greater recognition given to Basque cultural traditions over the last 20 years.

Basque villages can almost always be identified by the presence of the *fronton*, where the ball game of *pelota*, similar to fives, is played. Scenically the Basque country – Euzkadi to the Basques – is tremendously varied and beautiful; the peaks of some mountains rise to over 1,800 metres while below and between them stretch superb forested valleys with clear mountain streams, limpid pools and high mountain lakes. In spring and early summer the beauty of the western Pyrenees is breath-taking. The Atlantic coast scenery is a very different – long beaches of white and gold sand which attract sunworshipers to Biarritz and St-Jean-de-Luz.

Bayonne

Trains *13 daily from* **Paris** *(4 hours 40 mins by* TGV, *others 7 hours); 6 from* **St-Jean-Pied-du-Port** *(1¼ hours); 11 from* **St-Jean-de-Luz** *(30 mins); 10 from* **Bordeaux** *(1 hour 40 mins).*

Bayonne, the capital of the Basque country, is a picturesque and historic town, standing at the confluence of the rivers Adour and Nive, its old arcades streets a striking contrast to the appearance of nearby Biarritz. The station, in the Faubourg St-Esprit, on the right bank of the Adour, lies beneath Vauban's Citadel. The ramparts, built by Vauban and now laid out as a promenade, are perhaps the most attractive feature of the city.

What to see

Cathédrale Sainte-Marie

The much altered Gothic cathedral, built on the site of a Roman temple, is of interest to English visitors chiefly for the arms of the House of Plantagenet and the Talbot family. They serve as a reminder that Bayonne belonged to the English crown for nearly 300 years during the Middle Ages. The town grew rich under English rule, thriving largely on the flourishing wine trade with England and Ireland, and it held out for a long time against the French armies of Charles VII commanded by General Dunois, until it finally surrendered in 1451. Not only did Bayonne lose its lucrative English markets as a result but it was compelled to pay a large war indemnity to the French crown and French taxes proved to be significantly higher than those previously raised by the English. By the 18th century, however, the town was prospering again, trading extensively with Spain, Holland and the Antilles and sending fishing vessels to the Newfoundland fishing banks until French rights to fish there were lost in 1713.

Ste-Marie has superb stained glass but the building suffered during the 16th century when it was used briefly as a cemetery and during the Revolution a lot of the interior decoration was destroyed when a lot of the interior decoration was destroyed (Open Mon–Sat 8 am–7.15 pm, Sun 8.30–7 pm.)

Many of the Jews expelled from Spain in the late 15th century settled in Bayonne where they started up chocolate factories. It appears that the Jews were also responsible for the introduction to France and manufacture of marzipan, both products still being made in the town. Apart from the local chocolate and marzipan, the delicious hams and Izarra, the local liqueur, Bayonne's greatest attraction is undoubtedly the Musée Bonnat, in Rue Jacques Lafitte, one of the 2 greatest art galleries of south-western France.

Musée Bonnat

Leon Bonnat, a native of Bayonne, enjoyed exceptional fame in the 19th century, not just as a painter, mainly of portraits, but also as a teacher and art collector. Among his many distinguished pupils can be numbered Toulouse-Lautrec, Munch and Braque. His exceptionally fine collection of Old Master paintings and works by his contemporaries forms the nucleus of the bright modernised museum named after him. (Open Wed–Mon 10 am–noon and 3–7 pm; off-season Mon and Wed–Thurs 10 am–noon and 2.30–6.30 pm.)

Old Quarter

The old quarter surrounds the Cathédrale Ste-Marie, built between the 13th and 16th centuries, the most rewarding streets being the Rue du Port-Neuf, with its many chocolate shops, and the Rue Argenterie which runs down from the cathedral to Pont Marengo and the Musée Bonnet.

Izarra Distillery

Izarra, the extraordinary yellow and green local liqueur, can be tasted at the Izarra Distillery at 9 quai Bergeret, off Place de la République. The green herbal-based Izarra is even more potent than the yellow variety. (Open 15th July–Aug Mon–Sat 9–11.30 am and 2–6.30 pm; English tours available.)

Practicalities in Bayonne

Tourist Office Hôtel de Ville, Place de la Liberté, in Grand-Bayonne under arcade (Tel. 59 46 01 46); maps; list of festivals; guided tours of city (in French). Open Mon–Sat 9 am–7 pm; Oct–May Mon–Fri 9 am–12.30 pm and 1.30–6.30 pm; Sat 9 am–12.30 pm.
Railway Station Off Place de la République (Tel. 59 46 81 63); information office open 9 am–noon and 2–6.30 pm; luggage office open 10 am–noon and 2–6 pm; lockers.
Buses Place du Réduit beside river in Petit Bayonne (Tel. 59 59 04 61). **Markets** Marché Municipal, Market hour takes place Tues, Thurs and Sat mornings along the banks of the River Nive, on Quai de Chatio. There is also a junk market, Friday mornings, on place Paul Bert.
Festival Jambon de Bayonne and charcuterie fair: Easter week; Jazz aux Remparts: mid-end July.
Hotels Hôtel des Basques, 4 rue des Lisses, in Petit-Bayonne, overlooking Place Paul Bert (Tel. 59 59 08 02).
Hôtel des Arceaux, 26 rue Pont Neuf (Tel. 59

59 15 53). Newly renovated, 15 mins walk from station in pedestrianised heart of Grand-Bayonne.
☆ Hôtel Paris-Madrid, Place de la Gare (Tel. 59 55 13 98). Right next to the railway station, with plenty of rooms.
☆☆ Le Grand Hôtel, 21 rue Thiers (Tel. 59 59 14 61). Large, comfortable hotel right in the heart of the old town, not far from tourist office; good restaurant serving Basque specialities.
☆☆ Agora, ave Jean-Rostand (Tel. 59 63 30 90). Modern, with delightful garden and riverside terrace.
☆☆☆ Loustau, 1 Place de la République (Tel. 59 55 16 74). Comfortable, modernised hotel in good location beside the Adour bridge, but rooms at front can be noisy. Good cooking in restaurant.
Restaurants Le Moulin à Poivre, Place de la Gare, in St-Esprit (Tel. 59 55 56 91). Good simple food including riz basquaise.
☆ Le Saint Simon, 1 rue Basques, near the

Porte St-Leon and the Pont du Génie over the
Nive (Tel. 59 59 13 40).
☆☆ *François Miura*, 24 rue Marengo (Tel. 59

59 49 89). An excellent restaurant close to the
station and beneath the Citadel; reserve if
possible.

St-Jean-Pied-de-Port

Trains *4–5 trains daily from* **Bayonne** *(55 mins).*

From Bayonne the fertile valley of the Nive heads south-east through the delightful
foothills of the western Pyrenees with its varied cultivation and frequent villages
interspersed with fine stretches of forest which give the landscape a pleasant air of
domesticity. Beyond **Cambo-les-Bains** and the old village of **Itxassou**, renowned
for its cherries, lies the **Pas du Roland**, a defile in the mountains said by legend to
have been created by the sword of Roland. Higher up the valley of the Nive, and at
the end of the railway line, lies the fascinating little town of St-Jean-Pied-de-Port,
the capital of Basse-Navarre, so called from its position at the foot of the pass or
'port' of Roncesvalles.

Charlemagne pursued the Saracens over this pass into Spain in the year 778,
using a road originally created by the Romans, part of his army being led by
Roland, count of Brittany. According to the medieval chanson *Song of Roland*,
Roland and the 12 peers of the Emperor Charlemagne were crushed to death by
rocks flung down on them by the treacherous Basques. Ignobly ambushed, Roland
perished, unable to avail himself of his sword, the mighty 'Durandal' that, further
east in the Pyrenees, below Gavarnie, was responsible for the great split in the
rocks called the Breche de Roland.

What to see

Ramparts
With its double line of ramparts and lofty Citadel restored by Vauban in the 17th
century, St-Jean-Pied-de-Port is one of the most entrancing and delightful towns of
the western Pyrenees and an ideal jumping-off point for walks in the surrounding
mountains.

Throughout the Middle Ages the town was one of the most animated and
frequented pilgrimage stops in France, being the last resting-place in France on the
long and wearisome pilgrimage route to the great shrine of St James at
Compostela in north-western Spain. All the great pilgrimage routes heading for
Santiago da Compostela met at St-Jean-Pied-de-Port, not just those coming from
Cluny, Paris and Vézelay but also from eastern France and Provence. Religious
orders, such as the Clunians and the Knights of St John, supervised the provision

of accommodation on the recognised pilgrimage routes and provided guides to take groups across the Pyrenees and west to Santiago. The great heyday of the pilgrimages was the 13th and 14th centuries; by the beginning of the 16th century the numbers of pilgrims had dropped considerably, but the growing number of beggars and tricksters, taking advantage of genuine pilgrims, meant that a prison had to be built to deal with them. It still exists, adjacent to the bishops house where 3 bishops loyal to the schismatic popes of Avignon lived after having abandonned Bayonne.

The Citadel

The precipitous street leading to the Citadel contains many beautiful 16th- and 17th-century houses, largely built of fine red sandstone. The lower town is surrounded by ramparts built by Vauban while the old town, on the right bank of the Nive, retains much of its 15th-century defences, of which the fortified church of Nôtre-Dame-du-Pont and the Porte St Jacques formed a part. At the upper end of the Rue de la Citadelle lies the oldest site originally founded by Garcia IV of Navarre in the 11th century.

The town and surrounding country were ceded to France only in 1659 by the Treaty of the Pyrenees, following the Spanish defeats at Salses and Perpignan. From St-Jean-Pied-de-Port magnificent mountain scenery can be enjoyed from the sun-drenched terrace of a local café or explored on foot, following either the old pilgrim routes north or the Grand Randonée routes running east and west that intersect the town. Apart from the trout found in abundance in the river Nive, the town is famous for its crayfish cooked according to a local recipe in white wine and burnt brandy.

Practicalities in St-Jean-Pied-de-Port

Tourist Office 14 ave Charles de Gaulle, in the centre just outside the old city walls (Tel. 59 37 03 57); maps; hiking information; list of local festivals. Open Mon–Sat 9 am–12.30 pm and 2–7 pm, Sunday 10.30 am–12.30 pm and 3.30–6.30 pm.

Railway Station Ave Renaud (Tel. 59 37 02 00). Open 5.30 am–10 pm; from station up Ave Renaud to Ave Charles de Gaulle, then turn right.

Bicycle Rental Chez Steunou, Place du Marché, next to tourist office (Tel. 59 37 25 45).

Markets Mon, all day in Place du Marché; with many locally produced products including cheeses such as Ardiganza, a dry sheep's milk cheese.

Hotels Hôtel des Remparts, Over the Nive, along Ave Charles de Gaulle (Tel. 59 37 13 79) Clean and simple.

Hôtel Itzalpea, Place du Trinquet (Tel. 59 37 03 66). Quiet and pleasant, outside the old wall.

☆☆ Ramuntcho, rue France (Tel. 59 37 03 91). Comfortable hotel right in the heart of the Haute Ville.

Camping Camping Municipal, on banks of the River Nive (Tel. 59 37 11 19).

Restaurants Chocolainia, Place du Trinquet, at entrance to Haute Ville Superb local dishes, including local Pyrennean ham and fish from the River Nive.

☆ Arbillaga, 19 Place de Gaulle (Tel. 59 37 06 44), Excellent cooking; traditional Basque dishes, as well as local trout.

☆☆ Etche Ona, Place Floquet (Tel. 59 37 01 14). One of the best restaurants in St-Jean-Pied-de-Port; offers excellent regional dishes in delightful setting.

Orthez

Trains *trains daily from* **Bayonne** *(40 mins); 7 daily from* **Pau** *(35 mins).*

To reach Orthez it's necessary first to return to Bayonne and then take another train east through the foothills of the western Pyrenees. From St-Jean-Pied-de-Port the train descends the valley of the Nive, through a series of wild gorges and fertile flood-plains, to **Bidarray** with its 14th-century bridge, **Cambo-les-Bains** and **Ustaritz** which for 600 years was the capital of the Labourd. It is dominated by its vast seminary founded in 1753 which has played an important role in maintaining the study of the Basque language.

From Bayonne the undulating countryside of the Pays de Labourde stretches west to the village of **Peyrehorade** overlooked by the ruins of the 13th-century Château de Apremont. Further west stands **Hastingues**, a *bastide* founded and named after Lord Hastings in 1289 who at the time was the Lieutenant of Guyenne. The village of **Sorde l'Abbaye** on the River Gave retains its 13th-century abbey church with a remarkable mosaic floor in the choir originally created for a local Gallo-Roman villa. The River Gave then leads east through gentle and attractive countryside to the picturesque town of **Orthez**, the ancient capital of Béarn until the 15th century.

The old territory of Béarn was an independent viscountcy until the end of the 13th century when an heiress married the Count of Foix, the lord of the neighbouring territory, whereupon the houses of Foix and Béarn were united.

Gaston Phoebus

The town was a stronghold of Gaston Phoebus X, one of the most wayward sovereigns of medieval France. On account of his good looks he was given the name of Phoebus and adopted the blazing sun as his crest. Little given to a life of reflection, he soon established a reputation for lasciviousness and prodigality which he tempered by patronising the arts. He succeeded however in impressing Froissart who visited him in 1388 while in the course of writing a history of Gascony. Froissart's description of him as a 'prudent knight, full of enterprise and wisdom, constant at his devotions' who 'never allowed men of abandoned character to be about his person' is completely at odds with everything else known of him. He murdered his brother and his only son, together with 15 of the latter's companions, on the false charge that they were planning to murder him. 'Which was a pity,' Froissart remarked, 'for there were not in all Gascony such handsome and well-appointed squires.'

What to see

Tour Moncade

Of the mighty castle built by Gaston VII on the lines of the Château of Moncade in Catalonia, and described by Froissart in his *Chronicles*, little now remains, the town having been sacked in 1569 following its capture by Protestant forces. All that survives is a single 13th-century tower, the Tour Moncade, the former keep of the château which still dominates the town. With the death of Gaston Phoebus X, the fortunes of Orthez declined until Catherine of Foix and Béarn married Jean d'Albret of Navarre, thus uniting the 3 territories under the crown of Navarre.

Fortified Bridge

The town clusters beneath the Tour Moncade round one of the most remarkable bridges of southern France, a graceful 13th-century construction defended by a tall fortified tower pierced by a city gate. The gate-tower is one of the oldest surviving in France, its elegant arches bridging the rocky banks of the Gave de Pau at their narrowest point. The gate-tower was put to use as late as 1814 when Marshal Soult defended the town against the superior forces of the Duke of Wellington. With Soult's defeat 7 kilometres to the north-west on 27th February, the town was abandoned by the French forces. It was at this battle that Wellington received his first wound of the Peninsular War while on the French side, General Foy distinguished himself, being wounded 14 times in the course of the battle.

At the end of the bridge Rue Bourg-Vieux leads up to the Tour Moncade. The street is lined with old houses, of which the finest is the **Maison Jeanne d'Albret** at number 39.

Maison de Jeanne d'Albret

Jeanne d'Albret was the intolerant and merciless Queen of Navarre and mother of Henri IV, whose espousal of Protestantism was to spark a series of appalling massacres carried out on her orders by her faithful Scottish commander, Montgomery. On the death of her husband in 1562, Jeanne publicly embraced Protestantism, a declamation which forced her to flee for shelter to the Protestant stronghold of La Rochelle. Undeterred, she sent Montgomery to Orthez to convert her citizens by force, the latter compelling the Carmelites to jump into their own well until it could take no more and forcing the Cordelier friars to jump from their monastery windows to their deaths in the river below.

Practicalities in Orthez

Tourist Office Maison Jeanne d'Albret, 1 rue Jacobins (Tel. 59 69 02 75).
Railway Station Rue Paul Bailleres (Tel. 59 55 50 50). For town centre from station, walk left under bridge, first left down Ave Xavier Darget and right at Place de la Moutete.
Markets Tues; famous for its locally smoked hams.
Festivals *Mardi Gras* (Shrove Tuesday):

Carnival; *Orthez fête*: July
Hotels ☆ *Hôtel Au Temps de la Reine Jeanne*, 44 rue Bourg-Vieux (Tel. 59 67 00 76). In the heart of the old town.
Restaurants ☆☆ *Auberge St-Loup*, 20 rue Pont Vieux (Tel. 59 69 15 40). Close to the medieval bridge; excellent cooking in beautiful old hospice.

Pau

Trains 7 *trains daily from* **Bayonne** *(1¼ hours)*; 4 *daily from* **Biarritz** *(1½ hours)*; 15 *daily from* **Lourdes** *(½ hour)*; 8 *daily from* **Bordeaux** *(2 hours)*; 8 *from* **Toulouse** *(2 hours 50 mins)*; 2 *daily from* **Nice**; 8 TGVs *from* **Paris** *Montparnasse (5½ hours)*.

Just a few minutes before arriving in Pau, the train passes through the little town of **Lescar** where 12 members of the royal House of Navarre are buried in the 12th-century cathedral. The most distinguished amongst them is Queen Marguerite who gave refuge at the Château de Nerac to such Protestants as Calvin, Beza and Marot.

Pau itself has grown considerably in recent years but it still occupies the most idyllic site on a ridge overlooking the Gave de Pau with breath-taking views of the distant Pyrenees. Apart from its outstanding position, the town's glory is its 12th-century château with its magnificent Gobelin tapestries and ornate royal chambers with superbly decorated ceilings.

It was in Pau that on 13th December 1553, Jeanne d'Albret gave birth to a son destined to become Henri IV, King of France as well as of Navarre. A statue of him gazes from the shade of the Place Royale across the Boulevard des Pyrenees from where there is a panoramic view of the Pyrenees that, according to Lamartine, equalled that of the Bay of Naples. The view is indeed impressive, stretching from the Pic-Longue du Vignemale, the highest mountain in sight, and the Pic du Midi de Bigorre in the east to the Pic d'Anie in the west. Between the 2, and standing out prominently on a clear day, are the 2 peaks of Midi and Ossau that rise close to the Spanish frontier.

The mother of Jeanne d'Albret was the educated and distinguished princess, Marguerite de Valois, also known as Marguerite d'Angoulême and Marguerite de Navarre, the sister of King Francis I, and one of the most notable figures of the French Renaissance. Her beauty, intelligence and charm were widely recognised during her lifetime and were celebrated in verse by poets after her death. From Italy she summoned Italian artists and architects who introduced Renaissance concepts to France while at the same time she patronised and protected the leading figures of the French Reformation. Apart from religious verse, Marguerite also wrote 72 gallant tales, inspired by Boccaccio's *Decameron*, which were published posthumously under the title *Heptameron*.

Soon after the end of the Peninsular War, English visitors began to take up residence in Pau, finding its winter climate a great deal more congenial than that of the Shires and Home Counties. It was here that Alfred de

Vigny met and married an English girl while stationed with his regiment in the town. By 1825 the British had built an Anglican church and by the 1860s 3,000 of the population of 21,000 were British. In their inimitable fashion, the British soon began to organise everything on the lines of the country they had left behind. Regular fox-hunts were established, a golf-course was laid out in 1856 and Scottish balls were held. Numbers had already begun to decline however by the end of the 19th century and by the 1930s, the Blue Guide reckoned that its climate was most suited to 'overworked intellectuals'. Today it has recovered from the faded elegance characteristic of most fashionable 19th-century resorts.

What to see

Chateau de Pau

Under the direction of Marguerite de Valois, Italian architects transformed the rude castle erected by Gaston Phoebus in the 14th century into a fine Renaissance palace. Of Gaston's château only the massive red brick Keep at the south-east corner survives, the north-eastern Tour de Montauzet having been rebuilt in the 16th century. Today, the west wing and fine great staircase are all that remains of Marguerite's Renaissance palace, the exterior having been largely remodelled, to its great detriment, under Louis-Philippe and Napoleon iii. The Renaissance ornament of the courtyard is by the Italian craftsmen of Marguerite de Valois, wife of Henry iv.

The royal apartments are open to the public, the objects of greatest interest inside being the Gobelin and Flemish tapestries depicting hunting scenes and the labours of the months. The kitchen and dining-room with its gargantuan table are also very impressive. In the Grand Salon de Réception on the first floor Catholic prisoners held in the castle by Jeanne d'Albret and her commander Gabriel Montgomery were massacred after a banquet in the 1560s. In the castle is a 15th-century Gothic chest, the oldest piece of furniture in the castle, Henri iv's backgammon board inlaid with ivory and mother-of-pearl and, on the second floor, in the Chambre de Henri iv, the king's cradle, made of a single tortoise-shell, where Henri was laid after his birth in 1553. (Château open Apr – Oct, daily 9.30 – 11.30 am and 2 – 5.30 pm, Nov – Mar, daily 9.30 – 11.30 am and 2 – 4.30 pm.)

Musée Béarnais

On the fourth floor of the château the Musée Béarnais traces the history of the region with displays of local costumes and crafts. It also possesses a small collection of local cooking utensils and furniture. (Open daily 9.30 am-12.30 pm and 2.30 – 6.30 pm; off-season 9.30 am-12.30 pm and 2.30 – 5.30 pm.)

Henri iv, Pau's greatest native, married another Marguerite de Valois in 1572, and became King of France in 1589. Despite his many virtuous qualities his best remembered words were the cynical observation 'Paris is well worth a Mass'. In 1598, in his most memorable act, he issued the Edict of Nantes, extending religious toleration to Protestants, a far-sighted and noble deed that brought an end to 40 years of bitter religious war.

Musée des Beaux-Arts

Hidden in a hideous neo-Classical building dating from the 1920s in Rue Mathieu Lalanne is an unexpected delight – one of the best collections of paintings to be found in southern France. Thanks mainly to the wealth of its 19th-century visitors, the Musée des Beaux-Arts has an exceptionally good art collection for a small town, the Spanish school being particularly rich while the greatest treasures are French 19th-century paintings, notably by Daubigny, Fantin Latour, Henner and Degas. (Open Wed–Mon. 9 am–noon and 2–6 pm).

Despite its distance from the actual peaks, Pau is a delightful place in which to rest and enjoy the excellent climate and incomparable views. Most of the chief wine-producing districts of the Pyrenees are located around Pau and the cuisine is excellent. A short walk from Pau brings one to **Jurançon**, on the opposite bank of the Gave, noted for its wine, the best in the Pyrenees.

Practicalities in Pau

Tourist Office Next to Hôtel de Ville in Place Royale (Tel. 59 27 27 08).

Railway Station Ave Gaston Lacoste, at bottom of hill by château (Tel. 59 55 50 50); luggage storage open 8 am–8 pm; a free funicular takes you up to the Blvd des Pyrénées (7 am–9.30 pm).

Buses CITRAM, 30 rue Gachet (Tel. 59 27 22 22); buses to Gavarnie, Agen, Artouste and St-Jean-Pied-du-Port.

Markets Daily, also Mon markets devoted to poultry and cattle.

Festivals *Festival de Pau:* end-June to end-July; plays, concerts, ballet, firework displays, pelote tournaments, poetry readings, music in chateau courtyard and elsewhere; *Grand Prix de Pau:* June, motor race; *Theatre festival:* July.

Hotel *Hôtel Le Béarn*, 5 rue Maréchal Joffre (Tel. 59 27 52 50). Pleasant and right in the heart of the town.

Hôtel de la Pomme d'Or, 11 rue Maréchal Foch (Tel. 59 27 78 48). With rooms facing a courtyard near Place Clemenceau.

Hôtel d'Albret, 11 rue Jeanne d'Albret (Tel. 59 27 81 58). Nice, spacious rooms down a little street close to the château.

☆☆ *Roncevaux*, 25 rue L. Barthou (Tel. 59 27 08 44). Just off Place Royale.

☆☆ *Commerce*, 9 rue Maréchal Joffre (Tel. 59 27 24 40). A comfortable hotel-restaurant with quiet rooms just off the large Place Clemenceau; excellent value meals in restaurant.

☆☆☆ *Continental and Conti*, Rue Maréchal Foch (Tel. 59 27 69 31). Classic grand old hotel from Pau's heyday; excellent restaurant.

Hostels *Auberge de la Jeunesse*, 30ter rue Michel Hounau, from station take funiculaire, follow rue St Louis, Rue Maréchal Foch, rue Garet and then Rue Michel Hounau (Tel. 59 30 45 77).

Camping *Municipal*, 3 km from station. Bus 7 from station (direction **Trianon**) then change to bus 4 (direction **Bocage Palais des Sports**).

Restaurants *Le Panache*, 8 rue Adoue, next to St-Martin. An excellent little restaurant offering duck heart, a gastronomic Béarnais speciality.

Pyrénées, Place Royale (Tel. 59 27 07 75). Modest and informal restaurant with good cheap menus.

Brasserie le Berry, 4 rue Gachet (Tel. 59 27 42 95). A small brasserie offering good cooking at affordable prices.

☆☆ *St-Jacques*, 9 rue Parlement (Tel. 59 27 42 95). One of the most popular restaurants in town; offers a wide range of classic dishes.

Oloron-Ste-Marie

Trains *5 – 6 trains daily from* **Pau** *(45 mins).*

Leaving Pau, the railway crosses the Gave and quickly arrives at Oloron-Ste-Marie, an ancient feudal stronghold standing on a hill between the Gave d'Aspe and the Gave d'Ossau. In Roman times a road ran south from Pau to Oloron and over the pass of Somport to Zaragossa in northern Spain. Although Oloron Ste-Marie now straddles both banks of the Gave d'Aspe, in Roman times it occupied the promontory between the Aspe and the Ossau rivers. With the destruction of the city by the barbarians, a new town was built on the west bank of the Aspe.

What to see

Eglise de Ste-Marie
The church of Ste-Marie was erected on the west bank in the 12th century and it is almost unique in that its remarkable western porch survived unscathed from the usual desecration of the religious wars. Its central column is carved with the figures of 2 chained Saracens who have been put to work upholding the tympanum, sculpted with a scene of the Deposition and 2 lions symbolising the persecuted and triumphant church. To the right is an equestrian figure of Gaston IV, who departed on the Crusades only to return to find Arabs had invaded his kingdom in his absence, while on the left is a man being hungrily devoured by a monster. Above these stretch an arch with sculptures of the 24 Old Men of the Apocalypse engaged in playing musical instruments or adoring the Holy Lamb that carries the Cross, while Evil is represented by the dragon's head. Between the Old Men of the Apocalypse and the Deposition are scenes drawn from 12th-century peasant life – boar-hunting, fishing, the smoking of salmon, cheese-making, ham-curing and wine-making. Largely carved from Pyrenean marble, the doorway is one of the finest Romanesque sculptures to be found anywhere in the Pyrenees.

Apart from its massive 12th-century square tower, the cathedral is also of special interest for its 14th-century choir which is a masterpiece of the delicate rayonnant style.

Old Quarter
On the other side of the Gave d'Aspe is the domed church of Ste-Croix, built on the summit of a hill in 1080 by Centulle IV, viscount of Béarn, and surrounded by many 15th–17th-century houses. The central square, Place Gambetta, is also lined with old houses, some arcaded, while down along the river are quiet quays bordered by sleepy houses. Like Bayonne, Oloron Ste-Marie is renowned for its chocolate, which was originally produced by Jews expelled from Spain in the 15th century.

Practicalities in Oloron Ste-Marie

Tourist Office Place de la Résistance (Tel. 59 39 98 00).

Railway Station Ave de la Gare. To town centre from station, walk down Ave Carnot, over Gave d'Aspe, and Place Mendiondou to Place de la Résistance.

Markets Tues and Sun morning.

Festivals Cattle Fair; 1st May; Bi-annual International Folk Festival: Aug.

Hotels ☆ *Hôtel Paix*, 24 ave Sadi-Carnot (Tel. 59 39 02 63). No restaurant.

☆☆ *Hôtel Brun*, Place Jaca (Tel. 59 39 64 90). Comfortable hotel on attractive square; good restaurant attached.

☆☆ *Hôtel Le Béarn-Darroze*, 4 Place Mairie (Tel. 59 39 00 99). Comfortable, modernised, and smart hotel on central square, close to tourist office. Good cuisine from own restaurant.

Excursion from Oloron Ste-Marie
The Valley of the Aspe.

South of Oloron Ste-Marie lies the steep and narrow valley of the Aspe, its river flowing turbulently due south to the Spanish border. The gorge through which the river flows is clean and sharp, bordered on either side by high barren hills, opening out in places to fertile valley-plains devoted to maize and wheat interspersed with small oak and chestnut woods. Down this remote and silent valley run the old lines of the only railway line of the central Pyrenees which used to make the journey over the border into Spain where it led to Jaca and Zaragossa, a journey that revealed the whole beauty of the Pyrenees and the extraordinary contrast of the French and Spanish slopes. Today most of the journey can be made by bus from Oloron Ste-Marie.

After **Asasp** the valley enters the *defile d'Escot*, where the Aspe flows through a magnificent gorge formed by the peaks of Roumendares and Napayt. Further up the valley lies the little village of **Sarrance** situated in a bend in the Aspe. The village has been a pilgrimage site since the 12th century and was visited by Louis XI in 1461. The focus of the church is the 12th-century granite statue of the Virgin which was believed to have miraculous powers. It sheds some light on the 16th-century

mind to learn that having worshipped at the shrine of the miracle-working Virgin, Marguerite de Navarre sat down and wrote most of her *Heptameron* here, a collection of verse which borders on the obscene.

From the attractive little cloisters of the Praemonstratensian monastery next to the church a half-hour walk leads up a track to a large calvary overlooking the valley. Further up, the valley broadens out around **Bedous** into a fertile landscape overlooked by the peaks of Anchet, Arapoup, Labigouer and de Burcq. The little village of **Accous** was the capital of a valley-republic during the Middle Ages and to its south-west lies the valley of Lescun where local peasants successfully blocked an incursion by Spanish troops in 1794. Beyond **Etsaut**, a small village with a number of interesting old houses, lies an extremely narrow stretch of gorge beyond which the **Fortress of Portalet** is perched on a rock high above the river. **Urdos** is the French frontier town and beyond this the old railway line enters a tunnel before emerging at Les Forges d'Abel. To the west stretches the National Park of the Pyrenees, clothed with oak forests, the snow-capped peaks of Aspe and Garganta glimpsed from time to time.

Leaving Pau the train passes **Coarraze**, in whose château Henri IV was brought up *à la paysanne*, and the village of **Nay**. A little beyond is **St-Pé** and its 17th-century abbey, immediately beyond which comes the view of **Lourdes** and its basilica and castle-rock.

Lourdes

Trains 7 *trains daily from Pau (½ hour); 8 from* Bordeaux *(2 hours 10 mins); 5 from* Paris, *a few require you to change at Dax or Toulouse (7–9 hours); 9 from* Toulouse *(2½ hours); 3–4 from* Cauterets *(change at Pierrefitte, 1 hour); also* SNCF **buses** *from Cauterets.*

Lourdes is one of those places that seems to divide everyone, especially those that have never set foot in the place, into 2 vehemently opposed camps – those that decry the commercialism of religion, the ugliness of the basilica and the tawdriness of the religious souvenirs and those that, making allowances for the inevitable flotsam and jetsam that accompanies any religious endeavour, succeed in finding something spiritual to take away with them. As with so many other aspects of life, it is likely that people will take from it what they bring to it. In the summer Lourdes is phenomenally crowded and visitors must be ready to accept the throngs and bustle.

Briefly told, the story of Bernadette is that of an illiterate 14-year-old girl, Bernadette Soubirous, who claimed in 1858 that the Virgin Mary had appeared to her in the Grotte de Massabielle while out collecting firewood beside the Gave de Pau. The visions occurred many times and on one occasion Bernadette scraped away the soil to unleash a gush of water from a spot where no spring had previously existed. The church authorities reacted sceptically at first but after 4 years of enquiry, the authenticity of her claims was accepted by the local bishop, and the miracle was confirmed by the Papal authorities. A feast day was appointed on the anniversary of the first apparition and ever since there has been a phenomenal growth in the number of pilgrims, now numbering some 2 to 3 million a year, making Lourdes the greatest pilgrimage site in the world. In summer the town is quite literally packed with pilgrims and curious visitors. The old town is situated at the foot of the rock dominated by the castle while the pilgrimage town lies on the opposite side of the Gave de Pau.

What to see

Grotte des Apparitions

Apart from the grotto, known as the Grotte des Apparitions, the basilica of the Rosary and a vast subterranean basilica, which are now the focus of the town, Lourdes also possesses an austere and precipitously situated château. The basilica and the grotto are approached from the old town by the Esplanade des Processions, which extends from the Breton Calvary, a crucifix 40-feet-high made from Breton granite to the colossal statue of the Virgin. The basilica before the calvary is preceded by 2 curved approaches rising on arches on either side of the Church of the Rosary. The pass beneath the right-hand approach leads to the Miraculous Grotto, or Grotte de Massabielle, the scene of the Virgin's apparition, where the walls are now covered with the crutches of miraculously-healed pilgrims and with ex-votos of every description.

Château de Lourdes

On the other side of the Gave rises a grim fortress, the **Key of Lavedan**. This impressive castle, housing for the moment an eclectic collection of Pyrenean material, has the distinction of being the last stronghold in Guyenne to be held by the English, who did not surrender until 1418. Most of the present building dates from the 16th and 17th centuries but the Keep and Tour de Garnabie formed part of the English castle. Lord Elgin was briefly held prisoner in the castle, then in use as a prison, while making his way back to England from Constantinople in 1804. Apart from the Pyrenean exhibits, the castle retains the trough used for boiling the oil which was rained down on attackers at the moment when they thought they had victory within their grasp. From the medieval ramparts there are excellent views west over the town and the basilica, and there are 2 interesting gardens within the castle walls, one devoted to alpine plants and the other to plants with medicinal properties. (Open Easter–mid-Oct, daily 9 am–noon and 2–7 pm; mid-Oct–Easter, Wed–Mon 9 am–noon and 2–7 pm.

One kilometre south of the town a funicular climbs to the **Pic du Jer** at a height of 950 metres while another on the opposite side of the valley ascends to **Le Béout** from where there is a fine panorama of Lourdes, the Pic du Jer and the Valley of the Gave de Pau.

Practicalities in Lourdes

Tourist Office 1 Place du Champs Commun (Tel. 62 94 15 64). Open Mon – Sat, 9 am–7 pm, Sun 10 am–noon; maps; brochure; list of 400 hotels; accommodation service.

Railway Station Ave de la Gare (Tel. 62 37 50 50); luggage storage; lockers open 7.30 am–7 pm; information office open 8 am–1 pm and 1.30–7 pm; 10 mins walk from station to *centre ville*.

Buses Place Capdevieille, below tourist office (Tel. 62 94 31 15); SNCF buses to Cauterets, 3–5 daily (50 mins).

Festivals *International de Musique Sacrée*: Easter Weekend.

Hotels There are over 380 hotels in Lourdes to cope with huge influx of visitors and pilgrims; budget hotels are concentrated in the area around Rue Basse in the town centre, and in route de Pau.

Hôtel-Restaurant Paix et Continental, 3 rue de la Paix (Tel. 62 94 91 31).

☆ *Notre Dame de Lorette*, 75 Route de Pau (Tel. 62 94 12 16). Unremarkable but friendly and in nice location on far bank of river from the grotto; good French cuisine.

☆☆ *Albret et Taverne de Bigorre*, 21 Place Champ-Commun (Tel. 62 94 75 00). Pleasant little central hotel, good value; delicious cooking from chef Claude Moreau.

☆☆ *Majestic*, 9 ave Maransin (Tel. 62 94 27 23). Conveniently close to station.

☆☆ *Aneto*, 5 rue Félix (Tel. 62 94 23 19).

☆☆ *Beauséjour*, 16 ave de la Gare (Tel. 62 94 38 18). Comfortable hotel with decent rooms, very close to station.

Christian Hostel *Centre des Rencontres* 'Pax Christi', 4 rue de la Foret, 10 min walk from basilica (Tel. 62 94 00 66).

Restaurants There are numerous inexpensive restaurants all through the town. Better meals in the larger hotel restaurants.

☆☆ *L'Ermitage*, Place Mgr Laurence (Tel. 62 94 08 42). Good regional and classic French cuisine.

Excursion from Lourdes
Cauterets

Buses 4 – 5 *SNCF buses daily from Lourdes (55 mins).*

The land stretching south of Tarbes to the Spanish border and from Lourdes in the west to Luchon in the east was once the ancient county of Bigorre. Established in the 9th century, with Tarbes as its capital, Bigorre was frequently ruled by women, not conforming to the Salic law which predominated in the north and which precluded women from reigning as monarchs. By the Treaty of Brétigny in 1360 the English held Bigorre by right but were not chased out until 1418. The mountainous region of Bigorre, from south of Lourdes to the frontier, consisted of the 7 valleys of Lavedan which retained a wide margin of independence although nominally subject to the counts residing at Tarbes. Even the attempts by Colbert to impose a tax on the independent-minded Bigourdans led to an armed resistance which kept the royal tax-collectors out of the high valleys for 12 years.

Leaving Lourdes and passing the funicular stations of Le Beout and the Pic du Jer, the valley of the Gave de Pau is scattered with mounds of morraine left behind by retreating glaciers. On one such glacial deposit rise the ruins of the **Château Jalou** while above the head of the valley to the south can be seen the peak of Vignemale between those of Viscos to the east and Cabaliros to the west. The ruins of the tower of Vidalos are passed just before the little spa town of **Argelès-Gazost** situated at the confluence of the Gave de Pau with the Gave d'Azun. Just before the town lies the Château de Vieuzac while to the south stands the Château d'Ourout. The old quarters of the little town are clustered round the **Tour Mendaigne**, the thermal baths being located in the attractive new quarter adjacent to the circular park.

St-Savin was the great religious centre of the central Pyrenees for a thousand years before Lourdes came to prominence in the second half of the 19th century.

The Romanesque church was fortified in the 14th century and its sentry walk, used by defenders to repel attack, is still intact. The church is all that remains of the Benedictine abbey, whose abbot was also the temporal ruler of the valley during the Middle Ages. Passing the ruins of the 12th-century Château de Beaucens with its double ring of defences, once the seat of the Viscounts of Lavedan, the valley divides, the westerly valley following the Gave de Cauterets that runs swiftly through deep gorges cut by the river into the dark schist. **Pierrefitte-Nestalas**, just beyond a delightful stretch of chestnut woods, is the railway terminus.

Set in a beautiful valley on the edge of the **Parc National des Pyrénées Occidentales**, Cauterets is the ideal place from which to explore the nearby mountains. It has been fashionable since the 16th century when Marguerite de Valois, Queen of Navarre, composed some of the *Heptameron* here. Napoleon III's mother, Queen Hortense, and his future wife, Eugénie de Montijo, paid visits to the spa, the latter after her expulsion from the court of Isabel II of Spain. The great lure of Cauterets has always been the sulfuric hot springs which attracted Victor Hugo, Georges Sand and Châteaubriand amongst others to the town. Of all the different baths and waters to be tested the most off-putting and life-enhancing is the **Thermes des Oeufs** with its smell of rotten eggs. Not to be missed is the télépherique which climbs to the Col d'Ilhéou.

Information on the Parc National des Pyrénées can be found on the Place du Gare, the headquarters building for the park also housing a **Musée du Parc National** with excellent exhibitions on mountain climbing and the peaks in the area. (Open 9.30 am-noon and 3.30 – 7pm.) One of the best walks around the area is the GR 10 which passes through Cauterets and continues to Luz St-Sauveur by 2 separate paths. One passes over a plateau while the other twists past the Lac de Gaube, the icy peak of the Pic du Vignemale and the village of **Gavarnie** and **Gedre**. A 2-hour ascent leads one up the **Col d'Ilhéou** to the **refuge d'Ilhéou**. A shorter trip, taking 4 hours, leads to the **Pont d'Espagne**.

Practicalities in Cauterets

Tourist Office 2 Place de la Mairie (Tel. 62 92 50 27); accommodation service.

Bus Station To town centre, turn right, up Ave Général Leclerc to Place de la Mairie; buses also to Lourdes, Gavarnie, Luz-St-Sauveur.

Cable Car One block from station, to the Col d'Ilhéou. (Open 9am–12.15pm and 1.45–5.45pm in summer.)

Hiking Information *Maison du Parc*, Place de la Gare.

Markets Daily covered market *Les Halles*; open air market: *Place de la Gare*, Fridays, during July and August.

Festivals Motor-race: July.

Hotels *Hôtel-Restaurant Christian*, 10 rue Richelieu. Immaculates rooms and very friendly.

Hôtel du Béarn, 4 blvd Général Leclerc, opposite the covered market (Tel. 69 92 53 54). ☆☆ *Welcome*, Rue de l'Eglise (Tel. 62 92 50 22). Right in the heart of the town.

☆☆ *Etche Ona*, Rue Richelieu (Tel. 62 92 51 43). A short walk down Rue Richelieu from the former railway station; good traditional French cooking.

☆☆ *Trois Pics*. Ave Leclerc (Tel. 62 92 53 64). Good comfortable hotel with excellent facilities, including swimming pool.

Hostels Centre UCJC 'Cluquet', Ave Docteur Domer (Tel. 62 92 52 95). Cheap hostel accommodation on outskirts of town.

Labroquère/St-Bertrand-de-Comminges

Trains *7–9 trains daily from* **Lourdes**; *change at* **Montréjeau-Gourdon-Polignan** *(1½ hours);* SNCF **buses** *to* **Labroquère**, *from where 2km walk to St-Bertrand-de-Comminges.*

From Lourdes the train skirts the Foret d'Ossun to **Tarbes**, the ancient capital of Bigorre, but now an ugly town on the Adour that can be quietly overlooked. East of Tarbes the railway crosses the Plateau de Lannemezan, dissected by dozens of rivers draining north through the Gers to the Garonne river. From **Montréjeau** and St Gaudens SNCF buses head up the valley of the Garonne to **St-Bertrand-de-Comminges** and Luchon at the head of the valley of the same name. This is one of the most delightful and fascinating journeys to be made in the central Pyrenees. The intriguing town of St-Bertrand-de-Comminges is a 2-kilometre walk uphill, or a short taxi ride, from the station and a walk well worth making despite the gradient.

What to see

Cathédrale Notre-Dame

The Cathedral of Notre-Dame of St-Bertrand-de-Comminges is the most beautiful and interesting church in the French Pyrenees. Its setting is nothing short of extraordinary, crowning as it does, the summit of a small isolated hill against a backdrop of dark mountains. Surrounded by massive buttresses without which one feels the cathedral would inevitably collapse, it dominates the village and surrounding valley. The aisleless nave is uncluttered and elegant being executed in a pure rayonnant style while the magnificent Renaissance choir, begun in 1537, comes as a great surprise, contrasting so markedly with the cathedral's heavy and squat exterior. The rood loft, choir screen and stalls are exquisitely carved with a great sense of humour, the scenes including ones of a monk being birched and monkeys struggling for possession of a sturdy stick – an allusion to earthly rivalry within the church. The choir-stalls and the bishop's throne were carved in the 1530s at the expense of Jean de Mauleon and are amongst the finest of their age in France. On the outside of the choir are a superb series of heads of men and women, said to be those of Francois I's courtiers.

Originally founded by Iberians driven across the Pyrenees by Pompey's army, the original site of Comminges in the river valley was abandoned after it had been laid waste by the Vandals in the 5th century. One legend has it that 4 years after the death of Christ, Herod Antipas and his wife Herodias, those responsible for the death of St John the Baptist, were exiled to the Roman town, Lugdunum Convenarum which was then the capital of the Covenae colony, by the Emperor Caligula. It is estimated that the population of the town in the 1st century BC was around 60,000 compared to the 300-odd inhabitants resident there today. The hilltop fortress was sacked by the Burgundians in the late 6th century and remained deserted until work began on the construction of the cathedral in the 12th century. That such a large cathedral should be built in this remote location is due to the fact that Comminges was an important resting-place on the route from eastern France to Santiago de Compostela. Bertrand de Got, the Bishop of Comminges in the mid-13th century, used his influence and power to further enrich the cathedral, especially after becoming the first of the Popes resident at Avignon. The tympanum above the western portal depicts the Adoration of the Magi. The enchanting and tiny Romanesque cloister on the south side of the cathedral looks out tranquilly over the Garonne river.

Roman Settlement

The ramparts of the town are medieval but rest on Gallo-Roman foundations and the hillside below retains the outline of a Roman theatre. It was through the **Porte Majou** that the ancient Roman road reached the Citadel, which later extended down into the plain as far as the rivers Valcabrère and Garonne. Archaeological excavations of this area have brought to light the Roman forum, a temple dedicated to Augustus, thermal baths, a theatre and one of the earliest Christian basilicas in France, dating from the 4th century. A Roman imperial trophy of the 2nd century found on the site of the Roman forum can be seen in a small chapel in the square opposite the west façade of the cathedral. The figures of a Roman emperor and Barbarian prisoners are most probably the work of 1st-century Greek sculptors. Further north, towards the Garonne, more thermal baths, a civic basilica with a mosaic almost 46 metres in length and an amphitheatre have also been discovered.

Eglise St-Just-St-Pastor

Very close to these Roman vestiges, at Valcabrère, stands a fascinating church, St-Just-St-Pastor, which was the cathedral of the See until the 11th century and which incorporates in its structure many columns and stones taken from the adjacent Roman town. The walk to St-Just-St-Pastor from Labroquère takes one past vines, under a Romanesque gateway and into a tranquil cemetery that dates back to time immemorial. The earliest church, probably built on this spot in the 4th century, was dedicated to St-Just and St-Pastor, 2 boys martyred at the time of Diocletian.

Practicalities in St-Bertrand-de-Cominges

Hotels ✩✩ *Hôtel l'Oppidum*, Rue de la Poste (Tel. 61 88 33 50). Comfortable, modernised hotel with a good restaurant.

Excursion from St-Bertrand-de-Comminges
Luchon

Buses *3–4 SNCF buses or trains from Montréjeau-Gourdon-Pol (55 mins), and Labroquère/St-Bertrand-de-Comminges (50 mins).*

From Labroquère/St-Bertrand-de-Comminges the turbulent waters of the Garonne lead due south down a narrow valley past the ruined tower of **Fronsac**. Here the valley divides, the westerly valley widening to form the enchanting Vallée de Luchon, encircled by wooded hills, above which rise a number of peaks, snow-capped for half the year. The valley leads north to Luchon, the most fashionable of the Pyrenean resorts.

Luchon is a pleasant little place but is of little historical interest except for its Romanesque church which was sacked by the Huguenots in the 16th century, and for the fact that it was the birthplace of St Raymond, the founder of the Spanish military order of Calatrava. The old village clusters around the church of Notre-Dame but most of the town dates from the 18th century, having been rebuilt after a fire in 1723.

The thermal springs had been enjoyed by the Romans as early as the 1st century AD and to make access to the springs easier they constructed a road south to Luchon from their colony of Lugdunum Convenarum. Excavations have revealed the traces of 3 enormous **marble baths** that were once equipped with hot air and steam vents. Following their destruction by the Barbarians, the thermal waters flowed unutilised into the river Pique for over a thousand years.

Over 80 **thermal springs** flow today from the mountain of Superbagnères to the south-west of Luchon, the water emerging at temperatures ranging from 22 to 67 degrees centigrade. The thermal springs are amongst the most sulphurous and radioactive in the world and are extremely beneficial for the treatment of respiratory and rhuematic ills, not that one has to be unwell to enjoy them. The superbly run thermal baths, the **Etablissement Thermal**, are found at the southern end of the handsome street, Allées d'Etigny, behind which stretches the delightful **Parc des Quinconces**, from where a funicular descends to the railway station.

The chief attraction of Luchon is that it is high in the mountains, enjoys a superb climate and makes an excellent base for exploring the surrounding mountains. Part of the old town remains but even the new part with its tree-lined promenades and gardens, is attractive. Long distance Grande Randonnée routes lead off to west and east while close to the town are a number of short walks, the easiest and closest being that from the village of Montauban, east of Luchon, to the waterfalls known as the Cascades de

Montauban.

Practicalities in Luchon

Tourist Office Allées Etigny (Tel. 61 79 21 21).
Hotels ☆ *Hôtel Sports*, 12 ave Maréchal Foch
(Tel 61 79 02 80). Close to the old station,
almost opposite the church.
☆☆ *Deux Nations*, 5 rue Victor Hugo (Tel. 61

79 01 71). Nice, bright rooms in welcoming
hotel very close to centre.
☆ *Le Pailhet*, 12 ave Maréchal Foch (Tel. 61 79
09 60). The restaurant of the Hôtel Sport; good
simple Pyrenean fare.

LUCHON–TOULOUSE

Trains/Buses SNCF *bus or train to* Montréjeau-Gourdon-Polignan; *7 trains daily
from Montréjeau to* Toulouse *and* Lourdes.

Luchon lies at the end of the former railway line and unless one plans to hike
through the mountains along the Grande Randonnée route it is necessary to
backtrack to Montréjeau on the Pau-Toulouse railway line.

From **Montréjeau** the railway line follows the route of the Garonne and the old
Roman road north-east to Toulouse. Leaving **St-Gaudens** behind the line at first
skirts the Garonne giving a view south of the impressive ruins of the Renaissance
Château de Montespan. The Garonne is crossed just south of **St-Martory** with its
attractive 18th-century bridge, beyond which lie the 12th-century ruins of the
Château de Rocquefort on the far bank from the natural gas plant at **Boussens**.
Martres-Tolosane can be recognised by its 13th-century octagonal steeple, a
structure characteristic of the region. Leaving the low hills, known as Les Petites
Pyrénées behind, the Garonne broadens out into a wider, flatter landscape. A little
to the north of **Muret**, the former capital of the county of Cominge, an important
battle took place in September 1213. Here Simon de Montfort defeated the army of
Pedro II of Aragon who was himself killed in the course of the battle. Shortly
beyond lies **Toulouse**, the great capital of the Midi, characterised by the red bricks
which for a thousand years or more were virtually the sole building material to be
used in the construction of the city. (For Toulouse, see Languedoc-Roussillon, page
203.)

Index